FOUNDATIONS OF EDUCATION

PERSPECTIVES ON AMERICAN EDUCATION

■ **John Martin Rich** ■
University of Texas at Austin

Merrill, an Imprint of
Macmillan Publishing Company
New York

Collier Macmillan Canada, Inc.
Toronto

Maxwell Macmillan International Publishing Group
New York   Oxford   Singapore   Sydney

Cover art/photo: Leslie Bakshi
Editor: Linda A. Sullivan
Developmental Editor: Kevin M. Davis
Production Editor: Lucinda Ann Peck
Art Coordinator: Raydelle M. Clement
Photo Editor: Anne Vega
Cover Designer: Robert Vega
Production Buyer: Patricia A. Tonneman

This book was set in New Aster by Carlisle
Communications, Ltd., and was printed and
bound by Arcata Graphics/Halliday. The cover
was printed by Lehigh Press, Inc.

Macmillan Publishing Company
866 Third Avenue
New York, NY 10022

Macmillan Publishing Company is part of the
Maxwell Communication Group of Companies.

Maxwell Macmillan Canada, Inc.
1200 Eglinton Avenue East, Suite 200
Don Mills, Ontario M3C 3N1

**Library of Congress Cataloging-in-
Publication Data**
Rich, John Martin.
  Foundations of education : perspectives on
American education / John Martin Rich.
    p.   cm.
  Includes bibliographical references and index.
  ISBN 0-675-21265-0
  1. Education—United States.   I. Title.
LB17.R49   1992   91-22397
370′.973 —dc20   CIP

Printing: 1   2   3   4   5   6   7   8   9

Year: 2   3   4   5

Photo Credits: pp. xxiv, 146, 391, 509, UPI
Bettmann Newsphotos; pp. 2, 5, 82, 88, 359,
574, Robert Finken; pp. 8, 62, 91, 132, 144, 225,
245, 260, 267, 281, 296, 308, 318, 335, 339, 370,
443, 474, 479, 528, 536, 558, Ulrike Welsch; pp.
26, 80, 152, 160, 161, The Bettmann Archive;
p. 34, Macmillan; p. 58, Jim West; p. 65,
Frances M. Roberts, p. 92, Jean Greenwald/
Macmillan; pp. 104, 419, Richard B. Levine; pp.
120, 127, 202, 212, 408, 410, 454, 490, 587, AP/
Wide World Photos; p. 238, George Aleman;
p. 256, Steve and Mary Skjold; p. 290, Stuart
Spates; pp. 293, 328, 431, 457, Gale Zucker;
p. 352, Charles S. Hawkins; p. 376, Trinity
Photos; p. 398, J. Wiebe/CSU-LA; p. 499, Red
Morgan/Time Magazine; p. 506, Christopher S.
Johnson/Stock Boston; p. 572, Courtesy of IBM;
p. 592, Skjold Photographs.

■ **P R E F A C E** ■

This text is an introduction to the foundations of education. Its central aim is two-fold: to provide students with current information and research about our schools and to help students learn to think critically about the process of education and their role as educators in that process. The text strives to provide students not simply a catalog of the basic information about the history, philosophy, and social context of education in our country, but seeks, by examining basic themes across the foundations, to help students see the fundamental forces and concepts that have shaped our educational system and our ideas about what education is and should be. The central question that the text encourages students to ask and helps them explore throughout is what does or will this information I am reading mean to me as an educator. It is hoped that by offering students a thematic, integrated picture of the foundations and by assisting them to think critically about schooling and the education process that they will better retain and use this information to reflect on and understand what they do as professionals in their classrooms and school systems.

ENCOURAGING CRITICAL THINKING AND REFLECTIVE TEACHING ■

You will find a lot of questions in this text. In fact, some chapter sections are devoted to trying to answer with the student a single, specific question. For example, "Is Teaching a Profession?" in Chapter 2 and "Is Teaching Possible?" in Chapter 6. Certain basic questions about education informed the writing of much of this text, questions like: What is education? What is teaching? What are the aims (both professed and actual) of education in our country? Is a certain kind of knowledge of greater worth than another kind? These and other questions are usually posed directly in the text. Doing so accomplishes two purposes. First, it encourages students to enter into the text. Everyone who wants to be a teacher has some conception of what education and teaching are. Second, trying to answer such questions provides a meaningful framework within which to present and discuss what others have thought and/or what research has shown. Moreover, because students at times have, at least in a preliminary way, accessed their own thoughts about a topic or issue, students have an initial frame of reference from which to compare and contrast (i.e., think about) the information being presented. Not only does this encourage students to think along with the text, it also increases the chances that they will remember what they read.

■ SPECIAL FEATURES

Pause to Reflect

Throughout the text, an effort is made to get students to synthesize what they have read, to tie the information being presented to their own experience, and to show the relevance of material to actual practice. One of the ways this is accomplished is through the use of a feature called "Pause to Reflect." (See pages vi–viii for a list of these.) In this feature, students are asked questions relating to the section of text they just read. These also provide excellent opportunities for class discussion and highlight some key educational issues confronting teachers today.

Educational Issues

Though educational issues are raised throughout the text and in the "Pause to Reflect" features, several important issues are also pulled out into "Educational Issue" boxes, where opposing views on an issue are presented for consideration and discussion. (A list of these is presented on pages viii–ix.)

Pedagogy

To help students focus on and understand critical information, the text of each chapter contains a brief overview, with a topic outline; margin notes; and bold-faced key terms. At the end of each chapter are the following pedagogical features: a detailed and integrative summary; key terms; discussion questions; learning activities; suggested readings; and notes. The book also contains a comprehensive glossary.

ACKNOWLEDGMENTS ■

Among the Merrill editors, I wish to thank Jeff Johnston for his interest in my undertaking the project, David K. Faherty for able assistance during the project's early stages, Linda Sullivan for her recent involvement and support, Kevin Davis for his time and meticulous attention given the project, Key Metts and Cindy Peck for their excellent editorial and production help, and Anne Vega for her photo research. I am especially grateful to Jana Holzmeier for her considerable skills, judgment, and patience in preparing the manuscript; and to Audrey for her support.

The recommendations and criticisms of a number of reviewers helped improve the manuscript and avoid oversights and errors. Their names follow: Robert H. Baldwin, Clarion University; Myra J. Baughman, Pacific Lutheran University; Janet Boyle, University of Wisconsin, Stevens Point; JoAnne Buggey, University of Minnesota; Paul R. Burden, Kansas State University; Grace M. Burton, University of North Carolina—Wilmington; Alden L. Carlson, State University of New York; Duane Christian, Texas Tech University; Naomi T. Crumley, Delaware State College; Russell Doll, University of Missouri—Kansas City; Joseph L. DeVitis, State University of New York at Binghamton; Dorothy Huenecke, Georgia State University; Michael L. Jacobs, University of Northern Colorado; John H. Jensen, Boise State University; Michael H. Jessup, Towson State University; Tony W. Johnson, University of Texas at San Antonio; Robert W. Kinderman, Kurtztown University; Marcella L. Kysilka, University of Central Florida; A.G. Larkins, The University of Georgia; William Matthias, Southern Illinois University at Carbondale; John W. McClure, University of Iowa; Max H. McCullough, Southwest Missouri State (Professor Emeritus); Joseph W. Newman, University of South Alabama; Franklin Parker, Northern Arizona University; Marjorie P. Quimby, Ball State University; Leonard H. Roberts, Troy State University, Dothan; Robert C. Serow, North Carolina State University; Beverly D. Shaklee, Kent State University; Janice Streitmatter, University of Arizona; Joan Strouse, Portland State University; and Melinda Sysol, State University of New York, Fredonia.

■ SPECIAL FEATURES ■

■ BRIEF CONTENTS ■

■ C O N T E N T S ■

■ PART ONE

TEACHERS ∎

C areers in education have changed dramatically from those in the predominantly rural American schools of the nineteenth century to those in the large, complex educational systems of today's post-industrial society. The increased complexity of society has, in and of itself, necessitated many changes in the teacher's role and preparation. Helping to prepare individuals to function in and contribute to our complicated world is in some ways a different task than that faced by teachers a generation ago, to say nothing of 100 or 150 years ago. We will discuss these matters throughout this book. In this first section, we will look specifically at some of the career options available in education, describe some of the changing roles of teachers, and explore what it means to be a professional educator.

As in all professions, both internal and external rewards encourage people to enter education. We will look at some of these rewards. We also will discuss how being a professional educator involves much more than finding and holding a job in education. It entails not only competency in a number of areas but also a commitment to preserving the integrity of the education process. Finally, a teacher is in a position to greatly influence children's development and, as such, often is held to a higher standard of conduct and is granted less right to privacy than other members of a community. We will examine this challenge to personal freedom as well as challenges to academic freedom in the classroom. Both challenges are an integral part of this enterprise in which all of society has so high a stake—education.

CHAPTER 1

BECOMING A TEACHER ■

A LOOK AHEAD

The purpose of this chapter is to introduce you to the opportunities in teaching and to some of the other career choices available to professional educators. You will learn about:

- Some of the reasons teaching is chosen as a career
- Sources of teacher satisfaction and frustration
- Supply and demand in teaching
- Public and nonpublic school systems
- Alternative careers for educators
- Change and continuity in teacher status in our society
- Middle-class values and how they affect education

American education today is in a state of great ferment. Controversies over increased taxes to support school-board issues, minority dissatisfaction with the educational system, and debate about teacher salaries and merit pay are often in the news. Widespread changes are sweeping education at the state level, colleges and universities are reforming teacher education, and the technological revolution will have an ever-increasing effect on how schools are run and students are taught. These are only a few of the many controversies and developments stimulating change and unrest.

As one would expect, in the midst of all this change, the role of the teacher and the status of teaching as a profession are also changing and being re-examined. Teaching in America today is far different from the teaching that took place in the one-room schoolhouse. It is also far different from some images of the teacher perpetrated in the media and in literature. Teaching is undergoing modification largely as a result of societal changes. And just as you witness our world changing, you may very possibly see teaching as a career transformed within your lifetime. Teaching has never been, and certainly is not now, a career for the timid or fainthearted; it is demanding and challenging, and calls for intelligence, flexibility, and resourcefulness.

■ TEACHER EXPECTATIONS AND FRUSTRATIONS

Some students choose a teaching career because they genuinely like children and find it a joy to help them grow and realize their potential. They find a sense of intrinsic satisfaction in working with the young, and external rewards—tenure, fringe benefits, and vacations—play little, if any, role in their career decisions. Among secondary-education majors in particular, a fascination with the subject they plan to teach also can be a motivating factor, because they can continue studying the subject and are eager to convey their enthusiasm for it to their students. A very real reward for these teachers is seeing a student come to share the intellectual excitement the teachers themselves have found.

> Teachers communicate knowledge to students and facilitate learning. Wanting to be involved in this exciting process and wanting to work with young people are two key motivations for becoming a teacher.

Some students enter teaching to have a significant influence on the lives of others. Teaching is one of only a few occupations that offer such an opportunity. As Henry Adams said: "A teacher affects eternity; he can never tell where his influence stops."[1] The potential for teachers to influence the lives of their students is real, even though some teachers exert negative rather than positive influences and others have only a limited or transitory effect. Influential teachers can encourage able students to attend college, affect students' career choices, and instill desirable character traits and attitudes that can last throughout a student's lifetime.

> Effective teachers are also learners.

Teaching also provides opportunities for growth, both professionally and personally. In fact, the very nature of the profession demands growth. To maintain effectiveness as a teacher one must continually read, study, prepare, and gain vital new experiences. The challenge of young minds stimulates growth.

Considering today's relative lack of job security in the corporate world, it is understandable that some people might choose teaching for

Influential teachers manifest understanding and effective communication skills.

its relatively high degree of job security. Some states have **tenure** provisions whereby teachers, after successfully completing a probationary period, are automatically awarded continuing contracts. Teachers granted tenure then are considered permanent members of the school faculty and can be dismissed only for such serious offenses as immorality, incompetence, gross insubordination, unprofessional conduct, or for economic reasons.

Some students may choose a teaching career to avoid other features of the business world. If, however, they seek to escape from competition and bureaucracy (two features frequently attributed to business), they may be surprised at the extent to which these characteristics are also found in teaching.

Some people take a teaching position to supplement the salary of their spouses or to enable their family to live at a higher standard of living. In the past, when the qualifications for teaching were lower, people often taught for a few years to earn enough money for law or medical school, or until the right business opportunity came along.

Teaching also offers extrinsic rewards, not the least of which is job security.

The elevation of teacher certification standards, along with many social and economic changes, has caused this practice to decrease.

Generous summer and holiday vacations are another attraction. Having summers off gives teachers the time to continue formal studies, take inservice courses, travel, rest and relax, or catch up on chores put aside during the school year. Some teachers may take other jobs during the summers.

Unfortunately, some people who delight in controlling and exercising authority over others (often in the name of helping them) make their way into education. They covet a sense of power—perhaps because they themselves have often felt powerless. Whatever the motive behind their need for control, they see teaching as a quick way to gain power over others. They may be surprised to learn that teachers do not have much power and probably would be better off seeking a career that promises political or economic power.

■ PAUSE TO REFLECT
Examining Your Motives

- Why do you want to be a teacher? Which of the reasons presented here appeal to you? Why?
- Do you have reasons for entering the field other than those listed? What are they?
- How might your motives affect the way you teach and interact with your students?

In a survey of 22,000 teachers from every state, the Carnegie Foundation for the Advancement of Teaching asked teachers how satisfied they were in their job. Seventy-seven percent responded that they were satisfied; 23 percent said they were not.[2] But when questioned about their current career plans, of the 23 percent who expressed dissatisfaction, only 7 percent said they planned to leave as soon as possible. Six percent indicated that they might take some time off, and the remaining 10 percent were undecided about their plans.[3] The percentage of teachers who said their teaching experience was "worse than expected" gave the following reasons:

- Parents are unwilling to get involved (56 percent).
- Teachers do not receive the respect due them in the community (52 percent).
- Opportunities for advancement are lacking (36 percent).[4]

A Gallup poll compared the reasons teachers gave for resigning and the reasons parents thought teachers leave the profession (see Table 1–1). In contrast to the results of the Carnegie Foundation poll, teachers in the Gallup poll listed low teacher salaries, discipline problems, and the low status of teaching as the three most prominent reasons for their resigning. The seeming discrepancies between the results of the Carnegie study of disappointed teacher expectations

Factors outside the classroom can contribute to teacher frustration.

TABLE 1–1 Teacher opinion versus public opinion

The public, surveyed in 1982, differed from the teachers about why teachers leave the profession. Only 52 percent of the public mentioned low teacher salaries as one of the main reasons why teachers leave; 63 percent cited discipline as one of the main factors.

Paradoxically, the public was much more likely than teachers to see parents' lack of interest in their children's progress as a reason for teachers to leave the profession. Twenty-five percent of the public mentioned this reason, but only 11 percent of teachers do. Similarly, 37 percent of the public said that lack of support from parents is one of the factors causing teachers to leave the profession, whereas only 21 percent of teachers cite this as a reason.

Reasons for Leaving	All Teachers (Percent)	U.S. Public (1982) (Percent)
Low teacher salaries	87	52
Discipline problems in schools	46	63
Low standing of teaching as a profession	38	15
Students are unmotivated, uninterested in school	37	37
Lack of public financial support for education	26	24
Parents don't support the teachers	21	37
Outstanding teacher performance goes unrewarded	20	13
Difficulty of advancement	19	14
Parents are not interested in children's progress	11	25

Figures add to more than 100 percent because of multiple answers.

Source: Reprinted by permission of Alec Gallup, "The Gallup Poll of Teachers' Attitudes Toward the Public Schools," *Phi Delta Kappan* 66 (October 1984): p. 102.

and the Gallup poll on why teachers leave teaching can be explained, however. Although the problems identified by teachers as central sources of their frustration can certainly impair teacher effectiveness, these problems seem not to be primary reasons for their changing careers.

Some of the same teacher concerns have been revealed in other surveys. In a study by the Educational Research Service, for example, the biggest problems cited by teachers were salary concerns, paperwork, and lack of parental support—almost all problems that seem to be rooted in the value our society places on education and educators.

Working cooperatively with others on stimulating intellectual tasks makes teaching fulfilling.

Despite numerous shortcomings and frustrations, many educators find their work fulfilling. Teachers invest so much of their lives in their careers that they generally have high expectations from their work in terms of rewards and personal fulfillment. As psychologist Abraham Maslow has noted, self-actualizing persons view productive work as a cornerstone of their lives. Work is a part of the self, part of one's definition of self. Maslow believes that the path to happiness is, in part, a commitment to an important job and worthwhile work.[5] Erich Fromm took a similar position in his studies of human motivation, stating that the basic satisfactions of life are love and productive work.[6]

> Seeing your work as an educator as important and productive is central to your happiness in a career in education.

Whenever we have able people with good psychological health who can find in their work creative opportunities for personal expression, achievement, and advancement, and whenever we have educational leaders who are self-actualizing and take pleasure in the growth of other people, then good educational systems will develop and thrive. Teachers are the cornerstones of these educational systems. The great need today extends even beyond the improvement of school systems and teacher education programs. The need is to change the very image of teaching, and the problem is how to attract more capable people to educational careers.

■ PAUSE TO REFLECT

Your Motives, Expectations, and Possible Frustrations

- Look at the teacher responses in Table 1–1 and try to imagine how some of these problems might affect the rewards you hope to gain as an educator.

- If you are entering education, in part, to help children achieve their potential, how would a lack of parental interest affect your ability to reach your goal and enjoy the subsequent satisfaction?

- How would a lack of discipline and motivation among the students affect your attitude toward teaching?

> Achieving the goals that motivate you to enter education will bring satisfaction. Obstacles to your fully realizing those goals will be sources of frustration.

OPPORTUNITIES IN TEACHING ■

As in almost all situations, **supply and demand** directly affect the teaching opportunities you will find across the country. The demand for teachers depends on enrollment, changes in pupil/teacher ratios, and teacher turnover, including retirement. Higher birth rates after World War II rapidly increased elementary-school enrollment, bring-

> Changes in enrollments directly affect the demand for teachers.

ing about a shortage of teachers and school buildings from 1953 to the late 1960s. Overcrowded classrooms, double sessions in some metropolitan areas, and the employment of many teachers on emergency certificates were some of the problems resulting from the bulge in enrollments. Efforts to meet the shortage included recruiting more students for teaching careers, encouraging former teachers to return to the classroom, and encouraging those who had a bachelor's degree in an area other than teaching to begin teaching before completing the courses needed for certification.

The number of college graduates who were prepared to teach rose rapidly during the 1960s. Although many of these graduates chose not to enter teaching, by 1970, the teacher supply exceeded demand at the secondary level by 33,488 and by 16,137 at the elementary level.[7] More students during the 1950s and 1960s chose teaching careers at the secondary level than at the elementary level.

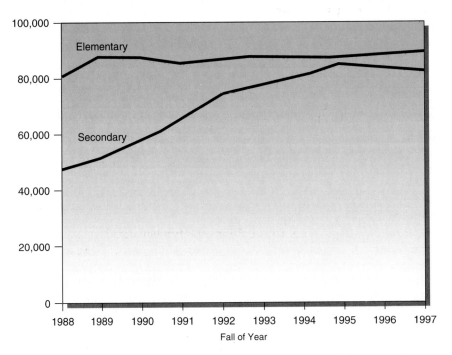

Source: National Center for Education Statistics, *The Condition of Education: Elementary and Secondary Education,* vol. 1 (Washington, DC: U.S. Department of Education, Office of Educational Research and Improvement, 1988), 44. Reprinted by permission.

FIGURE 1–1 Projected demand for new hiring of teachers, by level: Fall 1988–1997

While supply generally outstripped demand during the 1970s and into the 1980s, the picture today has changed. Demand for new teachers is expected to increase by 35 percent in the first half of this decade, peaking in 1995. Most of the increase will result from an increase in hiring at the secondary level of almost 80 percent between 1988 and 1995. Larger enrollments contributed to the hiring of more elementary teachers in the late 1980s. But elementary enrollments and, subsequently, hirings will level off slightly in the 1990s, with a projected increase in hiring of 11 percent during the decade (see Figure 1–1).

Though the general demand for teachers is rising, some of you will find it easier to get a job than others. A successful job hunt depends on several factors: where you live, what you are trained to teach, and the type of school in which you want to teach. Regional demand for teachers may differ. As some areas in the South and West grow in population, so will the demand for teachers. Obviously, the reverse is true as well: if a region loses a significant portion of its population, its demand for teachers drops. Teaching positions are likely to be more difficult to come by in a community viewed as more attractive than those surrounding it. This is also true in school districts that offer higher salaries and greater fringe benefits.

The relative demand by teaching field varies considerably across regions of the country (see Table 1–2). Demand is greatest for mathematics, some of the sciences, and some areas of special education. Some of these graduates are often able to find better-paying jobs in business and industry. The greatest teacher surplus is in physical education. If you are strongly interested in teaching in a surplus field, you might need to be willing to live in any part of the country and might have little control over the type and size of the community in which you will teach. To prevent this, you might consider a double major or, at least, a minor in a field that is in demand.

Finding and selecting a position are further complicated by the type of school and area in which you want to teach. In general, your choices of types of schools include public schools and nonpublic schools (which include parochial, or church-related, schools and secular private schools). To varying degrees, each can be found in several settings—rural communities, small cities, and metropolitan and suburban areas.

Competition from the business world for graduates in mathematics and science affects teacher supply in those fields.

Public Schools

Public schools offer the most consistent, varied choice of teaching jobs. If you opt to teach in the public schools, you are guaranteed availability of positions in your field. Some of you may choose to return to the community in which you grew up or to a similar one.

TABLE 1–2 Teacher supply and demand by field and region

Regions are coded: Alaska, Hawaii; **1** - Northwest; **2** - West; **3** - Rocky Mountain; **4** - Great Plains/Midwest; **5** - South Central; **6** - Southeast; **7** - Great Lakes; **8** - Middle Atlantic; **9** - Northeast. Alaska and Hawaii are not included in the national totals for years prior to 1990.
5 = Considerable shortage; 4 = Some Shortage; 3 = Balanced; 2 = Some Surplus; 1 = Considerable Surplus

Field	Alaska	Hawaii	1	2	3	4	5	6	7	8	9	National 1990
Agriculture	2.00	4.00	3.50	3.00	2.75	2.77	2.00	2.77	3.54	4.00	—	3.03
Art	2.00	1.00	1.25	2.28	2.00	2.52	2.05	2.48	2.18	2.00	1.86	1.96
Bilingual Education	4.00	4.00	4.13	4.79	4.75	4.36	4.76	4.00	4.50	4.53	4.00	4.35
Business	3.00	4.00	2.75	2.46	2.60	2.62	2.44	4.05	2.51	3.30	4.00	3.07
Computer Science	4.00	4.00	3.66	3.45	4.00	3.83	3.66	4.16	3.73	3.56	4.17	3.84
Counselor—Elementary	5.00	5.00	4.00	3.00	3.57	3.77	3.31	3.50	3.23	3.16	2.89	3.67
Counselor—Secondary	5.00	5.00	4.00	3.00	3.57	3.70	3.26	3.10	3.08	3.16	2.30	3.56
Data Processing	—	—	3.25	3.66	3.50	3.00	3.62	3.66	3.58	3.83	4.00	3.57
Driver Education	1.00	—	3.00	3.00	3.00	2.14	2.43	2.25	2.88	3.00	3.00	2.57
Elementary—Primary	5.00	2.00	3.14	3.26	2.57	2.16	3.40	3.48	1.80	2.26	2.08	2.83
Elementary—Intermediate	5.00	2.00	3.14	3.20	2.77	2.22	3.25	3.38	1.84	2.13	2.00	2.81
English	5.00	5.00	3.37	3.00	3.10	2.80	2.90	3.07	2.51	2.84	2.45	3.28
English as a Second Lang.	4.00	4.00	3.16	4.44	4.80	4.23	4.00	3.73	3.89	4.18	3.66	4.00
Health Education	1.00	4.00	1.28	1.83	1.71	1.78	1.86	2.36	1.69	1.94	2.83	2.02
Home Economics	4.00	4.00	1.66	2.30	2.00	2.23	2.55	3.05	2.04	2.75	3.00	2.69
Industrial Arts	4.00	5.00	3.00	3.00	2.16	2.41	3.33	3.09	3.00	3.20	3.33	3.23
Journalism	1.00	—	2.25	3.00	2.50	3.22	2.43	3.14	2.74	3.33	3.00	2.66
Language, Modern—French	4.00	3.00	2.71	3.00	3.20	3.22	3.33	4.04	3.10	3.24	2.57	3.22
Language, Modern—German	3.00	3.00	2.57	3.16	3.00	3.19	3.46	4.28	3.06	3.15	2.50	3.12
Language, Modern—Spanish	4.00	3.00	3.57	3.66	4.25	3.55	3.53	4.04	3.59	3.37	4.86	3.76
Language—Other	4.00	3.00	3.00	3.28	3.75	3.40	3.62	3.64	3.71	3.16	3.00	3.41
Library Science	5.00	5.00	3.20	4.14	3.00	3.78	3.70	3.35	3.89	3.33	3.00	3.76
Mathematics	4.00	5.00	3.37	4.35	3.37	3.61	4.10	4.21	3.71	3.71	3.54	3.91
Music—Instrumental	5.00	2.00	3.88	3.25	3.43	3.57	3.16	3.15	2.79	2.52	2.75	3.23
Music—Vocal	5.00	2.00	4.12	3.06	3.00	3.57	2.55	2.86	2.75	2.65	2.75	3.12

Others among you will prefer a school system different from the one of your childhood. You will no doubt want to consider the conditions in public schools in the various types of communities.

Life style and teaching environment should be part of your decision in choosing where you want to teach.

Rural Schools. An obvious advantage to teaching in a rural area is the less complicated life style and the ease of getting to know one's colleagues and neighbors. Some possible disadvantages can be a lack of advanced course offerings at the secondary level, an inadequate tax base to provide the school with the resources it needs, inadequate shopping, insufficient cultural experiences, and a lack of privacy.

TABLE 1–2 *(continued)*

Regions are coded: Alaska, Hawaii; **1** - Northwest; **2** - West; **3** - Rocky Mountain; **4** - Great Plains/Midwest; **5** - South Central; **6** - Southeast; **7** - Great Lakes; **8** - Middle Atlantic; **9** - Northeast. Alaska and Hawaii are not included in the national totals for years prior to 1990.
5 = Considerable shortage; 4 = Some Shortage; 3 = Balanced; 2 = Some Surplus; 1 = Considerable Surplus

Field	Alaska	Hawaii	Region 1	2	3	4	5	6	7	8	9	National 1990
Physical Education	2.00	1.00	1.43	2.27	1.43	1.41	1.94	2.05	1.56	1.70	2.14	1.72
Psychologist (School)	5.00	4.00	4.00	3.77	4.16	3.66	3.63	3.16	3.70	3.93	3.40	3.85
Science—Biology	4.00	2.00	2.75	3.60	2.66	3.12	3.60	3.78	3.29	3.13	3.00	3.17
Science—Chemistry	4.00	4.00	3.37	3.66	3.66	3.70	3.80	3.72	3.74	2.97	3.20	3.62
Science—Earth	2.00	3.00	3.12	3.60	2.62	3.24	3.68	3.81	3.20	3.25	3.14	3.15
Science—General	4.00	3.00	3.11	3.46	2.50	3.18	3.44	3.71	3.32	3.17	3.00	3.26
Science—Physics	4.00	4.00	3.71	4.10	3.70	3.95	4.05	4.37	3.77	3.89	3.66	3.93
Science—Other Areas	3.00	4.00	3.25	3.44	2.50	3.23	3.66	3.86	3.39	3.60	3.00	3.36
Social Sciences	2.00	1.00	1.43	3.26	1.44	1.54	2.17	2.08	1.73	2.03	2.10	1.89
Social Worker (School)	4.00	3.00	2.83	3.33	3.50	2.82	2.50	3.08	2.90	2.00	3.00	2.99
Speech	1.00	3.00	2.87	2.36	3.00	2.78	2.58	3.21	2.64	3.10	4.00	2.78
Special Ed—Deaf	5.00	4.00	4.20	4.62	4.80	4.38	4.71	4.38	3.85	3.50	4.33	4.34
Special Ed—ED/BD	5.00	4.00	4.57	4.69	4.80	4.62	4.54	4.61	4.27	4.10	3.86	4.46
Special Ed—Gifted	2.00	4.00	3.86	3.66	4.00	4.17	4.23	4.33	3.73	3.93	3.50	3.76
Special Ed—LD	5.00	5.00	4.66	4.33	4.66	4.43	4.46	4.54	4.23	4.05	4.00	4.49
Special Ed—Mental Hand.	5.00	5.00	4.75	4.35	4.66	4.19	4.63	4.52	4.10	4.10	4.00	4.48
Special Ed—Multi Hand.	5.00	4.00	4.75	4.50	4.83	4.25	4.54	4.47	3.88	4.05	4.00	4.39
Special Ed—Reading	5.00	3.00	4.00	3.13	3.66	3.19	3.93	3.77	3.27	3.32	2.80	3.55
Special Ed—Other	—	—	4.33	3.60	4.66	3.87	4.60	4.20	3.61	4.00	3.00	3.98
Speech Path./Audio.	5.00	5.00	4.60	3.76	5.00	4.47	4.33	4.00	4.18	4.21	4.00	4.41
COMPOSITE	3.74	3.54	3.30	3.42	3.35	3.28	3.42	3.57	3.19	3.25	3.20	3.39

Source: Reprinted by permission of the Association for College and University Staffing, *Relative Demand By Teaching Area and Year, Continental United States*, "Teacher Supply and Demand in the United States," ASCUS Research Report, Evanston, IL, 1990, p. 2.

Small-city Schools. In contrast, small-city schools (in communities of less than 100,000 people), while perhaps not offering the sense of community often found in rural settings, will be less likely to have the disadvantages of life in a rural area. Though small-city communities do not offer the range and diversity of cultural and educational opportunities that metropolitan areas do, life tends to be freer of the big-city stresses.

Metropolitan Schools. Many metropolitan inner-city schools have a preponderance of minority students and students from lower socioeconomic backgrounds. Teachers in these schools often are more likely to encounter students with learning, emotional, social, and health problems that require the services of skilled, experienced, caring teachers and an adequate supporting staff. Inner-city schools also may lack an adequate tax base, making the teachers' and students' tasks more difficult because of a lack of resources.

Suburban Schools. Suburban schools, which draw their students mainly from upper-middle-class backgrounds, usually provide larger per-pupil expenditures than inner-city schools. Also, in general, students enjoy more ample learning opportunities in the home and, therefore, tend to come to school better prepared for an academic curriculum. Although living in a metropolitan area offers more commercial, educational, and cultural opportunities than other communities, it has the drawbacks of greater congestion, pollution, crime, and isolation.

Nonpublic Schools

(Eldgridge, 1980)

Nonpublic or "independent" schools are considered private if they are not run by a government agency, even if they are partially supported by public taxes. Nonpublic schools comprise about 18 percent of the total number of elementary and secondary schools in the United States. They also enroll about 10 percent of all the students at these two levels, produce about 10 percent of all high-school graduates, and employ 11 percent of all elementary and secondary teachers. The largest enrollment in **parochial schools,** in order, are Catholic, Lutheran, Seventh day Adventist, Baptist, Jewish, and Episcopal. The number of Evangelical and Fundamentalist Christian schools has grown in recent years, while Catholic-school enrollment has declined from a high of 87 percent of all nonpublic schools in 1966 to 60 percent. Enrollments in **private secular schools** increased from 5 percent to 16 percent during the same period. *(Private Schools, 1989)*

Parents send their children to nonpublic schools for academic, religious, or social reasons. They might have doubts about the efficacy of public schools and want to provide their children with a more substantive academic education. They might want their children to receive religious education not available in public schools. Or they might want their children to interact with others of certain social backgrounds.

Nonpublic schools generally are smaller than public schools. Secular private schools, in particular, vary widely. Some have spacious campuses and large endowments; others assemble in abandoned storefronts or basements and struggle to make ends meet. Some are strict college preparatory schools; others emphasize student freedom and progressive ideas. Some of the better-funded schools have extensive extracurricular programs, advanced placement courses, and a variety of experimental courses. *(Rich, 1992)*

> Students who attend nonpublic schools tend to be more homogenous than those of some public schools.

EDUCATIONAL ISSUE 1–1

Is public-school teaching preferable to nonpublic school teaching?

Yes	No
1. One has an opportunity to teach a more diverse group of students in public schools.	1. Some of the diversity is undesirable because of learning problems; there is usually more homogeneity in nonpublic schools and fewer acute learning problems.
2. The number of job openings is greater in public schools.	2. Nonpublic schools are diverse in purposes and therefore may have better opportunities and expectations than public schools.
3. Salary levels are usually higher in public schools.	3. Most public schools have larger class size than nonpublic schools.
4. One's religion is not a factor in determining public-school employment.	4. Some applicants may prefer to teach in a school affiliated with their religious denomination; other nonpublic schools are nondenominational.
5. Fringe benefits for teachers are generally better in public schools.	5. Fringe benefits do not outweigh smaller classes, fewer bureaucratic regulations, and generally fewer discipline problems.
6. Certification generally is required for public-school employment, resulting in a better teaching staff.	6. Nonpublic schools are less restricted by certification requirements and other state regulations, which provide more opportunities for nontraditional applicants.

TABLE 1-3 Estimated average annual salary of teachers in public elementary and secondary schools, by State: 1969–70 to 1987–88

State	Current dollars						Constant 1987–88 dollars[1]					Percent change 1979–80 to 1987–88 in constant dollars
	1969–70	1979–80	1983–84	1985–86	1986–87[2]	1987–88	1969–70	1979–80	1983–84	1985–86	1986–87	
1	2	3	4	5	6	7	8	9	10	11	12	13
United States	$ 8,626	$15,970	$21,921	$25,198	$26,556	$28,044	$26,453	$23,830	$24,949	$26,825	$27,656	15.0
Alabama	6,818	13,060	17,682	23,090	23,200	23,320	20,908	19,488	20,124	24,581	24,161	16.4
Alaska	10,560	27,210	37,807	39,115	39,769	40,424	32,384	40,602	43,029	41,640	41,417	–0.4
Arizona	8,711	15,054	21,642	24,680	25,972	27,388	26,713	22,463	24,631	26,273	27,048	18.0
Arkansas	6,307	12,299	16,929	19,519	19,904	20,340	19,341	18,352	19,267	20,779	20,729	9.8
California	10,315	18,020	24,843	29,130	31,219	33,159	31,632	26,889	28,274	31,011	32,513	18.9
Colorado	7,761	16,205	23,276	25,892	27,387	28,651	23,800	24,181	26,491	27,564	28,522	15.6
Connecticut	9,262	16,229	22,627	26,610	28,902	33,487	28,403	24,217	25,752	28,328	30,100	27.7
Delaware	9,015	16,148	20,934	24,624	27,467	29,575	27,646	24,096	23,826	26,214	28,605	18.5
District of Columbia	10,285	22,190	28,667	33,211	33,797	34,705	31,540	33,111	32,627	35,355	35,197	4.6
Florida	8,412	14,149	19,497	22,250	23,833	25,198	25,797	21,113	22,190	23,686	24,821	16.2
Georgia	7,276	13,853	18,630	23,046	24,200	26,177	22,313	20,671	21,203	24,534	25,203	21.0
Hawaii	9,453	19,920	24,357	25,845	26,815	28,785	28,989	29,724	27,721	27,513	27,926	–3.3
Idaho	6,890	13,611	17,985	20,969	21,480	22,242	21,129	20,310	20,469	22,323	22,370	8.7
Illinois	9,569	17,601	24,191	26,897	28,238	29,663	29,345	26,264	27,532	28,633	29,408	11.5
Indiana	8,833	15,599	21,538	24,325	25,581	27,386	27,088	23,276	24,513	25,895	26,641	15.0
Iowa	8,355	15,203	20,149	21,690	22,615	24,867	25,622	22,686	22,932	23,090	23,552	8.8
Kansas	7,612	13,690	19,411	22,644	23,459	24,647	23,343	20,428	22,092	24,106	24,431	17.1
Kentucky	6,953	14,520	19,660	20,948	22,476	24,274	21,322	21,666	22,373	22,300	23,407	10.7
Louisiana	7,028	13,760	18,400	20,303	21,196	21,209	21,552	20,532	20,942	21,614	22,074	3.2
Maine	7,572	13,071	17,328	19,583	21,257	23,425	23,221	19,504	19,721	20,847	22,138	16.7
Maryland	9,383	17,558	23,870	26,800	28,893	30,933	28,774	26,200	27,167	28,530	30,090	15.3
Massachusetts	8,764	17,253	22,958	26,800	28,410	30,019	26,876	25,744	26,129	28,530	29,587	14.2
Michigan	9,826	19,663	27,104	30,067	31,500	32,926	30,133	29,341	30,848	32,008	32,805	10.9

State												
Minnesota	8,658	15,912	24,350	27,360	28,340	29,900	26,551	23,743	27,713	29,126	29,514	20.6
Mississippi	5,798	11,850	15,812	18,472	19,447	20,669	17,780	17,682	17,996	19,665	20,253	14.5
Missouri	7,799	13,682	19,269	21,945	23,435	24,703	23,917	20,416	21,931	23,362	24,406	17.4
Montana	7,606	14,537	20,690	22,482	23,206	23,798	23,325	21,692	23,548	23,933	24,168	8.9
Nebraska	7,375	13,516	18,785	20,939	21,834	23,246	22,616	20,168	21,380	22,291	22,739	13.2
Nevada	9,215	16,295	22,360	25,610	26,960	27,600	28,259	24,315	25,449	27,263	28,077	11.9
New Hampshire	7,771	13,017	17,376	20,263	21,869	24,091	23,831	19,424	19,776	21,571	22,775	19.4
New Jersey	9,130	17,161	23,264	27,170	28,718	30,720	27,998	25,607	26,477	28,924	29,908	16.6
New Mexico	7,796	14,887	20,571	21,817	23,850	24,351	23,907	22,214	23,412	23,225	24,838	8.8
New York	10,336	19,812	27,319	30,490	32,000	34,500	31,697	29,563	31,092	32,458	33,316	14.3
North Carolina	7,494	14,117	18,311	22,340	23,879	24,900	22,981	21,065	20,840	23,782	24,868	15.4
North Dakota	6,696	13,263	19,260	20,816	21,284	21,660	20,534	19,791	21,920	22,160	22,166	8.6
Ohio	8,300	15,269	21,290	24,518	26,288	27,606	25,453	22,784	24,231	26,101	27,377	17.5
Oklahoma	6,882	13,107	18,630	21,419	21,468	22,006	21,105	19,558	21,203	22,802	22,358	11.1
Oregon	8,818	16,266	23,155	25,660	26,690	28,060	27,042	24,272	26,353	27,317	27,796	13.5
Pennsylvania	8,858	16,515	22,703	25,853	27,422	29,174	27,164	24,643	25,839	27,522	28,558	15.5
Rhode Island	8,776	18,002	25,337	29,470	31,079	32,858	26,913	26,882	28,837	31,373	32,367	18.2
South Carolina	6,927	13,063	17,384	21,595	23,201	24,241	21,243	19,492	19,785	22,989	24,162	19.6
South Dakota	6,403	12,348	16,480	18,095	18,781	19,750	19,636	18,425	18,756	19,263	19,559	6.7
Tennessee	7,050	13,972	17,910	21,384	22,627	23,785	21,620	20,849	20,384	22,765	23,565	12.3
Texas	7,255	14,132	20,170	24,463	24,903	25,655	22,248	21,087	22,956	26,042	25,935	17.8
Utah	7,644	14,909	20,007	22,603	23,035	22,621	23,441	22,247	22,771	24,062	23,989	1.7
Vermont	7,968	12,484	17,606	20,796	21,835	23,397	24,435	18,628	20,038	22,139	22,740	20.4
Virginia	8,070	14,060	19,676	23,095	25,039	27,436	24,748	20,980	22,394	24,586	26,077	23.5
Washington	9,225	18,820	24,365	26,209	27,285	28,116	28,290	28,083	27,730	27,901	28,416	0.1
West Virginia	7,650	13,710	17,489	20,627	21,446	21,736	23,460	20,458	19,905	21,959	22,335	5.9
Wisconsin	8,963	16,006	22,811	26,347	27,815	28,998	27,486	23,884	25,962	28,048	28,968	17.6
Wyoming	8,232	16,012	25,197	27,224	28,103	27,260	25,245	23,893	28,677	28,982	29,267	12.4

[1]Based on the Consumer Price Index, prepared by the Bureau of Labor Statistics, U.S. Department of Labor. Price index does not account for different rates of change in the cost of living among States. [2]Data revised from previously published figures.

Source: Reprinted by permission of the National Education Association, *Estimates of School Statistics;* and unpublished data. (Latest edition 1987–88. Copyright © 1988 by the National Education Association. All rights reserved.) (This table was prepared December 1988.)

One of the best advantages of teaching in nonpublic schools is the generally lower ratio of teachers to pupils. Also, some of the sources of teacher frustration we discussed earlier in the chapter seem to be less acute in nonpublic schools than in public schools. Parents tend to be more actively involved in nonpublic schools, discipline problems are fewer, greater emphasis can be given to academic programs, and there are fewer bureaucratic regulations.[10] On the other hand, teacher salaries usually are about 40 percent lower than in public schools, and tenure and retirement provisions may be nonexistent (see Table 1–3). Some nonpublic schools lack sufficient financial support, and classroom materials can be scarce. Teachers also do not have an opportunity to work with students from a wide range of backgrounds. Moreover, some prospective teachers may object to certain church-affiliated schools because of their religious restrictions, censorship, or indoctrination.

■ **PAUSE TO REFLECT**
Choosing a School Environment

- What values might guide you to teach in a public school? In a private school?
- If the opportunity to teach a diverse group of students appeals to you, try to explain why.
- Do you think the compulsory nature of public schools has anything to do with any of the differences between public and private schools? If so, which differences?

■ ALTERNATIVE EDUCATIONAL CAREERS

Several options other than teaching exist for those interested in a career in education. Some of these careers usually require two or more years of successful teaching, while others require no experience in the classroom.

Administration

In addition to a superintendent and several principals, large school systems often have a director of business affairs, personnel director, curriculum director, public relations director, coordinators of elementary and secondary education, and a superintendent of buildings and grounds. In our brief overview of administrative careers, we will concentrate on the four most common positions: superintendent, assistant superintendent, principal, and assistant principal.

Superintendent. The superintendent, who is appointed by the school board and serves at its discretion, is the chief educational officer of the school district. Responsibilities include leading and directing the total instructional program, recruiting and developing quality personnel, maintaining effective community relations, and developing and managing the budget and the district's physical facilities.

Superintendents' salaries are usually two to three times higher than the highest paid full-time classroom teacher in the district. In major metropolitan areas, the superintendent's salary may exceed that of the mayor's. The average superintendent salary in 1989 was $71,190; the average classroom teacher salary was $29,608.[11]

Before you become too eager to become a superintendent, however, let us consider some other aspects of the position. The superintendent has a longer work day, less time off in the summer, and more varied pressures than teachers. Also, the superintendent is non-tenured and serves at the behest of the school board. Appointment may be for only one year, after which the board decides whether to renew the appointment. Or, the superintendent may be given a term contract for as much as three years. The superintendent can be discharged when the contract expires (or earlier, in some circumstances, if the salary for the remainder of the contract period is paid). Even though one may have served successfully as superintendent for many years, one still can be dismissed by the board and not have redress to the legal security of tenure.

The path to becoming a superintendent is long, and the preparation will usually eliminate those unsuited for the work. Two years of graduate study are required in some states, and many superintendents have Ph.Ds. Most of today's superintendents have moved successfully through the ranks: first as a classroom teacher, then as a vice principal and principal, and later as an assistant superintendent. Since there is usually a surplus of candidates for these jobs, most aspirants will have to seek other administrative positions.

Most administrators begin their careers as teachers.

Assistant Superintendent. The position of assistant superintendent is usually a training ground for the superintendency and serves an important function in its own right. Those with successful administrative experience, often as principals, usually are prime candidates. Large systems have several assistant superintendents, each of whom has a special area of responsibility, such as public relations, business management, curriculum, or personnel administration. Some are assigned special duties by the superintendent.

Principal. The principal is in charge of the total program of a particular school and manages that school's affairs. The principal implements the policies of the central administration and promotes effective teaching and good morale among faculty. The principal's primary responsibilities include resolving faculty problems, dealing with students and parents, handling the budget, maintaining and improving physical facilities, and guiding the instructional program.

After serving for several years as a successful teacher and earning a master's degree in educational administration, an individual would have fulfilled the formal requirements for becoming a principal. However, those who aspire to be principals also need desirable personal qualities, the most important of which is leadership.

Assistant Principal. In middle and secondary schools, and often in large elementary schools, one can find the position of assistant principal or vice-principal. The principal delegates responsibilities to the assistant principal in areas such as curriculum, instructional materials, club programs, and discipline. This experience prepares the administrator for promotion to principal.

Special Services

Education offers many opportunities other than teaching to work with students outside the classroom.

Guidance and Counseling. The school counselor is part of a personnel services team that may include school psychologists, speech and hearing therapists, and, in large school systems, social workers. Guidance counselors provide a range of services from overseeing students' schedules to helping students cope with the problems of growing up. Much of their work involves helping students assess their abilities and career interests. School counselors do not practice psychotherapy. Students with serious personality disorders generally are evaluated by the school psychologist or an outside professional; counseling deals more with normal developmental problems and normal ranges of behavior. To be certified, the counselor is expected to have teaching experience and a master's degree in guidance and counseling. The counselor also needs maturity, emotional stability, self-understanding, and an interest in working with young people.

School Psychology. The job of school psychologist is a recently created position that is found less frequently in the schools than the job of guidance counselor. The role of the school psychologist is to assess the abilities, aptitudes, interests, and personalities of students, particularly those whose academic performance or behavior falls outside the range normally expected for their peer group. The school psychologist uses various standardized tests and techniques, and, when appropriate, confers with teachers and parents about how to solve any problems in a particular case. The school psychologist also maintains liaison with other service specialists and confers on problems of joint concern. The American Psychological Association requires a Ph.D. in counseling psychology, which includes an internship program in schools or related institutions. Qualities needed are maturity, high intelligence, a desire to work with young people, and an interest in applying psychology in school settings.

School Social Work. The school social worker works mostly with truant students, unmarried pregnant girls, students with alcoholic or drug-addicted parents, and students from broken homes where the rift in the home affects school achievement. The school social worker examines the student's home and immediate environment to determine possible causes of the student's social and emotional problems. He or she then works with parents, teachers, and the student to try to improve the situation. Most time is spent on casework and consultation. Each social worker is assigned a number of cases and consults, whenever appropriate, with those directly concerned with the student's welfare. The school social worker is expected to have a master's degree in social work. Needed for the position are many of the same attributes of the counselor, especially skill in interpersonal relations.

Speech Therapy. Children with speech or hearing difficulties are the most common among students who require special services in the schools. The importance of the speech therapist in schools has developed rapidly in recent years. Speech therapists diagnose speech handicaps, recommend remediation programs, encourage the assistance and support of other parties concerned with the child's welfare, and provide teachers with information so that they can recognize and refer children who might have speech or hearing problems to other health-care professionals. The therapist, in addition to working with more serious disabilities, may establish screening programs and set up activities to help correct minor speech and voice deviations. To become a speech therapist, one is usually expected to complete a master's degree in the field.

Other Educational Careers. Your effectiveness at work and the degree of satisfaction you get from your job hinges in part on making the right career choice. Consider your own abilities and interests, study the requirements of different occupations, and use the career and placement services available to you at your college. At the very least, you will get a sense of what some of the other members of an educational team do and be more aware of the resources available to you and your students. Other educational opportunities are listed in Table 1–4.

1. Media specialist	10. Education journalist
2. School librarian	11. Private consultant to schools
3. Curriculum consultant	
4. State Department of Education	12. Museum program developer
5. U.S. Department of Education	13. Writer or researcher in professional organizations
6. Textbook editor, writer, or curriculum-materials developer	14. Trainer in a corporation
7. Foundations researcher or writer	15. Patient educator in hospitals and clinics
8. Adult educator	
9. Education specialist or teacher in foreign countries	

TABLE 1–4 Other educational positions

■ THE CHANGING ROLES OF THE TEACHER

An understanding of the history of teaching can enhance understanding of current attitudes toward teachers. We also can appreciate the progress teaching has made after many years of struggle for recognition, we acknowledge that current teacher roles, while exhibiting some continuity with the past, have changed in important ways.

The Colonial Period

Colonial America was not a miniature twentieth century. The colonists brought with them the social consciousness of the mother country and established a highly stratified society of distinct social classes. This social structure was fairly rigid and allowed for less upward mobility than does today's society. In general, three social classes were found in most communities: an upper class of gentlemen; a middle class who owned some property; and a lower class consisting of slaves and indentured servants. Colonial society was not democratic. One's role or place in society was clear, and public expectations were usually unambiguous. Traditions of rank and privilege, while perhaps not as rigid as those in the mother country, were distinctly evident in social and economic life.

Teachers were expected to be loyal to the civil government, religiously orthodox, and morally acceptable.[12] England ruled the colonies, and teachers and other officials were expected to take an oath of loyalty to the mother country. In addition to faithfully supporting the civil government, the schoolmaster also was expected to practice the dominant religion of the particular colony in which he taught. The moral character of teachers was closely watched during colonial times. (As we will discuss later in this chapter, this close watch on teacher mores persists in American culture even to the present day.) Being a moral person usually meant not doing certain things, such as drinking or gambling. Morality was not necessarily based on or concerned with any positive conception of what a moral person did, such as loving one's neighbor, but only with what one did *not* do. The content of this moral code of prohibitions differed to some extent at various times and places. Yet, in general, teachers were held to a more orthodox and restrictive standard than other citizens of the community—with the exception of the clergy. Teachers accepted these restrictions partly because many of them tended to be people who would abide by such codes. "Few teachers," according to Howard K. Beale in his discussion of teaching in colonial times, "had ever thought of differing from colonial views. Many regarded themselves as guardians of correct thinking."[13]

> The chief qualifications for landing a teaching job in colonial America often had little to do with the ability to teach academics.

Teachers came from all three classes, so it is difficult to generalize about colonial teachers. However, we can say that a fair number of those who taught in colonial classrooms were not motivated principally by a desire to teach and to help students learn. Some saw teaching as a temporary job until something better came along. Indentured servants often used teaching as a means to buy their freedom. And unfortunately, some adventurers and misfits, taking to teaching as a last resort, made their way into colonial schoolhouses.

The status of teachers varied considerably from one colony to another. (A more detailed discussion of the differences among the colonies in education can be found in Chapter 5.) However, a general pattern in status and salary did exist. This pattern, with some changes over time, continues today. Within the field itself, the college teacher had the highest status, followed by the secondary teacher, and then the elementary teacher. The gulf in status between these groups was greater during colonial times than it is now. A number of college professors were also clergymen or physicians—two of the groups with the most prestige in colonial America. These men tended to be the most learned in the community and had the knowledge necessary to teach Latin and Greek. There were some famous teachers in the Latin grammar school (the high school of the day, which offered a classical curriculum). Teachers in the Latin schools generally had more prestige

> Teaching credentials were considered more important at the secondary and university levels than at the elementary level.

than those who taught in the English school—the more common incarnation of the high school after the American Revolution. (We will look at both Latin grammar schools and English schools in Chapter 5.) Elementary teachers, however, were frequently indentured servants or people who combined teaching with church duties, such as the organists, sextons, and gravediggers.

To determine the teacher's status in the society as a whole, we can begin by comparing the salaries of colonial teachers with those of other occupational groups. Most clergymen in New England were members of the upper class and received a salary two to three times that of the schoolmaster. Physicians and lawyers also usually fared better than teachers. The New England schoolmaster's salary was most similar to that received by skilled laborers such as carpenters and bricklayers. In the Southern colonies, the schoolmaster's salary was not as good as that of the skilled artisan, unless the schoolmaster also was a clergyman. Women teachers, whose salaries were considerably lower than those of men, are not included in these comparisons because their numbers were proportionately small.[14] Due to the scarcity of currency, teachers sometimes were paid in commodities and livestock, or were provided with a dwelling and a few acres of land.

Even today, teacher salaries are often lower than those of skilled laborers.

The Nineteenth Century

The preparation of teachers began to be standardized during the nineteenth century. Teachers became better qualified, and those who had little interest in educating children were less likely to make their way into teaching. Despite these changes, however, the social restrictions, salaries, and, in general, teachers' status changed very little.

The standardization of teacher preparation improved teacher quality but had little effect on the salaries and status of teachers.

Communities still closely watched teacher conduct outside of school and held teachers to a code of prohibitions not imposed, at least to the same degree, on most other community members. A teacher could be fired for engaging in conduct the community deemed either offensive to public tastes or, more often, as setting a bad example for youth. The use of tobacco and liquor was usually forbidden; drinking almost always was grounds for dismissal. Gambling and profane language were also taboo. And teachers, especially in smaller communities, were expected to attend church regularly and to participate actively in church activities. The single teacher's dating behavior was watched carefully, and in some communities teachers had evening curfews or actually were forbidden to date. These prohibitions did not exist for non-teachers. For example, the practice of chewing tobacco was common among men in mid-nineteenth century America, and men and women of the higher social classes often drank at social gatherings. Gambling, in various forms, also was widespread.

Teacher salaries in the nineteenth century were still very low. For most of the century, country schoolteachers received salaries equal to those of common laborers, while the salaries of city teachers were similar to those of skilled artisans. However, from 1865 to 1890, teacher salaries rose more rapidly than these other two groups. This was most likely due to the extension of public education through the high-school years and to the higher qualifications of teachers. (We will discuss the development of public education in more detail in Chapter 5.) Still, the monetary value society placed on teachers' contributions was closer to that of semiskilled workers than of professionals.

Changing Social Attitudes and the Feminization of Teaching

As the qualifications of teachers improved throughout the nineteenth century, more and more teachers came from middle-class families who extolled community standards. In an age that witnessed the emergence of Darwinism and agnosticism and because of a growing alarm that "agnostic" professors in a few large universities were destroying the faith of students, elementary and high-school teachers almost without exception joined the chorus of parents and citizens who decried evolution and the attacks of science on religion. But change was coming, and while the voices raised against it might slow it down, they would not stop it.

Industrialization brought the migration of large numbers of people to the cities. With the growth of cities and urbanization, the homogeneity of communities began to break down. Many of the older standards began to erode after World War I. A growing secularization of culture and a willingness to entertain a scientific world view accompanied these changes. Modern science and critical studies of Biblical texts began to shake urban dwellers' faith in religious truths. Some lost faith in religion or became indifferent to it, while others sought a new basis for authority in human reason. The theory of evolution and other controversial scientific developments did not reach small towns and rural areas until after the first world war, and, in the absence of some of the forces acting in cities, took longer to be accepted. Censorship of what were considered noxious and evil doctrines was diligently pressed, as in the famous 1925 Scopes trial, in which John T. Scopes was prosecuted for teaching Darwinian evolution in school.

As a result of changing social attitudes, the onset of industrialism, the opening of the frontier, and social conditions like the depleted supply of males after the Civil War, women began to assume more active roles outside the home. Teaching was one occupation that was open to women. You will recall that teaching in colonial times was a

A number of social and economic forces made it possible for women to enter teaching in larger numbers.

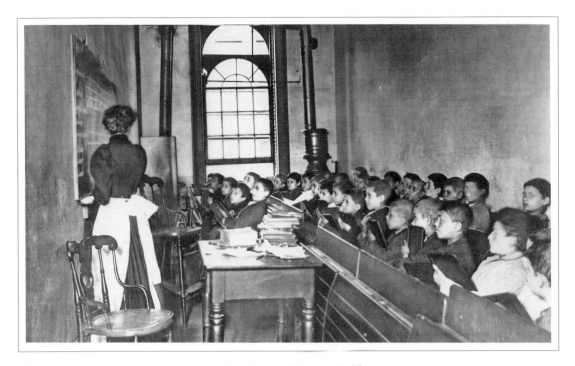

Many early classrooms were congested, grim, and inhospitable environments.

predominantly male occupation. By the latter part of the nineteenth century this was no longer the case. Not long after the Civil War, women became a scant majority in teaching. By 1880, women constituted 57 percent of the teaching force. At the turn of the century, 70 percent of all teachers were women, and almost 85 percent of the nation's teachers were women at the end of World War I.[15]

The ranks of male teachers, especially at the secondary level, grew after World War II. Some curtailment in the number of women teachers stemmed from administrative opposition to married women as teachers and efforts to make teaching more attractive to men. Despite this surge in male recruitment, however, women have remained the majority in the field of teaching.

Factors other than war, changes in belief and economic systems, and the expansion of the nation contributed to the **feminization of teaching** (the shift toward teaching's becoming a predominantly female occupation). Schools sought women to fill teaching positions. One reason was the belief that women's personalities were particularly nurturing. A less child-centered motive was that female teachers in the nineteenth century could be paid salaries one-half to one-third those of

Limited job opportunities outside the home, social views about the suitability of women for teaching, and the fact that women could be paid less than men contributed to the feminization of teaching.

male teachers because, though women's roles outside the home were expanding, their opportunities were limited to working in mills, on farms, or as domestic servants.

Only single females were allowed to teach from the 1850s to the 1920s; in fact, schools required women to resign once they married. This practice was based on the attitude that, once married, women would be supported by their husbands and jobs should be allocated based on financial need. Thus, in order to teach, women had to remain single or marry secretly. These constraints began to weaken after World War I. In 1923, 75 percent of urban districts refused to appoint married women, and rural districts were even more conservative. By 1941, the figure for urban districts decreased to 58 percent, and fell to 8 percent by 1951.[16] The widespread adoption of tenure systems (continuing contracts or permanent appointments of faculty) after 1925 contributed to these changes.

■ **PAUSE TO REFLECT**
Stereotypes of Teachers

- Do you see the origins of any stereotypes about teachers found in literature or elsewhere, the "spinster teacher," for example?

- What are some of the social and economic factors that might have contributed to this stereotype? Can you find the origins of any other stereotypes or examples of possible factors that contributed to current attitudes toward teachers?

- Do you think teachers today are subjected to a different set of standards than other members of a community?

Social Background of Teachers

To a large extent, teachers in this century have been part of the middle class. Many of those who entered the profession have tended to come from this group as well, but not all of them. A 1927 study of students attending teacher colleges in the Midwest found that more than half the students came from working-class and farm backgrounds.[17] A 1941 nationwide sample of 9,000 teachers showed that these teachers "[are] predominantly of native-white stock, invariably come from middle-class homes, [and] are of rural or small town origin."[18] These small-town and rural origins show up in other studies. In a nationwide survey of teachers by the National Education Association in 1957, 32 percent of the teachers were found to have come from farm communities.[19] And a 1950s survey of Texas teachers showed that nearly

As teachers you will most likely be members of the middle class.

three-quarters of the teachers were from communities of less than 20,000 people.[20] From his community studies in the early 1940s, Warner concluded that teachers in the East and South, where class lines were more deeply established, usually were part of the upper-middle class. Many of these teachers had apparently risen from lower-class families. In the Midwest and West, however, teachers were members of the lower-middle class and many had come from lower-class backgrounds.[21]

Carlson, in a 1961 study of teachers in the San Francisco Bay area, found that women teachers were from backgrounds of significantly higher status than men.[22] Teaching attracted four times as many affluent females as males and two and one-half times as many males as females from the lower class. Males who taught at either level and female secondary teachers gained in social status through teaching, though males made the greatest gains. Female elementary teachers, however, had a slight loss in status.

Recent studies show that teachers are drawn from all classes.[23] The largest portion comes from lower-middle class and upper-lower class backgrounds. The data also show, however, that 39 percent of new teachers, under age thirty, were raised in white-collar homes.[24]

People tend to be more favorably disposed to those who share their values. As a result, middle-class teachers may encourage more and have higher expectations of students who display middle-class values, even though this is certainly not the best thing for all students.

But what is the significance of **social class** for the teacher? Is it only of interest in the teacher's private life or does it also influence classroom effectiveness? Teachers tend to classify as brighter children who are quiet, clean, and show respect for the teacher. Teachers also favor students who share their values, regardless of the student's measured ability.[25] Teachers interact more with students for whom they hold high expectations, praise them more when they are correct, and criticize them less when they are wrong than they do students for whom they hold low expectations.[26] Teachers are also more likely to grant greater autonomy to those for whom they hold high expectations and punish them less for rule infractions. Teachers emphasize such middle-class values as hard work, orderliness, thrift, cleanliness, neatness, and sexual restraint. Middle-class teachers also tend to oppose long hair, unruliness, and aggressive behavior. The socialization process, which begins in infancy in the home, continues in the school in many forms. Children are taught to be orderly, to form straight lines and keep quiet when going to the playground or cafeteria, to sit quietly in their seat until recognized by the teacher, to turn in neat work and follow instructions carefully, and to respect the teacher's authority.

Schools also serve as a screening agency by selecting those best suited for the better jobs and positions in society and weeding out those who are less academically fit. The middle-class child has a greater likelihood than the lower-class child of succeeding in school not only because values are promoted at school and reinforced in the home but also because in middle-class homes more emphasis is placed on reading, learning, and getting ahead. Because public schools are essentially middle-class institutions, the middle-class child generally has an advantage over the lower-class child. The gap is closing, however, with the increase in compensatory education and related opportunities for disadvantaged children.

But middle-class values such as orderliness, punctuality, and honesty may very well be necessary for schools to operate. Determining and cultivating the traits needed to foster good learning environments are important, but fixation on any one trait to the exclusion of others can hamper teacher effectiveness and even prove harmful. Moreover, teachers who aspire to perfectionism in these traits often exhibit an intolerance of individual differences. For instance, a certain degree of orderliness is necessary in the daily operations of any school, but orderliness should facilitate learning, not become an end in itself. A fixation on values like orderliness and punctuality for their own sakes can lead to rigidity; and hard work, when carried to extremes, can lead to "workaholism" and eventually to "burnout." Teachers must examine their values thoughtfully, decide which ones promote desired educational objectives and which ones impede them, and take steps to keep the latter out of the classroom. Remember that your principal task is to help students learn and become better learners, and you will be able to keep the importance of social and personality traits in perspective within the larger framework of providing educational experiences.

Some middle-class values might be necessary elements of an effective learning environment.

Whatever a teacher's social background, there are significant values that should be promoted in the educational process: academic freedom for teachers, and equality of educational opportunity and freedom to learn for students. These values might be considered cornerstones of our educational system, even though they rarely are fully realized in practice. Academic freedom for teachers is necessary if teachers are to continue to investigate, to learn and inquire, to teach their subjects without interference, and to use the materials they think are most appropriate. Equality of educational opportunity is necessary if each student is to have a chance to realize his or her full potential. Students also need freedom to learn, or schooling could degenerate into a closed system of indoctrination of officially "approved" ways of thinking. Teachers should recognize students' freedom of expression in the classroom and their freedom of speech in general. Though creating the best learning environment for everyone in the classroom is difficult, it is one of the key tasks of an effective teacher.

The recognition of students' freedom of expression and freedom of speech is more important in teaching than the promotion of cultural values.

E D U C A T I O N A L   I S S U E 1–2

Should teachers instill middle-class values in their students?

Yes	**No**
1. Most teachers, being from the middle class, cannot avoid conveying their values through their behavior, even though they are not attempting to teach values directly.	1. The public-school population is socially and culturally diverse, and the values of each student's background should be recognized.
2. Certain middle-class values, such as orderliness and punctuality, are necessary for schools to operate successfully.	2. Equality of educational opportunity, academic freedom, and freedom to learn are more essential values to schools than middle-class ones.
3. Schools are also socialization agencies, and middle-class values are useful to prepare students for the workplace and their other adult responsibilities.	3. Those who get ahead in careers are innovative, creative people who develop new norms and ideas.

■ **Summary**

● Both intrinsic and external rewards encourage people to enter teaching. Many teachers do find the profession rewarding. A nationwide teacher survey showed 77 percent indicated satisfaction in their jobs. However, teachers do face some nagging problems. Chief among these seems to be displeasure over external rewards and school-community relations.

● Demand for teachers has fluctuated considerably over the past few decades, from overall shortages in the 1950s to oversupply in many fields during the 1970s. Job prospects for teachers look fairly positive today for teachers in some fields, less so for others. The demand is greatest at the secondary level until 1995. In addition to subject matter and grade level, opportunities in teaching vary depending on the type of community (rural, small cities, metropolitan areas, and suburban areas) and the type of school (public, church-related or private secular) one is interested in.

- Many alternative education careers within and outside schools are available to those who are qualified. Non-teaching careers in schools range from administration to special services. Those outside schools are either connected to government or in some independent agency or firm.

- Among teachers, status historically has been highest for college teachers, followed by secondary teachers, and lowest for elementary teachers.

- Numerous constraints were placed on the personal lives of teachers in colonial times and continued in place until nearly the present day. Female teachers, whose numbers rapidly increased during the nineteenth century, were particularly affected by these prohibitions.

- Middle-class values determine many of the public school's operations and directly influence teacher-pupil relations in positive and negative ways.

■ Key Terms

feminization of teaching   supply and demand

nonpublic schools   tenure

social class

■ Discussion Questions

1. What are the primary reasons that teaching is chosen as a career, and which do you believe are most important?

2. What are some reasons for teacher dissatisfaction? What can teachers do to improve the situation? How about the community? Education officials?

3. What factors must you consider when looking for a teaching position?

4. Compare and contrast teaching opportunities in public, parochial, and private secular schools.

5. What factors have brought about the changes in the status of teaching since colonial times? Do you think today's teachers are regarded highly enough? If not, what could be done to elevate their status?

6. How do social-class values affect teacher-student relations?

■ Learning Activities

1. Visit your teacher placement office on campus and review the job openings in your area of interest. Interview the placement director to find out what fields are in greatest demand and which areas of the country offer the most teaching opportunities.

2. Survey the public and nonpublic schools in your area, noting school characteristics, supply and demand for teachers, and teaching requirements.

3. Ask local teachers in your area of interest why they chose a teaching career and what about it is satisfying or disappointing.

Notes

1. Henry Brooks Adams, *The Education of Henry Adams* (Boston: Houghton Mifflin, 1907), 20.

2. *The Condition of Teaching: A State by State Analysis, 1988* (Princeton, NJ: the Carnegie Foundation, 1988), Table 81, 101.

3. Ibid., Table 82, 102.

4. Ibid., Table 80, 100.

5. Abraham H. Maslow, *Eupsychian Management* (Homewood, IL: Richard D. Irwin and the Dorsey Press, 1965).

6. Erich Fromm, *Man for Himself* (New York: Holt, Rinehart and Winston, 1947).

7. National Education Association, Research Division, *Teacher Supply and Demand in the Public Schools, 1970,* Research Report 1970, R-14 (Washington, DC: The Association, 1970), 47.

8. M. D. Eldgridge, "America's Nonpublic Schools: A Quantification of Their Contribution to American Education," *Private School Quarterly* (Fall 1980): 4–7; and D. H. McLaughlin and L. L. Wise, *Nonpublic Education of the Nation's Children* (Palo Alto, CA: American Institutes for Research, 1980).

9. *Private Schools and Private School Teachers: Final Report of the 1985–86 Private School Study* (Washington, DC: U.S. Government Printing Office, 1987), Table 1, p. 7; *United States Catholic Elementary and Secondary Schools, 1986–87* (Washington, DC: National Catholic Education Association, 1987), Table 1, p. 3.

10. For other differences, see James S. Coleman, Thomas Hoffer, and Sally Kilgore, *High School Achievement: Public, Private, and Catholic Schools Compared* (New York: Basic Books, 1982).

11. *Statistical Abstracts of the United States 1990, 110th ed.* (Washington, DC: U.S. Government Printing Office), 142.

12. R. Freeman Butts and Lawrence A. Cremin, *A History of Education in American Culture* (New York: Henry Holt, 1953), 131–32.

13. Howard K. Beale, *A History of Freedom of Teaching in American Schools* (New York: Charles Scribner's Sons, 1941), 38.

14. Willard S. Elsbree, *The American Teacher* (New York: American Book Co., 1939), 90–97.

15. Thomas Woody, "Entrance of Women into the Teaching Profession," *Educational Outlook* 2 (January/March 1928): 72–88, 138–63.

16. "Teacher Personnel Practices," *NEA Research Bulletin* (1952): 12–13; and C. N. Morris, "Career Patterns of Teachers," in Lindley J. Stiles, ed., *The Teacher's Role in American Society* (New York: Harper, 1957), 247–63.

17. Frederick L. Whitney, "The Social and Economic Background of Teacher College and of the University Students," *Education* XLVII (1927): 449–56.

18. Florence Greenhoe, *Community Contacts and Participation of Teachers* (Washington, DC: American Council on Public Affairs, 1941), 8.

19. "The Status of the American School Teacher," *NEA Research Bulletin* 35 (February 1957): 9.

20. Carson McGuire and George White, "Social Origins of Teachers in Texas," in *The Teacher's Role in American Society*, ed. Lindley L. Stiles (New York: Harper, 1957), 23–41.

21. W. Lloyd Warner, Robert J. Havighurst, and Martin B. Loeb, *Who Shall Be Educated?* (New York: Harper & Row, 1944), 101.

22. R. O. Carlson, "Variation and Myth in the Social Status of Teachers," *Journal of Educational Sociology* 35 (1961): 104–18.

23. National Education Association, *Status of the American Public School Teacher: 1958–1986* (Washington, DC: NEA Research Division, 1987), 162.

24. Ibid., 163.

25. F. I. Ortiz, "Hispanic-American Children's Experiences in Classrooms: A Comparison between Hispanic and non-Hispanic Children," in *Race, Class, and Gender in American Education*, ed. L. Weiss (Albany, NY: State University of New York Press, 1988), 63–87; and G. D. Spindler, "Beth Ann: A Case Study of Culturally Defined Adjustment and Teacher Perceptions," in *Education and Cultural Processes: Anthropological Approaches*, 2nd ed., ed. G. D. Spindler (Prospect Heights, IL: Waveland Press, 1987).

26. R. L. Allington, "The Reading Provided Readers of Differing Abilities," *Elementary School Journal* 83 (1983): 548–59; and L. Grant and J. Rothenberg, "The Social Enhancement of Ability Differences: Teacher-Student Interactions in First and Second Grade Reading Groups," *Elementary School Journal* 87 (1986): 29–50.

■ CHAPTER 2

PROFESSIONAL PROBLEMS ■
OF TEACHERS

A LOOK AHEAD

The purpose of this chapter is to explore what it means to become an educator and a professional. You will learn about:

- Seven common characteristics of a profession

- Whether teaching possesses these seven characteristics

- Issues relating to the professionalization of teaching, including professional ethics in teaching, efforts to improve teacher quality, and negotiation practices of teacher organizations

- Academic freedom in the classroom and the challenge of censorship

- A teacher's right to privacy and how it relates to and is affected by the public's right to know what goes on in its schools

IS TEACHING A PROFESSION? ■

What does it mean to be a professional educator? Are all teachers and administrators professional educators? Are they all educators? Some would claim that to be a teacher or an educational administrator automatically entitles one to be considered an educator. This is true, in the sense that the term *educator* is another name for teacher, instruc-

The term *educa-*
tor is more than a
job title.

tor, or educational administrator. But, if the term signifies a level of accomplishment or expertise, then not all teachers and administrators can rightfully claim to be educators. An **educator** may be considered someone knowledgeable in the theory and practice of education who can apply that expertise in the classroom. By this definition, only some teachers and administrators are educators, yet all should strive to be.

But what about being professionals? Is teaching a profession? Opinions differ on this question. There is a tendency at times to label as professions those occupations we consider prestigious. Though, as we will see shortly, being considered prestigious does not make an occupation a profession. Occupational prestige does give us a clue as to whether the public might (rightly or wrongly) consider the occupation a profession. Some studies show that people, when asked to rank occupations for prestige, rank medicine, law, dentistry,

Opinions vary as
to whether teach-
ing is a profes-
sion.

architecture, engineering, and optometry higher than elementary-school teaching (secondary teaching was not included in the poll).[1] Still other people—especially those within education—believe that teaching *is* a profession. In fact, educators have consistently sought to ensure that the field of teaching becomes more widely recognized as a profession.

Historically, teachers have believed that more widespread recognition of the professionalization of teaching would improve educational practice, enhance occupational status, provide larger salaries and fringe benefits, and offer teachers greater autonomy. Teachers are not alone in wishing to be accorded full professional status: workers in many occupations and semiprofessions have similar hopes. Occupations that have certain professional characteristics but fall short of meeting some of the criteria of a profession are considered **semiprofessions**. Librarians, social workers, nurses, pharmacists, optometrists, accountants, and a host of others all strive for professional recognition. In examining the question of whether teaching is or is not a profession, it is useful to see whether teaching fully possesses the basic characteristics of a profession. But before exploring these characteristics, some popular misconceptions should be dispelled. Just as a garbage collector might prefer to be called a "sanitary engineer" to dignify the work, others attempt to enhance the image of their jobs by referring to them as professions. It also is common to refer to those who earn their living as athletes as "professional" athletes. This popular usage merely distinguishes the full-time, salaried athlete from the so-called amateur athlete. A name change, however, does not necessarily change status. It has nothing to do, as we shall see, with the meaning of **profession**.

The Attributes of a Profession

Considerable overlap exists among various lists of professional criteria.[2] The following characteristics are those that professions have in common:

A High Degree of Generalized and Systematized Knowledge. Perhaps all occupations require some knowledge and technique,which, in many cases, may be conveyed orally rather than through books or the mass media. But most occupations require the novice to learn a set of skills and procedures to get the job done. In contrast, professions possess a base of theoretical knowledge that illuminates practice and provides governing principles that go beyond rule-of-thumb procedures in actual situations. The professional possesses this knowledge and is responsible for adding to it and expanding on it through continuing study. The public must be convinced that the professional has mastered this knowledge and will use it to solve problems that affect public welfare.

> Professionals are decision makers and problem solvers who apply theoretical knowledge and experience in concrete situations.

A Long Period of Specialized, Intellectual Training. Because the practice of a profession requires a considerable body of theoretical knowledge, students must spend many years in advanced study before being licensed to practice. Workers in other occupations, on the other hand, acquire their skills through relatively short training periods, an apprenticeship system, or through a shorter period of higher education (because the necessary theoretical knowledge and skills can be acquired without advanced study).

Practice Is Essentially Intellectual in Character. The work of professional practitioners is basically intellectual, demanding the ability to comprehend and apply principles to diverse situations, solve problems, reason logically, and draw warranted inferences from ideas. For example, architects and surgeons need highly developed physical skills, but they also must be able to judge intellectually how and when to use them. The basic intellectual nature of a professional's practice also draws on a broad background of systematic knowledge.

Professions Promote the Public Good by Providing a Unique Social Service. Professionals, in contrast to other occupational groups, generally serve the public good as well as their own interests. This means their services are valued by society and should be organized to provide sufficient services of high quality. In fulfilling this criterion, professionals are expected to provide a fair share of free or scaled services to those who cannot afford to pay the full fee. This expectation helps to distinguish professions from other organizational groups whose primary goal is financial gain (even though some professionals may fall short through an overriding pursuit of power and wealth). Professionals generally expect to be compensated sufficiently to pay off debts incurred during lengthy advanced study and to receive an income proportionate to the importance of the service they offer. (In actuality, supply and demand is often the greatest influence on income.)

Most professions are marked, at least in theory, by a sense of mission to serve the public good.

At times, professionals may be expected to risk their lives or reputations—for instance, physicians are expected to enter epidemic areas to treat the sick, lawyers may be expected to defend the rights of unpopular figures, and scientists are expected to publish their findings even if they are unpopular in the scientific community.

Ideally, a profession should provide a unique service that does not encroach upon other professions or semiprofessions. In reality, though, this is rarely the case. Lawyers compete with accountants for tax work and with banks to draw up wills. Medical doctors compete with osteopaths, chiropractors, chiropodists, and faith healers.

Control Over Standards of Entrance and Exclusion. Professions must be able to assure the public that their practitioners are competent if the public is to confidently grant them the freedom to exercise professional judgment.

Associations and the intellectual rigor of the professional education process limit the number of practicing professionals.

Because of the type of knowledge and the years of advanced study required by professions, entrance standards are high. Only a few individuals possess the intellectual abilities and personal characteristics that are likely to lead to a successful career. The ratio of those who enroll in a particular field to those who finally graduate varies according to the profession. Medical schools, for instance, emphasize selectivity in admissions rather than elimination of candidates after admission to avoid wasting high overhead and valuable faculty resources on students who will never graduate.[3] Some professions follow up after graduation with in-service programs and competency tests to encourage professional development. However, only in recent years have professions, such as medicine, made considerable effort in this area.

A code of ethics defines the mission of a profession and the standards of conduct for its members.

Enforcement of a Professional Code of Ethics. A profession controls its members through professional associations that establish standards of practice and ethical canons. It disciplines members who violate professional codes. For example, a physician who commits a serious offense could be discharged from the American Medical Association or the local medical society and be stripped of hospital privileges. An egregious offense can mean losing the license to practice.

Ideally, a standard code of ethics should be established for a profession unless the tasks among those in the profession are so diverse that a single code would be useless. Such is the case in engineering, which has numerous specialties and more than 100 national associations. The diversity makes it difficult for everyone to agree on a comprehensive code for all engineers. No matter what the codes or how many, though, they should regularly be evaluated in the light of any recent important cases to ensure that they still are clear and relevant.

When professions fail to uphold reasonable ethical codes, it may indicate a breakdown in the integrity of some practitioners or a failure of enforcement. In serious cases, the government may wrest control from the profession to prevent further offenses and to protect the public. Naturally, such actions would result in a serious loss of professional prestige and autonomy. In fact, if abuses were sufficiently widespread and there were no signs of improvement, it is likely that the group would not long remain a profession in the eyes of the public.

A Broad Range of Autonomy. The public usually does not consider itself qualified to judge the large amount of esoteric professional knowledge and decide how it should be used. To a certain extent, the public can evaluate the practices of professionals, but it is limited to its comprehension of professional standards and their possible applications.

Occupational groups with the least training generally are given the most supervision and the least autonomy, whereas those with higher skills traditionally have more authority over their tasks. No occupational group is wholly free of supervision and evaluation. There are also nonprofessional job situations—such as an automobile assembly line—where less supervision is required because tasks are highly routine and mechanical.

Licensed professionals should be capable of practicing without direct supervision in a range of diverse and complex situations. They need the autonomy, literally, to exercise their judgment and make the best decisions. A lack of autonomy erodes their ability to make decisions. While this leaves daily decisions in their hands, professionals still are subject to evaluation. Before the public is likely to grant extensive autonomy, professions need to develop and uphold high standards of entrance and exclusion and enforce a defensible code of ethics. If these conditions are not upheld sufficiently, or if the profession is judged to be motivated largely by the desire for wealth or power, then a nonprofessional public body probably will take control of the group.

> The freedom to evaluate situations and decide upon a course of action is central to the practice of a profession.

No single profession fulfills all the criteria of a profession; achieving the stature of profession is a matter of the degree to which an occupational group at any given time actually meets the criteria. Consequently some occupational groups that claim professional status ac-

No profession fully possesses all the attributes of the ideal profession. Occupations that possess most of these attributes are professions. Those that possess a limited number often are termed semiprofessions.

tually may be semiprofessions (nursing, for example), while other occupational groups have become professions only in recent decades (some areas of journalism), and still others have enjoyed professional status for many generations (the ministry).

Several occupations have been classified by some as semiprofessions. These include nursing, social work, and librarianship. Compared with professions, the semiprofessions have shorter training periods, less specialized and systematized bodies of knowledge, and less autonomy.[4] The professions are devoted to the creation and application of knowledge, usually enjoy privileged communication (confidential communication between professional and client), and often are concerned with matters of life and death. The semiprofessions are more concerned with the communication of knowledge, are not likely to enjoy privileged communication, and merely execute the decisions made by the professionals, even in life-and-death situations. Additionally, the semiprofessional has less autonomy than the professional and is more likely than the professional to use the position as a ladder for promotion into administration.

Does Teaching Possess These Attributes?

Let us apply each criterion of a profession to the field of teaching as we attempt to determine if it is, indeed, a profession.

Does Teaching Have a High Degree of Generalized and Systematized Knowledge of a Theoretical Nature?   The answer is far from simple. Through an accumulating body of research, much is known about educational institutions and the teaching-learning process although the quality of research in some cases may be questionable.[5] This vast amount of research has not always resulted in educational improvements, although recent studies of "effective" schools have identified the factors that make up sound school systems.[6]

Teaching probably contains a large enough base of theoretical knowledge to qualify it as a profession. However, this knowledge does not always guide practice.

As far as training is concerned, teachers need both subject matter knowledge and teaching abilities. A recent study shows that the knowledge base for beginning teachers includes (in addition to subject matter knowledge) classroom organization and management, assessment, child development, curriculum planning, the social and political environments in which teachers work, students with special needs, and the legal and ethical responsibilities of the profession.[7]

Does Teaching Have a Long Period of Specialized, Intellectual Training?   Historically, neither elementary nor secondary teaching has measured up to this criterion. In 1930 only two states enforced the degree requirements for elementary teachers, and only twenty-three states enforced the requirements for secondary teachers. In 1940 a majority of states (forty) enforced the degree requirements for secondary teachers, but it was not until 1960 that the majority (forty) enforced the requirements for elementary teachers.[8] Even today the length of specialized, intellectual training is not as extensive as in many professions (the ministry, medicine, psychiatry, and law, for example), though it is comparable to others (engineering).

Is Teaching Essentially Intellectual in Character? In many respects teaching fulfills this criterion. Teaching involves transmitting knowledge, dealing with abstractions, solving problems, and reconstructing knowledge. These and other cognitive tasks, though perhaps not all found in a single classroom, are characteristic of teaching as a whole. Of course, the public-school teacher has other responsibilities, such as advising students, developing curricular materials, serving on faculty committees, conferring with parents, and participating in workshops. Not all of these activities are strictly intellectual, but they are primarily so. As a whole, teaching often does not reach its full potential in fulfilling the criterion of intellectuality. Limitations in the body of systematized knowledge (as previously noted) restrict the intellectual character of educational practice. Moreover, classroom teachers do not always use the knowledge available, either in education or in their specialty. They also tend to be guided by what works successfully at the moment rather than by basic principles, an approach more often associated with semiskilled occupations.

Does Teaching Provide a Unique Social Service? Few professions meet this criterion because most share or compete for clients with other occupational groups, as we saw earlier in the cases of lawyers and physicians. The uniqueness of a service seems to have a direct bearing on the degree of respect a profession is accorded by the public. The higher the prestige, the more likely an occupation will be considered a profession by the public. The more alternative services there are in a particular field, the less respect that field commands, especially from those who choose an alternative service (chiropractors over physicians, for instance). And it is well known that some parents believe they can educate their children better at home than teachers can in a school.

If prestige is a measure of whether an occupation is viewed as a profession, a large portion of the public does not consider teaching a profession.

How does the public view the field of teaching? Elementary-school teachers placed eighteenth in a prestige ranking of sixty-three occupations (secondary teachers were not included in the poll).[9] A 1985 Gallup poll, commissioned by the National Education Association, asked participants to rate the prestige of various professions. Only 22 percent of the respondents said they perceived public-school teaching as very prestigious, while 30 percent said it had little or no status. About 50 percent thought the workload of public-school teachers was "very demanding."[10]

The public may be biased toward the teachers in their own communities, however. For example, a 1989 Gallup poll showed that 43 percent of the respondents gave their local public schools a grade of A or B; whereas only 22 percent gave the nation's public schools as a whole such high grades.[11]

Historically, some people entered teaching temporarily until a more lucrative or enticing career was available. But a profession is considered more than just a job; it is a lifetime career rather than temporary employment. More teachers must be realizing this, because in recent years the holding power of teaching has become among the strongest. The median tenure for secondary-school teachers is 12.5 years; for elementary-school teachers, it is 12.4 years. In contrast, two professions usually accorded higher prestige by the public have shorter median tenure: physicians (10.7 years) and lawyers (10.1 years).[12] Among professions with greater tenure than teachers are clerics (15.8 years), dentists (15.7 years), and civil engineers (13.0 years). Even though holding power may not in itself increase prestige (some nonprofessions have holding power, too), research does suggest that job tenure is necessary for the stability and continuity of professions.

Occupational rankings do not differ much cross-culturally or over time. Donald Treiman suggests that this is because similar technologies divide work in similar ways, and the greater the occupational power (the ability to control scarce resources and to give orders), the more prestige the occupation commands.[13] In the average prestige score from fifty-seven countries, high-school teachers rank eighth and primary teachers rank thirteenth out of forty-nine occupations.[14]

But prestige is not the complete picture when discussing the service provided by a professional. Professionals must practice **universalism** as opposed to **particularism**.[15] In other words, professionals may apply only general standards to their clients and must not judge their specific personalities or characteristics as attractive or unattractive. Although particularism is acceptable outside of work (as in choosing one's friends), it is wholly inappropriate in a professional relationship with a client. Thus, the professional must provide a service to anyone who requests it regardless of age, race, religion, sex, politics, social status, or personal preferences. A nonprofessional on the other hand, may act on particularism and withhold services with little or no censure.

Most professional educators do have a sense of mission to serve the educational needs of their students.

The professional also must be prepared to render service upon request, whether convenient or not. Moreover, the professional always must provide the highest quality services possible because the service is a vital one and to do otherwise would demonstrate less than full professional competence.

Does Teaching Control the Standards of Entrance and Exclusion?
To achieve professional status an occupational group first must recognize common interests that supersede competing interests, maintain performance standards, and control access to the occupation.[16] New students have easy access to the field of teaching—perhaps too easy.

Scholastic Aptitude Test (SAT) scores for prospective teachers are relatively low compared with the national average for all college students. The combined SAT scores of prospective teachers have been increasing since 1982.[17] (See Table 2–1.) Nevertheless, prospective teachers continue to score significantly below the average for all college students on SAT and Admissions College Testing (ACT) exams.[18]

> It is easier to enter teaching than to enter many professions, which might hinder recognition of teaching as a profession.

The National Council for the Accreditation of Teacher Education (NCATE) is doing its part to fulfill the criterion of controlling standards of entrance and exclusion by cracking down on substandard teacher education programs. After implementing more rigorous standards in 1989, the NCATE denied accreditation to over one-fifth of the programs it evaluated. It denied 20 percent of all 1990 accreditation requests. The NCATE wields a fair amount of power—it accredits about 550 of the 1,400 institutions that prepare teachers, and these institutions produce about 80 percent of the nation's teachers.[19]

> Efforts are being made to standardize and increase the rigor of teacher preparation programs.

Competency and accountability are being increasingly emphasized in the schools themselves. However, given the structure of many systems, weeding out an ineffective teacher is easier if the teacher is new to the system. While they must consider federal and state laws, court cases, and collective bargaining agreements, local school boards possess considerable power and flexibility in devising policies, such as personnel evaluation, hiring, and firing. Non-tenured teachers, for instance, can be dismissed without due process. On the other hand, teachers with **tenure,** a continuing contract awarded after a successful probationary period, can be terminated only for gross incompetence, insubordination or immorality, or in response to budget cuts or program reductions. Tenure provisions are not found in all school districts and it is not a constitutionally protected right, yet it is usually adhered to and protected by due process.

> Some see tenure as an obstacle to improving and maintaining teacher quality and accountability.

Tenure is more often attacked in higher education than in public elementary and secondary schools. Many critics believe that tenure protects incompetent teachers and should be abolished. For example, former Governor Richard D. Lamm supported elimination of tenure in Colorado schools and colleges and either longer probationary periods

TABLE 2-1 Scholastic Aptitude Test score averages, by intended area of study:[a] 1977-78 to 1987-88

Test and Year	Arts and Humanities	Biological Sciences and Related Areas	Business, Commerce, and Communications	Computer and Information Sciences	Education	Engineering	Mathematics	Physical Sciences	Social Sciences and Related Areas	Miscellaneous[b]
1	2	3	4	5	6	7	8	9	10	11
Verbal										
1977-78	439	436	409	420	396	448	464	499	448	422
1978-79	436	435	408	419	392	445	459	498	446	420
1979-80	434	433	406	417	389	444	455	495	448	419
1980-81	434	433	406	416	391	446	456	498	446	420
1981-82	436	434	409	417	394	449	455	496	450	424
1982-83	438	432	409	413	394	448	453	496	451	421
1983-84	440	434	410	411	398	453	457	501	451	423
1984-85	445	439	414	413	404	453	459	506	454	429
1986-87	447	438	415	403	408	456	475	507	452	410
1987-88	444	434	414	400	407	453	468	500	447	409
Change, 1977-78 to 1987-88	5	-2	5	-20	11	5	4	1	-1	-13
Mathematics										
1977-78	454	474	448	499	422	540	585	566	464	461
1978-79	452	472	448	498	420	536	580	561	463	458
1979-80	452	472	446	496	418	535	577	560	463	459
1980-81	453	472	446	492	418	534	572	558	463	459
1981-82	452	470	446	489	419	537	569	558	464	461
1982-83	454	470	445	484	418	539	572	560	466	460
1983-84	456	475	449	483	425	543	578	564	467	463
1984-85	462	480	455	488	432	545	578	569	471	469
1986-87	469	482	459	476	437	554	602	576	472	453
1987-88	471	482	462	470	442	547	596	568	472	455
Change, 1977-78 to 1987-88	17	8	14	-29	20	7	11	2	8	-6

[a]Students indicated their first and second choices of fields of study. Only their first choices are reported here.
[b]Includes "trade and vocational," "other," and "undecided" through 1984-85. Data for 1986-87 and 1987-88 exclude "other."
Note: Possible scores on each part of the SAT range from 200 to 800. No data are available for 1985-86 due to changes in the Student Descriptive Questionnaire completed when students registered for the test.

Source: Reprinted by permission of College Entrance Examination Board, *National Report on College-Bound Seniors*, various years. (Copyright © 1988 by the College Entrance Examination Board. All rights reserved.) (This table was prepared December 1988.)

or a new policy of "renewable tenure" (short-term contracts that are renewed as long as the teacher's performance continues to meet the standards of the field.)[20]

Tenure may have its drawbacks in the area of control, but it does serve a purpose. First, tenure provides job security, which may attract teachers who would otherwise be tempted by the higher salaries and generous perquisites of business and industry. Second, according to Parsons and Platt, tenure provides educational institutions with a pattern of stratification and competence necessary to perform educational and socialization functions.[21] Finally, tenure ensures academic freedom by allowing teachers to discuss unpopular but important subjects and issues in the classroom without fear of losing their jobs.

■ PAUSE TO REFLECT
The Advantages and Disadvantages of Tenure

- Do you think tenure should be protected, abolished, or modified?
- If tenure were abolished, would it be worth the loss of a valuable recruiting tool?
- Could schools function as efficiently without tenure?
- Do you think academic freedom would suffer without the protection of tenure?
- Is the idea of "renewable tenure" a reasonable compromise, or would it be essentially the same as no tenure?

Another characteristic of a profession is that the members themselves establish standards and decide cases. But classroom teachers do not have this power. Except for the state superintendent, local school boards and state boards of education are composed entirely of laypersons. Considering this lack of power and the lack of rigorous control over entrance and exclusion, elementary- and secondary-level teaching lacks full professional status.

Is a Code of Ethics Enforced in Teaching? This criterion will be discussed at greater length later in this chapter.

Does Teaching Grant a Broad Range of Autonomy? Through lay state and local boards, state curriculum guides, and the multiplication of bureaucratic rules and regulations, one might be led to believe that teachers have little autonomy. On the other hand, teachers can close their classroom doors and do what they believe to be best. Supervisors and principals seldom used to visit classes after a teacher's probationary period. However, with the increased use of merit evaluations, visits are scheduled regularly. Principals also require teachers to submit detailed lesson plans for approval, which also can threaten a teacher's autonomy. Moreover, even some teachers with tenure hesitate to discuss controversial issues because they fear repercussions from the community. Academic freedom is better protected today than during certain bleak periods in the past, such as the McCarthy era of the early 1950s when one could be personally and professionally ostracized for merely discussing an unpopular subject. Nevertheless, teachers do not yet have the degree of autonomy that is typical of professions.

> Though teachers often have limited input into what is taught, they do have some autonomy in deciding on how to teach.

Regardless of the professional status of teaching as a whole, individual teachers can approach their careers as professionals. Certainly, our educational system would need to undergo significant changes to overcome the obstacles to teachers' gaining some of the rights entrusted to members of other professions—autonomy, for instance. However, it is within your power to do the most you can for your students within the limits placed upon you by the system and society as a whole. Perhaps the best place to start is to think about what to do in the classroom. As much as possible, keep up with current research and try to apply in your classroom what seems to you of value in the research you read. Think about what your students (your clients) need from you as an educator and evaluate whether they are getting it.

> One need not be a member of a profession to act professionally.

In summary, teaching fulfills some professional criteria and falls short of others. Proposals for overcoming the weak spots will be presented in the section on certification and improving teacher quality a little later in this chapter. But first we will examine teaching and the criterion of professional ethics.

■ PROFESSIONAL ETHICS

Professional ethics have a higher profile than ever. Dramatic cases make headlines nearly every week: Watergate, Abscam, stealing documents for political advantage, lawyers bilking clients, corporate fraud and bribery, physicians billing Medicare and Medicaid for services not rendered, scientists falsifying research data, professors involved in conflicts of interest between their extramural activities and their university responsibilities, teachers propositioning their students with the promise of a high grade, and psychotherapists taking advantage of their clients in the name of emotional therapy.

Is teaching a profession?

Yes	No
1. Professions conduct research into methods of improving the field, and teaching is no exception.	1. The application of research findings to improve practice generally has been disappointing.
2. Teacher preparation requires a specialized period of intellectual training.	2. Historically, teachers have not had a long period of specialized training. Even today, their training is shorter than it is for many other professions.
3. The teacher's work is essentially intellectual in character, much like the work of doctors, lawyers, or engineers.	3. Teachers do not always use the available intellectual knowledge in the classroom, and some can tend to resort to a rule-of-thumb approach more typical of a semi- or nonprofession.
4. Teachers are the sole providers of a crucial social service.	4. Through home schooling and informal learning networks in the community, the public-school monopoly is breaking up.
5. Standards for teaching competence have been raised recently by use of entrance and exit exams and strengthened certification standards.	5. Teaching has not maintained as sufficiently high standards of entry and exclusion as have other professions, such as medicine, law, and engineering.
6. A professional code of ethics has been developed, widely disseminated, and periodically revised.	6. Codes of ethics are inadequately enforced in education.
7. Through collective bargaining and other means, teachers have greater decision-making power and autonomy than ever.	7. Teachers have less autonomy than other professionals.

A profession's code of ethics is established and enforced by the profession itself.

One of the distinguishing marks of a profession is a defensible and properly enforced code of ethics. A profession controls its members through standards of practice and ethical canons established by professional associations and other bodies. In turn, public trust and confidence in a profession depend upon the enforcement of high ethical standards.

Professional ethics means "all issues involving ethics and values in the role of the professions and the conduct of the professions in society."[22] The scope of professional ethics is broad and encompasses many activities, but it excludes strictly private acts as well as public acts performed as a citizen rather than as a professional.

A profession's code of ethics protects the public, the practicing professional, and the profession itself.

One function of professional ethics is to assure clients that professional services will be rendered in accordance with reasonably high standards and acceptable moral conduct. This confidence enables the professional to exercise relatively independent judgment in decisions that affect clients.

Second, ethical codes assure the public that the professional is serving the public interest and should continue to enjoy public trust, confidence, and support. The client's interest and the public interest usually coincide, but occasionally they may conflict, such as in decisions about the allocation of scarce, life-supporting medical resources.

A third function is to provide members of a profession with a code of rules and standards so that their conduct can be fairly and properly regulated. Such codes help maintain the integrity of professional organizations, especially when the code is developed by the organization. Codes also protect professionals from falling into undeserved disrepute and help avoid legal disputes such as lawsuits and license revocations. A code of ethics also deters increased government intervention into the profession and a consequent loss of autonomy and self-regulation.

Finally, a code is one of the hallmarks of a profession. This characteristic is especially important for semiprofessions that aspire to full professional stature.

Studying ethics codes for teachers can help you understand the principles and sense of mission that guide a professional educator.

The structure of professional ethics consists of the internal organization for implementation and the codes themselves. Knowing the source of a profession's control over ethical matters helps to identify the structure. Ethical control in education is divided among local school boards, state education associations, the National Education Association (NEA), and the American Association of School Administrators (AASA).

Teacher education programs need to teach professional conduct and instill desirable behavior during training, and professional organizations and school administrators should continue to emphasize professional ethics after the teacher has finished training and begun to practice. Teachers learn ethical behavior by acquiring adequate knowledge, pondering issues, and observing and practicing ethical behavior. They also embrace it by developing pride in the worth of their professional responsibilities and inviting perceptive supervision and adequate feedback.

Enforcement of ethical behavior requires a clear, well-regulated system that fully protects the rights of the accused. Both the NEA and the AASA have consistent and impartial enforcement procedures, but the number of cases heard is relatively small.

The other basic structure, or framework, of professional ethics lies in the codes themselves. Code structures are not identical but are likely to have certain generic similarities: general objectives, ideals, principles, standards, rules, and procedures. Not all codes need every aspect to function effectively.

NEA's "Code of Ethics of the Education Profession" (see Table 2–2) is divided into two parts: a preamble and the main body, which consists of two principles, each of which is followed by eight rules. The first principle pertains to the teacher's commitment to the student; and the second concerns the teacher's commitment to the profession. Unlike some other codes, and perhaps unfortunately, the sixteen rules are phrased negatively rather than positively. Stating what educators should *do* rather than what they should *not* do would provide a more effective and less restrictive model of behavior. Clarification and the precise application of the Code have been developed over many years by the NEA's Committee on Professional Ethics. Implementation and enforcement provisions are outlined in Review Board Procedures.[23]

Professional ethics grows out of the distinctive nature of professions, and the codes emerge from the requirements of the particular profession. Although many codes share certain principles—justice, altruism, freedom of inquiry—the actual application of these principles in terms of rules and standards differs from profession to profession, depending on their purposes, functions, and special activities. For instance, the law profession's interpretation and application of the right to privacy differs from education's interpretation because the privacy enjoyed by a lawyer's client is different from a student's right to privacy.

Development and Enforcement

The dissemination, interpretation, implementation, and enforcement of ethical codes deserve considerable attention. It is important to understand the machinery that fulfills these vital functions, what that machinery has accomplished, and what remains to be done.

Among other things, a teacher's code of ethics should cover classroom situations such as academic freedom, the ethical use of tests and testing, student dishonesty, the student's freedom to learn, and the student's right to privacy.

TABLE 2–2 Code of ethics of the education profession adopted by the 1975 New Representative Assembly

Preamble

The educator, believing in the worth and dignity of each human being, recognizes the supreme importance of the pursuit of truth, devotion to excellence, and the nurture of democratic principles. Essential to these goals is the protection of freedom to learn and to teach and the guarantee of equal educational opportunity for all. The educator accepts the responsibility to adhere to the highest ethical standards.

The educator recognizes the magnitude of the responsibility inherent in the teaching process. The desire for the respect and confidence of one's colleagues, of students, of parents, and of the members of the community provides the incentive to attain and maintain the highest possible degree of ethical conduct. The Code of Ethics of the Education Profession indicates the aspiration of all educators and provides standards by which to judge conduct.

The remedies specified by the NEA and/or its affiliates for the violation of any provision of this Code shall be exclusive and no such provision shall be enforceable in any form other than one specifically designated by the NEA or its affiliates.

Principle I—Commitment to the Student

The educator strives to help each student realize his or her potential as a worthy and effective member of society. The educator therefore works to stimulate the spirit of inquiry, the acquisition of knowledge and understanding, and the thoughtful formulation of worthy goals.

In fulfillment of the obligation to the student, the educator

1. Shall not unreasonably restrain the student from independent action in the pursuit of learning.
2. Shall not unreasonably deny the student access to varying points of view.
3. Shall not deliberately suppress or distort subject matter relevant to the student's progress.
4. Shall make reasonable effort to protect the student from conditions harmful to learning or to health and safety.

5. Shall not intentionally expose the student to embarrassment or disparagement.
6. Shall not on the basis of race, color, creed, sex, national origin, marital status, political or religious beliefs, family, social or cultural background, or sexual orientation, unfairly:
   a. Exclude any student from participation in any program;
   b. Deny benefits to any student;
   c. Grant any advantage to any student.
7. Shall not use professional relationships with students for private advantage.
8. Shall not disclose information about students obtained in the course of professional service, unless disclosure serves a compelling professional purpose or is required by law.

Principle II—Commitment to the Profession

The education profession is vested by the public with a trust and responsibility requiring the highest ideals of professional service.

In the belief that the quality of the services of the education profession directly influences the nation and its citizens, the educator shall exert every effort to raise professional standards, to promote a climate that encourages the exercise of professional judgment, to achieve conditions which attract persons worthy of the trust to careers in education, and to assist in preventing the practice of the profession by unqualified persons.

In fulfillment of the obligation to the profession, the educator
1. Shall not in an application for a professional position deliberately make a false statement or fail to disclose a material fact related to competency and qualifications.
2. Shall not misrepresent his/her professional qualifications.
3. Shall not assist entry into the profession of a person known to be unqualified in respect to character, education, or other relevant attribute.
4. Shall not knowingly make a false statement concerning the qualifications of a candidate for a professional position.
5. Shall not assist a noneducator in the unauthorized practice of teaching.
6. Shall not disclose information about colleagues obtained in the course of professional service unless disclosure serves a compelling professional purpose or is required by law.
7. Shall not knowingly make false or malicious statements about a colleague.
8. Shall not accept any gratuity, gift, or favor that might impair or appear to influence professional decisions or actions.

Note: Reprinted by permission of the National Education Association.

To be useful, a profession's code of ethics should apply directly to the daily situations encountered by its members.

A code also should address relations with colleagues and education officials, including issues such as recruitment, teacher evaluation, tenure, collegial relations, nepotism, retirement policies, and faculty dissent, strikes, and disobedience to institutional policies.

A code should offer guidance for the teacher in the community, covering the teacher's rights and responsibilities as a citizen, community misconduct and the grounds for dismissal, the teacher's relations with parents, the holding of public office, and conflicts of interest.

Once you have a solid understanding of professional ethics in education, the next step is to study and compare the ethical problems of other professions, profit from their achievements, and avoid their pitfalls. Many changes have been made in the professions themselves in the past twenty-five years. Professional ethics has received greater attention in law, medicine, and business than in education. The law profession has extremely rigorous procedures for prosecuting violators, the study of medical ethics has produced a huge body of literature,[24] and since the Watergate years, 322 business ethics courses have been added nationwide to the business curriculum in higher education.[25]

Comparatively little attention is accorded professional ethics in teacher education. The NEA has made much progress in developing, revising, disseminating, and interpreting its code of ethics since the initial code was drawn up in 1929. However, enforcement is difficult because of the large number of school systems across the country. Codes are better enforced at the state level through control of teaching certificates, and at the local level, through the disciplinary power of the school boards.

Enforcement of educational ethics remains weak, despite efforts toward improvement.

Despite the increasing attention to ethics, most professions show an estimated ethical violation rate of 10 percent to 20 percent of its membership every year—and educators are probably no exception.[26] Thus much important work remains in both the study and practice of professional ethics, not just in education, but in all professions.

■ CERTIFICATION AND IMPROVING THE QUALITY OF TEACHERS

Certification is designed to ensure competence.

Certification by the state is evidence that the applicant meets requisite standards for employment or further training, and students must be certified before they can teach. Certification protects children from unqualified teachers, ensures that public funds are used to employ only qualified personnel, and protects the value of a teacher's formal training by eliminating competition with unqualified applicants. Usually by fulfilling the requirements of an accredited teacher education program, a student will be certified to teach in the public schools of that state. If you plan to teach in another state, be sure to check on the requirements early in your program.

Certification is a relatively new practice. During colonial times, the towns, churches, or civic officials determined the fitness of a teacher, and standards were low or nonexistent. During the nineteenth century, most states left the responsibility of certification to the county or local school districts, which required new teachers to pass formal examinations. State governments began taking a regulatory role in public education in the middle of the nineteenth century, and expanded their powers appreciably during the twentieth century. Today states have complete authority over teacher certification. /stop

Each state's certification process is unique, although there are certain generic similarities in training and degree requirements. All states and the District of Columbia require at least a bachelor's degree for initial certification, and twelve states require a fifth year of training. Students in some states also must take the National Teachers Examination before they can be certified. The number of required semester hours in general education ranges from twenty to sixty, depending on the state. Teacher education requirements vary from twenty to thirty-three hours for elementary teachers, and from twelve to eighteen hours for secondary teachers.[27]

Requirements for becoming a teacher can differ significantly from state to state.

Each state determines which out-of-state personnel can work in its schools. Mutual exchange arrangements are possible with twenty-two states, which base their standards on those developed by the National Association of State Directors of Teacher Education and Certification (NASDTEC).

Generally, though, certification requirements can vary dramatically from state to state within a teaching specialty.[28] Many states allow students to begin teaching before they have completed the required course work, and some states have been known to grant emergency certificates to students who have not completed four years of college. In their continuing efforts to improve certification procedures, some states are increasing subject matter requirements, raising the minimum requirements for SAT scores and grade point averages, and seriously considering the implementation of five-year teacher education programs. States also are turning to tests as screening devices, and the courts have affirmed this practice while adding guidelines for states to follow.

In 1971, for instance, the United States Supreme Court held in *Griggs v. Duke Power Company* that tests used to screen applicants must clearly be related to the job and its tasks, a ruling that also applies to the use of screening tests for teachers. The court, however, upheld South Carolina's right to use the National Teachers Examina-

In an effort to improve teacher quality, many states are increasing the requirements to become certified as a teacher.

tion (NTE) to determine pay scales and eligibility for certification, even though blacks scored lower than whites, because the proportion of black teachers approximates the proportion of black citizens.[29]

Some states use the NTE as a certification requirement or as an alternate screening device. Other states require students to pass a test of teaching competence or mastery of subject matter. To ensure fairness and relevance, developers of such tests must be certain their test questions are valid and that test scores accurately reflect a student's achievement. Research into the usefulness of state-devised competency tests is limited, and studies of the NTE have yielded mixed findings. One study showed that teachers who scored well on the NTE generally had received high ratings from their supervisors during practice teaching.[30] On the other hand, an earlier review of NTE found no evidence of validity.[31]

Several education-related groups have offered further suggestions for improving the quality of teaching. The Bicentennial Commission on Education for the Profession of Teaching, for instance, has recommended that certification be renewable based on a teacher's continuing satisfactory performance, "and that states share certification responsibility with teacher groups and college teacher educators."[32] More recently, the Carnegie Task Force on Teaching as a Profession has proposed establishing a national board for professional teaching standards, with state and regional branches, to determine the standards and certification requirements for teachers.[33] To think that states would voluntarily relinquish control of education standards to a national board is perhaps naive. Such a board also probably could not be expected to respond well to the needs of local and regional districts. Nevertheless, a national board might correct the deficiencies in some states' certification plans. The task force also has suggested replacing undergraduate education programs with a broad liberal education curriculum and moving the more specialized teacher education programs to the graduate level.

The Holmes Group, a coalition of deans, has recommended eliminating the undergraduate degree in teacher education and replacing it with a program in which students concentrate on the subjects they plan to teach. The study of teaching itself would move to the graduate level and would include the concepts of cognitive psychology.[34]

States also could consider tightening the qualifications for entering a teacher education program, and schools could recruit more vigorously among the academically talented. Currently, teacher education does draw some students with high SAT scores, but it attracts a disproportionate number of low scorers as well. Unfortunately, the field of education will not attract the best and the brightest unless improvements are made in its occupational status, salary levels, working con-

---

Several states require candidates to pass competency tests before they can be certified to teach.

The Holmes Group advocates eliminating the undergraduate degree in teacher education.

To improve the overall quality of teachers the field also needs to attract qualified people.

ditions, and intellectual challenges during training and on the job. Improved working conditions could include greater autonomy for teachers, which strong professional organizations can negotiate.

PROFESSIONAL ORGANIZATIONS ■
AND COLLECTIVE BARGAINING

During the 1960s the image of the teacher began to emerge as that of a young, tough militant willing to take aggressive, concerted action to redress grievances in the field. This is an accurate image if we consider labor strikes militant. The Bureau of Labor Statistics recorded ninety-one teacher strikes from 1940 through 1962; a great contrast to the 131 teacher strikes in the single academic year 1968–69. The reforms of the 1960s stimulated a significant change in the politics of American education and fueled the struggle for teacher loyalty by the two major educational associations: the National Education Association (NEA) and the American Federation of Teachers (AFT).

Both groups have decades of experience behind them. In 1857 members of ten state teacher associations gathered in Philadelphia and founded the National Teachers Association. The new organization, inauspiciously formed just before the Civil War, and restricted to male public-school teachers, floundered during its early years. In 1870 it changed its name to the National Education Association and began aggressively recruiting members through federation. It brought in other organizations like the National Superintendents Association and the American Normal Association, and made them departments of the NEA. Still, total membership was only about 2,500 by the turn of the century. To boost membership the NEA established state associations and induced principals in some schools to pressure teachers to join.

The NEA moved its headquarters to Washington, DC, organized a research division, and began sponsoring important commissions like the Committee of Ten, the Commission on the Reorganization of Secondary Education, and the Educational Policies Commission. Membership in the NEA reached an all-time high of about 1.9 million in 1976, declined to 1.6 million in the early 1980s, and grew to 1.8 million by 1986.[35]

The American Federation of Teachers was founded in 1916 and attempted to organize teachers around economic and professional concerns. The AFT organized itself along labor union lines and affiliated with the American Federation of Labor, although it was a long time before it officially sanctioned teacher strikes. The AFT began with 2,500 members and grew to more than 30,000 by World War II.

Unlike the NEA, the AFT represents only teachers, not administrators, and sees the two as having conflicting interests, not unlike those of management and labor.

Its most rapid growth and greatest organizational victories, however, have occurred in more recent years. The great leap in membership occurred during the 1960s. The NEA outdistanced the AFT in growth and influence until the 1960s. At that time the more vigorous tactics of the AFT won it the right in many large cities to represent teachers as their exclusive bargaining agent with local school boards. In 1960 the AFT had 60,000 members; today it has more than 600,000 (unlike the NEA, the AFT does not offer membership to school administrators).

Although they are not as far apart on the issues as they used to be, the two organizations have many central differences, the most basic being their views on organized labor. The NEA believes that teachers cannot hope to become fully professional unless their organizations are independent, and that the AFT is hindering this possibility by affiliating with organized labor. On the other hand, the AFT charges that the NEA is dominated by administrators who control their teachers and discourage demands of which administrators and school boards might disapprove.

The NEA accuses the AFT of inhibiting the professionalization of teaching by being more of a labor union than a professional association.

The NEA also has accused the AFT of violating state laws and using unprofessional tactics such as strikes and collective bargaining, which the NEA believes are more appropriate for industrial workers. The AFT claims that the NEA speaks only for the educational establishment, coerces teachers into joining, and is racially biased because it failed to immediately require its Southern affiliates to comply with desegregation after the 1954 Brown case. (See Chapter 10 for discussion of this landmark case.) While representatives for both organizations have been known to exaggerate their claims against each other, by and large their charges are true.

As AFT victories piled up and membership grew, the NEA began to reconsider its approach. Without a doubt, the single greatest influence on the NEA's changing policies and practices in the past few decades has been the AFT.

As AFT popularity among teachers grew, the NEA began to sanction the use of some "labor" tactics.

When the AFT started gaining teacher loyalty in large cities through the power of collective negotiating, the NEA reluctantly adjusted its policies and announced it would engage in "professional negotiations" (as opposed to collective bargaining). The two procedures may be different in theory but are similar in practice.[36] By the end of the 1960s the AFT had made considerable gains in large eastern cities, and the NEA was strongest in suburban and rural areas throughout the nation. The tactics used by the NEA and AFT have become increasingly similar, and today both organizations can be considered labor unions.

Collective Negotiations

Collective bargaining is the attempt to resolve the conflict between two or more parties through compromise and concession. In teacher/school-board negotiations, the practical intent of collective bargaining is to gain more control for teachers, in the decision-making process. However, it does place teachers in an adversarial role and assumes a fundamental conflict between teachers and school boards. Proponents of collective bargaining say that successful negotiations can lead to greater autonomy for teachers and more control over instruction and work conditions. Critics insist that unionization (including collective bargaining) is incompatible with the field of teaching because unions belong in industry; schools are not factories, they say, and teachers are not laborers. Teachers are the largest unionized occupational group in the United States, although it has not always been so.

Before 1959 collective bargaining was not required of school boards in any state. Today, however, thirty-three states require bargaining, thirteen others permit it, and four states prohibit it.[37] About 88 percent of the nation's teachers belong to the AFT or NEA and 83 percent belong to local teachers associations.[38] Despite the high membership figures, interviews of nearly 200 teachers found that they generally are ambivalent about unionism and are selective about which militant actions they will support.[39]

Teachers are free to join professional associations or unions, and school boards are free to bargain with teacher organizations if they wish, as long as no statutory limitation is placed upon them. A school board can enter into a bargaining agreement for a stipulated length of time, but it cannot bind future school boards to that agreement. Bargaining usually involves matters like salaries, working conditions, grievance procedures, seniority, policies, and fringe benefits. Areas such as the budget, hiring practices, and the curriculum, however, are beyond the legal scope of collective bargaining.

Teacher collecting bargaining usually focuses on improving working conditions and benefits for teachers, not on giving teachers more say in educational policy.

When negotiations reach an impasse, a third party often is brought in to help resolve the dispute through fact-finding procedures. This usually staves off any extreme actions by both parties and gives the third party enough time to do its job. Teachers, for instance, would be in a weak position if they engaged in strikes or sanctions before a third-party decision is reached, and both teachers and the board would be vulnerable if they refused to abide by the third party's recommendations. The teachers' position still is considered militant while the third party is involved. Teachers can inform the board that they still expect some concessions. The board, too, is free to indicate which points it is unwilling to concede. Not all negotiation sessions reach a happy resolution, and strikes or sanctions may enter the picture.

Strikes and Sanctions

Though originally the NEA did not engage in strikes, which it labeled unprofessional, it did approve of imposing sanctions under certain conditions. **Sanctions** involve curtailing or withdrawing teacher services to a district or state in cases where teachers are not under contract. After reaching an impasse in negotiations, the teacher organization publicizes the matters in dispute, asks teachers in the district or state to not sign contracts for the forthcoming year, and strongly recommends that other members not accept a position in the boycotted area. Sanctions do not violate contracts and school districts are given notice before they are applied. However, sanctions can last well into the school year and they often last longer than strikes.

A **strike** is a work stoppage while under contract in an attempt to force an employer to comply with demands. While strikes occur more often among AFT membership, they have been used increasingly by local NEA affiliates as the NEA continues to adopt policies more characteristic of the AFT.

Teacher strikes are illegal in most states. Nine states allow teachers to strike, usually after they have exhausted all other avenues, but most other states explicitly prohibit strikes. Should teachers strike despite laws against it? One argument against strikes holds that citizens should obey the law, and that to do otherwise is immoral. When teachers strike illegally, therefore, they

Teachers strike to gain public or legislative support for issues they consider vital.

are committing an immoral act and setting poor examples for their students. Moreover, if each citizen could freely decide which laws to obey and which to disobey, society would soon collapse.

Another argument against strikes is that teachers have a monopoly on the market and should not be permitted to withhold their services. This actually is an argument in support of legislation against strikes, because it suggests that the public interest would be endangered by the inability to maintain the schools.

A third argument is that strikes are unprofessional and that teachers never will attain full professional stature as long as they engage in them. As we learned earlier in the chapter, one characteristic of a profession is that it requires its members to render service upon request, whether convenient or not, and to provide the highest quality service possible because it is vital to the clients.

The arguments against strikes are powerful: strikes are illegal and hence immoral, run counter to the public interest, and are unprofessional. The latter two arguments logically can be offered even in states that permit strikes.

Because the issue of strikes raises complex issues that deserve scrutiny, let us take a closer look at these three arguments. First, the belief that to violate a law against strikes is immoral assumes that the law is a higher form of morality than an individual's independently derived moral code. But is this necessarily the case? Is civil law a higher moral authority than our individual understandings of right and wrong? Did Rosa Parks, for example, commit an immoral act when she refused to give up her seat on a Montgomery, Alabama, bus to a white passenger?

In a democratic society, individual rights are secured by social recognition. One function of government is to offer a framework of laws through which social institutions and individuals can flourish. The laws that establish and protect these rights reflect society's definition of the common good and can be expanded or restricted as society's definition of that good evolves. According to this view, the state protects and reconciles citizens' rights through the legal system, and individuals may disobey a law only when the law runs counter to the common good. Obviously, one of the reasons a society might have such a law is that that society's concept of the common good has changed since the law was first enacted.

However, other reasons also exist for laws not reflecting all of society's sense of what is right. Even in democracies, legal systems sometimes establish a distribution of rights to maintain social stability. In these cases, the law is what legislators have stipulated as the normal condition for society; they attempt to maintain this condition by law and, if lost, to restore it by law. In other words, the law is no more just

> Critics say strikes are a breach of teachers' professional obligations to their students, to society, and to the profession.

> Moral obligations sometimes conflict with legal obligations.

or moral than those who make it. And when the law serves stability without concern for justice and morality, one could argue that citizens are morally bound to disobey the law.

The second argument against strikes—that the public interest is endangered by an inability to maintain the schools—overlooks the fact that schools are closed for holidays, inclement weather, sports events, and teachers conventions. So far, no one has complained that these closings harm children or society. Moreover, one can disagree with certain laws in a society and, therefore, not obey them, without rejecting the foundation upon which the society itself is constructed (as does the revolutionary, for instance). Teacher strikes, where illegal, fall into this category. Though they violate the law, they pose no threat to the perpetuation of society.

These two arguments tie into our earlier discussion of professionals' obligations to their fellow citizens and to society as a whole. The third argument against strikes addresses the question of strikes and professionalism head on.

Professionals, as a rule, do not strike. But there may be overriding conditions that warrant the withholding of services, such as changing conditions or policies. In these instances, teachers should make every effort to educate the public about the issues involved. They must prove the moral rightness of a strike by explaining the undesirable educational conditions that brought about the strike, and they must demonstrate that they have exhausted every avenue of negotiation, including repeated attempts at discussion and collective bargaining. Finally, they must reassure the public that a work stoppage will not have dire consequences.

Strikes usually are initiated over demands for higher teacher salaries and better working conditions rather than insufficient per-pupil expenditures, violations of academic freedom, unsafe buildings, or other serious deficiencies over which the public would be more likely to condone a strike. A case can be made, however, that the satisfaction of teachers' material demands can improve the learning environment and have a positive effect on student achievement.

If a strike were the only way to promote the welfare of students, society, or the profession, striking could be seen as a professional obligation.

We can see now that some strikes probably are morally and even professionally justified while others are not. Each situation should be examined individually before such a judgment is made. At least from a moral and professional standpoint, the success of a teacher strike is measured by whether it has promoted the public welfare.

How effective are strikes in getting teachers what they want? An early research study found strikes to be an effective union tactic,[40] but more recent studies have shown mixed results. Some strikes have resulted in large gains for teachers, but others have resulted in teachers having to settle for less than had been offered before the strike.[41] Also, a review of average salaries in states that permit teacher strikes shows no appreciable increase in pay for teachers.[42] As for the general effect of collective bargaining, though it has only modestly increased teacher salaries, if at all, it has enabled teachers to define and, in some cases, reduce the limits of their jobs. It also has provided protection for seniority and ensured better procedures for negotiating grievances.[43] But although teachers have won some improvements in working conditions and job security, they have not gained much influence over instructional policy. Overall, collective bargaining has been neither as harmful as its critics feared nor as effective as its proponents wished.

In an attempt to better address educational problems and avoid the need for strikes or bargaining, some school districts are experimenting with self-government. In Dade County, Florida, for instance, thirty-two of the district's 280 schools have instituted a program in which teachers and administrators work together to redesign programs and educational policy. The teachers have far more power to determine the number of faculty to be hired, how teachers will function, and how funds will be spent.

■ **PAUSE TO REFLECT**
Teacher Strikes

- Nine states permit striking as a last resort, but does that make it acceptable?
- Can teachers strike and still be considered professionals?
- It is argued that teachers need autonomy and decent working conditions to best serve their students. Should they be allowed to pursue those needs, even to the point of striking?

ACADEMIC FREEDOM AND CENSORSHIP ■

To thrive, democratic societies need an educated citizenry that can exercise independent judgment. To promote this free-thinking citizenry, certain freedoms are necessary in the educational process. However, some citizens ritualistically extol the virtues of a democratic society and the importance of education in maintaining and improving it, and then refuse to grant teachers the academic freedom they need to produce independent thinkers.

Academic Freedom

Academic freedom is the liberty needed to develop and communicate knowledge in an academic community without administrative, political, ecclesiastical, or other forms of interference. Unlike civil liberties, which apply to all citizens, academic freedom concerns only the faculty and students of educational institutions. Academic freedom is vital to the continuing search for truth, not only on "safe" topics but also on those likely to stir widespread controversy.

Education depends upon a free flow of ideas.

Support for academic freedom reaches back to Aristotle, who said, "All men by nature desire to know." To be fully human, individuals must develop and use their intellectual abilities. Whenever unnecessary and arbitrary restrictions are placed on inquiry, life becomes stunted and distorted. Thus, it is through free inquiry that people learn to sift truth from error and use their knowledge to enjoy more meaningful lives.

On more utilitarian grounds, progress in the arts and sciences probably would have been impossible if forward-thinking researchers had been denied the academic freedom to pursue controversial ideas. Additionally, progress in all social institutions, including schools, requires free and unfettered criticism.

Academic freedom, open debate, and discussion are essential in the pursuit of ideas.

Academic freedom, however, is not absolute; it carries with it cor-relative responsibilities. It also is surrounded by issues and questions that deserve some thought by those who, like you, intend to enter education:

- Should limits ever be placed on academic freedom?
- What are the basic rights and responsibilities of faculty per-taining to academic freedom?
- On what grounds should difficult cases involving the right to teach and learn be decided?

Howard K. Beale, in a comprehensive historical study of freedom of teaching in American schools, observed, "Teachers in each century and locality have been allowed to discuss subjects that did not seem to matter and been denied freedom on issues about which men did seri-ously care."[44] He concluded his study in 1939 with the doubt that teachers are any more free today than in the past. In fact, he found more violations of freedom from 1929 to 1939 than in the rest of history combined.[45] Conditions did not improve much during the 1940s and 1950s when America was seized by a consuming fear of communism. Many suspected that teachers might be "subversive," and attempted to root out those considered disloyal to the United States. This atmosphere of fear and suspicion discouraged any discussion of controversial issues in most schools and colleges. The height of this "Red Scare" came during the McCarthy era in the early 1950s, when the loyalty of individuals in certain occupational groups, teaching in-cluded, was seriously questioned by a Congressional committee. New York began requiring educators to take loyalty oaths, and the practice quickly spread throughout the country in the 1950s. The practice de-clined in the 1960s.

Historically, academic freedom has applied to research scholars, not to teachers whose main task is to transmit the resulting knowledge. Despite attempts by public-school teachers to establish their rights in this area, the courts have refrained from formulating any general prin-ciples, preferring to deal with the issues case by case.

Some people be-lieve that young children should be protected from controversial ideas.

When considering such cases, courts look at several factors. One is the general belief that older students need less protection from con-troversial or potentially dangerous doctrines than do younger ones, who are less experienced, more impressionable, and more likely to be hurt while their character and personalities are taking shape. Courts also consider whether a teacher has strayed from the course outline or from assigned readings—and do not look favorably upon that.[46] Ex-temporaneous discussions of sexual matters, for instance, usually are

Academic free-dom is not a carte blanche to dis-cuss ideas not specifically re-lated to the sub-ject at hand.

not considered protected by academic freedom.[47] In the case of a biology teacher whose contract was not renewed because it was decided that he had overemphasized sex in his health class, the court ruled that teachers do not have the right to disregard the text and syllabus[48] and that academic freedom is not a license for unrestrained expression that diverges from the curriculum. This includes material that is irrelevant as well as potentially controversial. For example, public-school teachers cannot preach their religion in class or recruit students for their religious organizations.

In most states, local school boards have considerable authority to establish curriculums, and teachers retain some discretion in choosing teaching strategies. Teachers usually can assign controversial materials if they are relevant to the subject, appropriate to the age and maturity of the students, and are not disruptive. If teachers follow these guidelines, school boards cannot interfere, even to placate irate citizens.

Censorship

Censorship in public education, a perennial problem, has increased sharply in recent years. The number of organizations devoted to censorship activities and attacks on public schools has grown dramatically.[49] **Censorship** is the deliberate attempt to exclude materials that offend the censor or that the censor believes may damage the young or harm society. The two dominant forms of censorship are conservative censorship and liberal censorship.[50]

Conservative censorship appears in two related forms. The aim of the first form is simply to promote virtue and prevent vice. It seeks no other justification than that virtue is good for the individual and vice bad. And since, if, as J. F. Stephen believes, the object of legislation is to promote a good moral system, then the promotion of virtue and the prevention of vice should be legislated.[51] The purpose of the second form of conservative censorship is to combat forms of immorality considered harmful to society. Patrick Devlin says that a community of political and moral ideas makes society possible, and that history shows societies will disintegrate without a common morality, a fundamental agreement about good and evil. He concludes that "it is not possible to set theoretical limits to the power of the state to legislate against immorality."[52]

Through the use of both forms, conservative censorship organizations endorse teaching creationism instead of evolutionary theory and advocate elimination of sex education, secular humanism, values clarification, and textbooks that run counter to the religious and moral values of parents. Some organizations go even further, demanding that

Censors limit what others can read, see, or hear.

schools use only textbooks that honor the family, monogamy, the woman's role as wife and mother, and the man's role as provider and protector.[53]

Of late, *secular humanism* has become the term used by conservative censors to embrace most of the "evils" they deplore. Secular humanism is alleged to be atheistic, human-centered, evolutionary, sexually permissive, and to advocate freedom to read whatever one desires.[54] In *Torcaso v. Watkins, Clerk* (1961), the United States Supreme Court added fuel to the fire when it deemed secular humanism a religion. Conservative censors have used this interpretation to argue that public schools are violating the First Amendment by attempting to establish a religion of secular humanism.[55]

Other groups engage in *liberal censorship*,[56] a term that usually refers to attempts by minority groups (meaning minority in either number or power) to censor materials they believe are prejudicial, stereotypical, or degrading. Blacks, for instance, have been offended by words or caricatures in *Little Black Sambo, Huckleberry Finn,* and *The Gold Bug;* Jews have objected to the characters of Fagin in *Oliver Twist* and Shylock in *The Merchant of Venice;* and women have taken offense at sexist stereotypes in textbooks and other materials.

Some censors charge educators with censorship when selecting course material. Some educators have themselves argued that censor-

> Censors, whether from the left or the right, seek to suppress ideas they think will harm society.

ship is, indeed, inevitable because no course of study can include all available material. Therefore, the process of "selection entails exclusion and thus censorship."[57]

Selection of course material involves value judgments about what students need to know.

Without adequate safeguards, selection could become a form of censorship. Obviously, as a teacher, you will need to consider carefully what you assign and why. Furthermore, to guard against selection turning into censorship, educators must allow students access to pertinent materials not included in the course, refuse to deny access to any materials, and help students to assess evidence for themselves so they can become independent thinkers and educated citizens.

Arguments Against Censorship. John Stuart Mill makes three trenchant points against censorship:

- Suppression of opinion may blot out the truth.
- Even if an opinion is false, truth is served by refuting error.
- No opinion is completely true or false; therefore, an unconventional opinion may be useful because it contains some truth.

Opponents of censorship believe that the suppression of ideas harms society more than exposure could.

Thus, he concludes, freedom of thought and opinion should not be curbed by authorities.[58]

Assuming that arbitrary censorship is to be avoided, educators should recognize students' rights to freedom of expression in the classroom and freedom of speech in general. Schools should be centers of inquiry where students are not limited to "safe" topics, but are free to read and examine all points of view. Only when it can be shown that introduction of controversial matter will likely disrupt the educational process should restrictions be considered.

Dealing with and Avoiding Censorship. To cope intelligently and consistently with would-be censors, schools should establish a policy for selecting instructional materials and define procedures for dealing with complaints. School libraries also should have such policies and procedures; they may elect to be guided by those of the American Library Association. Administrators and school-board members should be familiar with these policies and procedures. For their part, teachers should prepare written justifications for the use of controversial materials, including novels and short stories. These actions may not prevent censorship attempts, but they may ensure that challenges to school materials are resolved in a fair and orderly manner.

Selection committees should represent the community by including parents and other local citizens to encourage the airing of divergent viewpoints and to build a bridge to the larger community. Such representation may defuse some attacks on school materials, although the more extreme censorship groups usually are not swayed by such actions.

Good contacts with the local press can help, too. Educators can alert the newspapers to censorship threats and usually can count on them to take a stand against censorship on the editorial page when a dispute erupts and angry letters start pouring in. Local radio and television programs also can effectively inform the community of the school's position. Beyond that, educators can solicit the support of influential community members by speaking at meetings of local business and professional organizations.

Censorship groups have different ideological grounds for their attacks and some groups pose greater threats than others. But whatever the source of an attack, educators can meet it successfully with careful preparation, perhaps including some of the procedures just discussed. Consistent preparation can enhance school-community relations and promote a healthy, open atmosphere for learning.

■ **PAUSE TO REFLECT**
Censorship and Professionalism

- Can you see any connection between censorship and our earlier discussion of professionalism?
- Does censorship impinge upon teachers' autonomy as professionals? Try to explain the rationale for your answer.

A TEACHER'S RIGHT TO PRIVACY ■

As we discussed in Chapter 1, up through the early twentieth century, a teacher's right to privacy was severely restricted, especially in rural and small-town America. Today, while public-school teachers generally enjoy greater freedom from surveillance in their private lives, they are subject to widespread data collection and threatened by laws establishing the public's right to know. The potential conflict of these two ostensibly desirable values (the individual's right to privacy and the public's right to know) can pose problems for educators.

Privacy is "the right to be let alone, to enjoy solitude, intimacy, reasonable anonymity, and to reserve personal information."[59] Let us look at four important types of privacy:

- Privacy of information
- Privacy of personal physical access, contact, and intrusion

- Privacy from surveillance
- Privacy of personal possessions

Vast amounts of data are kept on all Americans, such as scholastic records, credit references, tax files, census data, and Selective Service data. Advocates of information privacy hope to restrict the collection of personal data without consent, to have access to the personal information that does exist, to have the right to challenge and ultimately delete inaccurate and damaging information, to oppose the collaboration of agencies in free exchange of information, and to prohibit the growth of centralized data banks.

Privacy of personal physical access, contact, and intrusion means the right to be free from interaction, touch, or interference. One has the right to be left alone, for example, and to enjoy freedom from being summarily accosted, freedom from socially interacting against one's will, and freedom from offensive sounds. It also may include freedom to maintain the overall privacy of one's body (which could include abortion rights). And it would include freedom from interference with one's actions, except when those actions violate laws or infringe upon the rights of others.

Privacy from surveillance means freedom from unwanted observation, listening, and recording. Most people do not want others to eavesdrop, "bug" their homes or offices, use electronic recording devices, or take photographs or televised shots without consent.

Finally, as written in the Fourth Amendment, people have the right "to be secure in their persons, houses, papers, and effects against unreasonable searches and seizures. . . ." Warrants can be issued only upon probable cause and must be supported by an oath or affirmation that describes the place to be searched and the person or things to be seized. Unlike the three other types of privacy, this type is constitutionally protected. At issue here, however, is whether the Fourth Amendment applies to public-school situations.

The right to privacy is supported on many grounds, including legal grounds based on the Bill of Rights, especially the First, Fourth, Fifth, and Ninth amendments;[60] psychological grounds based on the argument that people need to be free to develop a self-concept;[61] and moral grounds based on the duty to respect others.[62]

Privacy also can be supported by showing that it is embodied in the fundamental right to freedom. Free people should be able to choose the type of privacy they desire and to decide how that privacy shall be exercised. When citizens enjoy privacy, they actually enjoy a form of freedom.

Freedom is a necessary condition for privacy, but it is not the only condition, because one most likely must live under certain legal and political conditions to safeguard that right. An abridgement of freedom may result in intrusions into privacy through unauthorized use of one's personal information, physical intrusions, surveillance, and endangerment of one's private possessions. Such intrusions may constrain one's actions, as in notable figures refraining from certain public appearances because they fear their privacy will not be respected.

The Public Interest and the Right to Know

Educators' rights to privacy may be threatened by a growing recognition and advocacy of the public's right to know. Relatively recent federal guidelines, such as the Privacy Act of 1974, are designed to protect privacy, but federal antibias legislation, open meetings laws, and open records acts can conflict with that protection. In an attempt to preserve the protection of privacy, some of these laws, such as the Texas Open Records Act, exclude information considered confidential by constitutional, statutory, or judicial decisions. Nonetheless, the right to privacy is "a relatively new and evolving constitutional freedom that has not yet been adequately clarified by the courts to provide much protection for teachers' personal lives."[63]

Rights, however, are not absolute. Human beings do not automatically harmonize their purposes and activities with one another, so freedom may have to be curtailed occasionally to prevent interference with another's rights. Other values, such as equality, justice, or security, also may conflict with freedom. Because privacy is not absolute, it may have to be temporarily abridged when it conflicts with preeminent values. But the conditions under which privacy can be abridged have yet to be clarified. The Texas Open Records Act holds that "government is the servant of the people" and, thus, "all persons are, unless otherwise expressly provided by law, at all times entitled to full and complete information regarding the affairs of government and the official acts of those who represent them as public officials and employees."[64]

The public's right to know can be linked to the characteristics of public institutions. **Public,** as opposed to private, refers to that which concerns all members of the community without distinction. Thus, a town hall is said to be public because it is open to all, whether or not they choose to enter.

Public schools are public in terms of purpose, control, support, access, and commitment to civic unity.[65] A public school serves a public rather than a private purpose; it is not maintained for the personal advantage of teacher, proprietor, student, or parent. Public schools are designed to serve the welfare of a democratic society by assuring the imparting of knowledge and understanding needed to produce responsible citizens.[66]

Because teachers serve the public interest, the public has a right to certain kinds of information about individual teachers.

The public's right to know can be grounded in the public interest. Barry defines the public interest as "those interests which people have in common *qua* [as] members of the public."[67] And as an educated citizenry may be argued as being in the public interest in a democratic society, the public has the right to know what is taking place within our schools. Moreover, schools benefit from the constructive involvement of the public, and, for such involvement to take place, citizens need access to pertinent information. The issue becomes blurred when we try to determine what information is pertinent and who is best suited to make that determination.

Competency, Immoral Conduct, and the Right to Know

If public education is in the public interest, then the state must provide an effective school system. An effective school system requires a body of qualified educators. The public usually wants to know whether schools are performing effectively and whether the educators are competent. While basic employment and termination decisions may be left to school boards except in the most controversial cases, citizens may want access to specific information about some educators whenever questions arise about their competency.

Teachers can be dismissed for incompetence, immorality, insubordination, unprofessional conduct, and for economic reasons. It is easier to dismiss a teacher on probation than a tenured teacher, although both should expect to enjoy academic freedom. Most of the above grounds for dismissal are of greater concern to the administration and school board than to the public. Two notable exceptions are incompetence and immorality.

Among the legal grounds for judging a teacher incompetent are a lack of knowledge of one's subject, a physical disability that seriously impairs one's teaching ability, mental disability (such as a serious mental illness), and inability to maintain discipline in the classroom. In some states, failure to pass a written competency test is also grounds for discharge.

The public has the right to know whether a teacher is competent in the classroom. The right to information about a teacher's private life is less clear.

But the public's right to know is most likely to conflict with a teacher's right to privacy when the morality of a teacher's private life is in question. The public may admit, however grudgingly, that the decision to fire a teacher should be left up to the administration or school board in many cases because they have the expertise to judge the teacher's fitness. But most believe that no one is expert in morality and that each person has the right to make moral judgments, including about the private lives of teachers in the community.

Teachers generally are held to a higher moral standard in their private lives than most other community members, except perhaps religious leaders. The argument for this is that teachers influence young, emerging personalities and can inflict considerable harm if they are not good role models. Teachers historically have been subjected to surveillance—unwanted observation, listening, and recording—although keeping tabs on a teacher's private life is more difficult in today's larger cities. Teachers also do not enjoy full privacy of information: citizens may collect personal information about a teacher without consent.

The following acts, among others, often are considered immoral by all or segments of the public: homosexuality, pregnancy outside of marriage, excessive drinking, commission of a felony, possession of illegal drugs, use of vulgar or obscene language around students, and sexual advances toward students.

One might argue that immorality, if proved, is sufficient grounds for dismissal if the conduct can be shown to impair a teacher's professional responsibilities, yet still concede that the mere possibility of immoral conduct may not warrant infringing upon a teacher's privacy. Once teachers are screened during the initial hiring process, their rights to privacy should be honored so they have sufficient freedom and space for personal and professional growth. People who live in fear that their privacy might be violated at any time can only be inhibited in their individual development, which includes the opportunity to make choices, take chances, and shape a life plan of their own choosing.

The burden of proof should rest squarely on the one who enters the teacher's realm of privacy, whether school-board member, administrator, or individual citizen. One such realm is life style, and the question arises: should education officials concern themselves with a teacher's private life style? Probably not, unless it can be shown that some aspect of the teacher's private life seriously impairs his or her professional responsibilities (as in the case of alcoholism). When the behavior does not impair professional abilities as much as establish a poor role model, then the accusers must declare the moral principle that has been violated and prove that the activity has a negative influence on students. Education officials may consider the notoriety of the activity, whether it took place before or after the teacher was hired, and whether it occurred in the local community. Officials also may consider the negative effect the activity might have on students. That effect may be obvious in cases of drunken driving or armed assault but much less obvious in cases of homosexuality or unwed parenthood. That judgment would depend upon the mores of the community at the time. No matter what

One way to help protect teachers' rights to privacy is to decide that the public can concern itself only with information that affects the classroom.

the case, however, the burden of proof should rest with the school, and the teacher has a legal right to due process.

To sum up, the public has the right to know whether teachers and other public-school educators are qualified, but it has no right to invade the privacy of teachers to gather evidence in such matters. Administrators and school boards should safeguard teachers' private lives at all times, breaking that trust only in cases where a teacher's ability to fulfill professional responsibilities is seriously impaired by his or her life style. Furthermore, when an investigation is launched into a teacher's private life, the burden of proof rests with the school, and the teacher's constitutional rights must be observed. Such procedures are most likely to protect teacher privacy while safeguarding the public interest.

■ **PAUSE TO REFLECT**
What Is Expected of a Teacher?

- Teachers set critical examples for their students and generally are held to a higher moral standard than others. Do you think this is unfair? Or should you accept this higher expectation as a condition of being a teacher?

- Should teachers be accorded the same rights to privacy as other citizens?

- Is there a connection between what you do in your private life and what you do at work?

- Should education officials or others be allowed to delve into teachers' private lives to determine their moral fitness for teaching?

- If the public has a right to know about the education their children are receiving, should they be allowed access to private information about the teachers?

■ Summary

- Though we sometimes label as professions those careers we consider prestigious, they might not actually be professions in the precise definition of the word. True professions share a number of identifying characteristics: practice of a profession is essentially intellectual, is guided by a system of intellectual and moral principles, serves the public good in some significant way, and enjoys a fair amount of autonomy.

- Teaching possesses some of the characteristics of a profession. The act of teaching, for example, is essentially intellectual and is guided by a defined code of ethics. Teaching does not fully possess some of the other characteristics of professions. Teacher preparation is generally not as rigorous or extensive as preparation for many professions, and teachers lack the autonomy granted to many professionals. Still other professional characteristics can be found in the practice of only some teachers, not all being guided in practice by intellectual principles and a broad base of knowledge, for instance.

- The field of teaching is thorough in developing and disseminating ethical codes but needs improvement in the area of enforcement.

- Increasing the standards for teacher certification is seen as one possible means of improving the overall quality of teachers and pushing the career more toward full and recognized professional status.

- The NEA and the AFT both have been influential in promoting the cause of teachers. The two organizations originally were widely divided on whether teachers, as educators and professionals, should engage in collective bargaining, sanctions, and strikes to achieve their ends. This gap has narrowed in recent years.

- Academic freedom is vital to education, but a teacher's right to a free and open learning environment does not extend to unrestrained expression that diverges from the curriculum. Censorship, the chief threat to academic freedom, can come from conservative or liberal sources.

- As members of our society, teachers are entitled to the same rights as other individuals, one of the most basic of which is privacy. At the same time, however, the public has the right to know those things that affect its interests, one of the most basic of which is the education of its children. The public's justified right to information regarding a teacher's competence and moral character (the latter of which is often subjectively evaluated) can expose teachers to undue scrutiny and, in a sense, makes them less free than other members of society.

■ Key Terms

academic freedom	professional ethics
censorship	public
certification	sanctions
collective bargaining	semiprofession
educator	strike
particularism	tenure
privacy	universalism
profession	

■ Discussion Questions

1. To what extent does teaching measure up to the characteristics of a profession? Should it be considered a profession even though it falls short of some criteria? What steps can be taken to help teaching acquire full professional status?

2. How can the quality of prospective teachers be upgraded? Should the entrance requirements to teacher education programs be stiffer? Or should the weeding out process begin after training during the certification process? Can you think of other methods of improving teacher quality?

3. Should certification remain a duty of the state or should a national board be established to handle the applications? If teachers were required to reapply regularly for certification, would that ensure higher quality education?

4. Teacher organizations have done a thorough job of developing a code of ethics, but enforcement remains weak. How can that area be strengthened?

5. The AFT has influenced the NEA in many ways, especially in the area of negotiations, sanctions, and strikes. All in all, do you think that these groups have helped to improve the quality of education? How? Some argue that collective bargaining and the threat of sanctions and strikes belong in industry, not education. Do you agree? If so, what other methods can teachers use to improve working conditions?

6. How have the courts restricted the concept of academic freedom? Should students be protected from controversial ideas and discussions that do not fit the curriculum, or should they be exposed to as many different ideas as possible, whether relevant or not?

7. What is the difference between selection and censorship? Or is selection just a form of censorship? How can selection be protected from turning into censorship?

8. How does a teacher's right to privacy conflict with the public's right to know? What steps can teachers and education officials take to avoid this conflict?

■ Learning Activities

1. Gather information from the AFT and NEA and compare their positions on sanctions, strikes, and other controversial issues.

2. Debate the proposal: tenure for teachers should be abolished.

3. Find out local school-board policies on collective bargaining, sanctions, strikes, tenure, academic freedom, and censorship. Report to class on your findings.

4. Debate the proposal: teachers should not strike.

5. Invite a representative from the local teachers association to present the association's policies on some of the issues raised in this chapter, such as the professionalization of teaching, ethics in the classroom, unionization of teaching, academic freedom, and rights to privacy.

6. Interview a representative of a censorship group about the group's objectives, rationale, and tactics. Find out what materials are targeted and why.

Suggested Readings

AFT/NEA. *The Crucial Differences*. Washington, DC: American Federation of Teachers, AFL–CIO, 1984.

The characteristics and differences between the two organizations are explained.

Beale, Howard K. *A History of Freedom of Teaching in American Schools*. New York: Scribner, 1941.

An important historical study of the many and diverse restrictions placed upon teachers.

Creswell, Anthony M., Michael J. Murphy, and Charles T. Kerchner. *Teachers, Unions, and Collective Bargaining in Public Education*. Berkeley: McCutchan, 1980.

Explains the role and procedures of collective bargaining in education.

Eaton, William Edward. *The American Federation of Teachers, 1916–1961*. Carbondale, IL: Southern Illinois University Press, 1982.

Traces the emergence of the AFT and the early years of its development.

Feistritzer, C. Emily. *The Making of a Teacher: A Report on Teacher Education and Certification*. Washington, DC: National Center for Educational Information, 1984.

An assessment and critical analysis of certification and teacher education.

Fischer, Louis, David Schimmel, and Cynthia Kelly. *Teachers and the Law*. New York: Longman, 1981.

A readable book that explains teachers' legal rights.

Jenkinson, Edward B. *Censors in the Classroom: The Mind Bender*. Carbondale, IL: Southern Illinois University Press, 1979.

Lively case studies of censorship groups are presented.

Rich, John Martin. *Professional Ethics in Education*. Springfield, IL: Charles C. Thomas, 1984.

A systematic study of ethical codes, teacher and student rights, faculty relations with colleagues and other officials, the educator in the community, and other topics.

Wesley, Edgar B. *NEA: The First Hundred Years*. New York: Harper & Row, 1957.

A history of the NEA's early growth and activities.

Notes

1. *National Data Program for the Social Sciences: Cumulative Codebook for 1972–77 General Social Surveys* (Chicago: National Opinion Research Center, University of Chicago, October 1977), 224–35.

2. Among the different definitions of profession, see A. M. Carr-Saunders and P. A. Wilson, *The Professions* (Oxford: Clarendon Press, 1933), 491; Bernard Barber, "Some Problems in the Sociology of the Professions," in *The Professions in America*, ed. Kenneth S. Lynn (Boston: Houghton Mifflin, 1965), 18; William Goode, " 'Professions' and 'Non-Professions'," in *Professionalization*, eds. Howard M. Vollmer and Donald L. Mills (Englewood Cliffs, NJ: Prentice-Hall, 1966), 36.

3. Everett C. Hughes, "Professions," in *The Professions in America*, ed. Kenneth S. Lynn (Boston: Houghton Mifflin, 1965), 9.

4. Amitai Etzioni, ed., *The Semi-Professions and Their Organizations* (New York: Free Press, 1969), v.

5. See *Encyclopedia of Educational Research*, 5th ed., 4 vols.; and *Handbook of Research on Teaching*, 3rd ed. (New York: Macmillan, 1986).

6. "Effective Schools" (special issue), *Educational Researcher* 12 (April 1983): 1–35.

7. Maynard C. Reynolds, *Knowledge Base for the Beginning Teacher* (Elmsford, NY: Pergamon Press, 1989).

8. W. Earl Armstrong and T. M. Stinnett, *A Manual on Certification Requirements for School Personnel in the United States* (Washington, DC: NEA, National Commission of Teacher Education and Professional Standards, 1962), 10.

9. *National Data Program for the Social Sciences*, 224–35.

10. Blake Rodman, "Public Favors Pay Raises, Competency Testing for Teachers, N.E.A./Gallup Poll Indicates," *Education Week* (August 21, 1985): 52.

11. Stanley M. Elam and Alec M. Gallup, "The 21st Annual Gallup Poll of the Public's Attitudes Toward the Public Schools," *Phi Delta Kappan* (September 1989): 41–54.

12. "The Young and the Restless," *U.S. News & World Report* 106 (January 23, 1989): 66.

13. Donald J. Treiman, *Occupational Prestige in Comparative Perspective* (New York: Academic Press, 1977).

14. Ibid., 155–56.

15. Talcott Parsons and Edward A. Shils, eds., *Toward a General Theory of Action* (New York: Harper Torchbooks, 1951), 82.

16. Wilbert E. Moore, *The Professions: Roles and Rules* (New York: Russell Sage, 1970), 10.

17. Daniel Koretz, *Educational Achievement: Explanations and Implications of Recent Trends* (Washington, DC: Congressional Budget Office, 1987).

18. Jan Krukowski, "What Do College Students Want? Status," *Change* (May–June 1985): 21–28.

19. Debra Viadero, "NCATE Rejects Over One-Fifth of Accreditation Requests," *Education Week* (May 2, 1990): 5.

20. "Colorado Governor Seeks Re-examination of Tenure," *The Chronicle of Higher Education 27* (August 3, 1983): 3.

21. Talcott Parsons and Gerald M. Platt, *The American University* (Cambridge, MA: Harvard University Press, 1973), 364–65.

22. Michael D. Bayles, *Professional Ethics* (Belmont, CA: Wadsworth, 1981), 3.

23. National Education Association, *NEA Review Board Procedures* (Washington, DC: The Association, 1980).

24. Tom L. Beauchamp and Lawrence B. McCullough, *Medical Ethics* (Englewood Cliffs, NJ: Prentice-Hall, 1984).

25. "Board Room, Classroom Exploring Business Ethics," *The Christian Science Monitor 75* (October 25, 1983): 15–16.

26. *Encyclopedia of Education,* s.v. "Code of Ethics."

27. Robert E. Goddard, ed., *1989 Teacher Certification Requirements* (Lake Placid, FL: Teacher Certification Publications, 1989).

28. C. E. Feistritzer, *The Making of a Teacher: A Report on Teacher Education and Certification* (Washington, DC: National Center for Educational Information, 1984).

29. Griggs v. Duke Power Co., 401 U.S. 424 (1971).

30. J. W. Andrews, C. R. Blackman, and J. A. Mackey, "Preservice Performance and National Teacher Exams," *Phi Delta Kappan 12* (1980): 358–59.

31. T. J. Quirk, B. J. Witten, and S. F. Weinberg, "Review of Studies of the Concurrent and Predictive Validity of the National Teachers Examinations," *Review of Educational Research 43* (1973): 80–113.

32. Robert Howsam et al., *Educating a Profession* (Washington, DC: American Association of Colleges for Teacher Education, 1976).

33. Task Force on Teaching as a Profession, *A Nation Prepared: Teachers for the 21st Century* (New York: Carnegie Corporation of New York, 1986).

34. Holmes Group, *Tomorrow's Teachers* (East Lansing, MI: Holmes Group, 1986).

35. For a history of the NEA, see E. B. Wesley, *NEA: The First Hundred Years* (New York: Harper & Row, 1957).

36. T. M. Stinnett has attempted to highlight the differences in *Turmoil in Teaching* (New York: Macmillan, 1968), 90.

37. M. Finch and T. W. Nagel, "Collective Bargaining and the Public Schools: Reassessing Labor Policy in an Era of Reform," *Wisconsin Law Review* 6(1984): 1580–1670.

38. Ibid., 1580.

39. S. M. Johnson, *Teacher Unions in Schools* (Philadelphia: Temple University Press, 1984), 149–53.

40. R. E. Doherty and W. E. Oberer, *Teachers, School Boards, and Collective Bargaining: A Changing of the Guard* (Ithaca, NY: New York School of Industrial and Labor Relations, 1967).

41. L. McDonnell and A. Pascal, *Organized Teachers in American Schools* (Santa Monica, CA: Rand, 1979).

42. Finch and Nagel, "Collective Bargaining."

43. Susan Moore Johnson, "Unionism and Collective Bargaining in the Public Schools," in *Handbook of Research on Educational Administration,* ed. Norman J. Boyan (New York: Longman, 1988), 603–22.

44. Howard K. Beale, *A History of Freedom in American Schools* (New York: Charles Scribner's Sons, 1941), xiii.

45. Ibid., 263–64.

46. Pictrunti v. Bd. of Education, 319 A.2d 266 (N.J. 1974).

47. Moore v. School Bd. of Gulf County, 364 F. Supp 355 (N.D. Fla. 1973).

48. Clark v. Holmes, 474 F. 2d 938 (7th Cir. 1972), *cert. denied,* 411 U.S. 972 (1973).

49. Barbara Parker and Stefanie Weiss, *Protecting the Freedom to Learn: A Citizen's Guide* (Washington, DC: People for the American Way, 1983), 10–11.

50. Two other forms—totalitarian censorship and radical censorship—are found infrequently in the United States today. Totalitarian censorship is represented by Nazism, fascism, and Soviet Communism. Radical censorship is expressed by Herbert Marcuse's "Repressive Tolerance" in *A Critique of Pure Tolerance,* ed. Robert Paul Wolff et al. (Boston: Beacon Press, 1969), 81–123.

51. James Fitzjames Stephen, *Liberty, Equality, Fraternity* (Cambridge, MA: Cambridge University Press, 1967), 190.

52. Patrick Devlin, *The Enforcement of Morals* (London: Oxford University Press, 1965), 12–13.

53. Edward B. Jenkinson, *Censors in the Classroom: The Mind Benders* (Carbondale, IL: Southern Illinois University Press, 1979), chs. 8 & 9.

54. Parker and Weiss, op. cit., Appendix C.

55. Torcaso V. Watkins, Clerk, Vol 367 of U.S. Reports (1961) p. 488.

56. Spencer Brown, "The Dilemma of Liberal Censorship," *The Education Digest* 30 (September 1964): 4–6; Jack Nelson and Gene Roberts, Jr., *The Censors and the Schools* (Boston: Little, Brown, 1963), ch. 10.

57. Louis Fischer, "Social Foundations" in *The Teacher's Handbook* (Glenview, IL: Scott, Foresman, 1971), 567.

58. John Stuart Mill, *On Liberty* (Indianapolis: Liberal Arts Press, 1956), 64.

59. W. H. Hornby, "On Balancing Rights" in *The Right to Privacy*, ed. G. S. McClellam (New York: Wilson, 1976), 198.

60. J. F. Westin, *Privacy and Freedom* (New York: Atheneum, 1970).

61. J. W. Chapman, "Personality and Privacy" in *Privacy*, eds. J. R. Pennock and J. W. Chapman (New York: Atherton Press, 1971).

62. S. I. Benn, "Privacy, Freedom, and Respect for Persons" in *Privacy*, eds. J. R. Pennock and J. W. Chapman (New York: Atherton Press, 1971).

63. Louis Fischer, David Schimmel, and Cynthia Kelly, *Teachers and the Law* (New York: Longman, 1981), 226.

64. Frank R. Kemerer, *The Educator's Guide to Texas School Law* (Austin: University of Texas Press, 1986), 196.

65. R. Freeman Butts, "The Public Schools: Assaults on a Great Idea," *The Nation* (April 30, 1973): 553–60.

66. Ibid.

67. Brian Barry, *Political Argument* (London: Routledge & Regan Paul, 1965), 190. For a different approach, see John Martin Rich, "The Public Interest and Educational Policy Decisions", *Education and Society*, vol. 7, no. 2 (1989): 71–75.

■ PART TWO

"Stretching and Yawning"

S T U D E N T S ■

P art Two relates to students—their rights and responsibilities, their individual and social problems. Historically, our society has treated the young significantly different from adults. Adults have rights—but do children?

Popular in the nineteenth century, the *in loco parentis* (Latin for "in place of parents") doctrine empowered schools to exercise the same control over students as parents did at home. Parents have extensive control over their children, the doctrine held, and school officials should have similar control. In addition to controlling academic and extracurricular activities, schools attempted to control the dress, manners, and morals of their students.

Since the mid-twentieth century the courts have increasingly recognized that the young have rights, and that they do not leave those rights at the school door. Judicial decisions have substantially changed and restricted the *in loco parentis* doctrine. Today, courts generally recognize that students are entitled to basic constitutional rights just as adults are.

In exercising our rights, though, we all must be aware that rights are not absolute; limitations exist despite the difficulties in establishing them. For example, how do we respect freedom of speech yet prevent slander? Also, what if your rights conflict with mine?

For the young growing up is a time of fears and tears, hope and exuberance, illusions and intoxications. For the adults who observe them it is a time of joys and exasperations. In a complex postindustrial society growing up involves more social problems than ever. With rapid social and economic changes, the erosion of community norms, the breakdown of the nuclear family, and the lack of universal values, many young people find their lives adrift. Some turn to drugs, promiscuity, crime, or even suicide. Others drop out of school or run away from home.

What responsibilities do educators have for helping students cope with such problems? How can aid best be given? To answer these questions, Chapter 3 explores student rights and responsibilities in philosophical and legal contexts. Chapter 4 then presents several urgent individual and social problems that inhibit students' well-being and healthy development and proposes some solutions.

■ C H A P T E R 3

STUDENTS' RIGHTS AND ■
RESPONSIBILITIES

A LOOK AHEAD

The purpose of this chapter is to present the issues surrounding the
rights and responsibilities of students. You will learn about:

- The concept of rights in a democratic society

- The responsibilities that accompany those rights

- A model to guide the sanctioning of student behavior in the
classroom

- The concept of freedom and how it relates to education

- Three different views of student freedom

- Children's rights versus paternalism in the school system

Since the mid-twentieth century, the United States Supreme Court
has recognized that students do not lose their constitutional rights by
going to school, and that, in fact, schools are a good place to teach
respect for rights. At the same time, however, rights carry with them
certain responsibilities that students must learn in their journey to
adulthood and independence.

■ CONCEPTS OF RIGHTS AND RESPONSIBILITIES

Rights

In a democratic society, a person's rights extend to various freedoms, including freedom of speech, press, appearance, and privacy; free access to opportunities in the society (equal opportunity); and the right to due process of law. In a way, we can define **rights** as freedoms or, more specifically, as entitlements to freedoms.

Rights are, in essence, freedoms to do what you wish and freedoms from having the will of others imposed upon you.

Rights serve two basic functions; they give us the freedom to do certain things and they protect us from the actions of others. In a society, rights generally are defined legally; that is, legal guidelines describe what a person can and cannot do. Different societies provide for different degrees of freedom for their citizens. The more free individuals in a society are, the more rights we say they have. Even in free, democratic societies, however, certain citizens sometimes are granted **privileges** (rights or immunities granted as benefits, advantages, or favors that are not universally given to all). The grounds for giving out these privileges can vary. Some privileges, such as a driver's license, are earned. Others come with a particular position, such as a political or executive office.

The most basic concept of rights transcends societal/legal conventions. This is the idea that certain basic **human rights** are to be enjoyed by all people. These rights are not based on merit or privilege. Central to this idea is a belief in human equality. As Vlastos points out, the concept of universal equal human rights is based on the assumption that human worth is equal and universal and not tied to talent, character, or personality traits.[1]

Some believe that, to develop, people must be free and that a society of developed individuals is essential.

Arguments supporting the value of societies' granting their citizens these basic rights are many. One of the most compelling is that basic rights should be protected so that people can fully develop their humanness and individuality. Without certain fundamental rights like freedom of speech, press, assembly, and religion, one cannot become fully human. Moreover, allowing such development benefits a society as well as the individual. Of course, how people who have these rights shape their lives is an individual matter limited only by social circumstances, social norms, the legal system, and individual initiative and ability.

Is education one of our basic human rights? Education is not guaranteed by the United States Constitution.[2] But some state courts, such as those in California and Wyoming, have concluded that education *is* a fundamental right. In contrast, a New York court declared that education, though not a fundamental right, constitutes a substantial interest that deserves some special judicial protection. In other states, courts have not answered the question of whether education is a right; instead they have deferred to state legislatures to determine educational services and their funding.[3] Though a fundamental right to an education is not recognized in many states, all states except Connecticut have made provisions in their constitutions for education.

Responsibilities

Rights and responsibilities often are correlated. Individual rights place an obligation—a **responsibility**—on members of a society to respect the rights of their fellow citizens. If a person has a right to act, others have a duty not to restrain that person. At the same time, however, members of a society have the right not to have the actions of others impinge upon their rights. So, though you and I might have the right to speak freely, we do not have the right to incite people to riot and violate the rights of others. In fact, we have a responsibility not to do so. In short, we have an obligation to make sure that in exercising our rights we do not impinge upon or limit the rights of others.

Living in a group requires mutual respect among individual group members.

But aside from this, all rights do not necessarily carry with them corresponding responsibilities, and many responsibilities do not correspond to specific rights. For example, students have the right to attend classes, but are they responsible for paying attention? Young children and animals are granted certain rights; but because of their dependent state, they are not expected to have corresponding responsibilities. Adults, on the other hand, often have more responsibilities than rights. That one can have duties and obligations without correlative rights is evident in the numerous responsibilities of family life, occupation, and citizenship.

Accountability is an active feature of responsibility. Elected officials are expected to be accountable to their constituents; governmental checks and balances are designed to hold different aspects of government accountable; you and I, if we speak in public, are accountable for what we say. The general meaning of accountability is to entrust something to someone and to call on that person to render an account of how that trust has been executed.

One who acts responsibly uses discretion, assesses the consequences of his or her actions, and tries to act rationally. The ability to make intelligent moral judgments is necessary to determine whether one is acting responsibly. At times, acting responsibly means simply fulfilling one's duties and obligations. Yet responsibility in its widest sense involves more than this. We can fulfill some duties by following orders without even using our moral and rational abilities. One needs to understand the moral features of an act to be truly responsible.

True responsibility involves choice.

The moral features of responsibility are easier to understand when we consider responsibility as a form of responding to others positively. As Dewey has noted: "One is held responsible in order that he may *become* responsible, that is, responsive to the needs and claims of others, to the obligations implicit in his position."[4] You show care and concern for others by understanding that your actions can affect another or that another depends on you to act responsibly. Each of us is responsible to those who are legitimately dependent upon us. If my actions can affect someone, I am responsible toward that person. Employees are responsible to their bosses and vice versa. If you are a member of a study group, you are responsible to the other members of the group. By the same token, offspring depend upon parents, students upon teachers, patients upon doctors.

Individual Versus Collective Responsibility

Responsibility can be ascribed to individuals and to groups.

Responsibility is either individual or collective. **Individual responsibility** ascribes to one person the sole or primary responsibility for an act. For instance, individuals are responsible for paying debts, keeping promises, and disciplining their children. **Collective responsibility** ascribes responsibility to a group, organization, firm, or governing body for acts that affect individuals, groups, or society as a whole. In education, organized teachers strikes and sanctions, school-board policy decisions, and state and federal education legislation are examples of collective responsibility.

Each person in a school has responsibilities. The school system as a whole also has responsibilities—to individual members of the school and to the broader society.

Any educational process requires at least minimal forms of individual and collective responsibility. Educational systems are regulated by rules, standards, policies, and performance evaluations. Common also to educational systems is a network that structures and defines levels of authority and gives them corresponding levels of responsibility. This responsibility brings predictability to relationships in the school system and assures fairness and respect for all. Responsibility, when spelled out in institutional policies and standards, helps guarantee fairness and consistency by clearly stating what actions will or will not be tolerated, who will be held responsible, and what the consequences of a given action will be.

Sanctions in the School System

Whenever students fail to abide by a rule, sanctions may be applied. A sanction is a reward in favor of, or punishment against, a certain act. In deciding whether a sanction is warranted against a student, the teacher must consider several factors: the relationship of sanctions to the use of rules, and the designation of responsibility. A *rule* is a type of generalization used to govern conduct, action, or usage. The term *responsible* is used in this context to apply to cases of student behavior in which teachers can justifiably use sanctions. Sanctions may not be necessary in certain cases because some students are motivated by variables such as a desire to achieve in school or respect for authority. But whether sanctions or other measures are employed, sanctions cannot rightfully be applied unless the student can be held responsible for the act. The application of sanctions is outlined in the sanctions model (see Figure 3–1).

Teachers seek to encourage responsible student behavior and discourage irresponsible behavior through sanctions.

Type 1: A is a desirable act; X did A.
Type 2: B is an undesirable act; X did not do B.
Type 3: C is a desirable act; X did not do C.
Type 4: D is an undesirable act; X did D.

FIGURE 3–1 Sanctions model

Types 1 and 2 usually lead to sanctions in favor of the act—a reward or good word. Types 3 and 4 usually lead to sanctions against the act—punishment or reprimand.

Rewards are more likely to be provided for Type 1 than for Type 2, because it is expected that the student will avoid breaking a rule. For example, a student obeys the teacher's instructions (Type 1); a student does not create a classroom disturbance (Type 2). Reward would more likely be given for performing the desirable act than for *not* committing the undesirable one.

Teachers generally apply sanctions against a student who commits an undesirable act. Thus the most common application of sanctions against an act would be Type 4 (as when a student creates a classroom disturbance). Sanctions occasionally may be applied against students who fail to perform a desirable act (as when a student watches passively rather than helps a teacher lift a heavy load of books and supplies—Type 3).

Two types of sanctions can be identified in teacher-student relations: academic and policy. **Academic sanctions** frequently are applied when students learn or fail to learn subject matter according to the teacher's rules for mastering content. **Policy sanctions** are employed when a student obeys or disobeys the rules of the classroom and the school.

Academic and policy sanctions are not mutually exclusive; they often reinforce or inhibit one another, or sometimes both. A policy rule, for example, that requires students to raise their hands and be recognized before speaking can enhance the effectiveness of academic rules for mastering content. On the other hand, a policy rule that

A teacher has to be firm and caring in inculcating responsible student behavior.

Teacher responses should be constructive.

prohibits talking in the library can inhibit academic rules requiring collaboration by students for mastering content. Ideally, though, academic and policy rules should reinforce one another.

Academic sanctions are used primarily to encourage the ability to understand, manipulate, and apply cognitive content in accordance with academic rules. Policy sanctions deal primarily with behavior in relation to others and are usually ethical in nature (in contrast to academic sanctions, which are largely nonmoral). Academic sanctions, for instance, are applied when a student works a mathematics problem correctly or incorrectly, follows or fails to follow verbal instructions on a test, draws or fails to draw correct inferences from data, or runs or does not run a laboratory experiment correctly. Policy sanctions can be applied when a student observes or fails to observe rules of conduct in relation to fellow students, school personnel, and school property.

Teachers usually are justified in rewarding desirable acts (Type A) when such acts are performed with an objective in mind and with an understanding of their consequences. Sanctions usually can be applied against students when they fail to perform a desirable act (Type C), though there are exceptions for which students should be excused.

Teachers probably are not justified in rewarding Type 1 or Type 2 acts if the act was accidental and beyond the ability of the student to anticipate the consequences (as in the case of a student who inadvertently works a math problem correctly but cannot explain it to the teacher's satisfaction). Teachers also are not justified in applying sanctions against acts (Types 3 and 4) when the act is caused by an uncorrectable condition (as in the case of mentally retarded students who do not have the capacity to understand or fulfill the expectations) or a correctable condition that the teacher is incapable of correcting (stuttering, for example). Third, sanctions are not justified when what is expected is beyond the student's ability to perform (for example, the teacher has not prepared the student adequately to master content or the student cannot comprehend or physically master a complex policy). Finally, most would agree that one is not justified in punishing actions that are compelled. If it was impossible for a student to act in any fashion other than he or she did, then the behavior was compelled. A psychological disorder that causes an irresistible impulse to steal (kleptomania) would be one example; another is a situation in which one student physically forces another to perform an undesirable act. Despite these notable exceptions, teachers generally can hold students responsible for their acts.

> Before responding to student behaviors, teachers should understand those behaviors as completely as possible. Only then can a teacher truly respond constructively.

■ **PAUSE TO REFLECT**

Sanctions in the Classroom

- Of the four types of sanctions discussed, which do you think best promote learning in a student? Think of two or three situations in which you would use such sanctions and explain why they would be effective.

- Which types of sanctions were most commonly used in your high school and under what circumstances? Were they effective?

- How could the use of sanctions have been improved?

STUDENT FREEDOM ■

In democratic societies there is generally a presumption in most matters in favor of freedom, and interference with it must be based on supportable grounds. One focal point of democratic education is the question of freedom in the classroom. A certain amount of freedom is essential if students are to learn effectively and to develop their abilities. These freedoms include freedom of self-expression, freedom to develop unique abilities, and freedom from autocratic imposition of subject matter.

Freedom generally can be expressed in two ways: "freedom from" and "freedom to." **Freedom from** is the absence of restraint or coercion that would compromise a person's freedom. Abolishing a dress code would be an example of expanding this type of freedom for students. Another example of freedom from restraint would be allowing students twenty-four-hour, unrestricted access to the library. The less interference, the greater the individual's freedom. Note, however, that circumstances are not hindering unless one wants to do something that those circumstances prevent.

Freedom to holds that one is not fully free to do something without the ability, power, and means to perform the act. Implicit in this type of freedom is "freedom from," the idea that you would not be prevented by rules or by another person from doing what you want. But added to this is your own ability to actually accomplish what you want to. For example, students who are able to read, write, and speak effectively have more choices in life and, thus, are more free. An individual needs the opportunity to choose among available alternatives, the ability to understand the alternatives, and the ability to arrive at informed choices.

> Freedom means not having to adopt others' choices; it also means having alternatives to choose from and the ability to make those choices.

Justifications of Freedom

The Means to an End. John Stuart Mill once noted: "The human faculties of perception, judgment, discriminative feeling, mental activity, and even moral preference are exercised only in making choice. . . . The mental and moral, like the muscular, powers are improved by being used."[5] Because freedom permits the individual to choose and thereby cultivate his or her intellect and character, many consider freedom essential for the improvement of the individual and, thereby, a democratic society. Those who hold this view see the value of freedom to be a means to an end; that is, its value is instrumental.

Freedom for Freedom's Sake. Another justification argues that freedom need not serve a utilitarian function, like improving society. Freedom has value in and of itself and without it, a valued way of life would not be possible.[6] For example, we often exchange thoughts and ideas as we determine what we are going to think or how we are going to act in any given situation. These deliberations would be pointless, though, if we had no freedom to act on the conclusions we draw from those deliberations. Just as we demand that freedom for ourselves, we must grant it to others, even if we do not agree with

The right to speak and to do so effectively embodies both "freedom from" and "freedom to."

their conclusions. If we do disagree, we can hope to change their minds through rational persuasion, not through force or restraint (such as limiting their freedom to speak or to act). This argument holds that freedom is not a means to an end, but rather is an end in itself; that is, its value is transcendental.

Views of Student Freedom

Progressivism. Accepting Rousseau's dictum that a child is born basically good, early child-centered advocates of **progressivism** leaned toward the "freedom from" approach. They believed that a child should be freed from stringent rules and regulations and permitted to

Progressives believe that, to develop, children need an unrestrictive environment.

develop naturally, to explore and create. This interpretation arose in
the early twentieth century as a reaction against the philosophy of
traditional education. The older education, progressives claimed, separated the learning of subject matter from the child's daily experience,
emphasized authoritarian control, and employed stern discipline that
failed to consider the needs and interests of the child.

The "progressive" teacher's role changed from disciplinarian and
taskmaster to facilitator of learning activities. Rugg and Shumaker,
two early, key proponents of progressivism and child-centered schooling in the United States, envisioned a school in which children were
free from rigid schedules, coercion, and lock-step methods; where
children would actively engage in self-expression and study real-life
interactions rather than subjects. Children no longer would respond
passively to what is being taught, but would learn how to learn by
themselves. The teacher no longer would have to worry about discipline because the child would become self-directed, self-disciplined.
The activity- or child-centered schools would eradicate the concept of
discipline and implant the concept of growth.[7]

The progressive teacher maintains good rapport with students and facilitates learning.

At Summerhill, a private British school based on progressive ideas, A. S. Neill built a program using children's own interests and their capacity to work and live cooperatively with their peers by developing and enforcing their own rules and regulations. Neill established a self-government plan at Summerhill in which he retained responsibility for overall administrative matters, diet and health, but turned the rest of the operations over to students, who met weekly to discuss rules and determine action to be taken against violators. All were encouraged to express their views, and each student older than eight had one vote. Neill claimed that self-government is therapeutic because it releases tensions, and children are more likely to abide by rules that they make themselves. He also believed that better relations are promoted between teachers and students because the teacher is no longer the disciplinarian.[8]

This is not to say that Neill never chastised students—he did believe that children should respect others' basic rights. If a child, for example, threw mud on a door Neill had just painted, he might be angry with the child. However, Neill would take into account the possible reasons for the child's action. If the child had thrown the mud just after transferring from a hateful, authoritarian school, rather than reprimanding the child, Neill might help the child sling mud so the child could release the pent up anger toward that authority. Neill said he observed a distinction in his policies between liberty and license, and that, while children generally should respect others' rights, occasionally some license was necessary for a cure.[9]

Although the progressive model seriously attempts to meet the child's needs and interests, and discipline is more closely related to instruction and the social life of the school, some problems remain. Critics of this model charge that progressives have been too permissive and have overemphasized "freedom from" before sufficient development of "freedom to." Although students are free to express themselves and develop naturally, critics believe that many students have not developed the judgment and skills they need to choose to act responsibly. Parents and educators have the right—and the responsibility—to curb a student's "freedom from" when it harms others or interferes with their rights. "Freedom from" also should be curtailed when the student exercising it could be harmed.

Critics believe progressivism does not provide enough guidance to children.

Essentialism. Essentialism provides progressivism with its chief opposition. Although expressed in various forms in early American education, it became an organized movement in the 1930s, dominated education during the Cold War era of the 1950s, and enjoyed a resurgence in the late 1970s and 1980s in the back-to-basics movement.

Essentialists insist that children lack the maturity and ability to guide their own development.

Unlike progressivism, which believes strongly in the child's ability for productive self-direction, **essentialism** emphasizes the external values of discipline, order, control, and industriousness. Michael Demiashkevich, an educational philosopher and a proponent of essentialism, defines discipline as an ensemble of rules and regulations governing student behavior. He believes it is important that students be made to see the significance of school rules and regulations so that they will accept them. Punishment is not in itself objectionable, and if a teacher has asked a student to change his or her behavior, but to no avail, the teacher may resort to punishment.[10]

William T. Harris, United States Commissioner of Education from 1889 to 1906, put forth four cardinal rules a student should follow in the classroom: regularity, punctuality, silence, and industry. Those rules, he said, should extend beyond school hours to everyday life so that the child will develop good character and learn responsibility through obedience to a higher will.[11] Ross L. Finney, an educational philosopher, shared this belief in the importance of social control. He claimed in the late 1920s that too much emphasis was being placed on individual initiative and independence as a result of misconceptions about democracy. He saw nothing wrong with drill and memorization. He believed there were occasions when regimentation is needed and believed resistance from the young should be expected because of the inevitable conflict between youthful instincts and social demands. Social stability requires that such resistance be overcome, because indulging children is not in their interest. And the alternative to control is not freedom but social chaos.[12]

Critics of essentialism believe that it is overly concerned with objectives and rules and that it inhibits student initiative and growth.

Essentialism provides structure, order, and regulated study habits by shifting the focus from the child's interests to the teacher's authority. The danger, critics say, is that the teacher's role can degenerate into authoritarianism. The student's "freedom from" is heavily restricted and "freedom to" is restricted by a required curriculum and many classroom rules and regulations that students usually do not participate in developing. The penchant for corporal punishment in schools that emphasize essentialism can be traumatic for children. It can restrict their "freedom to" by inhibiting their ability to fully and actively engage in the learning process and by damaging the student's self-esteem and motivation to learn.

An Alternate Approach

Progressivism risks focusing insufficient attention on responsibility and essentialism risks denying freedom to the extent that, as Mill would have it, self-directed responsibility cannot be developed. Too little adult control can result in immaturity and irresponsibility, while too much can lead to submissiveness or rebelliousness.[13]

Because autocratic or very lenient parents usually produce children with too little self-confidence and too much dependence or rebelliousness,[14] a middle ground suggests itself as the best path to take in rearing and educating our children. Some child-rearing practices support the development of greater self-determination within supportive conditions of parental warmth and concern and consistency in discipline.[15] The hope is that through caring but firm guidance, children will enjoy the freedom to explore and discover what life has to offer, and, at the same time, learn to monitor their own actions as responsible members of society. If a child is nurtured in a reasonable framework of authority, the child eventually will grow from dependence to independence. Coupled with this authority is the freedom to appeal rules and laws, to socialize freely, and to help shape models for codes of conduct.

Instead of battling each other, freedom and authority go hand in hand on this middle ground. Freedom always is found within a society regulated by a system of rules and principles (from simple traffic laws to complex principles of honesty and protection of human life). The authority, however, must be democratically established and responsive to the will of the people. It must be open to scrutiny and criticism and provide free elections to express the larger will.

■ **PAUSE TO REFLECT**
Progressivism and Essentialism

- Can the ideals of progressivism and essentialism be combined to provide a desirable environment for learning and growth while maintaining discipline and instilling a sense of social responsibility?
- What are those ideals and how can they best be combined?
- Consider your own experience: in what type of school system were you educated?
- What parallels exist between it and the approaches discussed here?
- How could your school system have been improved?

The goal for student freedom in education is to move from dependence to independence and increased autonomy tempered with social responsibility. Each individual who strives for independence must learn to think intelligently so as to arrive at sound judgments and decisions. The process of becoming independent also involves becoming one's own authority and eventually teaching these principles to the next generation.

To develop, students need teacher expectations and guidance to realize those expectations. They also need freedom to make choices.

However, to encourage greater independence and autonomy ("freedom to") it is necessary to reduce and, if possible, eliminate conditioning and indoctrination. Both processes bypass reflective thinking. Conditioning (training to respond automatically, on cue) stamps in unreflective behavior patterns, and indoctrination (the teaching of beliefs and principles) instills unexamined dogmas. If students are to move from dependence to independence, they need to learn reflective thinking so that they can arrive at their own judgments and decisions.

Effective school policies allow the maximum freedom for all, while assuring that such freedom does not impinge upon any student's right to learn. Such policies also support the goals of the school and do not violate student rights. Student participation in developing school policies and rules creates a shared responsibility for policy and a deeper student understanding of its purpose. This can only help promote a sound learning environment.

EDUCATIONAL ISSUE 3–1

Should students be allowed maximum freedom in the classroom?

Yes	No
1. Traditional education stifles students with authoritarian control and stern discipline.	1. Without firm control, classrooms would be chaotic.
2. Children should be free to develop naturally, to explore and create.	2. Children cannot be creative without acquiring a body of knowledge and developing self-discipline.
3. Children should learn to work cooperatively with their peers to develop their own rules and regulations.	3. Children lack the maturity and the responsibility to regulate themselves and others.

■ PATERNALISM AND CHILDREN'S RIGHTS

John Holt[16] and Richard Farson[17] generally believe that children and adults should have the same basic rights. Holt says we have created an army of people to tell the young what they have to learn and to make them learn it. Compulsory education, he says, "is such a gross violation of civil liberties that few adults would stand for being forced to go to school. But the child who resists is treated as a criminal."[18] Farson, too, opposes compulsory education and believes that the function of the current school system is not to educate but to maintain the system through indoctrination.[19] Farson would abolish compulsory schooling and its attendant indoctrination, while Holt would allow children to decide what they would like to learn and with whom they will study.

Farson and Holt espouse an extreme philosophy, but their ideas point up the need to examine what, if any, limits should be placed on the rights of children. This raises the issue of paternalism. **Paternalism** involves action in which "the protection or promotion of a [person's] welfare is the primary reason for . . . coercive interference with an action or state of [that] person."[20] Such an act is carried out in the person's "best interest" whenever the person is incapable of performing, or is considered incapable of performing, the act alone. Compulsory education is a dramatic example of paternalism in education, and it illustrates the core question regarding this issue: are teachers and administrators justified in interfering with or coercing a student for the student's educational welfare? The answer to this question lies, at least in part, in the answer to a second question: are children capable of making decisions about their educations?

Howard Cohen, another children's rights advocate, tries to solve the problem of the seeming violation of students' basic rights in the education process with the notion of "borrowed capacities."[21] Just as adults may call upon legal, financial, or medical experts for advice in exercising their rights, so can children. With the help of agents, children could, Cohen proposes, exercise their rights without harming themselves or others. But Cohen's agents, to be other than paternalistic relations, would need to be roughly equal to their child clients in intelligence, moral judgment, and experience for the child's wishes to be truly represented. In other words, Cohen's solution seems untenable in that it does not address the core rationale for paternalism in education—that children and adolescents lack the faculties and/or experience to make certain decisions.

In trying to expand children's rights, reformers like Holt, Farson, and Cohen might, in fact, sacrifice the welfare of children by overlooking the developmental differences between children and adults. Adult constraint, says Diana Baumrind, is a precondition for self-determination.[22] No child psychologist would agree that the child is equal to the adult in experience, intelligence, and moral competence, Baumrind says. Not even the child liberators can deny the immense differences in knowledge, experience, and power that separate the child from the adolescent and the adolescent from the adult. These differences, she adds, do not stem from adult exploitation but from

We could say that those who believe that children should have the same rights as adults take progressivism to an extreme.

Those who support paternalism in the schools would agree with at least some of the basic assumptions of essentialism.

laws of nature. The reformers fail to consider the fact that children depend on adults for survival and guidance through the years of growth and maturation that lead to the capacity for self-determination.

It would seem, then, that paternalism cannot altogether be avoided. But what types of paternalism can be justified, and on what grounds? The main argument against paternalism is that it interferes with the individual's freedom. And because democratic societies recognize freedom as a basic right, freedom should not be restricted without just cause. If it can be shown that some forms of paternalism lead to necessary states of well-being, then interference with freedom would seem to be acceptable. By so interfering, the understanding is that the capabilities of the children and, thereby, their opportunities and their freedom, ultimately would be expanded.

Acceptable Forms of Paternalism

The objectives of paternalism in education are to prevent harm and promote welfare. *Preventing harm* obviously consists of avoiding danger to life and limb; yet it might also include avoiding serious dangers to mental and emotional health and growth. Safety restrictions on the use of certain power tools in machine shop courses (even if students believe that the restrictions abridge their freedom) are rules that prevent harm. So are rules that prohibit sexual relations between teachers and students or curriculum guidelines that consider the cognitive level of students. Without curriculum guidelines, for example, children could be put in classes so difficult that they would be doomed to failure or so easy that they would not be challenged to learn.

Paternalistic acts for the purpose of promoting student welfare are designed primarily to achieve educational goals. A safe environment, free from physical, emotional, and mental harm, is a necessary but not a sufficient condition to the promotion of welfare. *Promoting student welfare* means providing specific opportunities and programs to achieve educational goals. A compulsory school attendance law is an example of a rule to promote student welfare, as is a compulsory curriculum that appropriately challenges students and is focused on promoting student growth.

Sometimes, letting students make their own decisions is the best decision a teacher can make.

But if the purpose of paternalism is to prevent harm and promote the student's welfare, not all acts in the name of paternalism can be justified. It is best for students to enjoy an absence of restraints whenever they are capable of performing an act without harming themselves or others or without violating others' rights. To repeat John Stuart Mill's position, freedom from restraint promotes development. The following conditions generally are considered justifications for school paternalism:[23]

- Mental disability
- Immaturity (physical or emotional)
- Lack of essential knowledge
- Serious emotional disturbance or mental illness
- Threats to safety of self or others

Mental Disability. Paternalistic intervention is more often seen with the disabled than with the normal student. The mentally disabled are usually slower to develop physically and emotionally, and teachers and other educational authorities often, in conjunction with the students' guardians, make programming decisions for these students. They also usually need to follow through on these decisions by providing special help and support to these students, sometimes in opposition to the students' wishes. Students with a mental disability may also exhibit visual and hearing impairment and language and speech retardation, which require additional special intervention. Student consent in these instances of paternalism, though desirable, is not required. However, care should be taken not to abuse the right of paternalistic intervention. Evidence must show that a particular paternalistic act is likely to prevent harm or promote the student's welfare. Teachers should, whenever possible, let disabled students perform for themselves, even though perhaps less ably than the teacher might like.

Immaturity. Many paternalistic acts are justified on the grounds of student immaturity; but some children's rights advocates believe this justification has been abused. Each student must be evaluated individually before a particular paternalistic practice is put in motion. In situations where the evidence is not compelling, the student should be given the freedom to act independently as long as serious injury or harm is not likely to result.

Lack of Essential Knowledge. A third ground for paternalism is the lack of essential knowledge. Such knowledge, considered necessary to live and reason independently, may include advanced ideas about physical and mental health, marriage, child care, personal finance, and occupational opportunities. Consent may not always be forthcoming because of a required curriculum and other restrictions on student choice. Again, educators must demonstrate that such paternalism is in the student's interest.

Emotional Disturbance or Mental Illness. A fourth reason for paternalistic intervention is emotional disturbance or mental illness. The only school intervention likely in the case of mental illness is to refer the student, with parental consent, for outside mental health services. Therefore, the chief concern is whether the student's judgment is so clouded by emotional disturbance that he or she is likely to endanger his or her educational welfare or pose a threat of serious harm to self or others. The disturbances may be temporary, in which case the student's freedom is restored once the disturbance is overcome. Whatever the student's behavior—aggressiveness, defiance, withdrawal—a compelling case must be made that the student actually suffers from emotional disturbance and that intervention is required to protect the student's interest or to prevent harm to others. Educators must guard against automatically classifying disruptive students or those who relate to others differently than the norm as emotionally disturbed. Instead they need to identify the cause of the disruptive behavior and take appropriate steps to deal with it. For instance, a disruptive student might be hyperactive and need medical treatment, or an unusually quiet student might simply be shy and need greater understanding and support from the teacher.

Threats to Safety.   Threats to safety of self or others is a fifth justification for paternalism. If a student is in serious physical danger and is either incapable of self-protection or fails to perceive an imminent danger, then intervention is justified. Such dangers as the potential for student violence, the power of electrical tools or chemicals, and the possibility that a contagious disease will spread would justify intervention.

In conclusion, children's rights advocates have made some important points, but because children are not as developed as adults in experience, intelligence, and moral competence, they cannot be granted all of the same rights as adults. Therefore, to prevent harm and to promote the student's educational welfare, paternalistic practices can be justified under certain conditions in cases of mental disability, immaturity, lack of essential knowledge, emotional disturbance or mental illness, and threats to safety.

■ Summary

- Rights are entitlements. They give us the freedom to do certain things and protect us from the actions of others. Certain rights, usually called human rights, are considered basic to all. Education is not considered a basic right under the United States Constitution, though most states have made provisions for it in their own constitutions.

- The rights we have are shared by other members of society, and we are responsible for respecting others' rights even as we exercise our own.

- Schools are governed by a set of rules designed, ideally, to promote and protect the rights of all students to learn. Teachers generally can hold students responsible for following those rules. If a student follows a rule, a teacher may apply a positive sanction (reward); if a student breaks a rule, the teacher may apply a negative sanction (punishment). Sanctions pertaining to mastery of subject matter are called "academic sanctions," while those pertaining to non-academic behavior are called "policy sanctions."

- Progressives believe students should be free from rules and regulations so they can develop naturally and independently. Essentialists emphasize social control and advocate discipline, order, and industriousness in and out of the classroom. Both of these can, in their own ways, inhibit the development of children into truly responsible and free adults. A middle-ground approach helps students learn independence as well as social responsibility.

- Paternalism in the schools involves intervening in the activities of students by teachers who know better (or believe they know better) what is in the student's best interest. While children's rights advocates argue that children should have the same rights as adults, developmental differences between adults and children do provide a basis for paternalism, which usually can be justified under five basic circumstances.

■ Key Terms

academic sanctions	paternalism
collective responsibility	policy sanctions
essentialism	privileges
freedom from	progressivism
freedom to	responsibility
human rights	rights
individual responsibility	

■ Discussion Questions

1. Most rights carry corresponding responsibilities. What are some examples of rights and their responsibilities? What rights, if any, don't have (or shouldn't have) attached responsibilities?

2. Under what conditions can teachers rightfully apply sanctions to students?

3. What arguments could students offer to demonstrate that their rights were violated in school?

4. Offer a rationale for protecting student freedom.

5. Contrast progressive and essentialist views on student freedom and assess their respective merits.

6. As a teacher, what forms of paternalism would you use? Explain why.

■ **Learning Activities**

1. Collect student handbooks from various school districts and evaluate the adequacy of provisions for student rights and responsibilities.

2. Conduct a study of a school district in terms of the major changes that have been made in the past thirty years in policies governing student rights and responsibilities.

3. Observe several classes and record the teachers' paternalistic practices. Sort out the justifiable ones from the unjustifiable ones and explain the basis of your decisions.

Suggested Readings

Baumrind, Diane. "Reciprocal Rights and Responsibilities in Parent-Child Relations." *Journal of Social Issues* 34 (Spring 1978): 182–84.

This article attempts to explain that children cannot be granted the same rights as adults because of the differences in developmental characteristics.

Feinberg, Joel. *Social Philosophy*. Englewood Cliffs, NJ: Prentice-Hall, 1973.

The author takes a philosophical approach to issues of rights, freedom, coercion, and harm.

Holt, John. *Escape from Childhood*. New York: E.P. Dutton, 1974.

A leader in the child liberation movement, Holt argues that children should enjoy the same rights as adults.

Price, Janet R., Alan H. Levine, and Eve Cary. *The Rights of Students*, 3rd ed. Carbondale, IL: Southern Illinois University Press, 1988.

Using a question-and-answer format, the book is addressed to students and covers a full range of legal rights, from personal appearance to grades and diplomas.

Notes

1. Gregory Vlastos, "Justice and Equality," in *Social Justice*, ed. Richard B. Brandt (Englewood Cliffs, NJ: Prentice-Hall, 1962), 31–72.

2. San Antonio Indep. Sch. Dist. v. Rodriguez, 411 U.S. 1 (1973).

3. Mary M. McCarthy and Paul T. Deignan, *What Legally Constitutes an Adequate Public Education?* (Bloomington, IN: Phi Delta Kappa Educational Foundation, n.d.), ch. 2.

4. John Dewey, *Theory of the Moral Life* (New York: Holt, Rinehart and Winston, 1960), 170.

5. John Stuart Mill, *On Liberty* (Indianapolis: Liberal Arts Press, 1956), 71.

6. H. P. Griffiths, "Ultimate Moral Principles: Their Justification," in *Encyclopedia of Philosophy* (New York: Macmillan and Free Press, 1967), vol. 8, 181; and R. S. Peters, *Ethics and Education* (London: Allen and Unwin, 1970), 180–82.

7. Harold Rugg and Ann Shumaker, *The Child-Centered School* (New York: World, 1928), 102, 314.

8. A. S. Neill, *Summerhill: A Radical Approach to Child Rearing* (New York: Hart, 1960).

9. A. S. Neill, *The Problem Child* (New York: McBride, 1927).

10. Michael Demiashkevich, *An Introduction to the Philosophy of Education* (New York: American Book Co., 1935), 306–13.

11. W. T. Harris, "School Discipline," in *The Third Yearbook of the National Herbart Society* (Chicago: University of Chicago Press, 1908), 65–66.

12. Ross L. Finney, *A Sociological Philosophy of Education* (New York: Macmillan, 1928), 468–70.

13. Urie Bronfenbrenner, "The Changing American Child: A Speculative Analysis," *Journal of Social Issues* 17(1): 6–18.

14. E. Douvan and J. Adelson, *The Adolescent Experience* (New York: Wiley, 1966); and G. H. Edler, "Structural Variations in the Child Rearing Relationship," *Sociometry* 25 (1962): 241–62.

15. Urie Bronfenbrenner, "Some Family Antecedents of Responsibility and Leadership in Adolescents," in *Leadership and Interpersonal Behavior*, eds. L. Petrullo and B. Bass (New York: Holt, Rinehart and Winston, 1961), 239–71.

16. John Holt, *Escape from Childhood* (New York: E. P. Dutton, 1974), 18.

17. Richard Farson, *Birthrights* (New York: Macmillan, 1974), 5.

18. Holt, op. cit., 2441–42.

19. Farson, op. cit., ch. 7.

20. Rosemary Carter, "Justifying Paternalism," *Canadian Journal of Philosophy* 7 (March 1977): 133.

21. Howard Cohen, *Equal Rights for Children* (Totowa, NJ: Littlefield, Adams & Co., 1980), ch. 5.

22. Diana Baumrind, "Reciprocal Rights and Responsibilities in Parent-Child Relations," *Journal of Social Issues* 34 (Spring 1978): 182–84.

23. This list, however, cannot be considered exhaustive because widespread changes in educational institutions may bring to light the need for other types of paternalistic practices or a decrease in paternalism, depending on the learners' maturity, institutional purposes, and related factors.

■ C H A P T E R 4

STUDENTS ■

The purpose of this chapter is to present several urgent social problems that affect the lives of students and offer some solutions. You will learn about:

- What constitutes a *social* problem and how these problems develop in a society

- Some suggestions for counteracting social problems in the school setting

- Peer groups and student subcultures and their influences on students

- Why some student subcultures degenerate into delinquent gangs

- How domestic abuse and neglect influence student behavior

- Television's effect on student behavior and academic achievement

- Drug abuse and suicide among teenagers and how educators can help fight these problems

- Discipline problems, violence, and delinquency in the schools

- The problems faced by school dropouts

- Sexuality among teenagers and the influence of sex education courses

The problems school-age children must confront in our society are not easy ones. Students may suffer physical or emotional abuse at home and unhealthy pressure from peers at school. Some live in fear of being attacked in the school hallways. Others must choose whether to join or defy a gang or whether to experiment with drugs and alcohol—all while struggling with emerging feelings and insecurities about who they are and how they fit in. Adding to the confusion are the conflicting messages students receive about how to deal with these problems: their parents or teachers tell them one thing, while their peers tell them something else. These problems can be overwhelming, and many students are at high risk of dropping out of school. An alarming number are even at risk for committing suicide. In this chapter, we will look at some of the key problems faced by students today as well as the influence wielded by the family and the media. We also will discuss some ways teachers, parents, and the community can help students navigate these treacherous paths in their lives.

▪ CHARACTERISTICS OF SOCIAL PROBLEMS

A **social problem** is a social condition that is widely considered undesirable. A social problem is distinguished from a personal problem in that it affects groups, organizations, or society as a whole rather than an individual. Economic recession, homelessness, drug abuse, and gang activity are examples of current social problems. Acts of nature (hurricanes, earthquakes, drought) are not in themselves social problems but may precipitate or aggravate existing social problems by causing homelessness, epidemics, or financial problems.

Problems are in the eyes of the beholders.

There is an element of perception and recognition in classifying a social condition as a social problem. A social condition becomes a social problem when the majority of people in a given society or its influential decision makers consider it seriously undesirable. Merton distinguishes between two types of social problems.[1] A **latent social problem** is a social condition that may go against a society's interests or values but which has yet to be acknowledged by the public as a problem. Once a latent social problem is denounced by the majority as a harmful problem in need of a solution, it becomes a **manifest social problem.** For example, most people are aware of the existence of white-collar crime (embezzlement, fraud) and even consider it undesirable. But they do not yet recognize it as serious enough to need an immediate solution, so it can be considered a latent social problem. Street crime, on the other hand, is generally recognized as harmful to society and in need of a solution—it can be considered a manifest social problem.

Social problems often are temporary and relative. A society's values and abilities change over time, and, therefore, what are perceived as social problems change, too. Earlier in this century, for example, child labor was widespread until a large enough group of people protested the practice. Child labor, once barely a latent social problem, became a manifest social problem. With the passage of child labor laws, the problem was solved. Another manifest social problem, high infant mortality rates, has been alleviated through advancements in medicine, sanitation, and hygiene. Drug abuse has long existed, but until a few decades ago, it was isolated enough that most people did not give it much thought. Today, of course, drug abuse is considered a major social problem that needs an immediate solution. Someday, if the right measures are found, drug abuse may follow child labor and high infant mortality rates into the category of largely solved problems.

Social problems also are culturally defined. Sex discrimination is perceived as a major social problem today in the United States but is only emerging as a social problem in some West European nations and is not recognized as a social problem in many Middle Eastern nations where women's rights are severely restricted. Prostitution is viewed as a social problem in America, but in ancient Athens prostitution was considered essential to preserve female virginity because most males would not marry before age thirty.

Social problems may be mistakenly equated with deviant behavior. **Deviant behavior** is a social behavior that violates social norms and is subject to social sanctions, including legal sanctions. **Norms** are guidelines for social action. Although some norm violations such as drug addiction, delinquency, and prostitution presently are considered social problems, other norm violations such as jaywalking, discourteous behavior, and profanity are not considered sufficiently serious to be classified as social problems. Moreover, some social problems may not involve norm violations at all—traffic congestion, epidemics, and economic depression, for example.[2]

> Social problems can include some violations of social norms by citizens, but they also can include more complex problems that have nothing to do with individuals going against the norm.

Because a social problem is a matter of perception and social recognition, the majority of the population or key decision makers must consider a certain social condition undesirable so that steps can be taken to correct it, whether lobbying for changes in the law or appealing for funds and other resources to fight the problem. But to best overcome a problem, we first need to understand how it became a problem in the first place and how the problem is likely to progress unless action is taken against it. These explanations will be helpful later in this chapter as we discuss some of the social problems faced by today's students and what educators and school systems can do to alleviate them.

■ PAUSE TO REFLECT
Latent Social Problems

- Can you think of any other examples of latent social problems in our society? How will they have to evolve to be considered manifest social problems? What changes will society have to make to find a solution?

- What are examples of latent social problems that have developed into manifest problems in the past fifteen to twenty years? How can they be solved?

Explanations for Social Problems

Social Disorganization. A successful social system is organized through a consistent set of norms and values that guide our behavior and social interaction with each other. We expect our leaders to live by those norms and to enforce them in our communities. But not everyone agrees on what those norms should be, and if the disagreement becomes so severe that orderly social interaction is impossible, the result is **social disorganization**—or anomie (literally, "a state of normlessness"). A disorganized society is unable to agree on or establish a clear set of goals or effective procedures for achieving those goals. It also is unable to cohesively enforce social control or teach proper behavior to its members. The members of a community plagued with broken families, shifting population, and a lack of neighborhood unity, for example, are not likely to have a set of common norms and values to live by, and, therefore, they suffer social disorganization.[3]

> A society that lacks the cohesiveness to establish norms is likely to suffer from problems rooted in a lack of direction or structure for social interaction.

The school system is a logical place to combat social disorganization. Educators can begin by creating a set of norms and values for students to follow, developing clear and compelling goals as well as consistent procedures for achieving them, and initiating effective **socialization** practices, or methods of teaching students proper behavior. The hope is that students can apply their positive school experiences to their home lives and community activities.

Conflict. Society can be viewed as a struggle between contrasting and opposing groups. **Conflict** develops whenever groups holding different values live in the same community and the laws and norms of the dominant group impinge on the other groups.

If the differences are deep enough, violence may erupt from such conflicts.[4] Each group pursues its own values, which may conflict with the values of other groups; therefore, from the perspective of one's group membership, other groups would appear to be deviant. But this does not mean that the other groups are disorganized or that overall social organization is threatened. A thriving society is not an integrated system in which everyone always agrees on the norms and values; rather, it is a balance of contending groups, each offering unique contributions. In any conflict, the dominant group defines deviance. It follows, then, for example, that deviance is usually defined in the public schools as breaches of white, middle-class values. Juvenile delinquents and criminal gangs are viewed as minority groups out of sympathy with the norms of the dominant majority. Those belonging to groups considered deviant may feel alienated, exploited, and unduly controlled. But if they somehow become dominant, they likely will consider the formerly dominant group as deviant because deviance is largely a matter of whose values will prevail.

A society that establishes norms that do not take into account the values of all its groups opens the door to social conflict.

Again, the public schools have an opportunity to teach different groups how to live in harmony by reducing or eliminating the sources of conflict, at least in the schools. Various ethnic, racial, and radical groups often find themselves in conflict with school rules (which, as noted earlier, usually are based on white, middle-class values). Educators can help reduce conflict by recognizing and enforcing student rights and inviting all students and parents to help develop the student codes. Educators also can support and encourage community control of the school system so that minority groups have as much say in developing and enforcing the norms and sanctions of the school. If each group is represented equally, it follows that none would be considered deviant.

Labeling. This explanation of social problems pertains only to deviance and holds that deviance is a self-fulfilling result of being labeled as a deviant by an authority figure. Negative labels include "drug addict," "alcoholic," "truant," "juvenile delinquent," "punk," and "vandal." Not all labels have a negative effect. Positive labels such as "honor student" and "star athlete" can promote pride and achievement. But for our purposes here, we will focus on the potentially damaging effects of negative labeling.

The power of labeling a person should not be taken lightly, particularly by teachers.

While a negative label simply might identify the deviant behavior at first, the label itself can aggravate the deviant behavior and reduce the chances that the person will change the behavior. "If that's what they expect of me," the person might say, "why should I change?" The stigma of a negative label also can contribute to deviance. Students labeled as "vandals" or "violence prone" tend to view themselves negatively, and others tend to react to them differently. Such people may rebel against any measures taken to control them and seek solace among others in their situation. Often they will band together and create a deviant subculture. A **subculture** is a system of attitudes, values, modes of behavior, and life styles that are distinct but related to the dominant culture. A **deviant subculture,** then, is a subculture that deviates from the norm. The creation of such subcultures is known as **secondary deviance.** So, ironically, the social control measures normally used to curb student delinquency, for example, may very well have the opposite effect by precipitating more widespread participation in deviant subcultures.[5]

School officials can break this cycle by eliminating the use of negative labels whenever possible. Labeling is rampant in our society and in our school systems. Eliminating it will mean making some major changes in our approach to education. Labeling and any classification schemes that have the same effect as labeling should not be used for instruction, guidance, or administrative purposes. This would restrict the use of various psychological and standardized tests, the handling of students who violate school rules, and the many other practices where labeling is common. Preservice and inservice education programs would need to include warnings of the dangers of labeling and encourage instead humanistic educational practices that treat the student as a whole person and eliminate the use of labels. Students who have suffered the negative effects of labeling may need extra attention and support to reverse those effects and discourage the student from further secondary deviance.

Differential Association. Edward H. Sutherland theorizes that deviant and unlawful behaviors both are learned by association with others who engage in deviant behavior.[6] Specifically, deviant behavior is learned within intimate personal groups—usually deviant subcultures—that have their own language and set of unique gestures. A person could fall in with such a group through secondary deviance (discussed in the previous section) or merely through proximity: a youngster who lives in an area populated by deviant groups probably is going to associate with them to some degree. Members of these groups learn techniques for violating rules or laws and develop the motives, attitudes, and rationalizations for such violations. The group member usually is isolated from law-abiding people and patterns that might counteract these tendencies. Whether individuals will become deviant depends on whether they associate more with law-abiding or deviant groups. Individuals who associate more with deviant or violent groups early in life or with greater frequency and intensity are at greater risk of becoming deviant or prone to violence.

To counteract the effects of differential association, educators must supervise school group relationships and student subcultures closely and provide sound, law-abiding role models for students to

Some experts believe that social deviance is principally spread through social contact. The same, of course, would hold true for socially affirming behavior and attitudes.

associate with. Outside the school system, administrators can establish after-school programs to continue students' positive associations by providing healthy recreational and learning activities. Finally, educators can support efforts to reach the root of the problem by encouraging government programs for neighborhood improvement and renewal.

All of these approaches may be faulty, or at least incomplete, in that they do not consider the possibility that deviancy is an inherited tendency, which some researchers have theorized. They also do not examine the effects of television on behavior, a topic we will discuss later in this chapter.

These explanations have in common the fact that deviant behavior starts or is maintained through supporting peer groups or subcultures. Many subcultures can be found among students who are at the age where approval and security from their peers is important.

STUDENT SUBCULTURES ■

Peer Groups

Children begin forming peer group attachments almost immediately, even at the preschool level. A **peer group** is an egalitarian group in which members share a common characteristic, such as age or ethnicity. Evidence indicates that these attachments grow throughout childhood and adolescence[7] and that by the time students are in secondary school, they are likely to belong to some sort of student subculture.

Interaction with peers plays a vital role in a child's social development,[8] and peer groups may enhance or detract from the process of socialization, the process by which we acquire the knowledge, skills, and behavior needed to become productive members of society and by which we also learn what are considered appropriate roles for our age, sex, and social class. In his early studies of adolescent subcultures, James Coleman postulated that in industrial society a great deal of the responsibility for training and guiding our children has shifted from the family to the school and, in turn, to student peer groups. He points out that the extended period of dependency in such societies has resulted in an adolescent social system in the high school[9] that guides behavior and defines desirable or undesirable traits among students. Coleman and his associates studied this informal social system in ten schools and found that the more highly esteemed students were friendly, popular, and attractive, were skilled in many areas, and pos-

A larger share of the socialization process has shifted from the home to the peer group, where value systems might not reflect the long-range perspective of adult experience.

sessed material goods such as cars, records, and clothes.[10] Athletic prowess was prized among boys, and activities leadership was admired among girls. Girls did not consider good grades important; in fact, they considered it important not to appear smarter than boys.

These findings seem to be supported in a more recent large-scale study by John Goodlad in which junior and senior high-school students were asked which types of students they considered most popular.[11] Sixty percent of junior high students and 79 percent of senior high students named athletes and students with good looks as most popular. Smart students were highly ranked by 14 percent of the junior high students and 7 percent of the senior high students. When asked to name the single best thing about their school, students at both levels most frequently answered "my friends." Choices of "classes I'm taking" and "teachers" ranked low.

It appears that the importance of academics is getting short shrift among the adolescent student subcultures. If the process of socialization is, indeed, shifting from the family toward the schools, and since we can hardly expect students to ignore peer group influence, how can educators use this influence to encourage academic achievement? To begin with, teachers can emphasize class activities that encourage students to work together. They also can promote projects and activities in which all students can participate, thereby discouraging student cliques. Some schools have initiated successful peer teaching and tutoring programs, which help promote group norms that encourage academic achievement.

So far, we have discussed aspects of student subcultures normally found in any adolescent group. Under the watchful eye of school officials, these subcultures are normal, relatively harmless, and even nurturing in the security and guidance they offer to students in their uncertain teenage years. Most members of these groups can be expected to emerge from high school well-prepared for their next steps in life. But some subcultures grow beyond the norm and can have dangerous influences on students. Some become involved in drug abuse (to be discussed later in this chapter), and others develop into delinquent gangs. Gang membership has become a manifest social problem in recent years and deserves a close look here.

Gangs

Gangs always have been a part of the American metropolitan landscape to some degree, but, after a period of relative inactivity in the late 1960s, they have arisen again in larger cities in the United States in more virulent, criminal forms. It is estimated that youth gangs are present in about 300 United States cities, and that two-thirds of these gangs are concentrated in ten large cities.[12] Murder, rape, robbery, drug trafficking, extortion, and vandalism are common gang activities, made easier by the members' access to weapons like pipe bombs, automatic rifles, and machine guns.

Most gang members are of school age and often are found near school grounds recruiting new members and generally stirring up trouble. A conservative estimate holds gangs responsible for more than half of the vandalism in Los Angeles schools.[13] The climate of fear created by gang presence in a schoolyard can be intense. Students become afraid to go to school, or if they do make it to class, find it difficult to concentrate on their studies.

Why do some student subcultures degenerate into delinquent gangs, and how can educators combat the trend? The four explanations for social problems that we discussed earlier may help us understand how gangs form and what can be done to dismantle or prevent them.

The social-disorganization approach explains the rise of delinquent gangs as a result of a breakdown of social norms. These youths have received little positive socialization from their families, schools, or communities. They turn to gangs in their search for continuity and security. Educators can attempt to divert youths from joining gangs by creating an organized atmosphere of learning and living at school. They should create a set of positive norms and values for students to follow, help students develop clear goals and means of achieving them, and improve techniques of positive socialization.

Gangs can offer youths a sense of belonging, but the values and norms in these gangs are often in strong conflict with the values and norms of the larger society.

The conflict approach suggests that a delinquent gang develops as the result of a conflict between the values of the larger society and those of a group of youths. This group, considered socially deviant, feels alienated from the mainstream of social life and follows the only path it finds open: the path to delinquency and crime. Educators might be able to intercept this group at its socially deviant stage by encouraging the members to express their values in school and giving them a greater voice in developing school policies. In other words, by allowing the youths into the mainstream, educators might be able to stop the group from developing into a delinquent gang.

The labeling approach suggests that a delinquent gang develops as a self-fulfilling result of its members being labeled "deviant" or "delinquent." Such labels probably are applied after the undesirable behavior is observed, so, while the label does not necessarily create the behavior, it undoubtedly worsens it. Educators can break this self-fulfilling cycle by eliminating the use of labels whenever possible and educating teachers and school officials about the dangers of labeling.

The differential association explanation holds that individuals become gang members through social interaction with other gang members or youths who practice deviant behavior. They learn the codes of gang membership and the motives and rationalizations for deviant or criminal behavior. Educators can modify this behavior by seeing that students have ample opportunity to associate with positive, law-abiding role models within the school system.

Since gangs usually grow out of conditions in the larger community, school officials should solicit the cooperation and support of community leaders and relevant agencies to battle the problem on all four fronts. In Philadelphia, for instance, a coordinated program has stemmed the tide of gang activity by involving school officials, community leaders, churches, recreational centers, neighborhood crisis intervention teams, and informal parents' councils.[14]

■ FAMILY INFLUENCES

Harmful values and norms in a family can be socially and psychologically destructive.

The four explanations of social problems deal with major social influences outside the family and the media. In this section, we will discuss the strong influence the family can have on an individual's behavior, and in the next section we will look at the social effects of television. While a family can have vital, positive influences on an individual, our concern here is with the social problems that a family can create for children, specifically through violence or neglect.

Violence

Family violence can take many forms, from corporal punishment to child abuse. **Violence** is a sudden and extremely forceful act that causes physical harm or suffering. The most common form of family violence is **corporal punishment,** which is defined as punishment inflicted directly to the body, such as spanking. Corporal punishment that causes excessive physical harm or threatens the child's life or safety becomes **child abuse.** Not all corporal punishment is necessarily violent. Milder or more deliberate forms that do not cause physical harm or suffering may be considered examples of **force.** Force involves the use of physical strength to cause someone to do something, such as picking up a rebellious child and physically forcing him or her to sit at the dinner table.

Our society generally approves of corporal punishment both at home and in school. At least 93 percent of all parents spank their children,[15] and the United States Supreme Court has ruled that paddling in the school does not violate either the Eighth Amendment's prohibition of cruel and unusual punishment or the Fourteenth Amendment's guarantee of the right to due process.[16] However, there is a fine line between corporal punishment and child abuse, and the courts will intervene if an adult causes excessive physical harm to a child in the name of corporal punishment or if the punishment is inflicted with a "malicious desire to cause pain."[17]

Physical child abuse can result in death or permanent brain damage, bleeding around the skull, severe bruising, mutilation, broken bones, and other severe injuries. Children under age four are most likely to be abused. Reported cases of child abuse range from 6,000 to 10,000 cases a year, but surveys that asked people about cases they know suggest that the figure exceeds two million each year.[18]

Why do so many adults resort to corporal punishment? A simple explanation is that it is sanctioned by the cultural norms of our society. But when parents cross the line from corporal punishment to child abuse, we need to take a closer look at the causes.

One psychological theory holds that it stems from frustration. A parent with several young children to care for might be unprepared for the demands of the job, and, in an attempt to stop a whining, crying, or misbehaving child, might hit the child to alleviate the frustration and regain control. Or the family breadwinner might be laid off and end up physically taking out anger and frustration on the child at home.[19]

> The inability to deal appropriately with stress is considered a key cause of child abuse.

This **frustration-aggression hypothesis** suggests that frustration leads to some form of aggression.[20] Little testing of this theory has been conducted in the home environment, however. Furthermore, the hypothesis does not offer an operational definition of "frustration." We all find different things frustrating to different degrees, and our reactions to frustrations also differ. In fact, some of us might choose to leave a frustrating situation rather than react aggressively.

Another psychological theory suggests that parents who abuse their children suffer from serious emotional or personality disturbances, such as schizophrenia, character disorders, impaired impulse control, gross immaturity, chronic aggressiveness, rigid and detached personalities, and jealousy.[21] However, most people do not fit neatly into a single psychological category, and few studies have attempted to test these hypotheses. Furthermore, even if an abusive parent suffers from one of these disturbances, he or she is still influenced by social and cultural factors, and those factors are likely to figure into the causes of child abuse.

Social Factors of Child Abuse. Parents from lower-class backgrounds are more likely to use corporal punishment than are parents from the middle class. Similarly, figures show that lower-class parents are more likely to abuse their children than are middle-class parents, although it is possible that middle-class abuse is more common than we know because it is not reported as often.[22]

The difference between abuse in the lower class and in the middle class might be explained by the fact that the two classes instill different values and settle disputes differently. For instance, parents in the middle class tend to encourage more autonomy for boys and greater decision-making power than do lower-class parents.

Child abuse generally is more common in families with unwanted children, single parents, or parents who were raised in violent homes and adopt the violent role model from their own early socialization. A parent's unemployment may create frustration and anxiety, which the parent then takes out on the child. Child abusers are more often women than men, perhaps simply because women generally spend more time with children than men do. A common complaint among women who stay home with their children is that they sometimes feel as if the children are interfering with their goals and freedom. When a parent feels trapped like this, frustration and anger can set in, and, in an abusive situation, the children are likely to bear the brunt of that anger.[23]

As we can see, the onset of child abuse is based on a complex set of interacting psychological and social factors. However, enough studies have been done on the causes of child abuse in the home that a pattern in the personalities of abusers often can be detected. If these people are recognized early on as being predisposed toward violence and are approached in a supportive and encouraging manner, they might be persuaded to get help for their problems before those problems explode into child abuse at home.

One theory holds that aggression should be expressed in the home rather than suppressed, because violence is a part of human nature and can only be controlled—not eliminated. Expression of anger relieves tension and diminishes the likelihood of further, more severe violence. Advocates of this theory believe that children should be allowed to participate in aggressive play activities, behave aggressively in psychotherapy playrooms, or watch aggressive acts on television. Many psychoanalysts and their followers subscribe to this theory of catharsis,[24] but several studies have failed to support the hypothesis. In fact, these studies suggest that a child's participation in aggressive activities actually might increase aggression.[25]

How can educators and school officials help stem the tide of child abuse? First, they can report signs of abuse to the proper child welfare agencies. In fact, they are legally obligated to do so. Most states impose

Abuse is often socialized (for example, passed on from generation to generation).

Educators can help identify child abuse. They also can model positive non-abusive values and norms.

criminal penalties for failure to report abuse, ranging from fines to prison terms. In addition, civil suits can be brought against someone for failing to report suspected abuse.

Schools and other public institutions can prohibit the use of corporal punishment as the first step toward changing the social norms that sanction the practice. Schools can offer parent education courses and sound sex education programs that might help reduce the incidence of teenage parenthood, and they can encourage the development of more extensive child care facilities to take some pressure off working parents. Also, teachers can be trained to spot children who exhibit signs of predisposition toward violence and alert parents or school officials in the hopes of breaking the pattern of violence early in the child's life.

Latchkey and Homeless Children

Educators also are in a good position to detect and provide for two other groups increasing in number across the United States: latchkey children and homeless children, including children who run away from home to escape abuse or conflict. The Census Bureau estimates that there are at least two million latchkey children in the United States,[26] and the National Coalition for the Homeless estimates that almost one million children can be counted as homeless.[27]

Latchkey children are youngsters who return to empty homes after school, usually because their parents work outside the home. While the parents may not have a choice, their latchkey children nonetheless can suffer the effects of being left alone. Researchers are divided over what those effects are, however. Some studies suggest that these children suffer abnormal levels of fear, but other studies find no significant differences between latchkey children and supervised children.[28]

Nevertheless, a significant percentage of students are latchkey children, and educators should keep this in mind when developing school programs and policies. For instance, latchkey children probably could benefit from counseling and a variety of after-school activities.

As the homeless population increases across the country, so does the number of homeless children. Studies show that these children rarely attend school and suffer poor health and learning disabilities.[29] Runaways account for at least one million of the homeless children in the United States and are likely to drop out of school, become addicted to drugs, or fall in with delinquent gangs. As with latchkey children, these homeless children also can benefit from counseling and after-school activities. In addition, educators can encourage the community to join in demanding improved governmental assistance

Providing a structured and supportive environment for children can help protect them from negative influences.

for these children, from providing temporary shelter and counseling to helping homeless families get back on their feet and into a more stable routine.

▪ THE INFLUENCE OF TELEVISION

Children under the age of eighteen spend more time watching television than doing anything else except sleeping.[30] This would suggest that television takes valuable time away from a child's educational and personal development. It also raises concerns about the possible adverse effects of television violence on children.

While excessive television viewing (more than five or six hours a day) might interfere with a child's development, there is little evidence to suggest that moderate viewing (less than three or four hours a day) has any adverse effect.[31] Moreover, the degree of influence that television has upon a child depends upon the child's attitude (frustration, anger, avoidance of school work) while watching a program.[32]

Because television viewing has no prerequisites, is oriented in the present, is image-centered and non-punitive, and is presented in short, complete doses, children do not have to think or participate in the activity. Some teachers complain that because of the undemanding nature of television, their students come to school expecting to sit back and be entertained. They say students are not interested in dealing with abstractions and symbolic material, which require effort and sustained concentration.

One of television's most negative effects on children might be that it stunts their cognitive development and their motivation to engage in the learning process.

While early studies have been inconclusive on the effect of television violence on children, later studies have detected a relationship between television violence and aggressive behavior in children.[33] Other controlled experiments have shown a small but consistent correlation between television violence and aggressiveness, but there is little evidence to show that this relationship carries over to situations outside the laboratory.[34]

Perhaps one of the main problems with violence in the media is that it is too quick, too easy, and gratuitously presented in unrealistic settings. Children can come away from a violent show with the idea that violence is an easy solution for everyday problems or a smart, efficient way to handle difficult people. To combat this potentially adverse effect, we should demand programs with less gratuitous violence, and that any violence that is portrayed should emerge naturally from the context of the story. We also should raise more questions about violence in the media in general (such as movies and news programs) and perhaps reconsider our values that stem from the history of violence in American society.

This is not to say that television does not offer valuable educational programming. Indeed, children who watch educational shows like "Sesame Street," "3-2-1 Contact," and "Square I" have exhibited positive academic achievement.[35]

■ **PAUSE TO REFLECT**
Television Violence

- We have discussed the effects of television violence on young people and on their achievement in school, but what other effects—negative or positive—can television have on children? For instance, can beer commercials entice a child to start drinking? Can nature programs teach a child to respect animals?

- What can be done to curb the negative effects of television and enhance the positive ones?

- Think back to your own experiences during elementary and secondary school. How much television did you watch? What kinds of shows? How did your viewing habits hinder your schoolwork, if at all?

EDUCATIONAL ISSUE 4–1

Does television viewing adversely affect student achievement and behavior?

Yes	No
1. Television viewing takes valuable time away from studying.	1. Moderate television viewing does not lower academic achievement.
2. Students expect to be entertained in school.	2. Teachers can learn techniques from television to make learning material more appealing.
3. Television violence tends to encourage violent behavior in children who already have tendencies toward aggressive behavior.	3. Experimental results in laboratory settings that demonstrate a small correlation between viewing violence and aggressive behavior do not carry over to settings outside the laboratory.

■ SUBSTANCE ABUSE

Few would disagree that substance abuse among the nation's youth has become a manifest problem in need of a solution. In this section we will look at the pattern of drug and alcohol use among young people, some reasons that children today turn to drugs and alcohol, and methods that parents and schools can use to fight the problem.

The National Institute of Drug Abuse reports that although marijuana use is declining (see Table 4–1), nearly two-thirds of American teenagers experiment with an illegal drug before they graduate from high school, and more than one-third use drugs other than marijuana. A nationwide survey of high-school students indicates that 20 percent smoke cigarettes daily, 6 percent drink alcohol daily, and 7 percent use marijuana daily.[36]

Teenage involvement with drugs generally follows a pattern. The first substances used are beer and wine, followed by hard liquor and tobacco, then marijuana. Though the use of psychedelics and heroin often is preceded by the use of marijuana, it is no longer believed that marijuana use invariably leads to use of hard drugs.[37]

Students sometimes smoke to test the effects of smoking on their bodies.

The first use of alcohol may occur as early as elementary school, and there is every indication that drinking continues into high school. Arrest rates for drunken driving among youth have increased dramatically since 1960, and one in six teenage deaths is alcohol-related.[38]

Among eighteen to twenty-four-year-olds, 2.51 million use cocaine once a month or more.[39] With the growing availability of "crack"—a cheaper, highly addictive, and potentially deadly form of cocaine—the incidence of addiction is likely to increase as the trend of drug use grows among high-school students (see Table 4–1).

Why do children turn to alcohol and drugs, and who are most susceptible? In some cases, students learn substance abuse through social interaction with peers who drink or use drugs (differential association). A study of 1,634 students in grades seven through nine showed that students became more susceptible to drugs and alcohol as they moved through these grades, but that variables such as age, sex, and the type of drug influenced individual decisions to use them.[40]

Some youngsters turn to drugs or alcohol for relief from the enormous stress they are under. A survey of 18,000 Kansas students through twelfth grade found youngsters who had been under stress since early childhood. A study of 4,000 Kansas students from kindergarten to third grade found youngsters who experienced "negative stress behavior," which included sleeplessness, short tempers, and nail biting. The sources of stress ranged from domineering parents to broken homes to a more competitive society. These stressed children were more susceptible to substance abuse, as well as teenage pregnancy, dropping out of school, obesity, and chronic heart disease.[41] Though the causes of the stress vary, the study suggested that the home environment is the primary source. Typical parents communicate with their children about fourteen minutes a day—and about twelve of those minutes are consumed with talk about unimportant matters. Another source of stress is parents who give their children conditional love: "We will love you if. . . ."

Children in our society are often under a good deal of stress. Substance use is one response to that stress.

Children prone to alcohol or drug abuse often share one or more of the following predictors:

- Family history of alcoholism, drug use, or criminality
- Lax supervision or constant criticism at home
- Early antisocial or aggressive behavior in school
- Low motivation or academic failure in elementary school
- First use of drugs before age fifteen
- Association with peers who drink or use drugs[42]

TABLE 4-1 Trends in drug use among high-school seniors, by type of drug and frequency of use: 1975 to 1986

Type of Drug and Frequency of Use	Class of 1975	Class of 1976	Class of 1977	Class of 1978	Class of 1979	Class of 1980	Class of 1981	Class of 1982	Class of 1983	Class of 1984	Class of 1985	Class of 1986
1	2	3	4	5	6	7	8	9	10	11	12	13
Percent reporting having ever used drugs												
Alcohol	90.4	91.9	92.5	93.1	93.0	93.2	92.6	92.8	92.6	92.6	92.2	91.3
Any illicit drug abuse	55.2	58.3	61.6	64.1	65.1	65.4	65.6	64.4	62.9	61.6	60.6	57.6
Marijuana only	19.0	22.9	25.8	27.6	27.7	26.7	22.8	23.3	22.5	21.3	20.9	19.9
Any illicit drug other than marijuana[1]	36.2	35.4	35.8	36.5	37.4	38.7	42.8	41.1	40.4	40.3	39.7	37.7
Use of selected drugs												
Cocaine	9.0	9.7	10.8	12.9	15.4	15.7	16.5	16.0	16.2	16.1	17.3	16.9
Heroin	2.2	1.8	1.8	1.6	1.1	1.1	1.1	1.2	1.2	1.3	1.2	1.1
LSD	11.3	11.0	9.8	9.7	9.5	9.3	9.8	9.6	8.9	8.0	7.5	7.2
Marijuana/hashish	47.3	52.8	56.4	59.2	60.4	60.3	59.5	58.7	57.0	54.9	54.2	50.9
PCP	—	—	—	—	12.8	9.6	7.8	6.0	5.6	5.0	4.9	4.8
Percent reporting use of drugs in the past twelve months												
Alcohol	84.8	85.7	87.0	87.7	88.1	87.9	87.0	86.8	87.3	86.0	85.6	84.5
Any illicit drug abuse	45.0	48.1	51.1	53.8	54.2	53.1	52.1	49.4	47.4	45.8	46.3	44.3
Marijuana only	18.8	22.7	25.1	26.7	26.0	22.7	18.1	19.3	19.0	17.8	18.9	18.4
Any illicit drug other than marijuana[1]	26.2	25.4	26.0	27.1	28.2	30.4	34.0	30.1	28.4	28.0	27.4	25.9
Use of selected drugs												
Cocaine	5.6	6.0	7.2	9.0	12.0	12.3	12.4	11.5	11.4	11.6	13.1	12.7
Heroin	1.0	0.8	0.8	0.8	0.5	0.5	0.5	0.6	0.6	0.5	0.6	0.5
LSD	7.2	6.4	5.5	6.3	6.6	6.5	6.5	6.1	5.4	4.7	4.4	4.5
Marijuana/hashish	40.0	44.5	47.6	50.2	50.8	48.8	46.1	44.3	42.3	40.0	40.6	38.8
PCP	—	—	—	—	7.0	4.4	3.2	2.2	2.6	2.3	2.9	2.4

TABLE 4–1 (continued)

Type of Drug and Frequency of Use	Class of 1975	Class of 1976	Class of 1977	Class of 1978	Class of 1979	Class of 1980	Class of 1981	Class of 1982	Class of 1983	Class of 1984	Class of 1985	Class of 1986
1	2	3	4	5	6	7	8	9	10	11	12	13
Percent reporting use of drugs in the past thirty days												
Alcohol	68.2	68.3	71.2	72.1	71.8	72.0	70.7	69.7	69.4	67.2	65.9	65.3
Any illicit drug abuse	30.7	34.2	37.6	38.9	38.9	37.2	36.9	32.5	30.5	29.2	29.7	27.1
Marijuana only	15.3	20.3	22.4	23.8	22.2	18.8	15.2	15.5	15.1	14.1	14.8	13.9
Any illicit drug other than marijuana[1]	15.4	13.9	15.2	15.1	16.8	18.4	21.7	17.0	15.4	15.1	14.9	13.2
Use of selected drugs												
Cocaine	1.9	2.0	2.9	3.9	5.7	5.2	5.8	5.0	4.9	5.8	6.7	6.2
Heroin	0.4	0.2	0.3	0.3	0.2	0.2	0.2	0.2	0.2	0.3	0.3	0.2
LSD	2.3	1.9	2.1	2.1	2.4	2.3	2.5	2.4	1.9	1.5	1.6	1.7
Marijuana/hashish	27.1	32.2	35.4	37.1	36.5	33.7	31.6	28.5	27.0	25.2	25.7	23.4
PCP	—	—	—	—	2.4	1.4	1.4	1.0	1.3	1.0	1.6	1.3

Note: A revised questionnaire was used in 1982 and later years to reduce the inappropriate reporting of nonprescription stimulants. This slightly reduced the positive responses for some types of drug abuse.

[1] Other illicit drugs include any use of hallucinogens, cocaine, and heroin, or any use of other opiates, stimulants, sedatives, or tranquilizers not under a doctor's orders.

—Data not available.

Source: U.S. Department of Health and Human Services, Alcohol, Drug Abuse, and Mental Health Administration, *Drug Use Among American High School Students and Other Young Adults, National Trends Through 1986.* (This table was prepared September 1987.)

What can parents and educators do to reduce substance abuse among young people? The most effective battle can be fought on the home front. Parents need to provide accurate information about alcohol and drugs long before their children reach adolescence. Children look to their parents as role models, so parents should refrain from using any substance they do not want their children to use. These suggestions, coupled with a supportive atmosphere in which children can develop high self-esteem and sound judgment can go a long way in the fight to keep children drug- and alcohol-free. If the family is unable to handle the problem, help can be sought from school counselors, the family physician, social workers, and adolescent drug treatment centers.

Perhaps the strongest source of help involves the peer groups themselves. Educators can encourage peer group leaders to promote substance abuse programs and initiate campaigns against drugs, alcohol, and cigarettes. Drug-free students serve as role models and can have strong positive influences on their peers. Most drug education programs, while well-intentioned, often only touch on the facts about substance abuse; they need to go further by developing strong role models and programs that teach students how to change their behavior.[43] And finally, schools can work together with the community to reach and help high-school dropouts, who are at high risk of substance abuse. They can launch joint efforts to establish neighborhood recreational and drug education programs to offer dropouts substantive and positive alternatives to substance abuse.

> Substance use is, to a certain extent, a socialized behavior. Adults can help a great deal by not modeling the behavior and encouraging peer groups to avoid substance use.

■ SUICIDE

Teenage suicide has been on the rise in the United States since the 1950s. Children whose problems do not seem, on the surface, to be worse than anyone else's can suddenly end their life with a bullet, an overdose, or a razor blade. Their stunned friends and family react with feelings of guilt, shame, fear, and confusion. How could this happen? What could drive a child to the point of such despair that suicide seems to be the only answer? And why are more children today choosing suicide? In this section we look at some philosophical discussions of suicide as well as some current social factors that might shed light on those questions. We also will discuss how educators and parents can identify children at risk of suicide and what can be done to help them.

> Teen suicide has risen sharply in recent years.

First, some statistics. One in ten young people might attempt suicide every year,[44] and 5,000 of them succeed. The suicide rate for people aged fifteen to twenty-six tripled between 1950 and 1980; suicide now ranks as the tenth highest cause of death in the United States and is the second highest cause of death for white males aged fifteen to nineteen years old. More than three times as many females attempt suicide as males, but more males succeed: the ratio of male to female suicide is 2.5 to 1. The available statistics may be skewed because family members often do not report the death as a suicide for fear of incurring the undesirable stigma that can accompany suicide.[45]

Many experts from philosophers to researchers have tried to explain the causes of suicide. Debate has centered on whether suicide is a rational or psychotic act; whether it is immoral or can be justified in some cases; or whether it is the result of complex historical, cultural, social, and personal relations.

Most experts no longer believe that every suicide is a psychotic act, but whether it is a rational one is open to debate. If one carefully explores the meaning and consequences of suicide, seriously considers the options, and then still chooses suicide, one could be considered to have made a rational decision.

Judging whether suicide is immoral depends partly upon one's ethical, religious, and cultural beliefs. Humans share the instinct of self-preservation and the belief that all individuals have the right to protect and preserve their lives. If the purpose of life is to become all one can be, or **self-actualizing,** then suicide is a violation of one's true self, and hence is immoral. But it also can be argued that if one truly believes that the goals of self-actualization have become impossible to achieve, that life is meaningless or suffering is unbearable, then suicide would appear to be justified. Others would say that we not only have the right to protect and preserve our lives but we also have the social obligation to do so, even if we believe life is meaningless or that suffering is unbearable. Suicide denies our responsibilities to our families, friends, and community, causing them unnecessary suffering by depriving them of our contributions and offending those who believe suicide is immoral.

Camus claimed that suicide is the ultimate philosophical problem: "Judging whether life is or is not worth living amounts to answering the fundamental question of philosophy."[46] While suicide usually is dealt with as a social phenomenon, Camus notes, his concern is with exploring individual thought that precedes suicide. He believes that, for some people, suicide is the only way to deal with **the absurd,** or the inconsistency between one's own beliefs and values and one's environment. The absurd is neither in the individual nor in the world but in the confrontation of the two. The absurd refers to life's meaninglessness, lack of structure, and inconsistency. Suicide, Camus believes, is a confession that "life is too much for you or you do not understand it."[47] A person might, for example, proceed day to day in a particular routine without questioning it and then one day suddenly become aware that the routine—and hence one's life—seems senseless. Camus' answer is that suicide is an unacceptable response, because a fundamental purpose in life is to fulfill one's humanity by confronting and accepting the absurd.

Using a sociological approach, Emile Durkheim analyzed 26,000 suicide cases and found that the propensity toward suicide varied among societies and depended upon the degree of integration within a society.[48] Societies with higher degrees of integration (people bound to each other by ties of affection and obligation, as in marriage) had fewer instances of suicide. Durkheim's summary of nineteenth century statistics from several countries suggested that married people were less likely to commit suicide than were unmarried people (single or widowed).

Jack Douglas, however, contends that any suicide statistics are suspect because coroners and medical examiners can mistake suicide for something else, usually an accident.[49] Douglas also suggests that suicides are more accurately reported in larger towns than rural areas, and that highly integrated groups are more likely to conceal suicides than poorly integrated ones.

A sense of hopelessness, that the future holds nothing positive, is a major cause of suicide.

Maurice Farber, in an attempt to pinpoint the cause of suicide, has concluded that hopelessness is the most important element in the decision to commit suicide.[50] **Hopelessness** is the feeling one arrives at if life's conditions are unbearable and one does not feel competent to change those conditions. For instance, an individual with a damaged sense of competence who is faced with difficult situations that he or she does not feel able to handle is at high risk of suicide, especially in societies with a lax attitude toward suicide. On the other hand, an individual with a strong sense of competence and self-confidence as well as optimism for the future is less likely to commit suicide, especially in societies where suicide goes against community norms and values.

Other social trends that can lead to suicide among young people are growing competition in schools and the work force, the inability to make friends in large school systems, media coverage of suicides among youth (which can give other young people the idea), family instability, and the declining role of organized religion in society.

What youths are at the greatest risk of committing suicide? How can parents and educators help youngsters deal with their problems before they decide suicide is the only answer? Youths in the most danger of committing suicide share some characteristics:

- They are in conflict with adults—for example, parents and their children seriously disagreeing on role responsibilities.
- They tend to be aggressive and delinquent.

'Samariteens' or suicide prevention hotlines may be the last desperate hope for some youth.

- They come from unstable homes in which alcohol or drugs are abused.
- They suffer from acute stress or depression.

Some common behavioral symptoms can alert watchful parents and teachers to a high-risk youth:

- Drug or alcohol abuse
- Withdrawal from friends or family
- Irregular sleep habits
- Involvement in high-risk activities, such as speeding or playing Russian roulette
- Giving away of favorite possessions
- Unusual neglect of personal appearance
- Abrupt change in eating habits[51]

Students contemplating suicide often exhibit warning signs that can alert teachers to a potential problem.

Educators who notice any of these signs in a student should alert the parents and encourage them to get their child professional help. Educators should not hesitate to intervene in such a case. In our society, an educator's obligation to protect the student's welfare generally outweighs the obligation to respect the student's freedom. Moreover, this situation falls under one of the five justifications for paternalism—to prevent harm.

■ VIOLENCE AND DELINQUENCY

Lack of discipline has been cited consistently by the public as the most significant problem in education.[52] And a survey of teachers found that 54 percent believe that student behavior interferes with their teaching.[53] While the problem ranges from everyday mischief to serious violence, we will focus in this section on discipline problems that lead to violence, vandalism, and delinquency. We will examine examples of school violence, possible causes of that violence, the effect it has on teachers and other students, and some things educators can do to curb the problem.

Although some of the most serious offenses peaked nationwide in the mid-1970s, the National Institute of Education (NIE) reports that 6,700 schools still are seriously affected by crime.[54] Much of that crime appears to be related to drug abuse and delinquent gang activity in the school.

The disruption and danger of physical harm has created an atmosphere of fear among students and teachers. The NIE study found that 20 percent of the students were sometimes afraid of being hurt in school, and 3 percent said they were afraid most of the time. The fear was so great in some cases that the students avoided restrooms and other areas where they expected to be attacked.

Violence in the schools can seriously undermine schooling by creating an environment where fear rather than learning preoccupies students and teachers.

Among teachers, 12 percent (about 120,000) said they were hesitant to confront misbehaving students for fear of being harmed. Morale can drop severely among teachers who are constantly afraid for their safety. A psychiatrist evaluated 575 teachers who had experienced extraordinary and sustained levels of stress related to the violence in their schools. They suffered symptoms ranging from disorganization to anxiety attacks. Much of the stress was related to the fact that many of these teachers had subconsciously expected their students to view them as wise parental figures and to treat them with respect and dignity. When the students reacted with disrespect and violence instead, shock and confusion set in. The psychiatrist compared the teachers' suffering to "combat neurosis" found among the psychiatric casualties of World War II.[55]

Unless there are signs of improvement, school systems can be in danger of losing their teachers—either through transfers or resignations. The stress tells on the students, as well. The threat of violence around every corner impinges severely on their freedom to learn and live as they choose. Some students may drop out of school rather than face daily danger and others might develop psychological disorders as a result of living in a sustained state of fear.

What are the causes behind this reign of terror in our schools? The level of violence in the schools appears to parallel the severity of problems in poor urban neighborhoods, especially family problems. The most common problems include lax discipline, especially by the father; insufficient supervision; and a lack of unity.[56]

The use of corporal punishment also can be a factor in student violence. It establishes a model of violence and perpetuates the idea that violence is an acceptable way to solve problems. As a solution, school officials might want to think twice about the example corporal punishment sets for students. If administrators are unwilling to ban the use of corporal punishment, they should at least make sure that students are given the right to due process (see Chapter 3) before they are punished.

Beyond that, teachers need the support and cooperation of school administrators in disciplining violent students, including suspension or expulsion if necessary, and in encouraging teachers to file official reports of assaults.

Other measures, already initiated by some of the more severely affected schools, include the installation of security guards, undercover police officers, electronic surveillance, guard dogs, paid community security aides, and voluntary security help. Some schools have made architectural changes in their buildings. These features include multistrength windows; electronic alarm systems; roofs with plastic domes instead of skylights; extra-strength hardware on doors and windows; and bricked-up entrances that are rarely used, especially in basements and storerooms.

Efforts to deal with crime in the schools have altered the school environment.

California has gone a step further in its efforts to protect students. In 1982 voters adopted a constitutional amendment known as the "victim's bill of rights," the only bill of its kind in the nation. The amendment guarantees students and school employees "the right to a school environment that is safe, secure, and peaceful."[57] As a result of this amendment, legislation is being considered that would require each school district in the state to develop a security plan. Whether this amendment means that school districts can be held liable for acts of violence against students or property remains to be seen. Depending on how the plan unfolds in California, it could have a major effect on how other states approach the question of school security.

The inherent problem with most measures designed to enhance school safety is that they can impinge on student rights, especially rights that protect them from physical restraint, search and seizure, and violation of confidentiality. But students also have a right to not be harmed by others and to be free to learn; and since one justification of paternalism is to prevent harm, school officials should attempt to strike a balance between the two. This may seem like an impossible task, but administrators should be able to strike this balance as long as they refrain from pursuing safety and order for their own sake (which can lead to unnecessary violations of student rights). Instead, they should remember that the purpose of safety and order is to protect students and enhance the atmosphere for learning. Keeping this in mind will ensure that school officials restrict a student's rights only when proven necessary to protect the rights of other students.

■ SCHOOL DROPOUTS

One of the most disappointing situations a teacher can face is that of a student who decides to quit school. Each year, 25 percent (700,000) of high-school students do just that;[58] without a doubt, the dropout rate in the United States has become a manifest social problem. In this section, we will look at some characteristics of dropouts, trends that can lead students to quit school, and suggestions for curbing the problem.

In the United States in 1987 the average of students who graduated four years after beginning their freshman year was 71.1 percent. A review of eighty-one studies of school dropouts between 1949 and 1972 found that minority students who came from lower-class families were more likely to drop out of school at some point.[59] Students who eventually dropped out were found to have lower overall intellectual ability, with most students in the bottom 25 percent of the student population and the least number of students in the top 25 percent. These students had low academic achievement, based on grade point average, retention of material, and achievement test scores. These characteristics persisted, even when the variables of socioeconomic status and ability were controlled in the studies. More recent studies support these findings, affirming that high-school dropouts usually are of lower socioeconomic status, exhibit higher hostility toward school, and tend toward delinquency, truancy, and other measures of alienation.

A persistent lack of success in school seems to be an important influence in the decision to drop out of school.

Other characteristics shared by dropouts included serious personal and social problems, like alcohol abuse, aggressiveness, and little interest in extracurricular activities. These students were frequently absent from school and tended to have less well-defined goals and lower occupational aspirations. Their parents tended to be indifferent toward the value of an education and often failed to supervise their children adequately.[60]

Dropouts face a host of problems in our society, including low self-esteem and an increased chance of ending up in prison, not to mention the inability to find a satisfying, well-paying job. A modern economy strongly favors college-educated, skilled workers; in fact, many companies often find it cheaper to import goods from other countries than to manufacture them here, cutting deeply into the opportunities for less-skilled workers.

Some progress has been made in thirty-eight states toward slowing the dropout rate.[61] Several programs, some of them rather innovative, have been initiated in the effort to discourage students from dropping out. West Virginia, for instance, was the first state to pass a law (in 1989) requiring teenage dropouts to surrender their driver's licenses. Wisconsin has followed suit and similar legislation is under consideration in other states. Critics complain, however, that the law does not address the sources of the problem and that the punishment does not fit the crime; that is, a driver's license regulates driving, not school attendance, and the two should not be related. In fact, the West Virginia law has been challenged in court by a seventeen-year-old father-to-be who claims he cannot support his family because he has no way of getting to his job.[62]

Solutions aimed at the sources of the dropout problem might include alternative schools that would offer special programs and counseling for potential dropouts, including students with behavioral problems and pregnant teenagers. In addition, schools could institute strong attendance policies that require immediate follow-up on absences. They also could introduce remedial measures by identifying problem students early and attempting to work with them in their home settings.

American educators also could learn from and adapt successful programs from other countries. Nearly three-fourths of West German students, for instance, receive up to three years of classroom instruction in one of more than 400 trades. The state-supported instruction is offered one day a week and includes on-the-job experience, for which employers pay wages. Perhaps as a result of this program, West Germany has a low rate of youth unemployment.

SEXUALITY ■

Because attitudes about sex vary dramatically in our society, teenagers receive widely conflicting messages about the subject. These messages often add to the fear and confusion of youngsters already dealing with the insecurities of growing up. Parents and educators face the difficult task of guiding teenagers through this period of uncertainty. In this section we will look at the social attitudes toward sex, statistics regarding sex and the teenager, some dangerous consequences of irresponsible sex, and how educators can teach youngsters to make responsible choices.

In today's society, we generally exhibit a much more casual attitude about sex than have past generations. The Victorian era, for instance, is known for its puritanical condemnation of any overt expression of sexuality. As studies by Freud, Kinsey, and others have led to a relaxation of sexual mores, the subject is generally more open today.

Teenagers today begin engaging in sex earlier than teens of previous generations. During the 1960s and 1970s, teenagers had gained a greater acceptance of such issues as abortion, intercourse, homosexuality, and having a child outside of marriage.[63] Some trends, however, show a decline in premarital intercourse from the early 1970s to 1987.[64] Yet still, the number of teenage pregnancies continues to increase, perhaps because of failure to use contraceptives or to use them properly and the more accepting attitudes toward single parenthood.

Adolescent girls may believe that they will not become pregnant, and this attitude suggests that they do not use birth control because they are not mature enough to plan for the future. Adolescent boys also may not believe that pregnancy will occur, and, consequently, may not assume any responsibility for contraception.[65] The National Center for Health Statistics reports the incidence of teenage pregnancy has risen 100 percent since 1975. Each year, more than 200,000 babies are born

Teenage parents have to assume parenting responsibilities before many are emotionally and intellectually ready to do so.

to girls under eighteen. And even more girls have abortions: in 1987, the number of abortions performed in the United States was 1.6 million.

Ninety-six percent of these girls keep their babies. Families headed by young mothers tend to be poor,[66] perhaps partly because teenage mothers often drop out of school before getting the education they need to find a well-paying job. Moreover, they cannot afford to hire a baby-sitter to watch their children while they look for work, and a vicious cycle ensues.

Youngsters who engage in irresponsible sex also run the risk of developing sexually transmitted diseases, like herpes, gonorrhea, syphilis, and AIDS (acquired immune deficiency syndrome). AIDS, which is acquired through the exchange of blood or body fluids, is considered epidemic in our society. It has claimed 70,000 lives and infected 130,000 others. Researchers predict that deaths from AIDS will reach 285,000 to 340,000 by 1993, becoming the fourth leading cause of death (it is currently sixth). The number of people with AIDS will more than triple by 1993 to between 390,000 and 480,000.[67]

> The personal and social costs of unprotected sex among teenagers is an increasingly serious problem.

Sex Education

Sex education, once mostly biologically oriented, has broadened in recent years to include discussions about sexuality, programs to help parents teach their children, single courses for students, and spiral curriculums that offer the topic in increasing levels of depth and comprehensiveness. However, only 50 percent of secondary students receive some sort of sex education, and less than 10 percent elect to take separate courses in the subject.

Furthermore, studies by the United States General Accounting Offices have found AIDS education lacking in most school districts.[68] A study of 232 randomly selected school districts found that 66 percent of the districts provided AIDS education, but that only 5 percent offered it at every grade level. More schools offered it in the seventh grade than in the eleventh or twelfth grades (when students are more sexually active). Among teachers, 17 percent of those who teach AIDS education had no special training. Furthermore, AIDS education was rare among the nine million young people aged fourteen to twenty-one who are not in school and are at especially high risk of being exposed to the AIDS virus.

Surveys of college students have shown that sex education in the elementary and secondary schools can increase a teenager's knowledge about the subject. And while teenagers' attitudes about sex may remain relatively unchanged as a result of sex education, their attitudes toward others tend to become more tolerant.[69] A national study has found that while sex education is not likely to influence a teenager's decision to engage in sex, it can have a positive influence on the use

> Sex education seems to be an effective way to encourage students to be more responsible sexually.

of contraception. Sexually active teenage girls who had taken some sort of sex education class were less likely to become pregnant.[70]

It's clear that sex education in the schools can serve a valuable function, but educators and parents need to work together to develop and improve that education. Sex education courses can supplement the values children learn at home and give teenagers the information they need to make responsible choices.

■ **PAUSE TO REFLECT**
Sex Education

- What sex education classes were offered in your school? Do you think they were worthwhile? What features did you find the most relevant? How could the curriculum have been improved?

- If you were a public-school administrator, what types of classes would you want to offer? If you were a parent, would you agree? Why or why not?

EDUCATIONAL ISSUE 4–2

Should sex education be taught in public schools?

Yes	No
1. Youth need sex education to gain vital knowledge that they may not receive in the home or elsewhere.	1. Attitudes about sex remain relatively unchanged after sex education.
2. Sex education fosters more tolerant attitudes toward others.	2. Despite attitudinal change, there is no clear-cut effect on behavior.
3. Teenage females who had sex education were less likely to become pregnant.	3. The decision by teenagers to engage in sexual activity is not influenced by sex education in school.
4. The public schools perform an important service for students and society by offering sex education programs.	4. Sex education in school usurps the family's prerogative and instills values in children that may conflict with those of their parents.

■ **Summary**

- A social condition becomes a social problem when a majority of society recognizes it as seriously undesirable. Social problems usually involve violations of a society's norms or values (prostitution, for instance), but others do not (traffic congestion). Merton distinguishes between latent social problems (conditions that run counter to a society's norms but are not yet considered problems) and manifest social problems (latent social problems that society recognizes as harmful and in need of solution).

- The development of social problems can be explained by four basic theories: *social disorganization,* which occurs when members of a society disagree on the norms and values of that society to the point that social interaction is impossible; *conflict,* which occurs when groups with different values attempt to live in the same society and the dominant group tries to force its values on the other groups; *labeling,* which is the practice of judging and then classifying an individual in a particular category; and *differential association,* which is the idea that individuals learn either proper or deviant behavior depending on the kind of people they associate with.

- Educators can combat the effects of these theories by ensuring that different groups are treated equally within the school system, eliminating the use of labels whenever possible and encouraging students to associate with positive, law-abiding role models.

- Students develop peer attachments and student subcultures that guide behavior and define desirable or undesirable traits for its members.

- Some student subcultures degenerate into delinquent gangs, which are more criminal in nature than ever. The four theories of social problems can help explain the development of a gang.

- Corporal punishment is widely sanctioned by society as an acceptable form of discipline both in the home and the school. However, there is a fine line between corporal punishment and child abuse, and educators should be trained to spot signs of family abuse. Furthermore, the sanctioned use of corporal punishment teaches children that violence is an acceptable way to solve problems.

- The effects of television on behavior and academic achievement are open to debate. Some studies indicate that excessive television viewing may inhibit academic achievement, but moderate viewing has not been proved harmful. In addition, while many people may complain about the level and manner of violence on television there is little evidence that it causes violence in children who do not already have tendencies toward aggression.

• Nearly two-thirds of the nation's students will experiment with an illegal drug before they graduate from high school. Students prone to alcohol or drug abuse share some characteristics that can be warning signs of a child's predisposition to addiction.

• One in ten young people may find life so unbearable that they will attempt suicide. Some social trends that can lead to this decision include growing competition in schools and the work force, the inability to make friends, media coverage of other suicides, family instability, and the decline of organized religion in society. As with children who abuse drugs, children prone to suicide share characteristics and behavioral symptoms that can serve as warning signs. Educators should not hesitate to intervene if they suspect a child is in danger of attempting suicide because the obligation to protect the child from harm outweighs the obligation to protect the child's freedom.

• The NIE reports that 6,700 schools are seriously affected by violence, most of which appears to be related to drug abuse and delinquent gang activity. The threat of violence hangs heavy over students, who cannot concentrate on their studies, and over teachers, some of whom have shown signs of "combat neurosis" after sustained periods of fearing for their safety. Suggested solutions include banning corporal punishment in the schools because it encourages the use of violence as an acceptable behavior, installing increased security measures, and commissioning architectural alterations to discourage vandalism.

• Each year, 25 percent of students drop out of school. These students tend to have low overall intellectual ability, low academic achievement, and serious personal and social problems. Suggested solutions to the problem include development of stronger attendance policies as well as special programs and counseling for potential dropouts.

• As sexual feelings awaken in teenagers, so do questions and insecurities. Without adequate support, guidance, and education from parents and teachers during this fragile period in their lives, teens may choose to engage in sex before they fully understand the possible consequences, which can include pregnancy and AIDS. Sex education in the schools appears to be helpful, but educators and parents need to work together to improve education both in the schools and at home.

■ Key Terms

child abuse	manifest social problem
conflict	norms
corporal punishment	peer group
deviant behavior	secondary deviance
deviant subculture	self-actualizing
force	social disorganization
frustration-aggression hypothesis	socialization
hopelessness	social problem
labeling	subculture
latchkey children	the absurd
latent social problem	violence

■ Discussion Questions

1. Of the different social problems faced by students, which can best be explained by social disorganization, conflict, labeling, or differential association? Which need other explanations (psychological or philosophical)?

2. Name some examples of social problems and deviant behavior. How do they differ? What role does deviant behavior play in creating social problems? Conversely, what roles do social problems play in creating deviant behavior?

3. What are some examples of student subcultures? What negative influences can they have on students? How about positive influences?

4. Identify some key socializing influences on the young in contemporary society (peer groups, for example). What are some of the positive and negative effects of these influences?

5. What are some ways teachers can capitalize on the educational uses of television to make learning materials more appealing?

6. How can media other than television influence the socialization of young people? What steps can be taken to curb the negative influences and enhance the positive ones?

7. As a teacher, how would you identify a child at high risk of dropping out of school, becoming addicted to drugs, or commit-

ting suicide? What would you do if you suspected a child was in such danger?

8. How would you react if a student threatened you with physical harm? What should the schools do to ensure your safety as a teacher and the safety of your students?

■ Learning Activities

1. Observe and describe the behavior of a local student subculture in terms of social background (race, social class, ethnicity), norms, activities, and their attitudes toward academic work.

2. Meet with social workers and discuss the problems of child abuse in your community. Find out what solutions they would propose. Visit a court hearing on a child abuse case and note the arguments and reasons behind the alleged abuse.

3. Collect student handbooks issued by school systems in your area and outline the rules or policies designed to regulate, modify, or solve social problems faced by students.

4. Invite to class a school administrator, a police official, and a criminologist to discuss the causes of and possible solutions to student violence and vandalism.

Suggested Readings

Kenniston, Kenneth, and the Carnegie Council on Children. *All Our Children: The American Family Under Pressure*. New York: Harcourt Brace Jovanovich, 1977.

A report on the social and economic crisis that the American family is living through.

Kirby, Douglas, Judith Alter, and Peter Scales. *An Analysis of U.S. Sex Education Programs and Evaluation Methods*. Atlanta: Bureau of Health Education, Centers for Disease Control, Department of Health, Education and Welfare, 1979.

A survey and assessment of sex education programs.

Pavalko, Ronald M. *Social Problems*. Ithasca, IL: F. E. Peacock, 1986.

Uses a social structural perspective to study the family, crime, substance abuse, and other social problems.

Postman, Neil. *Teaching as a Conserving Activity*. New York: Delacorte Press, 1979.

Shows how schools can function as a countervailing force to the media.

Rich, John Martin. *Discipline and Authority in School and Family.* Lexington, MA: Lexington Books, 1982.

Studies the interrelationships and conflicts between the public schools and the family in light of changing conceptions of authority, with emphasis on the effect of violence.

Saunders, Malcolm. *Class Control and Behavior Problems: A Guide for Teachers.* Berkshire, England: McGraw-Hill, 1979.

Deals effectively with disruptive behavior, emotional maladjustments, and other problems.

Smith, Ronald W., and Andrea Fontana. *Social Problems: Role, Institutional, and Societal Perspectives.* New York: Holt, Rinehart and Winston, 1981.

Assesses suicide, child abuse, substance abuse, family problems, and violence in society.

Notes

1. Robert K. Merton, "The Sociology of Social Problems," in *Contemporary Social Problems.* Robert K. Merton and Robert Nisbet, eds. (New York: Harcourt Brace Jovanovich, 1976), 13–15.

2. Allen E. Liska, *Perspectives on Deviance*, 2nd ed. (Englewood Cliffs, NJ: Prentice-Hall, 1987), 3.

3. Examples of the social disorganization approach include Robert K. Merton, *Social Theory and Social Structure* (Glencoe, IL: Free Press, 1957); Albert K. Cohen, *Deviance and Control* (Englewood Cliffs, NJ: Prentice-Hall, 1966); and Reece McGee, *Social Disorganization in America* (San Francisco: Chandler, 1962).

4. The conflict approach is presented in the following works: Thorsten Sellin, *Culture Conflict and Crime* (New York: Social Science Research Council, 1938); George B. Vold, *Theoretical Criminology* (New York: Oxford University Press, 1958); and Richard Quinney, *The Social Reality of Crime* (Boston: Little, Brown, 1970).

5. Examples of the labeling approach include Howard G. Becker, *Outsiders* (New York: Free Press, 1963); and Edwin M. Lemert, *Human Deviance, Social Problems, and Social Control* (Englewood Cliffs, NJ: Prentice-Hall, 1967).

6. The theory was first formulated in Sutherland's *Principles of Criminology*, 3rd ed. (Chicago: Lippincott, 1939) and revised in the fourth edition in 1947.

7. S. R. Asher, S. L. Oden, and J. M. Gottman, "Children's Friendships in School Settings," in *Current Topics in Early Childhood Education*, Vol 1, ed. L. G. Katz (Norwood, NJ: Ablex, 1977).

8. J. M. Gottman and J. T. Parkhurst, "A Developmental Theory of Friendship and Acquaintanceship Processes," in *Minnesota Symposium on Child*

Psychology, vol. 13, ed. W. A. Collins (Hillsdale, NJ: Lawrence Erlbaum Associates, 1979).

9. James S. Coleman, "The Adolescent Subculture and Academic Achievement," in R. Havighurst, B. Neugarten, and J. Falk, *Society and Education* (Boston: Allyn and Bacon, 1967), 109–15.

10. James S. Coleman, *The Adolescent Society* (New York: Free Press, 1961).

11. John Goodlad, *A Place Called School: Prospects for the Future* (New York: McGraw-Hill, 1984), 76–78.

12. W. Miler, "Youth Gangs," *Children Today* (March–April 1982): 10–11.

13. Committee on the Judiciary, *School Violence and Vandalism*, U.S. Senate, Subcommittee to Investigate Juvenile Delinquency (Washington, DC: Government Printing Office, 1976), 152.

14. Ibid., 341–69.

15. Rodney Stark and James McEvoy III, "Middle Class Violence," *Psychology Today* 4 (November 1970): 52–65.

16. Ingraham v. Wright, 430 U.S. 651 (1977).

17. Alan Sussman and Martin Guggenheim, *The Rights of Parents* (New York: Avon Books, 1980), 50.

18. Richard J. Gelles, "Child Abuse as Psychopathology: A Sociological Critique and Reformulation," in *Violence in the Family*, eds. Steinmetz and Straus, 1975, 205.

19. John E. O'Brien, "Violence in Divorce-Prone Families," in *Violence in the Family*, eds. Suzanne K. Steinmetz and Murray A. Straus (New York: Dodd, Mead, 1975), 65–75.

20. John Dollard, et al. *Frustration and Aggression* (New Haven: Yale University Press, 1939), 1.

21. Letitia J. Allan, "Child Abuse: A Critical Review of the Research and the Theory," in *Violence and the Family*, ed. J. P. Martin (New York: Wiley, 1978), 48.

22. E. Douvan and J. Adelson, *The Adolescent Experience* (New York: Wiley, 1966).

23. Richard J. Gelles, "Child Abuse as Psychopathology: A Sociological Critique and Reformulation," in *Violence*, eds. Steinmetz and Straus, 190–204.

24. See: Bruno Bettelheim, "Children Should Learn About Violence," *Saturday Evening Post* 240 (May 11, 1967): 10–12; William C. Menninger, "Recreation and Mental Health," *Recreation* 42 (1948): 340–46; and Dorothy W. Baruch, *New Ways of Discipline* (New York: McGraw-Hill, 1949): 35–45.

25. Albert Bandura and R. J. Walters, *Social Learning and Personality Development* (New York: Holt, Rinehart and Winston, 1963).

26. United States Bureau of the Census, *After-School Care of Schoolage Children*. Series P-23, No. 149 (Washington, DC: U.S. Government Printing Office, 1987), 145.

27. Kirsten Goldberg, "Many Homeless Children Reported Out of School," *Educational Week* (March 25, 1987): 6.

28. A. Bridgman, "Schools Urged to Seek Solutions to Troubles of Latch-Key Children," *Education Week* 3 (36; 1984): 10, 15.

29. Anne Pavuk, "Families with Children Constitute Third of the Homeless, Mayors Say," *Education Week* (May 20, 1987): 12; Kirsten Goldberg, "Many Homeless Children Reported Out of School," *Education Week* (March 25, 1987): 6.

30. Alice Sterling Honig, "Television and Young Children," *Young Children* (May 1983): 63.

31. Mark Fetler, "California Surveys of Home Television Viewing and School Achievement," *Educational Media International*, No. 4 (1984): 22–25.

32. Gavriel Salomon, "Media's Effects on Children's Thinking Patterns," *Educational Media International*, No. 4 (1984): 2–7.

33. United States Public Health Service, Panel of Scientists, *Report to the Surgeon-General on Television Violence* (Washington, DC: U.S. Government Printing Office, 1972).

34. Jonathan L. Freedman, "Effects of Television Violence on Aggressiveness," *Psychological Bulletin* 96, (1984): 227–46.

35. Milton Chen, *A Review of Research on the Educational Potential of 3-2-1 Contact: A Children's TV Series* (Washington, DC: U.S. Department of Education, 1984).

36. Columbia University College of Physicians and Surgeons, *Complete Home Medical Guide* (New York: Crown Publishers, 1985), 357.

37. Ibid.

38. Michael W. Sherraden, "School Dropouts in Perspective," *The Educational Forum 51* (Fall 1986): 18.

39. Carolyn Kitch, "On-the-Job Drug Tests: What to Know," *Good Housekeeping* (January 1987): 145.

40. G. J. Huba and P. M. Bentler, "The Role of Peer and Adult Models for Drug Taking at Different Stages in Adolescence," *Journal of Youth and Adolescence* 9 (1980): 203.

41. "Schoolkids' Lives Are Stressful, Too, Study Finds," *American Statesman* (May 5, 1989): E7.

42. "Drug Education Gets an F," *U.S. News & World Report (October 13, 1986): 63.*

43. "Teaching Kids to Say No: How Effective Are Drug-Awareness Classes?" *Newsweek* (June 5, 1989): 77.

44. Judy Folkenbert, "To Be or Not to Be: Preventive Legislation," *Psychology Today* (April 1984): 9.

45. "Suicide." *Encyclopedia of Bioethics* (New York: Free Press, 1978), vol. 4, 1618–27.

46. Albert Camus, "An Absurd Reasoning." In *The Meaning of Life*, eds. Steven Sanders and David R. Cheney (Englewood Cliffs, NJ: Prentice-Hall, 1980), 65.

47. Ibid., 66.

48. Emile Durkheim, *Suicide* (New York: Free Press, 1951). Originally published in 1897.

49. Jack D. Douglas, *The Social Meaning of Suicide* (Princeton, NJ: Princeton University Press, 1967).

50. Maurice L. Farber, *Theory of Suicide* (New York: Funk and Wagnalls, 1968).

51. "Suicidal Students," *NEA Today* (January/February 1985): 5; Deborah Burnett Strother, "Suicide Among the Young," *Phi Delta Kappan* 67 (June 1986): 759.

52. George H. Gallup, "The 16th Annual Poll of the Public's Attitudes Toward the Public Schools," *Phi Delta Kappan* 66 (September 1984): 23–28.

53. "NEA Survey Investigates Teacher Attitudes, Practices," *Phi Delta Kappan* 12 (September 1980): 49.

54. National Institute of Education, *Violent Schools—Safe Schools*, vol. 1 (Washington, DC: Department of Health, Education and Welfare, 1978).

55. A. M. Block and R. R. Block, "Teachers—A New Endangered Species?" in *Violence and Crime in Schools*, eds. K. Baker and R. J. Rubels (Lexington, MA: Lexington Books, 1980), 82–83.

56. James Q. Wilson, *Thinking About Crime* (New York: Basic Books, 1983).

57. Lisa Jennings, "California Court Weighs School-Safety Provisions," *Education Week* (May 31, 1989): 10.

58. Gary S. Becker, "Tuning in to the Needs of High School Dropouts," *Business Week* (July 3, 1989): 18.

59. Florida Department of Education, *School Dropouts: An Annotated Bibliography of Dropout Studies* (Tallahassee: Florida Department of Education, 1976), 152–54.

60. R. J. Havighurst, et al. *Growing Up in River City* (New York: Wiley, 1962); J. Combs and W. Cooley, "Dropouts in High School and After School," *American Educational Research* Journal 5 (1968): 343–63; and D. N. Lloyd, "Prediction of School Failure from Third-Grade Data," *Educational and Psychological Measurement* 38 (1978): 1193–1200.

61. "A Larger Crowd at the Finish," *U.S. News & World Report* (June 12, 1989): 69.

62. "Driver's License Dropouts Law Faces Challenge," *American Statesman* (June 1, 1989): A20.

63. Frank G. Bolton, Jr., *The Pregnant Adolescent: Problems of Premature Parenthood* (Beverly Hills: Gage Publications, 1980), 25.

64. National Research Council, *Risking the Future: Adolescent Sexuality, Pregnancy, and Childbearing* (Washington, DC: National Academy Press, 1987), Table 2–6.

65. W. G. Cobliner, "Pregnancy in the Single Adolescent Girl: The Role of Cognitive Functioning," *Journal of Youth and Adolescence* 3 (1974): 17–19.

66. Margaret C. Dunkle and Susan M. Bailey, "Schools Must Ease the Impact of Teenage Pregnancy and Parenthood," *Education Week* 4, no. 8 (October 28, 1984): 24.

67. Shirley Wilson, "Lifting Mask of Apathy Goal of AIDS Official," *American Statesman* (May 9, 1990): D1, D3.

68. Ellen Flax, "AIDS-Education Programs Fall Short, Auditor Reports," *Education Week* (May 9, 1990): 5.

69. H. S. Bernard and A. J. Schwartz, "Impact of a Human Sexuality Program on Sex-Related Knowledge, Attitudes, Behavior, and Guilt of College Students," *Journal of the American College Health Association* 25, no. 3 (1977): 182–83; A. Godow and F. E. LaFave, "The Impact of a College Course in Human Sexuality Upon Sexual Attitudes and Behavior," *Teaching of Psychology* 6, no. 3 (1979): 164–67.

70. Melvin Zelnik and Young J. Kim, "Sex Education and Its Association with Teenage Sexual Activity, Pregnancy, and Contraceptive Use," *Family Planning Perspective* (May/June 1982): 116.

■ PART THREE

PHILOSOPHY AND THE DEVELOPMENT OF EDUCATION ■

T eaching involves much more than technique or the mechanical dissemination of facts. It means becoming an educator and learning to develop educated persons. A true educator understands the significance of education throughout history and continually searches for meaning and purpose in the field rather than slavishly yielding to tradition, fads, or trends.

Part Three examines the historical aspects of education and highlights the influences of leading educators. We will discuss how the theories of the past have shaped the schools of today and how you can learn from these theories to help shape the schools of tomorrow. A look at the philosophical foundations of education will help you interpret the philosophical grounds for today's educational issues and policies, analyze some important educational philosophies, and begin developing your own philosophy of education.

Chapter 5 traces the development of elementary, secondary, and higher education from colonial times to the present and the related development of teacher preparation and minority education. Chapter 6 offers an intensive overview of philosophies of life and, in turn, education. Chapter 7 looks at the aims of education—how they have developed throughout history and how educators today can improve upon them.

■ C H A P T E R 5

HISTORICAL DEVELOPMENT ◾
OF AMERICAN EDUCATION

A LOOK AHEAD

The purpose of this chapter is to place American education in a historical perspective to better understand the development of education today. You will learn about:

- The development of colonial education

- How the strict influences of Calvinism and other religious doctrines shaped the structure of colonial education

- The rise of the common schools for elementary education and the influence of leading educators of the time

- How the liberalizing view of the child reshaped approaches to education

- The development of secondary education, from Latin grammar schools to the comprehensive high school

- The introduction of colleges and three basic structures of higher education

- How college education has evolved into the variety of choices available today

- The beginning of organized teacher preparation programs

- Some suggestions for improving the education of teachers

- The historical treatment of minorities in education

147

"The disadvantage of men not knowing the past is that they do not know the present. History is a hill or high point of vantage, from which alone men see the town in which they live or the age in which they are living." This observation by British essayist G. K. Chesterton offers solid justification for studying the history of education.

History gives us a perspective on our lives and institutions and lets us reappraise forces from the past still at work in the present. All our choices and judgments are based on assumptions about the past and beliefs about the future. The study of history can show us the problems that arise when tradition meets new conditions and demands and how people of other times have dealt with those problems.

Studying the history of American education gives you a sense of perspective and enables you to better understand the challenges of the present.

In this chapter, we will look at the history of education from colonial times to the present—including the development of elementary, secondary, and higher education—searching for any patterns that can help us solve the problems we face in education today.

■ ELEMENTARY EDUCATION

The early settlers, preoccupied with survival in a land of uncertainty and struggle, did not envision a formal system of public education. The family, the church, and the community were the cornerstones of colonial life and, as such, were the sources of education at the time. Large, extended families were common, and early marriage was the rule (girls by age sixteen, boys by age twenty). As a result, most families had numerous children and relatives in addition to servants to help with the work. The extended family was largely a self-sufficient economic unit and provided for most of its own religious, educational, recreational, and political needs (the latter being the function by which family members were protected from danger). Life for colonial children meant obedience and hard work to deter barbarism in the wilderness of the New World.

The family, which was the center of life in colonial society, provided for the educational needs of its members.

What education there was in colonial America was strongly influenced by European antecedents and experiences in the Old World, such as the Reformation. The **Reformation,** a religious reform movement, arose in Europe in the sixteenth century protesting scriptural interpretation in the Catholic church, clerical corruption, and abuse of authority. The movement began in 1517 when Martin Luther issued his Ninety-Five Theses attacking many practices of the Catholic church. Other religious dissidents, such as John Calvin, spread religious reform in various European nations, all of which gave rise to numerous Protestant denominations, including Puritanism.

Colonial education had its roots in the European experience.

One of the goals of the Reformation was to remove the priest as the intermediary between the average individual and God. Luther believed not only that the clergy was corrupt but also that the intermediary position between God and the members of the church, which the Catholic clergy was believed to serve, was theologically ungrounded. According to Luther, individuals were saved directly by God's grace, which was given as a result of individual faith in Christ. Luther and others believed that to be saved, people needed direct access to the Scriptures. Luther translated the Bible into German to make the Scriptures more available to the common people. But still, to experience the Scriptures directly, people had to be able to read. The Reformation's influence in colonial education can be seen as early as the first school law, the Massachusetts Act of 1642. This statute required parents and masters of apprentices to see that children learned to read the Scriptures.

> The Massachusetts Act of 1642 made it compulsory for parents to teach their children to read and thus brought an end to the voluntary system of education.

The law also required that children be taught to read the capital laws of the land. So, citizenship goals were established. An economic motive also might have been at work here: the colonists sought to prevent the development of the pauper class, so prevalent in England at the time. The Massachusetts Act, therefore, was also a relief measure that shifted the burden of caring for children from town government to the masters to whom the children were apprenticed. Adults to whom children were apprenticed were required to teach them a trade and reading skills. By 1650 Connecticut had adopted a similar law. Rhode Island's laws in 1655 were similar but made no reference to apprenticeship.

The earliest form of primary education was the **dame school**. These schools were open to boys and girls and were often the only instruction that girls received. Dame schools were run by spinsters or widows who charged small fees to take children into their homes and hear lessons while sewing and performing household chores. In the larger towns, the "reading-and-writing" schools de-emphasized writing and emphasized reading as necessary for religious purposes.

> Colonial education stressed religious objectives and fostered various religious beliefs.

Early Elementary Education in the Colonies

New England. The New England colonies considered education a civil responsibility of the state (as reflected by the Massachusetts Act of 1642). Church and civil authorities in the Massachusetts Bay Colony viewed schooling as a means for maintaining religious orthodoxy. These Puritan leaders were not interested in education as a means for promoting democratic government, since as theocratists they believed democracy to be the worst type of political system.

> In the New England colonies, education was the responsibility of the state and was a means of preserving religious orthodoxy.

Through the Puritans, Calvinism became a powerful force in the Massachusetts Bay Colony. Next to Martin Luther, John Calvin (1509–1564) was the most famous sixteenth-century Protestant leader. Calvin acquired complete political power in Geneva, Switzerland, by means of a constitution that made him ruler of the state and created a theocratic public in which religion merged with politics.

His *Institutes of Christian Religion* laid out the theology of **Calvinism**. Calvin claimed that God was omnipotent and omnificent and knew the past, present, and future. To Calvin, this meant that God knew—indeed, had predestined—those who were to be saved and those who were to be eternally damned. Calvin maintained that the outward sign of a person's election to grace is his moral behavior. Calvin and the elders spied upon citizens of Geneva to detect heretical and immoral acts, and some citizens were punished variously, including banishment and execution; Calvin was especially harsh to those whose religious views differed from his own.

Calvinism spread widely: to the Huguenots in France; to the Dutch Reformed Church in the Netherlands; to Scotland, where the zealous preaching of John Knox led to the rise of Protestantism; and to the Puritans in the Massachusetts Bay Colony.

Puritanism influenced American religious thought for 150 years.

The Puritan outlook permeated much of the religious thinking of the Americans for 150 years. The Puritans adopted Calvin's belief in predetermination and his view of a wrathful God, the belief that behavior indicated whether one was among the elected or the damned, the concept of original sin, the need for obedience to God's commandments and to the authority of parents and elders, and the value of hard work.

Calvinism shaped the nature of colonial education.

The New England Primer, which expressed Calvinistic teachings, appeared in 1690 and lasted 125 years through many editions and various changes. The *Primer,* used in both school and church, greatly influenced the New England character. A catechism in the *Primer* by John Cotton, a Boston minister and Protestant spokesman, titled "Spiritual Milk for American Babes . . . ," asked the child:

Q. Are you then born Holy and Righteous?
A. No, my first parents sinned, and I in them.

Q. Are you then born a Sinner?
A. I was conceived in Sin and born in Iniquity.

Q. What is your Birth Sin?
A. Adam's Sin imputed to me, and a corrupt Nature dwelling in me.[1]

In this era, known as the **Great Awakening,** Jonathan Edwards' orthodox Calvinism was expressed through the Congregational Church. Edwards declared: "That all are by nature the children of wrath, and heirs of hell; and they every one that has not been born again, whether he be young or old, is exposed every moment to eternal destruction, under the wrath of Almighty God . . ."[2] Edwards also observed that though children may seem to be innocent, they are not: "If they are out of Christ, they are not so in God's sight, but are young vipers, and are in a most miserable condition, as well as grown persons; and they are naturally very senseless and stupid, being born as a wild ass's colt, and need much to awaken them."[3]

This image of children as basically bad and in need of harsh discipline was widespread. In Connecticut the governor and any two magistrates had the power to sentence any incorrigibles to hard labor and severe punishment in the house of correction.[4] In Massachusetts any children older than sixteen and of sufficient understanding who cursed or hit their natural parents could be put to death, unless the parents were found to have been "unchristianly negligent" in educating their children, or to have provoked them by extreme and cruel correction.[5]

Because of the Calvinistic belief in original sin and predestination, there was not much that religious and moral instruction was expected to accomplish other than to teach children to place complete faith in God's will and mercy. To this end, Massachusetts and Connecticut schools required children to recite catechisms. Because obedience to parents and teachers was ordained by God, the Calvinists said, children were expected to obey their commands without exception and without question. Obedience to one's earthly father prepared one for obedience to the heavenly Father. Pupils were taught that school regulations were based on the office of the teacher, and severe punishment was considered not a last resort but "the first and the true remedy."[6]

In 1699 Cotton Mather wrote *A Family Well-Ordered,* in which he vividly outlined the dreadful consequences that would befall the undutiful child: God's vengeful curse would lead him into worse sins and "result in untimely and especially horrible deaths of hanging, suicide, and being eaten by vultures, and will result after death in eternal punishment in the utter darkness of Hell."[7]

The Middle Atlantic Colonies. Because of the variety of religious sects and the inability of those sects to agree on a single school plan, the Middle Atlantic colonies established different parochial schools based on particular religious denominations. The tolerant attitude of the Quakers and generous terms for land purchases attracted a large number of Germans to eastern Pennsylvania, while New Netherland (now known as New York) was predominantly Dutch for more than a century. Schools were slow to develop because of the lack of social cohesion in sparsely settled areas, religious and ethnic diversity, and

> The Puritan view of children as basically corrupt led to dogmatic teaching and harsh treatment for children in the classroom.

> While the New England colonies exhibited cultural and religious uniformity, the Middle Atlantic Colonies demonstrated diversity and a wider variety of educational practices.

The schoolmaster worked with a diverse group of students while other students socialized or slept.

the absence of a common language. Each religious group sought to overcome these handicaps by providing instruction in its parishes and opening charity schools for poorer children.

Unlike in New England, the religious denominations in the Middle Atlantic colonies did not use state authority to support schools, although schooling was, at least in part, religious. Both German and Quaker schools instilled religious beliefs while offering a practical education for a trade. Some nonsectarian private schools were established in Philadelphia for utilitarian studies. In New Netherland, religious values also were highly regarded; in fact, the schoolmaster was a church officer. And all but the poor were expected to pay tuition.

The Southern Colonies. An agrarian way of life and rural isolation characterized the Southern colonies after the first settlement at Jamestown in 1607. Southern planters exported tobacco to England, where it was processed and distributed at a profit in Europe and the Southern colonies. The cultivation of tobacco required a large labor force and, after the 1713 Treaty of Utrech opened the African slave market, a plantation system based on slavery developed from the Chesapeake Bay region to Florida. By the middle of the eighteenth century a planter aristocracy had developed in Virginia and Maryland. Many of these landed aristocrats were of English lower-class or middle-class backgrounds, as titled Englishmen were not likely to emigrate to America.

Landed aristocrats were determined that their sons receive a Renaissance education and sometimes sent them back to England for that purpose. More often, though, they hired tutors to avoid the hazards of the long ocean voyage. These tutors, usually indentured servants, taught classical subjects to the boys, and French and occasionally other subjects to the girls. The girls also were instructed in the social graces by their mothers.

As a result of the plantation economy in the Southern Colonies, there were few schools, and education lagged behind.

Southern philanthropic and religious societies founded several charity schools, and some private schools were also established. As the demand for skilled labor grew, apprenticeship programs were developed for poor and illegitimate children as well as for orphans. Slaves and American Indians received no formal education, although some missionary societies sought to teach them enough to read religious writings. Beyond that, however, education for slaves was discouraged and often illegal.

Rise of the Common Schools

After the Revolutionary War the responsibility for education was turned over to the states, because the new United States Constitution did not specifically mention education. In the early nineteenth century many people resisted the idea of public support for **common schools,** schools under state auspices designed to teach a common body of knowledge to students of different social backgrounds. The wealthy did not think they should be required to pay for the education of working-class children, and they argued that property should not be taxed to support schools. Moreover, they said, education had long been a family matter, not a public concern. Some people also feared that public education would conflict with parochial schools. A human nature argument was advanced as well: human ability is widely variable and traits are unevenly distributed, hence, most people cannot profit from schooling. Moreover, it was argued, children of the poor educated at taxpayers' expense were likely to lose their initiative and become indolent. Besides, if the poor were forced to attend school, they would not be free to work. Not everyone thought this way, of course, and a few rose up to demand improvements in education.

After the American Revolution, education became the responsibility of the states rather than the federal government and therefore remained decentralized.

James G. Carter (1795–1849) was an early leader in Massachusetts school reform. He was instrumental in establishing a state school fund that helped towns provide higher levels of education. As a member of the state legislature in 1835, Carter drafted a bill creating the first state board of education. The board was empowered to appoint a chief state school officer who would be responsible to the board. Some were surprised when Horace Mann, not Carter, was appointed to the post.

Mann (1796–1859) was a young, respected lawyer and senator who gave up a promising political career to pursue his broad humanitarian interests. His role as secretary to the state board, 1837–1848, was to assess school conditions and attempt to overcome any inadequacies. Mann discovered dereliction of school committees in performing duties, unqualified teachers, high rates of student absenteeism, substandard school facilities, an absence of libraries, and widespread public apathy. Mann tirelessly crisscrossed the state appealing to people's vested interests. He promoted education as necessary for a republican form of government; as an instrument for equalizing opportunity; and as a means for improving industry and conquering vice, crime, and poverty. Mann issued twelve annual reports that influenced public opinion not only in Massachusetts but also throughout the nation and abroad. He opposed sectarian teaching in the common schools and established the first public normal school in 1839 for teacher preparation. Although bitterly attacked by his opponents, by the time he resigned in 1848 the common schools were on a solid foundation. Five years later he became president of Antioch College. In his last address to the graduating class in 1859, the year of his death, he urged the graduates to heed his parting words: "Be ashamed to die until you have won some victory for humanity."

Henry Barnard (1811–1900), a lawyer with two years of European education, made similar contributions to education reform in Connecticut and Rhode Island. In 1838 he introduced a bill in the Connecticut state legislature establishing a state board of education. He became the board's first secretary and found even worse conditions in Connecticut than Mann found in Massachusetts. But conservative forces proved stronger than Barnard. After proposing sweeping educational changes and new taxes to support those changes, Barnard was removed from office and the board of education was abolished. Though discouraged after his four years of service, he accepted a similar post in Rhode Island where he remained until 1849. He launched a campaign similar to the one he led in Connecticut: gathering information, speaking, writing, and reporting to the legislature. His hard work led to reform of the school laws. In 1851 he returned to Connecticut to become principal of the newly formed normal school in New Britain, and in 1867 Barnard became the first United States Commissioner of Education, a post he held for three years. Table 5–1 lists some additional significant events in the history of American education.

As commissioner, Barnard urged the upper class to support public schools if for no other reason than to protect their interests by providing for better-trained workers and less crime and delinquency. Though more conservative than Mann and perhaps a less effective

During the early nineteenth century, Horace Mann fought and won the battle for public schools that were open to all.

TABLE 5-1 Significant events in American educational history

1635	Boston Latin grammar school established
1636	Harvard College founded, first American college
1642	Massachusetts Act requiring rudimentary instruction
1647	Massachusetts Act requiring Latin grammar schools
1751	Founding of Franklin's Academy in Philadelphia
1779	Jefferson's proposal for free schools of Virginia
1783	Webster's spelling book published
1787	Northwest Ordinance, first federal education law
1821	Boston English Classical School founded, first public high school
1836	McGuffey eclectic readers published
1837	Horace Mann appointed Secretary of Massachusetts State Board of Education
1839	First public normal school opened in Lexington, Massachusetts
1852	First state compulsory school attendance law ratified in Massachusetts
1860	First English-language kindergarten established in St. Louis
1862	Morrill Act passed, founded the land-grant college movement
1867	U.S. Department of Education established
1874	Kalamazoo decision gives schools the right to levy taxes for support
1881	Tuskegee Normal School founded by Booker T. Washington
1893	Committee of Ten report recommends that standardized high schools focus on college preparation
1896	*Plessy v. Ferguson*, the "separate but equal" decision
1909	First junior high school established in Berkeley, California
1910	First junior college established in Fresno, California
1918	*Cardinal Principles of Secondary Education* published
1919	Progressive Education Association founded
1925	*Pierce v. Society of Sisters*, Oregon court decision protects private schools
1932	New Deal programs for the poor
1944	G.I. Bill passed
1954	*Brown v. Board of Education of Topeka*, the desegregation decision
1958	National Defense Education Act
1965	Elementary and Secondary Education Act
1972	Title IX Education Amendment prohibiting sex discrimination in educational institutions receiving federal funds
1979	Department of Education established with cabinet status
1983	Publication of *A Nation at Risk*

Reformers throughout the United States advanced the cause of public education.

speaker, Barnard was a greater scholar, as evidenced by his editorship from 1855 to 1882 of the *American Journal of Education,* the only educational journal of national significance at the time and an encyclopedia of valuable information and ideas.

Other capable reformers included Calvin Wiley in North Carolina and Caleb Mills in Indiana. While they faced different circumstances, each sought to advance public education in his state.

Changes in Thought and Practice

With the influences of greater religious diversity from the Great Awakening and the use of reason from the Enlightenment (a philosophical movement based on the belief that reason is the path to knowledge), Calvinistic forces lost much of their power. One challenge to the belief in original sin came from John Locke (1632–1704), English philosopher, physician, and political theorist, who attacked the doctrine of innate ideas based upon his observations of infants.

One argument for the existence of innate ideas was universal assent to certain ideas. But Locke contended that even if there were any universally held ideas, they would not necessarily be innate because people could conceivably reach universal agreement without having to have been born with the idea. The point is irrelevant, anyway, he said, because no ideas exist to which universal assent is given. Take certain logical laws: "Whatever is, is"; and "It is impossible for the same thing to be, and not to be." These laws have been considered innate; but infants, children, and the mentally retarded have not the slightest comprehension or thought of them. It is unconvincing, he added, to claim that these truths are imprinted upon the mind but are not perceived; since to say something is imprinted is to signify that it is perceived.[8]

Locke declared that the mind at birth is a **tabula rasa,** a blank slate, on which experience writes. The origin of all ideas is experience, which is composed of sensation and reflection. Furthermore, if there is nothing innate in the human mind at birth, there can be no human depravity or original sin innate in the human heart. Since the mind is an empty vessel into which experiences can be poured, then all individuals are alike at birth—"all men are born equal."

A more liberal, positive view of children evolved from the philosophies of John Locke, Jean Jacques Rousseau, and others.

Anglicans, Quakers, several minority religious sects, and some secular groups also offered liberalizing views of the child. By the middle of the nineteenth century, newer views of child nature began to emerge from Rousseauian romanticism, growing humanitarianism, and political conceptions of democracy, which claimed that children need greater liberty to prepare for citizenship responsibilities.

The elementary curriculum expanded during the nineteenth century. One new direction was the study of one's own language and grammar rather than classical tongues. Another extension stemmed from the Herbartian idea that the moral ends of education could be served by a study of history and literature. Johann Friedrich Herbart (1776–1841), German philosopher and educator, believed that knowledge meant power and that knowledge and conduct could not be separated. He believed history and literature should be included in the curriculum as the chief sources of moral ideas. Herbart also believed that children should be under adult control until they had acquired sufficient knowledge of moral ideas. At that point, he said, adults should begin relinquishing control to avoid becoming tyrannical.

The introduction of nature study in the late nineteenth century curriculum can be attributed to Swiss educational reformer Johann Heinrich Pestalozzi (1746–1827). He stressed the importance of accurate observation of objects to promote effective thinking. He believed sense impressions of nature were the foundations of knowledge. Though earlier educators, such as Comenius and Basedow, had relied on pictures of objects, Pestalozzi held that, for the beginning of experience, objects themselves must precede pictures of them. Later, pictures would be introduced to help the child make the transition to drawing, writing, and reading.

In contrast to Locke's passive tabula rasa view of the mind, Pestalozzi viewed the acquisition of sensory experience as an active process that involved the whole mind. He believed children learned to discriminate, abstract, and analyze the qualities of objects. The child's inner being reached out to order the world of sense objects rather than waiting for them to impress themselves upon the senses. The art of instruction lies in selecting the right objects for observation and analysis.

Pestalozzi believed that the beginning of all instruction lies in form, number, and language. The characteristics of any object consist of its outline and its number and are brought to consciousness through language. As a consequence, Pestalozzi spent considerable time teaching children to observe, analyze, count, and name objects.

Another influence on children, one that affected the progressive education movement (discussed in the next chapter), was the growth of **romanticism,** a broad European movement that affected education, the arts, the humanities, and the tenor of thought. It sought a simpler life, elevated feelings and emotions over intellect, identified with the poor and downtrodden, deified the child, expressed a love of animals and nature, and contrasted these charms to the corruptions and cruelties of urban life. Jean Jacques Rousseau (1712–1778), the leading French romantic, was highly influential in political and educational thought. In contrast to Calvin's original sin and Locke's blank slate, Rousseau's belief was that humans are born free and basically good but remain in the chains of corrupt institutions. Rousseau

During the nineteenth century, the elementary curriculum expanded in a variety of areas based on the prevailing philosophies of education.

Different views of children affected the development of education. Locke's belief in a child's mind as a "blank slate" and Rousseau's idea that children are born good displaced Calvin's doctrine of original sin.

thought that children should be educated close to nature, away from society. Emile, Rousseau's imaginary pupil, grew up naturally as the tutor permitted the laws of nature to unfold and introduced new thoughts only when Emile was ready for them. Rousseau outlined different stages of growth, explained how the tutor related to Emile at each stage, and indicated the different materials and activities to be used as Emile's inner being developed. The program emphasized activities and experiences, de-emphasized book learning, sought to avoid bad habits and to instill good ones, and restricted desires to those that could be fulfilled. Rousseau's plan was that, by late adolescence, Emile would have the ability to return to the larger society and learn from it but not succumb to its corruption. This philosophy shaped the progressive view of the child and stimulated the creation of child-centered programs and activity curriculums. Progressives also emphasized natural development and readiness for learning, but in a public-school group activity setting rather than in the isolation of nature.

■ **PAUSE TO REFLECT**
Understanding the Child

- Which view of the child do you think is most defensible: Calvin's notion that the child is born with original sin, Locke's view that an infant's mind is a "blank slate" to be filled as he or she experiences life, or Rousseau's belief that the child is born basically good?

- Do you agree with each philosopher's approach to educating the child of his views? What would you change, and why?

The idea of a school for young children was advanced by Johann Amos Comenius (1592–1670), who proposed an infant school in conjunction with the home, and Robert Owen (1771–1858), who emphasized health, physical education, and moral training. Friedrich Froebel (1782–1852) founded a kindergarten system in Germany in 1837 that based physical activity upon play activities. Unlike the Calvinists, who considered playing games a mark of the devil, Froebel viewed children's games as a serious occupation; it was a form of self-development that moved toward a unity with God.

Froebel envisioned an underlying rationale to the child's activities. In playing with a ball, a child can gain a sense of unity (because the spherical shape symbolizes unity). Similarly, by playing with a large cube that could be divided into smaller cubes, the child can learn the relation of the whole to its parts. This relationship also was symbolized by the way the kindergarten was organized. The idea of unity was expressed by arranging children in a circle and introducing them to many activities, such as singing, clay modeling, drawing, and painting. Froebel saw the teacher as somewhat of a "gardener," who provided a fertile ground for child development and attempted to eliminate noxious influences. Though differing in details, both Rousseau's and Froebel's programs embraced an unfoldment theory. Unfoldment theories later were criticized for establishing a theme toward which things were to unfold (such as Froebel's unity), or else for encouraging passive teaching methods that neglected the need of the child to gain knowledge.

Kindergartens in the United States were privately operated until the first public kindergarten was established in St. Louis in 1860. The kindergarten was slow to be accepted as part of the public-school system because the materials were expensive, the required teacher-pupil ratio was smaller, and the emphasis on play conflicted with the rationale of later primary grades that focused more on study. (For an overview of significant events in American educational history, see Table 5–1.)

> Though not at first part of the public-school system, kindergartens were established in the nineteenth century.

Textbooks and Grading in the Common Schools

The lasting influence of *The New England Primer,* published in 1690, was joined by a series of books from Noah Webster (1758–1843). He published a spelling textbook in 1783, followed by two books devoted to reading and grammar. The speller contained the alphabet, syllables, lists of words, and fables. Nearly twenty-four million copies of the book in its various editions were sold during Webster's lifetime; and though its sales began to decline in the East, it continued to be popular in the South up to the Civil War and even after the Civil War in the West. The series was popular not only with students but with unenrolled children and adults as well.

McGuffey's readers became the most popular readers of their day. Written by William Holmes McGuffey (1800–1873), the first two were published in 1836 and three more were published by 1841. They later were made into six readers and revised several times. These readers were popular throughout the rest of the century, and it is estimated that one-half of the children attending school during this period used them.

Dividing students into grades was unheard of in the original one-room common schools. As the number of classes and students increased, however, grade levels were established to promote greater instructional effectiveness. Pestalozzian instruction and more effective divisions of labor that better used the special abilities of teachers also encouraged the use of grades. Yet with America still a rural, scattered nation, the use of grade levels did not become widespread until the second half of the nineteenth century, with increased urbanization and greater concentrations of population. As schooling became more complex—longer school terms, more years of schooling, and a wider variety of good textbooks—the single elementary school was divided

> In the nineteenth century many types of textbooks were developed and grade levels were established.

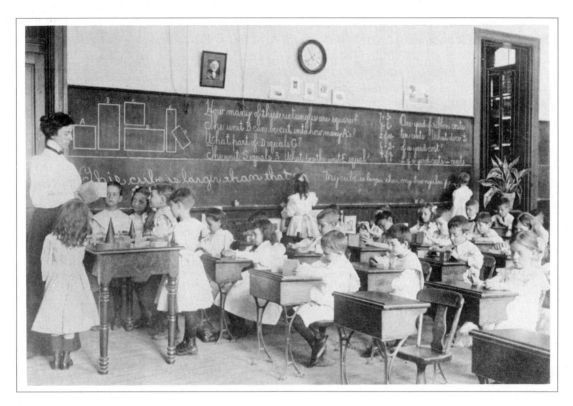

Early classrooms were formal, orderly, and highly structured.

into primary schools for beginners and more advanced schools for older pupils. Some cities had two divisions below the high school; other cities had as many as five. These divisions consisted of a graded curriculum and the classification of pupils into two to five grades. In school systems with two grades below high school, reading was emphasized in the lower division, with grammar, spelling, arithmetic, geography, and sometimes bookkeeping reserved for the upper divisions.

■ SECONDARY EDUCATION

Latin Grammar Schools

The ideals of the Renaissance heavily influenced the development of secondary education in the colonies. The **Renaissance** was a reawakening in learning and the arts that began in Italy during the fourteenth century and later spread throughout Europe. Scholars rediscovered

Greek and Roman works, considering them "classics," and Latin, Greek, and Hebrew came to be recognized as the languages of scholarship. To be able to read the classics and gain an understanding of them marked one as an educated person. This perspective led to the teaching of Greek and Latin to post-primary boys and to the establishment of Latin grammar schools to accomplish this task.

The first Latin grammar school in the American colonies, called the Boston Public Latin School, was established in Boston in 1635. It was "public" in that it was under public control and partly supported by public funds. Later, the Massachusetts Act of 1647 ordered the appointment of one teacher for every fifty families in an area and required the establishment of a Latin grammar school where there were 100 or more families. Girls rarely were admitted, although some were able to receive private instruction.

The colonists used the English Latin grammar school as their model. The English Latin schools followed the humanistic education practices of northern Europe rather than those of the Italian Renaissance, because boys were sent to the Latin grammar school not to cultivate aesthetic enjoyment of the humanities but to prepare for college and for service to church and state.

About one-third of colonial Massachusetts towns had Latin grammar schools by 1700. Of the remaining two-thirds, many towns were too small to fall under the law's provisions, some towns evaded the law, and others that would have liked to have had a Latin school had dif-

> The Renaissance reawakened an interest in the classics that led to the re-emergence of the Latin grammar school—the forerunner of the modern high school—which survived for 300 years.

> In 1647 the state of Massachusetts passed a law establishing schooling, primarily for young men, by outlining the conditions under which towns were required to set up Latin grammar schools.

Study halls were strictly supervised by schoolmasters who demanded that students concentrate and apply themselves to their studies.

ficulty finding a master (teacher). Some of the Latin grammar schools established in the middle colonies before the Revolution were religious in character.

The first three years of school were devoted to the elements of Latin, the fourth year was given to Ovid and Erasmus, Cicero was studied during the fifth year, Virgil was added in the sixth year, and several Greek authors were studied in the seventh year. The task of the Latin grammar school was to prepare boys for college.

Franklin's Academy

But conditions in America—where survival was uppermost, time was short, and the need for practical skill was great—did not promote enthusiasm for classical studies. Recognizing these needs, Benjamin Franklin founded an academy in Philadelphia in 1751. The academy bridged the differences between the Latin grammar schools and the public high schools, which were developed about seventy years later. Franklin emphasized the English language, physical exercise, handwriting, arithmetic, geometry, bookkeeping, astronomy, history, geography, oratory, logic, morality, and natural history. To gain supporters, however, he offered a classical course of study parallel to the more modern studies, because some people still did not believe that an education without Latin was a genuine education—a belief, incidentally, that continued well into the twentieth century.

The academy, a new kind of secondary school with a more practical curriculum, was set up to replace the Latin grammar school.

The academy movement grew at a moderate but steady pace during its first half century, and gained even greater popularity in the next twenty-five years due partly to the public support in New York. Still, academies usually were privately run and appealed to middle-class students who could afford the time and cost of schooling but who were not planning to attend college. Academies varied considerably both in student composition and curriculum. Many academies were boarding schools, others were church-related, and still others were military schools. Some academies were established for girls despite the prejudice that women did not need an education beyond the three Rs. The curriculum of academies included a diversity of subjects from Greek to modern languages, biblical studies to United States history, penmanship to painting, natural philosophy to chemistry, and arithmetic to trigonometry.

The Classical School

A third type of secondary school was founded in 1821 as the Boston English Classical School (renamed the Boston English High School in 1824). It is generally considered the first American public high school and was designed to teach boys what they needed to know "to become merchants and mechanics." Since Boston already had a Latin grammar school, classical studies were omitted from the curriculum and the program included courses usually offered in the English department of an academy. A separate high school was established for girls in 1826, but was closed two years later because it was too popular—it was publicly supported, and the mayor was afraid it would bankrupt the city. The school was reopened in 1852 as a teacher preparation institution.

More significant in its effect on the future of the high school was the Massachusetts Law of 1827 enacted mainly through the efforts of James G. Carter. This act, which revised and expanded the Massachusetts Act of 1647, required a high school to be established in all communities with 500 or more families, and Latin and Greek to be offered in districts with populations of 4,000 or more. Maine, New Hampshire, and Vermont soon followed with similar laws. By 1860 public high schools had spread to other parts of the country, concentrating in the cities.

> The public high school movement gained momentum with the establishment of the first American high school in 1821 and the passage of a law six years later that expanded the Massachusetts Act of 1647.

Public Support

Public support of high schools was affirmed in the historic Kalamazoo Case of 1874. An irate taxpayer objected to taxation to support a high school, arguing that one could gain employment without attending high school. The Michigan Supreme Court issued a unanimous decision that upheld the right of school boards to levy taxes to support public high schools. Since the state had already established elementary schools and a state university, the court said, it would be inconsistent to have to seek a private secondary education. The court recognized the intention of the legislature to create a complete system of schools that provided access to the university. Similar cases in eight other states were decided the same way.

Even though states had established public-school systems, compulsory school attendance laws and child labor laws were necessary for education to be truly universal. The motives for compulsory education included protecting immigrants and the poor from exploitation by avaricious manufacturers, promoting good citizenship, and advancing Protestant values. Massachusetts established the first compulsory-attendance law in 1852. Fourteen more states enacted similar laws in the 1870s, and Mississippi followed suit in 1918. Even though the laws were on the books, many states did not enforce them until after the turn of the century.

Reform movements to regulate child labor began before the Civil War but did not become a national movement until the end of the nineteenth century. Children worked on farms, in mills, and in facto-

Child labor laws enabled children at low socioeconomic levels to attend school.

ries for sixty or more hours a week, frequently under unsafe and unsanitary conditions. National committees were established to set minimum age requirements for workers and to regulate hours and working conditions. Codifying these aims in federal law proved difficult at first. The Keating-Owen bill of 1916 to regulate child labor was declared unconstitutional as an unwarranted infringement of states' rights, and a proposed Constitutional amendment with similar aims failed to be ratified. These outcomes left child labor regulations with the state. The tide was flowing toward reform, though, and by the 1930s all states had established either mandatory educational requirements before youth could be employed, or laws requiring continued education while at work.

Changes in Thought and Practice

Thomas Jefferson (1743–1826), third American president, author of the Declaration of Independence, and founder of the University of Virginia, was an innovator in the development of American education. In a plan for the education of youth in Virginia, he sought to diffuse knowledge among the masses because he considered education necessary to make a democracy work. As he said in a letter: "If a nation expects to be ignorant and free, in a state of civilization, it expects what never was and never will be."

Jefferson was an early proponent of education for the masses.

Jefferson proposed a bill designating small districts in each county of the state. Each district would establish a school for teaching the three *R*s, and supply a tutor. Everyone would be entitled to send their children there for three years free, and for as many more years as they chose if they paid tuition. One poor child of talent from each of the twenty districts would be chosen to attend that district's grammar school to study Greek, Latin, geography, and the higher branches of numerical arithmetic. Every one or two years one boy would be chosen to continue for six more years. When the system was fully under way, ten students would be completing grammar schools every year with expectations of continuing their studies at William and Mary; the other ten students would likely become masters in the grammar school.

Jefferson's proposal was ahead of its time and was never ratified, yet his educational thinking became an influential form of meritocracy. A **meritocratic system** offers rewards like scholarships and reduced tuition in return for achievements that fulfill the standards of the system. (This differs markedly from systems that provide such rewards on the basis of irrelevant factors such as race, religion, nationality, seniority, sex, family background, politics, and wealth.) Various types of tests, such as I.Q. tests, achievement tests, and personality tests, have been developed to sift and sort people in the educational system. Other meritocratic criteria include grades, scholarships, honor rolls, diplomas, and certificates, and awards of various types. By using screening devices, those who can profit from an undergraduate education or graduate and professional study are evaluated and selected for programs and future employment.

Andrew Jackson (1767–1845), seventh American president, had similar visions of education for the masses and sought to take the idea further. He joined a movement toward greater popular participation in government, attacking privilege and monopoly and attempting to broaden opportunity in many areas of life. Jackson appealed to the farmer, the artisan, and the owner of a small business; he was viewed with suspicion and fear by those in established positions.

Jacksonian democracy promoted an egalitarian movement in American government and education. **Egalitarianism** is a belief that all humans should have equal political, social, and economic rights. In the nineteenth century egalitarianism was expressed by public support of the common school and the high school, compulsory school attendance laws, and changes in the curriculum that made it useful to a wider range of students. In the latter twentieth century egalitarian influences include the Supreme Court's desegregation decision (*Brown v. Board of Education of Topeka*, 1954), the civil rights movement, civil rights laws, programs for the disadvantaged and disabled, bilingual education, and legislation to protect women's rights in education.

The National Education Association appointed a number of committees whose work greatly influenced secondary education. The 1893 report of the Committee of Ten on Secondary School Studies shaped the direction of secondary education in the United States. Led by Harvard president Charles W. Eliot, the committee asserted that the high school should be a college preparatory program and recommended a battery of courses designed to prepare a student for college. High schools were to teach English; the classical languages Greek and Latin; modern languages, usually French and German; mathematics; physics, chemistry, and astronomy; natural history; history; and geography, geology, and meteorology. It was assumed that studies that prepared one for college also best prepared one, at least mentally, for life.

> High schools began to adopt college preparatory programs in the late nineteenth century.

To standardize the wide diversity found throughout the nation in high-school curriculums, the committee recommended that every subject be taught the same way in all programs. It was proposed that each subject be equivalent to every other in seriousness, dignity, and efficacy. This led the Committee on College Entrance Requirements in 1899 to develop a formula that later resulted in the development of Carnegie units, the basis of the high-school credit.

Subsequent commissions appointed by the National Education Association were more flexible than the Committee of Ten. The NEA's Commission on the Reorganization of Secondary Education, for example, recommended in the 1918 "Seven Cardinal Principles of Education" that schools be set up to serve the practical needs of individuals and society, not just prepare students for college. The commission was influenced by the educational philosophy of British sociologist and educator Herbert Spencer (1820–1903), who sought to determine what knowledge is of greatest worth.

> In the early twentieth century most people favored a practical education for those who would not attend college.

He defined knowledge as being either ornamental or useful and declared that English education in his time was dominated by ornamental knowledge. For Spencer, study of the classics and languages, which dominated secondary education at the time, was of little real productive use and was principally employed by the upper class to demarcate themselves from the other social classes. What, then, was useful knowledge, and how did one determine the relative worth of knowing this thing or that? Heavily influenced by Darwin's theory of evolution, Spencer believed that those things that contributed most to the survival of humankind and to the progress of society (social evolution) were of the greatest real value. He classified in terms of their priority the leading activities that constitute human life: first, activities that directly minister to self-preservation; second, activities that do so indirectly, such as the gathering of scientific knowledge; third, activities that promote the rearing and discipline of offspring; fourth, activities that maintain proper social and political relations; and last, activities devoted to leisure. Ultimately, Spencer held that science is the knowledge of greatest worth because it is best equipped to enable us to survive and progress.

In formulating the Cardinal Principles, the Commission on the Reorganization of Secondary Education reflected Spencer's thought that education should serve the practical needs of the individual and of society. The commission put forth that students should receive an education in seven areas: health, command of fundamental processes (math, reading, thinking, etc.), worthy home membership (participation in the family), vocational education, civic education, worthy use of leisure, and ethical character. Only command of fundamental processes could be considered a direct preparation for college; the other six areas were directed more to personal and social competencies. In contrast to the Committee of Ten report, the Cardinal Principles were more concerned with preparation for life among students not attending college and exhibited more flexibility by designating broad competencies to be acquired rather than a standardized program to be mastered.

The Middle School and Junior High

The Committee of Ten and the Committee on College Entrance Requirements believed that the four-year high-school period offered insufficient preparation for college and recommended in 1899 that secondary education begin in the last two years of elementary education. William Rainey Harper (1856–1906), first president of the University of Chicago, boldly proposed that secondary schools should cover the eighth grade of the elementary school and the first two years of college. In 1912 the NEA's Committee on Economy of Time in Education advocated six years of secondary education. By 1918 a psychological rationale was proposed for the junior high school: youth of this age were undergoing physiological, social, and psychological changes that required different types of programs than those provided in the elementary school or the high school. In addition to the educational and psychological rationales put forth to advocate an interim program between elementary and high school, a rapid increase in high-school enrollment provided an impetus to act. Secondary school enrollment increased rapidly between 1880 and 1920. There were 110,000 students in secondary schools in 1880; 200,000 in 1890; 500,000 in 1900; 900,000 in 1910; 2,200,000 in 1920.[9] New buildings were needed to accommodate students; and junior high schools were advocated on this ground as well.

The junior high school has its roots in the early part of the twentieth century.

The first junior high school was established in 1909 in Berkeley, California. Some believed that the early junior high schools created an interest in secondary schooling and helped increase the holding power of the high school. Some critics of junior highs contended that they were principally an administrative reorganization of secondary education that only belatedly developed a curriculum rationale.

In the 1960s the middle school was developed not only as a new form for organizing school systems but also as a new approach for educating pupils in the sixth, seventh, and eighth grades (in some instances the fifth and ninth grades were included). In short, the middle school, its advocates claimed, was a curriculum response to the special needs of this age group. A sufficiently broad research base to validate the effectiveness of junior high school is lacking, whereas the middle-school movement has recently accumulated greater data to support its claims. The middle school, designed to serve as a bridge between childhood and adolescence, stresses such features as individualized study, team teaching, integration of extracurricular activities into the formal curriculum, use of a non-graded plan, and development of interdisciplinary programs.

The middle school concept is a curricular as well as an organizational approach.

Educators debated what to do with vocational education. In 1878 Emerson White called attention to the need for industrial education, and in 1912 the National Society for the Promotion of Industrial Education proposed that vocational schools be established separately from regular high schools. John Dewey spoke against separate systems, and many parents, convinced of the prestige of academic study, wanted a broader education for their offspring than a straight technical program. Consequently, both vocational and general education have remained in one system, leading to the comprehensive high school.

In an eight-year study that shed an interesting light on college-preparation programs, the Progressive Education Association, in the 1940s, tracked students in thirty progressive schools and thirty traditional schools throughout their high-school and college studies. A comparison of the two groups showed that those in progressive schools, who had been excused from meeting basic entrance requirements, were virtually as successful in college as those who had met the requirements. This, incidentally, led many colleges to lower their high-school requirements for admission.[10]

The comprehensive high school was given a boost by James B. Conant's influential study in 1959 of the American high school, which recommended diversified programs for the development of marketable skills. The study recommended the creation of comprehensive high schools with multiple curriculums, programs for the academically able, and more ample counseling services. High schools with fewer than 100 in the graduating class would be phased out.[11] The organizational structure of high schools has remained largely unchanged to this day. (For an overview of the contributions of the leading American educators, see Table 5–2.)

■ HIGHER EDUCATION

The first college to be founded was Harvard College in 1636. Boys admitted to Harvard had been well prepared for college in Latin grammar schools and were able to sight-read Cicero, speak Latin, make Latin verses, and decline and conjugate Greek nouns and verbs.

The nine colleges in existence during colonial times were small, traditional, and widely scattered. Some colleges were supported by religious denominations and others, such as Harvard, Yale, and William and Mary, received state aid as well as denominational support. Latin, Greek, and Hebrew were offered, and corporal punishment was frequently used for discipline. Emphasis on classical studies, high tuition, and lack of accessibility hurt the popularity of these colleges. At the time of the American Revolution, only about one out of every thousand colonists had been to college, and in 1776 there were only 3,000 living graduates of American colleges.[12]

The few who attended the country's first colleges received a thoroughly classical education.

In the middle of the eighteenth century, the **Great Awakening,** a series of religious revivals that spread through the colonies, resulted in doctrinal changes and modifications in social and political thought.

TABLE 5-2 Leading American educators

Educator	Influence
Benjamin Franklin (1706–1790)	Founded the Academy in Philadelphia in 1751
Thomas Jefferson (1743–1826)	Founded the University of Virginia and a state-wide plan for education
Noah Webster (1758–1843)	Developed a widely used spelling book and helped standardize spelling
Emma Willard (1787–1870)	Promoted higher education for women
James G. Carter (1795–1849)	Sponsored legislation for the first state board of education in Massachusetts
Horace Mann (1796–1859)	Considered the father of the common school
Mary Lyon (1797–1849)	Founded Mt. Holyoke College in 1837, first women's college in the United States
Catharine Beecher (1800–1878)	Promoted higher education for women
William Holmes McGuffey (1800–1873)	Developed readers that were standard texts in nineteenth-century American schools
Ralph Waldo Emerson (1803–1882)	Transcendentalist, essayist, poet, and education writer
Henry Barnard (1811–1900)	Education leader in Connecticut and Rhode Island, first U.S. Commissioner of Education, leading journal writer
Andrew D. White (1832–1918)	Led the college land-grant movement
Charles W. Eliot (1834–1926)	Developed the elective system at Harvard University
William T. Harris (1835–1909)	Leading Hegelian and U.S. commissioner of education from 1889 to 1906
Booker T. Washington (1856–1915)	Principal spokesman for blacks, founded Tuskegee Institute in 1881
John Dewey (1859–1952)	Pragmatic, progressive, and influential educational philosopher
W. E. B. DuBois (1868–1963)	Black civil rights leader and educator
Mary McLeod Bethune (1875–1955)	Black educator who founded Bethune-Cookman College

TABLE 5–2 *(continued)*

Educator	Influence
George S. Counts (1889–1974)	Leading social reconstructionist
James B. Conant (1893–1978)	Issued influential reports on secondary education, teacher education, and the disadvantaged
Robert M. Hutchins (1899–1977)	President of the University of Chicago and leader in the Great Books program
Mortimer J. Adler (b. 1902)	Editor of *Encyclopedia Britannica* and developer of the Great Books program
Carl R. Rogers (1902–1987)	Developed nondirective therapy and humanistic education leader
B. F. Skinner (1904–1990)	Leading behaviorist who developed programmed learning materials
John Holt (1923–1985)	Libertarian leader of informal education and home schooling

The movement increased opposition to the Anglican Church, encouraged a democratic spirit in religion, and led to the founding of such colleges as Dartmouth, Princeton, Brown, and Rutgers.

At about the same time, the **Enlightenment** also was influencing modern thought. The movement's extreme rationalism and skepticism led to **deism,** a belief in God on rational grounds without reliance on authority or revelation. During this period Thomas Jefferson sought to reorganize the course of study at William and Mary and at Kings College (now known as Columbia) to reflect the ideals of the Enlightenment and to better prepare young men for responsible citizenship in the wake of the American Revolution. As a result, studies in French, natural history, and economics were offered for the first time.

Numerous colleges were chartered in the early nineteenth century, but more than 700 failed before the Civil War. Colleges were opened even if there were no elementary or secondary schools in the area. Many college founders established colleges to express their belief in endless progress. The desire for a nearby college, missionary zeal, and religious denominationalism also contributed to the rapid increase in the number of colleges at the time.

Struggles Over the Curriculum

Americans generally admired a self-made man whose accomplishments were without benefit of formal schooling. To appeal to this down-to-earth public, colleges in the early nineteenth century began playing down intellectual rigor, genius, and brilliance in favor of the development of commonplace virtues. They began to de-emphasize social responsibility and elevate monetary gain as a desired end.

The Yale Report of 1828 sought to combat the new subjects and options developing in the curriculum. Seeking to strengthen classical studies, the report advanced the **formal discipline theory,** which held that the mind, like the muscles, can be strengthened by rigorous exercise through the study of difficult subjects like mathematics and Latin. The classical curriculum would provide a **massive transfer of training,** that is, it would enable young men to perform better in any undertaking by developing the proper habits of mind and character.

Advocates of the new sciences and proponents of the classics struggled constantly to dominate American higher education. The classicists aligned themselves with aristocratic tradition and resisted any attempts to dilute their required classical curriculum. Sporadic breaks in the strict classical pattern could be found in various parts of the country during the early nineteenth century as the new sciences gained footholds of popularity among the general public. Their popularity continued to grow, and by 1850, the scientific school was a fact of college life. By 1870 twenty-five colleges had opened scientific departments.

Classicists not only resisted the enlarged curriculum that the sciences were forging but also opposed the introduction of romance languages and other new disciplines in the humanities. The older classical notions began losing their position of dominance in the face of these new developments. The popularity of Latin slipped even further when the decision was made toward the end of the nineteenth century to model graduate education in America after the research model found in German universities (more about this shortly). To make matters even worse for the classicists, later psychological experiments by William James and by Edward Lee Thorndike suggested that the formal discipline theory was ineffective.

> Dispute about whether a college education should be grounded in intellectualism or practicality began nearly 200 years ago.

■ **PAUSE TO REFLECT**
The Practical Versus the Classical

- Has your general education so far consisted of a classical curriculum, a practical approach, or a combination? How could it have been made more useful to you?

- How would you structure the ideal curriculum for elementary school? High school? Higher education? How would such a curriculum be an improvement over current standards in education?

The Liberal Arts Education. Three dominant conceptions of higher education were found in late nineteenth-century America: liberal culture, research, and utility.[13] The liberal culture proponents, who were in a minority, advocated studying modern languages from a literary standpoint. The student would combine broad learning with aesthetic tastes and moral development. Ethics replaced religion as the basis for the formation of character. A study of literary models and philosophical works was considered the best path to character development.

The liberal culture proponents took pains to see that the breadth of learning did not degenerate into mere dilettantism. A broad but substantive education could be attained, advocates believed, by a study of the standards of past civilizations. In this quest, they opposed (1) the narrow religious fervor of the Fundamentalists, (2) the emphasis upon a utilitarian accommodation to the demands of a burgeoning economy (think back to Spencer), and (3) the German model of highly specialized studies found in the graduate schools. Both science and utilitarianism represented to liberal culture advocates an impoverishment of the human spirit.

The original aim of a liberal arts education was to produce a cultivated man.

The cultivated man, they believed, was a gentleman, a man of polish and style. They also believed that it was easier to develop a gentleman if the young man came from the proper upper-class background. As a result, they identified with certain aristocratic strains of thought and scorned the idea of attempting to reshape middle-class youth. The clash of the gentleman ideal with the dignity and worth of the common man was never truly reconciled, although many liberal culturists hoped that liberal culture studies eventually would trickle down to the masses and society would be uplifted.

The liberal culture ideal, though still present today in various liberal arts colleges, has declined in influence and has little appeal to the majority of today's college students, who are more influenced by the spread of vocationalism, the growth of professionalization, and the effects of science and technology. This ideal also has been challenged by the emergence of women's studies, minority studies, explorations of non-Western cultures, and other subjects usually ignored by liberal culture curriculums.

The Research Model. The emphasis on research in higher education, another salient influence, began about the 1860s. Germany had made considerable progress in developing graduate education and promoting scientific research and, as word of its accomplishments spread, several American students and scholars traveled abroad to study for their Ph.D. degrees. As young American scientists gained inspiration from German universities, they interpreted the German ideals in a unique fashion: German methods became wedded to British empiricism in the research activities of American scientists.

The founding of Johns Hopkins University in Baltimore in the 1870s symbolized the German ideal of research. Through the leadership of its president, David Coit Gilman, doctoral programs were established based upon the research ideal, and scientific research was espoused as a worthy role for the university. In light of these developments, the conception of science began to change. Science always had been considered any well-organized body of principles within an area of knowledge. Philosophers and classicists could speak of the scientific organization of subject matter in their disciplines. But science was moving beyond that and becoming associated with the search for evidence of nature's workings and the uncovering of basic laws that would explain the data of scientific investigation. Scientific research led to greater specialization in the university and encouraged scholars to consider it academically respectable to investigate minute topics exhaustively.

At Johns Hopkins, Gilman urged that only students sufficiently prepared to provide the faculty with challenging stimulation be admitted to the program. As the ideals of scientific investigation spread to other universities in somewhat diluted form, other faculties began to raise their standards. As a result, only the best of the best were admitted to the leading institutions, and because many of the students went on to teach in these universities, the quality of the faculty began to improve, also. By the turn of the century, the Ph.D. degree was mandatory for employment at the better institutions. The next step was to insist on scholarly publication as a requirement for advancement—the "publish or perish" doctrine was installed. By 1910 research was the emphasis of leading universities.

> Emphasis on scientific research led to policies of selective admissions.

As the role of research grew during the twentieth century in major public and private universities, so did the involvement of the university in the affairs of the larger society. Universities showed particular interest in the corporate structure and the military-industrial complex. Federal research funding in those areas rose dramatically from World War II through the 1960s. Funding declined in the 1970s, as the New Left, a humanist, neo-Marxist movement, began to seriously question the wisdom of these new alliances. Critics protested the control exerted by the military-industrial complex, including its influence over scientific research in the universities. As a result of this pressure, universities began to reappraise their policies governing secret research— indeed, they reassessed the priority of research in general over other functions. In the 1980s universities accepted fewer classified research contracts, but federal funding declined.

Utilitarianism and the Land-Grant Colleges. The utility ideal, although present to a minor degree before the Civil War, emerged with considerable strength during the land-grant movement in the 1860s.

The Morrill Act of 1862 made available to each state grants of land on the condition that the grants be used for the teaching of agriculture and mechanical arts, with a special provision for military science and tactics. The schools were expected to offer a well-rounded education, so other scientific and classical studies were not to be excluded. States used their grants in various ways. Eighteen of them added agricultural and mechanical arts to existing state institutions, other states established new colleges for this purpose, and a few states granted portions of the funds to private colleges and universities. Sixty-nine colleges and universities received funds under the act.

Utility educators became more common in the applied sciences and social sciences. Vocational preparation, once handled largely through apprenticeship programs with no connection to university responsibilities, was incorporated into higher education. Utility educators gained a place in the administration, substantially strengthening their position. The older colleges mainly had prepared men for the professions of law, medicine, and theology. But with the installation of new vocational programs, such as home economics, engineering, business administration, and agriculture, the distinction between vocations and professions blurred. As a result, occupations considered superior in social prestige because of the requirements for advanced study now were on more equal footing with the new vocations. Nevertheless, although all careers were equal in principle the older professions still retained some of their distinctive status.

> Utilitarianism provided a basis for offering vocational study at the college level.

Utility educators believed that the university could serve society by preparing practical men with technical competence and disseminating technical knowledge to the home, farm, and factory. Some even advocated that the university assume whatever functions were requested by the citizenry. Many educators often were pressured by politicians and vested-interest groups to lower their notion of "practicality" so that preparation for even more new trades, such as industrial trades, blacksmithing, and carpentry, would become part of the university curriculum.

Conflict arose among educators, administrators, and the public over what actually constituted utility and practicality. Some scholars wanted to concentrate on social reform and social efficiency. Some administrators interpreted "utility" as the ability to amass material goods, while others considered it an ethical term that encouraged a crusade for public service. Finally, many citizens wanted the universities to instill various civic virtues or develop civic leaders who would clean up politics.

All of these ideals have found a place in American higher education. Today, a wide array of vocational programs are securely a part of higher education, and programs preparing students for technical specialties can be found alongside the research ideal and a modified liberal culture ideal. As the opportunities increase in the universities, society has come to believe that a college education is necessary to find a good job. This was especially true in the 1980s as material desires increased and altruism declined. Undergraduates tended to turn away from the liberal arts and enroll in vocational and professional fields that promised the greatest pecuniary return.

In the late nineteenth century, Charles W. Eliot (1834–1926), president of Harvard University, introduced the elective system, later adopted in modified form by other universities. In addition to giving students the chance to study subjects outside their chosen fields, the elective system brought about greater parity among the sciences and the older disciplines as students began exercising their choices. The popularity of the elective curriculum has waxed and waned throughout the twentieth century, losing favor in the years before World War I, gaining it back in the late 1960s, and losing it again in the late 1970s.

Since World War I, higher education has undergone the same rapid changes as the rest of society. Between World War I and World War II the undergraduate program was similar to today's blend of free electives, liberal requirements, and concentration on a chosen field. But critics wanted more emphasis on general education, experiential education, honors classes, and independent study. General education was stressed during and immediately after World War II in an effort to promote national solidarity in the face of foreign enemies. The G.I. bill opened higher education to many older students and ushered in a period of rapid growth in enrollment. When the Soviet Union launched Sputnik in 1957, many leaders were alarmed that the United States had fallen behind in the space race. Pressure escalated to promote science, mathematics, and foreign languages in university curriculums, with special attention to accelerated study and education of the gifted.

Student activism during the 1960s led to student-centered education and the introduction of various courses that related to student concerns, such as courses about the Vietnam war, sexual relations, drugs, and civil rights. More emphasis was placed on the whole student and education that involved feelings and emotions.

Since then, universities have made an even greater shift toward vocationalism. Federal research funding also has declined, leaving some institutions with severe financial problems. In an attempt to avoid dependence on one or two main sources of revenue, many institutions have begun diversifying their offerings and opportunities. Several schools attempt to attract students from different backgrounds—minorities, the academically disadvantaged, adults, and the poor. Others have developed nontraditional adult education, competency-based curriculums, community-based education, and a

Because college curricula have grown out of many philosophical approaches to education, today there are schools that serve the needs of every student.

revitalization of the core curriculum. The diversity of American higher education today, as seen in the variety of community and junior colleges, state colleges, state universities, land-grant universities, municipal universities, private secular colleges and universities, and church-related colleges, assures that every student will be served.

■ TEACHER EDUCATION

Are teachers born, not made? For many generations teaching was considered a gift. Charlemagne (742–812), who could not find anyone fully suited to teach his children, finally turned to England and brought back Alcuin to direct the palace school. The belief that teaching was a gift created a shortage of qualified teachers, as one might imagine, and inhibited the development of teacher education. In the time of Pestalozzi (1746–1827), teaching had evolved to the point that it was based not only on a knowledge of one's subject but also on an understanding of pedagogy (teaching methods). Educators from both Europe and America visited Pestalozzi's schools to observe these principles of pedagogy in practice and later to test them in their own countries.

> Teachers at one time had only slightly more education than their students did.

In colonial times, most teachers had no training beyond what they learned in the elementary school in which they now taught. After the Revolutionary War, sporadic and inadequate attempts to prepare teachers emerged with the Lancaster-Bell monitorial system, the academy, and teacher institutes. The monitorial system, which originated in England, was a mostly economic measure that let one teacher handle large numbers of pupils by teaching the lesson for the day to several bright youngsters who, in turn, taught the lesson to the other children on their rows. The academy, which provided those who attended it with more than the three *R*s, was only able to prepare a small proportion of the teachers needed. The teacher institutes, influenced by Henry Barnard's work, offered short but intensive periods of training that, despite their limitations, lasted well into this century.

The Normal School

The first systematic and sustained attempt to provide teacher preparation emerged with the establishment of the first state normal school in Massachusetts in 1839. Since many students entered the normal school at the completion of elementary school (grades one through eight), they studied high-school level courses in addition to pedagogics. Normal schools offered one- to four-year programs, with two years of college study available for graduates. New forms of educational theory spread in the late nineteenth century from the normal school at Oswego, New York, which embraced Pestalozzian methods, and from the state normal school in Normal, Illinois, which was based on modified Herbartian ideas. By the late nineteenth century, normal schools had broadened their course offerings and were firmly established under state support; they were preparing most of the elementary teachers and some of the high-school teachers.

New York State upgraded the normal school to a teacher preparation school in the 1890s. But the first school established specifically as a teacher college was built in 1903 in Ypsilanti, Michigan. By 1930 most of the normal schools had been converted to teacher colleges; by the end of the 1960s, most of them had been reconstituted as state colleges and, in some cases, state universities. The usual four-year program in teacher colleges was designed to give students a general education as well as instruction in teaching methods and preparation in their teaching specialty.

Despite early opposition from scholars who considered normal schools and teacher colleges substandard and resisted the introduction of teacher education into the university, some state universities established chairs of pedagogy in the late nineteenth century. Other universities began offering courses in education within existing academic departments, and by the 1930s a large number of colleges and universities offered courses in education.

Criticisms of Teacher Education

A conflict over teacher education erupted in the 1950s and was conveyed to the public in a simplified form as "how to teach versus what to teach." Critics Arthur Bestor and other essentialists charged that the mediocre showing of the public schools was not due to a lack of effort but to inappropriate aims promoted by progressive education that emphasized life adjustment.[14] The low intellectual quality of American schools, they said, stems from educationists who prepare teachers with teaching methods that are out of touch with the world of scholarship. The critics had no reason to think the situation would change, because the educationists worked closely with educators and state departments of education to set the standards for teacher education. Bestor and his colleagues believed that citizens and liberal arts professors should participate more fully, exercise greater control over the preparation of teachers, and assume more responsibility in the accreditation of teacher schools and colleges.

James Koerner, in a national survey of teacher education in the 1960s, raised and extended the charges made by the critics of the

1950s.[15] He concluded that (1) those who prepare teachers are "incompetent," (2) undergraduates in education are some of the weaker students in the university, (3) the programs fail to weed out weak students, (4) a maze of interlocking agencies staffed by educationists control public education, and (5) educationists communicate in a distorted language that tends to exclude all but the initiated. The abolition of departments of education would be most attractive, he said, but unrealistic. Instead, he recommended that students be required to major in liberal arts and that education courses be fewer in number and higher in quality.

> Koerner believed that teachers should study primarily content and that specific training in methods should be minimal.

Koerner's message, similar to that of many of the 1950s critics, was that if teachers knew their subjects, they would automatically be good teachers. One easily could argue, however, that while knowledge of one's subject is indeed necessary, it is not a sufficient condition for good teaching. Teaching is a complex process that requires knowledge of the teaching-learning process and human development as well as one's subject. It also requires a critical understanding of aims, purposes, and the social context of education, as well as highly developed skills in interpersonal relations.

An important study of teacher education during the 1960s was conducted in a two-year period by James B. Conant.[16] In the first year, Conant and his associates visited seventy-seven public, private, and church-related institutions in twenty-two states. During the second year, they concentrated on state departments of education in the sixteen most populous states.

> Studies by Conant in the 1960s showed that there was no agreement about the best and most appropriate way to train teachers.

Conant found room for improvement in both education and liberal arts. He also found that though the need for liberal arts is generally agreed upon, there were wide differences of opinion as to what it should be. In short, he found "a complete lack of agreement" on what constitutes a satisfactory general education for future teachers.[17]

Conant concluded that teacher education should be an all-university responsibility and that a state-approved program of practice teaching is the most important requirement for adequate teacher preparation. The people who supervise practice teaching should have considerable experience and their roles should be considered analogous to those of clinical professors in some medical schools. Conant contended that state certification requirements have no demonstrable effect on the quality of teaching. Each institution should be permitted to develop its own teacher education program, he said, and be allowed to officially certify that candidates are qualified to teach as long as they had participated in a state-approved practice teaching program. While this proposal gives universities more control over their own programs, a laudable goal, it also creates even greater diversity of programs, discourages standardization, and makes it impossible to devise even a minimum set of requirements for all state institutions.

Probably the most influential national study of American public education and teacher education during the 1970s was a three-and-one-half year investigation by Charles E. Silberman, sponsored by the Carnegie Corporation.[18] The study was divided into an examination of current conditions and deficiencies in the public schools, how those deficiencies could be overcome, and the relation of those considerations to the improvement of teacher education.

Silberman, in distinct contrast to other critics, did not find a single culprit: he thoroughly and equally critiqued liberal arts colleges, schools of education, and the public schools. He outlined in vivid detail the failures of our "grim, joyless" public schools and found that what was wrong was not venality, stupidity, or indifference, but "mindlessness." He found the same condition in various forms in liberal arts colleges and schools of education. By mindlessness, Silberman meant that educators fail "to think seriously or deeply about the purposes or consequences of education."[19] Too seldom are teachers, at whatever level, committed to a clear sense of purpose and direction. He believed that schools and colleges should be infused with thought about purpose and how what they are doing fulfills clearly conceived purposes. Instead, he found a tendency to confuse daily routine with purpose and to transform routine, such as schedules and lesson plans, into ends in themselves. The central task of teacher education, he said, is to provide teachers with a sense of purpose or a philosophy of education. Hence, history and philosophy should occupy a central place in teacher education. While these studies have not directly enhanced practice, they have raised questions about the meaning of practice and the goals of one's activities to which all teachers should give great attention.

> Silberman believed the greatest weakness of teacher training was the failure to imbue teachers with a sense of the purpose of education.

Silberman held that the study of education itself should be placed at the center of the liberal arts curriculum because it involves our conception of the good person, the good life, and the good society; and one cannot fully consider such concepts separately from a study of education because education is our means of sustaining them. Of course, he did not mean that teacher education in its present form should become the core of liberal arts education, because, among other reasons, such questions are too rarely considered. (We will discuss this question of purpose in education when we get to Chapter 7.)

Efforts to Change Teacher Training

Other innovations in teacher education during the sixties and seventies were the Master of Arts in Teaching (M.A.T.) program, programs for culturally different learners, and competency-based teacher education. The Harvard M.A.T. program, which was instituted in 1936, is probably the best known of the M.A.T. programs. These five-year programs are designed for liberal arts graduates who have little or no background in teacher education. The fifth year consists of an internship in the schools and conference courses; teacher education courses and clinical experiences are closely related. Other five-year programs have been conducted at Stanford, Duke, George Peabody, Cornell, and UCLA.

Educators belatedly have recognized that teachers often must work with culturally different learners. The Cardoza Project in Urban Teaching was designed to prepare teachers for inner-city schools. The program recruited Peace Corps and VISTA veterans and, later, college graduates. Some institutions have attempted to provide multicultural education, and several states have mandated a multiethnic component to teacher education.

Performance-based teacher education (PBTE) or **competency-based teacher education** (CBTE) emerged during the late 1960s as an alternative to the prevailing system. The new system was based upon specifying learning goals and holding students accountable for achieving those goals or taking action to achieve them. The performance goals (in the form of knowledge, skills, behaviors) are derived from conceptions of teacher roles and formulated so that an assessment of performance can be made easily. Once formulated, the goals are stated clearly so that the students understand what is expected of them. Competencies would be determined depending on the level of mastery attained by students under specified conditions. Evaluation of competency would be as objective as possible and, while performance would be the basic source of evidence, some consideration would be given to the knowledge students need to teach effectively. Thus, this teacher education program emphasizes performance rather than the accumulation of course credits.

Proponents of C/PBTE claim a number of advantages for these programs: (1) in certifying candidates, state education departments will be able to see that the candidates demonstrate sound teaching abilities; (2) individual students can receive greater attention as they proceed at their own pace in acquiring competencies; (3) the program is systemic and provides feedback on performance; and (4) it reassures the public of teacher competency.

At the same time, critics have identified several weaknesses: (1) the programs are based on a behavioristic model that defines learning as only what is measurable and therefore deals only with what can be measured; (2) the program is technocratic because it concentrates solely on imparting skills and ignores the student as a person; (3) the program does not produce research findings to show what skills and behaviors a teacher must possess to be a successful teacher; and (4) competencies are derived from current, unquestioned teacher roles that might be ineffective.

Of 686 institutions surveyed in 1977, 58 percent reported that they were operating complete or partial CBTE programs, while an additional 26 percent were exploring CBTE.[20] Interest in CBTE, however, leveled off sharply by 1980 for a variety of reasons, probably including that it was difficult to implement.

The Holmes and Carnegie Reports.   Two reports on teacher education were especially prominent during the 1980s: the Holmes Report and the Carnegie Task Force on Teaching as a Profession. The Holmes group consists of education deans from several dozen research universities who invited 123 public and private universities to accept their goals and work collaboratively to achieve them. The Holmes Report recommended a program similar to the M.A.T. program of the sixties and seventies in that prospective teachers would earn a bachelor's degree in liberal arts and take a fifth year of teacher education.[21] The report proposed that undergraduate degrees be eliminated in specialized education fields. Instead, universities would work with public-school systems to create schools of professional development that would be locations for teacher training and applied research on teaching and learning. This could be accomplished by universities' developing close ties with a limited number of schools, or by focusing on a few subjects. In addition, a group of instructors with limited training in pedagogy could be recruited to teach in the public schools under supervision for up to five years during periods of teacher shortages.

Educators at some smaller colleges have objected strongly to five-year programs because the colleges do not offer graduate programs or they lack the needed faculty. The idea of hiring teachers who do not have special training has been challenged at NEA and AFT meetings.[22] Critics point out that in their efforts to quickly meet the demand for teachers, many school districts have only created further problems by hiring untrained and incompetent teachers.

The Carnegie Task Force on Teaching as a Profession called for the restructuring of teacher roles and school organization.[23] The plan seeks to attract highly qualified persons who otherwise might pursue different careers; in turn, teachers would agree to higher standards and accountability for student performance. Bureaucratic school systems would be replaced by systems grounded in the authority of professional competence.

To implement the plan, schools would be restructured to provide an improved professional environment and a new category of lead teacher would be created. A national board for professional teaching standards, with state and regional membership, would be established to develop high standards and certification requirements for teachers. To attract promising teachers and improve minority representation in

Proposals to improve teacher education could bring fundamental changes in university programs and the organization of schools.

the field, salaries and career opportunities would be made more competitive with other professions. Students would earn a bachelor's degree in arts and sciences and go on to a graduate school of education, which would offer a curriculum leading to a master of teaching degree based on a knowledge of teaching and a record of internship in schools.

The National Board for Professional Teaching Standards was established in response to the Carnegie report with expectations of being fully operational in the early 1990s. It recommended that certification not be linked to state licensing or to graduation from an accredited teacher education program. Current policies exclude many otherwise qualified teachers, the board said, and state program-approval standards are unfair because they vary widely. Dealing a serious blow to these recommendations, the American Association of Colleges for Teacher Education voted not to support the work of the national board.[24] The association, which represents 700 out of 1,300 colleges and universities that prepare teachers, claimed that such changes actually would lower the very quality the national board sought to raise.

We clearly have come a long way from the early belief that teachers are born, not made, but we must remember that the preparation of effective teachers remains a great and exciting challenge without definitive answers.

■ **PAUSE TO REFLECT**

Evaluating Current Teacher Education Programs

- Describe the teacher education program in which you are currently enrolled, reflecting on what you believe to be the purpose of the curriculum.

- Does the program cover everything you think it should? If not, what other courses or opportunities could be offered to help you become a more complete educator?

- Do you think teacher education should be part of the university or separated into professional training schools? Why?

■ MINORITY EDUCATION

The United States was built on the idea that people from different racial, religious, and ethnic groups make up the core of the country and our society. More diverse and pluralistic than most European nations, the United States has provided opportunities and faced conflicts that most nations have never experienced. America was and is supposed to be a land of equal opportunity, but these opportunities some-times have been unequally distributed and at other times denied. While numerous cultural differences have been seen by some as a way of enriching and improving society, others have perceived them as threats to be overcome. Generally, white immigrants from Western Europe have been received with the least prejudice, white immigrants from Eastern Europe usually have met with more resistance, and non-whites, both immigrant and native, have born the brunt of the greatest discrimination.

American public education generally has been most successful in educating white male middle-class youth and less successful in edu-cating girls, lower-class whites, certain ethnic groups, and non-whites. In this section, we will look at the educational treatment of three major minority groups: Native Americans, black Americans, and Mexican Americans. Further discussion of these groups will be found in Part Four of this book.

> The pluralism of American society has not always been successfully reflected in edu-cation.

Native Americans

Native American children in the precolonial period were taught by parents and relatives in an extended family. Children also learned through activities of the clan, secret societies, societal leaders, and the community. They were expected to develop economic skills, knowl-edge of the cultural heritage, and spiritual awareness.[25] Economic skills emphasized training for survival, which stressed the mainte-nance of a harmonious relationship with nature.

Knowledge of the cultural heritage was passed along through sto-ries told by the oldest generation to the youngest. The tales reinforced cultural ideals learned in daily lessons. Spiritual awareness was devel-oped through rituals and ceremonies, with the intensity of training increasing sharply at puberty. During this period, boys were tested to determine who would train for the priesthood; others were initiated into secret societies. Discipline was promoted through reward and punishment, ridicule, and fostering the ability to withstand pain.

Conflict between the Native Americans and the colonists arose, basically, out of divergent value systems and perspectives. Economic and material considerations were important to the colonists; courage and loyalty were more important to the Native Americans. The use and ownership of land became the major conflict between the colonists and the natives. The colonists wanted to control and exploit the natural environment; the Native Americans considered the environment holy, a gift from the gods to be worshipped and protected. The colonists believed that the Native Americans were making inefficient use of the land and therefore believed they were justified in taking the land away from them—peacefully if possible but violently if necessary. Some colonists regarded the Native Americans as savages who ought to be annihilated; others accepted their humanity, though not their equality with white settlers, and sought to Christianize and educate them. Still others sought to acculturate the Native Americans. **Acculturation** is the process of learning and adopting the cultural traits of another group.

The settlers' origi-
nal aim in educat-
ing Native
Americans was to
"civilize" them.

The earliest attempt to promote higher education for Native Americans was in Virginia in the early 1600s in which a fund was established to support Native American youth who were to be boarded in the homes of colonists and taught the "rudiments of civilized life." Several also were sent to England to be educated with the hope they would return and educate others in their tribe. The Puritans sought to educate the Native Americans to become preachers and teachers. Some colonists believed that Indian youth should be removed from their tribe to maximize exposure to "civilized life." Puritans, for example, believed that Christianity and the habits of civilization could best be instilled in boarding schools.

Native Americans were unable, ultimately, to resist the encroachment of white settlers for a number of reasons: the European population was far larger, the Native Americans had no immunity to European diseases, and intertribal rivalries were exploited by the colonists. Pontiac had preached that the Native Americans must turn away from the white ways, reject trade goods that destroyed their independence, and unite against the whites. Tecumseh had a similar message, urging tribal leaders to rise against the United States. He supported the British in the War of 1812, but after Britain lost the war, the Native Americans never again had the active support of the European powers against the policies of the United States.

To understand the attitudes of Native Americans today and the evolution of their educational opportunities in white society, some knowledge of the history of white denial of Native American rights is necessary. In the early 1800s, Georgia ceded its western lands to the United States in return for a promise that the federal government would extinguish the land claims of the Cherokees of Georgia. The federal government forced the Cherokees to relinquish most of sixty million acres by 1826. In *Cherokee v. Georgia,* the courts ruled that a Native American tribe is not a foreign nation and therefore does not have a constitutional right to bring court action against a state. The courts did rule, however, in *Worcester v. Georgia,* that Georgia could not pass laws that superseded the laws of the Cherokees.

The Indian Removal Act of 1830, sponsored by Andrew Jackson, was designed to move all Native Americans of the southeastern states to west of the Mississippi. Jackson signed ninety-four treaties with the tribes to induce them to move. Remembered as "The Trail of Tears," the transfer took three years, shattered the lives of tens of thousands of people, and killed thousands more. By the early 1840s, about 100,000 Choctaws, Creeks, Cherokees, Chickasaws, and Seminoles had been moved. The treaties had promised rations, weapons, and tools, but the goods either never arrived or were insufficient to fill the needs of the tribes. As the white frontiersmen encroached on the new lands, the Native Americans were forced to accept treaties even less favorable than before.

The Native Americans began shaping their lives around the horse and the buffalo, but competition among tribes for hunting grounds and the white slaughter of the buffalo herds led to a thirty-year conflict between the Native Americans and the whites for control of the land after the Civil War. By the late 1800s, the number of Native Americans had been reduced to 300,000. Most of these survivors were assigned to reservations, under military guard, and were required to live there.

The Bureau of Indian Affairs' (BIA) policies toward Native Americans have vacillated from attempting to isolate them as separate nations to treating them as wards of the government and "civilizing" them. From 1794 to 1868, the federal government signed 120 treaties with various tribes that contained educational provisions.[26] White American-style schools were established on the reservations, and many Native Americans lost their hunter-warrior ideals and developed a passive dependency on the BIA. Thousands of Native Americans turned to alcohol and peyote for relief from the pain of losing their independence and way of life.

Non-reservation boarding schools, such as Carlisle School in Pennsylvania, sprang up across the country in which missionaries taught Christianity, English, and various skills to the Native Americans. The BIA established day schools and boarding schools on reservations; those who did well in the day schools could attend the boarding schools. Basic skills were taught along with mechanical arts and farming in an attempt to help them earn a living by farming. Reformers sincerely believed that Native Americans would be better off learning to live as the whites did, so as these schools developed, they veered further away from Native American culture and became more oriented to the white community. Industrial training schools were created to combine skills in using tools and machinery with the study of English. As a result, Native American religious and cultural values were virtually trampled.

Native Americans fought back by organizing the Society of American Indians, campaigning for Indian citizenship, and denouncing the policies of the BIA. In 1923 white liberals created the American Indian Defense Fund to oppose further confiscation of Native American land. And in 1924 Congress passed the Indian Citizenship Act, which con-

> The emphasis on teaching trades and farming to Native Americans ignored their cultural heritage.

ferred citizenship on those born in the United States. Under the Hoover administration in 1929, day schools were opened near reservations so that children could be near their families. Bilingual education was introduced and traditional dances and crafts were encouraged. Under the Indian Reorganization Act in 1934, each tribe was granted the right to draft its own constitution and assume ownership of all reservation land. A movement to enroll Native American children in public schools began in the 1940s, and by 1970 two of every three Native American children were enrolled.

Many of the one million Native Americans attempted to accommodate white society by learning English, while striving to retain their ethnic identity. As a result, by the late 1960s only forty-five native languages remained in use of the more than 300 once spoken.

The education of Native American students has continued to suffer. Students have problems adjusting to school values that differ dramatically from the values of their homes, the curriculums rarely are relevant to Native American needs, language barriers often hinder the students in white schools, and a high turnover rate of educators in Native American boarding schools prevents a sufficient degree of consistency and planning.

> Despite reforms that began in the 1920s, the United States educational system still does not properly serve Native Americans.

EDUCATIONAL ISSUE 5–1

Should the purpose of education be to assimilate minorities into the mainstream culture?

Yes	No
1. They have chosen to live in this land and should adopt the ways of the majority.	1. Cultural differences add variety to life and should be encouraged.
2. The best job opportunities are in the mainstream and people need to understand the dominant ways to compete effectively.	2. Just because a culture is dominant does not mean it is superior, and minorities should not be required to adopt it.
3. People should at least learn the language so they can communicate with the majority of people in society.	3. Bilingual education programs easily can overcome language barriers between cultures.

Black Americans

The South, with its fertile soil, long growing season, and navigable rivers, was well suited for a plantation economy, but for tobacco, rice, and cotton crops to be truly profitable, plantation owners needed large supplies of cheap labor for planting, picking, and processing. The owners considered forcing the Native Americans into slavery, but rejected the idea because of insufficient population, their susceptibility to European diseases, their ability to escape because of their knowledge of the land, and their inexperience in agriculture. The plantation owners had to turn elsewhere.

Dutch traders delivered the first Africans to Jamestown in 1619. Although at first Africans were indentured servants who could be released after seven years, by the 1700s the Africans were considered property over whom their masters had absolute legal control.

A distinctive African American culture had developed by the eighteenth century in which slaves spoke English fused with their native tongues, developed extended kinship relations, and practiced, as much as was possible, their native customs.

The American Revolution released certain ideological forces that would eventually throw the concept of slavery into question: white Americans sought their freedom from England while 500,000 black Americans remained in slavery. But emancipation was still decades away, and the whites had devised many methods of keeping the slaves under their control, not the least of which was denying them an education. The system was organized so that slaves were forbidden to learn to read or write, and it was illegal to teach a slave these skills. Most slaves from the same tribe were separated or forbidden to speak to each other, and they were not permitted to retain their African names or speak their native tongues (to reduce the chances of insurrection).

> One way white Americans tried to maintain control over their slaves was to deny them an education.

Despite the laws against teaching slaves literacy skills, many plantation owners provided in their wills for the education of their slaves. Owning a large number of highly trained slaves was considered a status symbol, but often the owners did not have enough work for them and would hire them out to employers who needed them. Thus many slaves were hired as skilled workers, such as carpenters, barbers, and bankers. This practice eventually created an educated group of slaves who later led the struggle for freedom. Some slaves gained literacy through "play schools" in which slaves were taught by the plantation owner's children. To promote obedience, owners of large plantations established Sunday schools for slaves that often required Bible reading. But the slaves first had to learn to read. Despite the fear that literacy might expose slaves to abolitionist literature, a group of South-

> Initial reasons for teaching literacy to slaves were to enhance their owners' status and to enable the slaves to read the Bible.

ern religious leaders insisted the risk was worth it. These opportunities were not widely accepted in Southern society. Nevertheless, what little schooling the slaves did receive served them well as some escaped to the North and used their education to advance the antislavery movement.

As the Civil War approached, Lincoln's main goal was to save the union rather than abolish slavery. He and other Northerners shared white Southerners' attitudes that blacks were naturally suited to servitude. When Lincoln issued the Emancipation Proclamation in 1863, proclaiming slaves to be free, he gained a sizable source of soldiers inclined to fight against the South, and authorized the armed forces to enlist freedmen. Emancipation, of course, did not guarantee equal treatment, and in some ways the black struggle had only just begun.

Freedmen Schools. Because emancipated slaves no longer could depend on their masters for support, benevolent societies in major Northern cities sprang up in the form of freedmen associations to provide teachers and the necessities for survival. In the 1870s benevolent and religious groups from the North established educational systems in the South to help freedmen make the transition to freedom. Freedmen schools were found in fourteen states, with most located in Louisiana, Virginia, and North Carolina. White children began attending these schools and were given the same instruction and taught in the same classrooms as blacks. The curriculum not only emphasized the three *R*s but character and personality development as well.

> Private groups took on the task of educating blacks to help them make the transition to freedom when slavery was abolished.

Yet a private educational system for four million people could not be maintained indefinitely and a public educational system for blacks was proposed. Controversy raged over any kind of education for blacks. Southern whites resisted the employment of black teachers from the North to teach in the freedmen schools and insisted they be replaced by white teachers. The governor of North Carolina closed the freedmen schools in his state. In Alabama, black servants were not permitted to work if they attended school. Property owners generally were antagonistic toward establishing public schools because they believed that laborers did not need an education and that those worth educating would find some way to obtain it on their own. Many Southern states attempted to establish public schools in the early nineteenth century, but many of the appropriated school funds were used for other purposes. The few public schools in operation were for the white poor and were open only a short period each year. Although the South had many private schools, they were reserved for the affluent. By 1870 white Southerners had accepted the Fourteenth Amendment under duress but rejected racial equality as well as the idea that blacks should be educated at public expense.

> White Southerners resisted the development of a public educational system for blacks.

Obstacles of Intimidation and Segregation. Blacks who attempted to exercise their rights found immediate and often violent obstacles in their way. The Ku Klux Klan, formed in 1866, was quite effective in intimidating blacks through threats, assault, and murder. The rate of lynchings increased during the 1870s despite laws passed to curb the Klan. The landlord-tenant system was less violent but no less effective. It reduced many blacks to a status resembling slavery because many black tenants were illiterate and could not recognize when they were shortchanged in their crop sales. In 1870 Tennessee passed a law prohibiting interracial marriages and five years later adopted the first "Jim Crow" law mandating separation of the races in public transportation. Tennessee's lead was followed elsewhere in the South by laws banning blacks from white hotels, barber shops, restaurants, and theaters. By the late 1800s most Southern states had passed laws banning blacks from most white establishments. By 1885 most states had laws requiring separate public schools.Literacy tests and poll taxes were developed to prevent blacks from voting. A series of civil rights decisions by the United States Supreme Court from 1873 to 1898 reinforced segregation including a decision to separate citizenship rights in the federal government from rights in the separate states to the "separate-but-equal" doctrine that sanctioned segregated public transportation facilities (*Plessy v. Ferguson*, 1896).[27]

> The educational system that did develop for blacks was, by 1885, legally separate from white schooling.

Despite the enormous obstacles, black education began to advance with the establishment of several educational institutions. S. C. Armstrong, a Civil War general and an officer of black troops, founded Hampton Normal and Agricultural Institute in 1868. While accepting segregation, he appealed for more normal schools to prepare a sufficient number of black teachers. He also advocated industrial education to build character and emphasized the acquisition of skills.

> The earliest higher education for blacks was aimed primarily at teacher training.

Booker T. Washington. Armstrong's doctrine found a ready apostle in Booker T. Washington (1856–1915), a young black student at Hampton who served as Armstrong's secretary. In 1881 Washington opened a black normal school in Tuskegee, Alabama, which was modeled on the Hampton plan. Students cooperated in the creation of Tuskegee by sharing all the tasks such as constructing the buildings and raising the crops. Washington believed that blacks had to convince Southern whites that an industrial education for blacks was in the interests of the South. He advised his students to cooperate with whites and to obey the law. He encouraged thrift, good manners, high morals, patience, and intelligent management of farms. Though he did not disapprove of a study of the liberal arts, he believed blacks would better benefit economically through the development of vocational skills and the cultivation of the soil. At Tuskegee teachers were prepared in agriculture, gardening, and carpentry as well as grammar and arithmetic.

Washington came to national attention after his speech at the Atlanta Exposition in 1895 and remained in the public eye until his death in 1915. In that Atlanta address he said, "In all things that are purely social we can be as separate as the five fingers, yet one as the hand in all things essential to mutual progress." Washington's proposals for industrial education were applauded by whites in both the North and the South, because many believed that these proposals would not dramatically alter relations between the races. They may have been right, but Washington knew that blacks, starting with so little, would have to work up gradually to positions of status and power.

W. E. B. DuBois. Offering a striking alternative to Washington's industrial education programs was W. E. B. DuBois (1868–1963), a black educator who studied at Fisk, Harvard, and the University of Berlin. He acknowledged that manual training was of value for all youth, but insisted that true education is not to make men carpenters, but to make them men. To do this, liberally educated teachers and leaders should be cultivated to instruct students and their families and to provide students with the intelligence and technical skill to be good workers. To develop such teachers, he said, black colleges should be established to educate The Talented Tenth (top 10 percent of the student population) to assume positions of leadership, for it is the exceptional man who will advance the condition of blacks. DuBois championed the study of liberal arts and the humanities to help blacks develop and cherish their own culture. He insisted on not only economic equality but also civil and political equality for blacks.

Black educators disagreed about whether blacks should receive primarily vocational training or a liberal arts education.

DuBois accused Washington of preaching the gospel of work and money to such an extent it overshadowed higher goals, and he objected to Washington's dismissal of higher education for blacks. The attempt to pacify whites, DuBois claimed, had simply further disenfranchised blacks and pushed their status even lower. DuBois joined Atlanta University in 1897 and left in 1910 to assume a leading role in the National Association for the Advancement of Colored People. In his later years he devoted himself to the idea of Pan-Africanism, a movement started by American and West Indian blacks near the end of the nineteenth century to promote the interests of all blacks.

For every three dollars spent for the education of whites in the South in 1900, two dollars were spent on black education; in 1930 seven dollars were spent on whites for every two dollars spent on blacks.[28] The majority of black children during the first half of the twentieth century attended impoverished schools that lacked adequate facilities and well-trained teachers. As blacks migrated to urban areas in search of greater economic opportunities, they moved to areas with larger tax bases in which some of the income could be made available to education. But by mid-century, the inner-city tax base areas had begun to decline as industry and the more affluent families migrated to suburban areas leaving the poor to fend for themselves. Many Northern states provided separate schools for blacks, especially whenever whites pressured school officials for segregation; yet some states—Ohio, Illinois, Indiana, and New Jersey—had both segregated and integrated school systems.

The number of black colleges has increased from one in 1854 to more than 100 today. These colleges are either privately endowed, church-related, or public. Blacks also have been enrolling in predominantly white colleges in record numbers since the mid-1950s. Other changes since the mid-century include the addition of black administrators in black colleges and in some predominantly white colleges, and the growth of black enrollment in graduate and professional schools.

Despite the "separate-but-equal" (*Plessy v. Ferguson*) decision by the United States Supreme Court in 1896, by the 1940s the constitutional edifice of Jim Crow began to fall with a series of decisions. The first decision came with *Mitchell v. United States* (1941), which declared that the denial of a Pullman berth to a black traveler violated the Interstate Commerce Act. A. Philip Randolph, a black leader, issued a call in 1942 to march on Washington. President Roosevelt, eager to prevent unrest, issued an executive order banning racial discrimination in defense industries, government, and defense training programs. In 1948 Randolph took a strong stand against segregation in the armed forces; later that year, President Truman acted to end such segregation.

In *Brown v. Board of Education of Topeka* (1954), the historic desegregation decision, the United States Supreme Court ruled that "separate-but-equal" was inherently unequal and could not be made equal. The next year the court proclaimed that desegregation should proceed "with all deliberate speed." Desegregation proceeded more quickly in the border states but, as expected, was resisted in the deep South. Federal marshals were stationed at the University of Mississippi, and the national guard arrived at Little Rock High School and the University of Alabama to protect blacks seeking to enroll. Resistance to desegregation also took the form of gerrymandering the school districts, offering tuition support to private white schools, and reducing funds to integrated public schools.

Through the rest of the fifties and into the sixties, the black struggle for civil rights intensified under the leadership of Martin Luther King, Jr. In 1964 Congress passed the Civil Rights Act, which outlawed discrimination in education, voting, and public accommodation. It also provided funds to the Department of Health, Education and Welfare to pursue desegregation of schools. The threat by the United States Office of Education to withhold federal funds to segregated school districts provided a strong incentive to desegregate. Federal district courts attacked de facto segregation in the North and South and required districts to devise acceptable desegregation plans. (For a sample of how blacks have fared in the post-segregation schools, see Chapter 9.)

■ PAUSE TO REFLECT

Minority Education

- How might history have been changed if all slaves had been allowed access to the same education as whites?
- Do you think the power of an education could have contributed to earlier emancipation? If so, how?
- What lessons can be learned from the effects of denying some groups a full education?
- How do you think the educational system should be structured regarding minority education? For example, if you think schooling should be customized for different cultures, explain what kinds of programs you would propose.

Mexican Americans

Mexico has a long history of occupation by and conflict with other countries, including Spain (which had converted most of Mexico to Christianity by the time of Mexico's independence in 1821) and the United States (which defeated Santa Anna in 1836). The latest conflict virtually ended in 1848 with the signing of the Treaty of Guadalupe Hidalgo, which ceded half of the Mexican territory to the United States. For $15 million the United States acquired title to Texas and land that later became California, Nevada, Arizona, Utah, New Mexico, and part of Colorado.

The Spanish-Mexican-Indian group living in those areas were given the choice of either maintaining their Mexican citizenship or becoming American citizens. Those who did not declare their intention to remain Mexican citizens automatically became American citizens after one year. Despite their official acceptance, however, these new citizens were generally viewed as a defeated, inferior people whose rights need not be taken seriously. In fact, it has been estimated that the number of Mexican Americans who were killed in violent ethnic encounters from 1850 to 1930 was greater than the number of blacks who were lynched during that period.

In California, New Mexico, and Texas, Mexican Americans often were cheated out of their property through dishonest land deals. In Texas, especially, where antagonisms were more intense than in other states, the legislature and local townships imposed heavy taxes and banks charged high interest rates that many Mexican Americans could not meet, forcing them to default on their property.

Mexican Americans often were relegated to hard, dirty, and poorly paid jobs in mining, agriculture, and the railroads. Whites dominated politics and in some areas, such as South Texas, imposed the same poll taxes and literacy tests on the Mexican Americans that had been used to disenfranchise blacks. Children were often forced to work in unsafe conditions and were denied adequate schooling and health care. What schooling they did receive was segregated and patterned after white culture—children were discouraged from speaking Spanish, for example.

> Early education of Mexican Americans was as segregated as that of blacks.

Policies of repression continued as economic opportunities attracted Mexican immigrants to the United States. These workers were encouraged by trade associations, chambers of commerce, and fellow workers to work hard for low wages without complaint.

In the public schools, Mexican American children were forced to abandon Spanish, encouraged to enter vocational programs rather than college preparatory studies, and to replace their cultural heritage with Anglo-American ways. Protestant missionaries continued the efforts to "improve" the Mexican Americans by divesting them of their Catholicism, folk culture, extended family arrangements, and the use of alcohol.

To avoid conflict with the Anglos, the first political organizations for Mexican Americans emphasized assimilation into the new culture. But as discrimination and repression continued, more and more Mexican Americans began to protest. The League of United Latin American Citizens (LULAC) was founded in 1927 to oppose discrimination and promote higher education. Cesar Chavez, a proponent of nonviolent social change in the spirit of Martin Luther King, Jr., diverged from King in pursuing economic improvement rather than civil rights. He is perhaps best known for organizing a California grape boycott in the late 1960s to appeal to the conscience of America.

> As had been the case with Native Americans, education of Mexican Americans distanced them from their cultural heritage.

Mexican Americans today make up the largest Hispanic group and the second-largest minority group (blacks make up the largest). More than 80 percent of Mexican Americans live in urban areas, and 84 percent live in five southwestern states: Arizona, California, Colorado, New Mexico, and Texas. California has the largest number of Mexican American residents, while New Mexico has the largest proportion.

Mexican Americans were segregated in school until after World War II. Segregation was justified with parochial arguments, such as Mexican Americans could not speak English well enough to participate effectively in Anglo schools, they needed to be Americanized before mixing with Anglos, and their "slowness" would hold back Anglo children. Because schools generally were monocultural until the 1960s and 1970s, public schools did not reflect the values, language, heritage, and teaching styles characteristic of other cultural groups. **Monocultural** means reflecting the traditions of only one culture, usually the dominant one in the larger society. Mexican American children, forced to live and learn in a strange culture, have tended to fall behind other students academically and suffer higher attrition rates than non-Hispanic students. Two innovations may help alleviate these problems: bilingual classrooms and multicultural education.

Bilingual education is designed to provide schooling in two languages to enable students to acquire proficiency in the second language while maintaining their proficiency in the first. This approach has gained popularity in American education, marked by the testing of several programs during the 1960s and the growth and spread of bilingual education during the 1970s.

Multicultural education is designed to help all students function effectively in more than one cultural world. It emphasizes ethnic literacy so that different groups, including the white majority, can gain an understanding of cultural differences. Through multicultural education, minority students would acquire not only social and economic skills but also skills to promote social change. We will discuss bilingual and multicultural education in more depth in Chapter 9.

Educational innovations offer some hope of better serving Mexican American students.

Summary

- Colonial education was heavily influenced by the European Reformation as well as unique conditions of American colonial life. Children were expected to do as they were told at all times and corporal punishment was used freely to enforce obedience.

- Elementary educational methods varied from the strict Calvinistic approaches in New England to the more tolerant but still religious approaches of the Middle Atlantic colonies to agrarian-centered schooling in the South. Slaves received rudimentary reading lessons to enable them to read the Bible, but in general, education for slaves was prohibited.

- After the American Revolution, common schools supported by public funds began to emerge. In the early eighteenth century, James Carter, Horace Mann, and Henry Barnard led reform movements against substandard teaching, high absenteeism, and public apathy toward state-supported schools.

- John Locke dealt the first blow to the Calvinistic approaches to education by suggesting that children were not born with original sin but rather were blank slates awaiting the imprints of experience. Further liberalizing views of the child led to expanded curriculums in the nineteenth century, including the study of one's own language instead of the classical tongues and a gentle, self-paced method of learning known as "unfoldment."

- As the population grew and textbooks like Webster's speller and McGuffey's readers gained popularity, the common schools began dividing classes into grade levels.

- The Massachusetts Act of 1647 provided for teachers and Latin grammar schools in most populated areas. These secondary schools reflected the influence of the European Renaissance: boys studied the classics to prepare for college and for service to church and state. Girls rarely were admitted to these schools, but some received private instruction.

- Benjamin Franklin's academy, established in 1751, de-emphasized the classics and focused more on practical subjects like English, handwriting, history, and arithmetic. Some academies were established for girls even though many people believed that girls did not need an education beyond the three *R*s.

- The English Classical School, founded in 1821, was considered to be the first American public high school. It prepared boys "to become merchants and mechanics." The Massachusetts Law of 1827 called for the establishment of high schools in populated areas, and by 1860, public high schools were common in most parts of the country.

- The liberal influences of Horace Mann and Andrew Jackson fueled the growth of egalitarianism in education, resulting in compulsory attendance laws and changes in the curriculum to make it useful to more students.

- The Committee of Ten, appointed by the National Education Association, recommended that high schools be structured as preparatory schools for college. The Commission on the Reorganization of Secondary Education, in the "Seven Cardinal Principles of Education," held that high schools also should serve the practical needs of individuals not attending college.

- Rapid increase in high-school enrollment as well as the desire for an interim program between elementary school and high school prompted the creation of junior high schools and, later, middle schools. These schools ministered to the special needs of children between childhood and adolescence.

- Several colleges were established in the early nineteenth century, reflecting their founders' belief in endless progress. The curriculum generally included Latin, Greek, and Hebrew, and corporal punishment was a favored form of discipline. As the years passed, colleges played down intellectual pursuits and emphasized more commonplace virtues. In opposition to this trend, the 1828 Yale Report advanced the *formal discipline theory,* which held that the mind required vigorous exercise through the study of difficult subjects like math and Latin. The popularity of the new sciences endured, however, and colleges continued to add them to their curriculums.

- Three kinds of higher education dominated in the late nineteenth century: *liberal culture* (emphasizing the study of modern languages through literature), *research* (especially in the sciences), and *utility* (emphasizing agricultural and mechanical arts).

- Higher education in the twentieth century has changed as rapidly as society itself. Today students can choose from a variety of curriculums at a variety of schools from private colleges to state universities.

- Teachers once were thought to have been born with the gift of teaching, but that belief eventually gave way to the realization that teaching is a complex procedure that requires thoughtful preparation.

- Organized teacher education began with the nineteenth-century *normal schools* and has evolved into the detailed programs we know today.

- Suggestions for improving teacher education have included establishing five-year college programs, increasing emphasis on practice teaching, developing higher entrance standards, giving more attention to the purpose of education, and instituting competency-based teacher education programs.

- The Holmes group and the Carnegie Task Force on Teaching as a Profession each issued influential reports on the state of education in the 1980s. The Holmes Report recommended a five-year college program, the abolition of undergraduate degrees in the specialized education fields, and the creation of "schools of professional development" to train teachers. The Carnegie Task Force called for restructuring teacher roles and school organization to attract more highly qualified people into the field and establishing a national board for teaching standards.

- American education historically has been aimed at white middle-class males, while minorities generally have been ignored or denied access to education of similar quality.

- Educational opportunities for minorities, especially Native Americans, black Americans, and Mexican Americans, have improved in the past few decades, but much remains to be done in that area.

■ Key Terms

acculturation

bilingual education

Calvinism

common schools

competency-based teacher
    education

dame school

deism

egalitarianism

Enlightenment

formal discipline theory

Great Awakening

massive transfer of training

meritocratic system

monocultural

multicultural education

Reformation

Renaissance

romanticism

tabula rasa

■ Discussion Questions

1. How did the establishment of the common school shape the direction of elementary education in America?

2. How did the leading reformers contribute to changes in elementary education and our view of the child?

3. Why did the colonists feel so strongly about the study of the classics? Why did they begin to decline in popularity?

4. What were some distinctive characteristics of nineteenth-century American education?

5. Do you think the wide variety of higher-education opportunities is desirable? Why or why not?

6. Assess the educational opportunities of other minority groups in America and compare their treatment to the treatment of the groups discussed here.

7. How has American education changed for the better since colonial times? How has it changed for the worse?

■ Learning Activities

1. From historical documents and library research, try to construct a history of your local school district. Do any patterns emerge similar to the ones we have discussed?

2. Take your research a step further by interviewing older majority educators and citizens in the community about their experiences

in school and whether they think their education was satisfactory. Compare their impressions with the historical information you collected earlier. What conclusions can you draw about the quality of education in the past few decades?

3. Write a biographical sketch of a leading educator presented in this chapter.

4. Interview members from two minority groups, asking them to recount their educational experiences. Were their needs met? Did they experience discrimination of any kind? How do they view the state of education for minorities today? What would they like to see changed?

Suggested Readings

Button, H. Warren, and Eugene Provenzo. *History of Education & Culture in America*. Englewood Cliffs, NJ: Prentice-Hall, 1983.

A study of education in relation to American culture.

Lazerson, Marvin, ed. *American Education in the Twentieth Century: A Documentary History*. New York: Teachers College Press, 1987.

Vital documents that shaped twentieth-century American education, from Booker T. Washington's addresses to *A Nation at Risk*.

Olson, James Stuart. *The Ethnic Dimension in American History*, 2 vols. New York: St. Martin's Press, 1979.

An exploration of the lives, achievements, and conflicts of many American ethnic groups.

Randolph, Frederick. *The American College and University: A History*. New York: Vintage Books, 1965.

A stimulating account of the development of higher education within a broad social perspective.

Spring, Joel. *The American School*, 1642–1990, 2d edition. New York: Longman, 1990.

Focuses on ideological, social, and political forces that shaped education.

Notes

1. "The New England Primer," in *Readings in Public Education in the United States*, ed. Ellwood P. Cubberley (New York: Houghton Mifflin, 1934), 51.

2. "Jonathon Edwards Describes the 'Children of Wrath,'" in *Education in the United States: A Documentary History*, Vol. I, ed. Sol Cohen (New York: Random House, 1974), 478.

3. Ibid.

4. "Instructions for the Punishment of Incorrigible Children in Connecticut (1642)," ibid., 370.

5. Ibid., 370–71.

6. Pickens E. Harris, *Changing Conceptions of School Discipline* (New York: Macmillan, 1928), 79.

7. Quoted in R. Freeman Butts and Lawrence A. Cremin, *A History of Education in American Culture* (New York: Holt, 1953), 68.

8. John Locke, *An Essay Concerning Human Understanding*, Bk. I, Ch. 2.

9. *Biennial Survey of Education in the United States, 1944–1946* (Washington, DC: U.S. Government Printing Office, 1949).

10. Wilfred M. Aiken, *The Story of the Eight-Year Study* (New York: Harper, 1942).

11. James B. Conant, *The American High School Today* (New York: McGraw-Hill, 1959).

12. Frederich Rudolph, *The American College and University: A History* (New York: Vintage Books, 1965), 21–22.

13. Lawrence R. Veysey, *The Emergence of the American University* (Chicago: University of Chicago Press, 1965).

14. See: Arthur E. Bestor, *Educational Wastelands* (Urbana, IL: University of Illinois Press, 1953); Mortimer Smith, *And Madly Teach* (Chicago: Henry Regenery Co., 1949); and Albert Lynd, *Quackery in the Public Schools* (Boston: Little, Brown, 1953).

15. James D. Koerner, *The Miseducation of American Teachers* (Boston: Houghton Mifflin, 1963).

16. James B. Conant, *The Education of American Teachers* (New York: McGraw-Hill, 1963).

17. Ibid., 209.

18. Charles E. Silberman, *Crisis in the Classroom* (New York: Vintage Books, 1971).

19. Ibid., 11.

20. W. S. Sandefur and D. Westbrook, "Involvement of AACTE Institutions in CBTE: A Follow-up Study," *Phi Delta Kappan* 59 (1978): 344–36.

21. The Holmes Group, *Tomorrow's Teachers: A Report on the Holmes Group* (East Lansing, MI: Holmes Group, 1986).

22. "Putting Teachers to the Test," *U.S. News & World Report* (July 21, 1986): 58.

23. Carnegie Forum on Education and the Economy. *A Nation Prepared: Teachers for the 21st Century: A Report on the Task Force on Teaching as a Profession* (New York: Carnegie Foundation, 1986).

24. "AACTE Decides Not to Support Teaching Board," *Education Week* (September 20, 1989): 1, 21.

25. Margaret Connell Szasz, *Indian Education in the American Colonies, 1607–1783* (Albuquerque: University of New Mexico Press, 1988), 11.

26. American Indian Policy Review Commission, *Report on Indian Education* (Washington, DC: U.S. Government Printing Office, 1976), 30.

27. These cases and their effects are presented in Henry Allen Bullock, *A History of Negro Education in the South, From 1619 to the Present* (Cambridge, MA: Howard University Press, 1967), 66–70.

28. John Hope Franklin, *From Slavery to Freedom: A History of Negro Americans,* 4th ed. (New York: Knopf, 1974), 415.

CHAPTER 6

PHILOSOPHY OF EDUCATION ■

The purpose of this chapter is to introduce selected issues and concerns in the philosophy of education so that you can begin thinking about them and developing your own philosophy. You will learn about:

- Basic philosophical systems of thought
- How a philosophy of education can be derived from those basic systems
- Examples of philosophies of education
- How theories of human nature can affect those philosophies
- Whether teaching is possible in light of some human-nature theories
- Whether the norms and values of society should influence education, or vice versa
- How to build your own philosophy of education

Some students question the need to study philosophy because they think it will needlessly delay getting on with the business of teaching. Besides, philosophy is considered impractical in a world where people are expected to get things done, not speculate about remote ideas.

But philosophy can hardly be called impractical in view of its effect upon civilizations. It has been claimed that everyone is either a Platonist or an Aristotelian thinker. Confucianism has vastly affected the everyday lives of the Chinese. The way we think today has been shaped by the various forms of logic developed by Aristotle, Mill, Russell, Whitehead, and others. Descartes developed analytical geometry and Leibniz and Newton created calculus. Marxism has transformed governments and directly affected the lives of billions of people.

The list is by no means complete, but the point is that philosophy may influence both thought and action, determine the way we live, and affect our sense of beauty and value. Theory may guide practice just as the results of practice may help to revise theory. Educators need a compelling framework to structure, make meaningful, and give a sense of direction to their experience. A **philosophy of education**—a justifiable belief system regarding education—provides guidance in making everyday decisions in the classroom.

■ WHAT IS PHILOSOPHY?

Philosophy seeks to understand reality and values.

Philosophy began in ancient Greece before the time of Socrates and, in essence, relies on *reason* to explain the world and human nature. It posed an alternative to other approaches to explaining and coping with life, such as myth, superstition, tradition, mysticism, and dogma. The philosophic quest, generated by a sense of profound wonder about human life, attempts to sort, sift, and analyze phenomena in an effort to discover or create, depending on one's perspective, a logical framework that explains our world and what takes place in it. Establishing such a framework—and even just the process of trying to—enables the philosopher to see life in broader perspective and with greater depth and meaning; it makes possible the systematic organization of human experience. The philosopher traditionally has raised questions about the individual and the cosmos: what is mind and what is matter? Why are we here? Does the universe have a purpose, or does it seem to have purpose only because of our imaginations? Is there objective truth (independently verifiable fact) and, if so, can one ever gain it? How do we determine what is good and what is bad? What is beauty and how can it be recognized?

Philosophy has been viewed in numerous ways. Plato envisioned philosophy as the search for ultimates: a quest to discover ultimate reality or the general causes of all things. Whether there is a reality higher than what scientific discovery provides is a philosophical issue. But other philosophers, such as John Dewey, have seriously questioned whether philosophy can provide such knowledge.

With the advent of modern science and the division of knowledge into numerous disciplines, some view philosophy's role as limited to areas not investigated by science or areas in which philosophers have special competence in gaining knowledge. Philosophy, as with other disciplines, has become more specialized. Although some philosophers still attempt to formulate major systems of thought, there has been an increase in the number of specialists who operate with greater precision on more limited problems. The older view that philosophy is a search for the meaning and purpose of life is not accepted by analytic philosophers, who reject the notion of the philosopher as a sage. They envision the philosopher as an analyst of language and concepts because all philosophical problems, they believe, arise within ordinary language and must be resolved there. But other modern movements, such as existentialism, consider "human existence" and "the individual" as the starting points for philosophical inquiry.[1]

Among philosophers there are disagreements about what philosophy can or should investigate.

Despite these differences, philosophy traditionally has accepted certain fields of study as integral to the discipline (see Table 6–1). Disputes arise over the relative importance of the fields, which ones should be included in a philosophical system, the acceptable methods of inquiry, and the purposes the inquiry is to serve.

Metaphysics is the investigation of the nature of the world or reality through reason. It seeks to go beyond physics ("meta" means "beyond" or "after") to discover what is ultimately real. Metaphysics usually develops systems of ideas about the nature of reality or, if our knowledge of reality is limited, metaphysics may provide a method for gaining knowledge. It attempts to present a comprehensive, coherent, and consistent account of reality. It may take the position that reality is *transcendent*, that it lies beyond experience (as in a supernatural world view found in some religions), or *immanent*, the idea that reality consists only of what is discovered in experience. Metaphysics deals

Field	Area of Inquiry
Metaphysics	Studies the nature of reality and being
Epistemology	Inquires about the nature, presuppositions, and scope of knowledge
Logic	Studies correct thinking or rules of inference to arguments
Ethics	Inquires into morally right conduct and the morally good life
Aesthetics	Analyzes standards and values in art and aesthetic experiences
Axiology	Studies the nature, status, and types of values

TABLE 6–1 Fields of Philosophy

with such topics as mind and body, freedom and determinism, fate, space and time, time and eternity, God, causation, being, and nothingness.

A metaphysician might ask, "What is the meaning of life?" An epistemologist would ask, "How do we (or even can we) know what the meaning of life is?" A logician would investigate and evaluate the thought processes of the two as they tried to answer their questions.

Another field of philosophy is **epistemology,** which inquires about the nature, source, meaning, and limits of human knowledge. The epistemologist wants to answer questions such as these: What is knowledge? What are its sources? How is it formulated and communicated? What are the differences among belief, opinion, and knowledge? Epistemology investigates such topics as skepticism, perception, knowledge and belief, truth and falsity, evidence and justification, and memory.

Logic is the study of correct thinking or rules of inference to arguments. It is concerned with rules by which inferences that entail their conclusions (A = B, B = C, therefore A = C) may be distinguished from premises that do not (every part of a machine is light in weight, therefore the whole machine is light in weight). Logic is systematic and formal. From an abstract pattern of inference, many particular inferences may use the same logical form (for example, from "No A is B" you can infer "No B is A"). Topics in logic include language (in terms of its use, informal fallacies, and definitions), deduction, induction, and scientific method.

Ethics inquires into morally right conduct and the morally good life. Ethics is divided into normative ethics and metaethics. **Normative ethics** is concerned with what people ought to do (Should one always tell the truth?) and with systems of ethics (such as Epicureanism, Stoicism, Kantianism, utilitarianism, and situation ethics.) **Metaethics** analyzes ethical language and the justification of ethical inquiry and judgments (for example, what is meant by the terms *good, right,* and *ought?*).

Unlike metaphysics and epistemology, axiology studies the nature of values and value judgments, not the nature of reality or our knowledge of it.

Another field that deals with values is **aesthetics,** which analyzes standards and values in art and aesthetic experience. An aesthetic attitude is primarily concerned with neither factual information nor the practical uses of things, but rather with the immediate qualities of the contemplative experience. Aesthetics seeks to identify the values of aesthetic objects and experiences; it attempts to determine the difference between aesthetic perception and other types of perception, such as scientific perception. Thus aesthetics is concerned with aesthetic objects, artistic form, critical analysis and evaluation, representation and meaning in the arts, artistic truth, aesthetic value, and the role of the arts in human life.

Both ethics and aesthetics are axiological studies. **Axiology** is the study of values to determine their origins, meaning, characteristics, types, and epistemological status. Axiological studies may include political, technical, prudential, and hedonic values. The field is concerned with whether values are objective or subjective, cognitive or noncognitive, absolute or relative, natural or non-natural, justifiable or non-justifiable.

Philosophical Systems

The great number of philosophical systems of thought can be explained by the complexity of both the world and human nature, the variety of possible plausible explanations of phenomena, competition among philosophers, the inability to definitively refute a philosophical system as one can refute false scientific claims, changes in outlook during different historical periods, and the discovery of problems that cannot be adequately explained by existing philosophies. Thus, through the centuries philosophy has developed many prominent and plausible schools of thought that compete for human allegiance and seek to become the prevailing mode of thought within a historical period. An overview and outline of the leading philosophies is presented in the following sections.

Idealism.   Idealism began in ancient Greece before Plato and extends to leading philosophers in the early part of this century. Those who subscribe to **idealism** perceive the world as essentially mental; it is composed of Mind, Spirit, or Idea. A philosophy whose metaphysics depict the world as comprising essentially one thing, mental or otherwise, is known as **monistic**. One monistic position is found in major religions that hold that the world is spiritual. These religions differ from idealism mostly in their epistemology: idealism believes that truth is gained through reason, while many religions look for truth in sacred works, charismatic leaders, oral traditions, faith, and revelation.

Idealism holds that the world is an idea.

Idealism has more than one form. **Subjective idealism,** as represented by George Berkeley (1685–1753), Irish philosopher and bishop, holds that matter does not exist, as physical things are ideas in the minds of perceivers. Only minds are real, including God's supreme mind. Thus, for Berkeley, "To be is to be perceived." The room you are in is there because you perceive it. Once you leave the room and no human mind perceives it, the room could go out of existence unless God perceives it. In other words, material objects are nothing but collections of sensation, and sensations do not exist if they are not experienced and perceived. Berkeley's philosophy, however, is in danger of succumbing to **solipsism,** the theory that no reality exists other than oneself, and that everything is the creation of one's consciousness. Berkeley attempts to avert solipsism and this form of mental isolation by claiming that God perceives nature and thereby maintains its order. But the problem still remains to prove God's existence and powers as well as the existence of other minds.

Subjective idealism, taken to the extreme, holds that the world is my, or your, idea. Objective idealism holds that the world is the Absolute's (God's) idea.

In contrast, **objective idealism,** as represented by German philosopher Georg W. F. Hegel (1770–1831), as well as other idealists, holds that truth is mental and objective. That which is real is manifested in, but transcends, human minds. The mental and spiritual character of existence is more comprehensive than finite minds. To know is to progress toward greater conformity with the Absolute Mind. Thus, solipsism has been avoided, but there is danger instead that the individual's identity finally will conform totally with, and therefore be absorbed into, the Absolute.

Not all idealists subscribe to monism. French philosopher René Descartes (1596–1650) adopted a dualistic view in holding that both mind and body exist. **Dualism** asserts the existence of two independent, separate, and irreducible realms. Descartes held that mind and matter are separate and cannot influence each other. Matter is extended in space and time; mind is unextended thinking spirit. God is absolute substance and the creator of mind and matter.

Idealists believe that reason, not the senses, perceives reality.

Idealist epistemology advocates **rationalism,** the belief that reason is the primary source of knowledge and is superior to and independent of sense perception. Though Descartes, unlike some idealists, believed that matter as well as mind exist, he was a rationalist in his approach to knowledge. One activity of rationalism is uncovering *a priori knowledge,* which is prior to and independent of sense experience. This can be illustrated by the German philosopher, Immanuel Kant (1724–1804), who believed that some knowledge of the world can be gained *a priori* by using the categories of our mind that structure our understanding. One category is cause-effect. Phenomena are possible only because the mind can order them in space and time, and the mind can know such phenomena through causality. It is necessary to have concepts of space and time for experience to be possible; these concepts are *a priori.* (An example of *a priori* knowledge is that if a = b and b = c, then a = c. *A priori* knowledge depends not on sensory experience but on the meaning of symbols.)

Relying exclusively on reason and logic can lead to well-drawn conclusions, but it does not provide a way of evaluating premises.

Idealism proposes the **coherence theory of truth** that claims a statement or belief is true if it is logically consistent with other statements accepted as true. The theory attempts to develop a systematic and coherent body of knowledge that presents as complete a picture as possible of absolute reality. Thus if a system accepts the propositions that God is spiritual and that humans are created in God's image, then it would be logically consistent to accept the statement that humans have spiritual qualities. Thus the strength of this coherence theory is its systematic, coherent, and logical nature. One weakness is that if some general statements are false, then any other statements based upon those general statements are also false. For instance, if our basic statement about the world is that it is flat and composed of pancake mix, then all other accepted beliefs about the Earth must be consistent with this statement (the Earth will taste like pancake mix or if one travels a great distance, one will fall off the Earth). Another weakness is that it does not test beliefs in experience but only in terms of their logical consistency and coherence.

As for a school curriculum, the idealist believes that it should be focused on the ideal concepts to which students should aspire. All subjects should have mental, moral, and spiritual value. The curriculum should emphasize liberal study rather than vocational and professional study, and should offer broad, general courses to avoid overspecialization.

One desirable method of teaching is the **Socratic method** by which a series of questions is raised, points of view are elicited, and some conclusions are drawn leading to a general truth or ideal. Socrates frequently raised questions about virtues such as piety, temperance, and courage, but his method can be used with other basic questions, such as "Can virtue be taught?" Imitation is another idealist method in that the teacher is expected to set a worthy example for students. The teacher also can employ inductive and deductive reasoning as well as use Hegel's dialectic of thesis-antithesis-synthesis to explain change. Marx used such a theory, for example, to explain how societies move from capitalism to socialism to communism.

Realism. Realism began with Aristotle (384–322 B.C.) and extends into this century. It conflicts philosophically with idealism, and idealists and realists frequently have sharp debates over their differences.

Realism, in contrast to idealism, holds that there is an external world that exists independently of the observer and is not dependent on the mind for existence. Thus material objects exist independently of our sense experience. The realist believes in **empiricism,** the idea that all ideas are derived from observation and experience and must be established by reference to experience alone.

Realists object to idealism for many reasons: if it were true that things cannot exist apart from one's consciousness of them, then neither can other persons; this points up a weakness in the solipsism theory. Second, many idealists believe that when we have sensations about the world, these sensations are dependent upon mind. The realist would argue that the idealist is confusing "sensation" as in the act of sensing with "sensation" as in the object that is sensed; in the former case it is mental, while in the latter it need not be so.

There is more than one form of realism. **Naive realism** is the belief that the world is the way we perceive it. No distinction needs to be made between the way the world seems to be (appearance) and what the world really is (reality), because our senses impart accurate information about the world. This is also the common-sense view. A moment's reflection, however, will indicate that people do not always perceive accurately or objectively: the straight stick seems to become

> Realism holds that the world exists on its own and is not an idea.

crooked when immersed in water; witnesses to the scene of an accident usually offer different reports of the details; two persons involved in an argument have different ideas about what occurred; to our perspective, the Earth appears flat and the sun moves around the Earth.

Representative realism, first developed by English philosopher John Locke (1632–1704), distinguishes between sense data and the objects they represent. The objects, or things known, are independent of the mind or the knower insofar as thought refers to them and not merely to sense data. Ideas (round, square, tall) represent objects. Locke claimed that primary qualities (such as shapes) represent the world, while secondary qualities (such as colors) have their basis in the world but do not represent it. Representative realism, in contrast to naive realism, can account for error in terms of our formation of inaccurate ideas or primary qualities about the world.

The basis for truth in realism is the **correspondence theory of truth,** which claims that a statement is true if what it refers to (corresponds to) exists. That to which a statement truly corresponds is called a fact. The process of finding correspondence is called verification or confirmation. "The purse is on the table" is true if it corresponds to the observed fact that the purse is sitting on the table.

An idealist or other philosopher could criticize the correspondence theory for certain reasons. Do our *beliefs* correspond with facts in the sense that they copy or resemble them? Suppose we believe that a particular poem is beautiful. Does our belief resemble the "beauty"? And what would that mean? Some general objections to Realism are that it diminishes the importance of the individual and can ignore aspects of human life and human knowing, like emotion and intuition, that exist outside of the strictly rational.

The realist curriculum would consist of verified knowledge and basic skills. The realist emphasizes accurate and impersonal knowledge about the world that would include an objective study of human civilization. The curriculum—a "subject curriculum"—would consist of natural sciences, social sciences, humanities, and instrumental subjects (logic, particularly inductive reasoning; languages; and mathematics). Only objective subjects would have a place in the curriculum and subjects appealing to the subjectivity of students would be excluded. Since the sciences stress objectivity more than any area, their role would be central in the curriculum. The realist would use a subject curriculum rather than an interdisciplinary one.

Realists employ objective, experimental, and observational techniques. In the school setting, they would draw their psychology from behaviorism and would advocate and promote the testing movement. The realist teacher would be clear, logical, and objective and, when needed, would study child and adolescent psychology to adapt materials to the learner.

A Naive Realist looks at a tree and believes that she sees the tree precisely as it is. A Representative Realist looking at the same tree believes that she does not see the tree precisely as it is.

Pragmatism. Pragmatism is a late nineteenth-century American philosophy that affected education and social thought. It differs, first of all, from most forms of idealism and realism by a belief in an open universe that is dynamic, evolving, and in a state of "becoming." It is a process philosophy, which stresses "becoming" rather than "being." This outlook found a sympathetic home in a rapidly emerging industrial society that tossed aside some of its inherited European traditions and sought to forge a new world. The emphasis on the process and the emergent nature of pragmatism was augmented by American philosopher and leading educator John Dewey (1859–1952). Early in his philosophical development, Dewey related pragmatism to evolution by showing how to view ourselves as creatures who have to adapt to each other and our environment. American philosopher and early psychologist William James (1842–1910) combatted monism and dualism with his theory of **pluralism,** which holds that the world is composed of many things. Dewey viewed life as a series of overlapping and interpenetrating experiences and situations, each of which has its own complete identity. The primary unit of life is the individual experience.

Charles Sanders Peirce (1839–1914), the founder of pragmatism, held that belief is a habit of action undertaken to overcome indecisiveness. He believed that the purpose of thought is to produce habits of action and that the meaning of a thought is the collection of the results of actions. For example, to say that steel is "hard" is to mean that when the operation of scratch-testing is performed on steel then it will not be scratched by most substances. The aim of Peirce's pragmatic method is to supply a procedure for constructing or clarifying meanings and to facilitate communication.

For his part, Dewey rejected the view that logic is the study of the formal conditions of valid inference and interpreted it instead as the comprehensive theory of how people solve problems by conducting inquiries. Inquiry is a process of developing means to reach desired ends, and logic is the empirical study of this process. Dewey divides inquiry into five stages: (1) the indeterminate situation, (2) identification of the problem, (3) determination of a problem-solution through hypotheses, (4) reasoning, and (5) construction of judgment.

As an example, Mary feels uneasy and apprehensive but is uncertain of the sources of her distress (Stage 1). Mary eventually locates the source of the problem as a low grade on her first history test and her concern to improve the grade on the next test (Stage 2). She hypothesizes that reading over her notes after every class and studying one-half hour each day will yield better results than cramming as she did for the first test (Stage 3). Mary then elaborates the meaning of her hypothesis and how she will test it (Stage 4). After receiving the results from her second test, she decides whether to accept or reject the

Dewey would expect students to work individually and in groups to solve meaningful problems.

hypothesis—probably on the basis of the grade achieved. If she does not accept the hypothesis, she must develop a new one and test it. But if this initial hypothesis is accepted, Dewey would call it a *warranted assertion* and use the word *judgment* for the settled situation described by a warranted assertion (Stage 5). Thus *warranted assertion* is a term used for Dewey's version of truth. The five steps are Dewey's pragmatic test for truth. For Dewey, truth is changeable and depends upon its confirmation by an investigator. There is no absolute truth. In a way, you could say that truth does not *exist*, but is made.

Life, according to Dewey, is development and development is growth. Growth is relative to nothing but further growth, and education is not subordinate to anything except more education. Education, Dewey says, is a continuous reorganization, reconstruction, and trans-

Many idealists and realists see the world's fundamental nature as constant; pragmatists do not.

formation of experience that adds to the meaning of experience and improves the ability to deal with subsequent experience.

Dewey sought the relationship between organized bodies of knowledge and the emerging interests and curiosities of children. He agreed with child-centered educators that, in educating children, one should begin with the children's interests, but differed from these educators by stating that one should connect these interests to what they ought to become interested in. The method of education should be the scientific or problem-solving method (outlined in terms of Dewey's five steps of inquiry). Dewey's laboratory school emphasized social occupations that represented human concerns about food, shelter, household furnishings, and the production, consumption, and exchange of goods. Four- and five-year-olds learned about preparing lunch before going home at mid-day; by the age of seven, the focus had shifted from occupations in the home and neighborhood to a historical approach that traced the emergence of occupations beginning with earliest culture; finally, by the age of thirteen, the emphasis had shifted to current events.

Dewey achieved a wide following, and his disciples referred to their philosophy as **experimentalism**. Some critics, however, objected to this pragmatic approach because it espoused relativism rather than absolute truths and values; these absolutes, they asserted, should constitute the curriculum. Other critics wanted to concentrate more on specific learning outcomes that are testable and measurable. Those who advocated home schooling rejected Dewey's conviction that schools could be sufficiently improved to become fully educative institutions.

> Pragmatists establish truth through experimentation. What their experiments seek to uncover are the consequences of actions—testing steel, changing study habits.

Analytic Philosophy.   A reform movement arose in Vienna during the 1920s and 1930s involving a group of mathematicians, scientists, and philosophers known as the Vienna Circle. The movement was directed toward achieving a scientific philosophy initially known as **logical positivism,** and later, **logical empiricism.** The logical positivists believed that philosophy should be reformulated. Epistemology could become part of the empirical sciences by studying how people organize, formulate, and verify knowledge. In contrast, metaphysical statements, which cannot be verified would be shifted to the arts along with ethics, because ethical statements mainly express feelings and emotions and also cannot be verified. When one says, "Don't kill," one is expressing one's emotions that killing is upsetting and one wants it stopped. Yet there is no scientific way to verify or prove whether this statement reflects a truth. Philosophy is therefore left with logic and the philosopher's task is to become a philosopher of science, the logical positivists say, because science is the only verifiable knowledge. The

> Logical positivists are not interested in speculating on matters that cannot be proven to be true.

upshot of logical positivism is that no ethical system can be shown to be better than another, and philosophers have no reason to raise momentous questions about the meaning of life that has engaged thinkers since the time of Socrates.

The logical positivist's theory of truth is based on the *verification principle,* which holds that "a statement has meaning only if it is verifiable." But must it be technically possible in the present to verify the statement? Consider the statement, "There is intelligent life in the universe beyond the reach of our most powerful telescopes." Verifying this statement empirically is not possible, but we still know its meaning. This formulation was later changed to the thesis: "A proposition has meaning only if it is possible to confirm it." The conditions are now less stringent. For instance, if there were ten conditions needed to verify a statement and only three had been discovered, then the statement has been confirmed but not verified; all ten conditions would be needed for verification. The latter process is known as logical positivism.

If, however, the earlier verification principle was too limited, the confirmation version was too broad because it admitted as meaningful such metaphysical statements as, "Either the sun is shining or the Absolute is imperfect." A more supportable approach was offered by Karl Popper (b. 1902), an Austrian philosopher of science who was not a member of the Vienna Circle. He saw the problem as not that of distinguishing science from metaphysics but science from pseudoscience, as metaphysical ideas are often the forerunners of scientific ones. Popper seriously questioned the use of induction by logical positivists and others. Theories are not developed by inductive procedures, he said; they begin as imaginative conjectures. Knowledge, then, is not a structure built up by inductive inference from passively received sensation. The process is conjectural and theoretical, a way of putting imaginative questions to the world to see if they can be falsified or refuted. Thus Popper proposed the construction of theories and the attempt to falsify them rather than the logical positivism approach of induction and the verification of propositions. When a hypothesis survives serious attempts to falsify it, it can then be provisionally accepted but never conclusively established (because science is an open system).

A second branch of analytic philosophy is **ordinary language analysis.** It was originated by Austrian philosopher Ludwig Wittgenstein (1889–1951), who renounced his earlier position, a form of logical positivism, and developed conceptual or ordinary language analysis in the 1930s. Since philosophical problems and puzzles arise in ordinary language, he said, they must be addressed there. Wittgenstein suggested that the study of language and concepts can be grouped together because they share a family resemblance. Some phi-

> Popper held that speculation and creating theories are important means of advancing our knowledge and that not being able to prove something false is a kind of verification.

losophers have tended to think of all languages as words whose "meanings" consist of the objects, ideas, or activities that the words "stand for" or "name." But this is only one function of language, a naming function. One learns to name things by pointing to the thing denoted and pronouncing its name. But merely learning the names of things does not teach us how to use them; we learn the meaning of a word by learning its use. There are language functions other than naming, such as reporting an event, giving an order, testing a hypothesis, telling a joke, solving a problem, and describing an object. To understand how to use a language is to understand how to operate by the rules embodied in various language functions. Moreover, for Wittgenstein, words have no absolute or ideal meaning but, at least in part, take their meaning from the linguistic context in which they are used.

Our basic educational concepts are framed in a variety of ways and also may be expressed in an ambiguous or conceptually confused fashion. Conceptual analysis seeks to identify the uses of terms in educational discourse and to observe and describe their linguistic movement. It also examines educational assumptions and the criteria and adequacy of arguments. After this primary analysis is completed, the conceptual structure is logically reconstructed to remove any source of possible perplexity and to render educational discourse more adequate for carrying its conceptual load.

Conceptual analysis studies meaning in language, not in the world beyond language.

For example, the meaning ascribed to the concept of equality is of great importance. Different interpretations may lead to different policies, provisions, and forms of treatment. Much discussion also centers on "freedom" and "rights," and each party may assume different meanings. As for teaching, many concepts are not always distinguished from one another: teaching, telling, indoctrinating, socializing, training, and conditioning, for instance. One function of philosophy of education is to overcome our conceptual muddles (by clarifying concepts such as teaching, learning, indoctrination, and equality) so that progress can be made in educational theory and in the improvement of policy and practice.

Conceptual analysis can be a useful preliminary step if language needs to be reformulated, but it is only a preliminary step. The philosopher of education also needs to study educational issues and problems in their context outside of language, as well as analyze the metaphysical theories and assumptions in education. The problem with conceptual analysis is not only its restricted scope but also its reliance on ordinary language itself, which is filled with ambiguities, inconsistencies, and illogical constructions. It also appeals to common-sense ways of thinking and speaking despite the weaknesses that science has demonstrated in common-sense views of the world.

Existentialism.   Existentialism is a European philosophy that originated with the Danish philosopher-theologian, Soren Kierkegaard (1813–1855), and likely reached its peak around World War II. One theme found in **existentialism** is a distrust of reason erected by philosophers since Descartes and the Enlightenment who believe that civilization will lead to higher levels of human progress. Existentialism insists that this claim of the Enlightenment is ill-founded because reason has been used not only to create but also to destroy. Existentialism exhibits a skepticism that any metaphysical system can adequately encompass, and account for, the variety and richness of human existence. These systems, existentialists contend, are remote, abstract, and academic in dealing with actual experiences and therefore have failed to confront the predicaments of existence that should be central to philosophy.

Existential issues seem to move to the forefront during extreme situations like war, terror, and brutality, when the belief in God might be shaken, and when the normative fabric of society is disrupted. In such situations, humans can become more acutely aware of their existence and their inability to anchor their beliefs. They begin thinking not in terms of abstract philosophical ideas but in terms of their own existence and what it entails. And this awareness of existence can lead in turn to an awareness of nonexistence. For French philosopher and playwright Jean-Paul Sartre (1905–1980), it is through human consciousness that nonbeing or nonexistence comes into the world. Nothingness is dependent upon being for its existence. The category of nonbeing is existentially real. Sartre believed that, cut adrift from metaphysical constructs, humans discover their freedom, and, in this freedom, humans discover nothingness. German philosopher Martin Heidegger (1884–1976) believed that it is through anxiety that humans encounter nothingness and develop an awareness of their mortality.

A cornerstone of existentialism is the idea that humans have absolute freedom to determine their lives. The existentialist makes these choices in the face of the enormous weight that this freedom entails.

Sartre saw no difference between being free and being human. This opens great possibilities; yet it also creates feelings of dread and nausea as one recognizes the reality of nonbeing and death as well as the great responsibilities that accompany such a radical freedom to shape oneself out of one's choices. Humans are condemned to be free; they are responsible for everything they choose. As awesome and terrifying as it might be, individuals must assume responsibility for their choices without recourse to shifting the blame to others or to institutions. It is through existential choices that individuals make their nature. Even an attempt to evade or flee the situation is a choice for which one must assume responsibility. Choice always goes hand in hand with radical freedom. Deliberation is governed by criteria which the individual chooses, such as a sense of obligation, but there is no rational ground for such choices. The criteria may be related to a way of life, but the way of life cannot be justified by reason or logic. One cannot provide a sufficient reason for his choice and in that sense it is baseless.

Between anxiety over choice and the dread of nonbeing, traps exist to snare humans and diminish their ability to become authentic persons who affirm themselves through choice. "Bad faith" is an example, which Sartre calls an individual's tendency to deny freedom even while using it. It is a form of lying—not to others but to oneself. Individuals deny to themselves what they are doing, as in the case of a person who makes amorous advances toward another, but denies or distorts to himself what he is actually doing. Heidegger found another danger to the ability to become authentic in "fallness." This is the universal tendency of individuals to lose themselves in present possibilities, thereby alienating themselves from future possibilities. Individuals retreat from their genuine selves, from their past and future through gossip, curiosity, and ambiguity. Gossip, filled with clichés and repetitions of the conventional, represents a restricted view. Curiosity, when engaged for novelty rather than understanding, turns away from authenticity. Ambiguity constitutes a singleness of purpose and a lack of comprehension that sacrifices the self to a preoccupation with the present. In the face of these ensnarements, humans must affirm themselves by seeking an authentic existence.

But what the individual can become is limited by nonbeing that is imminent from the time of birth. One frequently tries to cope with the recognition of death by objectifying and externalizing it, speaking of it as if it is something that befalls humankind in general. To become authentic, individuals have to recognize their own death, something they must face by themselves.

In Sartre's view, everything is contingent; there is no sufficient reason for things being what they are rather than something else. Humans live in a senseless world that they continually try to make sensible without finding any ultimate reason for the way things are.

The existentialist educator should be a free personality engaged in projects that treat students also as free personalities. The highest educational goal is to search for oneself. Teachers and students experience existential crises that involve an examination of oneself and one's life purposes. Education helps to fill in the gaps needed to fulfill those purposes; it is not a mold to which the student must be fitted. Thus the teacher should be aware of the life goals that students set for themselves. Students define themselves by their choices and the things that they make and do. They need to identify their own authentic selves and incorporate formal knowledge into their own individuality. In other words, to learn science is to transform it from formal theories, laws,

If you are an existentialist, your educational goal would be to know yourself.

and hypotheses into meaning in an individual's life. The teacher needs to understand the uniqueness of each student and help students examine their life's purposes. The humanities and fine arts have a central place in such a curriculum, not merely for analysis or appreciation but for revealing the great themes—anxiety, suffering, death—that one must face. The existentialist favors the Socratic method (see page 209) because it has the power to test the inner life. For example, an art teacher using the Socratic method insists that the student portray life as he or she sees it, not as the teacher or experts see it.

Even if you possess a sense of your authentic self, as an existentialist you can ultimately be left with no direction.

Existentialists emphasize the importance of choice in becoming authentic persons, yet claim that, ultimately, choice is baseless. But without a framework, criteria, and methodology for making choices, it is questionable that choices will be made wisely. By emphasizing irrationalism and subjectivity, existentialists leave choice without direction or guidelines.

Kierkegaard spoke of a dread of nothing in particular as though dread had an object named "Nothing." And Heidegger treated Being and Nothing as substantial entities. But the fact that we can use the words *nothing* or *nonbeing* does not give them the status of an entity that is as substantial as human being.

In their attempt to repudiate nineteenth-century materialism that rules out freedom and responsibility for action, the existentialists deny that there are causal explanations for action because they believe they would annul human freedom. However, one's decisions and actions can be part of the cause of future events. The opposite of "free" is not "caused" but "compelled."

The existentialist objects to large metaphysical and rationalistic systems as being remote and academic, failing to confront genuine problems of existence. But what existentialists do, especially Sartre and Heidegger, is to reject other systems and then load themselves down with the weight of rationalistic systems by constructing complex systems of their own. (For an overview of the five major philosophies, see Table 6–2.)

■ **PAUSE TO REFLECT**
Looking at Your Own Philosophy of Life

- As you read about the five philosophical systems presented here, you probably recognized some of your own beliefs among the examples. Try to put them into words. Which system of thought—or combination of systems—most closely fits your outlook on life? How do your beliefs affect your everyday life? Think about some of the decisions you have made during the past week or two. What guided those decisions?

TABLE 6-2 Philosophies

Philosophy	Reality	Truth	Curriculum	Teaching Methodology	Proponents
Idealism	Mental, spiritual	Coherence theory	Liberal study involving mental, moral, and spiritual values	Socratic method, imitation, dialectics	Plato, René Descartes, Immanuel Kant
Realism	Material	Correspondence theory	Verified knowledge and basic skills	Objective, experimental, and observational techniques	Aristotle, John Locke, Bertrand Russell
Pragmatism	Pluralistic	Pragmatic theory	Unified studies based on social problems	Problem-solving method	Charles S. Peirce, William James, John Dewey
Analytic Philosophy	Verifiable entities and conditions	Verification principle	Sciences, logical, mathematical, and linguistic studies	Scientific inquiry or conceptual analysis	Rudolf Carnap, Ludwig Wittgenstein
Existentialism	Subjective	Through individual choices	Arts and humanities	Individual projects in search of self	Soren Kierkegaard, Martin Heidegger, Jean-Paul Sartre

WHAT IS PHILOSOPHY OF EDUCATION? ■

Philosophy of education in the West began with the writings of Plato, but as in philosophy itself, philosophy of education is undergoing reexamination to clarify its role in the study of education. Of the numerous ideas about what exactly philosophy of education is, or should be, and how to approach it, several will be briefly discussed here.

A long-standing interpretation, with several versions, views philosophy as the parent discipline and views philosophy of education as connected to it in some way. Philosophy of education may be thought

Philosophy of education is not just a subfield of philosophy.

to derive its theories, problems, and methodology from philosophy. Education is a field in which the findings from general philosophy or the abilities of a general philosopher could be applied. In short, a philosophy of education can be derived from general philosophical systems, including recommendations for policy and practice. It has been argued, however, that the problems of philosophy are not those of education and that the philosopher with little or no knowledge, experience, and interest in education has scarcely any contribution to make to the study of education. Neither are there plausible grounds for believing that the material of education can be reduced to problems of philosophy if there are distinctive features in the study of education. Moreover, there may not be a logically necessary relation between a metaphysical system and education, though there may be other possible connections.[2] In other words, one may not logically infer a specific educational practice from the belief that the world, is, say, mental. But a psychological implication could be drawn so that teachers' beliefs could be inferred by their actions, and their actions implied by their beliefs. Consistency between beliefs and practices would be assessed not in terms of rules of inference, but in terms of human behavior in a means-end relationship. For example, a teacher who believes that human nature is basically good will behave benevolently toward students.

A second approach is more inductive. Philosophical positions can be discerned from case studies of the teaching process or from examining the assumptions underlying educational problems. The advantage of this approach is that it focuses on the phenomena of education rather than philosophy. But it also misleadingly assumes that a close, direct relationship exists between certain teacher activities and a philosophy of education. For example, that a language teacher uses drill to teach parts of speech does not necessarily tell us anything about the teacher's beliefs about the world or even about the teacher's beliefs about education and learning. Perhaps the teacher teaches this way because that is how he or she was taught.

Some hold that, although philosophy of education shared with general philosophy the right to pursue theoretical issues and problems without immediate concern, its inquiry should have some "practical" outcome.

A third interpretation holds that the purpose of philosophy of education is to develop a doctrine for organizing and prescribing the course for educational policy and practice. The point that a philosophy of education should have some bearing on the process of education is well taken, but it would stifle inquiry if every philosophical investigation had to relate directly to practice or lead to policy changes. Theoretical and metatheoretical studies (studies of theoretical and conceptual problems) may not have an immediate effect on practice; they may instead clarify meaning or provide criteria for constructing theory. To insist that they do have immediate effect may leave the philosophical and theoretical side underdeveloped.

A fourth view, which arose from the application of analytic philosophy to education, envisions philosophy of education as a study of the language and logic of education. The area of inquiry of such an interpretation includes studies of the use and misuse of basic educational concepts and the logic of educational arguments. Such studies are ultimately designed to improve educational research and to refine the conceptualization of education. Examples would be the development of more sophisticated research models of teaching effectiveness and the clarification of educational concepts such as different forms of equality. One need not deny the importance of such investigations to believe that philosophy of education is not limited solely to this function. To deny other functions, it would be necessary to show that on logical grounds they are impossible, that on pragmatic grounds they will fail to achieve the desired results, or that for prudential reasons it would be unwise to undertake them (for example, policy makers will ignore such studies).

Finally, some hold that philosophy of education is not a directive doctrine but a subject that promotes a liberal education. In other words, its purpose is to serve as a liberal and humane study that needs no justification on utilitarian grounds. It should assume a respected place in the pantheon of letters, arts, and sciences, revered for its potential to liberate individuals from the idols of the mind. In addition to those who doubt that philosophy of education possesses such powers, others charge that such a view promotes the abdication of philosophy of education's function to influence the course and direction of education and to help develop a discipline of education.[3]

The approach taken in this chapter is to view philosophy of education as having three dimensions: speculative, normative, and analytical.[4] The speculative corresponds to metaphysics that deal with the nature of reality, human nature, human experience, and the individual's place in the world. The normative dimension is concerned with moral education, values, aims, and the grounds of policy. The analytical pertains to the conceptual basis of education and deals with concepts such as "teaching," "learning," and "curriculum." Let us now examine some of the different philosophies of education.

Perennialism

Perennialism, an educational philosophy represented by proponents such as Robert M. Hutchins and Mortimer J. Adler, seeks to give new life to great ideas and truths of the past. It draws heavily upon the philosophies of Plato, Aristotle, and Aquinas and holds that the core beliefs of ancient and medieval culture apply directly to our own age. The term *perennial* may be defined as "everlasting," and the perennialist seeks everlasting truths. To discover these everlasting truths, it is necessary to apply the philosophies of these three great figures to our present day.

Turning to Aristotle, the perennialist suggests that to know reality, one must examine individual things and objects around us to find their essence. To find the essence, one must discard the particulars and search for the underlying essentials. The essence of human beings lies not in what they wear or what they like but in what they have in common—their ability to reason. Thus the search for an essence is the most important search that can be undertaken; it is a search for universality, or the most real form among elements.

In the search for truth, the perennialist is an Aristotelian realist rather than a Lockean realist. Though there is an external world independent of the observer, the quest is not for objects, events, and data but for essences. Some propositions are self-evident: they are unquestionable and cannot be improved upon. An example is the self-evidence of mathematical axioms; another is the principle of causality, from which the existence of God can be proven. (Through the observation of universal facts—motion, order—one concludes that God is the origin of these facts.) Thus the task of metaphysics, as Aristotle suggested, is the establishment of first principles. The discovery of truth is promoted by the laws of reasoning, such as found in the syllogism (all A is B, all B is C, therefore A is C).

Hutchins claims that the functions of a citizen may vary from society to society but every person has a function as a human being. There is a common human nature: humans are rational, moral, and spiritual beings and the development and improvement of that nature is the purpose of education. Humans are also free and, by nature, social. Schools should be concerned with the development of the intellect; moral and spiritual development is best left to the family and the church, yet all three institutions should work in harmony. The object of education is to know what is good for human beings and to place the goods in their order. This means that there is a hierarchy of values.[5]

Perennialists believe there are absolute, universal truths and that these truths are embodied in the Great Books of the Western world.

Perennialism seeks to provide a liberal education through a study of the Great Books of the Western world. Such programs were developed by Hutchins and Adler at the University of Chicago and by Stringfellow Barr and Scott Buchanan at St. John's College in Annapolis, Maryland, and Santa Fe, New Mexico. The St. John's program consists of a study of the classics for four years, beginning with the ancient Greek classics and moving through different historical periods until reaching the early twentieth century in the fourth year of study. Other instruction includes laboratory seminars, language study, music, and visiting lectures. These great works, say perennialists, embody absolute truths, represent the best that has been thought and said, and develop the reasoning powers. Other Great Books programs are found in adult education and in junior programs that induce the young to read and think.

Perennialism can be summarized in an assertion by Hutchins: "Education implies teaching. Teaching implies knowledge. Knowledge is truth. The truth is everywhere the same. Hence education should be everywhere the same".[6]

Not only could serious questions be raised about the claims of the premises; no logical connection exists among them. The process of formulating educational aims should be informed by the type of culture and the stage of society in which they will be used if they are to address cultural and educational conditions. Yet by stating aims as absolutes, they ignore varying cultural conditions. As for absolute truth, truths about the world (synthetic statements) are considered by science to be probabilistic, not absolute. Analytic statements ("All bachelors are men") are another form of knowledge but are unenlightening because they are redundant. In fact, according to P. F. Strawson, all we do when we say that a statement is true is to give our assent. For instance, if Smith says, "Jones' coat is gray" and you agree that it is true, you are not saying something further about the subject matter of the statement; instead of saying "true," you could just as easily say "yes" or "ditto." Thus to say that a statement is true is not to *say* something but to perform something, that is, offer assent or dissent.[7]

Perennialism holds that human nature is everywhere the same; yet today the social and behavioral sciences disagree about whether there is a common human nature and many different and sometimes conflicting theories have been proposed. Even if it could be established that there is a common human nature, it would be necessary to show that this nature is desirable and should be nurtured through formal education. Some also would disagree with Hutchins that formal education should be limited to developing the mind. Progressives would argue that education involves the whole person. Others would claim that the family, church, and other institutions have been derelict in their duties and therefore schools have to assume their responsibilities.

As for the Great Books, if absolute truth is thrown into question, the case for such studies is weakened. It may be said that this is the best way to develop the mind; however there may be simpler ways to do so without committing to a specific body of knowledge, such as trying to solve difficult mathematical and logical problems. It also may be claimed that such studies develop liberally educated persons, but that claim rests upon accepting the perennialist's idea of liberal education. Some of the great minds studied in the program—Goethe,

Some who disagree with perennialism hold that there are no universal truths about human nature. Others believe that, even if there are, education's mission in a society is broader than cultivating reason and includes such things as preparing people for the workforce.

Rousseau, Shakespeare, Whitman, and others—were not primarily educated this way. Moreover, students have begun protesting the Great Books program because non-Western authors, women, and minorities are neglected or underrepresented.

Essentialism

Essentialism was present in early American education, but it did not become an organized movement until the 1930s when it emerged as a reaction against progressivism. It became a dominant movement in the 1950s and 1980s and is represented by historian Arthur Bestor, Adm. Hyman Rickover, and William J. Bennett, Secretary of Education during the Reagan administration.

Essentialism is not linked formally to any philosophical tradition, though it is somewhat compatible with objective idealism and representative realism. It holds that both values and truth are rooted in and derived from objective sources. Our established beliefs and institutions are not only real but also true and good. Though they have flaws, these flaws are ones of judgment and are not inherent or irreparable.

Essentialism's goals are to transmit the cultural heritage and develop good citizens. It seeks to do this by training in the fundamentals, studying the basic subjects, developing sound habits of discipline, and learning to respect authority. Students cannot always study what strikes their immediate interest, but must study what they need to enable them to assume responsible adult roles. This means that sound study habits as well as discipline are stressed to master the fundamentals. Essentialists believe that essential knowledge is best organized and presented in a subject curriculum rather than weakened in broad curriculums or interdisciplinary programs.

Essentialism stresses teacher-centered education, order in the classroom, and student mastery of subject content.

The back-to-basics movement, which began in the 1970s and has continued into the 1990s, is a truncated form of essentialism because it focuses primarily on the three *Rs* and discipline, but it does not stress a full subject curriculum. Fundamental schools, which may be secular or religious, stress the basics, discipline (which may include corporal punishment and detention), competition, letter grades, standardized testing, homework, dress codes, and grouping students according to ability. Such schools also emphasize moral standards, courtesy, respect for adults, and patriotism. Other characteristics include teaching logical reasoning, one's history and heritage, government structure, and—in parochial schools—religion. Some proponents see their work as a struggle against "permissive education" to preserve values and transmit vital knowledge of the national heritage. Others view declining

Essentialists seek a structured learning situation in which the teacher is in authority.

test scores as a principal motivation for establishing fundamental schools. The back-to-basics movement is, in a sense, a move by lay-people for greater accountability in public education.

Bestor claimed that the public schools of the 1950s (the time at which he was writing) were not as effective as the schools even in the first decade of this century in teaching the basic disciplines. The progressives, he believed, had "watered down" the curriculum with life-adjustment education that failed to develop the mind or give one a grounding in the disciplines. Rickover, who also believed that schools had failed, believed European education could offer new models for American secondary education.

Bennett advocated a four-year high-school curriculum consisting of four years of English and three years of mathematics, science, and social studies. The curriculum would have a core of essential subjects and fewer electives.[8] At the elementary level, he urged helping and encouraging parents to participate in the education of their children.

The elementary school must teach every child to read, learn about the history and traditions of their country through the study of history, geography, and civics.[9]

While essentialism restores curriculum content, discipline, and authority, it has certain weaknesses. The curriculum is organized into disciplines according to the way scholars have developed knowledge rather than the way the young learn. Young minds might be more easily able to pursue interdisciplinary studies, enabling them to pursue ideas across many fields; they also could benefit from their natural curiosity, exploring direct experiences out of which inquiry can be initiated. Essentialism, with its emphasis on the teacher's authority, can degenerate into authoritarianism in which the teacher is viewed as an infallible source of knowledge and direction. Essentialists can rely on drill and rote learning; these practices not only make learning tedious for many students but also fail to promote meaning in learning, application of knowledge, or inquiry. While student discipline is rightfully emphasized, it is more externally imposed by teachers and school regulations rather than internally imposed through the strength of self-discipline. Essentialism focuses on the development of cognitive abilities and not on the whole person. Some educators, especially progressives, would consider that an incomplete and limited education. Essentialists may also have trouble motivating students because they insist on teaching certain things they consider important, regardless of students' immediate interests. Students cannot be interested in subjects, essentialists add, unless they know enough about them—and that takes discipline and hard work.

> Critics of essentialism contend that it does not pay enough attention to how students learn and are motivated.

Progressivism

Progressivism was a reform movement that provided an alternative to traditional education and sought to address the needs of a rapidly changing industrial society. It was part of a larger progressive movement in American society that sought to improve the lives of people by recognizing their individuality and encouraging self-expression. "Progressivism," according to Lawrence Cremin, "implied the radical faith that culture could be democratized without being vulgarized. . ."[10] The progressive movement initially consisted of child-centered educators (Francis Parker), pragmatists (John Dewey), and social reformers (Jane Addams); but by the 1930s the Progressive Education Association, founded in 1919, consisted mainly of child-centered educators and few reformers. The movement reached its peak in the 1930s, and by 1955 the Progressive Education Association had closed its doors. Nevertheless, by then, progressivism had had a considerable effect on American life and education.

Progressivism, differing from essentialism and perennialism, holds that the "whole child" should be educated, not just the mind. This meant that the social, moral, physical, and cognitive aspects of the child would be given equal weight (the spiritual side would be developed in parochial schools, the home, and the church). This greatly expanded the responsibility of the school, because progressives believed that education involves the total person: it is not just a mind that comes to school but the entire person, who must be nurtured and whose needs and interests must be met.

Progressive teachers are expected to assess the needs and interests of students in their classes and keep up with the latest findings in learning and human development. Assessment of needs and interests can be through a teacher's own observation or through the student's stated desires. The teacher's role is to guide learning and provide the needed resources, but not to lecture, promote drill or memorization, or wield authoritarian powers.

The curriculum seeks to fulfill these needs and interests by focusing on what children are interested in and using this material to fulfill their needs. If children are interested in boats, they can work together on projects making boats; in so doing, they can learn arithmetic by calculating dimensions, geography by discovering where boats travel, meteorology by studying weather conditions for sailing, fine arts by drawing sketches of boats, and literature by reading stories about boats. Children also learn to fulfill social needs by working cooperatively on projects.

Progressivism stresses child-centered education, a flexible and responsive learning environment, and hands-on learning.

The curriculum may be an activity or experience curriculum based on the assumption that children learn best through experience rather than subject matter—experience that is constructed from a knowledge of their needs and interests. The curriculum also calls for teacher-pupil planning in which teachers can ask children about their needs and interests. In working together, a problem-solving approach is used to determine tasks.

The progressives experimented with many different types of curriculums, all of which broke with the subject curriculum. The life-function curriculum was organized around persistent life situations: protecting life and health, engaging in recreation, satisfying the desire for beauty, securing education, improving material conditions. By studying persistent life situations and how related tasks are performed in society, specific plans for learning can be designed. Health needs, for example, consist of satisfying physiological, emotional, and social needs as well as learning to prevent and care for illness and injury.

Progressives rejected ability grouping and did not compare children except in relation to their own abilities. Extrinsic rewards usually were eliminated in favor of learning based on interest and motivation.

"Readiness" was carefully considered so that whatever was introduced into the curriculum was based on the learners' maturity and developmental levels. Pressure on students was avoided, grades de-emphasized, and cooperation encouraged.

The child-centered progressives were influenced by sense realism and romanticism. Drawing on sense realism, learning activities were usually approached inductively and were based on concrete experience before any generalizations were drawn. Progressive classrooms usually had many sensory objects—children's drawings, photographs of historical figures, bulletin boards, and science displays. Progressives believed in firsthand experiences that included frequent field trips.

As for romanticism, child-centered progressives held that the child is born basically good and should not be restricted in self-expression. Although they did not educate the child away from society as Rousseau advocated (discussed more fully on page 239), they did believe in nature study and becoming ready for learning. Pupil-teacher planning was promoted not only as a democratic procedure but also as a method that would improve learning outcomes.

One problem seen in child-centered education is that it can follow the child's lead to the point of neglecting the child's educational needs.

Some criticisms of progressivism were directed against Dewey (as noted earlier); but other critics targeted the child-centered group. Essentialists charged progressives with neglecting basic knowledge, failing to discipline students properly, insufficiently developing their minds, and failing to prepare them adequately for citizenship responsibilities. Essentialism also rejected romanticism and the romantic view of the child, believing that children did not learn naturally, but rather through considerable direction and discipline.

During the 1930s Dewey warned child-centered educators that they could not develop a philosophy by merely doing the opposite of traditional education: by trading external imposition for self-expression; external discipline for free activity; and learning from textbooks and teachers for learning from experience. The danger remains that child-centered progressivism will develop its philosophy negatively rather than positively and constructively.[11]

Both Dewey and the essentialists criticized child-centered progressives for their emphasis on student interest, but for different reasons. Where child-centered educators believed that the teacher should focus and build on the child's interest, the essentialists claimed that interest is a function of effort—that students could not be interested in something they knew little about and should exert considerable effort to learn about a subject and therefore become interested in it. Dewey agreed with the child-centered educators that teachers should begin with student interests but believed they should take the concept further by attempting to expand student interests through organized bodies of knowledge.

EDUCATIONAL ISSUE 6–1

Is essentialism a more worthy philosophy of education than progressivism?

Yes	No
1. Essentialism emphasizes transmitting national heritage and history, which should be the focus of public schools.	1. Essentialism ignores the "whole child," whereas progressivism emphasizes the social and physical development of a child as well as the intellectual.
2. Students should be taught discipline and basic academic subjects. Subject curriculums provide this focus.	2. Essentialist curriculums do not consider the social needs and special interests of the child; progressive curriculums do.
3. Essentialism provides basic education by emphasizing moral standards, high values, clear educational goals, and clearly defined roles for teachers and students.	3. Progressivism often encourages students to participate in the development of their own schooling, which can enhance the effects of their education.

Libertarianism

Libertarianism is a political philosophy, a small but growing political movement in the United States, and an educational philosophy with distinctive programmatic ideas. Its roots lie in anarchism, a political movement and philosophy that emerged in France during the nineteenth century. Anarchism opposes the coercive power of the modern state and seeks the maximum possible freedom compatible with social life. "Libertarianism," however, was not promoted as a synonym for anarchism until the 1890s.

Libertarianism opposes big government and its alleged interference in people's lives. Libertarians generally believe that public schools largely have been unsuccessful and that the rights of parents have been usurped in their children's education. Their central contention is that parents, rather than the state, should have primary responsibility for education.

John Hospers has stated some essential libertarian principles:[12] All human beings should be free to make their own choices as long as they do not interfere with the choices of others. In other words, all individuals have rights to their own lives and property and a duty to refrain from violating the same rights of others. It is through property rights that the individual's work is rewarded, goals can be achieved, and the future can be confidently planned. Rights are violated through the use of force, and government is the principal culprit. Therefore, the role of government should be limited to the protection of life, liberty, and property. Libertarians reject laws that require people to help one another, such as unemployment compensation, Social Security, minimum wages, and rent ceilings. And they usually oppose laws regulating pornography, alcohol, and drugs.

Some libertarians object to compulsory education. Paul Goodman, while seeing a need for compulsory education in the primary grades, is opposed to extending it to the high school.[13] He recommends that the funds for compulsory secondary education be turned over to youth to establish their own learning communities and free them to experiment with their own life styles and seek their self-identity. The funds also could be used to promote apprenticeship programs.

Ivan Illich goes further by recommending that compulsory schooling be abolished, the whole system be dismantled, and society be "deschooled."[14] He proposed instead that everyone have free access to information and tools needed in their lives. This would include access to museums, laboratories, and libraries; to apprenticeship programs; and to peer matching, a system by which each person would teach the other their particular skills.

Goodman and other libertarians, however, might have misinterpreted the coercive characteristics of compulsory attendance laws. Laws create obligations and embody standards. The standards then justify compulsion to comply with the law; therefore compulsion is a secondary rather than a primary factor in the way that laws function. Some talk about the state's coerciveness only in connection with laws of which they disapprove; because most Americans accept compulsory schooling, they would use the standard built into the law to criticize those who deviate from it.[15] It is a mistake to connect compulsory school attendance and the substantive results of schooling, because the legal requirement itself does not tell us anything about the content of education, the operation of programs, or teaching practices. There is no logical connection between the two and, if there is an empirical connection, libertarians have not pointed it out.

If compulsory attendance laws were to be abolished, certain social outcomes would be probable. Some who have profited from advanced schooling may favor the repeal of these laws, because the benefits of

Libertarians believe individuals should be free to make their own choices, including whether to educate themselves and how.

Compulsory education is not the root of school ineffectiveness.

schooling would be less widely distributed, and competition would be reduced.[16] The poor and disadvantaged likely would suffer the most should compulsory schooling be abolished.

As for Illich's deschooled society, he has no assurance that it would provide the learning environments that he proposes because the larger society itself would remain essentially unchanged. Schools are a reflection of their societies and the objectionable features that Illich found in the established educational system would not be rooted out by the disestablishment of schools: they still would exert their influences over youth through other institutions and agencies. Illich's own criticism of educational systems largely fails to distinguish the different levels of development and their attendant problems among educational systems in Europe, Latin America, and the United States. Thus he has essentially the same prescription for all.

The libertarian formula for freedom is workable in a world in which human desires and choices rarely conflict. To apply the formula in our world, where conflict and rivalry are hardened facts, would result in greater freedom for the strong than the weak, and no stable freedoms for anyone.

Reconstructionism

Reconstructionism emerged in the 1930s under the leadership of George S. Counts and Harold Rugg, and was later brought to fruition by Theodore Brameld. It recognized that progressivism had made certain advances beyond essentialism in teacher-pupil relations and teaching methodology, but it charged that progressivism had become fixated on the child and had failed to develop long-range, compelling goals for a society that, at the time, was undergoing great social, political, and economic transformations. The crises that gave reconstructionism its urgency were the Great Depression of the 1930s and the earliest dangers of nuclear annihilation in the 1950s. **Reconstructionism** called for a new social order that would fulfill basic democratic values and harmonize the underlying forces of the modern world. Advocates believed that working people should control institutions and resources if the world was to become democratic. Their aim was the development of an international democracy of world government in which all nations would participate.

An education for a reconstructed society would recognize the interdependence of the world's population (as in cases of ecological and economic problems). Thus students would need to study the realities of the modern world and recognize that they live in a global village. Teachers, therefore, would critically examine cultural heritages, explore controversial issues, provide a vision of a new and better world,

Reconstructionists view education as a vehicle for social and even global change.

and enlist students' efforts to promote programs of cultural renewal. They would attempt to convince students of the validity of reconstructionist beliefs but employ democratic procedures in doing so.

Critical pedagogy is a more recent educational philosophy that draws on neo-Marxism and promotes some of the goals of reconstructionism. Henry Giroux envisions radical teachers within and outside of schools who might develop educative practices outside established institutions. He views schools as potent vehicles for social change and wants them to participate in creating a new society. Key players in the drama would be teachers and students. The school would seek to unite theory and practice as it provides unified cognitive and affective characteristics (by linking the construction of school knowledge to the concerns of everyday life) that would liberate the individual and bring about social reconstruction.[17]

Giroux shows the dangers of the technocratic approach to education in which knowledge is standardized and intellectual work by teachers and students is superseded by practical considerations. He proposes that these dangers can be overcome by restructuring the nature of teaching so that teachers become "transformative intellectuals." Teachers no longer would be professional performers but free persons dedicated to enhancing the intellectual abilities of students.[18]

Although reconstructionism undergirds its beliefs and proposals by drawing upon findings from the social and behavioral sciences, the established empirical conclusions from these disciplines may well be insufficient for developing a planned international order. Thus many of their assertions lack sufficient scientific backing. Reconstructionists also have been accused of promoting indoctrination of students. While Brameld denies the charge, Counts insists the question is not whether "imposition" takes place in education, but from which source it will come. Rather than allow ruling groups or classes to impose ideas on society, say Counts and even somewhat less militant critical pedagogists, teachers should take the lead in helping to build a new social order. But, one might ask, is this an appropriate goal for education? Reconstructionism and critical pedagogy demand a commitment of the educator who in turn tries to bring about strong student commitment. It therefore assumes—probably erroneously—that a consensus can be reached on guiding ideals, goals, and values.

Another problem that arises from Giroux's critical pedagogy is how to bridge the gap between theory and the constraints of the classroom. Much of his writing treats the classroom as a theoretical entity and does not draw sufficiently upon the classroom studies of educational sociologists and ethnographers. A democratic philosophy also must involve the wider community and seek a consensus on the overall direction for public education; yet Giroux does not develop plans for doing so. The call for teachers to become "transformative intellectuals" is a limited aspiration insofar as teachers do not control public education and, as an occupational group, possess insufficient political or economic power to effect such large-scale change. Moreover, teachers as a body, though more militant than earlier in this century, have shown little interest in radical social change. Both reconstructionism and critical pedagogy overestimate the power of educational institutions to effect radical social change and neglect the need to first reconstruct society's political and economic institutions.

The approach used in the rest of this chapter raises and pursues certain basic philosophical questions about education. By "basic" is meant a definite groundwork and a starting point for inquiry. Some basic questions were raised in earlier chapters (as in Chapter 3 in terms of rights, responsibility, and freedom), and other basic questions will be raised in the next chapter (in connection with the concept and aims of education). These basic philosophical questions are designed to promote critical thinking and encourage you to reconsider your own position. The use of basic questions resembles the problems-issues approach but also can draw upon other systems to formulate the questions. (For an overview of the major philosophies of education, see Table 6–3.)

> Critical pedagogists overestimate teachers' control of the curriculum and also probably their willingness as a group to buy into the social agenda of critical pedagogy.

■ **PAUSE TO REFLECT**

Examining Philosophy of Education in Today's Schools

- Which philosophy of education do you think is most widely practiced in American schools today? How does it limit or enhance the potential of a school system?

- Do you think aspects of several philosophies could be combined to produce a superior approach to education? If so, what are those aspects and how can they be combined? What changes would occur in education as a result of this new philosophy?

PHILOSOPHICAL QUESTIONS IN EDUCATION ■

Human Nature and Education

How Do Theories of Human Nature Affect Education? This is the basic question with which we wish to begin. Unfortunately, our knowledge of human nature is not as extensive or as exact as our knowledge of the physical world.

T A B L E   6–3 Philosophies of education

Educational Philosophy	Supporting Philosophies	Aims	Curriculum	Teacher Role/Methods	Proponents
Perennialism	Platonism, Aristotelianism, Thomism	To develop rationality	Great Books	Use reading, Socratic method, and dialectics	Robert M. Hutchins, Mortimer Adler
Essentialism	Objective Idealism, Representative Realism	To transmit the cultural heritage and develop good citizens	Subject curriculum of fundamentals	Emphasize discipline, hard work, respect for authority	Arthur Bestor, William J. Bennett
Progressivism	Sense Realism, Romanticism, Pragmatism	To develop the whole person	Experiential and life functions	Guide, facilitator, and problem-solver	Francis Parker, John Dewey
Libertarianism	Anarchism	To free individuals to develop fully	Based on parental and learners' interests	Liberator and facilitator	Paul Goodman, Ivan Illich
Reconstructionism	Democratic Socialism	To reconstruct the social order	Social science focus	Enlist students in reconstructing society	George S. Counts, Theodore Brameld

Ideas about human nature have long played an integral part in theology, metaphysics, and political and educational philosophy. In religion, for example, Christianity has been influenced by the notion of original sin. Metaphysicians have had to consider the nature of being and the individual's place in the universe before they could formulate a systematic philosophy. Early political philosophers tended to establish the foundations of the state on their conception of human nature and the limitations they believed human nature imposed on human relations.

Ideas about what education is and should be are by necessity rooted in ideas about what people are and should be.

Educators, whether consciously or not, also operate out of certain beliefs about human nature, and specifically about the individual learner. Before schools can be organized and programs established, one must know something about the nature of learners—what they *are*, what they *can become*, and what they *ought to become*. One problem with this approach is the danger of committing the **naturalistic fallacy**. This fallacy, although it takes several forms, is that of deriving ethical statements from nonethical statements.[19] For instance, human beings possess the trait of rationality (nonethical statement); therefore, schools should seek to develop rationality (ethical or value statement). The problem here is that some other propositions need to be established before this conclusion can be reached. It is necessary to indicate that rationality is good (value statement), that schools should promote those good outcomes which they are most suited to foster (value statement), and that schools are, more than any other social institution, best equipped to promote rationality (empirical statement). However, the purpose of our inquiry is not to make education and its aims conform to human nature, rather it is to discover what in human beings can be effectively enhanced by the educational process.

Questions about human nature in education cannot be resolved solely with empirical findings, even though empirical and experimental studies of human nature have recently advanced on many fronts: biochemists have made strides in unlocking the genetic code; social scientists have provided greater understanding of social organizations and group behavior; and psychologists have ranged in inquiry from studies of unconscious forces, to the effects of conditioning, to viewing the organism as purposive and goal-directed. Educators operate with a set of values and aims, and interpretations of human nature provide only frameworks within which to view possibilities that one finds in different designs of the educational process. The educator is interested in the illumination provided by different interpretations and the educational consequences of acting on a particular interpretation. Even if widespread agreement existed today about human nature and what humans can become, these findings would provide only the outer limits of human capacities. They would not tell us which among the many possibilities humans *should* choose. The establishment of educational programs constitutes a set of decisions about what possibilities people should choose and pursue. The ramifications of these decisions are not always carefully considered, although they have considerable effect on the types of individuals a society produces.

> As educators, we need to think carefully about the connection between our ideas about human nature and our educational practice.

Is What We Become Predetermined?   Many who believe that there is such a thing as human nature hold that humans have an essence that is fully formed at birth. The Calvinists are among those who hold this belief. Others, like Aristotle, believe that essence is the essential nature of a thing that makes it what it is at any given stage in its development and makes it become what it will finally be (as a seed develops into a plant). In both these cases, and especially the first, one would have to question what role, if any, education could play in shaping the individual.

A behaviorist is more likely than a Calvinist to believe that schooling can have a major impact upon how a child grows up.

Still others altogether reject speculation about human nature. **Behaviorism** prefers to focus on overt behavior and to study it scientifically. Further, behaviorists believe that one's behavior is determined by environment, not heredity. To take an environmental viewpoint, rather than a hereditarian one, suggests that education can contribute significantly to the shaping of the individual. Although behaviorists reject an inquiry into the innate nature of humans, they do have a theory of human nature that is environmental, based on stimulus-response patterns of an organism that reacts to the environment (rather than acts upon it) and is readily conditioned.

Existentialist Sartre rejected the idea that essence exists in any form at birth. He believed that existence precedes essence.[20] Humans come into the world and then define themselves; and since there is no God to conceive a human nature, there is no human nature. Because existence precedes essence, humans are free to create their own essence. They also are responsible for it. Each person chooses and creates what he or she is to become. By choosing, we affirm the value of our choice and seek to choose the good. The individual is aware that choosing opens up certain possibilities. This realization alone directs choice; no god or innate program compels the individual to make a particular choice.

Though behaviorism and existentialism share the fundamental belief that what a person becomes is determined solely during life, the role each would see a teacher playing to help shape students is radically different.

Sartre's existentialism is in sharp contrast to behaviorism. One difference pertains to the implications for freedom. For Sartre, the premise that what individual human beings become is determined during life implies a radical, individual freedom, and an individual responsibility. B. F. Skinner (1904–1990), an internationally known behaviorist, would question whether free will even exists.[21] Sartre placed the cause of what a person becomes within that person. Skinner, on the other hand, placed it externally, in the environment. For Skinner then, the individual does not control who he or she becomes. And not having control, the individual, it follows, is not responsible for who he or she becomes. Not being responsible, the individual cannot experience the anguish and anxiety of choice as Sartre defined it.

Skinner believed that to make people happy, we need to make better use of the reinforcers we already have. And any new techniques of control should not involve punishment. Since we are always under the control of our environment, anyway, and since control in a utopian plan benefits the person under control, the individual need not fear control. Control can arise from accident or design, but it would be better to design it. As behavioral technology advances, it can be used to design cultures that reinforce desirable behavior.

Thus behaviorism proposes a hard determinism. **Determinism** holds that all things in the universe are governed by causal laws. **Hard determinism** suggests that one could not act other than the way one did. As with behaviorism, the individual is a reactive (rather than a proactive) organism that responds to and is conditioned by the contingencies of reinforcement in the environment, which would explain both desirable and undesirable behavior and do away with the need to appeal to individual responsibility. In contrast, the existentialist, especially Sartre, believes **radical free will** is necessary to become an authentic person. That free will includes a great range of human choices and total responsibility for one's choices.

In general, and especially from the educator's perspective, both behaviorism and existentialism have problems. Skinnerian behaviorism does not explain cognitive functioning and complex learning, especially language learning, where simple conditioning seems inadequate to explain how children acquire language. Additionally, behaviorism makes no allowance for goal-directed behavior that serves a purpose. In a behaviorist model, the educator assumes full responsibility for the education process.

While Sartre's existentialism provides much that behaviorism excludes—free will, choice, responsibility, and moral autonomy—it also has its shortcomings. Sartre and other existentialists often treat the exceptional as typical; moreover, the boundary between the two has been obliterated. That people experience anguish and dread is true, but it may not be a typical situation; yet, the existentialist builds his philosophy upon such situations. In addition, the idea of choice needs further scrutiny in terms of criteria for judging between true and false, right and wrong. Existentialism leaves this relationship largely unexamined. Sartre's ideas are conveyed largely in metaphorical form, such as that consciousness is "a decompression of being," which makes it difficult to submit them to any kind of empirical or pragmatic test for assessment. Finally, social and behavioral sciences would deny that a radical free will exists and would indicate many genetic and environmental factors that shape human choices.

Morality. Our views of human nature also affect how we view morality and influence the educator's treatment of the student. This can be seen by comparing a number of theories, some of which were presented in Chapter 5.

The Calvinistic beliefs in original sin and fatalism do not leave much room for religious and moral instruction other than instilling faith in God's will. **Fatalism** holds that all events happen the way they do no matter how we try to avoid or prevent them. Despite educational efforts, some people cannot be saved because God has predestined their fate. The child must obey parents and teachers simply because they command it. Showing obedience to one's earthly father prepares one for obedience to one's heavenly Father. The teacher is a parental surrogate, and severe punishment is to be inflicted on those children who fail to obey.

Thus our theories of human nature, valid or not, have educational consequences. As discussed in Chapter 5, Locke challenged the doctrine of innate ideas and questioned the belief in original sin. He substituted the view that the mind at birth is a blank slate to be filled by life experiences. Thus there is no original sin or morality at birth; morality, instead, is learned behavior.

Would Locke be likely to advocate teacher-centered or child-centered education?

The upshot of Locke's philosophy is an environmental view toward education. Whereas the belief in innate ideas required only a limited curriculum because many of the most significant ideas were already in the mind waiting to be drawn out, an environmental view such as Locke's believes a large curriculum is needed to fill the large slate. Usefulness is the basis for curriculum selection, as each study must make its contribution to adult life. The guiding principle is a "sound mind in a sound body." Education is a moral discipline rather than a process of intellectual instruction. The habit of self-control is of paramount importance to regulate inner impulse and desire. Locke sought to develop a person who would know how to act properly in society.[22]

Rousseau believed that the child is born basically good; it is society that corrupts.

Jean Jacques Rousseau (1712–1778), French philosopher and father of Romanticism, believed that the environment could have a significant effect on a child. However, unlike Locke, Rousseau believed that the child entered the world not as a blank slate, but with certain innate qualities and tendencies. In the opening sentence of *Emile*, Rousseau's famous treatise on education, he insists that "God makes all things good; man meddles with them and they become evil." Thus Rousseau believed in basic human goodness at birth. He also believed that humans are born free, but become entangled in the chains of corrupt institutions. One approach to removing these shackles was to educate the child (Emile) close to nature by removing him from society. Emile would grow up naturally as the laws of nature unfolded and he would not be forced to perform tasks before he was ready. Nature, Rousseau urged, wants children to be children before they are adults. Childhood has its own way of seeing, thinking, and feeling and it would be foolish to substitute adult ways. Here, the tutor is a facilitator of learning.

Progressive educators took to heart Rousseau's dictum that the child is born basically good. This meant that it no longer was necessary to impose upon the child stringent rules and regulations and exact harsh punishments for disobedience. Instead, the child could be permitted to develop naturally, to explore, and to create. To carry out these changes, the teacher would no longer be an unyielding disciplinarian and taskmaster; rather, the teacher became a facilitator of learning, one who arranged stimulating learning environments for students, working with them individually and in groups.

The connections found so far between human nature and morality are the suggestions that human beings are inherently evil (Calvin), neutral at birth (Locke), or inherently good (Rousseau). A fourth approach is a developmental one. Although Rousseau offered a rudimentary developmental theory consisting of four stages—infancy, childhood, preadolescence, and adolescence—that some have compared to the progress made in the history of the human race, contemporary studies have provided more substantial empirical findings to support a developmental approach.

Swiss psychologist Jean Piaget (1896–1980) conducted influential studies of both cognitive and moral development. Our focus will be on the moral studies.[23] Piaget held that morality consists of a set of rules and that all morality is based on the respect that the individual acquires for the rules. Most rules are developed by adults and then transmitted to children. Piaget studied the game of marbles, which had a set of rules amenable to psychological study. He observed both the ideas that children of different ages form about the character of game rules and the way they apply the rules.

Which would Rousseau advocate, child-centered or teacher-centered education?

Several stages were found in the consciousness and practice of the rules. In the earliest stage, which is motor and individual in character, the rules are primarily those that grow out of the child's early neuro-muscular development. Between ages two and five, the child imitates the rules of others, but either he plays by himself or he plays with others without trying to win. Thus he imitates rules but practices them according to his own fantasies. At this stage, the child regards rules as sacred and eternal, and any attempted alteration is interpreted as a transgression.

Between ages seven and eight, a less egocentric and more socially oriented outlook develops. The child now tries to win, and he also shows concern for the mutual control and unification of rules, although his ideas about them are somewhat vague.

Mastery of the rules proceeds by degrees and, between ages eleven and twelve, the rules of the game become fixed with a high degree of consensus. Children at this age enjoy discussing rules and the principles on which they are based. They recognize the need for mutual consent and the need to observe it; they also understand that a majority can change the rules. At this age, children's practices and attitudes toward rules closely resemble those of adults.

According to Piaget, to reason with children we must understand how they themselves reason.

In applying these findings to moral education, one needs to consider the child's conception of rule behavior at various stages of development. Thus practices that are effective at one stage will not necessarily be effective at another stage. Children are likely to reject moral reasoning below their level and fail to assimilate that which is above their level.

But some critics have questioned whether Piaget was actually assessing issues in moral development.[24] Piaget seemed unable to separate implicit questions of cognitive process, especially memory, from explicit moral issues. Young children typically experience difficulty in making inferences; yet Piaget's experiments require them to make inferential references. It also may be unwise to extrapolate from Piaget's experiments because they focus solely on stories and the game of marbles.[25] Though the child may appear to be gaining autonomy in some areas of rules experience, he may not have come that far in applying rules in other areas of life.

One significant problem is Piaget's equating of cognitive and moral ability. Growth in moral development may have more to do with the influences of experience than with intellectual abilities. Also one may question the existence and effects of inborn cognitive structures that form the basis of moral development.

A cognitive development theory by Lawrence Kohlberg (1927– 1987) is indebted to Piaget's pioneering work and Dewey's psychological writings. Kohlberg's studies have yielded six developmental stages allotted to three moral levels.[26] These stages are based on ways of thinking about moral matters. Kohlberg believed that a necessary, but not sufficient, condition for morality is the ability to reason logically. His theory, he claimed, is both psychological and philosophical, and his findings generate a philosophy of moral education designed to stimulate moral development rather than to teach fixed moral principles. Kohlberg believed that a philosophic concept of morality and moral development is required, that moral development passes through fixed qualitative stages, and that moral development is stimulated by promoting thinking and problem solving. Justice, Kohlberg said, is the key principle in the development of moral judgment.

Kohlberg sought to overcome the deficiencies of Piaget's research by using a much larger sample with a broader social base and equal proportions of popular and socially isolated children. He also was concerned with the principle of justice rather than simple virtue and vices and concepts like cooperation and equity.

Kohlberg admitted that he committed one form of the naturalistic fallacy: asserting that what moral judgments ought to be should rest on an adequate conception of what actually is. He claimed that it has been shown scientifically that there are universal moral forms centering on the principle of justice; science, therefore, can determine whether a philosopher's conception of morality accords with psychological facts. In turn, normative ethical analysis (analysis of moral concepts and moral statements) can show whether a particular moral philosophy can effectively handle certain moral dilemmas.

The educational applications of Kohlberg's theory have been to promote classroom discussion of moral issues to stimulate moral growth and to restructure the school environment so that students can participate in decision making by interpreting and enforcing school rules. An attempt is made in discussion groups to arouse cognitive conflict among participants and expose them to moral reasoning of a stage higher than their own. No separate courses are needed; rather, discussions of this type could take place in social studies, law education, philosophy, and sex education classes.

Carol Gilligan notes that Kohlberg found women, in light of their strong interpersonal orientation, to favor Stage 3 (where the child conforms to avoid disapproval), a stage he held to be functional and adequate for them.[27] She laments that the traits that have traditionally defined the "goodness" of women—their care and sensitivity to the needs of others—are those that mark them as deficient in moral development. She suggests that Kohlberg's scoring system may be biased against women because of the disproportionate number of males in the research samples and that the developmental theories themselves tend to be formulated by men.

Position	Human Freedom
Calvinism	Fatalism, Predestination
Skinner's behaviorism	Hard determinism
Piaget's and Kohlberg's moral theories	Soft determinism
Sartre's existentialism	Radical free will

TABLE 6–4 Human nature and freedom

It also has been suggested that the stages lack any necessary connection with moral action, and, therefore, what has been provided are stages of general cognitive, rather than moral, development.[28] Furthermore, Jack Frankel observes a contradiction in stage formulation: if the higher stages are better, they should contain something not found in the lower stages. If this is the case, however, how will those at the lower stages understand the arguments of those at the higher stages, let alone accept such reasoning as better than their own? On the other hand, if the higher levels are not more advanced, there seems to be no justification for helping the young move through the stages.[29]

Because of these and numerous other criticisms, Kohlberg's theory has stimulated much research, opening new ways of thinking about moral development.

Piaget and Kohlberg's developmental theories can be classified as a form of **soft determinism,** which recognizes causality and multiple causal forces, including one's own decisions. In terms of human freedom, human nature theories can be represented in Table 6–4.

■ **PAUSE TO REFLECT**
Your View of Human Nature

● To which theory of human nature do you subscribe? How does education today fail or succeed in reflecting that view? How could the field of education be rearranged to better reflect it?

■ IS TEACHING POSSIBLE?

It is commonly assumed that teaching occurs in millions of classrooms daily. Yet this may very well be a misleading assumption. Let us see why. First, we need to raise one basic question: is teaching possible?

It would seem that one necessary condition for teaching would be that the teacher possess the knowledge that is to be taught. If the teacher did not know what is to be taught, how would teaching be possible? But there is an even more fundamental question: is there such a thing as knowledge? Can one know anything? Everyone may entertain some doubts about some aspect of knowing at one time or another. One may question whether a particular method—faith, revelation, public-opinion polls—is reliable in providing knowledge. Others may doubt whether moral certainty or absolute moral standards can be established. Still others are **complete skeptics**; that is, they believe it is impossible to have knowledge of any sort. The Greek philosopher Gorgias propounded a complete skepticism. He doubted whether anything exists and argued that if anything did happen to exist, we could not know it. And even if we did know it, we could not communicate it. Thus, if we accept Gorgias's position, teaching would not likely be possible.

Complete skeptics do not present a general theoretical argument against the existence of knowledge. Rather, they seem to challenge particular knowledge claims, such as claims about the ability to remember or to accurately perceive the world, and then to deduce that we cannot know in general. It is easy to show the fallibility of memory by providing independent observers who could testify, for instance, that one's recollection of a past event was not accurate in every detail. As for perception, our senses often do not accurately record the world; for example, railroad tracks seem to merge as one peers into the distance. We know, however, that in reality they remain parallel. Having successfully challenged particular claims about knowledge, the complete skeptic then concludes that knowing is impossible.

What complete skeptics ultimately reject is the concept of objective knowledge, or at least humans' ability to possess it. For them, one's "knowledge" is subjective. This assumption informs their attempts to show that those who claim to know a thing in reality do not. A sensory report is challenged by another's contradictory sensory report. Similarly, complete skeptics question a particular conceptual framework by pointing out another's different framework. If knowledge were objective, it would be the same for everyone, would it not? Moreover, only one way of looking at a thing would make sense.

The complete skeptic is involved in a contradiction when asserting that knowledge is impossible because he is implying the truth of this statement and wants us to accept it. The true skeptic would not even assert as true that there is no truth. So, at least from the point of logic, only a particular, rather than complete, skepticism is possible.

Let us assume that some knowledge claims can be substantiated. Where does that leave us with our question: Is teaching possible? It would seem that so long as teachers communicate knowledge, teaching takes place. But what does it mean to communicate? And how does one know when communication has occurred?

> Teaching, as we usually understand it, implies the teacher's communicating knowledge to the student.

Augustine held
that teachers do
not teach—as we
often define that
action—but re-
mind a student of
what he already
knows.

Augustine (354–430), an early father of the Roman Catholic Church, philosopher and Christian theologian, confronted the question of how teaching is possible.[30] In a dialogue with his precocious son Adeodatus, Augustine directed attention to the assumption that teaching is accomplished through speech. He began by exploring whether speech exists to teach or remind; that is, whether words provide new information to the listener or simply call up information the listener already possesses. Augustine believed that one "learns" a thing only after recognizing that it refers to a reality one already knows. Thus, by hearing the names of things, one recalls images in the mind. For example, the word *dog* calls up the image of a dog in the mind of the listener. For someone who had never seen a dog the word would not mean anything. It could further be argued that this phenomenon holds true not only just for objects and their names (couch, chair, pencil, teacher) but also for discussions of concepts and abstract ideas. For example, if you, the reader of this book, understand the discussion of the relationship between the word *dog* and its effect on a listener, I did not teach you this. It made sense to you because it fits your experience. I simply brought your attention to something you already knew. What the teacher does then is help pupils see or discover what they already know. At best, the teacher's words remind pupils to consult the truth that already resides in their minds. And parents do not send their children to school to learn the teacher's thoughts; rather, parents send their children so that teachers can help the children understand what they already know.

If nobody teaches it to them, how do students come to possess this knowledge? Each of the philosophies we have discussed to this point would have their own answer to this question. Empiricism would hold that experience in the world provides it. Plato believed that ideas are innate. For Augustine, truth and knowledge are in each person through divine illumination. By his doctrine of illumination there resides in each of us an interior teacher, who is God himself.

Even if one does not accept Augustine's doctrine of illumination, one still can appreciate his explanation of communication and its implication for our understanding of our question, is teaching possible? Augustine would not necessarily answer this question with a no, but he would disagree with what we usually think teaching is.

Which kind of
relationship
would Locke ad-
vocate? How
about the other
thinkers we dis-
cussed in the last
section?

If we accept Augustine's view of how communication works, the relationship between student and teacher must undergo a fundamental, psychological shift. If the teacher has knowledge that he or she gives to the student, the student-teacher relationship is necessarily hierarchal, with the teacher standing above the student. On the other hand, if the teacher helps students understand what they already know and the teacher believes that this is the role he or she plays, the teacher-student relationship becomes less hierarchal. The teacher and student, who "know" the same things, stand on the same level. And the teacher does not instruct but facilitates.

Carl Rogers explored this relationship between teacher and student and felt it to be a much more fruitful area of inquiry than the one we are currently pursuing: is teaching possible? Though Rogers did not question that a person could pass knowledge on to someone else, he believed that "teaching" is a highly overrated function.[31] Rogers stated that he was not interested in instructing another. For imparting knowledge or skill, he believed that books and program materials would be more efficient. Moreover, he was not interested in assuming the role of causing someone to know something or of showing, directing, or guiding another. According to Rogers the real goal of education should be the facilitation of learning. He saw the teacher-student relationship as the key to accomplishing this goal. Rogers held that certain interpersonal qualities needed to be present between the facilitator and the learner if the facilitation of learning was to occur. The two must meet in a direct personal encounter without erecting facades. The facilitator also must care for the learner in a non-possessive way, prizing the learner's feelings and opinions. The facili-

Carl Rogers believed that teachers should function as facilitators of learning rather than as authority figures.

tator should try to understand students from their own point of view, without evaluating or judging them, and should manifest toward them empathetic understanding.

■ **PAUSE TO REFLECT**
Is Teaching Possible?

- After considering the points of view in this section, do you think teaching is possible?

- Do teachers "teach" or merely "facilitate?"

- How would you design a course based on Augustine's belief that students "learn" by being reminded of something they already know?

- How would you set up a classroom based on Carl Rogers's goal of facilitating learning?

■ HOW DOES EDUCATION RELATE TO THE LARGER SOCIETY?

An educational system cannot help but play a role within the larger society. In some cases that role is determined in part by a society's political and economic systems and by what a society's leaders expect the school to accomplish. In some nations the school is controlled by a particular group or power elite and is used to perpetuate the values and ideologies of that group. But even in democracies, power is unevenly distributed, and it is not uncommon for some groups to have a disproportionate influence on the schools.

A society's schools usually reflect the interests of the most powerful groups in the society.

Often the educational policies of these groups are meant to promote or support the group's interests. For example, when societies are in the midst of change that has the approval of those in power, the schools can be used to accelerate and direct the change toward preconceived ends. On the other hand, if the changes prove disruptive and threatening to those in power, they are likely to use the school to provide stability by teaching patriotism and the virtues of the old order.

The role of a school can be questioned when a society undergoes change. Take as an example, a rapid expansion of knowledge and the resulting increase in the number of specialties and disciplines. Even though the schools are unlikely to be able to fulfill immediately all the demands arising from the knowledge explosion, a society confronted with these innovations may expect its schools to introduce new programs for developing special skills, such as driver training or computer programming. Moreover, a period of great change has an unsettling effect on people, because their cherished values and accepted ways of behavior are seriously questioned. At such times the role of the school becomes confused and ambiguous as numerous voices express different goals and values. The usual conflict in such cases centers on whether education should re-emphasize eternal truths and cultural traditions or concentrate on new values and behavior.

Several positions exist on the relation of education and society; four major positions are presented here.

Isaac L. Kandel (1881–1965), an early leader in the essentialist movement and comparative studies in education, believed it necessary to inquire why societies establish schools.[32] The most persistent reason is to conserve and transmit the cultural heritage to the young and to equip them with the traits and ideals that will enable them to promote the stability and perpetuation of society. Thus the school is an agency for promoting stability and adapting the individual to the environment. Should the school fail in its performance of this function, society either stagnates or is taken over by the elite.

Students, Kandel said, should be taught to understand the world in which they live and to understand controversial issues. The school also should provide students with an unbiased picture of the changes occurring in society and let them form their own opinions of these changes. Schools cannot, however, educate for a new social order, nor should teachers use the classroom to propagate doctrine. The history of education, Kandel insists, shows the impossibility of schools' playing such a role, for society establishes schools to sustain itself through the teaching of prevailing beliefs. Change occurs first within society, and schools follow the lead. However, a more reciprocal relationship can be established between school and society wherein schools develop in students the knowledge and understanding needed to create enlightened citizens.

> Kandel believed that schools cannot shape society other than indirectly by producing citizens capable of directing society.

Pragmatist Dewey believed schools have an important role in producing social change.[33] The question is not whether schools can influence society but whether they influence it blindly or intelligently. The society that a school reflects is constantly undergoing change, often without a single, clearly defined direction. Because they do not take a leadership role, schools too often simply respond to social conditions that are in a state of disorder. But in what direction should schools guide society? Educators can study the newer scientific, technological, and cultural forces that are effecting changes, estimate their direction and outcome, and determine how schools can promote or fight the changes depending on whether the changes are considered beneficial. Thus schools will need to develop in youth the insight and understanding they need to participate effectively in a changing society.

> Dewey and other thinkers who follow in this section, held that schools, if they want to, can directly facilitate social change.

Brameld differs with the previous authors on this topic with his reconstructionist philosophy.[34] Writing during the height of the Cold War, he insisted that we live in one of the greatest periods of crisis in history. But we also are approaching an opportunity to develop a life-affirming world civilization of abundance. Yet neither teacher education nor liberal arts is adequate because neither is directed by a philosophy of education geared to a world in crisis. Nor are they aware of the revolution in the behavioral sciences. Every educational system should help diagnose the causes of a world in crisis and help the young cope more effectively. It also means that education should reconsider its purpose and study new ways of formulating goals, organizing subject matter, and improving teaching. Brameld notes that a unified theory of man is emerging, embracing broad social-service concepts like culture, that should integrate fields of knowledge. This means that systems of education can be reconstructed using substantial new knowledge by which human goals can be formulated based on cross-cultural and even universal values.

Samuel Bowles and Herbert Gintis offer a position that is related to Brameld's reconstructionism but has more of a neo-Marxist tone.[35] They claim that a correspondence can be found between the social relationships of economic life and the educational system. They label their approach a "dialectical humanism," through which they explore the tension between individuals and their environments. This tension can be found especially in the educational system in terms of resolving the conflict between the reproductive needs of society and the self-actualizing needs of students, as these needs often do not agree. Thus within this tension is a struggle for both security and freedom. The contradiction between the individual and the community is mediated by informal institutions—churches and armies, guilds and factories, peer groups and town meetings. In American society the school has assumed a major role in fulfilling these functions, and schools that deny this role are hypocritical, say Bowles and Gintis. The dissident teacher should convey to students the truth about society, they say, and demonstrate that superior alternatives to capitalism exist. To carry out this strategy, teachers and students should press schools and colleges to develop a participatory democracy in which all interested parties could pursue their own interests and rationally resolve conflicts. The struggle should seek to undermine the correspondence between educational institutions and capitalism. Revolutionary educators must develop a dialectical educational philosophy (one that seeks a new synthesis, as between the individual and the community) and lead the creation of a unified class consciousness that allies itself with the working class. Socialist educators should strive for open enrollment, financial aid for needy students, and the development of antidiscriminatory and socialist content of education.

In retrospect, Dewey, Brameld, and Bowles and Gintis differ from Kandel in that education is no longer viewed exclusively as a conserving function for society but can serve as an agent of change. Yet significant differences exist in how they view education's role in this change. Dewey's approach is more open-ended and less definitive, leaving it to educators to observe, develop, and test hypotheses, and explore new relationships and directions in education. Brameld is more concerned with the imperious crisis with which we are faced and the available, but neglected new knowledge that will help create a new world order. Bowles and Gintis depict a correspondence between educational institutions and capitalism and seek to overcome this alleged connection to build a form of democratic socialism.

■ **PAUSE TO REFLECT**
Determining Society's Role in Education

- Where do you think education fits into society? Should it be a reflection of society's norms and values at the moment? If so, how can education fulfill this function and still maintain independence from groups who seek to influence curriculum for their own ends?

- Or, do you think that schools should take the lead in shaping or redirecting society? If so, who should decide the path society should take? How can we ensure that educators do not become the new "elite" with dangerously concentrated powers of influence?

BUILDING A PHILOSOPHY OF EDUCATION ■

Now that we have explored some philosophical responses to basic questions, you may wonder how to begin developing your own philosophy of education. Having a personal philosophy of education would be personally and professionally desirable, of course, but it also can help you in job interviews when you are asked about your educational philosophy.

The first step is to determine what you believe about education. The focus here is not on detailed beliefs, such as which chalk is the best, but on basic questions about education, some of which were raised in this chapter. Others are explored in the next chapter and elsewhere in this text. The first step is to list basic questions drawn from this chapter and Chapter 7, leaving sufficient space under each one to write what you presently believe in response to each question. This still is not your philosophy; it is only a starting point. What you will have created upon completing this exercise is a credo, or a statement of beliefs. But you need to become fully conscious and articulate in expressing your beliefs about the basic questions. So, the next step is to uncover sound reasons or evidence to support these beliefs. At this point it may not be easy to find the support you seek for your beliefs. To move beyond this sticking point, begin by consulting the ideas of leading educational philosophers (Chapters 6 and 7 and the Suggested Readings). There is no reason that you should not profit from specialists who have devoted many years to these questions. This will enable you to modify, amplify, and reconstruct your belief system and rationale. After that, you will need to organize it into a system that is connected and logically consistent. Although you may borrow ideas from various educators, it is important that your ideas be consistent. The order would start with the most general and abstract statements, as well as the questions that must be answered first because they form the basis for subsequent questions. The most general statements refer to the entire educational system; the more specific statements refer to a particular level of schooling or a subject. For example, a question about why one should choose a teaching career depends upon first answering the question whether teaching is possible. And a question about what should be the content of the curriculum must be preceded by asking about the purposes of education. This overall process is illustrated in Figure 6–1.

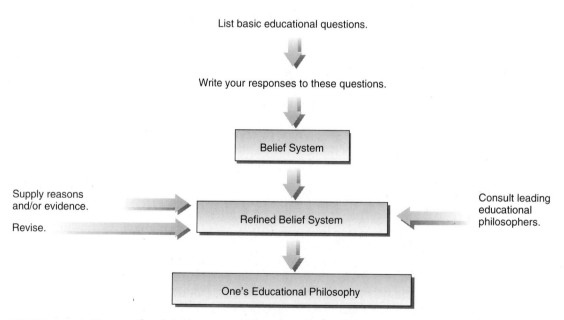

FIGURE 6–1 Process for developing a philosophy of education

■ Summary

- Philosophy has been viewed in several ways: as a quest for ultimate reality, an enterprise designed to develop a science of man, a search for the meaning and purpose of life, an analysis of language and concepts, and a study of human existence.

- Philosophy of education also has been envisioned in different ways: as the application of philosophy to education, the use of case studies from which philosophical principles can be drawn, a system for prescribing educational policy and practice, a study of the language and logic of education, and a subject that promotes a liberal education.

- Philosophy of education has three dimensions: speculative, normative, and analytical. The methodological approach used in the chapter is the analysis of basic educational questions.

- The topic of human nature can be related to education in terms of its effects on freedom and morality. Positions on freedom include radical free will (Sartre), hard determinism (Skinner), fatalism (Calvin), and soft determinism (Piaget and Kohlberg). As for morality, the views consist of original sin (Calvin), neutrality (Locke), and essential goodness (Rousseau).

- The question of whether teaching is possible arises from the theory of complete skepticism, which holds that it is impossible to have knowledge of any sort; from Augustine's studies, which question whether communication can occur without shared beliefs, and from Carl Rogers's assertion that teaching is a highly overrated function.

- The role of the school in relation to the larger society is discussed in four major positions: essentialism (Kandel), pragmatism (Dewey), reconstructionism (Brameld), and neo-Marxism (Bowles and Gintis). Though significant differences exist among the four positions, the first position views the school as a follower of society and the latter three see it as an agent of change.

- Developing an educational philosophy requires beginning with basic educational questions, stating one's beliefs about these questions, providing reasons or evidence for those beliefs, studying other educational philosophies, refining belief systems, and then organizing them coherently.

■ **Key Terms**

a priori knowledge
aesthetics
axiology
behaviorism
coherence theory of truth
complete skepticism
correspondence theory of
    truth
critical pedagogy
determinism
dualism
empiricism
epistemology
essentialism
ethics
existentialism
experimentalism
fatalism
hard determinism
idealism
libertarianism
logic
logical empiricism

logical positivism
metaethics
metaphysics
monistic
naive idealism
naturalistic fallacy
normative ethics
objective idealism
ordinary language analysis
perennialism
philosophy of education
pluralism
pragmatism
progressivism
radical free will
rationalism
realism
reconstructionism
representative realism
Socratic method
solipsism
subjective idealism

■ **Discussion Questions**

1. Which philosophical system of thought is most defensible? Give the reasons or grounds for your choice.

2. What are the functions of philosophy of education? How does it attempt to perform these functions?

3. Which of the five philosophies of education is most plausible and supportable? Explain why.

4. Why does the topic of human nature play an important role in education? Give examples of a system of education that could be developed to fit each theory of human nature presented in this chapter.

5. What do you think is the appropriate relationship between school and society? Define your position.

6. Why is it important for educators to develop their own philosophy of education? To what extent have you begun to develop yours?

■ Learning Activities

1. Review college catalogs and school district publications for a stated philosophy of education. Where stated, assess the adequacy of the philosophy. If a philosophy is not stated, try to infer what philosophy underlies the school's programs and policies.

2. Ask teachers in your local school district to discuss their philosophy of education.

3. Organize a debate in class on Sartre's view that "human nature" does not exist.

4. Review the progress you have made in developing your own philosophy of education. What else do you need to do to develop it to your satisfaction? When you are finished, show it to a classmate or your instructor and ask for constructive feedback.

Suggested Readings

Chambers, John H. *The Achievement of Education.* New York: Harper & Row, 1983.

An introductory analysis of educational concepts and issues, ranging from indoctrination to discipline and rights.

Dewey, John. *Democracy and Education.* New York: Macmillan, 1966.

Dewey's most complete statement of his educational philosophy.

Kneller, George F. *Movements of Thought in Modern Education.* New York: Wiley, 1984.

A critical summary of educational ideas in today's leading philosophical movements.

Ozmon, Howard A., and Samuel M. Craver. *Philosophical Foundations of Education,* 4th ed. Columbus: Merrill, 1990.

A systematic presentation of contemporary and traditional systems, including Eastern philosophies.

Peters, R. S. *Essays on Educators.* London: George Allen & Unwin, 1981.

Penetrating essays about leading educators along with a statement of the author's own influential position.

Russell, Bertrand. *Wisdom of the West.* New York: Crescent Books, 1989.

A clear, concise, and colorful introduction to Western philosophy by a leading twentieth-century philosopher.

Ulich, Robert, ed. *Three Thousand Years of Educational Wisdom,* 2nd ed. Cambridge, MA: Harvard University Press, 1963.

Original selections from Plato to Dewey, including Asian and Islamic sources.

Notes

1. Different viewpoints are presented in: *The Owl of Minerva: Philosophers on Philosophy,* eds. Charles J. Bontempo and Jack Odell (New York: McGraw-Hill, 1975); and *What Is Philosophy?* ed. Henry W. Johnstone, Jr. (New York: Macmillan, 1965).

2. Joe R. Burnett, "Some Implications of Philosophic Theory for Educational Theory and Practice," in *Proceedings of the Fourteenth Annual Meeting of the Philosophy of Education Society* (Lawrence: University of Kansas Press, 1958); and Hobart W. Burns, "The Logic of the 'Educational Implication'." *Educational Theory* 13 (1962): 53–63.

3. For other views and trends, see Christopher J. Lucas, *What Is Philosophy of Education?* (London: Macmillan, 1969); and Karen E. Maloney, "Philosophy of Education: Definitions of the Field, 1942–1982," *Educational Studies* 16 (1985): 235–58.

4. William K. Frankena, "Toward a Philosophy of the Philosophy of Education," *Harvard Educational Review* 26 (1956): 94–98.

5. Robert M. Hutchins, *The Conflict in Education* (New York: Harper & Row, 1958), 67–76.

6. Robert M. Hutchins, *The Higher Learning in America* (New Haven, CT: Yale University Press, 1936), 66.

7. P. F. Strawson, "Truth," in *Meaning and Knowledge,* eds. Ernest Nagel and Richard B. Brandt (New York: Harcourt, Brace & World, 1965), 160–66.

8. William J. Bennett, *James Madison High School: A Curriculum for American Students* (Washington, DC: Department of Education, 1987).

9. William J. Bennett, "First Lessons," in *Taking Sides,* 5th ed., ed. James Wm. Noll (Guilford, CT: Dushkin Publishing Co., 1989): 174–82.

10. Lawrence Cremin, *The Transformation of the School* (New York: Knopf, 1961), ix.

11. John Dewey, *Experience and Education* (New York: Macmillan, 1938), Ch. 1.

12. John Hospers, "What Libertarianism Is," in *The Libertarian Alternative,* ed. Tibor R. Machan (Chicago: Nelson-Hall, 1974), 3–20. Also see Hospers's *Libertarianism* (Los Angeles: Nash Publishing Co., 1971).

13. Paul Goodman, "What Rights Should Children Have?" *New York Review of Books* 17 (1971): 20–22.

14. Ivan Illich, *Deschooling Society* (New York: Harper & Row, 1971), Ch. 1 and Ch. 6.

15. Michael S. Katz, "Compulsion and the Discourse of Compulsory School Attendance," *Educational Theory* 27 (1977): 179–85.

16. Gerald M. Reagan, "Compulsion, Schooling, and Education," *Educational Studies* 4 (1973): 1–7.

17. Henry A. Giroux, *Ideology, Culture, and the Process of Schooling* (Philadelphia: Temple University Press, 1984).

18. Henry A. Giroux, "Teachers as Transformative Intellectuals," *Social Education* 49 (1985): 376–79.

19. Although G. E. Moore coined the term, the example used here is closer to the form pointed out by David Hume.

20. Jean-Paul Sartre, *Being and Nothingness* (New York: Washington Square Press, 1975); and his *Existentialism* (New York: Philosophical Library, 1947).

21. B. F. Skinner, "Utopia through the Control of Human Behavior," *The Listener* (January 12, 1967): 24–29.

22. John Locke, *Some Thoughts Concerning Education* (London: Cambridge University Press, 1934).

23. Jean Piaget, *The Moral Judgment of the Child* (New York: Free Press, 1965).

24. Joseph L. DeVitis, "Cooperation and Social Equality in Childhood: Adlerian and Piagetian Lessons," *Journal of Research and Development in Education* 17 (1984): 23.

25. Hugh Rosen, *The Development of Sociomoral Knowledge: A Cognitive-Structural Approach* (New York: Columbia University Press, 1980), 35.

26. Lawrence Kohlberg, *The Philosophy of Moral Development: Moral Stages and the Idea of Justice* (San Francisco: Harper & Row, 1981).

27. Carol Gilligan, "In a Different Voice: Women's Conception of Self and Morality," *Harvard Educational Review* 47 (1977): 43–59.

28. C. M. Beck and Others, eds., *Moral Education: Interdisciplinary Approaches* (Toronto: University of Toronto Press, 1971), 355–72.

29. Jack R. Frankel, "The Kohlberg Bandwagon: Some Reservations," in *Moral Education: It Comes with the Territory,* eds. D. Purple and K. Ryan (Berkeley: McCutchan, 1976), 291–307.

30. St. Augustine, *Concerning the Teacher (De Magistro),* trans. G. C. Leckie (New York: Appleton-Century, Crofts, 1938).

31. Carl R. Rogers, "The Interpersonal Relationship in the Facilitation of Learning," *Humanizing Education: The Persons in the Process,* ed. Robert R. Leeper (Washington, DC: Association for Supervision and Curriculum Development, 1967), 1–12.

32. Isaac L. Kandel, *Conflicting Theories of Education* (New York: Macmillan, 1938), 77–88.

33. John Dewey, "Education and Social Change," *The Social Frontier* III (1937): 235–38.

34. Theodore Brameld, "Imperatives for a Reconstructed Philosophy of Education," *School and Society* 87 (1959): 18–20.

35. Samuel Bowles and Herbert Gintis, *Schooling in Capitalistic America* (New York: Basic Books, 1975), 18–20.

■ CHAPTER 7

■ PART FOUR

SCHOOL AND
SOCIETY ▪

E ducational institutions are intricately related to the larger culture. The larger society creates the institutions and designs them to promote individual development and to serve society politically and economically. In Chapter 6 we discussed what the role of the school should be in relation to the larger society, but this section takes a different approach. We will place education within the framework of the larger culture by exploring the nature of culture, how cultures shape the individual, how cultures change, which cultural values are relative, and which are universal. Are individuals little more than the product of their cultural norms, or do they have the power to develop their individuality through freedom of choice? The school itself can be considered a subculture in which dominant cultural values are transmitted and sanctions are imposed on those who do not comply. The individual is further shaped by socialization, which begins in the home and continues in other social systems such as school, the job site, and the military.

In Chapter 8 we will look at these broad processes and at how communication, both linguistic and nonverbal, is involved in the socialization process. The way we think and conceptualize the world is partly determined by the language we use in terms of its grammatical and generative forms. We will explore the distinctions that are made in some languages but not in others, as well as different concepts of time, space, and number. We also will discuss how nonverbal communication supplements language by conveying attitudes and feelings and how it can conflict with verbal communication by betraying any insincerities in the verbal message.

In Chapter 9 we will discuss the crucial need of teachers to understand the different backgrounds of their students. Students' social class backgrounds affect their attitudes toward schooling and largely determine their value systems. Researchers in the past have advanced many spurious claims about the influence of race on academic achievement, and teachers today must assess carefully any such claims. They must also assess what policies schools should adopt regarding ethnic differences, the possibility of multicultural education, and the treatment of females.

In Chapter 10 we will look at different theories of education, including aristocratic systems, which offer education only to an elite group; meritocratic systems, which educate according to demonstrated achievement; and egalitarian systems, which offer education to all students regardless of performance. We will discuss the effect of the civil rights movement on equality in education and consider the effects of desegregation plans.

■ CHAPTER 8

CULTURE, COMMUNICATION, AND EDUCATION ■

A LOOK AHEAD

The purpose of this chapter is to show how broad cultural forces shape each individual's thoughts, actions, and potentialities. You will learn about:

- How culture helps shape the individual in a society

- How individuals become functioning, responsible members of society through the process of socialization

- The continuing debate about how children should be socialized

- How schooling fits into culture and socialization

- The role of schools in a pluralist society

- How education fits into a society's culture

- How verbal and nonverbal communication reflect a society's culture

- The use of bilingual education to preserve home languages and cultures

Much of what we think and do is the result of many years of social and cultural influences. We often are not conscious of the enormous effect these influences have on our lives. They shape our personalities and our value systems; they determine which language we use and how we use it; and they help determine how we relate to and function in the world around us. Culture even defines such fundamental aspects of our reality as our conception of time. For example, Americans think of time as fixed, an ever-present part of the environment. However, in Latin America time is less important and treated rather cavalierly: one hears the expression "our time is your time." In the Middle East everything beyond the present is placed in a single category or "future." Americans tend to think of the future in terms of the immediate future, whereas the future of the South Asian may involve centuries or an endless period. For the Navajo only the here and now is quite real, and Sioux have no word for time.[1]

Every culture has a multitude of **cultural traits,** the smallest unit of a culture that can be listed and described. The use of a stone ax to develop tools, the exchanging of gifts by bride and groom, and the shaking of hands when greeting someone are all cultural traits. Combinations of these traits form distinctive patterns that distinguish one culture from another.

SOCIETY AND CULTURE ■

A **society** develops when people form a group that is self-sustaining, has a definite geographic location, endures over time, shares a way of life, and is held together by the pursuit of common values embodied in that way of life. What these people create, in the broadest sense of the word, is their culture.

Every society has its ways of dressing, cooking, eating, raising and educating children, forming relationships, dividing labor among its members, and governing itself. These "ways" constitute a society's culture. A **culture** is a pattern of human behavior (including thought, speech, and action) shared by a group of people. It also includes the artifacts produced by those people. And, because a culture is passed from generation to generation, it depends upon the human capacity for learning and transmitting knowledge.

Culture sometimes is divided into material culture and non-material culture. *Material culture* consists of the artifacts, tools, clothing, housing, and technology created by a society—in other words, it is the objects a society makes and the methods it uses to make those objects and to sustain its material existence. *Non-material culture* consists of a society's values, belief systems, norms, ideologies, mores, and folkways. The young are taught appropriate behavior and belief systems and are told how the culture expects them to live their lives. The non-material culture determines the sacred and the profane and es-

A culture's capacity to endure depends on its members' ability to learn and to transmit knowledge.

tablishes desired personality traits and the dominant values to guide the life of an individual—for example, whether one should be materialistic or non-materialistic, individualistic or devoted to the group or clan, democratic or autocratic, religious or secular, benevolent or self-centered, egalitarian or elitist.

Socialization

Instilling cultural values is a fundamental aspect of socialization.

Socialization is the process by which individuals acquire the knowledge, skills, and behavior to make them functioning, responsible members of society. Individuals also learn culturally appropriate roles for their age, sex, and social class. By instilling roles, socialization processes help preserve social institutions. These processes differ from "education," which is usually designed to improve individuals and society by providing requisite knowledge and reflective abilities. Curric-

Through socialization, parents introduce their children to the stimulation of books.

ulums, particularly in public schools, reflect this distinction, though less so in the early grades, which emphasize the acquisition of skills and a rudimentary knowledge of the cultural heritage.

The chief socializing agents in our society are the family, schools, peers, and the media (see Table 8–1). Parents and guardians are the most important socializing agents during the years before school, followed—in varying order and degree of influence—by siblings, other relatives, playmates, and the media. Parenting chiefly involves socialization rather than education. Families do provide some degree of education, but their primary functions during early childhood are nurturing and socializing children to perform social roles such as son, daughter, or friend. The performance of a role depends upon knowledge, ability, and motivation; therefore, parents who are most effective in consciously directing this process let their children know what is expected of them, require them to do what they are actually capable of doing, and foster in them the desire to practice the appropriate behavior. Parents also need to practice what they preach. Parents who tell their children to consider other people's feelings but are frequently rude probably will find their children imitating what they do, not what they say.

Once children enter school, authority figures (educators) join in the socialization process. Ideally, other groups and institutions complement and reinforce the basic value system acquired in the family. But, as we saw in Chapter 4, peers and significant others (such as media personalities) tend to have more of a socializing influence on adolescents than do parents and teachers. When the influence of peers contradicts the influence of parents and teachers, conflict arises. Complementary value systems are more likely to be found in small, relatively homogeneous communities than in large metropolitan areas.

Socialization also takes place in other social systems—in college, on the job, and in the military, for example. When one starts college or takes a new job, one has to learn the rules and social expectations of the system. Young adults are socialized not only by authority figures but also through organizations and mentors. In a ten-year study of forty men using a multidisciplinary approach, Daniel Levinson and his

Parents cease to be the major socializing factor when children enter school.

TABLE 8–1 Socializing influences

Stage	Chief Influences
Infancy	Parents, siblings
Childhood	Parents, other authority figures, siblings
Adolescence	Peers, significant others, authority figures
Young adulthood	Mentors, authority figures, organizations

associates found that men ages twenty-eight through thirty-three tend to develop mentoring relationships.[2] The mentoring relationship is usually found in the work setting, the mentor is usually eight to fifteen years older than the protege, and the relationship lasts two or three years on the average. The mentor functions as a transitional figure and represents a mixture of parent and peer. The mentor can be a teacher, sponsor, host and guide, or counselor. Most importantly, the mentor facilitates the realization of a person's "Dream." The Dream is initially a vague vision, poorly articulated to reality, of what the person would like to make of life. The mentor helps the person more clearly define the Dream and find ways to realize it while providing needed moral support and encouragement.

Those being socialized also play a role in the socialization process, though young children, who generally are not aware of the process as it is taking place, are limited in their ability to participate in it. Older children or adolescents, who are cognizant of the process, can cooperate to foster their own social development. However, this growing awareness of the process also can thwart parental influence. As children turn to the judgment of their peers and to the values conveyed by media personalities, parents must find more compelling motivational devices to sustain their input into the socialization process and to stem the erosion of their authority.

> After a certain age, we begin to play a role in our own socialization.

The Socialization Process. Albert Bandura, in his **modeling identification theory,**[3] says that a principal way people learn is by observing others. Based on the principle of modeling and imitation, children observe a person (model) perform and act and, having seen the act, are likely to imitate it themselves. Experiments have been conducted in which children are placed in a room with a dummy. Before being placed in the room, some of the children saw the dummy being kicked; others did not. The children who had watched the dummy being kicked were more likely to kick the dummy than were the children who had not seen this behavior modeled. In addition, children kicked the dummy even more often after seeing the experimenter rewarded for kicking the dummy or being rewarded themselves for kicking it.[4] Parents aside, children are most likely to emulate models who can reward them, control the consequences of their behavior, and possess high status. Modeling teaches different kinds of behaviors, such as play patterns, aggression, language, and various social behaviors.

But, as Bandura himself would point out, children do not merely mimic the actions of those around them or take on the personalities and roles they see around them. They are, or become, individuals with a sense of self. Some sociologists and philosophers believe that the sense of self develops through social interaction. For example, C. H. Cooley offered the concept of the *looking-glass self,* in which individuals see themselves from the outside as though they were looking in a mirror. They imagine how others would view and react to them, and they are either pleased or displeased with the reflection.[5]

George H. Mead saw this ability to "take the role of the other" (to view ourselves from the perspective of others) as essential to the creation of the self.[6] He conceived this self as containing the "me," which arises as a set of attitudes acquired from others, and the "I," which responds to the "me." This self imitates the roles modeled for it in its environment, but it also reflects upon them and experiments and plays with them. Mead believes, for example, that children learn roles from those in their immediate environment, like mother, father, and grandparent, and then generalize these roles into archetypes for fatherhood, motherhood, and grandparenthood. A two-year-old who comes home from the doctor and "examines" a stuffed animal might at first be imitating the doctor's behavior, but as the child continues to play this game, the child generalizes the experience to form expectations of how all doctors act and what kinds of things they do. The child generalizes the other roles he encounters and, at some point, draws from all of these roles a picture of how people in general behave. Mead calls this picture "the generalized other."

Erving Goffman has shown that a person does not simply imitate roles but also can exploit the possibility for improvisation and play within a role beyond the necessities of correct behavior.[7] In other words, once children have embraced a role by showing attachment to it, exhibiting the capacity to perform it, and being actively involved in doing it, children, by the age of five, can begin distancing themselves from the role by showing that the task is too easy and that they can perform it in more than one way (as in assuming different postures while riding a merry-go-round).

The **symbolic-interactionist theory,** pioneered by Cooley and Mead, offers a compelling explanation of how the self-concept is formed and can be considered a more dynamic model than Bandura's modeling-identification theory. In the symbolic-interactionist theory, the child is as much an actor as a reactor. The newborn, then, gradually creates a social self through social interaction. Lack of support or response from parents can impede children's efforts to influence their environment and discourage children from acting. Such an environment can give children a sense of incompetence and inhibit the development of a strong and healthy self-concept. Schools and teachers can have the same negative effect on their students, especially in the area of a child's sense of academic competence.

In becoming socialized, we generalize what we see people do to others who operate in the same roles.

Methods of Socialization. Cultures use values, norms, folkways, mores, ideologies, and social sanctions to maintain stability and perpetuate themselves. **Value** is the quality of a thing, process, or relationship that makes it desirable or undesirable. For example, American society values optimism, individualism, materialism, and practicality; Chinese culture upholds the values of conformity, cooperation, and communal well-being.

Norms are the culture's basic prescriptions of what behavior is right and wrong.

Norms are rules that tell people what to do in a particular situation. Norms are more concrete than values, though the two are related. There are norms that prohibit behaviors such as cheating, lying, stealing, using obscenity, being rude, and being overly aggressive. Every cultural system is **normative** in that it contains requirements as to what one can and cannot do. Nearly all cultures permit nonconformity—though the amount and type of nonconformity permitted varies considerably from culture to culture. Some norms do not evoke strong emotion and their violation calls for only mild criticism or slight ridicule. These norms are called **folkways.** Wearing mismatched socks, putting a postage stamp in the wrong place on an envelope, or combing one's hair at the dinner table would be violations of folkways in American culture. In contrast, **mores** are stronger norms; violating them can lead to severe punishment within the cultural community. In American culture, mores exist that prohibit behaviors such as incest, rape, homicide, betraying one's country, and theft. Folkways can differ widely from one culture to another and even among segments within one culture, but mores seem to differ less across cultures. However, some differences can be found. For example, adultery in some cultures is punishable by death; in others, a host might offer his guest an opportunity to have sexual relations with his wife. In fact, not doing so can be taken as an insult to the guest.

An **ideology** (system of ideas regarding philosophic, economic, political, or social beliefs) also can provide social stability and control. An ideology like capitalism, socialism, communism, social Darwinism, or libertarianism can define and justify the interests of a group or culture.

Societies promote the cultural codes through sanctions. **Social sanctions** are forms of rewards and punishments used to exercise social control. These sanctions can be mild (a slight rebuke or mild ridicule when a folkway is violated) or severe (ostracism, imprisonment, or execution when a more is transgressed). Those who comply with the culture's norms might be rewarded through recognition, promotion, praise, awards or honors.

The relationship of social control mechanisms is indicated in Figure 8–1. Ideologies are listed at the top because they are more complex

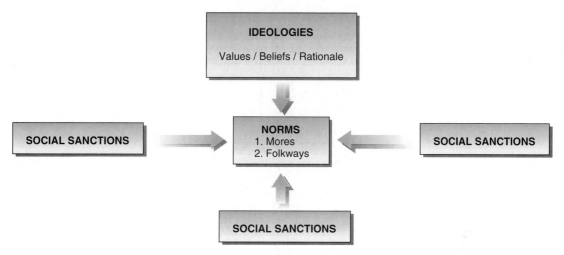

FIGURE 8-1 Social control mechanisms

in that they contain values, beliefs, and a rationale. They may contain, for example, beliefs about evolution as well as a rationale for justifying its use in structuring and interpreting social life. Social Darwinism, for instance, comprises such values as competition, survival of the most fit, and selective reproduction. **Normative consensus** exists when there is widespread cultural agreement on mores and folkways.

Norms are derived from values. For example, from the value of private property, norms ranging from prohibitions against walking on the grass to prohibitions against theft may be derived.

We could say that many of a culture's values, and thereby its norms, are embodied in roles, such as the role of the good son or daughter or the role of the good student. And so non-material culture is passed on both implicitly and, through actual rules, explicitly.

Some variation in the socialization of children in the United States has been ascribed to social-class background and the advent of new theories of child rearing. Middle-class parents shifted toward more permissive practices as new ideas of infant and child care emerged. The 1951 edition of the government's book *Infant Care*, for example, warned parents that too much pampering might result in the child becoming a "tyrant"; by the 1980s the book had taken a permissive attitude toward weaning, masturbation, thumb sucking, and toilet training. Middle-class mothers tend to use discussion and withdrawal of love as disciplinary measures while working-class and poor mothers are more likely to use physical punishment.[8] A comparison of the values of white-collar and blue-collar workers revealed that white-

Some parental socialization practices are attributable to socioeconomic status.

collar workers tend to prize internal standards of control for children, such as curiosity, self-motivation, and consideration for others; blue-collar workers tend to conform more to external standards.[9] Some of the differences in values can be attributed to what the parents have found useful in the occupational world. Blue-collar workers are more likely to punish their children immediately for misbehavior, while white-collar workers might first seek the child's motives or intentions.

For what roles should children be socialized? For the past century and a half, educators and philosophers have debated whether the socialization of children should focus on instilling childhood roles or on instilling roles similar to or continuous with those children will be expected to assume in adulthood. Some sociologists claim that because adult roles are mainly work roles of one form or another, socialization that develops attitudes and experiences favorable to work are likely to facilitate the formation of adult roles. If parents are extremely permissive and fail to provide work opportunities for children, childhood socialization will lack continuity with adulthood and can result in the child's refusal to accept adult roles or create trauma in the transition to adulthood.[10] Childhood and adulthood roles were more continuous when the home itself was an economic unit and children were sent to work in mines and factories alongside adults. One could argue that the advent of universal education, compulsory school attendance laws, and child labor laws actually have made the transition to adulthood more difficult for today's youth, because they break this continuity. In contemporary society, children have been increasingly segregated from adults and the period before they assume adult responsibilities has been lengthened. However, schooling can provide continuity with and preparation for adulthood. Academic study can be viewed as an occupation, a form of work, because it involves a specific set of duties and a highly structured time schedule. Moreover, much schooling is oriented to vocational preparation, as career education and related curricular developments demonstrate.

Educators since the time of Rousseau have counseled society against making childhood merely a preparation for adulthood. Warning fathers not to fill the fleeting days of childhood with bitterness, Rousseau urges parents to love childhood and indulge its pleasures, sports, and instincts.[11] Dewey notes that when education is conceived as a preparation for the future, it fails to consider the needs and possibilities of the present. Children naturally focus on the present; the future, for them, lacks urgency and they have little motive to prepare for it. The mistake is to make the future the basis of present effort rather than providing conditions for making best use of the present capabilities of the child.[12]

> Socialization was simpler when it was more exclusively a parental and economic process.

■ **PAUSE TO REFLECT**
How Should Children Be Socialized?

- Do you think children should be socialized primarily as preparation for adulthood, or should childhood consist of something more? If something more, what should it be?

- What adjustments could be made in American socialization practices to ease the transition from childhood to adulthood? For example, what could be done to close the "generation gap" that appears during adolescence?

The Subculture of the School

How does schooling fit into our survey of culture and socialization? If we consider the typical public school a subculture, it may become clear. A **subculture** or **microculture** is a system of attitudes, values, modes of behavior, and life styles that are distinct from but related to the dominant culture. The school can be thought of as a subculture in that the behavior and values of children differ from the larger adult culture yet embody many features of the culture.

While American public schools support the ideology of democracy as the best form of government, schools themselves are not democratically organized. They usually are organized bureaucratically with a hierarchal power structure. They also usually subscribe to the ideology of universal education and belief in government control of education, taxation for public schools, equal access to education, and compulsory attendance.

The values emphasized in public schools are largely middle class: achievement, hard work, competition, cleanliness, respect for authority, negotiation, orderliness, and control over impulses. Above all, emphasis is placed on the belief that people who apply themselves get ahead in school and in life. Seldom mentioned are those who rely on family connections, wealth, power, and influence to advance or maintain an important position or high status. The prevailing value is achievement; to achieve one must compete, but compete fairly. This is evident in the sorting and screening mechanisms used in the school system: grades, tests, honors, scholarships. Cleanliness and neatness are emphasized not only in dress but also in schoolwork, and children whose parents did not instill such values are at a disadvantage. Students also are expected to respect the authority of school personnel, and sanctions usually are imposed on those who fail to do so. Differences are to be settled by negotiation, discussion, and compromise rather than coercion or violence. Schools also have rules to maintain orderliness and promote a well-organized, safe, and reasonably quiet

> Schools promote the value that those who work hard will succeed.

atmosphere. Students are expected to control their impulses, which builds character and maturity and helps maintain an orderly school environment.

Schools have normative systems to govern behavior just as the larger culture does.

School values are reinforced and policies are fulfilled by a system of norms that regulates everyday school activities. Students are encouraged to, among other things, avoid tardiness, dishonesty, and running in the halls; to raise their hands and be recognized by the teacher before speaking in class; to form a line to go to the cafeteria or playground; to not push ahead of someone else in line, chew gum in class, or create a disturbance; and to use school equipment according to instructions. The norms and rules used to prevent disruption constitute what is sometimes called the hidden curriculum.

The **hidden curriculum** involves the covert and formal relations in home and school that influence learning, such as norms, grades, competition, social class background, and prejudice. Sometimes the hidden curriculum conflicts with the formal curriculum, as when the student's social class values conflict with school norms. The sanctions that would be imposed for violating the norm would depend upon the norm itself and the situation. Dishonesty on a test or assignment obviously would be subject to more severe sanctions than would tardiness; however, the sanction for tardiness probably would be more stringent if the problem were chronic. Students who persistently comply with school norms are likely to be rewarded with a good grade on deportment (in the early grades) and are likely to be treated more favorably by teachers and administrators.

As in the larger culture, some norms can be considered mores; others are folkways. Maintaining honesty in one's work is a more; not chewing gum in class is a folkway. Norms frequently are formulated as rules to render them more intelligible and applicable. A **rule** is a regulation governing conduct or procedure and usually takes an imperative form: "Do not run in the halls"; "Turn in all papers on time." The object of compliance is to reach a normative consensus by which school participants work together through a network of agreements and the orderly resolution of disputes.[13]

Such a description of school life emanates from the perspective of the school board and the professional staff; yet as we saw in Chapter 4, most schools also have student subcultures. These subcultures might support school norms or run counter to them, as when athletic prowess and good looks are accorded higher status among students than good grades. In an attempt to focus peer influence on academic work, some schools have started peer teaching and tutoring programs. To counter student cliques (another source of conflicting norms) teachers can promote subjects and activities in which all students can participate.

SCHOOLS IN A PLURALIST SOCIETY ■

The Interaction of Cultures

Because several cultures coexist in American society, many people object to the tendency of schools to reflect principally middle-class values because students from minority cultures are put at a disadvantage. Moreover, regardless of the utility of these values in the efficient running of schools and perhaps even in the students' lives as adult members of the larger culture, asking students to take on these values can be the same as asking them to abandon the culture into which they were born (or at least certain aspects of it) in favor of the dominant culture of the schools.

The culture of the schools may conflict with a student's home culture.

In an attempt to maintain and protect their way of life, some cultures reject the enterprise of public schooling. The Amish, for instance, strict Mennonite followers who settled in the United States in the eighteenth century, live a simple agrarian life based on their religious teachings with little contact with the larger society. Their religion teaches that education beyond the eighth grade is a detriment to salvation and a violation of their culture. In 1972 on the grounds of religious freedom, the United States Supreme Court ruled in *Wisconsin v. Yoder* that members of the Amish sect were not subject to the state's compulsory education laws.[14] The effort by the Amish to protect their culture from immersion into the larger society is an example of a **boundary maintenance mechanism.**

Many cultures, though they seek to maintain their stability over generations, might at times seek controlled change to meet new challenges, to discard obsolescent ways, or to compete more effectively with other cultures. Often, however, change is resisted and occurs only inadvertently, through force or through another culture's dominance. When change does occur, not all areas of culture always change at the same rate. William Ogburn held, for instance, that the material elements of a culture change more rapidly than the non-material elements. This can result in a **cultural lag,** inconsistence within a culture resulting from an unequal rate of change of cultural elements. The introduction of the automobile (material culture), for instance, eventually led to changes in people's beliefs about where they should live and work (non-material culture). Three general processes cause cultural change: invention, discovery, and diffusion. **Invention** is the process of creating new cultural elements. The invention of electric light, telephones, telegraphs, motion pictures, airplanes, and nuclear weapons has changed the way we live, work, and think about our lives. **Discovery** involves uncovering, recognizing, and understanding something that already exists, such as the discovery of penicillin through the microscopic observance of certain molds or discovery of radium by leaving a rock on a piece of photographic paper. **Diffusion** is the spread of cultural elements of one culture to another. For example, diffusion resulted from the beginnings of trade between Europe and Asia, the introduction of missionaries' religious beliefs into preliterate culture, and the influence of African art in Picasso's cubism. It is this process of diffusion that the Amish are resisting by segregating themselves from the larger society.

Despite the forces of change, people resist because of established ideology, values, norms, the application of sanctions, and ethnocentrism. **Ethnocentrism** is the belief that one's way of life, attitudes, and customs are superior to those of other cultures, that one's culture is "correct" and should be accepted uncritically and without question. Ethnocentric people look at other cultures as less advanced than their own, even benighted, and less moral. One may be taught that one's culture represents not only the best way of life, but also the only sensible and reasonable way to live.

Cultural Relativism

At the opposite end of the spectrum from ethnocentrism is **cultural relativism**—a method by which different cultures are studied objectively without using the values of one culture to judge the worth of another. This can be achieved by describing the practices of a culture from the viewpoints of its members. In separate studies, American anthropologists Margaret Mead and Ruth Benedict found that cultures varied in terms of personality development, child rearing, sex role behavior, and types of mental disorder.[15] Mead found that, while American adolescence is a period of crisis and search for identity, no such crisis occurred among Samoan girls, whose transition to adulthood was easy and without trauma. In New Guinea she found the Tchambuli females to be assertive and the Arapesh males to be passive, sensitive, and gentle. Mead attempted to relate her findings to the general educated public in America, even though some anthropologists rejected her view that there are no consistent sex differences in temperament.

Benedict observed that in American culture there is a break in the life cycle at which point a child is expected to become an adult and is treated differently. In other cultures, however, such as the Ojibwa, the life cycle is a continuous process in which children are given increasing responsibility and independence as they approach adulthood. Cultural relativism leads to the conviction that all cultures are equally valid and that every culture deserves respect. This position dispels ethnocentrism, develops more open-mindedness, and encourages people to observe and try to understand and appreciate cultural differences in the context in which traits function in a given culture. Cultural relativism also might have a moral side. It suggests that different societies have different moral codes and no objective standard exists by which one moral code can be judged better than another; right and wrong are matters of opinion that vary among cultures. The problem is that the conclusion does not always follow from the premise. In other words, if two cultures disagree on a moral matter, it does not necessarily mean that there is no objective truth about the issue.[16] For example, if two cultures disagree about the uses of slavery, that does not mean that no moral statement can be applied universally about slavery.

An even more serious problem is that from the perspective of the moral form of cultural relativism, one could not assert that Nazi Germany or Stalinist Russia were morally degenerate, because all cultures are to be considered equally valid and deserve respect. This leads to the question of whether there are any **cultural universals,** or practices and codes of conduct found in every culture. Humans have certain basic needs: cultures must clothe and feed their members, care for and teach the young, heal the sick, protect their members from harm. These activities, though the specifics of their performance may differ, are cultural universals. Moreover, all cultures disapprove of acts such as lying, stealing, incest, violence within the group, and failure to maintain control over one's impulses.[17]

Some essential values appear in every culture.

What Should Be the Role of Schools in a Culture?

Several theoretical approaches have been used to explain the complexities of culture and the role of education within a culture. Of these approaches, we will discuss structural-functional analysis, social-conflict analysis, cultural ecology, and sociobiology.

Structural-functional analysis is based on the view of society as a system of different parts that work together to develop a stable social system. Within the system, a cultural trait is understood with reference to the contribution it makes to the perpetuation of the culture as a whole. Values are considered the basis of the cultural system.[18] Common values bring about social cohesiveness. Cultural change can result from invention, discovery, or diffusion, but this theory emphasizes stability rather than change. Society is seen as composed of a social structure, which is a relatively stable pattern of social behavior, and social functions, which refer to the consequences for the operation of society as a whole. Each cultural trait helps the society persist. When the norms and values of a society are compatible, the society is more likely to be functionally integrated. When the cultural traits reinforce

One view of education is that it must prepare students to assume practical roles in society to perpetuate the culture.

Public schools have traditionally transmitted common values to a culturally diverse student body.

one another, the society can be said to be culturally integrated. When vocational skills taught in school are valued and used in business and industry, some evidence of congruence and integration in this area can be found among the different social systems involved.

Structural-functional analysis views the school's role as reproducing desirable norms and values of society by transmitting them to the young and encouraging them to internalize and exhibit them in their behavior. A common body of knowledge in the curriculum and a set of prescribed values are designed to promote social and cultural integration. Cultural traits that enable society to persist and prosper are taught. For instance, if computer skills are needed in the economy, then these should be taught in public schools. Transmission of a common knowledge base and a set of values promotes social and political stability.

The school also helps society allocate social roles in occupations by providing specialized knowledge and skills. Thus socialization is one of the school's most important functions in that it enables students to acquire desirable behavior patterns for gainful employment. Students who adopt the desired norms and acquire the requisite skills are rewarded with better jobs and higher socioeconomic status.

Though this theory accounts for social stability and cultural integration, it does not explain social conflict and other forms of instability; it also neglects the meanings that individuals give to their actions by focusing exclusively on the consequences of actions.

Social-conflict analysis depicts culture not as a well-integrated system but as a dynamic center of social conflict among categories of people. Unlike structural-functional analysis, this theory does not accept certain values as given. Rather, it critically asks about the forces that generate these values and seeks to discover what values support social inequality. Marx contended that values are shaped by the culture's system of economic production. The competitive and individ-ualistic values of American culture, for instance, are shaped by capitalism. Lewis Coser differed from Marx by citing the positive functions of conflict. He argued that conflicts in which someone who is an ally in one dispute and an opponent in another can prevent those very conflicts from dividing society. Complex societies have many interests and conflicts, which provide the balance that prevents instability.[19] The civil rights movement and women's liberation movement are two examples of the use of conflict to bring about change in American society.

This theory views the school's current role as a selecting mechanism for society's prestigious positions by sorting students according to ability and behavioral norms. The interests of the dominant and powerful are thereby served. The dominant class is able to maintain the social class structure by determining who controls the knowledge and skills needed in society. The upper class is able to influence key legislation and control school finance.

Another view is that some students must be socialized to roles that are subordinate to the dominant class.

Various ethnic, racial, and radical groups find themselves in conflict with school rules. Students are expected to conform to school rules not only to maintain order and discipline but also to prepare working class youth to conform to workplace norms imposed by the dominant group. But conflict is likely to develop whenever groups holding different values are expected to comply with one set of norms established by the dominant group.

To reduce conflict and alienation, school officials should identify those groups in which such tensions are likely to be found. Schools need to observe and enforce student rights and enable students and parents to participate in developing student codes. Parents and educators also need to expose the unequal nature of schooling and take measures to overcome it.

This theory does bring attention to the conflict overlooked by structural-functional analysis, the inequalities and unmet needs in society, and the dominance of some groups over others. But one problem with this theory is that it fails to explain adequately some crimes—theft, for instance. Theft is not sanctioned in any society and it cannot be explained by conflicting values. It also does not explain why some people deviate from their own group norms or become violent against members of their own group. The theory is much more suitable as an explanation of political and ideological conflict than of such common crimes and vices as theft, burglary, rape, arson, and alcoholism.

Cultural ecology is a theory that explores the relationship between human culture and the physical environment. It emphasizes how the physical environment—such as arable land, climate, and natural resources—influences the development of cultures. Marvin Harris agrees with Marx that culture is based on the material circumstances in which it exists.[20] Humans have to provide the basic necessities before they can participate in activities such as politics, art, and religion; consequently, the production of basic material goods limits the kind of government, laws, art, and religion that can be developed. Marx viewed the necessities for survival as the base of society and other cultural activities not directly related to survival as the superstructure. He insisted that the base determines the superstructure, not the converse. Harris attempts to account for customs on the basis of material circumstances. The prohibition in India against killing cows, he believes, is more than just a religious taboo; it is based on the need for oxen-driven plows in Indian agriculture because Indian farmers cannot afford farm machinery. Cows were not made holy in China because horses, donkeys, and mules were used as draft animals, and the Chinese did not need milk as a source of protein because their climate allowed them to keep pigs to supply meat.

The purpose of cultural ecology theory is to teach the importance of the natural environment on culture, which is generally neglected or overlooked in other theories. Teachers show that valued cultural patterns are determined by the natural environment rather than the prevailing view in developed societies that technology controls the natural environment and greatly influences non-material culture.

In preliterate cultures that are largely nomadic, the struggle for survival predominates and there is no formal schooling; instead, learning involves children in a direct, face-to-face relationship with elders through modeling and oral instruction. The types of institutions and social arrangements that preliterate cultures develop grow out of confrontation with the natural environment, and what is transmitted to the young is based on failures and successes in coping with this environment. In more developed societies as well, the necessities for survival shape the non-material culture.

The cultural ecological view holds that the population must be educated to meet its material needs before it can wrestle with the non-material values.

But, Harris's explanation overlooks that it is possible to survive without animal protein by eating a variety of vegetable proteins. Although the cultural ecology theory points out an important relationship between the natural environment and the culture that is largely neglected in other theories, it suggests that cultural patterns are always directly determined by the natural environment and never merely interact with one another. Additionally, some cultural elements–such as the arts and religion–are not directly linked to the natural environment in that they are derived through cognitive and creative processes.

Sociobiology seeks to explain the social organization of animals, including humans, in terms of biological characteristics. It draws on evolutionary theory, population ecology, genetics, and comparative ethology (the study of the characteristics of animal behavior). Whatever explanatory powers sociobiology may possess could stem from evolutionary theory, as the major advances in biology fit into broad outlines of Darwin's ideas. When new discoveries have conflicted with the theory, the theory has been modified to accommodate the discoveries.[21] Fitness in biology is a measure of one's reproductive success. Thus, the most successful living things are the best reproducers. Any older species consists of individuals who are descendants of the best reproducers of previous generations.[22] But as biologist Stephan J. Gould has indicated, chance factors can enter in: evolution can be interspersed with comparatively sudden and pronounced changes.

Cooperation and altruism are needed to maintain family stability and to socialize the young. Sociobiology, in contrast to the popular view of Darwinian competition and Spencer's "survival of the fittest," finds an important place for two kinds of altruism. One form is kin selection, which states that animals increase their fitness not only by choosing desirable mates that maximize reproductive success but also by sacrificing for relatives, with priority given to the closest relatives with whom one shares the most genes.[23] Nepotism is virtually a universal human trait. By treating relatives differently than strangers, inclusive reproductive fitness is maximized. It also could be inferred that the extended family and its internal roles grew out of kin selection. But this form of altruism, since it discriminates against non-relatives, can lead to blood feuds, tribalism, ethnocentricity, and a general lack of harmony within society and in international relations.

Reciprocal altruism, a second type, is in force when the return to the altruist is greater than its costs in units of inclusive fitness. Thus the act carries a low risk to the altruist while it confers a high benefit upon the recipient. Moreover, a high probability must exist that the beneficiary will reciprocate. Altruists must guard against those who cheat: namely, those who accept the benefits but refuse to reciprocate. Altruists inform one another about cheaters and sometimes punish them. Reciprocal altruism, therefore, is likely to evolve in intelligent, closely integrated social species with relatively long lifespans.[24]

Differing from social Darwinism that believes in "survival of the fittest," sociobiology recognizes not only struggle and competition for survival for humans and animals but cooperation and altruism as well. It claims there is a continuity between humans and animals (in contrast to the views of most major religions).

Sociobiology differs with ordinary views of progress that believe that human progress takes place within a given generation whenever significant economic, technological, or political advancements occur. Instead, progress is viewed in an evolutionary perspective over great periods of time with occasional sudden and pronounced changes. Thus the young would envision progress differently than did their ancestors and would be taught to increase reproductive fitness by choosing desirable mates, sacrificing for relatives, and promoting reciprocal altruism.

Kin altruism explains the role of the extended family's involvement in socialization, and reciprocal altruism explains the child's desire to help peers. The sociobiologist's explanation of altruism, however, could be improved. When the sociobiologist mentions altruism, the term refers to the consequences of individual behavior, not the intention or motivation of the actor. Yet a question exists whether these are cases of altruism if an intention to treat others in a certain way cannot be inferred.

■ LANGUAGE AND NONVERBAL COMMUNICATION

Communication consists of language and nonverbal behavior. **Language** is a system of formalized symbols and signs used as a means of communication. Language performs two functions. First, it supplies meaning to culture and helps a society accumulate the knowledge and experience of a culture's past that otherwise would be lost. Second, it organizes our perceptions of the world by enabling us to refer to past, present, and future; to describe sensory evidence and inner feelings; and to convey our thoughts and values.

A culture could not endure without language.

Nothing is known about the origin of language, but it is estimated to have been in use longer than writing, which originated 7,900 years ago. Language functions as a means of communication and a common bond for individuals. Languages are continually changing, but the direction of change is unpredictable. The languages spoken by simple, preliterate cultures are as complex as those of industrial societies, and all people belong to a **speech community,** a group of people who speak the same language. About 3,000 to 4,000 speech communities can be identified today, ranging from millions of speakers each to a few dozen. The languages presently spoken by groups of more than 50 million people, beginning with the most widely spoken language, are Mandarin, English, Hindustani, Spanish, Russian, German, Japanese, Malay, Bengali, French, Portuguese, and Italian.

The **linguistic relativity hypothesis,** proposed by linguists Edward Sapir and Benjamin Whorf, holds that the unique grammatical form of a language shapes the thoughts and perceptions of its users.[25] The different distinctions in time illustrate this point. Americans consider time to be scarce and precious; whereas the Hopi Indians have no words for "time," "late," "day," "hour," or "minute." They live in the present and suggest that things will happen when they happen.

Language both conveys culture and shapes it.

The more involved members of a culture are with a particular activity, the more linguistic distinctions there are. Eskimos, for example, have more than twenty words to describe snow. Arabs have hundreds of words to describe camels and camel equipment. Americans have hundreds of words for cars, which distinguish different types, various manufacturers, and different models.

The Yancos, an Amazon tribe, do not count beyond their word for three. The Temiar people of West Malaysia also end counting at three. Language enables us to make sense out of what we experience and to perceive differences among things. The lack of numbers in the Yanco and Temiar cultures affects the people's ability to perceive reality.

Whorf believed that people think of time, space, and color differently, depending on the culture's linguistic categories. Whorf probably would expect people to respond to color depending upon the shades named in the language. But in one experiment, people reacted in similar ways to color regardless of their language. The Dani, a tribe in Western New Guinea, has only two words for color: one refers to dark, cool colors and the other to light, warm colors. Eleanor Rosh-Heiden and D. C. Oliver tested Dani natives and American college students to see if there were any differences in their response to colors.[26] The researchers found that the two groups perceived color the same way.

Does language shape people's views of reality, or do people's views of reality determine the language structure? Perhaps what occurs is that language develops to help people to deal with their experiences. Once a particular language has evolved, it influences the world view of the speech community.

Harold Innis suggested that preliterate cultures have to be small because people must organize their culture within the short range of the voice.[27] The introduction of writing would change this arrangement because the culture could then disperse and remain in contact through writing. Reason replaces traditional sacred authority in a

A written language helps extend a culture beyond the range of the spoken voice.

culture that includes writing because people can examine records and develop consistent standards of judgment. As writing materials became more durable, cheaper, and more portable, a literate culture was able to spread more rapidly. Papyrus, a considerable improvement over clay tablets, was replaced by parchment and then by paper, which not only allowed written documents to become more commonplace but also provided one of the conditions for the invention of printing.

Marshall McLuhan depicted the media as extensions of the human body.[28] The media enable people to extend the power of their senses, just as movies permit the visualization of things distant in both time and space. Preliterate cultures focused on hearing, since it was the only way that they related to others' thoughts. But in literate cultures, people depend more on the eyes; it is as though literacy enlarges the eyes and shrinks the ears. A nonliterate person's senses are kept busy collecting impressions from various sources in no particular order, but a literate person experiences culture through words arranged in a logical order. With electronic media, a society enters a "postliterate" era in which television counters some of the effects of literacy by having us use our ears as much as our eyes. People in different parts of the world are being linked through electronic connections, and most of the literate world is becoming a "global village."

Nonverbal Communication

Nonverbal communication enriches and augments spoken language.

Nonverbal communication includes all forms of communication that are neither spoken nor written. Nonverbal communication relays messages (for example, through one's style of dress), augments verbal communication (by showing emotions that reinforce verbal communication), contradicts verbal communication (for example, displaying nervousness while saying "I feel quite confident"), and replaces verbal communication (for example, it allows two people who do not speak the same language to relate to each other).

Nonverbal communication extends to many areas, including personal space. For example, Americans are likely to feel uncomfortable when someone they do not know well moves within two feet of them. On the other hand, Latin Americans have a much smaller conception of intimate space.[29] Children may not be given explicit instructions about how close to stand when speaking to another person, but they nevertheless learn appropriate behavior by observing others—another function of nonverbal communication.

Nonverbal cues abound in every society:

- The way a person dresses communicates one's sex, nationality and ethnic background, socioeconomic status, mood, attitudes, and values.

- Some Native Americans and Hispanics teach their children to avoid eye contact, particularly with elders, because it is a sign of disrespect. White American teachers, on the other hand, typically insist on eye contact, because it presumably indicates that the student is paying attention. Teachers should be aware of such cultural differences to avoid misconstruing a student's intentions.

- Prejudices are attached to certain body types. The early Hawaiians equated obesity with beauty in women. In American culture the mesomorph (the muscular, athletic build) is preferred in men, while the ectomorph (the tall, thin, fragile build) is preferred in women. Attractive people tend to be judged more likeable, and taller men tend to be given higher status and to be considered smarter in school.[30]

- Teachers continually evaluate students not only by their verbal behavior but also by their actions and expressions. Yet teachers might not always be aware of the extent to and precision with which youth evaluate their teachers. Emerson observed in his essay on education that students "detect weakness in your eye and behavior a week before you open your mouth. . . ."

- A study by Basil Bernstein showed that lower-class youth depend more on nonverbal behavior of the teacher than other youth because they are less able to grasp abstract symbols and handle academic language with facility. Teachers tend to communicate through language in culturally restricted symbols that represent middle-class cultures.[31]

- Teachers use certain cues when they are about to make an announcement and want their students' attention. In one study, teachers tended to move to a space in the classroom empty of furniture, where groups assemble for meetings and which might have symbolic meaning as a place for teacher control.[32]

Charles Galloway divided nonverbal behavior into behaviors that encourage communication and those that inhibit it.[33] Observers used seven categories to record teachers' nonverbal behavior. Four categories represented encouragement and three represented an inhibition of encouragement. Behavior such as facial expressions, actions, and voice qualities that reinforce or inhibit behavior were studied. Teachers encouraged students by the way they listened, the emotional support they offered, and their responsiveness. Teachers who discouraged students acted uninterested in what students said, seemed more often to express disapproval by their behavior, and did not respond consis-

> Nonverbal communication has the power to encourage or to inhibit another's behavior.

tently to students. This study underlines the importance of nonverbal communication and suggests that teachers should make an effort to understand cultural differences not only in oral and written language but also in nonverbal behavior.

■ PAUSE TO REFLECT
Becoming Aware of Nonverbal Behavior

- Consider a few of your current teachers and focus on one who has a "commanding presence." What nonverbal behavior does this teacher use that gives you this impression?
- What nonverbal behaviors should you, as a teacher, guard against in the classroom? For instance, if you tend to focus on one or two students so that you can maintain your concentration, you probably would want to consider the inadvertent negative effect such behavior may have on the other students.

Teacher expectations tend to influence how they perceive and relate to students. Two psychologists administered intelligence tests and then gave teachers the names of "late-blooming" students who likely would exhibit a sudden growth in learning. Actually, the names of the students were randomly selected. After the intelligence tests were administered again in a year, the "late bloomers" had made considerable gains in scores compared to the rest of the students.[34] The study supported the hypothesis that once a child is labeled by teachers and others, a **self-fulfilling prophecy** comes into play: the teacher expects certain behaviors from the child and the child responds to the expectations. Critics have suggested that the study had several methodological weaknesses, because, they said, many variables can affect teacher expectations: test scores, academic achievement, social class, race, sex, and others.[35]

■ BILINGUAL EDUCATION

Bilingual education has become an important part of American education, marked by the testing of several approaches during the 1960s and the spread of bilingual education during the 1970s. Bilingual education is also a concern in such countries as Australia, Canada, France, the Netherlands, and the United Kingdom. Linguistically, the United States has tended to successfully assimilate people from European backgrounds, but not Native Americans, Puerto Ricans, or Mexican Americans.

Bilingual children usually have found that neither language served them well in coping with academic work. Educators, however, have generally underestimated the influence of home language and culture. Those students who survive academically are frequently asked to choose between their heritage and the dominant culture, a choice that can result in the child's isolation from his or her culture and family. Shirley Brice Heath has indicated that language arts curriculums are based on the assumption that language development is the same for all children, regardless of ethnic origin. But, she says, that research is based on middle-class English-speaking families.[36]

> Children of all cultures do not necessarily develop language in exactly the same way.

When schools had few bilingual children, school officials did nothing about the problems these children experienced or else perceived them as problems of low I.Q. Some early programs focused on vocabulary items without building a syntactical framework for using words. In the 1950s and early 1960s educators taught English as a second language using drill exercises; however, this approach had little place for the mother tongue. In 1968 the Bilingual Education Act developed curriculums and Spanish language instruction but gave little attention to the development of bilingual teachers.

The Bilingual Education Act marked the beginning of the federal government's role in bilingual education. The act was added to the Elementary and Secondary Education Act of 1965 and also was known as Title VII. The act recognized that children whose native language was not English needed different instruction than did native English speakers. In *Lau v. Nichols*[37] the United States Supreme Court rejected a lower court ruling that offering the same services to all students met the conditions of the equal-protection clause and Title VI of the Civil Rights Act. While the Lau decision did not mandate bilingual education, it directed the San Francisco Board of Education to explore options to overcome the problem of 1,790 Chinese students who suffered educationally because they received no services that met their linguistic needs. Two other decisions, however, did mandate bilingual education: *Serna v. Municipal Schools*[38] and *Aspira of New York, Inc. v. Board of Education of the City of New York.*[39]

> Early efforts to address the problems of non-English-speaking students overlooked the need for appropriate teacher training.

Bilingual education can be approached two ways: through transitional programs and through maintenance programs. Transitional programs use bilingual education to move from the culture and language of the home to mainstream American culture and language. The goal is to teach English so that the child can function effectively in English as quickly as possible. Teachers instruct students in their native language in social studies or science so they will not fall behind while learning English. As the child acquires greater English proficiency, the home language is gradually phased out.

Children may be assisted in learning another language through computer instruction.

The goal of maintenance programs is for linguistically different children to function effectively in both bilingual and bicultural environments. The child's native language and culture are taught concurrently with English and mainstream culture. The culture of the ethnic group is emphasized through art, history, and literature. Ideally, the student who completes such programs can function in two languages and two cultures.

Some critics object to bilingual education on policy grounds. As many as 56,000 foreign language instructors would have to be found nationwide.[40] Furthermore, a study of Title VII, whose project goals were more consistent with the maintenance approach than the transitional approach, found, after an analysis of second-grade through sixth-grade samples, that the program did not significantly affect student achievement in mathematics and English language.[41] R.C. Troike claims the lack of federal funding has resulted in a dearth of research data on the effectiveness of bilingual education. Of 150 evaluation reports surveyed by the Center for Applied Linguistics, only seven met the minimum criteria for acceptability.[42] Yet some programs have shown the effectiveness of bilingual education. Santa Fe Title VII students showed increased ability in English skills, mathematics, and especially reading; these students outperformed non-Title VII students in reading and mathematics.[43] Troike found that quality programs can provide equal educational opportunities for non-English speaking (NES) or limited-English speaking (LES) students, and that these students performed as well as, or better than, students in monolingual programs.[44] Other studies show that an LES student may need five to seven years to attain the nativelike control of the English language needed to perform well on academic tasks.[45] Although research may be insufficient in documenting the effects of bilingual education, research does not show that bilingual education is harmful. And most researchers agree that students with limited or no English proficiency should receive special assistance in school.

Despite criticisms, bilingual education at least seems to do no harm.

EDUCATIONAL ISSUE 8–1

Should bilingual education be offered in public schools?

Yes	**No**
1. Where bilingual education is not offered, bilingual children have to choose between their heritage and the dominant culture.	1. Schools can show respect for different cultures by focusing on multicultural education instead of offering bilingual education.
2. Bilingual programs promote greater student achievement.	2. Some studies show that bilingual programs in elementary grades do not significantly improve student achievement in mathematics and English language studies.
3. Bilingual education can promote greater equity and effectiveness.	3. Bilingual education confronts schools with unrealistic demands; it may require as many as 56,000 foreign language instructors in many different languages.

■ **Summary**

- A *society* is a self-sustaining group of people who live in a definite geographic location. The society endures over time, shares a way of life, and pursues a common body of values.

- *Culture,* a pattern of human behavior shared by a society, can be divided into *material culture* (the objects a society makes to sustain its material existence) and *non-material culture* (intangible aspects of a society, such as values, belief systems, and norms).

- Individuals acquire the knowledge and skills to function responsibly in society through the process of *socialization*. The primary socializing agents are the family, the schools, peers, and the media.

- Albert Bandura's *modeling-identification theory* holds that people learn principally by observing others and imitating their behavior while the individual sense of self develops. C. H. Cooley offers the *looking-glass self* concept in which individuals imagine how others would view and react toward them. The *symbolic-interactionist theory* holds that a child gradually creates a social self through social interaction.

- Cultures maintain and perpetuate themselves through the use of values, norms, mores, folkways, ideologies, and sanctions. *Norms,* which consist of mild *folkways* and stronger *mores,* are rules that tell people what to do in particular situations. *Ideologies* are systems of ideas regarding philosophic, economic, political, or social beliefs, and *social sanctions* are rewards and punishments used to maintain social control.

- Some sociologists believe that children should be socialized from the perspective of the roles they will be expected to assume when they become adults. However, others believe that childhood is not merely a preparation for adulthood and that children should be indulged in their pleasures and impulses of the moment.

- The typical public school can be considered a *subculture* or *microculture,* in that it includes a distinct system of attitudes, values, modes of behavior, and life styles that are related to the dominant culture. The values most often found in public schools are middle-class ideals such as achievement, hard work, competition, and, above all, the belief that if one works hard, one will get ahead in life. These values are upheld through a system of norms, often called the *hidden curriculum,* which regulates school activities.

- Many people object to the domination of middle-class values in public schools and some even reject the public school system outright. In an attempt to preserve their unique culture, the Amish, for instance, have activated a *boundary maintenance mechanism* by refusing to send their children to public schools.

- Cultures change, no matter how hard some members of society try to resist. Cultures sometimes seek controlled change to keep up with the times and to compete better with other societies. When change happens faster than individuals' adaptation to those changes, society can experience *cultural lag*. Cultural change occurs in three major ways: *invention* (the process of creating a new cultural element), *discovery* (the uncovering of something that already exists), and *diffusion* (the spread of elements from one culture to another). *Ethnocentrism,* the belief that one's way of life is superior to any other, can stand in the way of cultural change.

- Cultural relativism, the opposite of ethnocentrism, is the objective study and acceptance of different cultures. Cultural relativists believe that all cultures are equally valid and deserve equal respect. The main failing of this thought is that from such a viewpoint, one could not denounce the values of cultures such as Nazi Germany or Stalinist Russia. This leads to the possibility that there might be a set of cultural universals that apply to all societies—such as that cultures must feed and clothe their members, care for the young and the sick, and protect their members from harm.

- Several theories attempt to explain the role of education within a culture: *structural-functional analysis* (based on the view of society as a system of different parts that work together to develop a stable social system); *social-conflict analysis* (based on the view that culture is a dynamic center of social conflict among categories of people); *cultural ecology* (based on the relationship between human culture and the physical environment); and sociobiology (based on the explanation of social organization of animals in terms of biological characteristics).

- Communication consists of language and nonverbal behavior. *Language,* a system of formalized symbols and signs, gives meaning to a culture and helps a society accumulate knowledge and experience of its past. The *linguistic-relativity hypothesis* holds that the unique grammatical form of a language shapes the thoughts and perceptions of the user. *Nonverbal communication* is any communication that is not spoken or written. Nonverbal cues abound in all societies and convey emotions that augment (or contradict) verbal messages and, occasionally, replace verbal communication (as in the case of two people who do not speak the same language). Nonverbal communication differs from culture to culture, and the wise teacher takes pains to understand those differences to avoid mis-construing a student's intentions.

● Bilingual education is receiving more international attention as educators try to provide equal opportunity in education. Bilingual education can be approached in two ways: through transitional programs (which emphasize moving from one's native language and culture to the dominant language and culture) and mainte-nance programs (which attempt to teach children to function ef-fectively in both languages and cultures). Critics of bilingual education point out that 56,000 foreign language instructors are needed to fulfill the program's requirements and that one study suggested that the program had little effect on students' achieve-ment in mathematics and English language studies.

■ Key Terms

boundary maintenance mechanism

communication

cultural ecology

cultural lag

cultural relativism

cultural traits

cultural universals

culture

diffusion

discovery

ethnocentrism

folkways

hidden curriculum

ideology

invention

language

linguistic-relativity hypothesis

modeling-identification theory

mores

nonverbal communication

normative

normative consensus

norms

rule

self-fulfilling prophecy

social-conflict analysis

social sanctions

socialization

society

sociobiology

speech community

structural-functional analysis

subculture

symbolic-interactionist theory

value

■ Discussion Questions

1. What are the mechanisms by which American culture seeks to maintain itself? Promote change?

2. Compare and contrast how these same tasks are performed in another culture.

3. If values, norms, and various cultural traits differ to a certain extent in various cultures, is cultural relativism a sound explanation for this phenomenon? Defend your answer.

4. Contrast socialization tasks with educational tasks in schools.

5. Does language largely shape one's view of reality or does one's view of reality determine the language structure? Defend your answer.

■ **Learning Activities**

1. Study the subculture of a local school and identify the ideology, values, norms, and social sanctions. Show how they seek to maintain stability and order.

2. Sit in on two or three classes and record the different nonverbal cues that the teachers use. Which ones are especially effective in promoting learning?

3. Examine the bilingual programs in the local school district and determine their relative effectiveness.

4. Organize a classroom debate on the resolution "Bilingual education should be available in all public school systems."

Suggested Readings

Barash, David. *The Whisperings Within.* New York: Penguin Books, 1979.
Provides a perceptive account of sociobiology.

Benedict, Ruth. *Patterns of Culture.* New York: Houghton Mifflin, 1935.
A classic treatment of cultural relativity and cultural integration.

Berger, Peter L., and Thomas Luckman. *The Social Construction of Reality.* Garden City, NY: Doubleday, 1967.
Shows how our reality is shaped by our epistemology and cultural categories.

Gilligan, Carol. *In a Different Voice: Psychological Theory and Women's Development.* Cambridge: Howard University Press, 1982.
Suggests that, in contrast to men's language, women's language is one of caring and interpersonal relations.

Hall, Edward T. *Beyond Culture.* Garden City, NY: Doubleday Anchor, 1977.
Discusses many aspects of our culture that we have taken for granted.

Harris, Marvin. *Cannibals and Kings: The Origins of Culture.* New York: Random House, 1977.

Uses the cultural ecology approach to explain different cultural practices throughout the world.

Levinson, Daniel J., et al. *The Seasons of a Man's Life.* New York: Knopf, 1978.

A longitudinal study of men from late teens to late forties that provides valuable insights.

Slater, Philip. *The Pursuit of Loneliness.* Boston: Beacon Press, 1976.

A critical examination of conflicting American values showing how the longing for community is frustrated by the emphasis on individualism and competition.

Notes

1. Edward T. Hall, *The Silent Language* (Greenwich, CT: Fawcett Premier Books, 1967).

2. Daniel J. Levinson, et al., *The Seasons of a Man's Life* (New York: Knopf, 1978).

3. Albert Bandura and R. J. Walters, *Social Learning and Personality Development* (New York: Holt, Rinehart and Winston, 1963), and Bandura, *Social Learning Theory* (Englewood Cliffs, NJ: Prentice-Hall, 1977).

4. Albert Bandura, "Vicarious Processes: A Case of No-Trial Learning," in *Advances in Experimental Social Psychology,* vol. 2 ed. L. Berkowits (New York: Academic Press, 1965), 1–55.

5. C. H. Cooley, *Human Nature and the Social Order* (New York: Charles Scribner's Sons, 1902).

6. George H. Mead, *Mind, Self, and Society* (Chicago: University of Chicago Press, 1959).

7. Erving Goffman, *The Presentation of the Self in Everyday Life* (Garden City, NY: Doubleday Anchor, 1959).

8. Urie Bronfenbrenner, "Socialization and Social Class Through Time and Space," in *Readings in Social Psychology,* eds. Eleanor E. Maccoby, T. M. Newcomb, and E. L. Hartley (New York: Holt, Rinehart and Winston, 1958), 400–25.

9. Melvin L. Kohn, "Social Class and Parent-Child Relationships: An Interpretation," *American Journal of Sociology* 68 (1963): 471–80.

10. F. Ivan Nye and Felix M. Berade, *The Family: Its Structure and Interaction* (New York: Macmillan, 1973), 403–04.

11. Jean Jacques Rousseau, *Emile,* trans. by Barbara Foxley (New York: Everyman's Library, 1972), 43.

12. John Dewey, *Democracy and Education* (New York: Free Press, 1966), 54–56.

13. Granted that the characterization of public-school operations largely follows a structural-functional analysis; however, this is the way that most systems actually operate.

14. Wisconsin v. Yoder, U.S. Supreme Court (1972), 406 U.S. 205.

15. Margaret Mead, *Coming of Age in Samoa* (New York: William Morrow, 1928), and her *Sex and Temperament in Three Primitive Societies* (New York: Mentor Books, 1950); and Ruth Benedict, *Patterns of Culture* (Boston: Houghton Mifflin, 1934).

16. James Rachels, *The Elements of Moral Philosophy* (Philadelphia: Temple University Press, 1986), 15–17.

17. Metta Spencer, *Foundations of Modern Sociology*, 4th ed. (Englewood Cliffs, NJ: Prentice-Hall, 1985), 65.

18. Talcott Parsons, *The Social System* (New York: Free Press, 1954).

19. Lewis A. Coser, *The Functions of Social Conflict* (New York: Free Press, 1956).

20. Marvin Harris, *Cultural Materialism: The Struggle for a Science of Culture* (New York: Random House, 1979).

21. Boyce Rensberger, "Evolution Since Darwin," *Science* 82 (1982): 41.

22. Robert A. Wallace, *The Genesis Factor* (New York: William Morrow, 1979), 23.

23. W. D. Hamilton, "The Genetic Theory of Social Behavior: I and II," *Journal of Theoretical Biology* 7 (1964): 1–52.

24. Some sociobiologists also mention group altruism; but because this is a more controversial form, it will not be presented.

25. Edward Sapir, *Language: An Introduction to the Study of Speech* (New York: Harcourt, Brace and World, 1921); and Benjamin L. Whorf, *Language, Thought, and Reality* (New York: Wiley, 1956).

26. Eleanor Rosh-Heident and D. C. Oliver, "The Structure of Color Space in Naming and Memory in Two Languages," *Cognitive Psychology* 3 (1972): 337–54.

27. Harold Innis, *The Bias of Communication* (Toronto: University of Toronto Press, 1971).

28. Marshall McLuhan, *Understanding Media* (New York: McGraw-Hill, 1964).

29. Edward T. Hall, "How Cultures Collide," *Sociology* 81/82 (Guilford, CT: Dushkin Publishing Group, 1981), 28–33.

30. L. Knapp, *Nonverbal Communication in Human Interaction* (New York: Holt, Rinehart and Winston, 1972); and P. R. Wilson, "Perceptual Distortion of Height as a Function of Ascribed Academic Status," *Journal of Social Psychology* 74 (1968): 97–102.

31. Basil Bernstein, "Codes, Modalities, and the Process of Cultural Reproduction: A Model," *Language in Society* 10 (1981): 327–63, and his "Social Structure, Language, and Learning," *Educational Research* 3 (1961): 163–76.

32. J. Schultz and G. Florio, "Stop and Freeze: The Negotiation of Social and Physical Space in a Kindergarten/First Grade Classroom," *Anthropology and Education Quarterly* 10 (1979): 166–81.

33. Charles M. Galloway, "Nonverbal: The Language of Sensitivity," *Theory and Practice* 13 (1974): 380–83, and his "Nonverbal Communication in Teaching," *Educational Leadership* 24 (1966): 55–63.

34. Robert Rosenthal and Lenore Jacobson, *Pygmalion in the Classroom* (New York: Holt, Rinehart and Winston, 1968).

35. Ann Parker Parelius and Robert J. Parelius, *The Sociology of Education* (Englewood Cliffs, NJ: Prentice-Hall, 1978), 317.

36. Shirley Brice Heath, "Sociocultural Contexts of Language Development," in California State Department of Education, *Beyond Language* (Los Angeles: National Evaluation, Dissemination, and Assessment Center, California State University, 1986), 145.

37. Lau v. Nichols, 483 F. 2d 791 (9th Cir. 1973), rev'd 414 U.S. 563 (1974).

38. Serena v. Municipal Schools, 499 F 2d 1147 (10th Cir. 1974).

39. Aspira of New York, Inc. v. Board of Education of the City of New York, 423 F. Supp 647 (S.D.N.Y 1976).

40. "Bilingualism Is Not the Way" (Editorial), *Christian Science Monitor* (July 14, 1983): 18.

41. M. N. Danoff, *Evaluation of the Impact of ESEA Title VII Spanish/English Bilingual Education Program: Overview of Study and Findings* (Palo Alto, CA: American Institutes for Research, 1978).

42. R. C. Troike, *Research Evidence for the Effectiveness of Bilingual Education* (Arlington, VA: National Clearinghouse for Bilingual Education, 1978).

43. C. F. Leyba, *Longitudinal Study of Title VII Bilingual Program: Santa Fe Public Schools* (Los Angeles: California State University, National Dissemination and Assessment Center, 1978).

44. R. C. Troike, "Synthesis of Research on Bilingual Education," *Educational Leadership* (March 1981): 298–504.

45. Virginia P. Collier, "Age and Rate of Acquisition of Cognitive-Academic Second Language Proficiency," paper presented at the American Educational Research Association meeting, April 23, 1987.

■ CHAPTER 9

SOCIAL CLASS, RACE, ■ ETHNICITY, AND GENDER

A LOOK AHEAD

The purpose of this chapter is to examine how key social variables can influence learning opportunities and educational achievement. You will learn about:

- The social stratification systems that determine the degree of status individuals have in society

- The difference between ascribed status and achieved status and how they affect social mobility

- Some theories about why societies are stratified

- The characteristics of different social classes

- The principal social classes in the United States

- How social class, race, and ethnicity can affect educational achievement

- How the socialization of males and females in American society is manifested in the school systems

- The beginning of multicultural education and some suggestions for the future

Despite the emphasis in the United States on universal education, certain minority groups have not had equal access to a quality education and the social, economic, and political benefits such an education can provide. As we discussed in Chapter 5, one limiting factor is the prevailing set of attitudes in our culture toward race and ethnicity. But the problem involves more than just attitude. Minority education opportunities also are connected to socioeconomic status, gender, language, the academic and social goals of the schools, and the degree to which the values that students learn outside the school coincide with those promoted within. In this chapter we will look at several key variables in students' backgrounds and explore how these variables—and society's attitude toward them—can affect educational opportunity and achievement. We also will consider what educators can do to enhance these opportunities for all students.

■ SOCIAL CLASS

Social Stratification

Every society has a system of prestige by which some individuals are accorded more status than others. Societies, in other words, are socially stratified. **Social stratification** is a hierarchal system in which people are categorized in terms of the degree of superiority—or inferiority—that society accords them. These categories can include race, ethnicity, gender, and social class. Variables such as income, occupation, formal education, and organizational membership can contribute to another hierarchy of status within each social class.

Societies often have different stratification systems: preliterate cultures generally have fewer categories than complex industrial societies, and industrial societies can differ in their emphasis on particular categories. Many societies differ, for instance, in the importance they place on race and ethnicity.

The power of the highest level of a society helps to hold its stratification system in place.

Social stratification is supported by beliefs that are rationalized as accurate and just by those in power. People who enjoy higher status usually defend the system, whereas people of lower status might seek to change the system and increase their status. Examples of some beliefs defended by the majority in power are the now-debunked myth that women are not aggressive enough to succeed in business and the belief that boys are inherently better at math and science than girls are.

Groups of lower status who try to change the system often run into obstacles because resources, opportunities, and access to power are usually distributed in a way that reflects stratification: the highest classes get the largest share, and the lowest classes get the smallest.

Ascribed Status Versus Achieved Status and Social Mobility

Social stratification may persist over generations if the system is based largely on **ascribed status** (an involuntary social position assumed at birth or later in life) rather than **achieved status** (a voluntarily assumed social position that reflects a measure of personal ability and accomplishment). **Social mobility**—movement within a social stratification system—depends in large part on the degree to which status in a given society is ascribed or achieved. For example, a **caste system**, which is a social stratification system based almost entirely on ascribed status, allows almost no mobility. Examples of caste systems can be found in the Hindu villages of rural India and South Africa's system of apartheid. Caste systems often are sanctioned by religious beliefs (as in India) or by racial beliefs (as in South Africa). If you had been born into a caste, your birth would determine your occupation, who you would be permitted to marry, with whom you could interact, your religion, and what, if any, social privileges you would be entitled to. Before the Emancipation Proclamation in 1863, the United States had a caste system based on race, although it was not as rigid as those currently found in South Africa or India.

Whereas some agrarian societies may be based on a caste system, modern industrial societies are stratified, at least in part, in terms of **social class**, or the grouping of people based on their socioeconomic status. Such systems tend to be based largely on achieved status. The more a society's social classes are determined by achieved, rather than ascribed, status the greater the social mobility in that society.

> Social mobility is more likely in a system based on achieved rather than ascribed status.

Another distinction between class and caste is the degree of **status consistency** within individual castes or classes. Caste systems have high status consistency; class systems have less status consistency. Though sharp differences in wealth, power, and prestige often exist between castes, individuals within the same caste have nearly the same amount of money, power, and prestige. In contrast, within the same social class, features such as occupational prestige, income, and amount of formal education may differ widely. As a result, the social boundaries between classes are less marked than those separating castes, and, therefore, social mobility is easier.

> Caste systems are more rigid than class systems, where boundaries between classes tend to blur.

The terms *achieved status* and *ascribed status* can help us to understand the different levels in a society and to see how one comes to occupy a particular level in a social hierarchy. But the everyday world is never as neat as our explanations of it. For example, the United States is a society with a fair amount of social mobility. If people are talented and work hard enough, some believe, they can accomplish anything. They can move up the social ladder. In other words, many people view status in the United States as achieved. However, the reality is that one's opportunities are profoundly affected by what class one is born into. So, while status in the United States is achieved to a great degree, it also is ascribed. In our society, for instance, education is one of the key ways to move up the social ladder. But social class often affects educational opportunity and achievement—a situation we will discuss in depth a little later in this chapter. Let us first assess why inequalities persist in society.

Theories of Stratification

Why have inequalities developed in every society that ever existed? Why do inequalities persist in so-called classless societies and other societies that have sought to eradicate inequalities? Some theories seek to answer these and related questions.

Structural-Functional Theory. The **structural-functional theory** holds that not all jobs in a society are equally important and that the most important jobs are also the most demanding.[1] The most important jobs, such as professions and executive posts, require talents and abilities that are scarce and can be developed only through a lengthy education. These jobs also subject individuals to much pressure and responsibility. To motivate people to pursue these positions, society provides considerable rewards in terms of income, power, prestige, and leisure time. Social inequality has unconsciously evolved in the efforts to ensure that the most important positions are filled by the best qualified persons. Some degree of social stratification, therefore, is inevitable.

Structural-functional theory has been criticized on several grounds.[2] The importance of an occupation in a society is difficult to measure without considering the relative power of the occupational group in that society. In medicine, for example, stringent medical-college admission policies control the number of physicians produced each year; in other words, these policies ensure that physicians are in demand. Thus it is not clear how much of an occupation's importance is intrinsic or politically generated. Other occupational organizations propagandize, usually through advertising, to convince the public of the occupation's importance. Another criticism is that the functional importance of some jobs does not always ensure a high degree of income, power, or prestige. The great importance of garbage collectors is appreciated—especially when they go on strike—but the connection between the job's functional importance and a garbage collector's income is slight.

All occupations do not necessarily command prestige commensurate with their functional importance.

Another criticism of the theory is that social stratification is not functional at all; in fact, it is dysfunctional because it blocks the realization and utilization of some of the society's talent. Families transmit their socioeconomic position to offspring regardless of individual merit, so poor children with great talent probably will have little chance to realize their full potential. And the more rigid the system of social stratification, the more talent and ability will remain underdeveloped. Critics also point out that people in different occupations do not always receive rewards because they help society as a whole but because their work is valuable to the corporation that employs them. Finally, this theory ignores the fact that stratification has been a source of social conflict throughout history as people have struggled to overcome social inequalities and gain greater rights and opportunities.

Conflict Theory. Karl Marx's **conflict theory** envisioned an inevitable conflict in capitalistic societies between the capitalists (bourgeoisie) and the workers (proletariat) because of economic exploitation that would in time lead to the overthrow of capitalism. Marx believed that social classes emerge from the different positions that exist in a given system of production. The bourgeoisie own the factories and other means of production and their interests are inherently opposed to those of the proletariat. The bourgeoisie keeps the profits and the proletariat cannot do much about it because the bourgeoisie are in control. Moreover, the proletariat may not entirely recognize the basis of their plight. But Marx believed that the proletariat would, in time, develop a "class consciousness" that would enable them to understand the common interests of their class and eventually recognize the need to take over the means of production. Marx predicted that an intermediate stage of socialism would eventually be transformed into the classless society of communism.

Marx's analysis overlooks the possibility that unequal rewards can motivate people to pursue certain occupations. Moreover, the overthrow of capitalism did not occur in capitalistic industrial states, as Marx had predicted. Instead, the overthrow occurred in agrarian countries, like China and the Soviet Union. Capitalism has been transformed since Marx's time, but not in the way Marx predicted. Since the nineteenth century, capitalism has seen the rise of white-collar jobs, organized labor, service industries, the knowledge industry, legal protection of workers, and the collaboration of government, labor, and industry.

Whereas Marx believed that conflict was based on ownership of property, today's theorists believe that is not necessarily the case. Managerial employees, for example, receive high salaries, enjoy many benefits, and have a degree of power, but they do not own the factories or

Even socialist so-
cieties have some
form of stratifica-
tion.

businesses. Today's conflict theorists, according to Ralf Dahrendorf, are interested in studying power and its effects, whatever the source.[3] Randall Collins observed further that socialist societies do not have social classes based on property, but they still are stratified. He distinguished three social classes:

1. those who give orders to many, but take orders from few;
2. those who defer to some, but can give orders to others; and
3. those who only take orders.[4]

Collins believed stratification could be defined by observing the location of individuals or groups in a communication network and noting whether they mainly give or receive orders.

Lenski's Theory. Lenski's theory explains social stratification as a sort of sociocultural evolution.[5] Gerhard Lenski noted that small hunting-and-gathering societies had little food and what was available was divided nearly evenly. The goods were shared according to need. Because no single group of people was able to accumulate substantially more resources than any other, stratification was minimized. But in horticultural, pastoral, and agrarian societies, people were able to increase their material goods. Some were more successful in doing this than others, and eventually a small elite began to control the surplus, leading to social inequality. These differences finally became institutionalized and a social-stratification system was developed.

But in industrial societies, inequality began to decline and these societies have become less stratified than preindustrial ones. Lenski explains this change in terms of the distribution of power. Power in agrarian societies is concentrated among the few and they generally use it to benefit themselves. Industrial societies, on the other hand, tend to disperse power over a larger proportion of the population, which leads to a wider redistribution of wealth. Workers in industrial societies require considerable education and training, and, with technological advancements, a greater proportion of the population can command greater social resources as manual jobs are replaced by white-collar occupations. As a result, social inequality declines over time and this decrease becomes functional for the society.

Criteria for Determining Social Class

How is social class determined in the United States, and what are some of its basic characteristics? Exploring this question should supply some valuable information about the purposes of education and about possible reasons why social class seems to have such a profound effect on how our children do in school.

It is commonly believed, especially in capitalistic societies, that income is the sole or primary factor that determines socioeconomic status (SES). But SES is more complex than that. Housing, organizational membership, occupation, formal education, race, ethnicity, and gender all play roles in defining one's social class in the United States. For example, someone who has a fairly prestigious occupation that requires extensive formal education (for instance, a college professor) might make the same amount of money as someone with a less prestigious occupation and less education (a person in sales, for example), but the college professor is usually perceived as belonging to a higher social class than the salesperson.

Several of the criteria affect one another. Formal education plays a significant role in income, organizational membership, and occupa-

Many students enroll in college preparatory classes hoping to enhance their socioeconomic and social status.

tion. And income affects the type of housing one can find. Parents'
occupations, income, and organizational membership affect their children's formal education. So does where one lives, because schools vary
in quality depending on the local tax base and the kinds of social
problems faced by the students in different areas. Education can play
an important role in affecting the other criteria that determine social
class (except perhaps gender and race). And, it is important to note,
education is the one criterion that people can control. Certainly it is
the only criterion into which you, as an educator, will have any input.
We will discuss education's effect on social class in more detail later in
this chapter.

Income. Income in the United States is related to age, race, region of
the country, size of the household, marital status, educational attainment, and home ownership (see Table 9–1). Note in the table, for
example, that the median income of households in which the head of
the household has fewer than eight years of formal education is
$10,884, while it is $43,952 where the head of the household has four
or more years of college. Note also the education patterns in the column for households with annual incomes of less than $5,000 and the
column for households with annual incomes of more than $75,000.
The correlation between education and income is distinct.

■ PAUSE TO REFLECT
Social Class and Income

● Using Table 9–1 as a guide, what conclusions can you draw
    about the effect that one's race has on one's potential income
    in our society?

● How do you think the degree of educational opportunity
    available to minorities might affect those numbers?

● What conclusions can you draw about the effect that one's
    gender has on one's potential income? Would greater educa-
    tional opportunities make a difference? How?

Housing. This social-class criterion is defined in terms of type of
housing and location. The type of home includes the building material
(wood, brick, stone, stucco), the square-footage, and the upkeep of the
property. Factors that affect the desirability of location include the
types of homes in the neighborhood, the quality of the schools, the
quantity of traffic, and whether nearby areas are zoned for industry or
business. This criterion is considered so important in our society that

T A B L E 9–1 Money income of households—percent distribution by money income level, by selected characteristics: 1987

Characteristic	Total households (1,000)	Percent Distribution of Households by Income Level (in dollars)								Median income (dollars)
		Under 5,000	5,000–9,999	10,000–14,999	15,000–24,999	25,000–34,999	35,000–49,999	50,000–74,999	75,000 and over	
Total[1]	91,066	6.9	11.5	10.6	19.2	16.1	17.2	12.2	6.3	25,966
Age of householder:										
15–24 years	5,226	13.8	16.6	15.8	25.6	15.8	8.1	3.6	.9	16,204
25–34 years	20,583	5.7	7.8	9.6	22.2	20.3	20.4	10.9	3.0	26,923
35–44 years	19,323	4.3	6.1	6.6	15.7	17.5	23.5	17.5	8.9	34,929
45–54 years	13,630	4.9	5.6	6.6	14.0	15.3	20.5	20.0	13.1	37,250
55–64 years	12,846	7.5	9.9	9.5	18.8	15.2	17.0	13.7	8.3	27,538
65 years and over	19,456	9.9	24.5	17.8	22.1	11.5	7.9	4.1	2.3	14,334
White	78,469	5.4	10.7	10.2	19.2	16.7	18.1	13.0	6.7	27,427
Black	10,186	17.9	17.7	13.3	20.7	12.2	10.8	5.5	2.0	15,475
Hispanic[2]	5,698	10.4	15.5	14.2	21.7	14.9	13.4	7.0	2.9	19,305
Northeast	19,137	6.0	11.9	9.0	17.8	15.9	18.0	13.5	8.0	28,069
Midwest	22,402	6.7	11.9	10.7	19.3	17.1	17.5	11.8	5.0	25,722
South	31,047	9.0	11.7	11.6	20.0	15.3	16.3	10.9	5.3	23,719
West	18,480	4.6	10.2	10.6	19.5	16.3	17.7	13.5	7.7	27,914
Size of household:										
One person	21,889	15.6	25.2	15.8	20.9	11.6	7.3	2.5	1.2	12,544
Two persons	29,295	4.5	8.7	11.5	22.2	17.9	17.7	11.7	5.7	26,481
Three persons	16,163	4.8	6.1	7.7	17.8	17.6	21.4	16.6	8.0	32,348
Four persons	14,143	3.0	5.0	6.1	14.8	17.3	23.5	19.6	10.6	36,805
Five persons	6,081	2.9	6.6	6.7	14.9	17.2	23.1	17.9	10.7	35,825
Six persons	2,176	4.8	7.7	8.5	15.0	15.8	21.6	17.8	8.8	33,871
Seven persons or more	1,320	4.5	8.9	8.9	18.1	15.3	18.0	15.8	10.6	30,800

TABLE 9–1 (continued)

Characteristic	Total households (1,000)	Percent Distribution of Households by Income Level (in dollars)								Median income (dollars)
		Under 5,000	5,000–9,999	10,000–14,999	15,000–24,999	25,000–34,999	35,000–49,999	50,000–74,999	75,000 and over	
Marital status:										
Male householder	62,773	3.4	6.7	8.9	18.9	17.8	20.7	15.5	8.1	31,534
Married, wife present	48,748	1.7	4.6	7.7	18.0	18.3	22.7	17.7	9.3	34,782
Married, wife absent	1,230	10.9	14.9	14.5	21.6	14.1	13.3	6.6	4.1	19,496
Widowed	1,920	10.8	26.7	17.3	18.7	11.3	7.3	6.2	1.8	13,424
Divorced	3,957	8.4	10.8	12.1	20.3	17.5	16.2	9.7	4.9	24,005
Single (never married)	6,477	8.9	11.9	12.5	24.4	16.4	14.4	7.7	3.7	21,493
Female householder	28,293	14.5	22.1	14.4	20.0	12.4	9.4	4.9	2.2	14,600
Married, husband present	3,061	2.7	6.6	7.3	16.4	17.4	22.8	16.7	10.2	34,847
Married, husband absent	2,156	24.7	23.4	15.5	19.9	9.0	5.8	1.2	.6	10,517
Widowed	9,628	15.2	34.0	16.6	17.0	8.4	5.4	2.2	1.1	10,209
Divorced	6,527	12.1	16.2	15.2	23.8	14.7	11.2	5.0	1.7	17,597
Single (never married)	6,310	16.9	17.6	13.1	22.5	15.3	8.7	4.6	1.2	15,759
Education attainment of householder:[3]										
Elementary school	11,500	16.3	26.7	17.2	19.7	9.9	6.4	2.9	.8	11,730
Less than 8 years	6,437	18.4	27.9	17.3	18.1	8.9	5.9	2.7	.7	10,884
8 years	5,063	13.7	25.2	17.1	21.7	11.0	7.0	3.1	1.0	12,999
High school	41,037	6.8	12.4	12.0	21.8	17.8	17.0	9.5	2.8	23,382
1–3 years	10,476	10.9	19.4	14.9	22.2	14.2	11.2	5.6	1.6	16,727
4 years	30,561	5.4	10.0	11.0	21.6	19.0	18.9	10.8	3.2	25,910
College	33,301	2.6	4.3	5.8	15.1	16.3	22.7	20.1	13.2	38,337
1–3 years	14,294	3.6	6.6	8.1	18.7	18.1	22.6	16.1	6.1	31,865
4 years or more	19,007	1.8	2.5	4.1	12.4	14.9	22.8	23.0	18.5	43,952
Tenure:										
Owner occupied	58,214	3.8	8.1	8.5	17.5	16.8	20.4	16.1	8.7	31,903
Renter occupied	31,180	12.0	17.3	14.2	22.6	15.0	11.6	5.4	1.9	17,474
Occupier paid no cash rent	1,672	17.7	20.8	15.2	20.5	11.2	9.7	3.5	1.4	13,613

[1]Includes other races not shown separately. [2]Hispanic persons may be of any race. [3]25 years old and over.
Source: U.S. Bureau of the Census, *Current Population Reports*, series P-60, No. 161.

338

sociological studies of communities can map property values and sort out desirable areas from undesirable ones.

Organizational Membership. Some community organizations are composed of members of only one social class because of stated admission policies (usually those of the upper-upper class); other organizations are composed of two classes closely related in prestige (usually the upper- and upper-upper classes, as in some country club memberships); and still other organizations are less restrictive. But sociologists have found such class distinctions at other levels, too. Studies of small communities have found that different churches and different men's and women's organizations tend to be composed of persons of similar class backgrounds. Most adults tend to establish friendships with individuals at the same class level, especially if they are in prestigious occupations.[6] About three out of five people in the upper-middle class belong to some type of voluntary organization compared with two out of five in the lower-middle class. Studies show that members of the lower class belong to few or no community organizations, often because of their long working hours, low income, and lack of ease around people of higher status.[7]

The membership of many organizations tends to be homogeneous in terms of social class.

Youth tend to associate with others of the same social class.

Occupational Prestige. Since 1925 studies have been conducted to
assess occupational prestige as an indicator of socioeconomic status.
The rankings of occupational prestige have been remarkably stable
since the 1920s and are fairly consistent from one country to another.
The unskilled and semiskilled occupations have less prestige than the
skilled ones, white-collar workers generally are ranked higher than
blue-collar workers, and professions rank higher than semiprofessions
(see Table 9–2). Donald Treiman offers an explanation of why these
numbers do not change from culture to culture or from year to year:
similar technologies divide work in similar ways; and the greater the
occupational power (ability to control scarce resources and to give
orders), the more prestige the occupation commands.[8] Occupation is
one of the most reliable indicators of status in the United States even
though occupational prestige and income are not always closely correlated (teachers and the clergy, for example, often command higher
occupational prestige than income).

Formal Education. As we have already discussed, formal education
carries prestige because it can enhance income and improve occupa-

T A B L E 9–2 Occupational prestige score, average for 57 countries

Occupation	Prestige Score	Occupation	Prestige Score	Occupation	Prestige Score
Physician	77.9	Building Contractor	53.5	Mason	34.1
University Professor	77.6	Actor	51.5	Plumber	33.9
Trial Lawyer	70.6	Bookkeeper	49.0	Sales Clerk	33.6
Head of a Large Firm	70.4	Traveling Salesman	46.9	Mail Carrier	32.8
Civil Engineer	70.3	Farmer	46.8	Truck Driver	32.6
Banker	67.0	Electrician	44.5	Bus Driver	32.4
Airline Pilot	66.5	Insurance Agent	44.5	Miner	31.5
High School Teacher	64.2	Office Clerk	43.3	Barber	30.4
Pharmacist	64.1	Garage Mechanic	42.9	Shoemaker, Repairer	28.1
Armed Forces Officer	63.2	Shopkeeper	42.4	Waiter	23.2
Clergyman	58.7	Printer	42.3	Farm Hand	22.9
Artist	57.2	Typist, Stenographer	41.6	Street Vendor, Peddler	21.9
Primary Teacher	57.0	Policeman	39.8	Janitor	21.0
Journalist	54.9	Tailor	39.5	Servant	17.2
Accountant	54.6	Foreman	39.3	Street Sweeper	13.4
Minor Civil Servant	53.6	Soldier	38.7		
Nurse	53.6	Carpenter	37.2		

Source: Donald J. Treiman, *Occupational Prestige in Comparative Perspective.* New York: Academic Press,
1977, pp. 155–56. Reprinted by permission of Donald J. Treiman and Academic Press.

tional opportunities. Both the amount of education and the institution attended affect the ranking of prestige. The prestige hierarchy moves up from high-school dropout to high-school graduate to college graduate to holder of an advanced professional degree. Western Europeans and the Japanese consider it more critical to graduate from an elite university than do Americans, but a select group of American universities nevertheless carries inordinate prestige. Graduates of their professional programs are likely to command top positions with high-status corporations such as prestigious law firms and Wall Street securities houses.

Race, Ethnicity, and Gender.   Race and ethnicity are related to social stratification. Whites have higher overall occupational standing than blacks and Hispanics and slightly higher educational achievement. Significant differences in income also exist among whites, blacks, and Hispanics. Class differences also exist within races. For example, historically, the wealthiest and most powerful Americans have been of English ancestry.[9] Gender also has a significant effect on social position. Women generally have less income, wealth, occupational prestige, and educational achievement than men do.[10] And households headed by women are more than ten times as likely to be poor as those headed by men. We will take a closer look at race, ethnicity, and gender later in this chapter. For now, let us examine the characteristics of the principal social classes in the United States.

Principal Social Classes

The Lower-Lower Class.   About 20 percent of the United States population lives in poverty. The people who make up this lower-lower class usually have few skills and less than eight years of formal education. Families headed by women are the fastest-growing segment of this class. Many members are functionally illiterate and live in the poorest neighborhoods. This class includes the unemployed and employed unskilled workers who usually are the last to be hired and the first to be fired. While some are new immigrants who perform menial tasks at the beginning of their climb up the social ladder, others have been caught up in the cycle of poverty and have been at the bottom of the social structure for generations. Those generationally trapped in poverty sometimes are referred to as the **under class.**

Members of the lower-lower class have reduced **life chances,** that is, they have less access to goods, services, and opportunities throughout their lives. They have lower life expectancies and are more likely to be among front-line military troops, to be victims of violent crime, to become mentally ill, and to have lower self-esteem.[11]

The Upper-Lower Class. About 32 percent of the population composes the upper-lower class. The jobs available to this segment tend to be simple and repetitive and allow for little autonomy. Members of the upper-lower class tend to live in inexpensive suburban houses and have a high-school education. Because of their usually limited formal education and vocational skills, most members of the upper-lower class are restricted in their upward social mobility. They tend to believe education is the key to getting a better job.[12]

The Lower-Middle Class. The lower-middle class constitutes 30 percent of the population and consists of skilled craftsmen (electricians, plumbers, cabinetmakers) and white-collar clerical and sales workers. Their income is about at the national average and they often own modest homes. Most members of the lower-middle class complete high school, and one-third to one-half of them attend college—usually a junior college or a state-supported college. They tend to subscribe to the Puritan ethics of thrift, hard work, financial independence, cleanliness, godliness, honesty, respect for authority, and sexual restraint. Their children are expected to be obedient and to respect the authority of their teachers.[13] Like members of the upper-lower class, they tend to consider education important for acquiring a good job.

Social classes at the lower levels of stratification value education as a means toward better jobs.

The Upper-Middle Class. About 15 percent of the population are members of the upper-middle class, and one-half of them have gained their status through social mobility. Their income is well above average, and they tend to be business executives and professionals. They own medium to large homes in fairly expensive areas and tend to play important roles in local civic and political organizations. Education is considered extremely important; their children usually attend public schools and state universities or private liberal arts colleges to prepare for life-long careers. In interpersonal relations, they stress individual initiative and smooth group functioning.[14]

The Upper Classes. The upper classes consist of only 3 percent of the population and can be divided into the lower-upper class and the upper-upper class (about 1 percent of the population). Upper-class families have yearly incomes of at least $100,000 and control a disproportionate share of stocks and real estate. The primary source of wealth for the lower-upper class is earnings ("new money"), whereas the upper-upper class gets most of its wealth through inheritance ("old money"). Many members of the upper class are top executives and high government officials; some members of the upper-upper class are patrons of the arts and charities. Historically, the upper class has been almost exclusively white Anglo-Saxon Protestant, although this is becoming less true today as more leaders of society and members of the most highly esteemed professions come from varied backgrounds. Besides wealth, members of the upper-upper class have status based in part on family name, practice **endogamy** (marriage between persons of the same social class), and observe intricate codes of etiquette. They educate their children through nannies, tutors, finishing and preparatory schools, and prestigious private colleges in the United States and abroad. They instill in their children the concept of *noblesse oblige:* the moral obligation to express honorable and charitable behavior toward members of lower social classes.[15]

Social Class and Educational Achievement

Lower-class students traditionally have a more difficult time in school than do middle-class students, and several explanations have been offered in an attempt to find a way to improve their educational opportunities:

> Schools generally represent the values of the middle class.

- Lower-class students have less access to educational and cultural resources that can contribute to educational achievement, such as toys, books, travel, and field trips, and they tend not to receive much supplemental education at home.[16]

- Parents of lower-class students tend to lack the knowledge they need to help their children make wise choices about their educational futures.[17]

- Basil Bernstein found that middle-class students use an elaborative language that promotes cognitive development, while lower-class students tend to use a more restricted language.[18] Because most schools and teachers use this formal language of the dominant class, lower-class students are at a disadvantage because they cannot speak the formal language as well as middle-class students can.

- Whether they realize it or not, teachers tend to bring middle-class norms to school and to impose middle-class expectations on students. The socialization process, which begins during infancy in the home, continues in the school in many forms: children are expected to be orderly, form straight lines, keep quiet on the way to the playground or cafeteria, wait to be recognized by the teacher before speaking, turn in neat work, follow instructions carefully, and respect the teacher's authority. Because students also bring the norms of their own social class to school, conflicts can arise if the students' norms do not happen to be of the middle class.

- Schools serve as front-end screening agencies by identifying students likely to be best suited for the better jobs and positions in society and weeding out those who are less academically fit. The middle-class child has a greater likelihood than the lower-class child of succeeding in school not only because middle-class values are reinforced in the home, but also because more emphasis is placed on reading, learning, and getting ahead. Middle-class parents encourage their children to plan for the future. Because public schools are essentially middle-class institutions, the middle-class child, upon first entering school, has a decisive advantage over the lower-class child. (The upper class is not represented here because most do not send their children to public schools.)

- Regardless of a student's measured ability, teachers tend to favor students who share their own values. Studies have shown that children who are clean, quiet, and respectful of the teacher usually are classified as brighter than others and often are placed in high-track classes such as college preparatory programs. Teachers generally have a difficult time giving failing grades to students they like[19] and tend to interact more with those for whom they hold higher expectations. They praise these students more when they are correct and criticize them less when they are wrong.[20] They give them more autonomy in their school work and punish them less for rule infractions. In contrast, lower-class students tend to be given the minimum attention, are placed in lower tracks, such as vocational programs, and receive fewer hours of actual instruction. Teachers tend to interact with these students less than the higher-track students, offer less encouragement, and worry less about them when they drop out of school because they assume they probably will fail.[21] As a result, these lower-class students fall further behind in schoolwork, have lower self-esteem, and in extreme cases might not even consider themselves "students."

Teachers must make conscientious efforts to help students from the lower classes overcome the built-in social barriers they will encounter in the educational system.

To begin to overcome these problems, teachers first need to identify the values that stem from their own social-class background and recognize how these values might influence their attitudes and behavior toward lower-class children. Second, teachers can make special efforts to become more tolerant and understanding of social differences and the reasons for the differences. This deeper self-perception and greater understanding can lead to new, more sensitive teacher-pupil relations. Finally, educators can make sure that the curriculums address the concerns and problems of lower-class youth.

But what, specifically, can be done to promote a better education for lower-class youth, especially the lower-lower class? Here are some suggestions:

- Teachers can assess each student's abilities and frame the schoolwork around those assessments.

- Group activities can be introduced that are designed to involve all students in the class and provide structure for learning activities.

- A wide variety of teaching methods and materials can be used and adapted to different learning styles.

- Teachers can provide compelling and worthwhile role models to make up for the lack of models in lower-class students' backgrounds.

- Because many lower-class students suffer low self-esteem, teachers can provide tasks at which the students can succeed, thereby improving the students' self-concept.

- Teachers and educators can avoid labeling students as "slow learners" or "problem children," as it is commonly agreed that when a teacher harbors preconceived notions of a child's behavior, the child probably will live up—or down—to those expectations.

- Teachers can help each student develop a close, caring relationship with a significant adult.

- Teachers and administrators can make every effort to involve parents in their children's education and keep open the lines of communication with them.

- Teachers and school nurses can teach and encourage good nutrition and health care.

- Administrators can avoid tracking (see Chapter 13) and offer compensatory education (see Chapter 10).

■ PAUSE TO REFLECT
Examining Your Own Values

- As a teacher, what values would you bring into the classroom? How could those values affect your teaching methods or your attitude toward students—both those with similar values and those with different values?

- Think back to your favorite teachers in school—how did they treat you? Which of their teaching approaches would you like to adopt in your own classroom?

■ **RACE**

In addition to social class, race is also considered by some observers to influence student achievement. Whether these influences are biological or environmental is disputed. **Race** is a subspecies of homo sapiens usually distinguished by certain physical traits. The three major racial classifications are Caucasians, Negroids, and Mongoloids. Scientists, however, recognize that there are no pure races and that many of the world's people do not fit precisely into one of these three classifications. Racial mixing has been common for tens of thousands of years, making exact classification impossible. Many white and black Americans are genetically mixed, for example, as the genetic traits have combined over the years, and the Mongoloid traits of the Native Americans have spread throughout the United States population. Moreover, knowing the predominant race of a group provides little understanding of the group's culture, as is the case with different Caucasian nationalities in Europe.

One difficulty with using race to determine tendencies is that the race concept is purely arbitrary. It depends on who is doing the classifying and which traits are selected as distinguishing ones. Many traits—blood type, skin color, facial features—could be used, but anthropologists differ on this opinion. William Boyd has identified five races, Carleton Coon says there are nine, Joseph Birdsell recognizes thirty-two.[22] Other anthropologists—among them Ashley Montagu, Jean Hiernaux, C. Loring Brace, and Frank Livingston—claim there is no such thing as race. Although they do not claim that all people are physically the same, they do not employ the concept of race when studying physical variables.

But the significant point is that race has attained prominent sociological meaning in some cultures as society attributes different rates of intelligence, personality, character, and physical prowess to different races. Such has been the case throughout United States history, and sometimes this has led to **racism,** the belief that one racial group is innately superior or inferior to another. Racism usually goes hand in hand with **prejudice** (an unfavorable opinion formed without facts to support it) and **discrimination** (unfair or unjust treatment of minorities just because they are minorities). In some instances, racism against individuals develops into **institutionalized racism,** socially sanctioned practices that result in systematic discrimination against members of specific groups. Several cases of both forms of racism were presented in Chapter 5 in the history of minority education.

Several studies have suggested a relationship between race and educational achievement, but the causes remain in dispute. In this **"nature-nurture" controversy**, some researchers believe intelligence is inherited, while others believe it is affected by environment—either physical or cultural. In 1986 the National Assessment of Educational Progress (NAEP) tested reading performance in third, seventh, and eleventh grades of public and private schools (see Figure 9–1). Black and Hispanic students scored lower than white students. The NAEP also found that eleventh-grade students in an academic curriculum had higher reading scores than students in vocational and general programs, and that black and Hispanic students were less likely to be enrolled in academic programs than white students.[23]

High-school completion rates and the number of awarded higher-education degrees vary by race and ethnicity. Nationally, about one out of every four 18- and 19-year-olds has not completed high school. About 84 percent of 20- to 24-year-olds have completed high school, a number that has remained constant since 1974. Fewer 18- to 24-year-old black and Hispanic youths receive high-school diplomas or the equivalent (see Table 9–3), although the proportion has increased since 1974. About 10 percent more students complete their high-school education by ages 20 through 24 than by ages 18 through 19.[24]

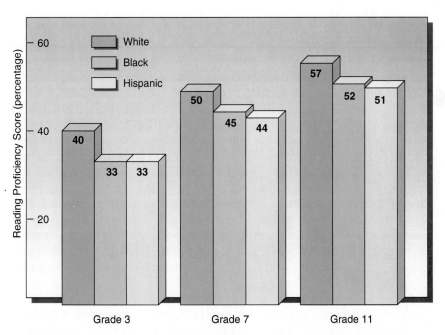

FIGURE 9–1 Average reading proficiency, by race and ethnicity: 1986

NOTE: The range of the reading proficiency scale was from 0 to 100. The average scores by grade were 38.1 for grade 3, 48.9 for grade 7, and 56.1 for grade 11.
Source: Adapted from National Assessment of Educational Progress, 1988.

TABLE 9–3 High school completion by race and ethnicity

Year	Age: 18–19			Age: 20–24		
	White	Black	Hispanic	White	Black	Hispanic
	Percent of age group			Percent of age group		
1974	76	56	49	86	73	59
1980	76	59	46	85	74	57
1986	77	65	55	85	81	62

Source: U.S. Department of Commerce, Bureau of the Census, "School Enrollment—Social and Economic Characteristics of Students, October [various years]," *Current Population Reports,* Series P–20; and unpublished tabulations.

In 1988 the percentage of the U.S. population with fewer than twelve years of formal education was highest for people age 65 and older and lowest for people age 25 to 34 (see Table 9–4). In 1988 more whites had completed four or more years of college than any other racial or ethnic group.

Intelligence testing has been a major instrument in classifying students into groups so as to organize and simplify plans for instruction and programming, a practice that has significantly affected students of all races and ethnicities. In general, minorities tend to score lower on such tests than whites, but again, the reasons for this are in dispute. Arthur Jensen believes that what I.Q. tests measure is 80 percent inherited and 20 percent cultural.[25] In Jensen's theory, intelligence comprises two levels: associated learning ability (Level 1) and conceptual learning and problem solving (Level 2). Level 1 is best tested by measuring memory span and rote-learning abilities, while Level 2 involves cognitive transformation of incoming data and is more similar to traditional concepts of I.Q. (intelligence quotient). Different ethnic groups score about the same on Level 1 tests, but black and disadvantaged children tend to score lower on Level 2 tests.[26] Jensen concludes that (1) blacks average about 15 points below whites on I.Q. tests; (2) blacks and disadvantaged children have more difficulty with abstract reasoning; (3) blacks and disadvantaged children do well on rote-learning tasks; and (4) compensatory education (programs to help disadvantaged children) has failed.

Jensen's studies have been criticized on several grounds: (1) he used relatively small samples; (2) the interaction between heredity and environment is impossible to separate and measure; (3) intelligence can be affected by several environmental factors that are difficult to measure, such as nutrition and prenatal care; (4) racial discrimination could account for differences in I.Q. scores; and (5) I.Q. tests are biased and do not necessarily measure intelligence.[27]

TABLE 9–4 Percent of population with less than 12 years of school and with 4 years of college or more, by age, race, and Hispanic origin: 1970 to 1988

Race and Hispanic Origin	Less Than 12 Years of School								4 Years of College or More							
				1988								1988				
	1970	1980	1985	Total	25–34 yr.	35–44 yr.	45–64 yr.	65 yr. and over	1970	1980	1985	Total	25–34 yr.	35–44 yr.	45–64 yr.	65 yr. and over
All races[1]	47.7	33.5	26.1	23.8	13.6	14.0	27.0	46.2	10.7	16.2	19.4	20.3	23.7	26.9	18.2	10.6
White	45.5	31.2	24.5	22.3	12.8	12.8	24.7	43.3	11.3	17.1	20.0	20.9	24.5	27.8	18.7	11.1
Black	68.6	48.8	40.2	36.7	19.5	22.8	46.8	76.5	4.4	8.4	11.1	11.3	13.2	15.4	9.2	4.7
Hispanic origin[2]	67.9	56.0	52.1	49.0	38.3	44.1	59.7	77.6	4.5	7.6	8.5	10.0	11.9	10.7	8.6	4.1
Mexican	75.8	62.4	58.7	55.4	45.7	48.6	68.7	84.1	2.5	4.9	5.5	7.1	8.4	8.7	5.2	1.4
Puerto Rican	76.6	59.9	53.7	49.2	32.4	44.3	67.9	83.2	2.2	5.6	7.0	9.6	11.3	11.2	7.3	2.2
Cuban	56.1	44.7	48.9	39.5	16.1	32.3	44.5	64.4	11.1	16.2	16.7	17.1	23.8	20.3	14.4	11.9
Other[3]	55.1	42.6	35.8	35.5	25.8	34.3	40.2	69.2	7.0	12.4	16.4	15.5	19.1	13.8	14.8	6.1

[Persons 25 years old and over. As of April 1970 and 1980, and March 1985 and 1988]

[1]Includes races not shown separately.

[2]Persons of Hispanic origin may be of any race.

[3]Includes Central and South American and other Hispanic origins.

Source: U.S. Bureau of the Census, *Census of Population: 1970,* vols. I and II, *1980 Census of Population,* vol. I, chapter C, *Current Population Reports,* series P–20, No. 438 and earlier reports; and unpublished data.

Richard Hernstein connected intelligence to social class by arguing that "(1) If differences in mental abilities are inherited, and (2) if success requires these abilities, and (3) if earnings and prestige depend on success, then (4) social standing will be based to some extent on the inherited differences among people."[28]

A strong argument can be made for the opinion that culture and environment, not heredity, most influence I.Q. scores. While, on the average, whites do score about 15 points higher than blacks on intelligence tests, a large number of blacks exceed the average test score for whites. Moreover, some blacks score as high as or higher than any whites on intelligence tests.[29] These exceptions to the "rule" would not be possible if intelligence were related solely to race.

Acting on the assumption that culture and environment can affect scores, some educators have attempted to construct "culture-fair" tests that skip mathematics and language and instead measure the observation of differences in pictorial details or spatial arrangements. But L. E. Tyler has suggested that minorities might be at even more of a disadvantage on pictorial than verbal items, because blacks tend to not score very high on pictorial tests.[30] Moreover, pictorial testing has less to do with achievement test scores and school grades than does verbal testing, although pictorial tests can be useful in assessing non-English speaking students or those from extremely different cultural backgrounds. But even if every student tested started out with the same advantages and disadvantages regarding knowledge of the material, a number of personal intangibles still are inherent in the tests and affect the cross-cultural validity of the scores—intangibles such as willingness to strive in the face of defeat, willingness to work for goals set by strange adults, and other traits associated more with the middle class.

> Measures of intelligence that are completely free of cultural bias are so far unavailable.

Some proponents of the "nurture" theory believe that the differences in I.Q. scores between blacks and whites can be attributed to prejudice and differences in social class. Others claim that scores can be affected by differences in social conditions (such as conditions faced by the poor compared with those faced by the middle and upper classes). J. McVicker Hunt summarized many studies on intellectual growth. While he recognized that heredity can set limits on human potential, he concluded that environment is extremely important and that schools should provide compensatory education to counteract disadvantaged backgrounds.[31] Christopher Jencks says we do not have an adequate definition of environment and its components, and we cannot measure the influence of genes on the environment or that of the environment on genes.[32] Heredity and environment interact and both contribute to human abilities, but the amount that each contributes cannot be stated precisely.

> The extent to which heredity and environment affect intelligence cannot be determined exactly.

EDUCATIONAL ISSUE 9–1

Do racial differences inherently affect intelligence?

Yes	No
1. Race is the most significant influence on intelligence.	1. The concept of race is arbitrary depending on what traits are selected and who does the selecting.
2. Whites score about 15 points higher than blacks on I.Q. tests.	2. Many blacks exceed the average I.Q. test score for whites, and some blacks score as high as any whites.
3. Blacks have more difficulty than whites in abstract reasoning.	3. I.Q. tests are not "culture-fair" and fail to consider environmental differences.

ETHNICITY ■

The Ethnographic Atlas identifies 892 ethnic groups in the world, with many cultures having more than five ethnic groups. A significant number of engineers, doctors, and technical workers in the United States have Asian backgrounds. In New York, 40 percent of elementary and secondary students belong to an ethnic minority; in California, white Anglos are in the minority. The United States, once a microcosm of European nationalities, is today a microcosm of the world. The unique and wide variety of cultural influences in our society cannot be ignored, and educators face stronger challenges than ever to ensure that all Americans have access to a good education, while respecting and preserving ethnic differences. The problems arise, especially, in trying to provide a multicultural curriculum; preparing teachers to understand and handle cultural differences; and avoiding ethnic and racial conflicts. The issue raises questions about how many cultures should be included and where the line should be drawn.

Ethnic groups can be viewed as serving three basic functions: (1) they promote group cohesion; (2) they sustain and enhance ethnic identity among their members; and (3) they establish social networks and communication patterns that help the group advance in society. A

The society of the United States today is the most culturally and ethnically varied of any society in history.

The United States is home to hundreds of ethnic groups. In some areas in California, people with Asian heritage are in the majority.

sense of unity and ethnic identity also can play an important political role as more ethnic groups begin to assert themselves in that arena.

Many ethnic groups also can be minority groups. A **minority group** is a category of people who are defined by physical or cultural characteristics and subject to social disadvantage. Examples of minority groups are some racial and ethnic groups, the disabled, political radicals, women, and homosexuals. The most prominent minority ethnic groups are Native Americans, Hispanics, Asian Americans, African Americans, and some European Americans.

While ethnicity serves many important functions, it can have disadvantages:

- Ethnic identity can create a parochial attitude that regards people who are not members of the group as inferior or untrustworthy.

- Ethnic groups might limit intergroup interaction to prevent cultural diffusion.

- Social conflict can be heightened in areas that contain several diverse ethnic groups as the differences in life styles and values are highlighted.
- Ethnic groups might restrict opportunities and autonomy by demanding conformity to maintain unity.
- They may reinforce stereotypical images of other groups, reducing the chances of ever settling any cultural differences.

The Treatment of Ethnic Groups

Several outcomes are possible when minority ethnic groups interact with the dominant group of a society.

Genocide and Expulsion. In extreme cases, members of the dominant group, seeking to quash dissent, might expel the minority groups (as Uganda's Idi Amin expelled several groups in the 1970s) or commit genocide (as the Nazis attempted to annihilate the Jews, and as the white settlers purged the Native Americans in their conquest of the frontier).

Ethnic Stratification. In less extreme cases, societies might engage in **ethnic stratification**, in which two or more ethnic groups maintain a dominant-subordinate relationship. Imperialism and colonialism are the most common means of ethnic stratification, as one nation seeks to extend its power over other territories. The European nations, for example, dominated the world at one time, exercising control over Africa, Asia, and the Americas and justifying their treatment of the natives on racist grounds. The United States also has been accused of imperialism and colonialism in several nations including Cuba, the Philippines, Panama, and Mexico.

Segregation and Partitioning. The dominant group also can maintain control through **segregation,** the forced separation of different groups and the establishment of rules or laws by which the dominant group can maintain its control. Segregation has been attacked in the courts as a violation of the Fourteenth Amendment, which guarantees equal protection under the law. As we discussed in Chapter 5, segregation (and its attendant institutional racism) often leads to separate school systems and other institutions for different races. If the tension among ethnic groups is especially high, sometimes the area will be split into different countries, known as **partitioning** (as in the partition of Palestine that created the state of Israel or the partition of Ireland into Protestant and Catholic regions).

Segregation is a formal means by which a society puts a minority ethnic group in a subordinate position.

Anglo Conformity.   Until about 1900 in the United States, **Anglo conformity** was a common form of domination in which the dominant group sought to maintain the social institutions and cultural patterns of England, especially in the school system. Protestant religious principles were taught in the public schools, the English language and British literature were preferred courses of study, and Anglo values dominated the school boards.

Amalgamation.   As the number of immigrants soared between 1870 and 1910, educators attempted to "Americanize" immigrant children by teaching them the ways of American democracy. Israel Zangwell's popular 1908 play *The Melting Pot* dramatized a society that Americanized immigrants by melding different cultures. This process is called **amalgamation**, a blending of different groups through a lengthy period of interbreeding. In other words, if groups A, B, and C amalgamated, a new group, X, would develop: A + B + C = X. A certain degree of amalgamation has occurred in Brazil, Hawaii, and Mexico.

Assimilation.   Members of the minority ethnic groups might renounce their ethnicity and strive to **assimilate** into, or adopt the culture of, the majority to escape discrimination, to advance more rapidly in their occupations, or because they are dissatisfied with their ethnic group. As they adopt the dominant culture, assimilated ethnic groups often lose their identity. In other words, if A, B, and C are different groups in a society (with A as the dominant group and B and C as the assimilated groups), then A + B + C = A. Assimilation was a feature of Anglo conformity as long as the Anglos were willing to accept the group if it relinquished its culture and adopted Anglo culture. (Less acceptable ethnic groups were segregated and not permitted to assimilate.)

Cultural Pluralism.   In an ideal society several different groups maintain their cultural differences and live in a state of peaceful coexistence after a period of adjustment. This form of **cultural pluralism** encourages respect for the rights of all groups in society. In school it involves appreciation for the contributions of all groups and a recognition of their histories and cultural backgrounds. Different groups work together in the community without trying to dominate or exploit one another, while maintaining their cultural distinctiveness and ways of life.

Appreciation of individual learning styles is a benefit of cultural pluralism.

Cultural pluralism means that teachers recognize different learning styles. A learning style, according to Dunn and Griggs, is "a biologically and developmentally imposed set of characteristics that makes the same teaching method wonderful for some and terrible for others."[33] Blacks, Hispanics, and Native Americans tend to be group-oriented; therefore, these students experience problems in the schools' highly individualistic learning environment.[34] These students tend to be field-sensitive, whereas Anglo Americans tend to be field-independent. Field-sensitive students prefer to work with others to achieve a goal, while field-independent students prefer to work alone. Teachers in a society based on cultural pluralism would work with field-sensitive students using cooperative teaching strategies that have been developed and tested.[35]

Integration. Another ideal situation, **integration** is a move toward greater equality among different ethnic groups by reducing the separation between them and encouraging them to work together. Amalgamation is a biological form of integration, but groups may integrate on a social and educational level as well. Instead of separate rules for different groups, the same rules apply to all. School systems and classes are racially and ethnically mixed in a nondiscriminatory manner, and emphasis is placed on common values and interests rather than on cultural differences.

GENDER ■

Socialization for male and female roles varies widely among different ethnic groups throughout the world. Margaret Mead found the males and females of the New Guinea Arapesh, for example, to be cooperative, nonaggressive, and responsive to others' needs. The Mundugumor males and females, on the other hand, were ruthless and aggressive. In a third tribe, the Tchambuli, the women were dominant and impersonal, whereas the men were less responsible and more emotionally dependent.[36] Mead's observations suggest that there is no basis for regarding aspects of behavior as either "male" or "female." But other anthropologists claim to have found universal cultural traits in sex roles. In all societies, for instance, men control the political and military institutions, and the traits of achievement and self-reliance are ascribed to men.[37]

Different areas of the home and community can be associated more exclusively with one sex than another. Women in some Middle Eastern societies are restricted to certain parts of the house and might have contact only with males who are family members. The marketplace and coffeehouses, on the other hand, are usually the male domains.

S. B. Ortner notes that men's work in all known cultures is assigned greater prestige than women's work regardless of the nature of men's work.[38] Among the Arapesh, for example, some men dress like women and perform female tasks. These men are referred to as "female men," with no notion of homosexuality or weakness implied.

In the United States socialization for masculine roles aims largely for self-reliance and achievement, and female roles tend toward nurturing and responsibility. Femininity usually is associated with cooperation, dependence, emotionality, passivity, and verbalness, while masculinity usually is associated with competitiveness, aggressiveness, independence, lack of emotion, impersonality, and spatial ability.[39]

Although many alleged differences between the sexes are unsupported, Eleanor Maccoby and Carol Jacklin conducted studies with results that support four basic differences[40]:

- Girls show greater verbal ability than boys. Their verbal skills are about the same until age eleven, when the girls tend to surpass the boys. This greater ability increases in high school.

- Boys show greater spatial ability (such as the ability to drive a car, fly a plane, or shoot at a moving object) beginning in adolescence and continuing throughout adulthood.

- Boys demonstrate superior mathematical ability, which manifests itself in adolescence and is unrelated to the number of math courses taken.

- Males in all societies studied are more aggressive, even from age two; this aggressiveness continues through the college years, and sometimes beyond.

In the academic realm, girls begin speaking, reading, and counting sooner than boys, and they perform as well as boys in math and science during the early grades. But boys' proficiency in math and science surpasses that of girls by adolescence; and by ages twenty-one to twenty-five, males have caught up with females in reading proficiency and literacy. Males substantially outperform females on all sections of the Scholastic Aptitude Test (SAT) and the American College Testing Program Examination (ACT), but girls receive better grades in school. This may be partly explained, looking back at an earlier discussion, by the tendency of some teachers to give higher grades to docile, cooperative students (usually girls) than to aggressive, independent students (usually boys).[41]

Mary Belenky and her colleagues discovered that women are more comfortable with personalized knowledge and knowledge from firsthand observation, but that most schools emphasize abstract, "out-of-context" knowledge instead.[42] Carol Gilligan claims that the dominant values of women in the United States tend to be those of caring, connecting, and being sensitive to the needs of others. Men, in contrast, tend to be characterized by separation and individualism. Women also experience more problems with competitive achievement and have more "fear of success" than do men.[43]

Can these differences, especially those that affect academic performance, be attributed to nature or nurture? Some researchers believe that learning differences exist between the sexes at birth and can be found in brain functioning.[44] Others think women perform poorly in math because they learn to fear such studies through socialization practices.[45] The debate continues, and all we can say for certain is that there is no definitive answer to the question. But that does not mean we cannot continue to study the differences and possible causes for those differences, and take care not to let unfounded opinions and stereotypes lead us into sexism.

Sexism is the belief that one sex is innately superior to another. In our society, the belief has historically persisted that men are superior to women. Examples can be found in textbooks and curricular materials as well as other aspects of schooling. Sexism can be manifested in the exclusive use of masculine pronouns, the presentation of females in only stereotypical roles, the failure to credit women for their contributions to history and society, and the reluctance to discuss issues of sex discrimination. In a study of 100 classrooms, teachers tended to give boys more academic attention, asking them more questions and providing them with clearer feedback. Girls, on the other hand, were more likely to be ignored or were given less precise feedback.[46] This treatment could be considered a subtle form of sex discrimination.

Sex discrimination is the denial of opportunity, reward, role, or privilege on the basis of sex. In 1972 an important series of educational amendments passed and included Title IX, an amendment that prohibited sex discrimination under any program that receives federal funding. Title IX protects students and employees in public schools and postsecondary schools from sex discrimination in admission, treatment, and employment.

Sexual harassment can be a form of sex discrimination and is a violation of many state laws and institutional regulations as well as of Title VII of the Civil Rights Act. The Equal Opportunity Commission defines **sexual harassment** as "unwelcome sexual advances, requests for sexual favors and other verbal or physical conduct of a sexual nature." These actions are illegal if they substantially interfere with work performance or create an intimidating or offensive work environment, or when a person's response to such advances becomes the basis for employment decisions.

The types of knowledge the schools emphasize may not be what female students are most comfortable with.

Differences in males' and females' intelligence cannot be definitively attributed to heredity or environment.

School sports programs also have been required to curtail what many viewed as discriminatory practices. Courts have generally ordered school districts to allow female athletes to compete with male athletes if no comparable programs exist for females. This has allowed women to compete with men in tennis, track, cross-country skiing, and other non-contact sports on the grounds that women were being denied the same benefits men were receiving. In other words, women were being denied equal protection of the law. Furthermore, several courts have ruled that women must be provided the opportunity to participate in contact sports either through sex-segregated or co-educational teams.

Laws against sex discrimination have enhanced opportunities for both students and educational professionals.

As we can see, much progress has been made since the 1970s and the institution of Title IX to curb the practice of sex discrimination. Educators have made concerted efforts to rid textbooks and other curricular material of sexism; affirmative action has led to the development of goals and timetables to eliminate employment discrimination—for example, more women are becoming principals (26 percent) and superintendents (10 percent); the courts have promoted opportunities for women athletes; and sexual harassment has been reduced by actions of the Equal Opportunity Commission and regulatory codes. More women today seek and obtain employment than ever. In 1890 fewer than one in seven workers were women, compared with almost one in two in 1989. The percentage of women professionals in 1950 was 40 percent, compared with 50 percent in 1987. The percentage of women managers in 1950 was 14 percent, compared with 38 percent in 1987.[47]

■ PAUSE TO REFLECT
Sexism in Our Society

- Chances are that you have been the victim of sex discrimination or sexual harassment, however subtle. Can you think of an example in your own life? How did it make you feel? How do you wish you had been treated?

- As a teacher, what steps can you take to ensure that your students enjoy maximum educational opportunities no matter what their gender?

■ MULTICULTURAL EDUCATION

Multicultural education grew out of the civil rights and women's liberation movements of the 1960s. Blacks and other ethnic groups demanded that curriculums be transformed to better reflect their history, culture, and experiences. About the same time, women began demanding revisions in textbooks to highlight women's contributions to American history and culture and to encourage readers to overcome stereotypical roles. Other groups, such as the disabled, also began to battle discrimination, demanding, among other things, easier physical access to public buildings and institutions, including schools.

At first, multicultural programs began to take note of ethnic holidays and special events, and offered elective courses that focused on the history and culture of African Americans and Hispanics. These courses usually were electives and were taken by students whose ethnic backgrounds were the subjects of the courses. Today, **multicultural education** is far more than a series of courses—instead it has become a total school reform involving a wide variety of programs and

Multicultural education began as a response to discrimination and has become a pervasive theme in curricula.

It is important to educate children about the contributions of others cultures and ethnic groups.

practices related to educational equity, ethnic groups, women, low-income groups, language minorities, and the disabled.[48]

An understanding of James Banks' typology of six stages of ethnicity (see Figure 9–2) lends itself to a multicultural approach in education. Each person is identified at one of the six stages, and the objective in education would be to help the individual move to a higher stage, toward Stage 6. In Stage 1 (Ethnic Psychological Captivity), individuals have low self-esteem and negative feelings about their ethnic groups. In Stage 2 (Ethnic Encapsulation), outgroups are regarded as enemies and racists; genocide might be contemplated. By Stage 3 (Ethnic Identity Clarification), ethnic pride is no longer based on hate or fear of other ethnic groups. In Stage 4 (Biethnicity), individuals are able to participate in two cultures, as is often the case with non-white minorities living in a predominantly white society. By Stage 5 (Multiethnicity and Reflective Nationalism), individuals have advanced to the point where they can function within several ethnic groups in their nation. In Stage 6 (Globalism and Global Competency), individuals can function within several ethnic groups in their nation and in other countries as well.[49]

Teachers must help minority students adapt to the school culture at the same time that they enrich their teaching with elements of the students' cultures.

What can educators do to ensure that students of minority ethnic groups get a full education without trampling their cultural heritage? Multicultural advocates claim that the school culture is alien to many minority students because it conflicts with the culture of their home life. Because this alienation can lead to low achievement, advocates say, the school culture should reflect the diverse cultural backgrounds represented in the student population. Teachers should be aware of and understand the values of different groups to better relate to the students and their communities. Different teaching styles could be developed to meet the needs of a wider variety of students. For example, some students respond well to field-independent teachers, who promote independent student achievement and competition between individual students. Other students respond better to field-sensitive teachers, who use more personal, conversational techniques and employ more oral and nonverbal communication.

At the elementary level, teachers could focus on concepts accompanied by concrete examples, concepts such as similarities, differences, race, and ethnic group. More advanced concepts then would be introduced at the secondary level, including culture, assimilation, discrimination, and racism. These concepts could be centered on a theme such as socialization, which would deal with self-concept, indoctrination, prejudice, and discrimination.

Not everyone believes that multicultural education is the best direction for education. Critics believe the concept undermines shared purposes and beliefs by depriving schools of a common set of traditions and a basic historical understanding of our nation. The school is

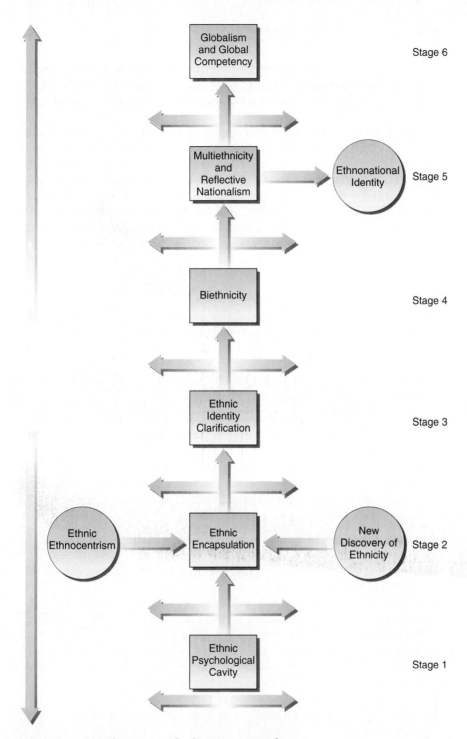

Stage 6

Stage 5

Stage 4

Stage 3

Stage 2

Stage 1

FIGURE 9–2 The stages of ethnicity: A topology

From James A. Banks, *MULTIETHNIC EDUCATION: Theory and Practice,* 2nd ed. Copyright © 1988 by Allyn and Bacon. Reprinted by permission.

Some believe that multicultural education is asking too much of the schools.

diverted from its central purpose by making it difficult to teach a common body of knowledge, because, at the present level of funding, it is impossible to serve the needs of everyone. The school system, they say, cannot be expected to meet the various needs of every ethnic group, assist with the numerous language difficulties, and solve social and political problems at the same time. These demands lead to moral relativism, which claims that all values are of equal worth.[50] Critics also point out that research in the area of multicultural education is inadequate for the development of a thoughtfully prepared program. For example, of the 3,000 titles on the subject, nearly 95 percent are essays that exhort the value of multicultural education but provide little research-based justification for various instructional approaches.[51]

▪ Summary

- All societies are socially stratified to some degree; that is, people are placed in categorics that are ranked in terms of the degree of superiority or inferiority that society accords them. The dominant class, usually the one in power, seeks to defend the system, while the subordinate classes usually seek to change it.

- Social mobility, or the movement within a socially stratified system, depends in large part on whether status is *ascribed* (assumed at birth or by decree) or *achieved* (assumed through ability and accomplishment). The more that social classes are determined by achieved status, the more social mobility is evident in the society. Status in the United States is generally considered to be achieved, but to some degree it also is ascribed.

- Several theories attempt to explain why a society becomes stratified, even societies that struggle to eradicate inequalities. The *structural-functional theory* suggests that society offers rewards (income, power, prestige, leisure time) to entice people to pursue important jobs in society. Social inequality becomes inevitable as the society seeks to ensure that the most important positions are filled by the best-qualified persons. Karl Marx's *conflict theory* holds that different social classes emerge from the different positions that exist in a given system of production (bourgeoisie versus proletariat). Lenski's theory holds that social stratification is the result of sociocultural evolution. As people in horticultural, pastoral, and agrarian societies increased their material goods, a small elite began to control the surplus, leading to social inequality. Industrial societies have less inequality because power—therefore, wealth—tends to be dispersed over a larger proportion of the population.

- Several criteria exist for determining social class in the United States, including housing, organizational membership, occupation, formal education, race, ethnicity, and gender. Many of the criteria interact and affect each other—formal education affects income, organizational membership, and occupation, for example.

- The principal social classes in the United States are the lower-lower class, the upper-lower class, the lower-middle class, the upper-middle class, the lower-upper class, and the upper-upper class. Lower-class students tend to have a more difficult time in school than do middle-class students, and several possible reasons have been offered. Lower-class students have fewer resources for learning outside the home, they don't speak the same elaborative language as teachers and middle-class students, and their norms and values can conflict with those of their teachers. Studies have shown that teachers, who bring their middle-class values to the classroom, tend to favor students with similar values and ignore students with different values.

- Suggestions for improving education for the lower classes include framing schoolwork around each student's abilities, introducing group activities in which all can participate, adapting a wide variety of learning materials to students with different learning styles, providing worthwhile role models and significant adult relationships, boosting self-esteem, avoiding labeling, involving parents, promoting health care, abolishing tracking, and offering compensatory education.

- Observers consider race to have a significant effect on student achievement, although whether those influences are due to biological or environmental factors ("nature or nurture") is disputed. Minorities tend to score lower on reading-performance and I.Q. tests than whites, and a strong argument can be made for the opinion that culture and environment might be a reason. Some educators have attempted to create "culture-fair" pictorial tests that de-emphasize mathematics and language, although critics say such tests have little to do with achievement test scores or school grades.

- As a microcosm of the world, the United States faces a great challenge in ensuring that minority ethnic groups have access to a good education, while respecting and preserving ethnic differences.

- When minority ethnic groups interact with the dominant group in a society, the dominant group might respond to them using one or more of these methods: genocide or expulsion, ethnic stratification, segregation and partitioning, conformity, amalgamation, assimilation, cultural pluralism, and integration.

- Although many alleged differences between the sexes are unsupported, some supportable differences have been discovered. In general, girls show greater verbal ability than boys; boys show greater spatial and mathematical abilities; boys show more aggressiveness than girls do. Some researchers believe these and other differences are inherent; others believe they are caused by different socialization practices.

- Society has had a tendency to use the results of such studies as a rationale for sexism, or the belief that one sex is innately superior to another. In education, sexism can be manifested in the use of masculine pronouns, stereotyping of female roles, failure to recognize women's contributions to history and society, and the lack of discussion of sexism issues.

- Many strides have been made in the past two decades to reduce the incidence of sex discrimination and sexual harassment, two common results of sexism. Title IX of the Educational Amendments of 1972, for example, prohibits sex discrimination under any program that receives federal funding. Sexual harassment is considered a violation of many state laws and institutional regulations as well as Title VII of the Civil Rights Act.

- Multicultural education attempts to meet the different cultural needs of minority groups in the classroom and to better reflect their history, culture, and experiences in the curriculum.

■ Key Terms

achieved status	integration
amalgamation	Lenski's theory
Anglo conformity	life chances
ascribed status	minority group
assimilate	multicultural education
caste system	"nature-nurture" controversy
conflict theory	partitioning
cultural pluralism	prejudice
discrimination	race
endogamy	racism
ethnic groups	segregation
ethnic stratification	sex discrimination
institutionalized racism	sexism

sexual harassment
social class
social mobility
social stratification

status consistency
structural-functional theory
under class

■ Discussion Questions

1. Of the three theories of social stratification, which do you think best explains stratification? Defend your choice.

2. Where else, besides in a caste system, can institutionalized racism be found? How is it manifested?

3. What problems can emerge from a teacher's social-class background in working with students of different social classes? What can be done to overcome these problems?

4. What can be said with confidence today about the relationship between race and student achievement?

5. What are the most desirable outcomes for minority groups when they interact with a dominant group? What can be done to increase the chances of these outcomes?

6. How can multicultural education improve education for all students?

■ Learning Activities

1. Visit several local schools and identify the social-class issues that they are dealing with.

2. Visit several public and private schools in your community and collect data on the composition of the student body in terms of SES, race, ethnicity, and gender. Compare the data with the curriculum and services provided by each school. What influences might be at work?

3. Organize a class debate on the following resolution: "_____ has more influence on educational achievement than _____ and _____ ." (Fill in the blanks with the following terms in any order you choose: *social class, race, ethnicity.*)

4. Interview classmates of different ethnic and racial backgrounds to discover whether they have experienced prejudice or discrimination in their schooling and, if so, how it has affected their education and achievements.

Suggested Readings

Banks, James A. *Multiethnic Education,* 2nd ed. Boston: Allyn and Bacon, 1988.

An introduction to ethnic movements, ideologies, theories, educational programs, and practices.

Gilbert, Dennis, and Joseph A. Kahl. *The American Class Structure.* Homewood, IL: Dorsey Press, 1982.

A comprehensive sociological text on American social classes.

Levine, Daniel U., and Robert J. Havighurst. *Society and Education,* 7th ed. Boston: Allyn and Bacon, 1989.

A systematic sociological treatment of American education.

Sadker, M., and D. Sadker. *Sex Equity Handbook for Schools.* New York: Longman, 1982.

Focuses on sex differences, sexism in education, sex bias in classroom interaction, sex bias in instructional materials, and sex equity in school organizations.

Schaefer, Richard T. *Racial and Ethnic Groups,* 4th ed. Boston: Little, Brown, 1990.

A study of prejudice, discrimination, and the problems of prominent racial and ethnic groups in American life.

Notes

1. Kingsley David and Wilbert Moore, "Some Principles of Stratification," *American Sociological Review* 10 (1945): 242–49.

2. Melvin M. Tumin, "Some Principles of Stratification: A Critical Analysis," *American Sociological Review* 18 (1953): 387–94.

3. Ralf Dahrendorf, *Class and Class Conflict in Industrial Society* (Stanford, CA: Stanford University Press, 1959).

4. Randall Collins, *Conflict Society: Toward an Explanatory Science* (New York: Academic Press, 1959).

5. Gerhard Lenski, *Power and Privilege: A Theory of Social Stratification* (New York: McGraw-Hill, 1966); and Gerhard Lenski and Jean Lenski, *Human Societies: An Introduction to Macrosociology,* 4th ed. (New York: McGraw-Hill, 1982).

6. Joseph A. Kahl and James A. Davis, "A Comparative Index of Socioeconomic Status," *American Sociological Review* 20 (1955): 317–25.

7. Lucile Duberman, *Social Inequality: Class and Caste in America* (Philadelphia: J. B. Lippincott, 1976), 154–55.

8. Donald J. Treiman, *Occupational Prestige in Comparative Perspective* (New York: Academic Press, 1977).

9. Charles Hirschman and Morris G. Wong, "Socioeconomic Gains of Asian Americans, Blacks, and Hispanics: 1960–1976," *American Journal of Sociology* 90 (1984): 584–607.

10. Patricia Madoo Lengermann and Ruth A. Wallace, *Gender in America: Social Control and Social Change* (Englewood Cliffs, NJ: Prentice-Hall, 1985).

11. Charles Bates Doob, *Sociology: An Introduction* (New York: Holt, Rinehart and Winston, 1985), 215–18.

12. John T. Macionis, *Sociology* (Englewood Cliffs, NJ: Prentice-Hall, 1987), 243.

13. Dennis Gilbert and Joseph A. Kahl, *The American Class Structure: A New Synthesis* (Homewood, IL: Dorsey Press, 1982).

14. Macionis, *Sociology,* 243.

15. Susan A. Ostrander, *Women of the Upper Class* (Philadelphia: Temple University Press, 1984).

16. Lawrence J. Schweinhart and David P. Wirkhart, "Education of Young Children Living in Poverty: Child-Initiated Learning or Teacher-Directed Instruction?" *The Elementary School Journal* 89 (1988): 213–25.

17. Wanda E. Fleming, "Program for Disadvantaged Youth: Efforts in the Middle Grades," *Educational Horizons* (Winter 1990): 82–87.

18. Basil Bernstein, *Class, Codes, and Control. Vol. III: Towards a Theory of Educational Transmission* (London: Routledge & Kegan Paul, 1977).

19. F. I. Ortiz, "Hispanic-American Children's Experiences in Classrooms: A Comparison Between Hispanic and Non-Hispanic Children," in *Race, Class and Gender in American Education,* ed. Lois Weis (Albany, NY: State University of New York Press, 1988), 63–87.

20. L. Grant and J. Rothenberg, "The Social Enhancement of Ability Differences: Teacher-Student Interactions in First and Second Grade Reading Groups," *Elementary School Journal* 87 (1986): 29–50.

21. S. A. Valverde, "A Comparative Study of Hispanic Dropouts and Graduates: Why Do Some Leave School Early and Some Finish?" *Education and Urban Society* 19 (1987): 311–20; and H. Borko and M. Eisenhart, "Student's Conceptions of Reading and Their Reading Experience in School," *The Elementary School Journal* 86 (1986): 589–612.

22. Theodosius Dobzhansky, *Mankind Evolving: The Evolution of the Human Species* (New Haven, CT: Yale University Press, 1962), 266.

23. National Center for Educational Statistics, *The Condition of Education 1989,* vol. 1: Elementary and Secondary Education (Washington, DC: U.S. Government Printing Office, 1989), 8.

24. Ibid., 24.

25. Arthur R. Jensen, "How Much Can We Boost I.Q. and Scholastic Achievement?" *Harvard Educational Review* 30 (1969): 1–123.

26. Arthur R. Jensen, "Jensen's Theory of Intelligence: A Reply," *Journal of Educational Psychology* 60 (1969): 427–31.

27. "How Much Can We Boost I.Q. and Scholastic Achievement: A Discussion," *Harvard Educational Review* (Winter 1969): 1–123; and Zena Smith Blau, *Black Children/White Children* (New York: Free Press, 1981), 26, 77, 181.

28. Richard J. Hernstein, "IQ," *The Atlantic* (September 1971): 58.

29. S. Dale McLemore, *Racial and Ethnic Relations in America*, 2d ed. (Boston: Allyn and Bacon, 1983), 89.

30. L. E. Tyler, "Human Abilities," *Annual Review of Psychology* 23 (1972): 177–206.

31. J. McVicker Hunt, "Psychological Development: Early Experience," *Annual Review of Psychology* (1979), 103–43.

32. Christopher Jencks, "Heredity–Environment Debate," paper presented at American Sociological Association meetings, Boston, August 1979.

33. Rita Dunn and Shirley A. Griggs, *Learning Styles: Quiet Revolution in American Schools* (Reston, VA: National Association of Secondary School Principals, 1988), 3.

34. Manual Ramírez and Alfredo Casteñeda, *Cultural Democracy, Biocognitive Development and Education* (New York: Academic Press, 1974); and Janice E. Hale-Benson, *Black Children: Their Roots, Culture, and Learning Styles*, rev. ed. (Baltimore: Johns Hopkins University Press, 1986).

35. See: Robert E. Slavin, *Cooperative Learning* (New York: Longman, 1983); and Elizabeth G. Cohen, *Designing Groupwork: Strategies for Heterogeneous Classrooms* (New York: Teachers College Press, 1986).

36. Margaret Mead, *Male and Female* (New York: William Morrow, 1949).

37. Clyde Kluckhohn, "Universal Categories of Culture," in A. L. Kroeber, *Anthropology Today* (Chicago: University of Chicago Press, 1953), 507–23.

38. S. B. Ortner, "Is Female to Male as Nature Is to Culture?" in *Women, Culture, and Society,* eds. M. Z. Rosaldo and L. Lamphere. (Stanford, CA: Stanford University Press, 1974).

39. Donna M. Gollnick and Philip C. Chinn, *Multicultural Education in a Pluralistic Society*, 3d ed. (Columbus, OH: Merrill, 1990), Ch. 6.

40. Eleanor E. Maccoby and Carol Nagy Jacklin, *The Psychology of Sex Differences* (Palo Alto, CA: Stanford University Press, 1974).

41. Jeanne H. Ballantine, *The Sociology of Education*, 2d ed. (Englewood Cliffs, NJ: Prentice-Hall, 1989), 257.

42. Mary F. Belenky, et al., *Women's Ways of Knowing: The Development of Self, Voice, and Mind* (New York: Basic Books, 1986), 200.

43. Carol Gilligan, *In a Different Voice: Psychological Theory and Women's Development* (Cambridge, MA: Harvard University Press, 1982).

44. Sandra E. Witelson and Janice A. Swallow, "Individualized Differences in Human Brain Function," *National Forum* (Spring 1987): 17–24.

45. Jacquelynne S. Eccles, "Gender Roles and Women's Achievement," *Educational Researcher* (June–July 1986): 15–19.

46. David Sadker and Myra Sadker, "Is the O.K. Classroom O.K.?" *Phi Delta Kappan* 66 (1985): 361–81.

47. *Statistical Abstract,* 1989 (Washington, DC: U.S. Government Printing Office, 1988), 388–89.

48. James A. Banks, "Multicultural Education: Characteristics and Goals," in *Multicultural Education: Issues and Perspectives,* ed. James A. Banks and Cherry A. McGee Banks. (Boston: Allyn and Bacon, 1989), 2–26.

49. James A. Banks, *Multicultural Education: Theory and Practice,* 2d ed. (Boston: Allyn and Bacon, 1989), 194–201.

50. M. Donald Thomas, "The Limits of Pluralism," *Innovations in Education: Reformers and Their Critics,* 5th ed., ed. John Martin Rich (Boston: Allyn and Bacon, 1988), 238–41.

51. Alma G. Vasquez and Henry T. Ingle, "Multicultural and Minority Education," in *Encyclopedia of Educational Research,* 5th ed. (New York: Free Press, 1982), 1267–69.

CHAPTER 10

370

EQUALIZING EDUCATIONAL OPPORTUNITY ■

A LOOK AHEAD

The purpose of this chapter is to explore the characteristics and influence of the movement toward equality in American education. You will learn about:

- Aristocratic education and its ascriptive mission of preserving education exclusively for the highest classes

- The rise of meritocratic education and its focus on achievement rather than privilege

- The concept of equality in education and the assumption that all people have a right to an education

- Three basic theories of egalitarian education

- How the civil rights movement precipitated great change in educational practices

- Some far-reaching proposals from education reformers

- The importance of school effectiveness in providing an equal education

- Attempts to desegregate the schools to equalize educational opportunities

- Special education possibilities for the disabled

Equal educational opportunity presents society with one of its greatest challenges. The issue is so complex, and the number of people affected—students, parents, teachers, administrators, the community—is so high, that it is almost impossible to devise a plan that will be completely fair to everyone. But efforts continue, and education today—for all of its faults—is far different from the unequal aristocratic education that prevailed until the late nineteenth century.

Although establishing equal educational opportunities for everyone is difficult, students cannot achieve full development without it.

A salient difference exists between student freedom to learn (see Chapter 3) and the right to equal educational opportunities. When freedom to learn is restricted, it is restricted for all students, either as a result of bureaucratic systems or the official values of the school. When the right to equal educational opportunities is restricted, on the other hand, it usually is restricted for certain groups based on artificial distinctions, such as race, social class, or gender. Students cannot develop fully if they are denied equal opportunities.

Many surveys of industrial nations during the 1980s showed that independence and individuality are highly valued in the United States. Americans generally are opposed to the government redistributing income from rich to poor or providing jobs for all. A survey of 1,200 adults in each of eight countries (the United States, Japan, and six western European countries) asked whether personal freedom or equality was more important. Of the U.S. respondents, 20 percent chose equality and 72 percent chose freedom (8 percent responded "neither" or "don't know"). The figures for freedom were highest in the United States sample; the figures for equality were lowest in the United States.[1]

This relative lack of interest in equality can be seen throughout America's history. The destruction of the Native American culture and the enslavement of blacks, as we discussed in Chapter 5, are only two examples of many instances of discrimination in the United States. In 1968 the President's National Advisory Commission on Civil Disorders said, "White racism is essentially responsible for the explosive mixture which has been accumulating in our cities since the end of World War II."[2] The commission concluded that the nation was moving rapidly toward two Americas—blacks in the central city and whites in the suburbs and peripheral parts of the city. "Within two decades this division could be so deep that it would be almost impossible to unite."[3]

This dire warning has not fully materialized, but the problems nevertheless are substantial, if somewhat different from those of the late 1960s. Today the central cities are composed of not only blacks but also other minorities and whites as well. The growing number of homeless and the increasing drug problem also contribute to social problems. Black progress, specifically, has been a journey of mixed results. Today the health of blacks in general has improved, more blacks are completing college (see Table 9–4), blacks are moving into better jobs, and more blacks are being elected to office. On the down side, the average income for blacks is 57 percent to 59 percent of the income for whites, blacks are more likely than whites to use hard drugs, and 47 percent of the prison population is black even though blacks constitute only 12 percent of the population.[4] This situation is similar for Hispanic Americans. A study by the National Council of La Raza found that the majority of the nation's 20.1 million Hispanics made no significant economic gains during the 1980s. United States Census data from 1979 to 1989 showed that nearly 27 percent of all Hispanic Americans lived in poverty in 1989, up from 25.7 percent in 1979. In comparison, about 31 percent of blacks and 10 percent of whites live in poverty.[5]

Since the Declaration of Independence, the importance of equality has been extolled as a cornerstone of our society. Social realities, however, are a different matter. As Christopher Jencks observed: "Almost nobody really wants to make America an egalitarian society. Ours is a competitive society, in which some people do extremely well and others do equally badly, and most people are willing to keep it that way. For as long as anyone can remember, for example, the richest fifth of the population has earned ten times as much as the poorest fifth. The ability to influence political and personal events is probably even less equally distributed."[6]

Despite the evidence that equality is not deeply rooted in the American conscience, equality is a basic principle of democracy, and equal treatment before the law is guaranteed in the Fourteenth Amendment. The problem is how to bring about equality when it is not highly valued in the general population. Specifically, for our discussion here, the question is how do the schools provide educational support for those who are socially disadvantaged. In this chapter we will discuss different forms of education and the influence that educational reformers have had on the system.

Egalitarianism can better be understood by contrasting it to two other influential forms of education with which it has had to compete: aristocratic and meritocratic education. Although both forms can be considered "elitist," the term is nebulous and tells us nothing about their significant differences.

> Despite the fact that equality has traditionally been glorified in American society, most Americans value personal freedom more.

ARISTOCRATIC EDUCATION ■

The history of education both in the West and East is largely a history of aristocratic education. **Aristocratic education** is rooted in a belief that a certain class or group is superior and should be the only group to receive the benefits of a formal education. This class or group may

Until the nineteenth century, in both the East and the West, aristocratic education, with its aim of preserving education for the highest classes, was the dominant form of education.

Social class, race, gender, and citizenship have determined who had access to formal education.

Friedrich Nietzsche's philosophies provided a rationale for aristocratic education by rejecting equal rights and calling for a society ruled by "supermen" who would control the masses.

be defined by royalty, nobility, social class, race, citizenship, or gender. In virtually all cultures, members of the highest class have had access to a superior formal education, which helps them maintain their status and prepare to perform their appointed functions. Invariably, the upper class has enjoyed the fruits of an education through exclusive private schools and tutors. (The rise of a sizable middle class, most of whom have access to a quality education, is more a phenomenon of late industrial societies, as in nineteenth-century America.) Race, gender, and citizenship also have significantly affected individuals' access to education. In ancient Athens, only male citizens were eligible to pursue a formal education. Comenius advocated universal education as early as the seventeenth century, but the United States did not subscribe to the idea until the late nineteenth century—and even then, certain minorities still did not receive an equal education. In the United States, formal education was withheld from races considered inferior—slaves were forbidden to seek schooling. The Emancipation Proclamation of 1863 may have guaranteed blacks their freedom, but not an equal education. Most European countries did not start offering universal education until this century.

The rationale behind aristocratic education can be clarified by two leading statements. German philosopher and classical philologist Friedrich Nietzsche (1844–1900) claimed that a morality in which all persons are treated as equals, however unequal their merit and attributes, is a slave morality detestable to the person of knowledge and integrity.[7] One has duties to one's equals, he said, but one may treat beings of lower rank as one chooses. The masses, with their slavish mentalities, may be sacrificed in the pursuit of knowledge and higher ideals. Their sacrifice will bring about a higher civilization led by the *ubermensch,* the higher man, or superman. Nietzsche viewed compassion and charity as the products of a herd mentality. Sympathy and pity are weaknesses, not marks of virtue. To be hard of heart, to be severe with oneself, is the mark of a virtuous man. Christianity and socialism are the faiths of "little men" where excuses for weakness are paraded as moral principles. Furthermore, the masses should learn to fear the higher classes, who by right should control them and use them for their own purposes. The idea of one morality for all is an illusion and detrimental to the higher man. Nietzsche believed that his era was a transitional one and that the best one could do was to prepare for a more fortunate age in which the higher man is a creator and has developed his will to power, using his abilities fully to overcome obstacles of self and others. Clearly, Nietzsche thoroughly rejected the concept of equal rights and advocated the derogation of the majority of people.

An aristocratic view more directly related to education was formulated by American-British poet and critic T. S. Eliot (1888–1965). Eliot was interested in creating the cultured man, an aristocratic figure, and found culture incompatible with equality. He believed that most men are incapable of distinguishing between good and bad and advocated a Christian education based upon classical studies—an education that would consist of considerable drudgery because students would have to interest themselves in subjects for which they lack aptitude. A Christian education would teach people to think in Christian categories, although it would not require belief in Christian dogma. Eliot believed it would be a serious mistake to use education to equalize opportunity or to prepare an intellectual elite, because such meritocracies would lack social and cultural unity, traits actually transmitted through the family. Eliot believed that universal education is dangerous because it lowers standards, causes unhappiness, and adulterates and degrades culture. Complete equality would be universal irresponsibility. The purpose of education, then, is "to preserve the class and select the elite."[8]

Eliot's aristocratic education would preserve the culture and the rightful place and standards of the aristocratic class, and Nietzsche's would erect a bridge to a higher man of culture who would create values far above those of the masses. Aristocratic education is obviously incompatible with democracy and principles of equality; it fails to respect and educate everyone except aristocrats—and probably male aristocrats at that. In such a system, *ascription* prevails over *achievement*, privilege prevails over right. In other words, one's position in society is inherited and education is a privilege of birth, not a right.

American-British poet T. S. Eliot favored the elitist idea of aristocratic education as an instrument used to preserve class.

MERITOCRATIC EDUCATION ■

Since the days of Jeffersonian democracy, meritocracy has played an important role in American life. Advanced industrial societies increasingly seek mechanisms by which a highly trained work force can be screened and developed, and a meritocratic system is designed to be fairer and more impartial than an ascriptive system. Such a system of screening and development would be executed through public education, usually under the heading of "equal educational opportunity."

A **meritocratic system** is based on achievement rather than ascription. In a meritocracy, awards, recognition, and the apportionment of goods and services are based on demonstrated ability rather than on

Meritocratic education uses testing to sort and select students.

Unlike aristocratic education in which ascription prevails, meritocratic education is based on achievement. seniority, race, religion, nationality, gender, or other artificial distinctions used to mete out the perquisites of life. The abilities and skills deemed most desirable and worthy of rewards are determined by the priorities and values of the institution. Meritocratic values include competitiveness, willingness to learn, and ability to adapt quickly to new situations and tasks. Gregariousness and advancement through political manipulation are devalued, although perhaps not eliminated. Education is of vital importance because one cannot depend on artificial distinctions for advancement.

"The partial triumph of the meritocracy," say Christopher Jencks and David Riesman, "brings with it what we call the national upper-middle-class style: cosmopolitan, moderate, universalistic, somewhat legalistic, concerned with equity and fair play, aspiring to neutrality between regions, religions, and ethnic groups."[9] Daniel Bell defines meritocracy as a system that advocates the elimination of "social differences in order to assure an equal start, but it justifies unequal results on the basis of natural abilities and talents."[10] A meritocracy is a "credentials society" in which certification through degrees and licensing becomes a condition for employment. But a meritocracy should not be confused with a technocracy, as a technocracy emphasizes technological efficiency and credentials that specify only minimum achievement. Meritocracy, Bell says, is more than a technocracy because it stresses individual achievement and earned status confirmed by one's peers.[11]

The meritocrat opposes an equality of condition based on income, wealth, position, power, or influence in society, because anything other than equal opportunity would threaten our fundamental liberties. Furthermore, it would be based not on fairness or justice but on envy and resentment. Some inequalities, however, are unavoidable and desirable, such as the degree of talent each person possesses. The point is to determine which inequalities are fair, an assessment that can be made while ascertaining "which [equalities] have been earned . . . and which kinds of equalities are necessary to preserve the natural rights of men and the social rights of citizenship."[12]

A meritocratic system is based on equal access to education so that students with potentials most valued by society would be in a better position to develop them and subsequently be rewarded for them. Future leaders are sorted out through the competitive system of grading, promotion, honors, and awards. Those who do not make the cut are reminded that they were given a fair chance and are expected to assume roles in society commensurate with their demonstrated abilities.

Programs for the gifted and talented are encouraged, and competency education, if constructed broadly enough, assures that certain measurable outcomes are achieved. **Competency education** focuses on developing the skills, abilities, and experiences needed by every high-school graduate to function successfully in society. Meritocrats occasionally join forces with essentialists (who advocate discipline and teaching the basics) in attempting to uphold standards, though the meritocrat is more likely to consider the effects of various sectors of society—government, business, industry, the military—when it comes to setting standards.

> The meritocratic system, with programs for the gifted and competency education, attempts to ensure equal opportunity for all.

The Case Against Meritocracy

Meritocracies and meritocratic education have been subjected to several searching criticisms. John Schaar, for example, points out that the meritocratic formula focuses on developing talents that are highly regarded by a given people at a given time.[13] Every society has a system of values organized in a hierarchy, with the system of evaluation varying from one society to another. The problem with the meritocratic formula, Schaar says, is that it is highly conservative and leaves little room for challenging the status quo (the current system of values). Before one subscribes to the formula, one should be certain that the values, goals, and institutions of society are actually desired.[14]

One might argue, however, that the meritocratic approach is not inherently conservative because it does not commit one to rewarding a single, unchanging set of values or talents: new and neglected talents can be identified and rewarded, leading to social change. Those who determine and enforce meritocratic standards can decide whether they wish to preserve existing values or to shape new ones; the only requirement is that the system be based on equal opportunity and demonstrated performance.

Critics of the meritocratic system also believe such a system promotes undesirable interpersonal relations. Schaar believes it encourages cruelty and competitiveness.[15] An example would be a footrace in which nine physically unprepared people compete with a track star, with the same rules applying to all. "But life," says Robert Nozick, "is not a race in which we all compete for a prize which someone has established; there is no unified race, with some person judging swiftness. . . . No centralized process judges people's use of the opportunities they had. . ."[16]

A meritocracy is competitive. But, one might argue, competition is not necessarily undesirable and cooperation is not necessarily inherently good. Competition can provide firms with the incentive to develop new safety and health products; a gang of thieves can cooperate with one another to swindle others. Furthermore, competition and cooperation are not mutually exclusive; they can exist side by side in various activities, as with two teams who cooperate to establish rules for a competitive game or competing companies who seek agreement on trade policies. What is more important is whether the competition is fair and designed to achieve an acceptable set of purposes. In the classroom, a race to finish a blackboard math problem first can develop quick thinking and the ability to work under pressure. Cooperative discussion afterward lets everyone share their approach to the problem and learn from others' experiences.

Other critics of the meritocratic system believe meritocracy has more serious related weaknesses. "It [meritocracy] is a dehumanizing society," says Kai Nielsen, "because it destroys any notion of fraternity or solidarity or even belonging to a common community of which we are all members; as equal members of a Kantian kingdom of ends."[17] John Rawls, in a related criticism, charges that a meritocracy discounts self-respect, one of a person's most important possessions.[18]

These are serious charges that can only partly be mitigated in a strict meritocracy. But if protection of self-respect and solidarity means ensuring the satisfaction of the less talented at the expense of opportunities for the more talented to realize their abilities, then one could argue that society is not necessarily better off. Besides, even the less talented probably will achieve more under a system, such as a meritocracy, that encourages them to excel.

But critics claim that meritocratic competition is not genuinely fair. Charles Frankel asks that if it is unfair that a person cannot take a test because he cannot afford to travel to the testing center, why is it fair for the person to have less opportunity to get the education that he or she needs to prepare for the test? If it is unfair for the person to be deprived of such an education, is it not also the mark of unequal opportunity to permit the person to remain in any environment that discourages the individual from seeking such an education?[19]

> Critics of the meritocratic system say that it preserves current societal values whatever they are, encourages cruelty and competition, and dehumanizes students.

To push the argument further, each person would not only need similar resources and educational opportunities for self-improvement, but would need to come from a similar type of home environment. Moreover, the size of the family and the quality of interpersonal relations among its members would have to be regulated to remove inequalities that might affect learning. And even this might not be enough: breeding also would have to be controlled to avoid genetic differences that might affect achievement.

But societies that espouse equality place certain limits on intervention and what conditions are worth modifying. Since equality is neither a sole nor absolute principle in most philosophies and social systems, it must be compromised in situations where its application infringes on other values. For example, regulating the interpersonal relations of family members or controlling breeding likely would restrict liberty, cause suffering, and ignore respect for others. Because most egalitarians believe in principles like liberty and respect as well as equality, they probably would accept some restrictions in policies to eliminate inequalities. But they should be ready to answer the meritocrat who asks why the egalitarian places limits at some points but not at others.

> Equality is one among many values in a society and may have to be compromised in situations where it infringes on other values.

Enough weaknesses have been pointed out in the strict meritocratic system to suggest that a modified system would make better use of a meritocracy's strengths and offer clearer distinctions between meritocratic and non-meritocratic criteria. Additionally, the use of non-meritocratic criteria might humanize some meritocratic criteria. Meritocratic criteria, for instance, can be tempered by the avoidance of unjust behavior.

What are the major injustices? **Invidious discrimination**, one type of injustice, involves arbitrary unequal treatment in developing and enforcing rules or in distributing burdens and benefits. Rules or programs that arbitrarily exclude people from benefits or treat people unequally on the grounds of race, gender, ethnicity, or religion would

---

EDUCATIONAL ISSUE 10–1

Should American education be based on meritocratic principles?

Yes	No
1. Meritocratic education is desirable because advancement is based on demonstrated achievement rather than on artificial distinctions.	1. The poor and disadvantaged do not have an equal opportunity to achieve.
2. A meritocracy awards students with abilities most valued by society and therefore better develops talent and leadership than any other system.	2. The values of society at any given time might neglect a range of human abilities.
3. Meritocracy promotes equality of opportunity, not equality of condition, because some inequalities are unavoidable, desirable, and fair.	3. Meritocrats ignore the social background of students, thereby fostering unnecessary and unjust inequalities.
4. Meritocratic values include competitiveness, willingness to learn, and ability to adapt quickly to new situations and tasks.	4. Meritocratic systems can destroy fraternity, lower self-respect, and dehumanize students.

---

be invidiously discriminatory, such as intelligence tests that are inherently biased against minorities. Discriminatory rules could include **de jure segregation** (segregation by law) or **de facto segregation** (segregation enforced not by law, but by fact, as in segregated patterns of residential housing—and therefore school districts).

Judgmental injustice consists of unfairly judging people, either as individuals or by their activities and achievements. Teachers who expect less from students with lower-class backgrounds, for example, would be guilty of judgmental injustice. This form of injustice is common enough that the American Association of School Administrators warns administrators to make every effort not to let position, rank, popularity, or social standing of a member of the school staff cloud their judgment when dealing with accusations of incompetency or unethical conduct. Administrators also are cautioned against letting strong and unscrupulous persons seize power and responsibility that is not theirs to seize.[20]

Exploitation, a third type of injustice, involves using others for one's own advantage by violating their trust, manipulating their natural disabilities, or deliberately undermining their efforts in a joint undertaking. Sexual harassment, a sort of violation of trust, is one of the most significant forms of exploitation.

These modifications would provide a mixed system by avoiding the major injustices. Nevertheless, an egalitarian system still might be preferable, and we will examine three theories of egalitarian education later in this chapter. First, let us analyze the concept of equality.

> Even if the strict meritocratic system were modified to avoid discrimination, unfair judgment of people, and exploitation, an egalitarian system may still be more viable.

THE CONCEPT OF EQUALITY ■

Some interpret equality to mean "sameness," as in similarity in physical or intellectual characteristics, such as height or I.Q. Under this definition people who are alike should be enrolled in the same curriculum, have the same teachers, and use the same texts. This approach is descriptive in the sense that certain observable characteristics are noted and compared before determining who should be treated identically.

Equality, however, is more a prescriptive than a descriptive concept in that certain actions and policies are based on a prescriptive principle, such as the assumption that people should be treated similarly. With such a concept, the burden of proof is on those who claim that people should be treated differently. In other words, that one is a human being is reason enough to expect similar treatment; when we make distinctions between people and propose to treat them differently, we should have supportable grounds for doing so. If differential treatment is justified, then equality is not being denied. Before deciding to treat a person differently, one must examine the context of the situation, the individuals involved, and the circumstances surrounding the situation. Any differential treatment one decides upon must comply with previously formulated rules, such as those that prohibit discrimination on the basis of race, religion, gender or disability. Thus, whether we are evaluating the treatment of juvenile delinquents, extraordinarily bright students, job applicants, or candidates for professional school, we must be certain that we observe the rules relevant to

> The concept of equality assumes that people should be treated similarly just because they are human beings unless different treatment is justified (e.g., modifying requirements for a disabled student).

the situation. Suppose, for example, that a school requires all students to take a course in physical education to graduate. How should this requirement apply to a physically disabled student? A student with a hearing impairment would be in a similar situation with a required music appreciation course. Differential treatment, such as modifying the course requirements, would seem to be called for in both cases and would not violate nondiscrimination rules.

■ PAUSE TO REFLECT

Justifications for Differential Treatment

- Under what circumstances could you justifiably treat a student differently? For example, if you had students who were visually impaired, you might give them their homework assignments orally after class rather than expect them to copy the assignments off the chalkboard.

- In a more complex situation, what if you had a student who continually interrupted the class? Would you be justified in giving that student extra attention (or less attention) in an effort to correct the situation?

- Were you or any students you knew in your high-school classes treated differently than everyone else? What were the situations? Was the differential treatment justified? What could the teacher or administration have done differently?

These examples are clear-cut enough that the actions taken are not likely to invite criticism. But other situations are more complex, and interpreting the rules can be difficult. One solution is to formulate rules for situations with appropriate qualifications built in rather than stated categorically. For example, the rule that all students, except those with medical proof of a disability, must take physical education to graduate would be a rule with a built-in qualification. Such rules are based on certain principles; even without full knowledge of a particular rule's underlying principles, one still could make some assumptions about the rule. For example, if a particular college does not practice racial discrimination in its admissions, one could assume that the rules of the college are based, in part, on the principle that racial discrimination is legally or morally wrong. If, when looking at a company, we find that men and women with similar qualifications earn similar pay and hold positions of similar importance, we can assume that the rules are based on the principle that sex discrimination is legally or ethically wrong.

While equality is essentially a prescriptive principle, certain descriptive aspects can be observed. The descriptive aspects found in the examples of the students with physical disabilities involve noting the disabilities and determining the extent to which they prevent the students from participating in the required courses. In this case, the student cannot be treated identically to students with no disabilities. Nevertheless, decisions about equality are essentially prescriptive in that they are based on the rules (and the underlying principles of those rules) that govern the situation.

THEORIES OF EGALITARIAN EDUCATION ■

Egalitarian education has different meanings depending on how various advocates and researchers have conceptualized the field of inquiry and the types of policies needed. The effect of egalitarian ideas in education can be seen as early as the 1920s, when state financing plans diverged from the conventional use of a flat grant to each school district. The movement has grown and modified over the years, and by the 1960s and 1970s three leading explanatory theories of egalitarian education had emerged: equal resources, equal outcomes, and substantive equality.

> The three basic theories of egalitarian education— all of which vary widely—are Equal Resources, Equal Outcomes, and Substantive Equality.

Equal Resources Theory

The **equal resources** theory emphasizes the equalization of the inputs of all school districts, which often involves increasing the funding to poorer districts. In the 1970s, a school-financing reform movement began that since has spread to many states. Broad changes in school support appear imminent in the wake of several court decisions, fiscal need at the local level, rapid increases in the cost of operating a school, rising voter resistance to school-bond issues and inequities among school districts.

> The Equal Resources Theory proposes the equalization of resources (funding) to all school districts.

Presaging these changes was a study by Coons, Clune, and Sugarman,[21] which focused on the inability of poor school districts to provide adequate education. The authors of the study, influenced by earlier investigations of Paul R. Mort and others, advanced the proposition that the quality of public education should not depend on the wealth of individuals, but rather on the total wealth of the state. A "power-equalizing" system of finance was designed to ensure that each district would receive proportionally equal funding with proportionally equal fiscal effort (tax assessments). This process would thereby assure equivalent educational offerings. Rich districts, for example, do not have the right to enjoy better schools with less effort (lower tax assessments), therefore, all districts in the state should be raised to the level of the rich districts, or rich districts should be equalized downward by contributing to funds to be distributed equally throughout the state. Rich districts could tax beyond the equalized base, the authors said, but it might be wise to place a ceiling on these efforts to prevent wealthy districts from having the ability to acquire so many resources that there are none to be had for the poorer ones. To bring about equalization of school funding, either property assessments should be uniform throughout the state or the state should institute a system of state property equalization.

The legal argument for funding reform was based on the Fourteenth Amendment, which guarantees equal protection of the law. Widely unequal taxing and allocation, reformers said, violated that amendment as well as comparable provisions of state constitutions. Some state courts have mandated state funding reforms: California, Connecticut, Kentucky, Texas, Washington, and West Virginia. Five states have adopted full state funding as a result of reforms. In contrast, the highest courts in Colorado, Georgia, Maryland, New York, and Oregon did not find funding disparities unconstitutional. In some states, the equal resources approach is the primary means of equalizing education. It rests on providing more equal inputs to school districts (such as better facilities, smaller classes, larger school library collections, and higher teacher salaries) so that poorer districts can compete for better teachers, provide a more comprehensive curriculum, offer more support services for students (such as counseling, vocational planning, evaluation, and health services), and provide more adequate equipment and facilities. This cannot be accomplished if the wealthiest school districts can spend many times more per pupil than the poorer districts for the same fiscal effort, hence, courts have ordered many state legislatures to devise suitable equalization plans.

Equal Outcomes Theory

The Equal Outcomes Theory focuses on equalizing opportunities for all students through such methods as integration of the schools.

When the United States Supreme Court decided in 1954 that "separate but equal" education was inherently unequal, states began desegregating their schools in the hopes of providing **equal outcomes** by equalizing the opportunities and achievements of all students. But what effect has desegregation had on the equality of education? The United States Office of Education sought an answer to that question and commissioned a study of equality, commonly called the Coleman Report. It was the largest study of its kind and has turned out to be one of the most influential.[22] The report included data on 645,000 children at five grade levels and 60,000 teachers in 4,000 schools. The findings of the study cast considerable doubt on the effects that increased inputs have on outputs (standardized verbal and mathematical achievement test scores) as the effects were considerably less than had been assumed. Results of standardized tests of verbal and mathematical skills suggested that the most significant determinant of academic success is the social and economic background of students. The study also found that the test performance of children from disadvantaged backgrounds increased as the proportion of white students increased (but only when white students constituted more than 50 percent of the school population). Also, contrary to popular belief, the performance of white students did not drop when they were placed in an integrated learning setting. The achievement of average Puerto Rican, Mexican American, Native American, and black students was much lower than that of average Asian American or white students at all grade levels, and the differences tended to widen at higher grades.

The report interpreted equality in terms of outputs rather than inputs. In attempting to bring about equal opportunity, the aim is not to make the achievement levels of all students identical, but rather to make identical the average levels of the lower-achievement group and the higher-achievement group. Inputs like school facilities and curriculum had the least effect on white and minority-group achievement and teacher quality had some influence. But achievement as a whole seemed to depend more on the social background and aspirations of the student body.

The schools did not seem to affect the average relative academic standing of pupils, leading one researcher who reanalyzed the report's data to conclude, "The strong relationship between the average scores of entering and graduating students suggests that the principal function of the schools is to serve as an allocation and selection agency rather than an equalizing agency."[23] As noted earlier, schools long have been a screening service to sort out the people who will receive the better jobs and the more important positions in society. But since the 1954 desegregation decision, educators have become increasingly concerned with improving the equalizing function of education.

The Coleman Report has been criticized for looking only at differences among districts (school and class size, levels of teacher training, per-pupil expenditures) and ignoring differences among schools *within* districts, and for not examining patterns of teacher-student interaction. Critics also have found fault with the study on various methodological, procedural, and substantive grounds and because it was not longitudinal (it was not conducted over a lengthy period of time).[24] The findings, however, have been tested and retested by researchers and, despite some variations in results, the general conclusions of the Coleman Report have been upheld.[25] A significant

The U.S. Government's Coleman Report found that though overall achievement seemed to relate more to social and economic background, desegregation was helping to bring about equality of opportunity.

conclusion of the report held that one way to improve the achievement of minority and poor children was through integration of the schools, providing impetus to desegregation efforts, particularly busing.

Substantive Equality Theory

A study published in 1972 by Christopher Jencks and his colleagues throws many of our conventional ideas about education to the winds. The study, in which data from several sources were analyzed and re-interpreted, concluded that neither family background, occupational status, cognitive skill, nor educational achievement adequately explains much of the variation in income in the United States.[26] These conclusions formulate the **substantive equality** theory. The authors also concluded that increased spending, compensatory education, integration, and preschool programs all have failed to significantly equalize cognitive skills. Distinguishing equality of opportunity from equality of results, the authors further claimed that equality of opportunity in an economic sense already exists because inequalities in family background, schooling, and test scores are not strongly related to differences in income. They recommended that inequalities in income between the top and bottom fifths of the population be reduced by raising the taxes of the rich and increasing the minimum income of the poor to achieve equality of results. This can best be accomplished, they said, by transforming society into a form of democratic socialism. The authors said that luck and personality make the biggest difference, accounting for three-fourths of the variations in income.

The Substantive Equality Theory states that luck and personality, rather than background or educational achievement, affect current earnings. Supporters of this theory advocate democratic socialism to equalize income.

This study has been criticized for its interpretation and treatment of the data that led the authors to their conclusions. According to Henry Levin, previous studies by economists have shown that schooling and family background do significantly affect earnings.[27] He claims that the Jencks study omits data on age (which can affect earnings) and place of residence (the cost of living can account for differences in income among various regions). He also claims that the study includes data that weaken the relation among schooling, family background, and income, and fails to consider non-cognitive personality traits.

In a subsequent study Jencks and eleven co-authors altered some interpretations and conclusions from the earlier study.[28] This new study found that the bachelor's degree can be expected to add an average of 30 percent to 40 percent to a man's lifetime earnings. (Women were not included because of insufficient data.) But for those who do not attend college, Jencks said, economic success is not affected by whether they complete high school or drop out at the legal minimum age. The study also found that intelligence, as measured by I.Q. tests, has little effect on an individual's economic success. A fifteen-point difference in intelligence test scores will, on average, produce only a 14 percent difference in lifetime earnings—a small gap compared with the overall earnings gap between wealthy and poor Americans. Jencks also concluded this time that family background is responsible for 48 percent of the variance in men's occupational status, although *family background* is defined broadly as everything that makes men with one set of parents different from men with another set of parents. Finally, while the earlier study cited luck as the explanation for many of the variations in men's income, the newer study barely mentioned it.

As we can see, the theories of egalitarian education vary widely. The equal resources theory probably can be considered the most influential in terms of affecting policy changes, because this is the area most often targeted in decisions by the courts and state legislatures. On the other hand, the call for democratic socialism under the substantive equality approach probably is the most radical and the least likely to be acted upon. With increased emphasis on competency testing and accountability, the equal outcomes theory also exerts influence, although many educators are likely to believe that schools can have a greater effect on achievement than the Coleman Report suggests. These three theories can be compared with aristocratic and meritocratic education to assess their explanatory power and relative value (see Table 10–1).

> Of the three theories of egalitarian education, the Equal Resources Theory and the Equal Outcomes theories have had the greatest impact on American education.

■ **PAUSE TO REFLECT**

Assessing the Theories of Education

- Of aristocratic education, meritocratic education, and the three theories of egalitarian education, which do you think is more easily defended? How would you defend it?

- If some aspects of meritocratic education are unfair, what can be done, besides avoiding major injustices, to modify the approach so that it offers the most students the most benefits? For example, how could the funding approach of the equal resources theory help establish the policy proposals of the meritocratic approach?

CIVIL RIGHTS AND THE SCHOOL-REFORM MOVEMENT ■

Until 1954 attempts to advance the causes of minority groups in the United States usually lacked boldness, organization, and national cohesiveness. But after the Brown decision in 1954, the civil rights move-

TABLE 10–1 A comparison of educational theories

Educational Theories	Underlying Principles	Allocation of Resources	Policy Proposals
Aristocratic Education	Only the superior few can benefit from formal education.	Unequal	Provide a superior education for society's leaders and upholders of culture.
Meritocratic Education	Advancement and rewards are based on demonstrated ability, not extraneous variables.	Provide equal access to education to compete for rewards.	Offer equal access, gifted education, competency education, standardized testing, scholarships and other honors, and screening for talent.
Equal Resources	The quality of public education should be a function of the total wealth of the state.	Each school district will receive equivalent allocations for similar fiscal efforts.	Courts should mandate state legislatures to develop funding reform plans and supervise their implementation.
Equal Outcomes	Educational equality between races is to be measured by outcomes on standardized achievement tests of verbal and mathematical skills.	Desegregate school systems.	Provide integrated schools, improve learning opportunities in the family, early childhood education, and standardized testing.
Substantive Equality	Income is more strongly affected by variables other than schooling and I.Q. scores.	Raise taxes of the wealthy and increase the minimum income of the poor.	Transform society into a form of democratic socialism.

ment gained momentum, becoming a struggle for the minds and hearts of the American people forged of conflict, dislocation, and the reweaving of the social fabric. The nation was transformed.

The proximate cause was the Brown decision, in which the United States Supreme Court declared that "in the field of public education, the doctrine of 'separate but equal' has no place. Separate educational facilities are inherently unequal." The next year the court ruled that schools should desegregate with "all deliberate speed." The National

Association for the Advancement of Colored People (NAACP) had supported the case of the Brown family before the court, taking a legalistic approach in advancing civil rights. Others, however, took different approaches, from civil disobedience to violence.

When Rosa Parks sat down in the white section of a Montgomery, Alabama, bus in 1955, she precipitated a yearlong bus boycott led by the Rev. Martin Luther King, Jr. The boycott resulted in a Supreme Court decision declaring bus segregation unconstitutional. King, drawing upon the teachings of Gandhi and Thoreau, emphasized civil disobedience, encouraging peaceful organized protests and nonviolent resistance based on moral principles to focus public attention on unjust laws and practices.

School segregation was blatantly unjust. *De jure segregation,* or segregation by law, was prevalent in the South, while *de facto segregation,* or segregation in fact and not by right, was common in the North as a result of segregated housing patterns. Resistance to school desegregation was nationwide, but the southern segregationists, especially, were intransigent, and several critical incidents illustrated the depth and intensity of the feelings against desegregation:

- In 1957 President Eisenhower sent 1,000 army troops and paratroopers to Little Rock, Arkansas, to quell mob threats and guarantee the safe enrollment of nine black students at Central High School.

- In 1961 two busloads of Freedom Riders (civil rights protagonists from the North) were attacked by white mobs in several Alabama cities.

- In 1962 federal marshals escorted black law student James H. Meredith to the registration office at the University of Mississippi.

- In 1963 Alabama Governor George Wallace exclaimed, "I say segregation now, segregation tomorrow, segregation forever." Also that year twin bombings of the homes of black leaders in the region led to a riot and, later, to an agreement to desegregate public facilities. And 200,000 civil rights demonstrators took to the streets of Washington.

- In 1965 King and more than 2,600 protesters were arrested in Selma, Alabama, during the three-day demonstrations against voter registration rules. The state police gassed, clubbed, and whipped the demonstrators as they prepared to leave Selma for Montgomery. Also that year, Malcolm X, a militant black separatist and Black Muslim leader, was shot to death as he prepared to give a speech in Manhattan.

The civil rights movement—beginning with the Brown Decision (1954) that separate educational facilities were unequal and the subsequent order to the schools to desegregate—precipitated great changes in American education.

Resistance to desegregation was nationwide but was especially extreme in the South.

Civil rights struggles ranged from civil disobedience to outright violence.

● In 1968 King was assassinated in Memphis, Tennessee, where he had traveled to support a workers' strike.

Society could not ignore the years of unrest, and significant legislation grew out of the civil rights movement. The Civil Rights Act of 1964 prohibited discrimination in public accommodations, public education institutions, voting opportunities, and hiring and promotion practices. Title VI of the act required the withholding of federal funds from institutions that practiced racial discrimination, and required all federal agencies to establish guidelines to fulfill the policy. The threat of withheld funds led to greater school desegregation in the South. The North, which had desegregated with less resistance, nevertheless promoted de facto desegregation through federal district court decisions. (See Chapter 13)

The Elementary and Secondary Act (ESEA) of 1965 was the largest single grant to date of federal aid to education. Schools received allocations for library resources, textbooks, and other instructional materials; funds for stimulating special programs and educational innovations in local school districts; funds for educational research leading to the development of national and regional laboratories; and grants to the states to strengthen state departments of education. But the bill is best known for its aid to the disadvantaged, especially through the compensatory education programs that were established as a result.

> The civil rights movement culminated in significant legislation — the Civil Rights Act of 1964 and the Elementary and Secondary Education Act of 1965, which prohibited discrimination, granted funds to schools, and established compensatory education.

Compensatory Education

Title I (later called Chapter I) of the ESEA, which accounted for nearly 80 percent of the $1.25 billion initially appropriated for the act, called for **compensatory education** "designed to meet the special educational needs of educationally deprived children in school attendance areas having high concentrations of children from low-income families." Project Head Start and Project Follow Through, two compensatory education programs established under the act, served millions of children throughout the country. New York City Schools sponsored a significant compensatory program known as the More Effective Schools project.

Educators held out great hope that these programs would overcome the academic difficulties that many children had experienced in regular school programs. One observer noted, "It has been predicted that Head Start and other preschool education programs will result in some of the most revolutionary developments in elementary education that this country has ever known."[29]

Many of the programs were conducted in schools under de facto segregation. Head Start, sponsored by the Office of Economic Oppor-

Elizabeth Eckford was one of the first black students to gain entrance to Little Rock's Central High School in 1957, in spite of threats from angry protesters.

tunity, attempted, through special preschool programs, to compensate for early deficiencies and help the child better prepare to enter school. The Head Start curriculum emphasized experiences assumed to be lacking in the home and neighborhood of lower-class children—verbal experiences, free play with a variety of materials, familiarization with the shapes of letters—and were based on the latest practices in preschool education. Some Head Start programs later were lengthened to extend through the entire school year. Project Follow Through, initiated in 1967, was designed to pick up where Head Start left off after evaluations showed that the gains from early childhood programs were not being maintained after kindergarten and first grade.

Despite the high hopes for these programs, a study by the United States Commission on Civil Rights found that compensatory programs in segregated schools did not achieve their goals.[30] Black children made greater gains in achievement in desegregated schools than in compensatory programs in segregated schools. Among the reasons given for the failures were the segregated nature of the programs and

Compensatory education—including Project Head Start and Project Follow Through, which were designed to meet the special educational needs of children in low-income areas—had flaws which have since been corrected, enhancing their effectiveness.

inadequate financing. And lengthening the program did not appear to affect the results.[31] Other explanations for the failures included a lack of uniformity, standards, and structure among the programs and the discovery that some of the teachers were not equipped to handle the tasks for which they had been hired.

Since 1975, however, some of the more serious of these mistakes have been rectified. Improved federal and state monitoring of the programs, increased funding in some states, and better evaluation of the programs have enhanced the effectiveness of compensatory education. Frequent monitoring of pupils, more time spent on tasks, and more parental involvement also have been found to contribute to the success of these programs.[32] School achievement in the early grades has increased among students who participated in Head Start, and other compensatory-education programs have had long-lasting effects, such as higher scores on I.Q. and reading tests.

Educational Reform

Key reformers in the late 1960s and early 1970s proposed far-reaching changes that placed the learner in new educational settings. As we saw in Chapter 7, Charles Silberman's national study of public education and teacher education found the schools to be "grim, joyless" places and concluded that "mindlessness" was the main problem with public schools, as well as with liberal arts colleges and schools of education. Too seldom are teachers at any level committed to a clear sense of purpose and direction. He recommended that history and philosophy should occupy a central place in teacher education, and cited the English primary schools, which favor an open classroom approach, as promising models for American elementary schools.[33]

Jonathan Kozol, another reformer, advocated "free schools."[34] These schools, popular during the late 1960s and early 1970s, were small, secular private schools that sought to provide a humanizing experience and an atmosphere of greater freedom of learning. They used progressive methods, Piaget's child development ideas, and some practices from the English primary schools such as creating the informal learning environment of the open classroom.

Edgar Friedenberg was more concerned with the insecure status of youth in today's society where they are pressured by an adult community that seeks to control and force them into desired patterns. He railed against the compulsory nature of schools, the restrictions on student choices and the system of authority, all of which reflect and reinforce society's attitude toward youth.[35]

Ivan Illich, as we saw in Chapter 6, proposed the deschooling of society and the development of informal learning networks.[36] Everyone would have free access to museums, laboratories, and libraries, and could participate in peer matching—the process of two people teaching each other their particular skills.

John Holt's educational ideas evolved over a more extended period and held the spotlight longer than those of other reformers. During the 1960s he said that children should have the freedom to live and think about life for its own sake. Schools should become a smorgasbord of artistic, intellectual, creative, and athletic activities from which students take as much as they want.[37] During the 1970s Holt focused on educational resources, pointing to the many resources in the community: mini-libraries in storefronts, multilith presses, bulletin boards, tape recorders, photographic equipment, language tapes and texts, toys, games, and puzzles. He believed that communities should be places where people share what they know, ask questions, and satisfy their curiosity.[38] He also insisted that children should have basically the same rights as adults, and they should have the right to decide about their own education and whether they want to attend school or learn elsewhere. Compulsory school attendance, he said, is a gross violation of civil liberties.[39] During the 1980s Holt focused on home instruction, a shift stemming from his criticisms of the educational system and his belief that home instruction can offer significant advantages over organized schooling wherever there are concerned and able parents.[40]

Various educational reforms have been proposed, such as making history and philosophy key courses in teacher education, setting up "free schools," abolishing compulsory education, deschooling society, having children decide on their own education, and focusing on home instruction.

Effective Schools

What is the point of school reform, however, if the schools are not effective in teaching all children what they need to know to live fully in society? Equality of education means equal access not just to classrooms and school materials but to the best education possible. Studies have found several factors present in effective schools, including strong, caring administrators, attentive teachers, and motivated students.

These studies, which challenge the findings of Coleman and Jencks, found several school characteristics that appear to promote higher achievement in basic skills:

- A school climate that is conducive to learning—it is free from disciplinary problems and embodies high expectations for student achievement
- Schoolwide emphasis on basic skills
- A system of clear instructional objectives for monitoring and assessing student performance
- A principal who is a strong programmatic leader, sets high standards, frequently observes classrooms, and creates learning incentives.[41]

To be meaningful, each element of school effectiveness must be considered in relation to the other elements within each situation. Researchers cannot say whether these characteristics actually cause school effectiveness, and they have not ranked the characteristics in importance. But it probably can be assumed that a combination of these characteristics need to be present for schools to be effective.

The characteristics of generally effective schools (not just schools that are effective in teaching basic skills) can be stated a little differently:

- A principal who exhibits leadership ability and emphasizes the quality of instruction
- A broad and pervasive instructional focus
- A safe, orderly climate conducive to teaching and learning
- Teachers who promote at least minimum mastery
- Program evaluation based on measures of student achievement[42]

Effective schools provide a climate conducive to learning, an emphasis on basic skills, a broad instructional focus with clear objectives, a strong principal, teachers who promote minimum mastery, program evaluation based on measures of student achievement, and high staff morale and control.

Other studies of school effectiveness, especially those that emphasize program evaluation, found the same five characteristics and added three more: high staff morale and expectations; a high degree of staff control over instructional and training decisions; and clear goals for the school.[43]

A promising longitudinal study by Michael Rutter and others examined twelve inner-city secondary schools in London in terms of students' in-school behavior, attendance, examination success, and delinquency.[44] Scholastic achievement was found to be affected by the school attended, but less affected by school size or age, or available space. The implication was that good outcomes can be achieved despite less-than-ideal physical surroundings. The study suggested that effective schools were the result of, among other things, teachers who were punctual and who prepared lessons in advance and directed attention to the class as a whole. Students had higher achievement rates when homework was assigned and graded regularly and when they were told that they were capable of learning and would, indeed, learn.

George Madus and others found that "schools, particularly at the secondary level, make a difference in subject-specific instruction. Further, this difference is to a large extent independent of home background and is related to structure, discipline, homework, and general press to achieve in school."[45]

As we can see from the results of these studies, it is clear that, despite the Coleman Report's suggestions, certain inputs do have a significant effect on student achievement.

Busing. Acting on the fundamental premise that some schools are more effective than others, and that desegregation can offer disadvantaged students a chance to attend these better schools, many federal district courts turned to **busing** as a means of equalizing educational opportunity by balancing the distribution of races throughout the school system. Even before desegregation, busing was a common feature of the educational landscape. As many as 40 percent of all students rode a bus because the nearest school was too far for them to reach on foot. But these were the days of segregation, and it was common for white children to be bused past an all-black school to an all-white school on the other side of town. Such busing raised little controversy and parents seldom complained about the inconvenience—until the district courts modified the busing system to achieve desegregation. Parents, especially parents who believed their children were being forced to attend inferior schools, began protesting the system and demanding that school districts find other ways of desegregating. The evidence on the effects of busing has been mixed. Some researchers have found that busing has done nothing to improve the achievement of minority children, while others claim that it has had a strong positive effect.[46]

Open Attendance. Some cities have instituted **open attendance** plans, which permit parents, at their own expense, to have their children transported to schools with less-than-capacity enrollment. These plans have not met with much success, which is not surprising because the financial burden of transportation falls upon the parents rather than the school district, and poor parents are rarely able to afford such costs.

Educational Parks. Another proposal for desegregation is the development of **educational parks**, which would consolidate or cluster existing schools, broadening their attendance areas so that the school population becomes racially and economically mixed. The idea is similar to busing in that it moves children away from their section of the city, but different in that all children are affected, not just one group. The grouping of schools in this way permits the development of more diversified curriculums and the employment of expert personnel to develop consistent diagnostic and remedial programs for the entire area.

Pairing. This plan calls for the **pairing** of two schools in a particular area so that they share the same attendance district. For example, a district would take two elementary schools, one predominantly black and the other predominantly white, and turn one into a kindergarten through third-grade school, and the other into a fourth- through sixth-grade school. All children from both areas would attend both schools. In a small community, one school building might become a central facility, but for the most part, both schools would have equal attendance. A similar arrangement can be developed in larger communities by turning the entire district into a single-attendance zone where each school would serve all students in one or two grades. Pairing guards against de facto segregation because school attendance remains the same even when residential housing patterns change within a district.

Magnet Schools. In an attempt to attract students from various racial and ethnic backgrounds and to voluntarily desegregate the schools, many districts have developed **magnet schools** that emphasize certain programs. Some magnet schools emphasize academics and college preparatory programs, others focus on the performing arts, and still others offer programs for the gifted. Elementary magnet schools might focus on a particular approach to learning, such as the Montessori methods, the open classroom approach, or an emphasis on learning basic skills. Some evidence shows that the overall quality and effectiveness of magnet schools is good,[47] although, at best, they can only supplement larger desegregation measures. Because magnet schools are selective, students who are low achievers (and therefore most in need of assistance) are not able to attend. As a result, the remaining public schools end up with a larger proportion of low achievers.

Various plans to accomplish desegregation include busing, open attendance, educational parks, magnet schools, pairing, and building-site selection, the last two of which achieve natural, large-scale desegregation over time with the least resistance.

Building-site Selection. Segregation is intensified by residential housing patterns and choice of school-building sites. The neighborhood school is the product of residential housing patterns, and in some cases, the gerrymandering of school districts. Before the Civil Rights Act of 1964, discrimination in public housing was not prohibited. Judging from the large number of cases prosecuted since 1964, such discrimination has been widespread. And the poor, of course, are severely restricted in their choices of housing whether or not discrimination is involved. Building sites chosen by school boards have tended to reinforce segregated housing patterns and, therefore, segregated schools because they often are located clearly in the middle of a given neighborhood. Desegregation can be promoted by building schools between neighborhoods, so that children from different neighborhoods can go to the same school.

Of the different desegregation plans reviewed here, the pairing and building-site approaches promise natural, large-scale desegregation over a long period of time; while busing promises more immediate desegregation, but meets with more resistance. Consequently, unless a school district is under court orders to desegregate through busing, districts might find one of the other plans more successful in the long run.

SPECIAL EDUCATION ▪

The education of students with disabilities poses a special challenge for schools that strive to provide equal opportunity to education. The problem is to give these children an education equal in quality to that of non-disabled children without restricting the rights or experiences of either group. In the nineteenth century students with disabilities were sent to state or private schools specially designed for them. By the turn of the century experts thought that if these children were to live in the community, they should not be segregated from it, and public schools began offering special programs for students with mild disabilities. Since that time, research in medicine, sociology, psychology, and education have contributed substantially to the understanding of disabling conditions and to the development of treatment and educational procedures.

In 1973 Congress passed the Vocational Rehabilitation Act, prohibiting discrimination against the disabled in the work environment and in any education program receiving federal aid. A *disability* was defined as a health condition or impairment that limits one's ability to perform a major life activity for an extended period of time. In 1975 the Education for All Handicapped Children Act (P.L. 94–142) was passed, requiring special educational services for the disabled. These special services include speech pathology and audiology, psychological services, physical and occupational therapy, recreation, counseling services, and medical services for diagnosis and evaluation. The act also provides due process in the assignment and placement of pupils, and requires that education take place in the "least restrictive" environment.

The "least restrictive" provision promoted **mainstreaming**, a plan by which children with disabilities would receive special education in the regular classroom as far as was possible. The justification for mainstreaming is the belief that children have a right to and can benefit from participation in the least restrictive educational program they can manage. Educators also believed that such integration can help break down any prejudices that non-disabled children might have about children with disabilities. Mainstreaming can entail anything from integrating the child with other students only for non-academic work (such as physical education) to assigning the child to a regular

Equalizing opportunities also involves education for disabled students, which has evolved from segregating to mainstreaming them, where they receive special education in the regular classroom.

P.L. 94–142 required that children with disabilities receive their education in the regular classroom.

classroom and providing general and special education, as well as support services, as needed within that classroom.

More than four million people in the United States between the ages of three and twenty-one have disabilities and receive special education services. Disabilities include speech, learning, orthopedic, and visual disabilities; mental retardation; and serious emotional disturbance. Those selected for mainstreaming usually have only mild disabilities, although the courts so far have decided that children with disabilities have a right to participate in public education regardless of the classification or the severity of the disability.

Mainstreaming does have drawbacks. Regular classroom teachers need special preparation and assistance working with children with disabilities; the children themselves might not be accepted by their classmates and therefore might not be able to depend on them for help in routine school activities; many school buildings might need extensive modifications; special programs need additional funding; and changes in curriculum and class size might be necessary to accommodate children with disabilities. Studies to determine the effectiveness of mainstreaming versus segregation in special schools have suggested that children with disabilities might profit in regular classes in terms of academic achievement, but that their social ad- justment is poor.[48]

In fulfilling P.L. 94–142 in general, it could be argued that educators have relied too much on testing and not enough on clinical data or on direct observation. Some educators are concerned that full implementation of P.L. 94–142 might result in preferential treatment of the disabled at the expense of the non-disabled, especially since the cost of educating a child with a disability is more than twice that of educating a non-disabled child. During the Reagan administration this concern was addressed through attempts to eliminate the mildly disabled from mandated programs and restrict the application of P.L. 94–142 to the more severely disabled. Some educators also point to the disproportionately high number of minorities, especially Hispanics, who are classified as retarded or learning disabled, raising concerns that they might be misclassified, trapped in the wrong program, and needlessly segregated from their peers.

The concept of equality suggests that schools should do everything possible to provide students with disabilities with the same quality of education that non-disabled students enjoy. The same concept also suggests, however, that such education should not be at the expense of opportunities for non-disabled children. It also suggests that educators should take great care to ensure that minority or disadvantaged children are not classified as disabled simply because they are different or have possible learning difficulties. As a rule of thumb, schools can promote equality of education by treating the child with a disability as a student first and as a person with a disability second.

One special education movement currently being debated is Regular Education Initiative (REI). It seeks to provide special services within regular classrooms, collaborate between regular and special education, and serve all students with learning problems. Many students have learning problems but are not eligible for special education. Special educators could assess the needs of these students and develop a learning plan for them in cooperation with regular educators.

Mainstreaming has many drawbacks in the area of resources as well as adjustment on the part of both the teacher and the students.

While schools should do everything they can to accommodate the disabled, it should not be at the expense of the other students.

Schools should treat the disabled child as a student first and disabled second.

REI is largely concerned with students with mild disabilities and adapting regular classrooms to them, although it still seeks to maintain special education services. The REI movement, however, has been criticized because not all students can be managed and taught effectively in the regular classroom, and a range of services, from mainstreaming to total segregation, is necessary. Another concern is that students with disabilities might be placed in regular classrooms without adequate support. More resources are needed because the regular classroom has a growing number of students at risk for school failure. Additionally, more effective instructional technologies are essential, and special educators need to take greater responsibility for low-performing students, including making placement decisions on an individual basis.

■ Summary

- Until the late nineteenth century aristocratic education was the dominant form of education in the East and West. Friedrich Nietzsche believed that only the highest classes should receive an education, at the expense of the masses if necessary; T. S. Eliot believed that the purpose of education was "to preserve the class and select the elite."

- A meritocratic system, on the other hand, espouses equal educational opportunity and is based on achievement rather than ascription. Students with potentials most valued by society, no matter what their class background, have the opportunity to develop them and subsequently be rewarded for them. Critics say the meritocratic approach is inherently conservative and perpetuates the accepted values of society, even if they are undesirable. Critics also believe such a system encourages cruelty and competitiveness, dehumanizes society, discounts self-respect, and is not genuinely fair. American education today is a mixed system consisting of meritocratic elements tempered with egalitarian principles.

- Equality is more prescriptive (prescribed by principle) than descriptive (based on analysis of similarities), although it does have some descriptive features. That one is a human being is reason enough to expect equal treatment, and the burden of proof rests on those who would treat someone differently.

- Egalitarian education has three basic theories: *equal resources*, which emphasizes the equalization of resources for all school districts; *equal outcomes*, focusing on equalizing the achievements of all students; and *substantive equality*, which advocates transforming society into a form of democratic socialism. The first two theories, especially the equal resources theory, have had the most influence on education.

- The civil rights movement of the 1960s culminated in the Civil Rights Act of 1964 and the Elementary and Secondary Education Act of 1965, mandating desegregation, more funding for all schools, and compensatory education, although de facto segregation and unequal allocations and education have persisted to some degree.

- Education reformers have proposed far-reaching changes in the school system, such as placing history and philosophy at the center of teacher education, developing "free schools," abolishing compulsory education, deschooling society altogether, giving children the freedom to live and think about life for its own sake, involving the community in the constant education of all, giving children the right to choose how they want to be educated, and focusing on home instruction.

- Equality of education means little in an ineffective school system. Studies have found that schools that successfully teach the basics share certain characteristics: a school climate conducive to learning; emphasis on basic skills; clear instructional objectives; and a strong principal. Schools that are generally effective share similar characteristics: a strong principal; a broad instructional focus; a safe, orderly climate; teachers who promote at least minimum mastery; and program evaluation based on measures of student achievement.

- Attempts to desegregate the schools include busing, open attendance plans, educational parks, pairing, magnet schools, and strategic selection of school building sites. Pairing and strategic building-site selection promise natural, large-scale desegregation over time, while busing provides immediate desegregation but meets with resistance.

- Education for students with disabilities has evolved from placing these students in special classes or institutions to integrating them into the mainstream, as called for by the 1975 Education for All Handicapped Children Act. The act also mandated special services for the disabled, and due process in the assignment and placement of pupils. Mainstreaming has drawbacks, especially in the area of resources and student adjustment, although some of the problems can be minimized by treating the child with a disability as a student first and a disabled person second.

■ Key Terms

aristocratic education	exploitation
busing	invidious discrimination
compensatory education	judgmental injustice
competency education	magnet schools
de facto segregation	mainstreaming
de jure segregation	meritocratic system
educational parks	open attendance plans
equal resources	pairing
equal outcomes	substantive equality
equality	

■ Discussion Questions

1. In view of the findings in this chapter and in Chapter 9, why do you think inequalities persist in our society?

2. How do Nietzsche and Eliot's positions promote aristocratic thinking?

3. How can we interpret Thomas Jefferson's statement, "All men are created equal . . ." to fit today's society?

4. At what point does it become futile to increase some types of school inputs?

5. In terms of studies by Coleman and Jencks, to what degree can formal education influence one's lifetime income and overall life chances?

6. Why has the civil rights movement met significant resistance in some areas? How successful has the movement been in achieving its aims?

■ Learning Activities

1. Organize a class debate on the resolution: "A meritocratic system should (or should not) be the basis for American education."

2. Examine the history of your community and prepare a report on how it was involved in, and affected by, the civil rights movement.

3. Find out what desegregation plans are used in your local school district and assess their relative effectiveness, through interviews with school officials and some parents and children who are directly affected by the plans.

4. Interview teachers in your area who were teaching during the civil rights movement about the perceptions of the era and its effect on their teaching responsibilities.

5. Organize a debate on the question: "Should disabled students be mainstreamed?"

Suggested Readings

Ballantine, Jeanne H. *The Sociology of Education: A Systematic Analysis*, 2nd ed. Englewood Cliffs, NJ: Prentice-Hall, 1989.

A sociological approach to problems of equality of opportunity.

Bell, Daniel. "On Meritocracy and Equality." In *The New Egalitarianism*, ed. David Lewis Schaefer. Port Washington, NY: Kennikat Press, 1979.

A defense of meritocracy by a leading proponent.

Coleman, James S., et al. *Equality of Educational Opportunity*. Washington, DC: U.S. Government Printing Office, 1966.

Full details of the equal outcomes position.

Coons, John E., William H. Clune, III, and John D. Sugarman. *Private Wealth and Public Education*. Cambridge, MA: Harvard University Press, 1970.

A statement of the equal resources theory.

Jencks, Christopher, et al., *Who Gets Ahead: The Determinants of Economic Success in America*. New York: Basic Books, 1979.

An expression of the substantive equality position.

Nash, Paul, ed., "The Cultured Man: Eliot." In *Models of Man*. New York: Wiley, 1968, 385–405.

T. S. Eliot's ideas about aristocratic education.

Pennock, J. Roland and John W. Chapman, eds. *Equality*. New York: Atherton Press, 1967.

Essays about the concept of equality, political and legal equality, and the implications of egalitarianism.

Strain, Philip S. and Mary Margaret Kerr. *Mainstreaming of Children in Schools: Research and Programmatic Issues*. New York: Academic Press, 1981.

Explores a full range of problems and issues about mainstreaming.

Notes

1. Ben J. Wattenberg, "The Attitudes Behind American Exceptionalism," *U.S. News & World Report* (August 7, 1989): 25.
2. *Report of the National Advisory Commission on Civil Disorders* (New York: Bantam Books, 1968), 203.

3. Ibid., 407.

4. "The Halting Progress of Blacks in the Last Generation," *U.S. News & World Report* (January 22, 1990): 28.

5. "Few Gains Made in 'Decade of Hispanic,'" *American-Statesman* (December 16, 1989): A1, A9.

6. Christopher Jencks, "Is the Public School Obsolete?" *The Public Interest* 2 (1966): 20.

7. Friedrich Nietzsche, *Beyond Good and Evil*, transl. by Walter Kaufmann (New York: Random House, 1966).

8. "The Cultured Man: Eliot." In *Models of Man*, ed. Paul Nash (New York: Wiley, 1968), 385–405.

9. Christopher Jencks and David Riesman, *The Academic Revolution* (Garden City, NY: Doubleday Anchor Books, 1969), 12.

10. Daniel Bell, "On Meritocracy and Equality." In *The New Egalitarianism*, ed. David Lewis Schaefer (Port Washington, NY: Kennikat Press, 1979), 41.

11. Daniel Bell, *The Coming of Post-Industrial Society: A Venture in Social Forecasting* (New York: Basic Books, 1973), 414, 453.

12. Daniel Bell, "A 'Just' Equality," *Dialogue* 8 (1975): 3.

13. John H. Schaar, "Some Ways to Think About Equality," *Journal of Politics* 26 (1964): 867–95.

14. Ibid., 871.

15. John Schaar, "Equality of Opportunity and Beyond," in *Equality*, eds. J. Roland Pennock and John W. Chapman (New York: Atherton Press, 1967), 233.

16. Robert Nozick, *Anarchy, State, and Utopia* (New York: Basic Books, 1974), 235–36.

17. Kai Nielsen, *Equality and Liberty* (Totowa, NJ: Rowman & Allanheld, 1985), 161.

18. John Rawls, *A Theory of Justice* (Cambridge, MA: Harvard University Press, 1971), 106–8.

19. Charles Frankel, "Equality of Opportunity," *Ethics* 81 (1971): 203–4.

20. American Association of School Administrators, *AASA Code of Ethics* (Washington, DC: The Association, 1966), 25.

21. John E. Coons, William H. Clune III, and Stephen D. Sugarman, *Private Wealth and Public Education* (Cambridge, MA: Harvard University Press, 1970).

22. James S. Coleman, et al., *Equality of Educational Opportunity* (Washington, DC: U.S. Government Printing Office, 1966).

23. Marshall S. Smith, "Equality of Educational Opportunity: The Basic Findings Reconsidered," in *On Equality of Educational Opportunity*, eds. Frederick Mosteller and Daniel P. Moynihan (New York: Vintage Books, 1972), 312.

24. Samuel Bowles and Henry M. Levin, "The Detriments of Scholastic Achievement—An Appraisal of Some Recent Evidence," *The Journal of Human Resources* 3 (1968): 3–24; Edmund R. Gordon, "Equalizing Educational Opportunity in the Public Schools," *IRCD Bulletin* (November 1967); and U.S. Commission on *Civil Rights, Racial Isolation in the Public Schools,* 2 vols. (Washington, D.C.: U.S. Government Printing Office, 1967).

25. Mosteller and Moynihan, *On Equality;* Harvey Averch, et al., *How Effective Is Schooling? A Critical Review and Synthesis of Research Findings* (Santa Monica, CA: Rand Corporation, 1972).

26. Christopher Jencks, et al., *Inequality: A Reassessment of the Effect of Family and Schooling in America* (New York: Basic Books, 1972).

27. Henry M. Levin, "Schooling and Inequality: The Social Science Objectivity Gap," *Saturday Review of Literature* LV, No. 46 (1972): 49–51.

28. Christopher Jencks, et al., *Who Gets Ahead: The Determinants of Economic Success in America* (New York: Basic Books, 1979).

29. Annie L. Butler, "Will Head Start Be a False Start?" *Childhood Education* (November 1965): 166.

30. U.S. Commission on Civil Rights, *Racial Isolation,* vol. 2.

31. *A Study of the Full-Year 1966 Head Start Program,* Washington DC: Planning Research Corporation, 1967).

32. Benjamin D. Stickney and Virginia R. T. Plunkett, "Closing the Gap: A Historical Perspective on the Effectiveness of Compensatory Education," *Phi Delta Kappan* (December 1983): 290.

33. Charles E. Silberman, *Crisis in the Classroom* (New York: Vintage Books, 1970).

34. Jonathan Kozol, *Free Schools* (Boston: Houghton Mifflin, 1972).

35. Edgar Z. Friedenberg, *Coming of Age in America* (New York: Random House, 1965).

36. Ivan Illich, *Deschooling Society* (New York: Harper & Row, 1971).

37. John Holt, *How Children Fail* (New York: Pitman, 1965) and *How Children Learn* (New York: Pitman, 1969).

38. John Holt, *Instead of Education: Ways to Help People Do Things Better* (New York: Dutton, 1976).

39. John Holt, *Escape from Childhood: The Needs and Rights of Children* (New York: Dutton, 1974).

40. John Holt, *Teach Your Own* (New York: Delacorte, 1981).

41. Brian Rowan, Steven T. Bossert, and David C. Dwyer, "Research on Effective Schools: A Cautionary Note," *Educational Researcher* 12 (1983): 24.

42. Ronald R. Edmonds, "Programs of School Improvement: An Overview," *Educational Leadership* 40 (1982): 64–69.

43. Stewart C. Purkey and Marshall S. Smith, "Too Soon to Cheer? Synthesis of Research on Effective Schools," *Educational Leadership* 40 (1982): 64–69.

44. Michael Rutter, et al., *Fifteen Thousand Hours: Secondary Schools and Their Effects on Children* (Cambridge, MA: Harvard University Press, 1979).

45. George F. Madus, Peter W. Airasian, and Thomas Kellaghan, *School Effectiveness: A Reassessment of the Evidence* (New York: McGraw-Hill, 1980), 174.

46. Wayne Sage, "Loaded School Bus," *Human Behavior* 7 (1978): 20–21.

47. Rolf K. Blank, "Magnet Schools Offer Diversity and Quality," *Educational Leadership* 41 (1984): 72.

48. L. Corman and J. Gottlieb, "Mainstreaming Mentally Retarded Children: A Review of Research," In *International Review of Research in Mental Retardation*, ed. N.R. Ellis, Vol 9 (New York: Academic Press, 1979), 235–56.

■ PART FIVE

INFLUENCES ON ■ SCHOOL DECISIONS

Part Five deals with the political, economic, legal, and curricular influences on school decisions and examines schools in terms of their interaction with the larger society and other social institutions. We also will look at the changing political and economic conditions that influence schools and their inner operations at different levels.

In Chapter 11 we will discuss two theories of democracy and their educational implications. Through an understanding of power and authority in bureaucratic school systems, we will examine the politics of education at federal, state, and local levels and discuss the relative roles and influences of each level.

In Chapter 12 we will explore the sources of public-school funding, the desirable characteristics needed for levying a tax, the growth of the state's role in educational financing, and alternative financial plans. While not all public officials believe that more funding is the only answer to public-education problems, many educators and others believe that some funding problems are critical. In this chapter we also will look at how economists view education in terms of its contribution to economic growth and its rate of return for the individual, as well as three plans for teacher compensation.

In Chapter 13 we will look at the role of law in education and society, the legal responsibilities of teachers, and the rights of students. We will discuss the legal issues surrounding church-state relations in education, minimum competency testing, tracking, and desegregation.

In Chapter 14 the focus will be on curriculum development and evaluation, including deriving aims from which objectives can be drawn, adopting elements for structuring the curriculum, sequencing material, and choosing the appropriate organizational pattern. We will discuss how evaluation of a curriculum can help educators make decisions and form educational policies, and assess six curricular innovations.

■ C H A P T E R 11

POLITICAL AND ■
ORGANIZATIONAL INFLUENCES

A LOOK AHEAD

The purpose of this chapter is to explain the relative influence of diverse political and organizational forces on education. You will learn about:

- Two theories of democratic education: representative democracy and participatory democracy

- How a bureaucracy attempts to maintain control and encourage innovation within a democracy

- Some inadequacies of bureaucracy in education

- The use of power on a national level, including the pluralist model and the power-elite model, and how they affect education

- Three basic types of authority as legitimate forms of power

- The use of power and authority to control people and institutions

- The advantages and disadvantages of the federal government's role in education

- The state's primary role in education

- The movement toward stronger local involvement in the school systems

A knowledge of the principles of organization on a federal level as well as a local level can help us understand how they affect education, especially in areas such as curriculum, teaching, working conditions for teachers and students, and operational policies. Each school's organization and administration determine the school environment; the school system can limit learning activities, or it can provide an experimental, open arrangement in which teachers and students are free to develop innovative programs.

An organizational structure should promote the attainment of goals.

The function of any organizational structure in education is to help a school reach its goals in an ethical manner. The structure should not be sacrosanct or considered an end in itself and should be altered if it persistently impedes the attainment of system goals. The ideal structure uses and apportions scarce resources effectively and places personnel in positions for which they are best suited. Much of today's organization is based on historical patterns, though, and during periods of rapid change, it can become antiquated or dysfunctional. To fully appraise the effectiveness of a school system, we need to understand how the system is organized and how it carries out various functions in terms of its organizational structure.

In this chapter we will explore the federal, state, and local levels of the organizational structure of education and how each functions. But first, let us provide some background to place these findings in a broader theoretical perspective. A democracy, for example, might expect its citizens to commit to certain arrangements to be consistent with democratic principles, but the rise of bureaucratic school systems and concentrations of power and authority also shape organizational structures and often influence political decisions affecting education.

■ PHILOSOPHIES OF DEMOCRATIC EDUCATION

Two major positions on democratic participation are significant in educational policy: representative democracy and participatory democracy. Representative democracy is found in most school districts, while participatory democracy is advocated in the literature of political science and politics of education. **Representative democracy,** which stems from Jeffersonian democracy, envisions citizens determining who shall represent them as a result of the election process. Such a democracy could be defined as an elective system in which majority influence is assured by elective and competitive minorities to whom the system is entrusted.[1] Political leaders, says Robert Dahl, are more likely to defend democracy even if voters prefer some other system because democratic procedures regulate conflict and protect their position of leadership.[2] V. O. Key, Jr. agrees that the health of democracy depends on the standards and competence of influential citizens and political activists.[3]

The philosophy limits the citizen's role to the selection of political leaders. And because it is assumed that each citizen wants to make wise political choices, the purpose of education should be to enhance one's knowledge about government and prepare new political leaders. This position, held by several groups, can be seen clearly in essentialism. Essentialists generally agree that the basic task of the schools is to develop the mind by transmitting the cultural heritage and equipping the young with the knowledge, skills, and ideals needed to contribute to the stability and perpetuation of society. They oppose turning schools into miniature democracies, whether by expanding the social studies, introducing life-adjustment education, or by injecting socializing procedures into an expanded vocational program.

Schools help to prepare leaders by screening and sorting people for political and economic life. Both essentialism and pragmatism have contributed to these meritocratic goals—essentialism by emphasizing the preservation of the culture through preparation in basic subjects and pragmatism by stressing the use of experts in evaluating truth claims.

> Representative democrats view education as a way to train citizens to perpetuate society.

Proponents of **participatory democracy,** which stems from Jacksonian democracy, say that while the representative theory is largely an accurate description of American politics today, this is not the way the system *should* operate.[4] The system should offer the widest possible participation to all citizens, because individuals should participate in decisions that significantly affect their lives. Politics, they say, is not limited to government but extends to any institution and agency in which power is used. Representative theory, however, would reject such an extension of the meaning of politics because government is different from any other institution: it is the only institution that has the right to use or authorize force, for example. Besides, to extend the term *politics* so widely tends to weaken it.

Participatory democrats believe that, to survive, democratic institutions must redistribute power and decision making. They also deny that representative democrats are more interested than the average person in preserving the system—especially if doing so conflicts with their interests.

One type of participatory democracy in education is built around the view that democracy is a way of life. Even though John Dewey's cultivation of knowledge experts may have contributed to the growth of a meritocracy, Dewey's ideas are more in the participatory vein. Dewey viewed democracy as more than a form of government; he saw it as primarily a mode of associated living.[5] He established two tests for the worth of social life: the number and variety of interests shared by a group and the freedom of interplay with other groups.[6] Undesirable societies establish barriers to the free exchange of ideas, whereas a democratic society has a place for all members and uses their thinking to help make changes in social life.

Dewey believed that schools should provide an understanding of social forces and the resources needed to cope with social problems. People need to know how things work and how to make them work properly. Knowledge, therefore, has to be connected to social action. This could be accomplished in the curriculum through social studies courses that show how society operates and what changes are needed; through science classes that consider the social consequences of scientific discoveries; and through vocational education, which provides an understanding of industry and the professions.[7]

Dewey also believed that teachers, either directly or through a representative, should be able to participate in forming educational policy. In the late 1930s he found that democratic methods of dealing with people had been more successful with students than with teachers and urged that teachers be encouraged to develop decision-making skills by having an opportunity to use them.[8]

A more recent form of participatory democracy is found in critical theory as expressed by Henry Giroux.[9] He believes that social and economic justice can be realized by democratic movements working through government. History is a continuous expansion of human rights as a result of struggles against oppression.

Giroux envisions radical teachers working within and outside of schools to develop educative practices outside of established institutions. He views schools as potent vehicles for social change and considers teachers and students important participants in this concept. Schools should seek to unite theory and practice by providing unified cognitive and affective characteristics to liberate the individual and promote social reconstruction.

> *A participatory democratic viewpoint is that education should help the citizenry understand the workings of society.*

■ BUREAUCRACY

Educational organizations, like other types of organizations, need properly operating internal functions if they are to attain their goals. After an organization has established its goals, it tries to maintain sufficient control over its operations to prevent disorganization and attempts to introduce innovations to bring about needed improvements. Ideally, an organization should strike a balance between the two objectives. If the administration is too concerned about control,

> *Control* is an essential feature of an organizational structure.

innovation may be suppressed. On the other hand, if innovation is too heavily stressed, the organization can lose control.

A **bureaucracy** is a large-scale organization designed to carry out complex tasks. It is generally assumed that an office holder, at least in an industrial state, is a member of a bureaucracy. According to Max Weber, the objectives of bureaucracies are to eliminate irrational and emotional elements, to elevate precision, speed, continuity, and unambiguity, and to encourage the subordination of personnel to the administrative hierarchy to reduce friction and to minimize material and personnel costs.[10]

True to Weber's interpretation, bureaucracies organize their offices according to a hierarchal principle in which each office is supervised and controlled by a higher one, although the lower office has the right to appeal and issue statements of grievance to the higher one. Qualifications and rules of authority for each office are specified in writing. To meet qualifications for the office, one needs specialized training, which ensures that appointments are based on merit rather than wealth, influence, or other extraneous factors. Promotion is based on seniority, achievement, or both; employment in the system constitutes a career; and the office holder is protected from arbitrary dismissal.

A school system can be considered a bureaucracy, although the teacher's position is not entirely bureaucratically organized. The teacher, while under the authority of the principal, is not usually closely supervised and cannot be thought of as following orders or implementing policy decisions because the goals of the school system cannot be readily quantified and measured. Moreover, most administrative rules (other than requirements to perform tasks such as taking attendance and monitoring students) do not apply to teaching, which contains many unpredictable factors and requires teachers to rely on their own judgment much of the time. Finally, unlike objective quality control in a factory, evaluation of teachers is subjective and difficult to devise and interpret.[11]

The teacher's role does not fit neatly into the concept of an educational bureaucracy.

Research has shown that bureaucracies are inefficient in many ways that Weber did not anticipate. Robert Merton suggests that, because of their structure, bureaucracies can become inflexible.[12] Office holders often follow rules slavishly and elevate those rules above the organizational goals the rules were designed to achieve. As a result, subordinates tend to follow orders even if those orders are misguided.

The undesirable aspects of bureaucracies may intrude on the teacher's functions when some techniques of industry are applied to school systems. Frederick Taylor advocated the scientific study of jobs in industry based on time study of tasks, leading to the establishment of a standard time for each job and payment of wages according to output.[13] More systematic studies later dealt with the division of labor, specialization and departmentalization of functions, and managerial supervision.[14]

In the early twentieth century American businessmen, from their positions on school boards, pressured educators to adopt industrial management principles in the operation of school systems, insisting that such procedures would result in greater efficiency and economy. From 1910 to 1929 these values and techniques were common in American education.[15]

Industry and education, however, are not parallel in their objectives or their methods. Forcing education to follow an industry model of management can lead to abuses and distortions of the teaching-learning process. Teachers often are expected to humanize education, which runs counter to the impersonality fostered by bureaucracies; they also are expected to individualize instruction, which can conflict with the bureaucratic norm of applying the rules to everyone or to classifying students into predetermined categories. Certain aspects of education, however, such as the business operations of school systems, can operate effectively on the industry model.

The social structure of future organizations, according to Warren Bennis, will be rapidly changing "temporary systems."[16] Groups will be organized on the basis of problems to be solved. Individuals will not be differentiated according to rank or status but in terms of abilities and professional training, and the executive will coordinate different task forces. This form of social organization, which Bennis calls "organic-adaptive" structure, involves the team use of specialized talents to attack specific problems. The transitory nature of the teams lacks the more enduring relations of bureaucracies and calls for more flexible and adaptable individuals.

Bennis's organic-adaptive model fulfills the need of professionals for greater autonomy. Lloyd Bishop has suggested that greater teacher participation and autonomy can be brought about by establishing a "professional teacher core."[17] The core would consist of teachers in specific disciplines as well as teachers with interdisciplinary responsibilities. Some of the teams would be temporary task forces formed by the professional teacher core to treat specific curricular problems.

In an organic-adaptive model, principals would reconceptualize their roles as collaborative ones. Effective principals encourage extensive involvement of faculty in decision making, and teacher leadership can play an important role in school systems. Even though research indicates that shared leadership and teacher involvement in problem solving are found in effective schools, few school systems provide an organizational structure for such activities.[18]

The bureaucratic model is appropriate to the more administrative aspects of an educational system.

Effective schools tend to feature collaboration between principal and teachers.

▪ **PAUSE TO REFLECT**
Effective Leadership in the Schools

- Do you think schools operate best under traditional industry management techniques, or would they run more efficiently under an organic-adaptive model?

- If a school were structured on an organic-adaptive model, what do you think your role as a teacher would be? For example, what input would you want to have in discipline and policy decisions?

- If schools used a temporary task force approach to solve problems, what kinds of problems would such a task force be ideally suited to handle? For example, if a school had a serious vandalism problem, how could a temporary task force help formulate a solution?

Power, Authority, and Control

Power. A person has **power** if he can get someone to carry out his will despite resistance. In other words, *A* has power over *B* if *B* resists *A* but still acts in the way *A* prescribes. Power also can take the form of influencing or controlling the other party's decision making. If the power figure controls a sufficient number of key decisions—as in parent-child relations—then the power figure (parent) dominates the subject (child) by determining his or her life plan. Other examples of such power would be found in a totalitarian state, in prison, or in a prisoner of war camp.

Power can employ coercion or force. A distinction can be made between the two processes.[19] The coerced person becomes the tool of another but still has the choice, under the constraint, of choosing the least undesirable course of action. Or, in the case of coercive laws, one can choose not to obey the laws. But when force is used, individuals can be excused because they are not responsible for their actions. Individuals can, however, be held partly responsible for acts committed under coercion—responsibility would be determined by the circumstances of each case.

In addition to its use through coercion or force, power also can be employed in conditioning, behavior modification, hypnosis, personal charisma, propaganda, and other instances in which the subject's will yields to the power figure's commands.

Power is closely related to influence. A person with **influence** sways, affects, or alters another by indirect or intangible means; influence can be exerted consciously or unconsciously. In contrast, power is exerted consciously, is tangible, and is usually direct (though there are exceptions, as in the case of propaganda). Power also differs from influence in that the power figure can invoke sanctions but the influential figure cannot. For example, a movie star influences countless fans to see his latest motion picture without invoking sanctions; the influential personality features of the star, which create a wide following, frequently can be intangible or ineffable.

Teachers usually cannot use force and must exert their will through influence, expertise, and the status of their office. Notable exceptions occur whenever teachers are legally permitted to use corporal punishment and other forms of physical control over recalcitrant students. If propaganda, behavior modification, and conditioning are also considered forms of power, one might think that teachers exercise considerable power; but, for the most part, the conception of power we discussed earlier applies primarily to legislative bodies, law enforcement machinery, and key administrative positions. For instance, state officials designated to enforce compulsory school attendance laws would have considerable power.

The federal government has various ways to exert power in determining educational policy.

Because educational policy is made by the federal government through methods such as the allocation of revenues, federal aid-to-education bills, and national commission reports sponsored by government agencies, a look at the use of power on a national scale can put educational control in perspective. Two different models have been used to explain power at this level in the United States: pluralism and the power elite.

The **pluralist model** is built on the idea that a complex organization is likely to have several centers of power. Many different groups have power and usually pursue somewhat different goals, with few groups attaining all of their goals. Government officials are constrained by laws in the exercise of power and are responsible to the voters and a wide range of special interest groups. Key decisions that affect society are not made by any one organization or group of people; and because numerous groups can exercise veto power, American politics is a process of negotiation and compromise. The process of negotiation among different power centers allows politicians to learn how to reach peaceful decisions beneficial to all parties involved.[20] Some pluralists, however, acknowledge that American democracy has been plagued with abuses of power (during the Vietnam War and the Watergate scandal, for instance), and an inability to resolve some serious social problems.[21]

The **power-elite model** holds that a small proportion of the population at the top of the social hierarchy holds most of the power, while those at the bottom have very little. C. Wright Mills, who introduced the term *power elite*, argued that the key decision makers in politics are in the upper class.[22] Mills claimed that the power elite is a coalition of

The pluralist model holds that many different groups participate in governance.

people who control corporations, the military, and the government. Retired generals become directors of corporations that bid on defense contracts, executives move to top government agencies and back to private companies, and members of the board of directors of one corporation are also on the boards of other corporations. Mills claimed that the pluralist model applies only to the middle sector of the social stratification system—such as Congress, where one pressure group can counteract another to establish countervailing power. But within the power elite, there is no countervailing power because the power elite is a single unified group. The power elite is a self-conscious cohesive unit; its cohesiveness is based on psychological similarity (values are determined by the institutional positions held), social interaction, and coinciding interests. Members of the power elite have at their disposal instruments to influence the masses in the form of television, public relations firms, and propaganda techniques. Some evidence appears to support Mills's thesis, especially since World War II, though it does not explain the frequent disagreement between corporations and the government, or between the military and the executive branch.

William Domhoff constructed a power-elite model based on "governing class."[23] This class (about one-half of 1 percent of the population) owns a disproportionate share of the nation's wealth and contributes a disproportionate number of its members to the controlling institutions and key decision-making groups. Domhoff contends that the governing class controls the executive branch of the federal government, the major corporations, the mass media, universities, foundations, and the important councils for domestic and foreign affairs. Domhoff's position is, in a sense, a refinement of Mills's model with a major difference in the ascendancy of the upper class to the apex of power. The executive branch, according to Domhoff, is not an equal partner with financiers and industrialists, as Mills saw it, but rather is controlled by them. Domhoff also believes the military has much less power than Mills contends and is dominated by the corporate rich through the executive branch. Social legislation, such as collective bargaining, Social Security, and worker's compensation, are tolerated because the upper class believes it is in its long-range economic interest. One could argue, however, that Domhoff has ignored the activities of labor unions and other pressure groups in his theory. Much of Domhoff's proof involves listing the upper-class pedigrees of key decision makers in government, yet he offers no evidence that these people actually promote the interests of the corporate leaders.

The pluralist model is a form of representative democracy in which citizens determine who shall represent them in areas such as government and education. The power-elite model and the governing-class variation suggest that an elite group holds most of the power and makes decisions that benefit it, but is able to convince the masses that the system is democratic by clever manipulation of the media and the use of propaganda. Universal education is supported only because the power elite desires a docile work force and citizens who will be content to develop a small stake in their community and not feel driven to revolt against the governing class. In the field of education the pluralist model generally is supportive of democratic decision making and democracy in education; the power-elite model is not. Domhoff's governing class is based on ascription and would impose an aristocratic model on the control of education.

Authority.   The state has a monopoly on the use of force in a given territory, but coercive force can generate fear, terror, or resistance unless the state's power is perceived by the populace as legitimate. An enduring society is based on agreement about cultural norms and a recognition of the state's right to use power to maintain social stability.

Authority is power perceived as legitimate rather than coercive. Weber identified three ideal conditions under which power is transformed into authority.[24] One type of authority is created when a leader is granted legitimate power because custom dictates that he or she is the one who should hold such status. This **traditional authority** is based on respect for established cultural patterns. The powers of the Chinese emperors of antiquity, the pharaohs of ancient Egypt, and the nobility in medieval Europe depended on traditional authority. When industrialization and greater cultural diversity permeate a society, traditions are no longer widely shared and traditional authority declines. But such authority, though not the basis of governance, still can be found in parent-child relations and male-female relations where traditional roles prevail.

Changes in society tend to weaken traditional authority.

Charismatic authority is the ability to inspire obedience and devotion in others as a result of extraordinary personal characteristics. Such a leader gains power on the basis of magnetic personal qualities and can inspire a people to pursue a new way of life—Hitler, Mao, Gandhi, and Napoleon were charismatic leaders. Weber argued that the survival of a charismatic movement after the departure of the leader depended on "routinization of charisma," or the transformation of charismatic authority into a combination of traditional and rational-legal authority.

Rational-legal authority (sometimes called bureaucratic authority) grants a leader power under a constitution or other legal system. Although all three types of authority have been important at one time or another, rational-legal authority is more common today and is the form vested in all public officials through formal rules and regulations often originating in law. Unlike traditional authority, rational-legal authority is based on achievement rather than ascription.

Although teachers might have some traditional authority, most of their authority rests in their office (rational-legal authority). Most teachers do not have charismatic authority, but they can appeal to students through their expertise. If students do not respect the office of teacher, for example, they might respect the teacher's expertise; and if they lack respect for expertise, they might respect or, more likely, fear negative sanctions. It is usually more promising, whenever possible, for the teacher to establish trust and goodwill through positive interpersonal relations.

Most of a teacher's authority comes from having achieved the role of teacher.

Control. In education, as elsewhere, power and authority are methods of control. **Control** requires authority or power to restrain or regulate persons and things. Teachers who have lost control of their classes, for example, have reached a point at which students no longer recognize their authority. The means by which a system is regulated usually varies: it might consist of judicial decrees, statutes, formal policies, guidelines, and the use of authority. Compliance to authority, if not voluntary, can be gained through the use of sanctions (rewards and punishment). Some personnel may respect the authority of the administrator's office; others may not comply with administrative directives unless they know the administrator has the power to enforce the directive.

Most controls, except in cases of personal deviance, are not directed at specific individuals but at certain categories (for instance, youth, women, minorities, foreigners) or role relationships (teacher-student, teacher-administrator, teacher-parent). Laws, regulations, and directives are used by official bodies to impose certain controls on certain groups.

Those in positions of authority are more likely to gain compliance when the controls take advantage of the values of people. This is likely to occur in school systems when teachers and students believe that a regulation is for the mutual benefit of everyone. Regulations also are more likely to be accepted when those directly affected have a voice in their formulation.

The organizational forms of American education are the structural aspects through which control is exercised to maintain the system and encourage innovation. To fully consider the system of controls and the use of authority, we must understand not only the organization at different levels of the structure but also how the officials entrusted to lead the system operate. To do this, we will examine in turn the organization and politics of education at the federal, state, and local levels.

■ **PAUSE TO REFLECT**
Control and Authority in the Classroom

- As a teacher, what form of authority do you think will best suit you—traditional, charismatic, rational-legal, or a combination? How would you use that authority to control your classroom, and what benefits would you hope to achieve? For example, if you rely on charisma, you might use jokes or anecdotes to keep your students' attention while teaching them useful information.

- What form of authority did your favorite (and least favorite) teachers in high school employ? Which forms of authority worked best? Why, in your opinion?

■ FEDERAL FUNCTIONS IN EDUCATION

Although the United States Constitution contains no direct reference to education, the federal government has exerted a significant influence on schools and colleges. Since power over education was neither delegated to the federal government nor prohibited to the states, it was, according to the Tenth Amendment, left to the states. Article I, Section 8, of the Constitution empowered Congress "to lay and collect taxes, duties, imposts, and excises, to pay the debts and provide for the common defense and general welfare of the United States." This General Welfare Clause has been interpreted by the Supreme Court as allowing Congress to tax and spend monies for a variety of purposes related to the general welfare, including federal aid to education. The Commerce Clause under Article I, Section 8 empowers Congress to "regulate Commerce with Foreign Nations, among the several States, and with Indian tribes." This has been interpreted by the Supreme Court as allowing some federal authority over school transportation, safety, and labor policies.

Today the federal government is involved in five major areas of education: (1) promoting equal educational opportunity; (2) stimulating educational reforms; (3) supporting educational research; (4) promoting educational preparation for employment; and (5) providing limited general support.[25] This involvement can be seen in a variety of federal legislation and programs.

The federal government has been involved in public education since 1785, so the debate over the constitutional authority to augment state educational expenditures is mainly of historic interest. The federal government has long operated its own schools with the establishment of the Military Academy at West Point in 1802, the Naval Academy in 1845, and the Air Force Academy in 1955. It also has educated residents of special federal areas on government reservations and federal districts, Native Americans and other indigenous peoples, peoples in outlying possessions, and armed forces personnel.

Federal grants to the states began with the Northwest Ordinance in 1785 and 1787 in which the sixteenth section of each township (one square mile out of thirty-six) was given to the states for educational purposes. The policy was not officially put into operation until 1803, when Ohio was admitted as a state. These unconditional grants of land were followed by the Morrill Act in 1862, which provided for land grants for the establishment of agricultural and mechanical colleges. This act and the Morrill Act of 1890 resulted in the establishment of sixty-nine land-grant universities, some of which have become distinguished universities that have made important contributions to science, technology, and agriculture.

The federal government also provides **categorical grants** (aid for specific purposes), which frequently require the state to match the federal funds. This was the case with the Smith-Hughes Act in 1917, which provided federal funds for vocational education on a matching basis. The interest in vocational education was sustained in the George-Reed Act of 1929, which provided a supplemental appropria-

Federal involvement in education has been in the form of financial and land grants and extensive legislation.

tion for the teaching of agriculture and home economics. The George-Deen Act of 1936 extended federal aid to include distributive education; and in 1946 the George-Barden Act increased the amount of aid for all areas of vocational education.

During the Depression the federal government passed emergency legislation that usually took the form of non-matching grants for specific purposes. These programs provided valuable relief during some of the bleakest years in American history. The National Youth Administration provided work experience and financial assistance for students so that they could continue their education. The Civilian Conservation Corps provided useful public work for young men in helping to conserve the nation's natural resources. The school lunch program also began during the Depression as an emergency measure but, unlike the other two programs, it became a continuing program with the passage of the school lunch act of 1946. Under this program the federal government provides the states with surplus food products and funds to distribute the products. Notable legislation during World War II was the Vocational Rehabilitation Act and the Servicemen's Readjustment Act of 1944, supplemented by other legislation after the war, and popularly known as the "G.I. Bill of Rights." The G.I. Bill provided subsistence allowance, tuition fees, and supplies for veterans of World War II who wished to continue their education.

The most far-reaching legislation since the war was the passage of the National Defense Education Act (NDEA) in 1958 and the Elementary and Secondary Education Act (ESEA) in 1965. The NDEA included aid to strengthen instruction in science, mathematics, and foreign languages; funds for the preparation of school counselors; and loans to prospective teachers. Congressional emphasis on science and mathematics stemmed largely from the Soviet Union's launching of Sputnik and fears that they were passing the United States in the space race. ESEA, as outlined in Chapter 10, had many provisions, the most notable of which were Title I, providing for compensatory education, and Title VII, the Bilingual Education Act of 1968. Table 11–1 shows the extensiveness of federal programs and aid to education.

The federal role in stimulating educational reform has been promoted by the support of educational research in the Department of Education, grants to individual researchers, and the encouragement of state departments of education to upgrade their research capabilities. Other activities include the targeting of funds to specific curriculum areas, technical assistance to state departments of education to upgrade planning and management activities, subsidies for instructional materials and library resources, investment in evaluation activities, and the development of small-scale experimental and demonstration programs.

TABLE 11–1 Selected federal programs and aid to education

1785	Ordinance of 1785—provided a survey of the Northwest Territory, which divided land into townships and sections
1787	Northwest Ordinance—reserved the sixteenth section in each township for education
1862, 1890	Morrill Land Grant—subsidized the establishment of agriculture and mechanical arts colleges in each state
1867	Department of Education Act—authorized the establishment of the Office of Education
1887	Hatch Act—promoted agricultural, mechanical, and scientific education in higher education
1914	Smith-Lever Agriculture Extension Act—distributed services of land-grant colleges to the people through extension services
1917	Smith-Hughes Vocational Act—provided for high-school vocational programs in agriculture, trades and industry, and homemaking
1929	George-Reed Act—expanded services and funds for vocational education
1930	Civilian Conservation Corps—provided relief and vocational training to unemployed youth
1933	School lunch programs—provided lunches in public and nonpublic schools; made permanent in 1946
1936	George-Deen Act—provided aid for education in the distributive trades of marketing and selling
1944	G.I. Bill of Rights—provided financial aid and counseling services for veterans to continue their education
1946	George-Barden Act—supplemented and broadened the Smith-Hughes Vocational Act to include distributive education and nursing
1958	National Defense Education Act—strengthened instruction in mathematics, science, foreign languages, and counseling and vocational programs
1965	Elementary and Secondary Education Act—provided omnibus legislation best known for its compensatory-education provisions
1972	Educational Amendments of 1972—established a National Institute of Education and a bureau-level Office of Indian Education
1979	Department of Education Organization Act—established a cabinet-level Department of Education

Department of Education

The chief educational agency of the federal government is the Department of Education (DOE). Educational programs, however, are not confined to this agency but are distributed among eleven departments and fifteen other agencies and units. Less than one-half of federal expenditures for education are made through the DOE; the majority of funding is distributed from the Office of Economic Opportunity, the Office of Emergency Planning, the Atomic Energy Commission, the Office of Science and Technology, the Smithsonian Institution, the National Foundation of the Arts and Humanities, and the CIA.

Historically, DOE has lacked status and power. In 1867 Congress established the Department of Education for the purpose of gathering and distributing statistical information about education, but did not give the department cabinet status. The act further provided for the appointment of a commissioner of education. The agency was part of the Department of Interior until 1939, when it was transferred to the Federal Security Agency, where it remained until 1953, when it became part of the newly established Department of Health, Education, and Welfare.

The collection of statistical data occupied the agency's early years; since then, it has administered grants, encouraged experimental and innovative work in education, and provided professional services for other governmental agencies and departments. The DOE controls land-grant institutions through the distribution of funds under the Morrill Act, through its authority for administering funds for earlier vocational acts, and through its administration of ESEA. Since 1918 educators concerned with the lack of visibility of education have called for a separate agency and for the secretary of education to be a member of the president's cabinet. As a result of campaigning by the National Education Association and other organizations, USOE gained cabinet status in 1979 during the Carter administration. (The USOE was the predecessor of the DOE, established in 1980.) The position of secretary of education was given cabinet status in 1980.

The research functions of the DOE have continued to grow. Since 1954 the department has implemented the Cooperative Research Act, which supports research in higher education and other agencies. The act was amended and expanded by Title IV of the ESEA by establishing new programs for training educational researchers, disseminating research findings through research clearinghouses, and supporting national and regional research laboratories. A National Institute of Education was created in 1972 to conduct and support scientific inquiry into the educational process. Its functions also include building an effective educational research and demonstration system and strengthening the scientific and technological foundations of education.

> The DOE administers educational programs, disburses funds, and engages in research.

Influences on Education Legislation

The most striking feature in the long history of federal aid-to-education bills is the lack of success in achieving ratification. Not until the ESEA in 1965 was a general aid bill for elementary and secondary schools passed, even though major federal aid bills were proposed as early as 1870 and were introduced steadily for decades. From the fortieth Congress (1867–1889) to the eighty-seventh Congress (1961–1963), federal aid bills were introduced in thirty-six of the forty-seven sessions.[26] In most cases, many different pieces of legislation were introduced at once. In fact, in the seventy-third Congress (1933–1935), twenty-five to thirty education bills were proposed, and between thirty and forty were offered in the seventy-fourth Congress.[27] While these figures exceed the norm, almost invariably several education bills were offered during a legislative session. Bills differed in their targeted area (vocational education, school-building construction, teacher salaries); in the extent to which they attempted to equalize opportunities among states; in the issue of categorical aid versus "block grants"; in the amounts to be funded; and in the length of time the funding should last. Differences in opinion resulted in bills with countless provisions, and these divergent and conflicting views usually meant that no single bill could gain the votes needed for passage.

Aid to education also has lacked support because of the habit of legislators to wait for a crisis or emergency before ratifying a bill. Congress did see emergencies in the high rate of failures to pass the mental test for induction into the armed forces in World War I; the financial crisis of many school districts that were unable to raise funds for teacher salaries during the Depression; the higher birthrates after World War II that created a shortage of school facilities; and fears during the late 1950s that the United States was being beaten by the Soviet Union in the space race.

The picture of federal aid is complicated by the array of organizations supporting or opposing legislation on several diverse grounds. The National Education Association (NEA) and the American Federation of Teachers (AFT) are the two major national organizations that lend their support to federal aid. Despite questions of constitutionality, the AFT has been willing in the past to grant aid to parochial schools, but the NEA has been adamantly opposed to such aid. The AFT has also requested large annual sums of aid; the more cautious NEA believes that very large requests will assure the defeat of a bill.

Many other groups who have varying degrees of influence with Congress have supported federal aid to education, but they do not necessarily agree on the most desirable types of federal aid. Organizations such as the PTA, the NAACP, the National Federation of Business and Professional Women's Clubs, the Young Women's Christian

Association, the American Association of University Women, and the National Council of Jewish Women all have supported federal aid.

Several other influential organizations oppose federal aid for various reasons. These organizations include the U.S. Chamber of Commerce, Daughters of the American Revolution (DAR), the National Association of Manufacturers, the American Legion, and the Farm Bureau. These organizations have not always opposed federal aid. The Farm Bureau, the DAR, and the American Legion supported some form of federal aid earlier in the century, but have fought against such legislation during the past several decades. Usually these associations object because they believe federal aid leads to federal control. The John Birch Society and other right-wing groups adamantly oppose federal aid for this reason. Catholic organizations generally oppose bills that do not provide grants to parochial schools. And various organizations representing minorities generally object to bills whose guidelines they believe to be discriminatory.

> The most common objection to federal aid is that it enables the federal government to control local schools.

The politics of education is illustrated in the activity leading to the passage of ESEA. President Johnson, in power at the time and very much in favor of the bill, had received a landslide election victory that provided a strong popular mandate and changed the composition of Congress and some of its key subcommittees. Because of his strong popular following, Johnson was not hamstrung by church-state issues as President Kennedy was, and he used his considerable political skills to greatest advantage. His support of the bill and his popularity were vital to the passage of the ESEA. But his influence was not the only factor: the NEA was willing to shift its position from general to categorical aid for the poor; economists convinced legislators and the public that education should be considered an investment rather than a consumption function; and Commissioner Francis Keppel and his deputies skillfully promoted federal education legislation. Adroit handling of the legislation in Congress helped to assure its passage. Provisions were added for aid to "impacted areas" and also for aid to urban areas in the North and rural areas in the South (to attract support from both wings of the Democratic Party). Title II, which provided public and nonpublic schools with library resources, textbooks, and instructional resources, was a major concession to Catholic educators who withdrew much of their resistance.[28] This process, incidentally, could be a case study in the mechanics of the pluralist model of organizations (as opposed to the power-elite and governing-class models).

> Power, authority, and control combined to ensure passage of the Elementary and Secondary Education Act.

The high priority President Johnson gave to education and his record of gaining congressional support for it were exceptions. Most presidents generally believe that active support of federal aid to education entails greater political risks than advantages and as a result, are willing to offer only limited leadership resources.[29] Under the Reagan administration, for instance, domestic responsibilities were shifted from federal to state and local governments as well as the private sector; the "bully pulpit" was used to cajole and galvanize states and local districts to improve education; and block grants returned federal funds for education to the states—**block grants** are federal allocations that states or municipalities may spend as they like as long as the intent of the legislation authorizing the grant is satisfied.

As we have discussed in previous chapters, the Supreme Court has had a great influence on education. The Court's influence on equality, academic freedom, freedom of students, loyalty, censorship, and church-state relations will be explored more fully in Chapter 13.

STATE FUNCTIONS IN EDUCATION ■

While the state always has been an agent of education legislation, the control over education during the seventeenth and eighteenth centuries resided almost exclusively at the local level. The state's control over schools was evident in several court cases in which city officials sought to control schools just as they controlled municipal government. The courts consistently maintained that public education is a function of state rather than local government. The state's role in education began to grow during the late nineteenth century, and in this century, it assumed a primary role in public education. The states' greater involvement resulted from a dereliction in local responsibility as well as from the need to assure minimum standards, eliminate irregularities and erratic local practices, and to secure a more equitable financial base for the schools.

The state exercises its authority by passing compulsory attendance laws, certifying teachers and other personnel, regulating the minimum length of school term, and providing foundation programs to reduce inequities between wealthy and poor districts. The state also institutes retirement provisions for educators, tenure laws (in most states), minimum salary standards, curriculum guidelines, and approved textbook lists (in some states). State education officials periodically inspect schools to assure that they comply with approved standards, consult local administrators, and collect and disseminate state school statistics. The state has the ultimate power to create and abolish school districts; hence the consolidation of school districts is regulated by the state.

In keeping with the powers delegated to the states by the U.S. Constitution, each state has a constitution that embodies the provi-

Originally, control of education tended to reside at the local level, but the states assumed greater authority in the nineteenth century.

sions for state governance. Many early state constitutions contained general sentiments concerning the importance of education. Subsequent constitutional revisions have specified and strengthened state powers in education, although the provisions vary from one state to another.

Each state legislature establishes schools and regulates their operation. State education laws are generally of two types: mandatory and permissive. Mandatory legislation is expected to be followed uniformly throughout the state and applies to such matters as compulsory attendance, certification, districting, school taxation, pupil transportation, required budgets and audits, teacher contracts, and tenure and retirement provisions. Permissive legislation grants local districts the right, within state-established limits, to interpret and judge some needs in light of local conditions. Legislation of this type includes leaves of absence, mergers of school districts, salary provisions, school-building requirements, and location of building sites. State school laws are compiled and published so that administrators and school boards understand their legal responsibilities. The laws, along with judicial decisions, constitute the school code for the state.

All state laws are subject to judicial review to determine their constitutionality. Cases can be carried to the highest state court and, in some instances, to the U.S. Supreme Court. The state supreme court not only may declare a law unconstitutional but also may invalidate acts of the state board of education and the state department of education. Cases have been heard in several states challenging state authority over local school districts and, in every case, the state courts have upheld the concept that education is a state function and that local districts operate by state consent.

> Whenever there has been a dispute over state versus local control, the courts have sided with the state.

The leadership of governors varies widely among states. Governors can be effective in defining educational issues, but have little effect on the enactment of policies. Where there is a traditional political climate that supports education by creating much revenue, the governor can have considerable power on some issues (as in Wisconsin, Minnesota, California, and New York).[30] Governors can initiate new education bills or veto those they disapprove. Their influence is affected by variables such as their popular mandate, their ability to marshal legislative backing, their skill in shaping public opinion and influencing special lobbies, and whether their party has a majority in the legislature.

State Boards of Education

The state board of education is the highest education authority in the state and formulates educational policies designed to control, supervise, and implement statewide functions. The board arranges the appointment or election of the chief state school officer, defines the duties of that office, and designates the term of appointment and the salary. In most states, the board supervises only elementary and secondary schools, but in other states, jurisdiction extends to publicly supported colleges and universities. Separate boards may be established to regulate vocational education, state universities, community colleges, vocational rehabilitation, and special education. Some states also have a textbook commission for selecting books to be used throughout the state, a board of examiners that prepares certification exams for teachers, and a retirement board that regulates teacher pensions. The trend is toward a reduction of the number of boards by placing their diverse functions under a single state board of education and empowering the chief state school officer to coordinate the different educational activities.

All states have boards of education, except for Wisconsin, which handles education through other government agencies. Thirty-four boards are appointed by the governor, thirteen are elected by popular vote, and two are made up of legislative or school-board members in a regional convention. The number of state board members varies from three to twenty-four, with nine being the most common. Several commission studies have recommended that the ideal board should have

Legislators, educators, and laypersons participate in decision making at the state level.

five to seven members. The length of term varies from three to twenty years, with four to six years being the most common. Laypersons with a strong interest in education are most likely to be chosen for the board.

The Chief State School Officer

The chief state school officer or state superintendent of education is the top executive position in state educational affairs. The position can be filled in one of three ways: appointment by the governor (seven states), appointment by the state board of education (twenty-nine states), and by popular election (fourteen states). Appointment by the board is considered by many to be the best method, because it keeps the office freer of partisan politics. Furthermore, the board is likely to be in a better position to appraise the professional qualifications of candidates and to make a wise choice. States are unlikely to switch to appointment by the board anytime soon because some states have constitutional provisions for election by popular vote.

The term of office in most cases is four years, although in some states the superintendent must stand for election every two years. Superintendents appointed by a state board usually are granted indefinite tenure. Educators generally believe that appointment by the board, a long term of office, and a choice among candidates from other states will most likely assure the appointment of a capable professional with strong leadership qualities.

The duties of the office are many and varied. The superintendent is the chief executive officer of the state board, assumes responsibility for organizing the state department of education, interprets school laws in a collaborative relationship with the attorney general's office, and authorizes the use of state funds as provided by law. The superintendent often delegates important activities to directors in the state department of education, but the final responsibility rests with the superintendent. These responsibilities can include the dissemination of information about local school districts, supervision of teacher certification, development of curriculum guides, and the proposal of education legislation. Professional educators probably are the best qualified to handle the tasks and responsibilities of the state department of education.

The State Department of Education

The state department of education or state department of public instruction is staffed with professionals who, under the jurisdiction of the chief state school officer, perform regulatory, administrative, and leadership functions in conducting state educational activities. State department responsibilities include areas such as administration and finance, curriculum and instruction, vocational education, and rehabilitation services. In the area of administration and finance alone, state departments administer state school funds and federal funds, regulate school lunch programs and transportation, develop reports and statistics, initiate audits, and establish standards for school-building construction. But state departments vary greatly in their effectiveness. In some states, the state superintendent is weak and is unable to exercise needed leadership in the department; in other cases the state superintendent is embroiled in partisan politics.

Keeping the superintendent and the department free of political patronage can be a major challenge. To avoid any problem, appointments to the state department can be made on the basis of merit and approved by the state superintendent. To maintain quality education in the states, the departments of education must be free of partisan politics and vested with the authority to assume the necessary regulatory and leadership functions.

State Politics in Education

State control over education has continued to increase in recent years, resulting in a substantial reduction of local control over funding levels, patterns of expenditure, and program structure. Yet, despite this increased state authority, D. E. Mitchell reports that the "vast bulk of legislative decisions are made by a tiny handful of people."[31] It is rare to find more than a dozen or so legislators with more than a casual understanding of the issues. Most legislators adopt a passive stance while only a few policy makers carefully deal with the issues.

Much information about state politics in education comes from studies in New York State,[32] in eight states in the Northeast in terms of state aid to education,[33] and in Michigan, Illinois, and Missouri in terms of how state politics affect education.[34] Great differences exist among some states, but other states exhibit generic similarities.[35]

The first type of organizational structure can be found in Vermont, New Hampshire, and Massachusetts. This structure is locally based and is characterized by provincialism, jealousy, and stalwart defense against the encroachment of outside forces. Superintendents of local districts defend their own interests and unite with great difficulty only to dissolve the union immediately after the common threat is overcome. Parochialism and lack of cohesion among educators hinder the passage of legislation and might, in fact, contribute to the ease of blocking unfavorable legislation.

The second type of organizational structure is characterized by a statewide pattern of interaction and can be found in New York State,

> Political arenas within which the states formulate educational policies range from those characterized by provincial and local infighting to those that evince democratic representation.

New Jersey, and, to some extent, Rhode Island. Massachusetts also could fit into this type. The statewide interest groups representing education enjoy a high degree of consensus, which conveys the appearance of a statewide monolithic structure and gives legislators the impression that a single public group represents education interests. The organizational structure is successful in both initiating and blocking legislation. The tendency is to avoid open conflict by working behind the scenes to gain legislative support.

Michigan has a fragmented statewide structure, a third type. Different education interest groups usually come separately to the legislature: the governor and legislative interests are frequently at odds; public-school interests are divided; the state has no procedure for resolving disputes, and no group has the ability to act as an intermediary. Because of the disunity and open conflict among education groups, hostility often develops in the legislature toward some of these groups. Even more stalemates probably would result without the widespread debate on educational issues that brings the power of educators to legislative attention.

The fourth type of organizational structure is found in Illinois and can be characterized as a statewide pattern of representation. The legislature has created the Illinois School Problems Commission, a formal governmental unit that functions like a legislative council. The commission plans its proposals before the legislative session to save time and expense and to improve the knowledgeability of the legislators in their deliberations. The commission represents the major education interests in the state and has a direct stake in the outcome of education decisions. Although interest groups in education are represented, ten of the commission's seventeen members are legislators. Statewide interest groups, therefore, form a focal point in this coalition created by the legislature. Because basic education decisions are made by the commission, conflict on the legislative floor tends to be minimized, simplifying the legislator's task.

State education associations, which are affiliates of the NEA, are influential in some states. The AFT's influence is primarily in large metropolitan areas because, as we discussed earlier, the AFT has concentrated on developing strong local rather than state affiliates.

In states such as Illinois, Michigan, and Missouri, the state affiliate of the NEA is relatively well organized, has gathered a wealth of information about the state's schools, and enjoys reasonably favorable access to the legislature. These associations seek to present objective information about schools in the state that legislators need in reaching decisions. They avoid overt pressure on legislators and refrain from aligning with other groups that are not directly concerned with education. By behaving in this manner, the affiliates can claim to be objective and believe their cases can be presented in more favorable light.

LOCAL FUNCTIONS IN EDUCATION ■

While public education clearly is a function of the state, the state can delegate some functions to local school districts through its discretionary authority. It is only in this sense that we can speak of control at the local level. And there is evidence of continuing, but diminished, local authority in education.

Local control extends only as far as the state allows.

The basic policy-making unit at the local level is the school board and the superintendent of schools. Nationally, 91 percent of school board members are elected in nonpartisan elections, 4 percent are elected in partisan elections (on a party ticket), and 5 percent are appointed (more common in large urban areas).[36] U.S. citizenship and residence in the school district are the only qualifications for board membership. Interest in school improvement, knowledgeability, and nonpartisanship are not formal qualifications, but are preferred. Board members usually serve without pay, except for reimbursement of expenses incurred in their work. The payment of salaries, without more stringent qualifications for the positions, could lead to undesirable patronage and attract incompetent or unscrupulous candidates. It also could lead board members to try to "earn" their salaries by assuming administrative responsibilities best left to the superintendent. The term of office varies, but the ideal term is at least four years with overlapping tenure among the members to ensure that there always will be at least one experienced member on the board.

School-board functions include selecting the superintendent, establishing educational policy, developing the school budget, determining salary schedules, allocating funds for buildings and equipment, and, in some school districts, selecting textbooks and courses of study. Most school boards concentrate their energies on budgetary matters, school buildings, and the formulation of general policy; they tend to leave decisions about curriculum and related professional matters to the superintendent and the administrative staff. Considerable variation in the authority of school boards is found throughout the nation, ranging from rural districts where the board assumes full authority for the educational program to large metropolitan districts where the board limits its function to the formulation of basic policy and delegates all other operations to the superintendent and the staff.

Theoretically speaking, the board represents the community will and is empowered to fulfill that will. However, besides the difficulty of determining community will in large urban areas of mixed social backgrounds, the board is constrained by the state. It must comply with state standards whether or not these standards coincide with community interests. Hence, the school board can forge its own distinctive program only within the framework of minimum standards and permissive, rather than mandatory, legislation. In short, the function of

The school board's first responsibility is compliance with the state rather than the local community.

the board and the superintendent is to provide quality education for the district using the resources at their disposal. Whenever resources are insufficient, they are responsible for seeking additional resources, whether at the local, state, or federal level.

The board is expected to seek the best qualified candidate for superintendent in terms of formal preparation, professional experience, and leadership ability. Superintendents are assisted in the daily tasks of administration and supervision by a staff, which varies considerably depending upon the size of enrollment and the funds available for staff positions. Small school systems have only a maintenance staff and a clerk or secretary to help the superintendent, whereas schools of moderate size have principals for each school, a business manager, an attendance officer, and several supervisors. In addition to these personnel, large city systems have assistant superintendents with different responsibilities for school operations, such as business affairs, personnel, curriculum and instruction, and special services (special education, adult education, school-community relations). Figure 11–1 indicates the line and staff relations and the relation of each public school (P.S.) to the administrative hierarchy. Staff personnel advise the superintendent and thereby influence teachers indirectly through the policy recommendations that the superintendent accepts. All but the smallest school systems have line personnel as well as staff personnel. Line personnel can be arranged in a pyramid of authority in which responsibilities are delegated to those below them in the hierarchy. At the top of the pyramid is the board of education, followed by the superintendent, who, as the executive officer of the board, is empowered to execute policy approved by the board and has discretionary authority in several areas. The school board might hire an assistant superintendent for instruction whose responsibility is to maintain close contact with principals, those next in line on the hierarchy, and supervise them on major instructional matters. Teachers are immediately responsible to the school principal.

Community Power Structures

What types of power structures can be found in local communities? Who are the principal players in the power structure and how do they use power to achieve their ends? How widely is power distributed? In what way and to what extent does the power structure influence educational policy decisions?

As discussed earlier in the chapter, a principal debate among scholars is whether the community power structure is pluralistic or controlled by an elite. In local community studies, Floyd Hunter's findings were the first to suggest the elitist position.[37] Hunter studied the power

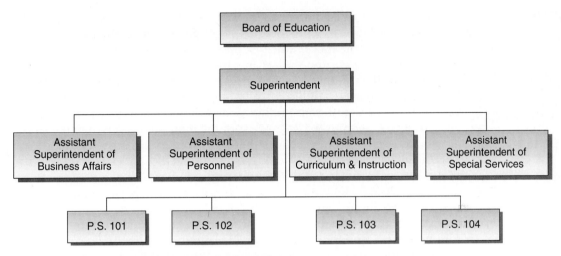

FIGURE 11-1 Organization of local school district

structure of a city of 500,000 using a reputational technique: citizens active in community life were asked to list people whom they believed to be the most important community leaders. The lists then were submitted to a cross-section of judges to determine leadership rank, and interviews were conducted with the people listed as well as others.

Hunter found that the more conspicuous and active citizens, while they made the lists in the study, were not the ones who made the key decisions. Key decisions were made by the top leaders behind the scenes. The power of these figures was not only evident in the policies they chose to establish but also in the projects they elected to block. Only forty people in the city were found to be in a position of influence at the top of a power pyramid.

The concentration of power and the lack of visibility of those who wield the power would seem to indicate that school administrators have been dealing with persons other than the power elite, or their representatives. The reasons for the defeat of school-bond issues, then, may lie deeper than administrators imagine and administrators probably need to become more astute in their understanding of community power.

Robert Dahl, on the other hand, believes that community power is pluralistic.[38] Dahl's study of New Haven indicated that leaders were much more visible than those in Hunter's study. Leaders also exercised power in just one sphere of community activity, such as education, city government, or economics. If Dahl's conclusions are correct, perhaps school administrators do know who wields power.

A lengthy debate ensued in the 1960s over the elitist versus the pluralist position and which of the two approaches is more acceptable

Whether the community power structure is elitist or pluralistic, school administrators must ultimately deal with those who wield power.

for the study of community power structures.[39] The debate took on ideological overtones as liberals generally espoused the pluralistic position while the more radical supported the elitist conclusions. Pluralists tend to examine the actions in the decision-making process and observe the influence exercised by the principal decision makers. As this methodology differs considerably from the reputational approach, it can lead to different findings when the two approaches are used in the same community. Regardless of the methodology used in the study, there is no reason to believe that all communities have the same type of power structure.

Roe Johns and Ralph Kimbrough studied 122 school districts of more than 20,000 population in Illinois, Kentucky, Georgia, and Florida.[40] Of these districts, twenty-four (six in each state) were studied in depth. Four different power structures were found in different communities: monopolistic elite; multigroup noncompetitive; competitive elite; and segmented pluralism. The monopolistic elite appears to be similar to Hunter's monolithic power structure. It consists of a dominant power group, hierarchically organized, that remains in power for more than one election and has few internal conflicts. At the other extreme is the segmented, pluralistic distribution of power similar to the arrangement Dahl found in New Haven. This structure has many competing groups separated by different interests with little overlap in group membership. Unlike in the monopolistic elite power structure, voter participation is high.

The two power structures between these extremes are the multigroup-noncompetitive and the competitive-elite structures. As the name implies, the multigroup-noncompetitive structure differs from the monopolistic elite in that the community has more than one power group. However the groups are partially separated, permitting open communication and a greater likelihood that a consensus will be reached on major issues. The competitive-elite structure has limited overlapping of groups and less communication and consensus among groups; nevertheless, one can find more overlap than in the segmented, pluralistic type.

The argument over whether power in local communities is elitist or pluralistic probably is too simplistic. Several possible patterns with somewhat different characteristics can be found. Knowledge of these systems might give educators the information they need to be able to influence favorable educational decisions.

The Politics of Local School Governance

Considerable evidence suggests that school-board members are not drawn from a representative cross-section of the local community. George Counts showed in his study of several thousand school-board members that three-fourths of them were business and professional men.[41] The only change in composition from the time of Counts's original investigation in 1927 to studies conducted in 1958 and 1959 was the decline of farmers on school boards, reflecting farm closures and school district consolidation. The income of members was well above average for the nation, and the proportion of women on boards remained stable at about 10 percent.[42] More recently, a 1987 survey showed minority representation was 5 percent (higher in Southern states: 11 percent black and 3 percent Hispanic), and the number of women had increased to 39 percent.[43] In comparison with the overall population, school-board members are older, wealthier, have more formal education, and hold a higher proportion of managerial or professional positions.

School-board membership tends not to be highly representative of the community population.

While school boards ideally should represent the interests of different community groups, many boards simply perform the function of legitimating school system policies. In a study of two suburban communities near a large northern city, it was found that the superintendent played the key role in socializing board members and converting them to a social role of legitimating school policies.[44] In an investigation by L. H. Zeigler and M. K. Jennings based on interviews with 581 school-board members and 94 superintendents in 96 school districts, it was found that board members and school personnel actively recruited more than 40 percent of new board members.[45] H. J. Tucker and Zeigler, in studying school-board meetings, administrative cabinet meetings, and other formal meetings in eleven school districts, found many conflicts in some districts; few in others.[46] In most districts, educational professionals used their expertise to control the decision-making process.

School officials are more likely to attempt to anticipate the demands of community groups when formulating educational policy if the community is homogenous. But community demands in a heterogeneous area are diverse and often in competition, making it difficult to anticipate them. School authorities in heterogeneous communities, therefore, can become unresponsive to community demands.[47] Unless a community is experiencing a crisis, citizen participation in school governance tends to be minimal and reactive. But citizens can be influential when they become activated. School construction, facilities, and finance issues are more likely to activate citizens than decisions about curriculum and personnel policy.[48] Educators are likely to have more influence on the latter policy decisions, especially in larger and more heterogeneous communities.

Community members tend to leave policy decisions about curriculum and personnel to school administrators.

Superintendents and school boards in large urban districts are often controlled by the bureaucracy. Studies of Boston schools[49] and New York City schools[50] illuminated the power that education bureaucrats had over the systems. Both studies found neither the superintendent nor the school board able to control the large, specialized bureaucracy that maintained the system so that bureaucratic interests flourished while those of the superintendent, school board, and public were diminished.

Community Participation and Control

Some communities have emphasized decentralization and directed a rising chorus of criticism at large city school systems. Decentralization would delegate more authority to people closer to the schools themselves. As early as the late 1960s, some blacks instead called for *community control of schools* whereby lay school boards in the neighborhood, rather than the central administration, actually would run the schools. Black parents, proponents contend, would be given authority over the education of their children and have the chance to instill black pride and overcome the failures experienced in the education of blacks when their education is controlled by a centralized white bureaucracy.

Many blacks feel that bureaucratic control makes the schools unresponsive to the needs of black students.

The complexities of metropolitan life have led to the development of large-scale organizations to provide essential services in the areas of health, welfare, education, police and fire protection, waste disposal, and transportation. Bureaucratic organizations have expanded correspondingly in size and complexity. Bureaucracies also frequently have failed to attain the standards Max Weber envisioned for them. Advocates of community control believe that by bypassing central bureaucracies, the inefficiencies, neglect, and favoritism commonly attributed to bureaucratic school systems will be overcome and black children will receive a better education.

Community-control leaders cite discriminatory policies in the employment of black teachers and administrators, a curriculum that fails to relate to black needs, and the employment of white teachers unprepared to teach black children. The clash of black interests with the central school administration and the local teachers' union became a bitter struggle during the late 1960s in New York City's Ocean Hill-Brownsville dispute.[51] Though the community-control plan advocated by blacks was not implemented, the controversy did lead to decentralization of authority. The school board appointed district or field administrators that would be more in touch with community needs. Similar struggles occurred in Detroit, Los Angeles, Philadelphia, and Washington, DC.[52]

Critics have several arguments against community control:

- Community control can undermine personnel standards and violate professional autonomy. Central administration can develop and enforce uniform and equitable personnel standards; small school districts historically have had the lowest standards and were most likely to employ unqualified personnel. Moreover, community-control proposals place teachers and administrators under the close supervision of laypersons. While schools should be responsive to community needs, such supervision can abridge professional autonomy, lower the educator's effectiveness, and create serious morale problems.

- Community control also can duplicate services and increase costs. One of the biggest advantages of centralization is the greater efficiency it provides. While these efficiencies have not always been realized in practice, they can be realized whenever sound principles of school management are used. It would appear to be unavoidable that some services, such as providing resource staff, equipment, and educational materials, will be duplicated under community-control plans.

Community control might introduce whole new problems rather than solve old ones.

- Community control not only runs against the tide of school-district consolidation but also would require state legislatures to create new school districts. Such legislation is unlikely to be passed anytime soon, because since the 1930s, the trend has been toward consolidating school districts rather than creating new ones.

- The most serious charge is that community control can further engender a separation of the races. A democratic society strives for integration and full participation by its diverse groups. An intensification of racial segregation would exacerbate the obdurate social and ethnic problems of American society. Some blacks, however, believe that American society will not be integrated in the immediate future, and they believe that they should be able to control their schools to instill black pride, gain better understanding of their heritage, and promote greater educational achievement.

Some decentralization proponents say that administrative decentralization poses fewer problems than community control. In such plans, principals and field administrators are granted more authority for planning and program design. Legislative action has divided New York City and Detroit school systems into several separate and relatively autonomous districts. These decentralized school districts, however, still might serve a population as high as 300,000 to 400,000. Parents may find that decentralization adds another level of administrative bureaucracy and, by creating further confusion as to where decisions are actually made, interferes with effective participation. Advocates, however, would claim that this is administrative decentralization, not political decentralization, and that it would not be any more difficult to trace the lines of authority.

Research evidence fails to show that decentralization or community control raises achievement test scores.[53] And not surprisingly, a survey of superintendents in 399 school systems showed that the superintendents were more positive about the idea of citizens advising professionals on school policy rather than actually determining school policy.[54] Despite this reluctance to turn school affairs over to the citizens, many cities are trying variations of the idea.

A new experiment in community control began in Chicago after the Illinois legislature in 1988 ordered the school councils to transfer power from the Board of Education to the neighborhoods. Each of the city's nearly 600 schools will answer to an elected local council made up of six parents, two community residents, two teachers, and a principal. The councils will have the power to hire or fire the principal, develop a school-improvement plan, and decide how discretionary funds will be allocated. More than 17,000 candidates vied for 5,410 slots on the local school committees, and voter turnout—16.1 percent—exceeded most suburban school committee elections. The plan has not been without problems or criticisms. Training thousands of ordinary citizens in parliamentary procedures and the intricacies of school affairs has been a daunting challenge. And principals, who will be placed on four-year contracts, have expressed concern that the councils will undermine their authority. Others fear that special-interest groups will dominate the councils. The plan has just begun, and the success or failure of the experiment remains to be seen.[55]

Decentralization may help make school systems more responsive to the needs of students and the local community.

Schools in Dade County, Florida, and Rochester, New York, have been experimenting with school-based management that takes decentralization to the school-building level. Unlike the Chicago experiment, these schools participate in school-based management on a voluntary basis, and governance is still controlled by the professional staff. **School-based management** involves managers and teachers in joint planning, goal development, and redefinition of teacher roles. Thirty-two of Dade County's 280 schools are involved in school-based management. Participating schools are expected to devise ways for principals and teachers to run the school together, and any changes must have measurable benefits for students. In Rochester schools, with much greater teacher participation in decision making and larger salary increases, teachers are held more accountable for student achievement, attendance, and related outcomes. The New York City school system divides authority among a central board and thirty-two community boards. It also has added a school-based management plan, involving 117 of the city's 984 schools, in which committees comprising the principal, teachers, and parents share the decision making.[56] Though most teachers are likely to prefer school-based management to community control, other communities are watching the Chicago experiment and, if it is reasonably successful, might implement their own community-control plans.

Public Schools of Choice

Public-school choice plans are open enrollment plans that permit parents to enroll their children in public schools outside the geographical district, with state funds allocated depending on the number of students enrolled in a system. Minnesota's school-district borders were opened under a law passed in 1987 so that dissatisfied students could transfer to schools in other districts. Arkansas, Iowa, and Nebraska

Schools of choice seek to expand the options and learning opportunities for students.

approved similar programs in 1989, and eleven other states have been considering this approach.

"Choice has worked," President George Bush proclaimed, "almost without exception, everywhere it has been tried."[57] And Governor Bill Clinton of Arkansas said, "Choice will encourage districts to do better. Competition will improve quality."[58] Political conservatives and businesspeople view schools of choice as injecting free-market competition into the educational system, liberals see it as a way to extend to the poor the options that the wealthy enjoy, and parents and educators perceive it as a means to encourage diversity in educational programs. Thus, according to proponents, it would reward schools that attract the most students, and thereby improve schools by forcing them to compete for students. Parents would be more motivated and involved by becoming consumer activists. Poor children would enjoy greater access and more variety.

But in the 1989 fall term, only 3,790 of Minnesota's 735,000 public school students had applied to transfer to different schools.[59] One problem is that parents have little information to use in deciding whether to transfer their children; another is that Minnesota provides no bus service for those who choose to leave their district. One plan that does seem to be working, however, is the "postsecondary options" program that permits juniors and seniors to attend classes in Minnesota's colleges and universities and earn both high school and college credits. About 10,000 Minnesota students have used this option so far and have done as well as or better than the average college freshman. Nine other states have adopted similar programs.

The choice-plan proposal has raised some objections. First, classroom space can limit choice unless provision is made to accommodate the extra students. Second, unless the state is willing to provide transportation, low-income families cannot afford the transportation to send their children to schools far from their area. Third, some parents are unwilling to send their children to a distant district no matter how weak their local schools may be. Fourth, parents do not always choose schools for educational reasons: some select schools near their home or work, and others sometimes deliberately transfer their children to schools with lower graduation standards. A capable agency that can disseminate information about public schools in the state might help overcome some problems of choice, but might not substantially alter misguided parental attitudes. A fifth objection is that the marketing concept applied to public schools is inappropriate because so-called competition will not force school improvement. Rather, the schools that are abandoned will deteriorate because they will lose their most vocal and influential parents. Moreover, improving schools and devising special programs require expertise that many schools lack; thus

Open enrollment plans raise practical problems that limit choice.

the marketing concept fails to supply weak schools with any means of improvement. In fact, it erroneously assumes that weak schools are willfully that way and that the loss of students will stimulate improvement.

▪ PAUSE TO REFLECT
Local Involvement in the School System

- How can communities become involved in their own school system without endangering the efficiency and standardization of central control or inviting patronage and corruption?

- Can you think of any ways that the public-school choice plans can be altered to allow parents to choose where to send their children without further damaging the weaker schools in the system?

EDUCATIONAL ISSUE 11-1

Should states adopt public-school choice plans?

Yes	No
1. Choice plans will promote school improvement by injecting free-market competition into the system.	1. Choice plans fail to offer any special means to improve weak schools.
2. It will offer the same options to the poor that some wealthy families enjoy.	2. Limited classroom space and transportation will prevent many poor families from participating in choice plans.
3. It would encourage greater diversity of educational programs.	3. Parental selection of schools is not always based on educational grounds.
4. Parents would become more motivated and involved.	4. Some parents are unwilling to send their children to other districts regardless of the weakness of local districts.

■ Summary

- Two theories of democratic participation can influence education: *representative democracy*, in which citizens select representatives, and *participatory democracy*, in which power is widely redistributed among the citizens themselves.

- Many educational systems are built on a bureaucracy, which ideally should allow the system to establish goals, maintain control, and encourage innovation. Max Weber's bureaucratic model involves organizing offices in a hierarchy, specifying qualifications and rules for each office in writing, and basing promotion on seniority or achievement.

- Critics of bureaucracy in education say that bureaucracies can become inflexible and intrude on a teacher's functions. For example, teachers are expected to humanize and individualize instruction, which runs counter to the impersonality and standardization inherent in a bureaucracy.

- Warren Bennis suggests that future organizations should be temporary systems, or *organic-adaptive systems*, organized depending on the problems to be solved. Such a system gives professionals more autonomy and allows greater teacher participation.

- Two models of power in our society are the *pluralist* model, a form of representative democracy which holds that a society has many smaller centers of power, and the *power-elite* model, which holds that power is concentrated in a small group of upper-class citizens who make decisions for the rest of us based on their own interests.

- Authority is a form of legitimate power and can be *traditional* (based on respect for established cultural patterns), *charismatic* (based on the ability to inspire obedience or awe through extraordinary personal characteristics), or *rational-legal* (based on a constitution or other legal system). Rational-legal authority is the most common form of authority found in today's educational system—most teachers rely on rational-legal authority and expertise to control their classrooms.

- Although the Tenth Amendment delegates responsibility for education to the states, the federal government is involved in five major areas of education: promoting equal educational opportunity, stimulating educational reforms, supporting educational research, promoting educational preparation for employment, and providing limited general support. The Department of Education is the federal government's chief educational agency.

- Despite criticism of federal involvement in education, many federal programs and aid-to-education bills have been instituted in the past two centuries. Two of the most influential pieces of federal legislation are the National Defense Education Act of 1958, which provided aid to strengthen instruction in science, mathematics, and foreign languages; and the Elementary and Secondary Education Act of 1965, which provided for compensatory education and, later, added the Bilingual Education Act of 1968.

- Since the late nineteenth century, education has become primarily a function of the state, which controls such areas as attendance laws, certification of teachers, length of school terms, and distribution of funds. The state board of education is the highest education authority in the state, and is responsible for controlling, supervising, and implementing statewide functions of education. The state school officer or state school superintendent is the top officer of the board and leads the state department of education.

- The state can delegate authority to local districts through mandatory and permissive legislation. Mandatory legislation deals with topics such as attendance, certification, districting, budgets, and tenure and is expected to be followed uniformly throughout the state. Permissive legislation allows local districts to use their judgment in interpreting the needs of their schools, particularly in areas such as leaves of absence, mergers of school districts, salaries, and building-site locations.

- The basic policy-making unit at the local level is the school board. Most school-board members are elected in nonpartisan elections, although some are appointed or elected on a party ticket. The school board has responsibilities such as choosing the superintendent of schools, establishing educational policy, allocating funds, and, in some districts, selecting textbooks.

- The power structure of a community can significantly affect the formulation of local educational policy. In a study of a city of 500,000, Floyd Hunter found that much of the power was wielded behind the scenes. Robert Dahl, on the other hand, found pluralism at work in other places. Other structures fall between these two extremes, such as the *multigroup-noncompetitive* structure (which has more than one power group and more open communication among them), and the *competitive-elite* structure (which has more than one power group but less communication among them).

- Some communities have lobbied for decentralizing schools, dismantling ineffective bureaucracies, placing more authority with the local districts, and providing children with a better education. Critics of decentralization argue that community control can undermine standards, duplicate services, require the establishment of new school districts, and, most importantly, foster segregation of the races.

● An innovative suggestion for the decentralization and improvement of schools is the *public-school choice plan*, which allows parents to choose the school they wish their children to attend. State funds would be allocated depending on the number of students enrolled in a system. The hope is that schools would be motivated to improve so as to attract more students. Critics say that limited classroom space and transportation costs can limit a parent's choice; that some parents might be unwilling to send their children to distant districts; and that abandoned schools will not improve but rather will deteriorate because they will have lost their most influential parents.

■ Key Terms

authority	pluralist model
block grants	power
bureaucracy	power-elite model
categorical grants	public-school choice plans
charismatic authority	rational-legal authority
control	representative democracy
influence	school-based management
participatory democracy	traditional authority

■ Discussion Questions

1. Is representative democracy or participatory democracy largely operative in American public education today? Cite evidence to support your position.

2. Although Weber believed that bureaucracies would invariably be more efficient than other organizational forms, why is this not always the case?

3. When students refuse to comply with school or classroom rules, what steps can teachers take in terms of power, influence, and authority?

4. Distinguish the different forms of authority and how these forms differ from power and influence.

5. What are the possible consequences for American education if the power-elite model prevails? The pluralist model?

6. Summarize why such a small percentage of federal aid-to-education bills introduced in Congress in the past several decades were ratified.

7. Of the four different local community power structures described by Johns and Kimbrough, which are most likely to support and enhance public education? Why?

8. What are the duties of the local school superintendent, and how would one determine the superintendent's effectiveness?

■ Learning Activities

1. Gather data about the administration of local school systems from public records, school-board meetings, and interviews with teachers and administrators. Do the systems fit into Weber's bureaucratic model or a different form of organization?

2. Organize a classroom debate on the resolution: "The power-elite model is more accurate than the pluralist model in portraying the use of power in American society."

3. Write a paper about how your state handles one of the following areas: teacher certification, accreditation, or curriculum guidelines. Identify the state agencies and state officials whom you contact for information.

4. Organize a classroom debate on the resolution: "Most states should implement public-school-of-choice plans."

Suggested Readings

Campbell, Roald F., Lavern L. Cunningham, and Michael D. Usdan, *The Organization and Control of American Education*, 6th ed. Columbus: Charles E. Merrill, 1985.

A systematic study of organization and governance at all levels, including the influence of interest groups, educators, and students.

Coons, John E., and Stephen D. Sugarman, *Education by Choice: The Case for Family Control*. Berkeley: University of California Press, 1978.

The authors advocate parental control over their children's education and explore how these changes could be implemented.

Dahl, Robert A., *Pluralist Democracy in the United States: Conflict and Consent*. Chicago: Rand McNally, 1967.

The pluralist model of power presented by its leading proponent.

Domhoff, G. William, *The Higher Circles: The Governing Class in America*. New York: Vintage Books, 1971.

An update of Mills's power-elite model by focusing on the upper class use of power.

Gerth, H. G., and C. Wright Mills, eds. *From Max Weber: Essays in Sociology*. New York: Oxford University Press, 1958.

Includes selections from Weber's ideas about bureaucracy, power, and charismatic authority.

Spring, Joel, *Conflict of Interests: The Politics of American Education*. New York: Longman, 1988.

Explores policy making in terms of interest groups, knowledge industry, courts, and different levels of government.

Wirt, Frederick M., and Michael W. Kirst, *Schools in Conflict: The Politics of Education*. Berkeley: McCutchan, 1982.

A systematic study of the politics of education that treats major policy issues.

Notes

1. Giovanni Sartori, *Democratic Theory* (Detroit: Wayne State University Press, 1962), 126.
2. Robert A. Dahl, *Who Governs? Democracy and Power in an American City* (Chicago: University of Chicago Press, 1956), 311–25.
3. V. O. Key, Jr., *Public Opinion and American Democracy* (New York, Knopf, 1961), 558.
4. Robert Paul Wolff, *In Defense of Anarchism* (New York: Harper Torchbooks, 1970); and Peter Bachrach, *The Theory of Democratic Elitism: A Critique* (Boston: Little, Brown, 1967), Ch. 7.
5. *Democracy and Education* (New York: Macmillan, 1966), 87.
6. Ibid., 83.
7. "Challenges of Democracy to Education," *Progressive Education* 14 (1937): 79–85.
8. "Democracy and Educational Administration," *School and Society* 45 (1937): 457–62.
9. Henry A. Giroux, *Ideology, Culture and the Process of Schooling* (Philadelphia: Temple University Press, 1981); and his *Theory and Resistance in Education* (South Hadley, MA: Bergin and Garvey, 1983).
10. *From Max Weber: Essays in Sociology*, transl. and ed. by H. G. Gerth and C. Wright Mills (New York: Oxford University Press, 1958); and Max Weber, *The Theory of Social and Economic Organization*, transl. by A. M. Henderson and Talcott Parsons (New York: Free Press, 1957).

11. Robert Dreeban, "The School as a Workplace," in *Second Handbook of Research on Teaching*, ed. Robert M. W. Travers (Chicago: Rand McNally, 1973), 452–53.

12. Robert K. Merton, *Social Theory and Social Structure* (New York: Free Press, 1957).

13. Frederick W. Taylor, *Scientific Management* (New York: Harper, 1911).

14. James D. Monney and Alan C. Reiley, *Onward Industry* (New York: Harper, 1931).

15. Raymond E. Callahan, *Education and the Cult of Efficiency* (Chicago: University of Chicago Press, 1962).

16. Warren Bennis, *Changing Organizations* (New York: McGraw-Hill, 1966).

17. Lloyd K. Bishop, *Individualizing Educational Systems* (New York: Harper & Row, 1971) Ch. 13.

18. Patricia Cloud Duttweiler, "Changing the Old Ways," *Journal of Research and Development in Education* 22 (1989): 7–12.

19. F. A. Hayek, *The Constitution of Liberty* (London: Routledge & Kegan Paul, 1960), 336.

20. Robert A. Dahl, *Pluralist Democracy in the United States: Conflict and Consent* (Chicago: Rand McNally, 1967).

21. Robert A. Dahl, *Dilemmas of Pluralist Democracy* (New Haven: Yale University Press, 1982); and Charles E. Lindblom, "Another State of Mind," *American Political Science Review* 76 (1982): 9–21.

22. C. Wright Mills, *The Power Elite* (New York: Oxford University Press, 1956).

23. G. William Domhoff, *Higher Circles: The Governing Class in America* (New York: Vintage Books, 1971).

24. Weber, *The Theory of Social and Economic Organization*, Part III.

25. *The Federal Interest in Schooling*, ed. M. Timpane (Cambridge, MA: Ballinger, 1978), 4–7.

26. Frank J. Munger and Richard J. Fenno, Jr., *National Politics and Federal Aid to Education* (Syracuse, NY: Syracuse University Press, 1962), 4, Fig. 1.

27. Ibid., 6–7.

28. The political activities surrounding the passage of the ESEA are detailed in Philip Meranto, *The Politics of Federal Aid in 1965* (Syracuse, NY: Syracuse University Press, 1965). Political problems encountered in administering ESEA are treated in Edith K. Mosher and Stephen K. Bailey, *The Office of Education Administers a Law* (Syracuse, NY: Syracuse University Press, 1968). For the effect of the ESEA on the states from 1968 to 1971, see Frederick M. Wirt and Michael W. Kirst, *The Political Web of American Schools* (Boston: Little Brown, 1972), Ch. 8.

29. C. E. Finn, Jr., *Education and the Presidency* (Lexington, MA: Lexington Books, 1977).

30. M. Milstein and R. Jennings, *Educational Policy Making and the State Legislature: The New York Experience* (New York: Praeger, 1973).

31. D. E. Mitchell, *Shaping Legislative Decisions: Educational Policy and the Social Sciences* (Lexington, MA: D. C. Heath, 1981), 457.

32. Michael Usdan, *The Political Power of Education in New York State* (New York: Institute of Administrative Research, Teachers College, Columbia University, 1963).

33. Stephen K. Bailey, et al., Schoolmen and Politics (Syracuse, NY: Syracuse University Press, 1962).

34. Nicholas A. Masters, Robert H. Salisbury, and Thomas H. Eliot, *State Politics and the Public Schools* (New York: Knopf, 1964).

35. Laurence Iannaccone has developed a typology of the organizational structure that links educators to the legislature in his *Politics in Education* (New York: Center for Applied Research in Education, 1967).

36. "Tenth Annual Survey of School Board Members," *American School Board Journal* (January 1988): 17–19.

37. Floyd Hunter, *Community Power Structure* (Chapel Hill: University of North Carolina Press, 1953).

38. Robert A. Dahl, *Who Governs?* (New Haven, CT: Yale University Press, 1961).

39. For a review of the debate, see *The Search for Community Power*, eds. Willis D. Hawley and Frederick M. Wirt (Englewood Cliffs, NJ: Prentice-Hall, 1968).

40. Roe L. Johns and Ralph Kimbrough, *The Relationship of Socioeconomic Factors, Educational Leadership Patterns, and Elements of Community Power Structure to Local School Fiscal Policy* (Washington, DC: Bureau of Research, Office of Education, HEW, 1968).

41. George S. Counts, *The Social Composition of School Boards* (Chicago: University of Chicago Supplementary Monographs, No. 33, 1937).

42. John J. Hunt, "Politics in the Role of the Superintendent," *Phi Delta Kappan* 49 (1968): 348–50.

43. "School Board Profile: Who You Are," *American School Board Journal* (January 1988): 20–25.

44. Normal D. Kerr (pseudonym), "The School Board as an Agency of Legitimation," in *Governing Education*, ed. Alan Rosenthal (Garden City, NY: Doubleday, 1969), 137–72.

45. L. H. Zeigler and M. K. Jennings, *Governing American Schools* (North Scituate, MA: Duxburg, 1974).

46. H. J. Tucker and L. H. Zeigler, *Professionals versus the Public* (New York: Longman, 1980).

47. R. F. Lyle, "Representation and Urban School Boards," in *Community Control of Schools*, ed. H. M. Levin (Washington DC: Brookings Institution, 1970), 138–68.

48. Zeigler and Jennings, *Governing American Schools*, 125–28.

49. Philip Schrag, *Village School Downtown* (Boston: Beacon Press, 1967).

50. Marilyn Gittell, *Participants and Participation* (New York: Praeger, 1967); and David Rogers, *11 Livingston Street* (New York: Random House, 1968).

51. Differing interpretations of this dispute can be found in Maurice Berube and Marilyn Gittell, *Confrontation at Ocean Hill-Brownsville* (New York: Praeger, 1969); and Martin Mayer, *The Teachers Strike, New York 1968* (New York: Harper & Row, 1969).

52. Harry L. Miller, *Social Foundations of Education: An Urban Focus*, 3rd ed. (New York: Holt, Rinehart and Winston, 1978), 374–81.

53. Allan Ornstein, "Research on Decentralization," *Phi Delta Kappan* (May 1973): 610–14; and David Selden, "The Future of Community Participation in Educational Policy Making," in *Community Participation in Education*, ed. Carl A. Grant (Boston: Allyn and Bacon, 1979), 76.

54. Harriet Talmadge and Allan C. Ornstein, "School Superintendents' Attitudes Toward Community Participation and Control," *Educational Research Quarterly* (Summer 1976): 37–45.

55. "Can Parents Save Schools?" *Newsweek* (October 16, 1989): 74; and "School Decentralization at Work," *Houston Chronicle* (July 10, 1990): A10.

56. "The Big Plunge on School Reform" (editorial), *The New York Times* (July 20, 1990): A12.

57. "The Uncertain Benefits of School Choice," *U.S. News & World Report* (November 6, 1989): 79–82.

58. Edward H. Fiske, "Choice of Public Schools May Be Wave of Future," *The New York Times* (June 4, 1989): Y13.

59. "The Uncertain Benefits of School Choice," 79.

■ C H A P T E R   1 2

ECONOMIC INFLUENCES ■

A LOOK AHEAD

The purpose of this chapter is to examine how schools are financed and to determine the chief economic and financial problems facing public education. You will learn about:

- The major objectives of taxation in the United States, including education

- Four principal sources of public-school funds and their basic features

- The school financial-reform movement and efforts to equalize funding

- Alternative financial plans that give parents a wider choice of schools

- The value of education as an investment in future earnings and the economy

- Methods of teacher compensation and the differences between salary scales and pay-for-performance

A cornerstone of public education is a belief in the importance of education in fostering good citizenship and sound government; consequently, public support is vital to the realization of these goals. Financial support is necessary to maintain adequate curricular offerings, facilities, learning materials, and teacher salaries. While funds alone do not guarantee quality programs, school districts with too little financial support are destined to offer inadequate educational programs and opportunities.

But government officials, interest groups, educators, and the public frequently disagree on education expenditures. Does the United States spend enough to educate its children? Does it spend too much? President George Bush said that the United States "lavishes unsurpassed resources on (our children's) schooling." Former Secretary of Education Lauro Cavazos added that whatever is wrong with our schools, "funding is truly not an issue." And Michael Boskin, chairman of the President's Council of Economic Advisers, said, "We spend more, per pupil, than most of the other major industrialized economies."[1]

It seems, then, that a paradox bedevils the educational system: international comparisons of student achievement indicate deficiencies among American students, but the United States spends more on education per pupil and as a share of national income than virtually all of their major industrial rivals.[2] A new study by economists M. Edith Rasell and Lawrence Mischal of the Economic Policy Institute attempts to solve the puzzle by suggesting that the nation's financial commitment to education is exaggerated because higher-education spending is included in the international comparisons.[3] Of the nations studied, the United States had the highest percentage of its population enrolled in higher education (5.1 percent compared with an average of 2.4 percent in the other fifteen nations). By subtracting public and private spending for higher education from the total national educational expenditures, the United States lags badly in funding for kindergarten through twelfth grade. The study ranks the United States fourteenth among sixteen nations studied in percentage of national and per-capita income spending on kindergarten through twelfth-grade education. To bring this education up to the average level of the other fifteen nations, the United States would need to increase spending by $20 billion a year—which is roughly equal to the entire Department of Education budget.

Officials in the Department of Education responded that absolute expenditures per pupil are the appropriate standard of comparison, not a percentage of national or per-capita income. Mischal defended this approach by claiming that comparisons of direct per-pupil expenditures do not take into account the higher costs of goods and wages in wealthier nations. Clearly, widespread agreement does not exist on whether the United States is spending too much or too little for education.

Arguments about our financial investment in education are complicated by apparent differences in student achievement in other countries.

SOURCES OF FINANCIAL SUPPORT ■

Taxation in the United States has three major objectives: (1) to raise revenue to support government; (2) to redistribute income and wealth; and (3) to regulate and protect the general well-being.[4] Revenues finance public schools, a government operation. Taxes also redistribute wealth and income by subsidizing various public social programs. And taxes protect the general well-being through the use of import tariffs and levies to protect domestic producers and stabilize the economy by, for example, imposing higher taxes to discourage consumption or to reduce the size of corporations.

The four principal sources of public-school funds are the federal income tax, state income tax, state sales tax, and local property tax. Before we can determine the adequacy of these sources or examine each tax individually, we need to understand certain features of taxes.

Four criteria are considered in levying a tax: wealth, income, consumption, and privilege.[5] A tax on wealth is based on property ownership, with the size of the assessment based on the value of the property. Another example is the federal estate tax, which is based on the value of the deceased person's estate. An income tax is based on the income of individuals and corporations after subtracting expenses and

School boards must ensure that school districts have an adequate tax base.

deductions. A consumption tax is usually a sales tax but is called an excise tax when it is a federal or state tax on the sale or manufacture of a commodity, usually a luxury item. Import duties or revenue tariffs also are considered excise taxes. A privilege tax, also called an occupation tax or license fee, is a fee exacted by the government from a person engaging in a certain occupation or profession. Such a license could be a medical license, a license to operate a retail store, or a license to offer transportation services. Part of the fee covers the cost of government regulation.

Everyone who pays taxes contributes to educational funding.

Taxes are levied equally whether or not the citizen has children in the public schools on the grounds that the public schools promote the common good. Taxes can be considered in terms of benefits received or sacrifices made. The benefit theory was rejected with the rise of the common schools in the nineteenth century because taxes were no longer based on the number of children the family had in school. The benefit theory, however, does apply to such taxes as motor vehicle license taxes and motor fuel taxes on the grounds that highways should be paid for by users. But the sacrifice theory has been applied to the public schools in terms of government expenditures for the public good that should be determined by the ability to pay based on rates that equalize burdens.[6]

The economic and social effects of a tax vary with the type of tax. If a particular tax is only for the purpose of raising revenue, then it should not affect social well-being or the economic decisions of people or leave a firm substantially worse off than before the tax. The property tax, while it does raise revenue, nevertheless has had some negative social effects: some cities have abandoned low-rent housing because property taxes (in addition to other expenses) exceeded rental income. Unlike property taxes, other taxes, such as import taxes, are designed to have an economic effect by controlling the rate of imported goods into the domestic market.

Ideally, taxes treat all parties equitably. It might seem that two persons with the same income should pay the same rate of income tax, and two persons who own property of equal value in the same neighborhood should pay the same property tax. But individuals have different incomes and different property values, so it is necessary to devise formulas by which they would pay taxes in terms of the benefits received or in proportion to their use of the service supported by the tax.

Tax systems are either progressive or regressive. A **progressive tax** increases the rates as the base amount taxed increases. For example, a rate of 2 percent applied to a base of $1,000, 4 percent to a base of $10,000, and 6 percent applied to a base of $100,000 would be progressive. A **regressive tax** increases the rates as the base amount taxed decreases. If the percentages were reversed in the previous example so that 6 percent applies to a base of $1,000 and 2 percent applies to $100,000, the tax would be regressive. A tax can have a regressive effect even when rates are uniform, as in the case of a sales tax, which takes a larger percentage of income from low-income groups than from high-income groups.

A **tax yield** is the revenue generated by a tax. Ideally, taxes should be adequate to supply essential public services. For example, federal income taxes yield an amount that covers only about half of federal operating costs. Tax yields also should be sufficiently stable to supply necessary services without resorting to deficit spending. The property tax yield is relatively stable except during a long economic depression. Yields should also be flexible to accommodate changes in government services and the purchasing power of the dollar. Income taxes and sales taxes are more flexible than property taxes because they change with the economy, although property taxes can be made more flexible by establishing flexible rates.

A tax yield with a rate that increases more rapidly than incomes is **elastic;** whereas a yield that increases at a slower rate is **inelastic.** The consumer demand for luxury items may slow dramatically as prices increase, and the tax yield from such items is said to be elastic because of such a response to changes in prices. In contrast, the yield from such necessities as food and telephone service is considered inelastic because demand usually does not drop dramatically when prices go up. The elasticity of supply is the responsiveness of output to price changes. Supply usually increases through greater production as prices move up; if supply does not increase, it is said to be inelastic. A progressive tax is elastic and a regressive tax is inelastic, because a progressive tax collects a higher percentage of a wealthy person's income than of a less wealthy person's income.

Ideally, taxes should be adaptable, not rigid. A tax system is considered rigid whenever restrictions on the rates or types of taxes prevent them from being adapted to essential needs. State government, for example, through rigid constitutional provisions that protect special interests, often prevents legislatures from developing adequate revenue systems. Similarly, constitutional and statutory provisions can prevent local school boards from producing sufficient revenues.

The cost of administration and compliance with tax provisions should be reasonable. The administration and collection of taxes is the government's cost; the cost of compliance falls on the taxpayer. The cost to city, county, and school governments of collecting the property tax can be reduced by using a joint system of assessments and collection. Some taxes, such as the retail sales tax, can be readily paid on each purchase; whereas the income tax had little ease of payment until

Local districts may be hampered in applying revenue sources to education.

payroll deductions begin, and the property tax's ease of payment can be improved by using quarterly or monthly payments rather than an annual one. On the other hand, individual and corporate income taxes require the most effort for the taxpayer to handle because careful records must be kept and accountants may be needed to prepare returns and provide tax advice.

Federal Income Tax. As for the four sources of public school funds, federal taxation not only provides revenue but also helps to regulate economic activity. Economic regulation is accomplished by reducing taxes during recessions to encourage greater investment and consumption and by raising taxes during inflationary periods to reduce demand on goods and services. Of the four taxes, the federal tax is the most progressive and therefore the most equitable. Studies before the tax-code revision of 1986, however, showed that the federal income tax process was filled with loopholes that enabled corporations and high-income individuals to pay little or no taxes.[7] In fact, Ferdinand Lundberg argued that America's propertied elite deals itself substantial tax advantages and the labor force, absolutely as well as relatively, shoulders the national tax burden.[8] This would explain, at least in part, why a tax that is progressive for more than 90 percent of the population results in little redistribution of income.[9]

The 1986 Tax Reform Act repealed most of the tax brackets in the income-tax laws in an effort to make taxation more equitable. Before 1986 the United States tax system was highly progressive, with fourteen tax brackets ranging from 11 percent to 50 percent. Congress repealed twelve of them, leaving a 15 percent bracket and a 28 percent bracket and phasing in a third bracket of 33 percent that applies to those with relatively high incomes. The list of items that could be excluded from income was shortened, and the number and types of tax shelters were curbed.[10] Under the provisions of the Tax Reform Act, the federal income tax became less progressive, but tax shelters were restricted, suggesting that wealthy individuals and large corporations could no longer avoid taxes altogether, although they would pay lower rates. The cost of administering the federal income tax is high, but the yield is so great that administrative costs are proportionally low. The cost of collecting federal taxes is less than the cost of collecting state and local taxes.

State Income Tax. Forty-five states levy a corporate income tax and forty-three states assess an individual income tax.[11] Some states are reluctant to adopt an income tax for fear it would drive the wealthy out of the state or that tax supporters in the legislature might have difficulty getting re-elected. State individual income taxes are graduated, but to more modest levels than the federal income tax. The brackets are narrow at the lower income levels (about $1,000) and the rate of progression is steep but begins to level out and down at about $15,000.[12] States have begun to index tax brackets to prevent increases in taxes because of inflation rather than higher income.

State Sales Tax. A general sales tax is levied in forty-five states, with rates ranging from 3 percent to 8 percent, and is the largest source of state revenue. States also can levy more at the local level,[13] such as counties and municipalities and, rarely, school districts. The sales tax is elastic in that it responds to changes in the economy, although substantially less so than income taxes. Some states include selective sales taxes on motor fuels, alcoholic beverages, tobacco products, and license fees, and severance taxes, which are paid upon the removal of natural resources from the land.

Many states do not tax essential items such as food and drugs, because the burden falls more heavily on low-income families who must spend a larger percentage of their income for these items. Yet even with these exemptions, poorer families spend more of their income for consumption, and in this sense sales tax is inequitable and regressive. To reduce the inequity, states can refund sales-tax payments to the poor (as Indiana and Hawaii have done) or give them credit on their state income tax.

> States must look for ways to make sales taxes less burdensome to the poor.

Local Property Tax. Since tuition income, gifts, and bequests constitute only a small source of local school revenue, school districts depend primarily on the property tax. Three types of property can be taxed: real property, tangible personal property, and intangible personal property. **Real property** includes land and buildings and improvements on the land, all of which are fixed in one location. More than 80 percent of the property tax yield comes from real property.

Tangible personal property such as automobiles, jewelry, appliances, and household furniture has a value of its own and can be moved from place to place. Commercial and industrial property, which includes machinery, is also in this category. Some people have argued that tangible personal property should be removed from the tax rolls because most of it is subject to a sales tax at the time of purchase and another tax would result in double taxation. Tax assessors also have difficulty identifying and assessing the value of items to be taxed.

> Property taxes are the main source of revenue for most school districts.

Intangible personal property includes such items as stocks, bonds, bank deposits, accounts receivable, insurance policies, and mortgages. This tax source is difficult to identify and already is subject to federal taxation, which again would result in double taxation.

Other possible local taxes include a local non-property tax collected through payroll deductions. Cities, more often than school districts, have been authorized to use local non-property taxes. Since many taxpayers are subject to federal and state income taxes, in such cases the local non-property tax constitutes triple taxation.

At one time, real property holdings were an indication of the wealth of an individual or family; more recently, however, intangible personal high-income property such as stocks and bonds have become the mark of wealth. Moreover, a family with many children needs a larger house than does a smaller family. The large family may have less taxable income than the smaller family, but its larger house might carry a larger tax assessment. The tax itself is not based on the taxpayer's equity. In other words, one family might have its house mortgaged to full value and another family with a house of the same value might own its home outright; yet both families pay the same amount of tax even though their taxable capacity differs.

Traditionally, real property tax is considered regressive because the lower the income class, the higher the percentage of property tax owed. Revisionists, however, believe that the property tax is progressive.[14] The traditional view holds that the property owner is unable to shift the tax burden, and renters bear tax burdens through higher rent payments. But the revisionists claim that the property tax is mainly levied on capital and is shared by all owners of capital in proportion to their holdings. It would seem, however, that the property tax on individual or family housing tends to be regressive because wealthy people spend a smaller proportion of their income on housing than do the less affluent.

Property is supposed to be assessed at a uniform percentage of full market value, but this is not done in some communities. Assessments also vary within the same state and even the same district. Other problems include the extended time period between assessments in some communities and the lack of training of local assessors (who are usually elected officials).

To its credit, the property tax is inelastic during depression and elastic in periods of prosperity. Except in cases of major natural catastrophes, the tax base of a community is not expected to decrease sharply.

Limits on property taxes require infusions of funds to education from other sources.

Of the different forms of taxation, the real property tax seems to be the most unpopular in some states. Proposition 13, approved by California voters in 1978, amended the state constitution to limit local property taxes and restrict local government in its efforts to increase other taxes. To offset Proposition 13, the state increased appropriations from a state general fund surplus. The influence of Proposition 13 was felt in other states—most notably Massachusetts, where school revenues were drastically reduced in 1980 as a result of a constitutional amendment to limit taxation.

Suggested property tax reforms include providing adequate training for tax assessors; consolidating tax districts, which then would be managed by full-time assessors; instituting 100 percent assessment that is kept current; ending exemptions and deductions to special interest groups that constrict the tax base and place an unequal burden on the rest of the population; adjusting the tax rolls whenever property values change; and providing a review board to hear taxpayer grievances.

The relative percentage of public school support from the different levels of government has changed dramatically since the 1919–1920 school year (see Table 12–1). The percentage of federal support grew from 0.3 percent in that year to 9.8 percent in 1978–1979 and declined to 6.4 percent by 1986–1987. The state's share has dramatically increased from 16.5 percent in 1919–1920 to 49.8 percent in 1986–1987; whereas the local share declined during the same period from 83.2 percent to 43.9 percent. This shift from local to state support reflects the trend of moving control of public education to the state level (as we discussed in Chapter 11).

Funding for public education is shifting to the states, along with a greater share in control.

The percentage of federal contributions varies widely among the states, with Mississippi receiving a high of 17.0 percent and Wyoming receiving a low of 2.3 percent. Local revenue contributions also vary widely, from a high of 91.2 percent in New Hampshire to a low of 0.2 percent in Hawaii, which has a statewide school district.

Another factor to consider when discussing school financing is the effect of collective bargaining. School districts involved in bargaining spend more both overall and on instruction.[15] Greater union power is related to higher salaries, benefits, and pupil expenditures. These influences are generally small (a maximum of $72 per pupil), but larger in districts with declining enrollment.[16] Budget decisions are coordinated with bargaining and frequently control budget choices,[17] except in school districts that face fiscal adversity, where economic conditions tend to control bargaining.[18] Salary increases from bargaining are financed by tax increases in wealthier districts, but by budget reallocation in less wealthy areas.[19] Although bargaining does affect other school financial decisions, labor concerns are not usually dominant. And schools that receive large increases in outside funds do not usually apply them proportionately to teacher salaries.[20] Thus bargaining is one of many influences on local school finance.

State Foundation Programs and Related Plans

States originally issued a **flat grant,** which specified the amount granted to local districts for each pupil. The flat-grant provision, however, proved insufficient to cover operating costs. Some educators recognized these inadequacies, and a **foundation program** was

TABLE 12-1 Revenues for public elementary and secondary schools, by source of funds: 1919–20 to 1986–87

School year	In thousands				Percentage distribution			
	Total	Federal	State	Local (including intermediate)[1]	Total	Federal	State	Local (including intermediate)[1]
1	2	3	4	5	6	7	8	9
1919–20	$ 970,121	$ 2,475	$ 160,085	$ 807,561	100.0	0.3	16.5	83.2
1929–30	2,088,557	7,334	353,670	1,727,553	100.0	0.4	16.9	82.7
1939–40	2,260,527	39,810	684,354	1,536,363	100.0	1.8	30.3	68.0
1941–42	2,416,580	34,305	759,993	1,622,281	100.0	1.4	31.4	67.1
1943–44	2,604,322	35,886	859,183	1,709,253	100.0	1.4	33.0	65.6
1945–46	3,059,845	41,378	1,062,057	1,956,409	100.0	1.4	34.7	63.9
1947–48	4,311,534	120,270	1,676,362	2,514,902	100.0	2.8	38.9	58.3
1949–50	5,437,044	155,848	2,165,689	3,115,507	100.0	2.9	39.8	57.3
1951–52	6,423,816	227,711	2,478,596	3,717,507	100.0	3.5	38.6	57.9
1953–54	7,866,852	355,237	2,944,103	4,567,512	100.0	4.5	37.4	58.1
1955–56	9,686,677	441,442	3,828,886	5,416,350	100.0	4.6	39.5	55.9
1957–58	12,181,513	486,484	4,800,368	6,894,661	100.0	4.0	39.4	56.6
1959–60	14,746,618	651,639	5,768,047	8,326,932	100.0	4.4	39.1	56.5
1961–62	17,527,707	760,975	6,789,190	9,977,542	100.0	4.3	38.7	56.9
1963–64	20,544,182	896,956	8,078,014	11,569,213	100.0	4.4	39.3	56.3
1965–66	25,356,858	1,996,954	9,920,219	13,439,686	100.0	7.9	39.1	53.0
1967–68	31,903,064	2,806,469	12,275,536	16,821,063	100.0	8.8	38.5	52.7
1969–70	40,266,923	3,219,557	16,062,776	20,984,589	100.0	8.0	39.9	52.1
1970–71	44,511,292	3,753,461	17,409,086	23,348,745	100.0	8.4	39.1	52.5
1971–72	50,003,645	4,467,969	19,133,256	26,402,420	100.0	8.9	38.3	52.8

TABLE 12–1 *(Continued)*

School year	In thousands					Percentage distribution			
	Total	Federal	State	Local (including intermediate)[1]	Total	Federal	State	Local (including intermediate)[1]	
1	2	3	4	5	6	7	8	9	
1972–73	52,117,930	4,525,000	20,843,520	26,749,412	100.0	8.7	40.0	51.3	
1973–74	58,230,892	4,930,351	24,113,409	29,187,132	100.0	8.5	41.4	50.1	
1974–75	64,445,239	5,811,595	27,211,116	31,422,528	100.0	9.0	42.2	48.8	
1975–76	71,206,073	6,318,345	31,776,101	33,111,627	100.0	8.9	44.6	46.5	
1976–77	75,322,532	6,629,498	32,688,903	36,004,134	100.0	8.8	43.4	47.8	
1977–78	81,443,160	7,694,194	35,013,266	38,735,700	100.0	9.4	43.0	47.6	
1978–79	87,994,143	8,600,116	40,132,136	39,261,891	100.0	9.8	45.6	44.6	
1979–80	96,881,165	9,503,537	45,348,814	42,028,813	100.0	9.8	46.8	43.4	
1980–81	105,949,087	9,768,262	50,182,659	45,998,166	100.0	9.2	47.4	43.4	
1981–82	110,191,257	8,186,466	52,436,435	49,568,356	100.0	7.4	47.6	45.0	
1982–83	117,497,502	8,339,990	56,282,157	52,875,354	100.0	7.1	47.9	45.0	
1983–84	126,055,419	8,576,547	60,232,981	57,245,892	100.0	6.8	47.8	45.4	
1984–85	137,294,678	9,105,569	67,168,684	61,020,425	100.0	6.6	48.9	44.4	
1985–86[2]	149,127,779	9,975,622	73,619,575	65,532,582	100.0	6.7	49.4	43.9	
1986–87	158,827,473	10,145,899	79,022,572	69,659,003	100.0	6.4	49.8	43.9	

[1]Includes a relatively small amount from nongovernmental sources (gifts and tuition and transportation fees from patrons). These sources accounted for 0.4 percent of total revenues in 1967–68.
[2]Revised from previously published figures.
Note: Beginning in 1980–81, revenues for State education agencies are excluded.
Because of rounding, details may not add to totals.

Source: U.S. Department of Education, National Center for Education Statistics, *Statistics of State School Systems; Revenues and Expenditures for Public Elementary and Secondary Education;* and Common Core of Data survey. (This table was prepared November 1988.)

instituted to overcome some inequities in local support and assure that all school districts can meet minimum standards. The foundation program is not a substitute for local efforts to collect revenue; in fact, districts must prove a mandatory effort to provide quality education before such grants are made by the state. The measure of ability to support local schools is determined in most states by a stipulated millage on property valuation. This procedure has serious limitations because real property is no longer the best measure of wealth in a district. Median household income might be a more reliable measure of local resources. Some southeastern states use an index of economic factors that includes personal income; retail sales receipts; and the value of farming, mining, manufacturing, and automobile vehicle registrations.

In lieu of a flat grant per pupil, some states consider average daily attendance as one basis for allocating school funds, hoping to increase school attendance. Other states use the total number of days of attendance by all pupils, which promotes a longer school year. The state can estimate a school's need by multiplying average daily attendance by a figure that represents an adequate expenditure per pupil. The figure obtained is the amount of money per pupil needed to purchase the essentials of an education program. The state then determines the ability of the school district to meet these costs and closes any gap in revenue with a state subsidy.

Nearly all states provide aid for special provisions beyond the foundation plan. These programs and provisions include classes for the disabled, vocational education, transportation, purchase of textbooks, health examinations, supervision of instruction, and school-building construction. Wealthy districts have an advantage because they need only a small increase in millage to provide matching funds for a state grant; whereas poorer districts usually need substantial millage increases. Special aids usually cannot be incorporated into foundation programs because some special aids include federal funds earmarked for special purposes.

Deficiencies in foundation programs have prompted the development of other plans. The **power-equalizing plan,** for example, guarantees to each local school district in a state the same assessed valuation per pupil. Equalization is accomplished mathematically rather than by redrawing school-district lines. If local taxes do not raise the per-pupil amount specified, general state funds subsidize the differences. If local taxes raise more than the per-pupil amount, the surplus is recycled to other districts. Such recycling has been unpopular and, where used, has been at less than the full rate. Florida, Maine, and Michigan have used this plan, although it has not been popular and not all of the funds have been recycled.

The **full-funding plan** calls for the state to specify per-pupil funding levels for each classification of student and then to impose a uniform property tax to fund the plan. If local districts fail to generate sufficient revenue to fund the plan, the state subsidizes districts directly. As a result of equal-protection lawsuits, California, New Mexico, Washington, and West Virginia adopted this plan. Hawaii also adopted the plan when it became a state in 1969.

■ **PAUSE TO REFLECT**

Fair Taxation for Public Schools

- Do you think everyone should be taxed equally to fund public schools? Or should people pay taxes depending on the number of children they have in school?

- If school-funding taxes are paid by the users only, what benefits, if any, should the non-users have to give up? For example, would a non-user have to pay a fee to attend a public event staged in a public-school building?

SCHOOL FINANCIAL-REFORM MOVEMENT ■

Court decisions in the 1970s prompted a school financial-reform movement that continued into the 1980s. Presaging these changes, as we discussed in Chapter 10, was a study conducted by Coons, Clune, and Sugarman,[21] which focused on the inability of poor school districts to provide adequate education. The authors suggested that the quality of public education should not be a function of wealth other than the total wealth of the state. The authors' "power-equalizing" system of finance was designed to ensure that each district could secure equal educational funds for the same fiscal effort (equal tax assessment), thereby assuring equivalent educational offerings. Rich districts do not have the right to better schools with less effort (lower tax assessment), the authors said; therefore, all districts in the state should be brought up to the level of the rich districts, or rich districts should be equalized downward by contributing to state funds. Rich districts could tax beyond the equalized base, but a ceiling should be placed on these efforts to prevent wealthy districts from commanding resources from the poorer ones. Property assessments should be uniform throughout a state to bring about equalization, or else there should be a system of property equalization by which the value of property in different communities can be compared to reach an assessment.

In 1971 the California Supreme Court handed down a historic decision in *Serrano v. Priest*.[22] The court concluded that the state's public-school financing system produced substantial disparities among school districts in the amount of revenue available for education. These disparities denied pupils the equal protection of the law (as stated in the Fourteenth Amendment). The court cited two school districts within the same county where the local assessed property valuation per child was thirteen times greater in the wealthier district. The court found education to be a "fundamental interest" that cannot be conditioned on wealth. "Education," the court said, "is the lifeline of both the individual and society." While the court declared the present system of school finance unconstitutional, it did not prescribe solutions or strike down the school finance system. Instead, it remanded the case to the trial court to determine whether the facts were as alleged, and, if so, to find the system unconstitutional.

The California legislature responded to the state supreme court decision by substantially altering the state's school finance system. The most important change was the imposition of a revenue limit in which school districts were restricted in the amount they could raise through local taxes and state aid. But to promote equalization, districts below the state average were allowed to increase their limits faster than districts above the average.

In 1973 the Supreme Court of New Jersey went a step further than the California court and struck down the state school finance program.[23] The court relied on a constitutional clause that required the state legislature to provide "a thorough and efficient system" of public schools to declare the system unconstitutional, concluding that the system did not provide equal opportunity.

In a 1973 decision that shifted financial reform to the states, the U.S. Supreme Court in *San Antonio v. Rodriguez* reversed a three-judge federal panel that had ruled that the Texas school financing system violated constitutional guarantees of equal protection.[24] Justice Lewis F. Powell, Jr., speaking for the five-to-four majority, said, "It is not the province of this court to create substantive constitutional rights in the name of guaranteed equal protection under the law. . . . Education is not among the rights afforded explicit protection under our Constitution. Nor do we find any basis for saying it is implicitly so protected." This decision is important also because the Supreme Court decided for the first time that education was not even an implicit right under the U.S. Constitution. While the majority denied that their decision in any way detracted from their "historic dedication to public education," they noted that it had never been the constitutional prerogative of the court to nullify statewide systems for public services because the burden fell unevenly upon the population.

Not all state courts overturned their finance systems. The highest courts in Michigan, Ohio, Oregon, New York, Maryland, Georgia, and Colorado were not persuaded that school taxes and funding disparities were unconstitutional. However, in addition to California and New Jersey, courts in Arkansas, Connecticut, Kansas, Kentucky, Montana, Texas, Washington, Wisconsin, West Virginia, and Wyoming declared their finance system unconstitutional and mandated the legislature to undertake reforms. Five states have adopted full state funding as a result of these decisions, and eighteen states have adopted some form of power-equalizing plan. These reforms were highly significant; in fact, James Guthrie declared that the "period between 1970 and 1980 saw more and farther-reaching changes in school finance distribution formulas and associated taxation plans than any other decade in U.S. history."[25]

> Many states have sought to establish equitable systems of taxation for school funding.

Alternative Financial Plans

Dissatisfaction with public education, its financial burden, and limited options for parents have led to three alternative financial plans: family power equalizing, tuition tax credits, and voucher plans. Coons, Clune, and Sugarman proposed a **family power-equalizing plan** after recognizing that expenditures still might depend on the decisions of a community even though expenditures should not be based statewide on local wealth.[26] A rural family, for example, might be willing to pay for an excellent education for its children, but its neighbors might be unwilling to make such provisions. Coons, Clune, and Sugarman proposed that several levels of quality be available in a community's schools, with each family free to choose the level it wants for its children and be taxed accordingly. The children would attend the school linked to the parent's choice of tax rate. Every school would be required by the state to establish an expenditure per pupil falling into one of four categories, and a school's expenditure could not rise above or below its chosen level. Critics object to the plan because, they say, wealthy districts would be required to return a large share of locally raised taxes and receive nothing in return. Wealthy districts, to compensate, might decide to transfer some school functions, such as libraries and athletics, to unequalized municipal tax rolls.

Tuition tax credits would enable parents who send their children to private or parochial schools to receive federal income tax credit for tuition expenses. The idea is based on the belief that parents should have a greater voice in their child's education by promoting parental choice and greater diversity in education. Although tuition tax credits were first proposed in the 1950s, the most significant recent bill (which failed to pass) was the 1978 Packwood-Moynihan bill, which included tax credits for college and university costs and allowed a refund for people who claimed tuition tax credits in excess of their tax liability.

The Reagan administration's Educational Opportunity and Equity Act of 1982 —which was vetoed by Congress—proposed to credit up to 50 percent of each child's tuition to private or parochial schools. Maximum credit, which would have been phased in over three years, would have provided $500 per child. A ceiling on income for qualified families attempted to ensure that benefits would go to working families, and a nondiscriminatory provision excluded families who send their children to schools that discriminate on the basis of race. The credits, proponents said, would have benefitted not nonpublic schools but taxpaying citizens.

Proponents of tuition tax credits believe that public schools constitute a monopoly not only over the poor but also over all who cannot afford to pay property taxes for public schools and pay private tuition as well. Tax credits are in the national interest, they say, because they free children of lower and middle classes to seek a more challenging educational environment. Furthermore, with easier access to a larger private sector, parents who want their children exposed to prayer in schools would have plenty of private schools to choose from and no longer would have to lobby for prayer in public schools.

The push for tuition tax credits has stirred much controversy. Former Attorney General Griffin Bell concluded in 1978 that the Packwood-Moynihan bill was unconstitutional because it violated First Amendment guarantees against the establishment of religion. He believed the bill would lead to divisive church-state entanglements and benefit sectarian schools more than nonsectarian ones.

In 1979 the U.S. Third Circuit Court of Appeals rejected the argument that parents whose children are enrolled in nonpublic schools have greater expenses and should be entitled to relief. Private schools already enjoy tax-exempt status, the court said, and receive considerable benefits under federal aid programs. The credit of $500 per child in nonpublic schools would contrast sharply with direct federal aid of $145 per pupil in public schools.

In what could be considered a compromise of sorts, the Supreme Court ruled, five to four, that states may give tax benefits to parents to offset some of their children's school expenses.[27] The justices upheld a Minnesota law granting parents a tax deduction up to $700 per child for the costs of elementary and secondary education, whether public or private. The Minnesota law differs from the Reagan administration proposal, which would have provided tax benefits only for those paying private-school tuition. Most of the benefits, however, still go to parents of children in private schools because public-school families pay no tuition and have fewer school-related expenses.

Some believe that tuition tax credits would enable students to seek a quality of education beyond what their local district offers.

Another alternative is the **voucher plan,** which would finance elementary and secondary education through certificates given by government to parents of school-age children. The parents select the school of their choice—public, private, or parochial—and present the certificate as payment for instruction in the chosen school; the school then presents the voucher to the government and receives a check for a stipulated amount based on a formula.

The voucher plan is not a new proposal, but earlier plans were essentially unregulated, leading to such dangers as violation of the separation of church and state and the intensification of segregated schooling.[28] Christopher Jencks and his colleagues developed a highly regulated voucher plan designed to overcome the substantial shortcomings of earlier proposals.[29] The plan would create an Education Voucher Agency (EVA) at the community level for receiving government school-financing funds. It would be locally controlled and would resemble a board of education except that it would not operate schools of its own; such responsibility would be retained by public and private school boards. The EVA would determine the eligibility of public and nonpublic schools to participate in the plan.

The voucher plan would provide more education options, break the "monopoly" of the public schools, and enable poor parents to have the same choice of schools as wealthy parents. Each school would announce openings every spring and would be required to take all applicants. If the number of applicants exceeded the number of places, a lottery would be used to fill half the places. The other half would be filled on a first-come, first-served basis. Each school would be required to accept the voucher as full payment, which would avoid discrimination against the poor. To prevent increased segregation, each school would be required to show that it had accepted at least as high a proportion of ethnic-group students as had applied. EVA would pay transportation costs of all children, and would disseminate information about all schools in the area.

The Office of Economic Opportunity offered grants to several communities to study the feasibility of the voucher plan, but only Alum Rock, California, tried the plan. Alum Rock's plan, however, differed from Jencks's plan in that it affected only public schools. Officials provided alternative programs within the public schools, and used the board of education in lieu of EVA. After four years of operation it was found that teachers, students, and parents liked the plan but that standardized test scores were either equivalent to national norms or, in some instances, had dropped below them.[30]

Except for the Alum Rock plan, voucher plans have several deficiencies.[31] Advocates believe that vouchers would do for public schools what free enterprise has done for the economy—increase healthy com-

Voucher plans put schools in competition with one another without providing them with all they may need to compete successfully.

petition. But schools, the critics say, are relatively decentralized as it is, and they already compete with private schools and with each other for teachers, appropriations, and special projects, and in their sports programs. The market analogy is misleading, they say, because profit-making firms sell their products to anyone who has the cash or credit, whereas private schools are not open to everyone. Nonpublic schools also would need to be far more innovative in their offerings to provide the benefits claimed from vouchers.

Some critics fear that if nonpublic schools accept substantial state funds, the state might try to regulate them more thoroughly. Parochial schools, for example, might no longer be able to offer sectarian religious courses, and all nonpublic schools might be subject to desegregation rulings and judicial standards of academic freedom. Critics also note that voucher plans make no provision to eliminate discrimination in the hiring of teachers. And public schools probably would not receive additional tax funds but nonpublic schools would be free to increase their endowment, which could lead to even greater inequities. The voucher plan would increase public costs to pay nonpublic-school tuitions, staff and operate the EVA, and create new buildings and facilities for private schools. Public-school facilities might not be used to their full capacity because of decreased enrollment, increased transportation costs, and inefficient use of tenured public-school teachers.

▪ EDUCATION AS AN INVESTMENT

Fiscal Effects of Federal Legislation on Students with Disabilities

Where enrollments decrease, per-pupil costs will probably rise.

Although student enrollment is expected to decrease in some school districts in the Great Lakes, Mid-Atlantic, and New England areas during the 1990s, costs will continue to rise because of factors such as a large influx of minority, bilingual, gifted, and disabled students, which raises the average cost per student. Since American education endorses the principle of providing equity and equality of opportunity for all students, the question is how to secure adequate financial resources to provide such opportunities.

Section 504 of the Rehabilitation Act of 1973, whose regulations became official in 1977, prohibits discrimination against disabled persons in all federally assisted programs and activities. Section 504 requires that facilities be barrier-free and that programs and activities not discriminate against the disabled in any way. Structural building changes were expected to be completed within three years of legislation. Funds, however, were not appropriated as part of this legislation, which meant that school districts had to come up with the extra money required to comply with the law.

Public Law 94-142 (Education for All Handicapped Children Act of 1975), on the other hand, which provided disabled students with access to a free education, appropriated federal funds for these programs. With Sections 504 and 503 of the Rehabilitation Act of 1973, the disabled have been redefined to include the severely and profoundly disabled and the age range has been broadened to include children from three through twenty-one years old. Public Law 94-142 covers a broad area and can include expenditures for transportation and medical expenses; developmental, corrective, and support services such as therapy and speech pathology; early identification and assessment; and parental counseling and training. The law authorized expenditures to cover 40 percent of the excess cost of educating a disabled child. But even though allocations rose steadily from the time the law was passed—from $152 million in 1976 to more than $1 billion by 1982—these amounts covered only 9 percent to 15 percent of the cost of educating a child with a disability.

The law's provisions included: (1) the development of procedures for identifying all children with disabilities; (2) the preparation of individual educational plans (IEPs) for each student in consultation with parents and, where appropriate, with the students themselves; (3) the mainstreaming of students with disabilities in as many regular school activities as feasible; and (4) the establishment of regular procedures by which parents could contest school-district decisions. The IEP provision established a mechanism that brought together parents and school officials to determine the needs of children with disabilities without regard for the cost to the district. Needless to say, Public Law 94-142 increased the cost of educating children with disabilities.

To provide for these increased costs and improve the equity of school finance formulas, school districts can use the **weighted-pupil approach.** These weightings compensate for the higher cost of educating some students, such as disabled students. When budgets are cut, the high-cost programs are usually the first to be cut back, but under this approach all programs suffer or prosper comparably when funds are reduced or increased. This approach also tends to reduce the number of categorical grants required to finance educational programs. Minnesota, Utah, and Washington have used this approach, and other states are expected to adopt similar financing methods.

Even when federal funds are appropriated for programs, the states may still face shortfalls.

Education and Earnings

What effect does education have on earnings? Is a college education worth the money? Do college graduates really have a significant edge over high-school graduates? Economists have attempted to measure the effect of formal schooling by comparing earnings of high-school and college graduates. In making their computations, economists count as a cost the earnings that college students must forgo during the four years they are out of the labor market. By choosing to attend college for four years students will earn nothing (assuming they do not take a part-time job) and also have the costs of tuition, books, and related expenses that they would not have if they had entered the job market directly from high school. High-school graduates who take jobs upon graduation have no further monetary outlays for schooling and begin immediately to acquire work experience that increases their earning power. And in some cases, when college graduates take full-time jobs, their earning power might not be as great as if they had been working for the past four years. Usually fairly soon, however, their earnings are greater than if they had taken a job after finishing high school. The earnings of high-school graduates are about two-thirds those of college graduates.

Gary Becker studied the rate of return from the investment in a college education.[32] He found that the rate of return of a college education before taxes in 1950 for urban white males was about 10 per-

Graduates need to make a realistic assessment of the effects of higher education on income.

cent to 12 percent. Making allowances for the generally higher ability of college students, these rates of return were scaled downward one or two percentage points and, after figuring for taxes, the total rate of return was 8 percent to 10 percent for people who did not attend college. Becker estimated the rate of return on physical capital in business and industry at about 8 percent and concluded that the return on educational investment was roughly equal to that of physical capital investment.

Other investigators have shown that the highest rate of return exists for those who complete the eighth grade, with lesser returns for a high-school and a college education.[33] Theodore Schultz computed a 35 percent rate of return for an elementary education, 10 percent for a high-school education, and 11 percent for a college education.[34]

These rate-of-return studies invite criticism on several grounds, some of which the investigators have acknowledged. College graduates, as compared with high-school graduates, are likely to have greater native ability, stronger motivation, and more financial resources, which could positively affect their earning power. It has been difficult so far to calculate precisely the effect of these factors on earnings, but some studies have estimated that individual ability accounts for 12 percent to 40 percent of the difference in earnings between high-school and college graduates.[35] On-the-job training also tends to raise earnings, but its influence is difficult to separate from the influence of formal education. More knowledge is needed of both the costs and benefits of this type of training, as well as other informal postgraduate training, before its influence can be calculated.

Many economists believe that earnings tend to reflect productivity rates, but this might not exactly be the case in view of the lack of competition in some labor markets. Ivar Berg also has argued that the alleged correlation between educational training and job performance is a myth.[36] His empirical data support the conclusion that there does not tend to be a *direct* relation between the amount of a person's education and training and the amount of that person's earnings.[37]

Clearly, a positive relationship exists between length of schooling and earned income, but does education itself result in the higher income or does inborn capacity or other factors among those who have more schooling have an additional effect? Various studies show conflicting and inconsistent results, but the prevailing opinion is that education accounts for 60 percent of earnings differentials, and factors such as family background and I.Q. account for 40 percent.[38]

Rates of return also can be estimated according to intended occupation. McMahon and Wagner report an expected return of 14 percent for physicians and dentists. An undergraduate engineering degree is expected to yield 25.5 percent and a master's in engineering another 12 percent. An undergraduate degree in elementary or secondary teaching is expected to return 12.3 percent and a master's degree another 0.8 percent.[39]

Educational Expenditures and Economic Growth

Is the support of education a burden to the economy? Until the 1960s economists tended to treat economic growth as a result of changes in labor and capital: output increases as the labor force grows. When new investments are made in machines and factories, total output can be expected to increase. For many years economists advised underdeveloped nations to increase physical capital if they wanted to increase their growth rate.

This conventional viewpoint was first challenged by an article that suggested that less than one-half of the increase in productivity could be attributed to increase in the volume of capital goods.[40] The stage was now set for Theodore Schultz[41] and Edward Denison[42] to demonstrate the contribution of education to national income. Denison studied the growth rate of the gross national product (GNP) between 1929 and 1957 and identified both positive and negative contributions. Positive factors contributed 109 percent, and negative factors contributed −9 percent for a net of 100 percent. Increased inputs of capital and labor accounted for 49 of the 109 positive percentage points, or 45 percent of the total, and increased education inputs accounted for 43 of the 109 percentage points, or 39 percent of the total—a significant contribution.

Other economists, while differing in details, also have concluded that investment in education positively affects economic growth.[43] Still, some questions could be raised without negating these conclusions. Denison's approach focuses rather exclusively on formal education and tends to ignore the effects of on-the-job training.[44] And because individuals' educational programs and the types of jobs that they take are not always closely related, the upgrading of positions in industry might not always be related to educational prerequisites but rather to such factors as the employer's desire to hire high-school graduates rather than dropouts. However, one effect of increased education is that it produces better decision makers in the allocation of resources, including the use of time. The greater the decision-making functions associated with a job, the greater the potential positive effect of education on productivity.[45]

Increased educational expenditure can lead to various social benefits as well, including a reduction in the amount of public revenues for health, welfare, and the penal system. Lower crime rates also can result, because a portion of crime can be attributed to low education

> Although there are differences among formulas, investment in education tends to have a positive effect on economic growth.

> Investment in education provides social benefits as well as increased productivity.

levels. A rise in family income also shows a corresponding decrease in delinquency; and because greater education and higher incomes are related, a similar relationship can be found between education and delinquency.[46]

It would seem, then, that the economy can only benefit from sound investment in human capital, and several measures can be taken to improve policies for such investments. Tax laws allow deductions for depreciation and replacement of nonhuman capital such as equipment and facilities, but offer no similar deductions for human capital. Skills, for instance, can deteriorate from a lack of use because of unemployment—tax deductions would be one way to offset the cost of such deterioration. Long-term loans for students, the elimination of discrimination in employment and advancement, the development of programs for people who have been discriminated against and for providing improved education for economically depressed areas all are investments that could prove to be in the best national interest.

TEACHER COMPENSATION ■

Even the best funding programs will not mean a thing if the teachers we hire to educate our children cannot or will not do the job. To attract the best and the brightest to the field, discourage them from leaving for more money, and motivate them to improve their professional competencies, schools need to be able to offer adequate salaries and fringe benefits. Expenditures for certified and noncertified school personnel constitute 80 percent to 85 percent of the funds spent for school operations.[47] But do monetary incentives attract and retain sufficient teachers? Though many teachers speak of the intrinsic reward of teaching, including helping students learn and develop, evidence suggests that salary is an important reason for entering—and leaving—teaching. An analysis of total supply and demand in the nation found that the number of people available to teach rises when teacher salaries are comparable to or higher than salaries in alternative occupations.[48] An analysis of trends also indicates that more people enter teaching when they expect salaries to rise because of growing enrollment.[49] The likelihood that an individual will leave teaching for another occupation is positively related to the amount a teacher is underpaid compared to potential earnings in other fields.[50]

Salary levels appear to have a subtle effect on teacher supply and demand.

The supply of teachers changed in the early 1970s as women began pursuing a wider range of occupations, with some of the top female talent choosing fields other than teaching. The state's activities also can affect supply and demand by raising or lowering certification standards or expanding services to the disadvantaged or disabled, which leads to a greater demand for teachers. The state also can raise or lower the required teacher-pupil ratios and create or delete programs that directly affect demand for teachers.

Other factors can influence teacher attitudes toward compensation. Teachers need adequate, sound retirement plans, group life insurance, comprehensive medical programs, and disability insurance. Salary itself might not be a sufficient consideration apart from fringe benefits, although a decent salary is an important foundation.

Since the 1980–1981 school year, average teacher salaries adjusted for inflation have risen almost 19 percent after declining 14 percent between 1972–1973 and 1980–1981. Teacher salaries at both elementary and secondary levels have risen at about the same rate (19 percent and 18 percent) since 1980–1981. The buying power of teacher salaries in 1987–1988 was the highest in 30 years.[51] The average teacher salary for 1988–1989 was $26,629, according to an AFT survey of fifty states, with salaries ranging from $41,832 in Alaska to $20,525 in South Dakota.[52] Affirmative action requirements have affected salaries in that female teachers must be paid on the same scale as males and be treated equally in hiring practices.

The traditional teacher salary system is a single-salary scale based primarily on formal education and years of experience with few or no distinctions among grade levels or subject areas. In defense of salary schedules, they are an important instrument of collective bargaining in that agreements reached between a teachers' organization and a school board are negotiated not for individual teachers but for the total staff. Salary schedules, then, can be used when negotiating with school boards to improve the overall economic standing of teachers in a school district.

On the other hand, salary increments are essentially automatic each year as the teacher's experience increases. The increases have little to do with teaching quality. During the probationary period, the principal or supervisor is likely to evaluate a teacher's performance quality, but once the teacher has been granted tenure, evaluations tend to drop off and salary raises become automatic. There is no room in a salary schedule to employ differential rewards based on teaching quality. (Teachers also are moved to a higher scale if they have formal education beyond a bachelor's degree, although, as we saw earlier, the salary benefits for a master's degree are not substantial.) When raises become automatic, supervisors can tend not to enforce minimum standards for tenured teachers, which undermines the rationale for basing pay partly on seniority. No improvement in teacher performances can logically be expected if minimum standards are not enforced. Enforc-

Single-salary schedules leave no room to reward teachers for high-quality teaching.

ing standards not only benefits students but also helps the morale of successful teachers who no longer see poor teaching rewarded.

The use of salary scales, which are found in most school districts, is not a true merit system. **Merit pay** rewards teachers with higher salaries for doing the same or a similar job better than their colleagues. Though plans differ, merit pay basically rewards teachers for outstanding performance with a raise or a bonus. The advantages of merit pay are that it encourages superior teachers to remain in the field by recognizing and paying them more, stimulates teachers to improve their performance, attracts high-quality people who seek a profession that rewards competence, and encourages more public support for higher salaries. The objections to merit pay are that objective evaluative procedures and accepted criteria of teacher merit are not available, overall faculty morale can be hurt, competition rather than cooperation is promoted among teachers, politics and patronage are encouraged, and the cost of the higher salaries might be prohibitive.

The teacher compensation plan employed by the school district should be clarified in the job interview.

Another pay-for-performance plan is the career ladder. **Career ladders** offer teachers higher salaries for performing duties different from those of their colleagues. As with merit plans, career ladders use systematic, periodic assessments of faculty, but differ in that they designate separate teacher categories, such as beginning teachers, senior teachers, and master teachers. Merit plans usually have only one category. Usually a certain percentage of teachers can advance in a given year on a career ladder, with master teachers sometimes used as consultants or to train beginning teachers. Teachers might spend up to five years on a rung before being eligible to apply for the next level of the career ladder. Teachers who reach the two top rungs of the career ladder might be employed ten to twelve months a year, as opposed to nine months for teachers on lower rungs, and supervise beginning teachers, evaluate other teachers, and develop curriculums.

The career ladder can break the lockstep of traditional plans, allow better use of staff based on ability, offer greater incentives and rewards for superior teaching, and provide a wider variety of educational services. The disadvantages of career ladders include the lack of an adequate evaluation system, insufficient teacher involvement in developing career ladders, the lack of openings on the top rung, inadequate funding, and possible adverse effects on teacher morale and collegiality.

A Louis Harris poll in 1986 indicated that of 72 percent of teachers who said they were familiar with merit pay, 71 percent were opposed to such systems, and 55 percent of the principals concurred. As for career ladders, 49 percent were in favor of them and 46 percent were opposed.[53]

One of the thorniest problems is the evaluation of performance. If standardized test scores are used, some teachers might teach almost exclusively for that test. The test might not be coordinated with the curriculum, and the more difficult to measure items probably would not be included. Classroom observation can encourage bias and favoritism, and the use of limited models of teaching effectiveness. It also is costly and time-consuming.

> *Merit pay and career-ladder plans are not widely accepted among teachers and administrators.*

■ **PAUSE TO REFLECT**

Weighing Teacher Compensation Plans

- Which teacher compensation plan do you think offers the most benefits for teachers, students, and society: salary scale, merit pay, or career ladder? What are those benefits?

- What would you consider to be the advantages and disadvantages of each plan? Which would you choose for yourself? Why?

EDUCATIONAL ISSUE 12–1

Should pay-for-performance be used in teacher compensation?

Yes	No
1. It will encourage superior teachers to remain in teaching.	1. Adequate evaluation systems are not available.
2. Career ladders offer opportunities to assume new responsibilities.	2. Merit pay can promote politics and patronage.
3. Career ladders provide a wider range of educational services.	3. It can damage teacher morale and collegial relations.
4. Merit pay, especially, will eliminate incompetent teachers.	4. Inadequate funding of career ladders leads to dysfunctions and lack of upward mobility.
5. Pay-for-performance will more likely receive public support than salary schedules.	5. Most teachers prefer salary schedules.

■ Summary

- Public-school financing is a complex, controversial issue upon which few people agree. Some studies suggest that the United States spends more per pupil than other major industrial nations. Others say the United States lags badly in expenditures for kindergarten through twelfth grade.

- Three major objectives of taxation in the United States are to raise revenue to support the government, including public schools; to redistribute income and wealth; and to regulate and protect the general well-being.

- The four principal sources of public-school funds are the federal income tax, state income tax, state sales tax, and local property tax. Four criteria are used to determine taxation: wealth (property owned); income; consumption (usually taxed through sales or excise taxes); and privilege (usually taxed through license fees).

- Taxes are levied equally, whether or not a person has children in the public schools, on the ground that public schools promote the public good. Ideally, taxes should treat everyone equitably, and because individuals have different incomes and different property values, formulas are used to determine the amount of tax owed in terms of benefits received or in proportion to the use of the service supported by the tax.

- Taxes are either *progressive* (the rate increases as the base amount taxed increases) or *regressive* (the rate increases as the base amount taxed decreases).

- *Tax yields* can be *elastic* (they increase faster than income) or *inelastic* (they increase more slowly). Regressive taxes are inelastic and progressive taxes are elastic (because they collect more of a wealthy person's income than of a less wealthy person's income).

- Federal taxation provides national revenue and helps to regulate economic activity (for instance, by reducing taxes during a recession to encourage consumption). The 1986 Tax Reform Act closed many of the loopholes in the tax code that enabled the very wealthy to pay few or no taxes and repealed most of the tax brackets.

- Most states levy an individual income tax, a sales tax, and a property tax. The property tax is the primary source of funding for the public schools and can include *real property* (land, fixed buildings), *tangible personal property* (jewelry, furniture), or *intangible personal property* (stocks, bank deposits).

- In distributing funds to public schools, states originally depended on a *flat grant* per pupil, but, when that system proved insufficient, many adopted a *foundation program* to fill the gaps and overcome the inequities of the flat-grant system. Other states allocate funds depending on average daily attendance and subsidize any insufficiencies.

- Deficiencies in foundation programs have prompted the development of other plans, such as the *power-equalizing plan*, which guarantees the same assessed valuation per pupil to every district in the state, and the *full-funding plan*, which specifies per-pupil funding levels for each classification of student and imposes uniform taxes to fund the plan.

- As studies began to show that poor school districts were unable to provide adequate education and courts began to require changes in funding plans, a school financial-reform movement emerged. California, for instance, imposed limits on the funds that districts could raise through local taxes and state aid, allowing districts below average to raise their limits faster than other districts. In all, five states have adopted full state funding and eighteen states have adopted some form of power-equalizing plan.

- Three suggestions for alternative financial plans have emerged in response to dissatisfaction with public education, its financial burden, and the limited options for parents. The *family power-equalizing plan* offers several levels of education quality for parents to choose from and taxes parents accordingly. *Tuition tax credits* offer federal income tax credit for tuition expenses to parents to send their children to private or parochial schools. The *voucher plan* finances elementary and secondary education through certificates redeemed by parents for public, private, or parochial education.

- Despite expected decreases in enrollment, school costs will continue to rise because of a large influx of children who need special services, such as minority, bilingual, gifted, and disabled students. Some districts use the *weighted-pupil approach* to compensate for the higher cost of educating these students.

- As an investment, education appears to have a good rate of return. College graduates earn about one-third more than high-school graduates, although education might not be the only contributing factor. College graduates are likely to have greater native ability, stronger motivation, and more financial resources, which could positively affect their earning power.

- Studies have suggested that education also has a positive effect on economic growth, perhaps partly because education makes better decision makers in the allocation of resources, including the use of time.

- Expenditures for school personnel constitute 80 to 85 percent of the funds spent on school operations, and evidence suggests that salary is an important factor in the decision of teachers to enter— and leave—teaching, although not the only factor. Adequate retirement plans, group life insurance, comprehensive medical programs, and disability insurance also are significant.

- Traditionally, teachers are paid on a single-salary scale dependent on amount of education and years of experience. Salary scales are useful in negotiations for higher pay, because all teachers benefit from the results. But critics say such scales provide for automatic raises each year with little room for differential rewards based on teaching quality.

- The *merit-pay* system rewards teachers with higher salaries for doing the same or a similar job better than their colleagues. Advantages include encouraging superior teachers to remain in the field, stimulating teachers to improve their performance, attracting high-quality candidates to teaching, and encouraging greater public support for higher salaries. Disadvantages include a lack of objective evaluative procedures and criteria of teacher merit, prohibitive costs of the higher salaries, and the potential for hurting faculty morale, promoting competition rather than cooperation among teachers, and fostering politics and patronage.

- *Career ladders* provide teachers with higher salaries for performing duties different from those of their colleagues. Different teacher categories include beginning teachers, senior teachers, and master teachers. Systematic, periodic assessments determine whether a teacher is ready to move to the next rung on the ladder. Advantages include better use of teachers based on ability, greater incentives and rewards for superior teaching, and the ability to provide a wider variety of educational services. Disadvantages include the lack of an adequate evaluation system, insufficient teacher involvement in developing career ladders, a lack of openings on the top rungs, inadequate funding, and the possibility of low teacher morale and collegiality.

- One of the biggest problems in pay-for-performance plans is the lack of adequate means of evaluating performance. If standardized tests are used, teachers might teach exclusively for the test; if subjective classroom observation is used, bias and favoritism might enter into the results.

■ Key Terms

career ladders	power-equalizing plan
elastic	progressive tax
family power-equalizing plan	real property
flat grant	regressive tax
foundation program	tangible personal property
full-funding plan	tax yield
inelastic	tuition tax credits
intangible personal property	voucher plan
merit pay	weighted-pupil approach

■ Discussion Questions

1. What are the desirable features to look for in any tax used for public-school revenues?

2. Compare the four different sources of public-school funds in terms of their desirable and undesirable features and determine the most preferable sources.

3. What type of state plan would best overcome inequities among school districts?

4. Should any of the three financial alternatives be tried on a more widespread basis? Why?

5. If a student were trying to maximize his or her rate of return through formal education, what advice would you offer?

■ Learning Activities

1. Organize a classroom debate on the resolution: "American education has many serious problems, but greater funding will not solve them."

2. Write a paper on public-school funding in your home state by gathering information on the sources of funding (local, state, and federal) and the state plan used. Then evaluate the adequacy of funding by applying the criteria presented in this chapter.

3. Develop and present to the class an argument on the topic, "The voucher should/should not be more widely used to allow greater parental choice."

4. Research the type of teacher compensation plan in your local school district and interview teachers and administrators about their opinions of the plan.

Suggested Readings

Benson, Charles S., *The Economics of Public Education*, 3rd ed. Boston: Houghton Mifflin, 1978.

A basic text that discusses education as an investment, sources of revenue, and problems in the allocation of educational resources.

Calhoun, Frederick S., and Nancy J. Protheroe, *Merit Pay Plans for Teachers: Status and Descriptions*. Arlington, VA: Educational Research Service, 1983.

A review of different programs.

Coons, John E., William H. Clune III, and Stephen D. Sugarman, *Private Wealth and Public Education*. Cambridge, MA: Harvard University Press, 1970.

An important study that spearheaded the financial-reform movement.

Guthrie, James W., Walter I. Garms, and Lawrence C. Pierce, *School Finance and Education Policy*, 2nd ed. Englewood Cliffs, NJ: Prentice-Hall, 1988.

Uses the principles of equality, efficiency, and liberty in analyzing finance, school productivity, and educational reform.

Johns, Roe L., Edgar L. Morphet, and Kern Alexander, *The Economics and Financing of Education*, 4th ed. Englewood Cliffs, NJ: Prentice-Hall, 1983.

A basic text that deals with education as an investment and finance at local, state, and federal levels.

Madus, George F., Peter W. Airasian, and Thomas Kellagan, *School Effectiveness: A Reassessment of the Evidence*. New York: McGraw-Hill, 1980.

This book describes, evaluates, and integrates studies of school effectiveness in readable form.

Notes

1. William Raspberry, "Lavish Funds for Education Is Fiction," *American Statesman* (January 23, 1990): A11.

2. "How America Is Shortchanging Its Schoolchildren," *Business Week* (January 20, 1990): 22.

3. Ibid.; and Julie A. Miller, "Study Puts U.S. Near Bottom on School Spending," *Education Week* (January 24, 1990): 1,22.

4. Roe L. Johns, Edgar L. Morphet, and Kern Alexander, *The Economics and Financing of Education*, 4th ed. (Englewood Cliffs, NJ: Prentice-Hall, 1983): 83.

5. Walter I. Garms, James W. Guthrie, and Lawrence C. Pierce, *School Finance: The Economics and Politics of Public Education* (Englewood Cliffs, NJ: Prentice-Hall, 1978), 119.

6. Philip E. Taylor, *The Economics of Public Finance* (New York: Macmillan, 1961), 292.

7. Louis Eisenstein, *The Ideologies of Taxation* (New York: Ronald Press, 1961); and Philip M. Stern, *The Great Treasury Raid* (New York: Random House, 1964).

8. Ferdinand Lundberg, *The Rich and the Super Rich* (New York: Bantam, 1969), 389.

9. Charles S. Benson, *The Economics of Public Education*, 2nd ed. (New York: Houghton Mifflin, 1968), 102.

10. Michael Savage, *Good News Bad News: The Concise Tax Guide* (New York: Workman Publishing, 1986).

11. *The 1990 Information Please Almanac* (Boston: Houghton Mifflin, 1990), 83.

12. James A. Maxwell and Richard Aronson, *Financing State and Local Governments*, 3rd ed. (Washington, DC: Brookings Institution, 1977), 95.

13. *The 1990 Information Please Almanac*, 83.

14. A summary of this controversy can be found in Joseph A. Peckman and Benjamin A. Ockner, *Who Bears the Tax Burden?* (Washington, DC: Brookings Institution, 1974), 25–43.

15. F. McDonald and A. Pascal, *Organized Teachers in American Schools* (Santa Monica, CA: Rand Corporation, 1979); S. M. Barro and S. J. Carroll, *Budget Allocation by School Districts: An Analysis of Spending for Teachers and Other Resources* (Santa Monica, CA: Rand Corporation, 1975).

16. R. W. Eberts and L. C. Pierce, *The Effects of Collective Bargaining in Public Schools* (Eugene, OR: University of Oregon, Center for Educational Policy and Management, 1980).

17. C. R. Perry, "Teacher Bargaining: The Experience in Nine Systems," *Industrial and Labor Relations Review* 33 (1979): 3–17.

18. M. Derber and M. Wagner, "Public Sector Bargaining and Budget-Making Under Fiscal Adversity," *Industrial and Labor Relations Review* 33 (1979): 18–23.

19. D. G. Gallagher, "Teacher Negotiations, School District Expenditures, and Taxation Levels," *Educational Administration Quarterly* 15 (1979): 67–82.

20. M. W. Kirst, "What Happens at the Local Level After School Financial Reform?" *Policy Analysis* 3 (1977): 301–24.

21. John E. Coons, William H. Clune III, and Stephen D. Sugarman, *Private Wealth and Public Education* (Cambridge, MA: Harvard University Press, 1970).

22. Serrano v. Priest 96 Cal. Rptr. 601, 487 p. 2d 1241 (1971).

23. Robinson v. Cahill 62 NJ 473, 303 A. 2d 273 (1973).

24. San Antonio Independent School District v. Rodriguez 411 U.S. 1 (1973).

25. James W. Guthrie, "Educational Finance: The Lower Schools." In *Handbook of Research on Educational Administration*, ed. Norman J. Boyan (New York: Longman, 1988), 380.

26. Coons, Clune, and Sugarman, *Private Wealth and Public Education*, 200–42.

27. Mueller v. Allen, 463 U.S. 388 (1983).

28. For some of these early plans, see Virgil C. Blum, *Freedom of Choice in Education* (New York: Macmillan, 1958); and Milton Friedman, "The Roles of Government in Education," in *Economics and the Public Interest*, ed. Robert A. Solo (New Brunswick, NJ: Rutgers University Press, 1955).

29. Christopher Jencks et al., *Education Vouchers: A Preliminary Report on Financing Education by Payment to Parents* (Cambridge, MA: Center for Study of Public Policy, 1970).

30. Jim Warren, "Alum Creek Voucher Project," *Educational Researcher* 5 (1976): 13–15.

31. See George R. LaNoue, "Vouchers: The End of Public Education?" *Teachers College Record* 73 (1971): 304–19.

32. Gary S. Becker, *Human Capital* (New York: Columbia University Press, 1964).

33. W. Lee Hansen, "Total and Private Rates of Return to Investment in Schooling," *Journal of Political Economy* 71 (1963): 128–41.

34. Theodore W. Schultz, "Education and Economic Growth," in *Social Forces Influencing Education* (Chicago: National Society for the Study of Education, 1961), 46–88.

35. Edward F. Denison, "Appendix to Denison's Reply," *The Residual Factor and Economic Growth* (Paris: Organization for Economic Cooperation and Development, 1964), 86–100.

36. Ivar Berg, *Education and Jobs: The Great Training Robbery* (Boston: Beacon Press, 1971).

37. Eli Ginzberg claims in the book's foreword that the author leaves several important questions unanswered.

38. Charles S. Benson, "Economics of Education: The U.S. Experience," in *Handbook of Research on Educational Administration*, ed. Norman J. Boyan, 360–61.

39. W. W. McMahon and A. P. Wagner, "The Monetary Returns to Education as Partial Social Efficiency Criteria," in *Financing Education: Overcoming Inefficiency and Inequity*, eds. W. W. McMahon and T. G. Geske (Urbana: University of Illinois Press, 1982): 150–87.

40. Robert M. Solow, "Technical Changes and the Aggregate Production Function," *Review of Economics and Statistics* (August 1957): 312–20.

41. Theodore W. Schultz, "Capital Formation by Education," *Journal of Political Economy* 68 (1960): 571–83.

42. Edward F. Denison, *The Sources of Economic Growth in the United States and the Alternatives Before Us*, Supplementary Paper no. 13 (New York: Committee for Economic Development, 1962), 67–79.

43. Benson, "Economics of Education: The U.S. Experience."

44. Demitri T. Koulourianos, *Educational Planning for Economic Growth* (Berkeley: Center for Research in Management Science, University of California, 1967), 39.

45. F. Welch, "Education in Production," *Journal of Political Economy* 78 (1970): 35–59.

46. Johns, Morphet, and Alexander, *The Economics and Financing of Education*: 55.

47. Ibid.: 294.

48. G. A. Zarkin, *The Importance of Economic Incentives in the Recruitment of Teachers*. Final report to the National Institute of Education (NIE-G-83-0068) (Durham, NC: Duke University, 1985).

49. G. A. Zarkin, "Occupational Choice: An Application to the Market for Public School Teachers," *Quarterly Journal of Economics* 100 (1985): 400–46.

50. W. J. Baugh and J. A. Stone, "Mobility and Wage Equilibrium in the Educator Labor Market," *Economics of Education Review* 2 (1982): 253–74.

51. National Center for Education Statistics, *The Condition of Education 1989: Elementary and Secondary Education*, vol. I (Washington, DC: U.S. Government Printing Office, 1989).

52. "Teachers' Rising Pay Barely Keeping Up With Inflation," *American Statesman* (June 22, 1989): A8.

53. J. M. Rich, ed., *Innovations in Education: Reformers and Their Critics*, 5th ed. (Boston: Allyn and Bacon, 1988), 191.

CHAPTER 13

LEGAL INFLUENCES ▪

A LOOK AHEAD

The purpose of this chapter is to examine the effect of significant legal decisions on American public education. You will learn about:

- The role of laws in society and how those laws function
- The rights of students to enjoy due process of law
- Substantive rights as they pertain to compulsory attendance, freedom of expression, appearance, and privacy rights
- The responsibility of educators in the realm of liability and negligence
- The relationship of church and state in education
- The state's right to regulate the curriculum
- The legal foundation of school desegregation

In recent years the courts have had a significant role in defining and protecting student rights, clarifying and determining the parameters of educators' responsibilities, and assuring greater equality of opportunity. But what is the basis of the legal system, its functions, and its operations in society? How does education fit into the legal system? Where do state rights end and individual rights begin? In this chapter we will look at the role of law in society in general and examine several court challenges in an effort to understand how the law has affected the shape of education.

491

■ LAW AND SOCIETY

A **law** is a prescribed rule of conduct or action formally recognized as binding by a controlling authority. It takes the form of rules and norms. A **legal system** is a network established for enforcing the laws. Laws have coercive power and are an exercise of force by duly constituted authorities through the use of sanctions. According to H. L. A. Hart, a legal system consists of primary and secondary rules.[1] **Primary rules** impose duties and secondary rules confer powers. Primary rules are commonly equated with laws, such as those regulating property and persons. **Secondary rules** are rules *about* rules: they provide procedures for creating, modifying, and repealing primary rules.

Rules, as used in legal reasoning, depend upon the facts of a particular case for their meaning. If Roe borrows fifty dollars from Dokes, is there an applicable rule to show that Dokes has a right to demand repayment of the debt? The case is the basis of legal reasoning; therefore, law may be thought of as the accumulation of cases. Rules are derived from particular cases and, as cases pertaining to certain types of conflicts over rights accumulate, the rules derived from earlier cases are enlarged upon. The full scope of a rule cannot be given at any one time, because a rule's scope is modified, enlarged, or restricted with additional cases. In the Roe-Dokes case the applicable rule would depend on whether Roe is solvent and negligent in repaying the debt, is bankrupt, or had extorted rather than borrowed the funds. A legal decision represents what certain judges consider right and just at a given time and place under particular circumstances. In another court (as cases appealed to higher courts sometimes indicate) the decision might be different. Rules do not "decide" conflicts over rights and obligations, but they are useful in the process of legal decision making. Their relevance and application, however, are not always self-evident; because rules are derived from earlier cases that might have divergent claims, their relation to a case under consideration must be re-evaluated.

The Function of Laws in Society

Is the law based on morality? One school of thought holds that as societies evolved, mores were developed to regulate them and, as societies became more complex, legal systems arose that embodied the mores. Laws enabled individuals to gain justice without taking matters into their own hands and attacking their enemies, and enabled nations to settle disputes without resorting to war. But if law is based on morality, how did legal systems permit slavery, apartheid, the burning of heretics at the stake, the torture of political prisoners, and genocide in concentration camps?

Legal science, according to Hans Kelsen, is a descriptive science and questions about values cannot be scientific.[2] He therefore posits a sharp separation between "is" and "ought" questions and believes that questions of justice rest upon intuitions rather than rationality. Not all jurists and legal philosophers accept this approach, known as "positivism." Jurist Lon Fuller criticized positivism[3] and emphasized the purposive element in the law: only rules that serve human purposes of furthering certain basic values can be counted as law. The overlap between law and morality can be seen by considering the conditions that a legal system must fulfill to regulate social life. Fuller believes that the conditions necessary for such regulation are attributes of the concept of justice; therefore law is necessarily connected with minimal notions of justice.

Two different perspectives—functionalism and conflict theory—offer explanations as to how law functions in society. **Functionalism** perceives the legal system as having vital societal functions. The legal system exercises social control by prescribing proper behavior and sanctioning those who disobey. Sanctions can include fines, civil penalties, arrest, and imprisonment. The legal system is responsible, first, for determining deviant behavior and the grounds for the penal code. It executes social control through the use of police, courts, and penal systems. Second, the legal system settles disputes in situations such as failed marriages, contested wills, and labor and management relations. A third function is innovation, as when laws are passed to protect the environment or to promote better labeling of foods. Finally, the legal system determines who is to receive benefits and who is to lose them. Those who comply with the system are considered good citizens and those who do not, when apprehended, are punished and, occasionally, deprived of some services and rights (incarceration). Thus, according to functionalists, law promotes order and stability and provides justice impartially.

> One function of a legal system is to exercise social control.

The **conflict theory,** however, questions for whom the legal system functions. When certain groups continually lose out in the distribution of rewards and punishments, the system is not functional for them. The law does not so much control conflicting interests as it expresses certain interests. The law was created by certain individuals and groups to protect their interests and to shape policy to reinforce those interests. Law can be used by one social class to protect its interests from claims by another social class, as in legislating tax regulations that shelter the holdings of the upper class. Certain groups (minority groups, the poor, the mentally ill) fare worse under the law because they tend to be harassed more by the police and receive less police

> As is the case with socialization, one view of the legal system is that it promotes the interests of the dominant class.

protection, less impartial treatment from judges and juries, and stiffer prison sentences. Conflict theorists propose that the legal system be made more just and impartial and that the larger society undergo large-scale reform to empower people to deal more effectively with their affairs.

■ DUE PROCESS

Students' rights in the educational system are now roughly parallel to a citizens' legal rights in a democratic society.

In the seventies student rights gained more recognition in the courts, and some school disciplinary practices were restricted, especially in areas involving due process. Schools had been allowed to develop rules and determine and administer punishment based on decisions by school officials. But courts have ruled that due process must be observed in cases of serious offense. The form that due process would take would depend upon the seriousness of the offense.

The rights to due process are embodied in the Fourteenth Amendment, which guarantees that no state shall "deprive any person of life, liberty, or property without due process of law." These safeguards apply not only to judicial proceedings but also to school boards. **Procedural due process** prohibits states from depriving anyone of "life, liberty, or property" without following fair procedures. **Substantive due process** offers protection against laws or rules that are overly vague, arbitrary, capricious, or unreasonable.

In Columbus, Ohio, several students were suspended from school during the 1970–1971 academic year without a hearing.[4] The United States Supreme Court declared in *Goss v. Lopez* (1975) that, though the Constitution does not require states to establish schools, once schools are established, students have a "property" right in them that may not be withdrawn without "fundamentally fair procedures." Schools must respect a student's constitutional right to due process in infractions that might lead to suspension or expulsion from school. The Court declared that students should receive some kind of notice and hearing, although the type of notice and hearing would depend on the need to protect the student without placing an unreasonable burden on school objectives. The disciplined student facing suspension should be advised of the charge and given an opportunity to respond. Only students whose presence poses a continuing danger to persons or property or who are disrupting the academic process can be removed without a hearing. But even in these cases, hearings are required as soon as practicable.[5]

Serious cases require written notice of the charges, the time and place of the hearing, and a description of procedures to be followed at the hearing. Students should have the names of the witnesses who will testify, a list of the evidence to be used against them, and the substance of the witnesses' testimony. Students also should have the right to cross-examine witnesses and to present evidence and witnesses in their own behalf. A record of the proceedings should be available, and the right of appeal should be clearly stated.

The Court has found no right to due process for students subjected to corporal punishment[6] or discharged for academic failure.[7] The Court held that academic judgments of educators should not be subjected to outside interference unless fraud or bad faith on the part of the school authorities could be proven.

Generally an expulsion cannot exceed the end of the academic year, unless it takes place near the end of the term. Teachers and administrators can initiate expulsion proceedings, but only the school board can expel a student. Suspensions, which are less severe than expulsions, include the short-term denial of school attendance or the denial of participation in courses and activities (in-school suspension). Courts have resisted attempts to spell out due-process requirements for short-term suspension, arguing that such formalization might weaken it as a disciplinary tool and diminish its effectiveness in the teaching process.

■ **PAUSE TO REFLECT**
Due Process for Students

- Do you think students should have a right to due process in disciplinary situations? Or should the school have the same arbitrary rights as do parents?

- How should a student accused of an infraction be treated? For instance, if a student were suspected of spray-painting graffiti on the walls, what procedures should school officials follow?

- Do you think students should be accorded due process before being expelled for academic failure? Why?

SUBSTANTIVE RIGHTS ■

Compulsory Attendance

All fifty states have compulsory school attendance laws with penalties for noncompliance. The state has the authority to enact reasonable laws for protecting its citizens; and since an enlightened citizenry is considered necessary for the well-being of the state, the state can reg-

Compulsory attendance laws are rooted in the notion that education is necessary for the public good.

ulate education. Parents can be prosecuted for failing to ensure that their children abide by compulsory attendance laws. In some cases, excessively truant children can be made wards of the court to be supervised by probation officers.

In 1922 Oregon's nonpublic schools were threatened when the state required every child between the ages of eight and sixteen to attend public schools. Three years later the United States Supreme Court, in *Pierce v. Society of Sisters* (1925), invalidated the statute on the grounds that it would destroy the property of private schools without the due process of law. The Court also declared that the Oregon statute interfered "with the liberty of parents and guardians to direct the upbringing of children under their control. . . ." The state could require all children to be educated and could supervise and inspect all schools, but parents were free to choose whether they preferred public or private education for their children.[8] Today each state has its own laws governing nonpublic schools.

Many states also provide for and regulate home education. The home-education movement has spread since the 1970s and now includes as many as 800,000 children. More than half of the states and the District of Columbia allow home education; four states require certified tutors in the home, and five states require students to be tested for mastery of basic skills.[9] States differ as to whether the state or parents have the burden of proving that home instruction is equivalent to public-school offerings. It would seem to be in the state's interest to develop enlightened citizens who will impose standards on the education of children at home.

Freedom of Expression

Teachers and students have the right to distribute handbills and petitions on school property. Students also have the right to wear buttons, insignias bearing slogans, and armbands. In Des Moines during the late 1960s, several students were expelled for wearing black armbands as a symbol of mourning for those on both sides who died in the Vietnam War. The students were expelled because their actions were

Schools may not deny the right to nondisruptive speech.

thought to be a disruptive influence. The United States Supreme Court held in *Tinker v. Des Moines Independent Community School District* (1969) that the wearing of armbands is "symbolic speech," and that the expulsion of the students was an abridgment of speech.[10]

A school policy cannot favor a particular viewpoint or bar the expression of opposing views. For example, students in Chicago successfully challenged the denial of access to antiwar activists after the board of education permitted military recruiters to visit schools.[11] The federal district court held that the school had denied free speech and equal protection rights. In another case a federal district court ruled that a homosexual student had a right to take another male to the senior prom, as the student's choice was an ideological message that constituted protected speech.[12] Students, moreover, cannot be disciplined for nondisruptive activities that are critical of school personnel or policies.

School authorities, however, can place certain restrictions on student activities, especially activities that are likely to disrupt the educational process. Student rallies can be confined to reasonably assigned times and places, and speech activity mixed with disruptive conduct can be punished.[13] Though nondisruptive speech is protected, speech that incites disruptive action, such as a call for a student strike or the takeover of the school building, is not protected by the First Amendment.[14]

> Schools retain the right to prohibit disruptive speech or activities.

The Supreme Court also has supported the authority of public-school personnel to restrict students' vulgar, lewd expression. Speech protected for adults under the First Amendment is not necessarily protected for children, as the sensibilities of fellow students must be considered. The Court noted that the remarks at issue were not protected political expression because the speech did not convey a political message. School authorities may protect students from sexually explicit, indecent, or lewd speech on grounds of fundamental values of civility.[15]

In terms of student publications, the Court has ruled that a school, as publisher of a student newspaper or producer of a school play, has a right to disassociate itself from speech that would interfere with school functions or impinge on the rights of other students, as well as speech that is poorly written, vulgar, or profane.[16] A student publication, the Court held, is not a public forum, but a supervised learning experience for journalism students as a part of a curriculum.

> School newspapers are not entitled to the same degree of freedom of speech as is the popular press.

Student Appearance

The United States Supreme Court has declined to address the issue of student appearance, but some federal Circuit Courts of Appeals have upheld the authority of public schools to regulate student hairstyles; other appellate courts have declared that hairstyle regulations violate students' constitutional rights. However, schools may regulate student hairstyles in special circumstances, such as the hairstyles of football players during football season. Attempts to overturn hair regulations on grounds of sex discrimination have been unsuccessful, except in Alaska, where the regulation was considered a violation of student rights under its constitution, and in Oregon and Ohio where such regulation was not authorized by state school codes.[17]

Court rulings about student appearance often reflect prevailing community standards.

Though a minority of cases reject students' constitutional rights in their choice of dress, most cases recognize such a right as either a general liberty or a specific right of expression. School regulations can be overturned if they do not recognize this right, which can be the case if regulations are overly vague, too broad, or unclear in their connection to a disruptive influence.[18] Cases from different states vary as to the length of girls' skirts and whether girls should be permitted to wear jeans to school. These variations might reflect divergent community mores rather than any legal conflict.

Privacy Rights

Search and Seizure. The surveillance activities of school officials have increased as drugs and other contraband have become more prevalent in the schools. Conflict arises between student claims of immunity from search without a warrant (Fourth Amendment) and the interest to protect the school environment. Lower courts have been divided over the application of the Fourth Amendment to the public schools, but they usually have upheld warrantless searches by school officials if there is reasonable suspicion that such searches will uncover a violation of law or school disciplinary rules.[19]

A student's right to privacy must be balanced against possible danger to the school or community.

In 1985 the United States Supreme Court held, in *New Jersey v. T.L.O.*, that the Fourth Amendment applies to school officials.[20] The Court decided that requiring a teacher to obtain a warrant to search a child believed to have violated school rules interferes with informal disciplinary procedures; consequently, the legality of a search depends upon its reasonableness under the circumstances.

Courts usually have held that lockers are school property and that students do not retain exclusive possession of their lockers. School officials are allowed to search lockers if there is reasonable evidence that they will uncover contraband disruptive to the educative process. But a search warrant is required if the purpose is to uncover criminal evidence.

In personal searches there must be reasonable cause to search and the search itself must be reasonable. Whether a strip search can be justified on the basis of reasonable suspicion is debatable. The Ninth Court of Appeals found a "pat-down" search and a subsequent strip search to be unlawful after a bus driver saw a student exchange money for an unidentified object.[21] The court, however, implied that a more dangerous situation, such as the probability of drug possession, might warrant such intrusions. Nonetheless, it would appear that except under emergency circumstances, few situations would justify such actions.

Most courts have held that because a reasonable expectation of privacy does not extend to the air surrounding objects, the use of dogs

Dogs may be legally used to search students' lockers and cars.

sniffing objects is not a search. The Fourth Amendment, therefore, does not apply to canine sniffing of student lockers and cars in public view. But the sniffing of individual students by dogs does intrude on an individual's privacy and constitutes a search.[22] Though the court did not prohibit such searches, it held that the intrusiveness of the search must be weighed against the school's need to search. When police are involved in school searches, a higher standard involving probable cause must be applied. Police involvement has the potential for violating students' Fourth Amendment protection.

Issues surrounding drug testing were pinpointed in a New Jersey case, in which, as part of a comprehensive medical examination, the school board had required students to submit to a urine test to detect illegal drugs.[23] School officials argued that drug abuse is an illness and that the test was a medical procedure; therefore, the Fourth Amendment did not apply. The court held that the test was unreasonable because all students were required to be tested whether or not they were suspected of drug use, and that suspending, without due process, those students who refused to take the test was unconstitutional.

Student Records and Other Privacy Issues. Indiscriminate and uncontrolled use of information about individuals restricts their freedom by endangering their educational, vocational, or social opportunities and, in turn, their personal development. The release of defamatory statements or inaccurate or obsolete information restricts an individual's life chances. Whenever possible each individual should grant consent for the release of personal information; if a student is too immature or inexperienced to grant consent, paternalism is warranted.

Before 1974 student records in some places were open to government inspectors, employers, and non-school personnel, but not to parents. In that year Congress passed the Family Educational Rights and Privacy Act (FERPA), which required school districts to develop procedures for parents to inspect student records and to inform parents of their rights under the act. To protect the confidentiality of student records, parental permission is required before the records can be shared with outsiders. The act also establishes procedures by which parents can challenge questionable information in the records.

But FERPA contains no procedure for monitoring implementation or assuring compliance by local school districts. Although federal funds can be cut off if compliance cannot be obtained, the Department of Education is not obligated to monitor abuses and states are not required to report compliance. On the other hand, FERPA does not prevent states from adopting more vigorous rules. FERPA also does not affect the release of statistical, non-personal data from student records. The potential for conflict between FERPA and federal or state Freedom of Information Acts has not been tested in the courts.

To date, the confidentiality of student records depends on the schools' voluntary compliance.

Students do have other rights in terms of their educational records. In *Goss v. Lopez,* for example, students who were found to have been suspended without due process were allowed to have the expulsion removed from their records. Furthermore, to reduce the danger of abusing cumulative records, the records should pertain only to educational decision making and exclude personal matters about sexual development, friendships, personal characteristics, and home stability.

Students also have the right to be alone or to interact quietly with another away from the hubbub of daily school activities. One can be constantly in contact with others only so long before symptoms of stress and other maladies develop. S. D. Webb found in a study conducted in urban centers in New Zealand that a perceived lack of privacy is associated with psychosomatic stress.[24] Students vary in their perceived lack of privacy and, consequently, the "glass bowl" atmosphere of many schools has different effects. Nevertheless, schools need to provide spaces where students can take a break from the busy routine.

When determining whether to monitor students without their knowledge, school administrators should decide whether definitive evidence exists that students cannot act responsibly in certain types of situations. In some schools, classroom activities are under surveillance by principals who leave the public address system turned on. More frequently students are watched not only in hallways, lunchrooms, and school grounds but also in rest rooms and athletic facilities. The operative principle probably should be that students cannot grow in judgment unless given opportunities to exercise judgment in everyday decisions. Safeguarding privacy protects the student's freedom and is likely to lead to a more clearly defined self-concept, greater respect for other people, and a more nurturing environment for educational growth.

LIABILITY AND NEGLIGENCE ■

Can teachers be held responsible for student injuries? Can they be held negligent when students fail to achieve at an acceptable level? Tort law offers remedies to individuals for harm caused by the unreasonable conduct of others. A **tort** is a wrongful act that causes damage, loss, or injury to another. A tort consists of a legal duty that the defendant has toward the plaintiff, the breach of that duty, and the causal relationship between the defendant's conduct and the damage to the plaintiff. For instance, if an industrial arts teacher (the defendant) did not instruct students (plaintiffs) in the proper use of hazardous equipment but permitted them to use it anyway and without supervision, the teacher could be charged with negligence.

Tort action can be classified into three types: negligence, intentional torts, and strict liability. **Negligence** is a failure to exercise a degree of care that a reasonable teacher would exercise under the same circumstance. The term refers to the standard established by law to protect people from unreasonable risks of harm. **Intentional torts** are committed with the desire to inflict harm, such as assault, battery, and false imprisonment. **Strict liability** refers to the creation of an unusual hazard, such as storing dynamite that results in an injury; the plaintiff does not need to establish that the injury was knowingly or negligently caused. Some school injuries stem from negligence, some occasionally from intentional torts, but rarely from strict liability.

Schools are generally permitted to use corporal punishment as long as it is not excessive.

Tort law permits teachers and administrators to use reasonable corporal punishment and to use necessary force in self-defense without being accused of committing an intentional tort. School boards usually are authorized to establish regulations for administering corporal punishment. Only a few courts have allowed corporal punishment for instructional purposes (as in coaching sports and related physical education programs).[25] In any case, such punishment must be reasonable in its purpose, the method used, and the amount of force employed. The United States Supreme Court ruled that corporal punishment does not constitute "cruel and unusual punishment" under the Eighth Amendment, nor does it violate the due process guarantees under the Fourteenth Amendment.[26] If students are excessively punished, remedies are available, such as lawsuits for assault and battery.

Courts generally have been reluctant to interfere with a school's right to discipline students and have sanctioned the use of reasonable force. Some courts have dismissed assault-and-battery charges against teachers who were found to have used reasonable force.[27] Battery has been upheld in cases where the teacher used excessive force, as in the case where a student suffered a fractured clavicle when the teacher threw the student into a movable chalkboard.[28] School personnel also can bring assault-and-battery suits against students, and in Oregon parents can be held financially responsible for damages.

Because educators have a duty to care for students in their charge, care that falls below an acceptable standard can constitute negligence. An acceptable standard would be what a reasonably prudent teacher would exercise. School personnel should maintain equipment and facilities and warn students of any known dangers. When a student is injured, the teacher is expected to provide assistance commensurate with his or her training. Improperly administered first aid can result in liability.[29] The degree of care involved should be determined by the age of the students, the environment, and the instructional activity. In places where risk is greater—gymnasiums, laboratory classes, industrial arts—a higher level of care is required. Even if a teacher is negligent, legal action cannot be sustained unless physical or mental injury occurs and a causal connection can be established between the teacher's action and the student's injury.

Another factor in determining liability is whether the circumstances causing the injury were foreseeable and could be guarded against by prudent judgment. Teachers are expected to provide adequate and appropriate instruction before letting a student participate in a risky activity.

For example, a physical education teacher was found negligent for permitting two students to engage in boxing without proper training when, as a result, one of the students was fatally injured.[30]

School personnel and school districts charged with negligence do have some defenses: assumption of risk (the student was aware of and accepted the risks involved in the activity); contributory negligence (the student contributed to his or her own injury); and comparative negligence (several parties held varying degrees of risk for the injury).

Educational Malpractice

Because all but one state have constitutional provisions for education and all have mandated school attendance, do the states and, by delegation, the local school boards have a responsibility to guarantee a minimum level of student achievement? Some students who did not reach a minimum level of achievement have filed lawsuits charging educational malpractice. Two forms of educational malpractice should be distinguished: (1) failure of a school to enable a student to attain satisfactory levels of achievement in basic courses, with consequent injury to the student's development; (2) failure of school authorities to exercise due care in the testing, evaluation, and placement of any student, with similar consequences.

In the first educational malpractice suit, the complaint combined three elements: charges of misdiagnosis, negligence in the operation of the educational program, and fraudulent representation.[31] Peter W. claimed that the school district was negligent in teaching, promoting, and graduating him from high school at a fifth-grade reading level. He also asserted that his performance was misrepresented to his parents, who were unaware of his condition until he was tested by a private agency.

Both the trial court and the appeals court dismissed the charges against the school district. The appellate court stated, "Classroom methodology affords no readily acceptable standards of care or cause of injury. The science of pedagogy is fraught with different and conflicting theories of how and what should be taught." Second, how can judges determine that the teacher's conduct was responsible for the student's injury when literacy is affected by factors outside the teaching process? These influences include the family, the media, and neurological, emotional, cultural, and environmental factors. Third, because schools have been charged with responsibility for many of society's needs, to hold schools liable would expose them to countless tort claims of dissatisfied students and parents.

While the courts made some valid observations in the case, their opinion can be criticized on several grounds. Courts do make judgments on standards of care when reviewing the dismissal of teachers for unprofessional conduct or incompetence. Additionally, schools should not be immune to liability because of the probability that factors outside of school contribute to student injury.[32] Finally, the courts might have overestimated the chance for frivolous or malicious suits.

In *Donahue v. Copiague Union Free Schools* (1979) the New York Court of Appeals dismissed a suit by a high-school graduate who claimed he was unable to complete job applications and cope with everyday life problems.[33] He maintained that the school had negligently failed in that it did not evaluate his mental ability, hire proper teachers, teach him adequately, use accepted professional methods, or advise his parents of his difficulties.

The court concluded that the school could not be held accountable for all students, with their varying abilities to learn, attaining a specified reading level upon high-school graduation. The courts, it maintained, are inappropriate forums for evaluating the conflicting theories of how best to educate. Moreover, even if it were possible to decide the best way to teach an individual, tension exists between satisfying the needs of individuals and those of the student body as a whole; the school is in the best position to determine how best to use scarce resources. Finally, failure to learn in this case did not indicate failure to teach, as there was no evidence that the graduate's classmates were illiterate; illiteracy, the court held, must have resulted from other causes.

Hoffman v. Board of Education (1979) was a case based on the second type of educational malpractice—misclassification. The New York Court of Appeals overturned a state appellate court that had awarded $500,000 for negligently diagnosing the needs of a public-school student and erroneously maintaining him in a program for the mentally retarded.[34] Hoffman scored one point below the required score for placement in a regular class, and he was placed in a class for the mentally retarded. His I.Q. was never re-evaluated during twelve years of public school, and the negligence claim rested on the psychologist's report that recommended that the student be retested within two years. Upon high-school graduation he was required by Social Security to take an intelligence test to continue receiving payments after his eighteenth birthday. He scored more than 100 on the test, and became ineligible to continue in the occupational training program for the retarded. The lower court distinguished this case from previous ones by noting acts of negligence (ignoring the psychologist's report) that had harmed the student. The New York Court of Appeals, however, reversed the lower court, ruling that instructional negligence claims should be handled within the administrative appeals network of the state educational system. If parents believe that a student has been misclassified, it is their responsibility to appeal the misclassification to the state commissioner of education.

In *B.M. v. State* (1982), however, the court remanded for trial a case of a child who had been misclassified as mentally retarded.[35] The child had been placed in a resource room for the educable mentally retarded for 40 percent of the school day without her foster parents' knowledge. In *Snow v. State of New York* (1984) a deaf child who was given an intelligence test inappropriate for deaf children was misdiagnosed as mentally retarded and placed in a class for the retarded.[36] The court affirmed the lower court's ruling that it was medical, not educational, malpractice and upheld the award of $1.5 million. A distinction was made between medical and educational malpractice claims on the basis of the child's age upon entry (Donald Snow was three years old when he was first misdiagnosed), the nature of the institution (he was in a state institution), and the kind of care administered (patients received medical and psychological treatment).

Cases of misclassification (*Hoffman* and *B.M. v. State*) rather than achievement failure (Peter W.) are more likely to be treated sympathetically by courts. In cases where harm is significant and avoidable, causes can be traced to the action or inaction of school officials, standards for care are readily ascertainable, and judicial involvement is held to a minimum, it is likely that courts will increasingly rule in favor of plaintiffs.

> School districts are more likely to be held liable for misclassifying a child than for a student's failure to achieve.

Though most states do not recognize a legal right to an education, some states recognize the need for educational adequacy (which has a direct bearing on student achievement). The notion of an adequate education was highlighted in the 1970s and 1980s by activities of state courts and state legislatures. The New Jersey legislature enacted a law to provide all children within the state "the educational opportunity which will prepare them to function politically, economically and sociably in a democratic society."[37] It specified major provisions of an adequate education. The state of Washington Supreme Court declared that students in every school district have the right to an adequately funded basic education program.[38]

Other state courts also have ruled on adequacy, emphasizing finance, programs, or a combination. These states have declared that educational adequacy is a responsibility of the state and local school districts, even though consensus is lacking on what is needed to achieve adequacy. Competency testing might be one way to achieve educational adequacy. Whether success on competency tests signifies educational adequacy is debatable, but it does indicate that educators are attempting to assure the public that students are acquiring basic academic skills. The question is whether the courts will construe com-

> The move toward competency testing may affect the schools' legal liability in cases of failure to achieve.

Competency testing has appreciably increased in many states since the 1980s.

petency testing as a guarantee of a minimal level of educational achievement or as a mark of reasonable, best-effort teaching. If the courts see it as a guarantee, then more suits over failure of student achievement are likely to succeed.

What can educators do to reduce the number of educational malpractice suits? First, they can avoid stating lofty educational goals and making claims not likely to be fulfilled with available resources and personnel. Next, diagnostic and placement tests can be developed that are appropriate to the learner and re-administered periodically. Whenever needed, suitable remedial action can be taken. Third, competency tests can allow educators to see that content is aligned more directly with the curriculum and used more for diagnosis rather than screening purposes. Next, education personnel should be carefully selected and frequently evaluated. Fifth, all educators can make sure they are fully insured with a reputable agency and that they understand the issues surrounding negligence, liability, and their professional responsibilities. Finally, educators can make extra efforts to adequately convey to the public the accomplishments of their local schools and the vital role of public education in American society.

■ PAUSE TO REFLECT

Examining Educational Malpractice

- Do you think students or parents should be allowed to sue educators for malpractice? How could the possibility of a lawsuit help or hinder the quality of teaching?

- What other methods can citizens use to ensure that they receive a quality education?

- Do you think competency tests are an adequate measure of student achievement, and therefore, of teacher quality? Why? What others means could be used to gauge achievement?

EDUCATIONAL ISSUE 13–1

Should educators be held responsible for the quality of education they dispense?

Yes	No
1. If the state requires citizens to be educated for the good of society, the state should be held responsible for the quality of that education.	1. The threat of lawsuits discourages educators from developing new ideas that might benefit students.
2. The public-school system is a monopoly, and parents have no alternative for free schooling.	2. Citizens have other, less drastic avenues for expressing discontent and promoting change in educational quality
3. Parents put their trust in educators to provide the best education possible.	3. Educators are only human and should not be held responsible for reasonable mistakes.

CHURCH-STATE RELATIONS ■

Organized religion has played a significant and tendentious role in United States history, and public schools often have become battlegrounds for those of different religious persuasions. Citizens are free to believe in any religion, to participate in any religious organization, or to subscribe to no religion at all. The state cannot prescribe or coerce in matters of religion. The First Amendment states, "Congress shall make no law respecting the establishment of religion or prohibiting the free exercise thereof." These establishment and free-exercise clauses constitute the grounds on which the United States Supreme Court rules in such cases. While the First Amendment does state that the restriction is placed on the Congress and, by implication, not on the states, in *Cantwell v. Connecticut* (1940), the Court held that the First Amendment's protection of religion applied to the states as well as to the federal government.[39] Sectarian religious practices have been widespread ever since the beginning of public education in the United States. It was not until 1940 that the Supreme Court was in a strong position to rule against some of these practices.

The Free Exercise of Religion

In 1940 the West Virginia legislature ratified a law establishing programs in citizenship education which required that all teachers and pupils recite the pledge of allegiance; failure to comply would be treated as insubordination and dealt with accordingly. Members of Jehovah's Witnesses sought to prevent enforcement of this law, claiming that, for them, the Bible was the supreme authority and that saluting the flag was forbidden by the scriptures. The United States Supreme Court claimed in *West Virginia v. Barnette* (1943) that the central issue was whether the state had a right to compel students to declare a belief by officially imposing the ceremony.[40] The Court held that the flag salute is a form of utterance; it did not question whether national unity was a desirable end, only whether the compulsory pledge of allegiance was a permissible means of achievement. "Those who begin coercive elimination of dissent," the Court stated, "soon find themselves exterminating dissenters. To believe that patriotism will not flourish if patriotic ceremonies are voluntary and spontaneous instead of a compulsory routine is to make an unflattering estimate of the appeal of our institutions to free minds. If there is any fixed star in our constitutional constellation, it is that no official, high or petty, can prescribe what shall be orthodox or force citizens to confess by word or act their faith therein."[41] This decision overturned a precedent established by the Court three years earlier when it held that "the promotion of national cohesion" through the compulsory flag salute in the public schools is a more important interest than that of religious freedom.[42] Lower courts have held that teachers have a right to refuse the pledge as a matter of conscience.[43] But, they said, teachers do not have the right to eliminate the flag salute from their classroom or to deny students the right to participate.

In other free-exercise cases Fundamentalist parents in Tennessee secured an exemption for their children from a reading series that offended their religious beliefs.[44] The parents claimed that the mandatory use of the series violated their free-exercise rights and their constitutional right to control the rearing of their children. The court did not order a separate school program for the dissident parents' children, concluding that doing so might violate the establishment clause by advancing religion. Instead, they excused the children from the prescribed program and allowed them to study reading at home as long as they were able to pass a standardized reading test. Religious exemptions, however, have not been honored when it was found that the exemptions were unnecessary to the practice of religion or disrupted the school program.[45] Statutes requiring students to be immunized against communicable disease, for example, have been upheld against students who claimed their religious tenets were violated.[46]

Court rulings do not favor religious exemptions if they would be disruptive to the educational process or against the interests of public safety.

Teacher-led prayers in public schools violate the establishment clause.

Religious Exercises in Public Schools

Beginning in the early 1950s the New York State Board of Regents required that a state-composed prayer be said aloud each day in the presence of a teacher. Even though it was argued that the prayer was non-denominational and that observance on the part of students was voluntary, the United States Supreme Court held in *Engel v. Vitale* (1962) that the state prayer was wholly inconsistent with the establishment clause because it established the religious beliefs embodied in the regent's prayer.[47] The Court also noted that the purposes underlying the establishment clause "rested in the belief that a union of government and religion tends to destroy government and to degrade religion."

The next year the U.S. Supreme Court heard *Abington School District v. Schempp* (1963), a Pennsylvania case in which students at Arlington High School were chosen to read ten verses from the Bible each day during their homeroom period. The readings were broadcast into each classroom and were followed by the recitation in unison of the Lord's Prayer.[48] The Court stated that even though students did not have to participate, the exercises still were unconstitutional under the establishment clause. That the exercise was only a "minor" encroachment on the First Amendment was not considered a defense, either. "The breach of neutrality that is today a trickling stream may all too soon become a raging torrent and, in the words of Madison, 'it is proper to take alarm at the first experiment on our liberties'."

Some construe the avoidance of religious observations in schools as advancing secularism as a religion.

The defendants also claimed that prohibiting these religious exercises constituted the establishment of a "religion of secularism." The court agreed that if "religion of secularism" meant that the schools became hostile to religion by giving preference to those who believe in no religion over those who are believers, then the state may not do so. However, the Court concluded that ruling the exercises unconstitutional did not develop a religion of secularism. Furthermore, it said public schools can offer studies in comparative religion or the history of religion in relation to the advancement of civilization.

Lemon v. Kurtzman (1971) raised questions about statutes in Pennsylvania and Rhode Island designed to improve secular education in nonpublic schools by supplementing the salaries of teachers of these subjects.[49] The decision led to the development of standards for the application of the establishment clause in church-state issues. To be valid under the establishment clause, a statute must (1) have a secular purpose; (2) neither advance nor inhibit religion; and (3) not foster "an excessive government entanglement with religion."

The courts have ruled on a variety of other cases related to religion. In 1980 the Supreme Court struck down a Kentucky statute that required the Ten Commandments to be posted in all public-school classrooms.[50] It found that the material was not integrated in a secular study of comparative religion, history, and civilization and therefore found that it violated the establishment clause. The Supreme Court in 1985 ruled that a 1981 Alabama law requiring a daily period of voluntary prayer or silent meditation violated the establishment clause.[51] The Court, however, indicated that laws calling for silent meditation or prayer without legislative intent to impose prayer probably would be upheld. In 1987 the California Court of Appeals, First District, held that invocations at public high school activities, like graduation ceremonies, are a form of prayer and violate the three standards under the establishment clause (cited in the Lemon case), and are therefore unconstitutional.[52]

The issue of creationism raises even more questions about the establishment of religion. A 1968 Arkansas statute prohibited public schools from teaching the Darwinian theory of evolution. The Supreme Court invalidated the statute because the purpose was to eliminate all subjects from the curriculum that Fundamentalists considered antagonistic to their religious beliefs; consequently, the Court ruled, the statute did not observe neutrality and violated the establishment clause.[53] By 1981 Arkansas had passed a law requiring both biblical and evolutionary theories to be taught in the public-school curriculum. The state argued that teaching a creator concept in "creation science" was not a religious exercise and that the literal Genesis view is not necessarily religious; the federal district court disagreed and held that the law was designed to advance religious beliefs.[54]

Courts have upheld the use of public-school facilities for religious purposes during non-school hours, provided the activities are not sponsored by the school. The use of public-school buildings by religious groups for civic or cultural activities was found not to violate the state constitution in New York.[55] However, offering religious groups lower rates than other groups does violate the establishment clause.[56] A federal law passed in 1984 requires schools that receive federal funds to provide equal access to students who desire to meet during non-school hours for religious purposes.

Released Time for Religious Instruction

In 1948 in Champaign County, Illinois, a taxpayer charged that, in violation of the First and Fourteenth Amendments, the local public schools were permitting religious teachers to engage in religious teaching during school hours.[57] The religious instruction was provided at no charge to the schools and was under the jurisdiction of the school superintendent. The United States Supreme Court held that the practice not only used the public schools to disseminate religious doctrines but also afforded sectarian groups an invaluable aid through the use of compulsory schooling; therefore, the practice violated separation of church and state.

In a related case in New York, released time was provided for religious instruction during the school day but off the school premises.[58] Once again, no public funds were involved. The Court noted that no religious instruction was brought into the classroom and that no student was required to attend. If teachers had been using their office to coerce students to take religious instruction, an entirely different case would be presented. While government may not finance religious instruction, blend secular and sectarian training, force religion on a person, or require religious observance, it should not be hostile to religion. The Court concluded that though the program might have been unwise from an educational or community viewpoint, it was constitutional.

Other cases have further clarified what is constitutionally permissible during released time. The Utah Department of Education allowed credit for released-time classes such as Bible history as long as the classes were not primarily denominational. The United States Court of Appeals, Tenth Circuit, upheld released-time classes but not the course credits on the grounds that public-school officials had to assess the religious content of parochial-school classes, thereby entangling the state in religion.[59]

Some states allow shared-time programs involving agreements between public and private school officials in sharing school facilities. A sixth-grade girl who was a full-time private-school student sought to enroll in a band course in her local public school, but was denied enrollment because the public schools required their students to attend full-time.[60] The Michigan Supreme Court ruled that the student be allowed to take the course, because to prevent her from doing so would penalize her for exercising her religious freedom by attending a private school.

Public Aid to Religious Schools

Decisions may be based on the welfare of students rather than on a constructionist view of separation of church and state.

In the 1920s Louisiana lent textbooks purchased by the state to children attending private and religious schools. Citizens sought to stop the practice. The United States Supreme Court held in *Cochran v. Louisiana State Board of Education* (1930) that the purpose of the appropriations was to make textbooks available without cost to all school children of the state.[61] The books were for secular, not religious, instruction. The Court concluded that the children, not the schools, were the beneficiaries of the appropriations. This case marked the beginning of the Court's "child welfare" theory, which has been used as a basis for decisions in subsequent cases.

A New Jersey statute authorized local school districts to contract for transportation to carry children to and from schools. A township board of education reimbursed parents of private-school students for the cost of using the public transportation system to send their children to attend school. A taxpayer filed suit challenging the right of the board to reimburse parents of parochial-school students. In *Everson v. Board of Education* (1947) the Supreme Court recognized a collision between the establishment and the free-exercise clauses, but said that New Jersey could not hamper its citizens in the free exercise of religion by preventing them, because of their faith or lack of it, from receiving the benefits of public-welfare legislation. The Court concluded in a five-to-four vote that the First Amendment does not prohibit New Jersey from allocating funds to parents for transportation to parochial schools.[62]

In a case involving the lending of public-school textbooks to parochial schools in New York State, the plaintiffs argued that the practice violated the First and Fourteenth Amendments.[63] In upholding the state's position, the Court of Appeals ruled that the practice benefitted all children regardless of the school attended, and that, because the textbooks were secular in nature and not instrumental in the teaching of religion, the practice was constitutional.

But in applying the three standards from the Lemon case, the Supreme Court ruled that state allocation of funds to nonpublic schools for building repair and maintenance unconstitutionally advanced religion. The practices of tuition reimbursements at state expense and state income-tax credits for parochial-school parents also effectively advance religion and foster excessive entanglements.[64]

The Court did uphold a Minnesota tax-benefit program that allows a state income-tax reduction for parents of children in public or private schools. The Court noted that the law was "vitally different" from others that had been struck down, as the others bestowed benefits only on private-school students. Providing state assistance to a broad spectrum of citizens does not have the primary effect of advancing religion.[65]

The Court has struck down provisions for direct aid to religious schools and any other arrangements that would require extensive government monitoring of parochial schools to ensure that funds only support secular activities. These arrangements include the loan of instructional materials, support of field trips, public funds for parochial teachers to provide "community education" courses for children and adults after school hours, auxiliary services on private-school premises, and field-trip transportation. While direct subsidies to religious schools have been found to violate the establishment clause, criteria are not clear on what would be permissible aid to the child.

■ **PAUSE TO REFLECT**
Religion in Public Schools

- What place, if any, do you think religion has in public schools?
- Should the state maintain complete separation from the church, or could some exceptions be made? For example, should the state be allowed to allocate funds to private schools? What kinds of funds? And should the state then be able to follow up on the use of those funds? If so, to what extent?

■ CURRICULUM ISSUES AND REGULATIONS

States have the right to regulate the curriculum as long as federal constitutional provisions are upheld. Lacking expertise in curricular matters, the judiciary is reluctant to intervene and leaves related decisions to state departments of education and local school boards unless constitutional rights are infringed. State statutes usually specify the courses offered and the grade level and make detailed provisions for such programs as special education, vocational education, and bilingual education. State laws usually require local school boards to adopt the state's minimum curriculum and may supplement it at the state's discretion. Some states permit local boards to develop their own courses of study. Local schools can establish admission criteria for particular courses as long as the requirements do not discriminate against particular groups of students. School officials have the authority to eliminate courses or activities not mandated by the state. Unless reductions in services are arbitrary and capricious, they generally are not overruled. Declining enrollment is a common reason for eliminating courses. Many states provide textbooks for free; others assess fees, a practice that has been legally challenged. The Supreme Court has not ruled on this matter, so it has been settled by the states. Arizona, Colorado, Indiana, and Virginia have allowed fees to be charged for public-school textbooks, while New Mexico allows fees only for books for elective courses. A waiver usually is provided for students who cannot afford to pay the fees.

Competency Testing

States have the right to establish standards for high-school diplomas and minimum performance standards for students. Courts also have approved the right of local school boards to use standards higher than the minimum in testing for promotion.[66] Twenty states require students to pass a **minimum competency test** (MCT) to receive a diploma; a few states allow the test to be developed at the local level; and other states permit the local board to decide on such tests. Courts generally have upheld the use of the MCT unless the test is found to be discriminatory or unconstitutional. Students are entitled to notice of test standards and an opportunity to satisfy those standards before a school can withhold diplomas. Courts have prohibited the use of the MCT as a graduation prerequisite until all students subject to the requirement have entered first grade under desegregated conditions.[67] Also, courts have ruled that students with disabilities need more notice of the MCT requirements than non-disabled students to ensure them adequate opportunity to prepare for the test.[68]

> The states are subject to legal constraints, particularly antidiscrimination laws, in adopting minimum competency standards.

Plaintiffs in Florida claimed that the state's competency test violated the due-process and equal-protection clauses of the Fourteenth Amendment. The Fifth Circuit Court of Appeals placed the burden of proof on the state of Florida to show that the test actually covered instructional material presented to students.[69] The court found that the test was valid in terms of both the curriculum and instruction, and that any causal link between the disproportionate failure rate of black students and past discrimination had been severed. Consequently, Florida was allowed to deny diplomas to those who failed the test, beginning with the 1983 class. Critics say there is a danger that teachers will teach to the test to make the test valid, which reduces the teacher's discretion and flexibility, narrows the curriculum, and might cause the minimum requirements to become the maximum.

Tracking

Tracking is the practice of subdividing students by ability or achievement level within and among curriculum groups. These groups are academic, general, and vocational curriculums. In 1967 the use of tracking in a Washington, DC, case was ruled unconstitutional in federal district court (*Hobson v. Hansen*).[70] The plaintiffs contended that some children were erroneously assigned to lower tracks and had little opportunity to advance to higher tracks because of the limited curriculum and the absence of remedial instruction. The court ruled that the plan denied equal opportunities for students in lower tracks. The court emphasized that it was not abolishing the use of track systems; classifications reasonably related to educational purposes were constitutionally permissible unless they discriminated against identifiable groups of children.

> Classification systems must also be nondiscriminatory.

The Fifth Circuit Court of Appeals struck down a tracking plan in Jackson, Mississippi, and held that students could not be placed in classes on the basis of standardized test scores until a desegregated school district had been developed to the court's satisfaction.[71] In a Louisiana case the federal district court held that the classification of students on a nondiscriminatory basis is permissible, but that tracking could not be used to perpetuate racial segregation.[72] The Fifth Circuit Court of Appeals concluded in an Alabama case that an ability grouping, which had been initiated shortly after a court desegregation order and resulted in a continuation of segregated schools, violated protected rights.[73]

Not all grouping plans are struck down, as seen in a San Francisco case involving the assignment of students to an academically elite senior high school based on student achievement. Blacks, Hispanics, and students from low socioeconomic backgrounds were underrepresented, resulting in a lawsuit. The Ninth Circuit Court of Appeals found that there was no clear evidence of an intent to discriminate and deemed the use of ability grouping to be educationally justified.[74]

The courts generally appeal to the due-process and equal-protection clauses of the Fourteenth Amendment. Courts are concerned that tests used for assignment purposes are unbiased and valid; that scores on both standardized reading and mathematics tests are used; and that the grouping plan help the school achieve its educational objectives rather than foster racial discrimination.

▪ SCHOOL DESEGREGATION

The legal basis in the struggle for desegregation of public schools begins with *Plessy v. Ferguson* (1896), although there was an unsuccessful desegregation case in Boston as early as 1849. The Plessy case involved the right of the state of Louisiana to provide separate railway carriages for whites and blacks. What has become the famous "separate-but-equal" doctrine was upheld. In 1896, the Supreme Court argued that it was a fallacy to assume that the enforced separation of the two races ". . .stamps the colored race with a badge of inferiority. If this be so, it is not by reason of anything found in the act, but solely because the colored race chooses to put that construction upon it."[75]

The separate-but-equal doctrine was applied in considering the constitutionality of a Georgia school board converting a black secondary school to a black elementary school to solve overcrowding at the elementary level. The move eliminated secondary education for blacks while it still was available to whites. The Supreme Court saw no need to intervene, as it envisioned its role solely as that of ensuring that the school-tax burden was equitably distributed.[76]

After World War II the Supreme Court rejected Oklahoma's defense that it had not been given sufficient time to establish separate facilities for a black law school applicant and held that such facilities should be provided for blacks as soon as for applicants of any other groups.[77] Two years later the Court rejected the practice at the University of Oklahoma of admitting a black graduate student but segregating him in facilities within the university.[78] The Court recognized that intangible factors could affect equal opportunity. The Court also found that the separate law school established for blacks at the University of Texas was unequal in library resources and faculty.[79]

The momentous 1954 decision *Brown v. Board of Education of Topeka* was unanimous.[80] The decision included cases from Kansas, South Carolina, Virginia, and Delaware. The plaintiffs contended that segregated public schools were not equal and could not be made equal, and they argued that they were being denied the equal protection of the laws. Because the separate facilities had been or were being equalized, the case became a direct challenge to the separate-but-equal doctrine. The Court decided that it would have to consider the effect of segregation on public education in light of the place of public education in American life. Chief Justice Warren, speaking for a unanimous court, stated:

> Does segregation of children in public schools solely on the basis of race, even though the physical facilities and other "tangible" factors may be equal, deprive the children of the minority group of equal educational opportunity? We believe that it does . . . , to separate [children] from others of similar age and qualifications solely because of their race generates a feeling of inferiority as to their status in the community that may affect their hearts and minds in a way unlikely ever to be undone.[81]

The Court also cited a Kansas case which noted that when the separation of the races has the sanction of law it exerts an even greater effect. The Court said that segregation was likely to retard the segregated students' educational and mental development and deprive them of the benefits they would receive in racially integrated schools. The Court observed that these consequences were amply documented by contemporary research and rejected any language in *Plessy v. Ferguson* contrary to its finding. The Court concluded that "in the field of public education the doctrine of 'separate-but-equal' has no place. Separate educational facilities are inherently unequal."[82] The following year, 1955, the Court in *"Brown II"* assigned lower federal courts the task of enforcement and declared that school systems were to desegregate "with all deliberate speed."[83] As indicated in Chapter 10, the civil rights

The basic premise of desegregation laws is that "separate" cannot be inherently "equal."

movement met considerable resistance. In 1969 the Court recognized that its all-deliberate-speed mandate had been ineffective and ordered segregated school systems to be terminated "at once."[84]

In 1971 the Supreme Court sought to determine the characteristics of an unconstitutional dual school system and to outline the steps needed to bring about a nonracial system.[85] The Court required school authorities to prove that such arrangements were not caused by previous discrimination. If local desegregation plans proved inadequate, courts could implement their own plans. In this case the Court approved a lower federal court's plan of forced busing to achieve school desegregation, although it cautioned that the soundness of any transportation plan must be based on the distance traveled, time involved, and the ages of the students.

The Supreme Court addressed northern segregation by considering the differences between **de jure segregation** (according to law or by government intent) and **de facto segregation** (segregation by fact, such as segregated housing patterns). The Court held that, in a school system like Denver's where no dual system had previously existed, the plaintiffs must prove not only that segregated schooling exists but also that it is intentionally maintained by state actions.[86] The Court found that the Denver Board of Education, although not operating under *de jure* segregation, effectively segregated black and Hispanic schools. But it refused to become involved in the issue of *de facto* segregation for the core city area because the plaintiffs had to prove *de jure* segregation in each part of the city in which they sought relief.

In another northern school-segregation case, the Supreme Court struck down an interdistrict desegregation plan ordered by a lower federal court to break the pattern of inner-city schools composed of minority students and suburban schools composed of white students.[87] The Court held that the plaintiffs did not prove purposeful discrimination by suburban districts, and therefore those districts could not be compelled to solve segregation problems in other districts.

The Supreme Court reversed an appellate court's endorsement of a busing plan to desegregate Dayton schools because it had not been determined whether official acts were discriminatory and how much segregation would have existed without these acts.[88] But, after reviewing the case a second time, the Supreme Court agreed with the appellate court.[89] The school board, therefore, had a responsibility beyond abandoning previous segregation practices; it had an obligation to ensure that its subsequent actions did not re-establish segregation. The Court allowed consequences of actions to be considered in determining discriminatory intent.

The Rights of Non-Citizens

A federal district court held that the Fourteenth Amendment protected "persons," not just citizens, in a case involving the rights of West Indian children to receive public-education benefits.[90] The children were wards of non-citizens legally residing in American territory. But would illegal aliens be treated the same way? Texas, which had passed legislation excluding illegal aliens from public education, claimed that the legislation sought to protect the state's interest by preserving limited resources for legal residents. In 1982 the United States Supreme Court observed that many illegal aliens would remain in the country indefinitely and some would become citizens. Through its legislation, the Court said that Texas was creating a subclass of illiterate residents that would add to the problems of crime, unemployment, and welfare. Any savings on educational costs were insubstantial compared with these problems.[91]

But the Supreme Court upheld a Texas statute in a case involving a United States citizen by birth who lived in Mexico with his Mexican parents but returned to Texas to live with his sister for the primary purpose of attending school.[92] The statute denied free schooling to minors living apart from their parents or guardians, and the Court held that the residence requirements of the school district represented a substantial state interest. The decision contradicted a ruling eight years earlier in which the Eighth Circuit Court struck down the exclusion of children from public education who did not have a parent or guardian in the district.[93] The Court held that the requirement violated the equal-protection clause.

The courts allow students who are not citizens to enjoy the benefits of a free public education.

■ Summary

- *Laws* take the form of rules and norms, and a *legal system* is a network of rules designed to enforce the laws. A legal system consists of *primary rules* (which impose duties) and *secondary rules* (which confer powers). Legal reasoning is based on case studies through which rules are derived.

- How the law functions in society can be explained through two different perspectives. *Functionalism* holds that the legal system has vital roles to play in society, including prescribing proper behavior and imposing sanctions on those who disobey. The *conflict theory* questions whether the law is impartially functional for all and suggests that law is created by certain individuals to protect their interests from other individuals.

- Since the 1970s the courts have increasingly recognized students' rights to due process of law as put forth in the Fourteenth Amendment. *Procedural due process* prohibits states from depriving anyone of "life, liberty, or property" without following fair procedures. *Substantive due process* protects individuals from laws or rules that are overly vague, arbitrary, capricious, or unreasonable.

- Because it is assumed that an enlightened citizenry is necessary for the well-being of the state and because the state is responsible for protecting its citizens, all states have compulsory attendance laws. Parents are free, however, to choose public, nonpublic, or in some cases, home education for their children.

- Teachers and students have the right to free expression on school property, including passing out handbills, wearing armbands, and criticizing school policies. They do not have the right to engage in activities that disrupt the educational process or endanger others. Student publications in the public schools are considered materials for learning and are not protected by free-expression laws.

- Courts generally recognize the rights of students to dress as they please, although schools can regulate appearance in certain circumstances, such as imposing a particular hairstyle on football players during football season.

- Students generally are not immune to searches by teachers if there is a reasonable suspicion that the searches will uncover a school or legal violation. Lockers are considered school property and are subject to searches; personal searches, however, are more strictly regulated. Testing all students for drugs has been deemed unconstitutional because reasonable suspicion of drug use does not exist.

- Student records are not as strictly protected, although the Family Educational Rights and Privacy Act (FERPA) requires schools to develop procedures to give parents access to their children's records.

- If students are to develop into responsible individuals, they should have access to quiet areas in the school building where they can get away from the hubbub of daily school activities, and they should expect to be free of constant surveillance.

- Tort action can be divided into three classifications: *Negligence* (the failure to exercise a degree of care that a reasonable teacher would exercise under the same circumstances); *intentional torts* (wrongs committed with the intent to cause harm, such as assault, battery and false imprisonment); and *strict liability* (the creation of a hazard that results in an injury).

- Teachers can use reasonable corporal punishment and force in self-defense without being accused of committing an intentional tort. To avoid charges of negligence, school personnel should keep buildings and equipment in good repair and warn students of known dangers. Teachers also should be sure that students have adequate training in an activity before letting the students participate.

- Some defenses against negligence charges include assumption of risk (the student was aware of and accepted the risks involved in the activity); contributory negligence (the student contributed to his or her own injury); and comparative negligence (several parties held varying degrees of responsibility for the injury).

- Two forms of educational malpractice can be distinguished: failure of a school to enable a student to reach satisfactory levels of achievement, thereby injuring the student's development; and failure of authorities to exercise due care in evaluating and classifying students. Courts probably are more likely to rule in favor of the plaintiffs in cases of misclassification rather than in cases of inadequate education, because consensus is lacking on what is considered an adequate education.

- The First Amendment states, "Congress shall make no law respecting the establishment of religion or prohibiting the free exercise thereof." The United States Supreme Court relies on this clause when ruling on cases regarding religion and public education. Under the establishment clause, a statute must have a secular legislative purpose, neither advance nor inhibit religion, and not promote excessive government entanglement with religion. In general, Supreme Court decisions have upheld the separation of religion and public education. Regarding public aid to private schools, the Court has allowed the lending of secular textbooks to private schools as long as all children benefitted from the loan but rejected the state allocation of funds to private schools, as that would be considered advancing religion.

- The courts generally leave curriculum decisions up to the states, stepping in only if constitutional rights are infringed. Schools can eliminate courses or activities not mandated by the state and some states charge fees for textbooks.

- Some states require students to pass a minimum competency test before they can graduate, and the courts have upheld this practice except when it is found to be discriminatory or unconstitutional. Critics say that competency testing induces teachers to teach to the test only, reducing their discretion and flexibility; narrowing the curriculum; and possibly causing the minimum requirements to become the maximum.

- In deciding whether to allow *tracking* (the classification of students into curriculum groups according to ability and achievement), the courts appeal to the due-process and equal-protection clauses of the Fourteenth Amendment. Tracking generally is allowed if the tests used for assignment purposes are unbiased and valid, if both reading and mathematics scores are used, and if the grouping plan helps the school achieve its educational objectives rather than foster racial discrimination.

- The legal basis for school desegregation can be followed from *Plessy v. Ferguson* (1896), which upheld the separate-but-equal doctrine, through *Brown v. Board of Education of Topeka* (1954 and 1955), which deemed separate facilities inherently unequal and ordered school systems to desegregate "with all deliberate speed."

- The courts have upheld the rights of non-citizens legally or illegally residing in the United States to a public education, but have denied free schooling to minors living apart from their parents or guardians.

■ Key Terms

conflict theory	negligence
de facto segregation	primary rules
de jure segregation	procedural due process
functionalism	secondary rules
intentional tort	strict liability
law	substantive due process
legal system	tort
minimum competency test	tracking

■ Discussion Questions

1. To what extent is law based on morality and vice versa?

2. What is the relation of law to educational policies and school rules?

3. What can teachers do to avoid negligence and malpractice suits?

4. What changes could improve students' substantive rights?

5. If members of a religious group decided that they did not want their children to participate in a curriculum activity for religious reasons, on what basis would courts likely decide the issue?

6. What sorts of religious activities, if any, are permitted in public schools? On what grounds are these activities allowed?

7. Under what conditions would tracking likely be approved by courts?

8. What are the weaknesses of MCT and how can these weaknesses be overcome?

9. Trace the changes in legal thought from the Plessy decision to the Brown case.

■ Learning Activities

1. Invite a legal expert to class to discuss current legal provisions for student rights.

2. As a group project, develop an outline and basic principles for a model student handbook that would recognize students' rights and responsibilities consistent with the latest legal decisions.

3. Find two spokespersons for religious denominations that have divergent views about religion and public education. Invite them to class to debate the issues.

4. Organize a debate on the resolution: "All public schools should use MCT."

5. Write a report about a local school system that has at one time been under court order to desegregate. Trace the history of the decision by considering segregation problems, the parties involved, the legal grounds for the decision, and the school board's response to it.

6. Outline a program in which religion could be studied in the public schools without violating the establishment clause.

Suggested Readings

McCarthy, Martha M., and Nelda H. Cambron-McCabe. *Public School Law: Teachers' and Students' Rights,* 2nd ed. Boston: Allyn and Bacon, 1987.

Provides a systematic treatment of public-school law.

Menacker, Julius. *School Law: Theoretical and Case Perspectives.* Englewood Cliffs, NJ: Prentice-Hall, 1987.

Relates school law to educational policy and provides key cases.

1989 Deskbook Encyclopedia of American School Law. Rosemount, MN: Data Research, 1989.

Provides accurate and authoritative information on the latest cases.

Price, Janet R., Alan H. Levin, and Eve Carey. *The Rights of Students*, 3rd ed. Carbondale, IL: Southern Illinois University Press, 1988.

Written clearly and concisely to inform students about their rights.

Van Geel, Tyll. *The Courts and American Education Law*. Buffalo: Prometheus Books, 1987.

Offers a summary, analysis, and commentary on new education laws at the federal and state levels.

Notes

1. H. L. A. Hart, *The Concept of Law* (New York: Oxford, 1961).
2. Hans Kelsen, *What Is Justice?* (Berkeley: University of California Press, 1957).
3. Lon Fuller, *The Morality of Law* (New Haven, CT: Yale University Press, 1964).
4. Goss v. Lopez, 419 U.S. 565 (1975).
5. McClain v. Lafayette Cty. Bd. of Ed., 673 F. 2d 106 (5th Cir. 1982) (carrying a deadly weapon to school).
6. Ingraham v. Wright, 430 U.S. 651 (1977).
7. Bd. of Curators v. Horowitz, 435 U.S. 78 (1978).
8. Pierce v. Society of Sisters, 268 U.S. 510 (1925).
9. Patricia Lines, "Home Instruction," *Issuegram* No. 49, Education Commission of the States (1984).
10. Tinker v. Des Moines Independent Community School Dist., 393 U.S. 503 (1969).
11. Clergy and Laity Concerned v. Chicago Bd. of Educ., 586 F. Supp. 1408.
12. Fricke v. Lynch, 491 F. Supp. 381 (D.R.I. 1980).
13. Lipkis v. Caveney, 96 Cal. Rptr. 779 (1971).
14. Williams v. Spencer, 622 F. 2d 1206 (4th Cir. 1980).
15. Fraser v. Bethel School Dist. No. 403, 755 F. 2d 1356 (9th Cir. 1985), *rev'd* 106 S. Ct. 3159 (1986).
16. Hazlewood School District v. Kuhlmeier, 86-836 S. Ct. (1988).
17. Breese v. Smith, 502 P. 2d 159 (Alaska 1972); Jacobs v. Benedict, 316 N.E. 2d 898 (Ohio 1974); Nehaus v. Federico, 505 P. 2d 939 (Ore. 1972).
18. Crossen v. Fatsi, 309 F. Supp. 114 (D. Conn. 1970); Wallace v. Ford, 346 F. Supp. 156 (E.D. Ark. 1972).
19. Tarter v. Raybuck No. 83-3174 (CA6, Aug. 31, 1984); Bilbrey v. Brown, 738 F. 2d 1462 (CA9 1948).
20. New Jersey v. T.L.O., 469 U.S. 325 (1985).
21. Bilbrey v. Brown, 738 F. 2d 1462 (9th Cir. 1984).

22. Horton v. Goose Creek Independent School Dist., 690 F. 2d 470 (5th Cir. 1982).

23. Odenheim v. Carlstadt-East Rutherford Regional School Dist., No. 4305-85E, December 9, 1985.

24. S. D. Webb, "Privacy and Psychosomatic Stress: An Empirical Analysis," *Social Behavior and Personality*, 6 (1978): 227–34.

25. Hogenson v. Williams, 542 S.W. 2d 456 (Tex. 1976).

26. Ingraham v. Wright, 525 F. 2d 909 (5th Cir. 1976), aff'd, 430 U.S. 651 (1977).

27. Thompson v. Iberville Parish School Bd., 372 So. 2d 642 (La. App. 1979).

28. Sansane v. Bechtel, 429 A. 2d 440 (Wis. App. 1983).

29. O'Brien v. Township High School Dist., 392 N.E. 2d 615 (Ill. App. 1979).

30. LaValley v. Stanford, 70 N.Y. S. 2d 460 (App. Dir. 1947).

31. Peter W. Doe v. San Francisco Unified Sch. Dist., 60 Cal. App. 3d 814, 131 Cal. Rptr. 854 (1976).

32. John Elson, "A Common Law Remedy for the Educational Harms Caused by Incompetence or Careless Teaching," *Northwestern University Law Review* 73 (1978): 641, 696, 747–54.

33. Donahue v. Copiague Union Free Schools, 407 N.Y. S. 2d 874 (App. Div. 1978), aff'd 418 N.Y. S. 2d 375, 391 N.E. 2d 1352 (N.Y. 1979).

34. Hoffman v. Bd. of Educ., 49 N.Y. 2d 121, 124, 400 N.E. 2d 317, 424, N.Y. S. 2d 378 (1979).

35. B.M. v. State, 649 P. 2d 425 (Mont. 1982).

36. Snow v. State of New York, 64 N.Y. 2d 745 (1984), affirming, 98 A.D. 2d 442, 469 N.Y. S. 2d 959 (A.D. 2d Dept. 1983).

37. Public School Education Act of 1975. N.J.S.A. 18A: 7A-1, et. seq.

38. Seattle Sch. Dist. No. 1 of King County v. Washington, 585 P. 2d 71 (Wash. 1978).

39. Cantwell v. Connecticut, 310 U.S. 296 60 Ct. 900, 84 L.Ed. 1213 (1940).

40. West Virginia v. Barnette, 319 U.S. 624 (1943).

41. Ibid., at 642.

42. Minersville School Dist. v. Gobitis, 310 U.S. 586 (1940).

43. Russo v. Central School Dist. No. 1, 469 F. 2d 623, 634 (2d Cir. 1972), *cert. denied*, 411 U.S. 932 (1973).

44. Mozert v. Hawkins County Public Schools, 765 F. 2d 75 (6th Cir. 1985), *on remand*, CIV-2-83-401 (E.D. Tenn. 1986).

45. Davis v. Page, 385 F. Supp. 395 (D.N.H. 1974).

46. Jacobson v. Massachusetts, 197 U.S. 11 (1905); Mosier v. Barron County Bd. of Health, 215 S.W. 2d 967 (Ky. 1948).

47. Engel v. Vitale, 370 U.S. 421 (1962).

48. Abington Sch. Dist. v. Schempp, 374 U.S. 203, 225 (1963).

49. Lemon v. Kurtzman, 302 U.S. 602 (1971) at 612.

50. Stone v. Graham, 449 U.S. 39 (1980).

51. Jaffree v. Wallace, 705 F. 2d 1526 (11th Cir. 1983), *aff'd* 105 S. Ct. 2479 (1985).

52. Bennett v. Livermore Unified School Dist., 238 Ca. Rptr. 819 (App. 1st Dist. 1987).

53. Epperson v. Arkansas, 393 U.S. 97 (1968).

54. McLean v. Arkansas Board of Education, 529 F. Supp. 1255 (1982).

55. Lewis v. Bd. of Education, 385 N.Y. S. 164 (1935).

56. Resnick v. E. Brunswick Twp. Bd. of Education, 343 A. 2d 127 (N.J. 1982).

57. McCollum v. Bd. of Education, 333 U.S. 203 (1948).

58. Zorach v. Clauson, 343 U.S. 306 (1952).

59. Smith v. Smith, 523 F. 2d 121 (4th Cir. 1975).

60. Snyder v. Charlotte Public School Dist., 365 N.W. 2d 151 (Mich. 1984).

61. Cochran v. Louisiana State Board of Education, 281 U.S. (1930).

62. Everson v. Board of Education, 330 U.S. 1 (1947).

63. Board of Education v. Allen, 392 U.S. 236 (1968).

64. Committee v. Nyquist, 413 U.S. 756 (1973).

65. Mueller v. Allan, 676 F. 2d 1195 (8th Cir. 1982), *aff'd,* 463 U.S. 388 (1983).

66. Sandlin v. Johnson, 643 F. 2d 1027 (4th Cir. 1981).

67. Debra P. v. Turlington, 644 F. 2d 397 (5th Cir. 1981).

68. Brookhart v. Illinois State Bd. of Educ., 697 F. 2d 179, 187 (7th Cir. 1983).

69. Debra P. v. Turlington, 644 F. 2d 397 (5th Cir. 1981).

70. Hobson v. Hansen, 269 F. Supp. 401, 492 (1967).

71. Singleton v. Jackson Municipal Separate School Dist., 419 F. 2d 1211, 1214 (5th Cir. 1969).

72. Moore v. Tangipahao Parish School Bd., 304 F. Supp. 244 (E.D. La. 1969).

73. United States v. Gadsen County School Dist., 572 F. 2d 1049 (5th Cir. 1978).

74. Berkelman v. San Francisco Unified School Dist., 501 F. 2d 1264 (9th Cir. 1974).

75. Plessy v. Ferguson, 163 U.S. 527 (1896).

76. Cumming v. Richmond County Board of Education, 175 U.S. 528 (1899).

77. Sipuel v. Board of Regents of University of Oklahoma, 332 U.S. 631 (1948).

78. McLaurin v. Oklahoma, 399 U.S. 637 (1950).

79. Sweatt v. Painter, 339 U.S. 629 (1950).

80. Brown v. Board of Education of Topeka, Kansas, 347 U.S. 482 (1954).

81. Ibid., at 494.

82. Ibid., at 495.

83. Brown v. Board of Educ., 349 U.S. 294 (1955).

84. Alexander v. Holmes County Bd. of Educ., 396 U.S. 19, 20 (1969).

85. Swann v. Charlotte-Mecklenburg Bd. of Educ., 402 U.S. 1 (1971).

86. Keyes v. School District No. 1 Denver, Colorado, 413 U.S. 189 (1973).

87. Milliken v. Bradley, 418 U.S. 717 (1974).

88. Dayton Board of Education v. Brinkman (Dayton I), 433 U.S. 406 (1977).

89. Dayton Board of Education v. Brinkman (Dayton II), 433 U.S. 526 (1979).

90. Hosier v. Evans, 314 F. Supp. 316 (1970).

91. Plyer v. Doe, 456 U.S. 202 (1982).

92. Martinez v. Bynum, Slip Opinion No. 81-857 (1983).

93. Hart v. Community Bd. of Educ., N.Y. Sch. Dist. No. 21, 512 F. 2d 37 (2nd Cir. 1975).

■ C H A P T E R 1 4

CURRICULUM INFLUENCES ■

A LOOK AHEAD

The purpose of this chapter is to provide an overview of the field of curriculum and its effect on the teaching-learning process. You will learn about:

- The conception of a school's curriculum and the influence of the curriculum development system.

- Four perspectives of curriculum and how each affects the development of a curriculum

- Five criteria used to select the content of a curriculum

- The common elements used to structure a curriculum

- Different organizational patterns of a curriculum

- Evaluating curriculums to determine needed changes and improvements

- The advantages and disadvantages of several curricular innovations

The curriculum, the heart of a school's activities, distinguishes one school system from another. The curriculum reflects the pivotal ideas that a school system has determined are important for youth. It reflects the knowledge and experiences of organized disciplines and world cultures that a school considers most essential. While financial constraints (discussed in Chapter 12) limit the curriculum in many ways,

*Within certain
limits, curriculum
can reflect a
school district's
uniqueness.*

the curriculum still expresses what educators can do with scarce resources. And while state curriculum guidelines can significantly influence local curricular patterns, most states allow local districts to offer special programs. An overview of a school's curriculum can reveal much of the character of a school system.

■ CONCEPTIONS OF CURRICULUM

The **curriculum** traditionally has been defined as courses of study. This definition has the advantage of pinpointing tangible material that can be observed, studied, and assessed. Yet to determine a school's curriculum fully, one must observe not only courses of study but also patterns, interrelationships, continuity, and articulation within the curriculum as a whole from the elementary grades through high school. While examining a program—say, social studies in the third grade—is important, seeing how the concepts and principles are carried forward into later grades and how the complexity and ramifications are increased also are important. Through such examination, the experiences gained by the student can be viewed in a broader temporal perspective. Thus, a course of study is only one part of a curriculum, and one can scarcely refer to the total of courses of study as a curriculum if one does not observe the principles by which the curriculum is developed.

*Curriculum in-
cludes not only
courses of study
but also the con-
text in which the
courses are
taught.*

Because of the influence of the progressive movement, the term *curriculum* tends to be defined as all the experiences a learner has while under the guidance of the school.[1] Most progressives consider the traditional notion of education as intellectual development as being far too limited; instead, they tend to conceive education as the development of the total person or "the whole child." They believe that to develop the whole child, it is necessary to consider all the experiences within the school that influence learning, even experiences that do not take place within a formal classroom setting. Learning is a joint product of the experience and activities of the child. The child gains knowledge through interaction with the world. Classroom learning activities are influenced by outside learning activities, which progressives call the **co-curriculum** (see Figure 14–1). Convinced of the merits of coordinating these diverse experiences to relate them to classroom activities, the progressives have broadened the definition of curriculum to make it consonant with their outlook. Their definition could be considered programmatic in the sense that it attempts to employ a familiar term in a different way to re-channel practice.[2] It fits into their plan of extending the school's responsibility to "the whole child."

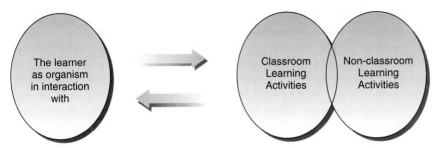

FIGURE 14-1 The progressive conception of curriculum

The strength of this conception is that it recognizes the total person, views the person within the context of a variety of learning environments, and depicts the curriculum as emerging and fluid rather than fixed and ready-made. This conception also recognizes the influence of out-of-class learning experiences and seeks to capitalize on these experiences by relating them to classroom activity.

The progressive view of curriculum is that it is not a static, in-school program.

This definition has several difficulties, however. It lacks precision because it abolishes the distinction between activities within and outside the classroom. When a term stands for almost all phenomena within an area of inquiry, it does not make distinctions among types of activities, processes, and products; hence it has little functional value.

Of more serious concern, it tends to combine the concept of learning with that of curriculum. For purposes of analysis and observation, curriculum, instruction, and learning, can be distinguished from one another. While instruction is associated with the actual teaching process, the total instructional dimension also includes planning and evaluating to achieve desired learning outcomes. The teacher, while interested in out-of-class learning that can affect instruction, generally concentrates on the learning outcomes that can be attributed to the instructional process.

A problem with such a broad definition is that it doesn't allow examination of curriculum components.

A curriculum cannot be evaluated exclusively in terms of learning outcomes because the teacher is a variable that affects to what extent the curriculum can be used in a particular class. Factors such as teaching ability, class composition, and educational resources influence learning outcomes.

A third way to conceptualize the curriculum is to consider it a systematic body of material and an organized plan for promoting formal instruction. The material is in the form of knowledge to be mastered, skills to be acquired, and experiences to be gained. The plan or plans in a curriculum translate content into instructional guidelines. In other words, a curriculum is inert until the material is made ready for instructional purposes. The plan consists of appropriate instructional activities and resources that can be used in implementing the curriculum.

A third definition of curriculum includes the body of knowledge to be taught and how it will be conveyed.

The advantages of this concept of the curriculum process are that it is not as limited as courses of study and does not combine curriculum, instruction, and learning (as does the progressive conception). Moreover, it distinguishes organized knowledge from extracurricular activities. Its weaknesses from the progressive viewpoint are that it emphasizes organized knowledge over learning experiences, does not offer an equal place for non-classroom learning experiences, and separates rather than integrates curriculum, instruction, and learning. Despite these possible shortcomings, this third conception is the main one we will use in this chapter. It also will be defended and further clarified as we progress.

The curriculum process can be depicted in terms of several relationships (see Figure 14–2). As seen in Chapter 11, education authority is established in local school districts through an elected school board, an appointed superintendent, and an appointed administrative

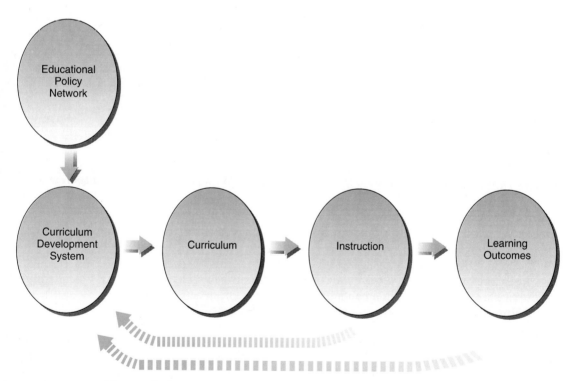

FIGURE 14–2 The curriculum process

Source: Influenced by a diagram in Mauritz Johnson's article, "Definitions and Models in Curriculum Theory," *Educational Theory,* 17 (1967), 127–40. It differs especially in the definition of the term *curriculum.*

staff. Through these organizational structures, authorities develop locally derived policy and implement state and federal mandates. A body of policy is developed over time to guide the daily operations of schools in the district; this body of policy is a **policy network,** which regulates curriculum decisions and determines who will participate in those decisions. The policy network also regulates other operations of the school district, including finance, personnel, and student regulations.

The policy network establishes and regulates the **curriculum development system,** an organizational framework for ongoing development, implementation, and evaluation of the curriculum. Curriculum specialists are regularly assigned to this system, and some teachers also are asked to participate, especially master teachers in the career ladder (as presented in Chapter 12). Others who participate periodically or provide input are administrators, curriculum specialists at state and federal levels, local school-board members, and interested citizens. Legislators (both state and federal) and national commission studies also can influence curriculum decisions through education legislation and significant reports that provide innovative ideas.

Through the curriculum development system, curriculums are created, implemented, evaluated, and revised. Thus, a body of material is selected and an organized plan for promoting formal instruction is implemented. The body of material is organized into an overall pattern that may be disciplinary, interdisciplinary, or experiential in structure. The organized plan translates the material into usable form for classroom instruction.

What happens to the curriculum depends on what the teacher does with it. The organized plan usually provides alternate ways to present the material and includes objectives and a variety of learning activities to enliven the material, as well as concrete applications. Instruction consists of planning, executing, and evaluating. In planning, the teacher takes curriculum plans and adapts them to a particular classroom situation to fulfill a particular set of objectives. These plans are carried out in the teaching process. During and after the process, the teacher evaluates the appropriateness of the material and teaching methodology, as well as student responses and achievement.

The teacher is responsible for implementing the curriculum.

Learning outcomes can be determined by several measures: classroom participation and responses, projects, group activities, performance tests, teacher-generated written tests, and standardized achievement tests. The measures should be appropriate to the objectives. For example, if greater aesthetic appreciation is an objective, the evaluative measures probably would include classroom participation and group activities as well as paper-and-pencil tests.

The members of the curriculum development system can solicit feedback from the results of instruction and learning outcomes to ascertain the effectiveness of a curriculum. In light of these data members can decide what revisions are needed to improve the curriculum's effectiveness. The curriculum can be evaluated in terms of content; that is, whether the material is systematic, accurate, and up-to-date. It also can be evaluated in terms of curriculum organization; that is, whether the curriculum pattern fits the way students learn. Evaluation also can determine how well the curriculum is articulated and provides continuity from one grade to the next. Finally, the implementation plan can be judged by how complete it is, how easily it can be operationalized, whether it is free from ambiguity, and what its range of application is (does it apply to one particular type of student or to many different students?).

■ CURRICULUM DEVELOPMENT

An educational philosophy must underpin curriculum.

Before curriculum developers begin, they must consider the goals or general objectives that will form the basis of the curriculum. Without such goals, the curriculum will lack purpose and clear direction. Let us assume that an educational philosophy is adopted for guiding curriculum development. General objectives for the curriculum would be derived from the aims contained in the philosophy.

If a philosophy holds to absolutes, its epistemology probably would identify a body of eternal truths that would likely result in a required curriculum for all students. If the adopted philosophy is more relativistic than absolutistic, the philosophy would recognize that no one curriculum is entirely suitable for all students. Therefore, the curriculum would consider the social framework in which it operates. The types of goals selected and the priorities assigned them would be influenced by the social and educational conditions in which they would be used. For instance, if the adopted philosophy were relativistic and flexible, the goals for an inner-city school (such as, learning about one's ethnic history) probably would differ from those of a wealthy suburban school (such as learning how people from advantaged backgrounds can help those less fortunate). Even if the two school systems had several common goals, the priorities assigned those goals might differ. Additionally, the curriculum content and the experiences that most likely would fulfill the goals also would vary.

The basis for justifying a set of objectives (as we discussed in Chapter 6) is its instrumental or intrinsic value. Objectives with instrumental value, for example, might enable students to become gainfully employed, fulfill their citizenship responsibilities, or gain admittance to a recognized university. In contrast, intrinsic value suggests that studying the material is worthwhile for its own sake and not for something outside the educational process. Those who hold to the intrinsic value of education believe that an educated person should have a broad understanding of science, history, and literature. Some educators would give precedence to objectives with intrinsic appeal, while other educators and key political figures might insist that schools adopt instrumental objectives in an effort to address pressing social, economic, and political problems.

Curriculum Perspectives

In developing a curriculum, educators usually choose one of four perspectives: (1) the learner; (2) the subject matter; (3) the larger society; or (4) eclecticism.

The Learner. Many progressive educators believe that priorities in the curriculum can be established by studying the characteristics of the learner to identify needed behavioral changes. Such studies can reveal the needs and interests of students, and because we teach children, not subjects, progressives insist, the learner's needs and interests should frame the curriculum. Learning experiences would be provided to meet students' needs and capitalize on their interests. For instance, if many students are absent because of illness, the teacher might introduce material about desirable health habits. If most students are interested in sports, spelling instruction could focus on learning to spell sports terminology and equipment, the cities and states in which teams are located, and the names of the players.

Curriculum may center around learners' "needs."

Although interests can be used as a starting point before moving students into broader areas of knowledge, an exclusive emphasis on interests is likely to result in a highly limited curriculum because the child's interests are limited. A value commonly attributed to a sound education is its power to broaden the range of human interest and stimulate students to become interested in areas of organized knowledge and cultures that they know nothing about.

Some progressives speak of "felt needs," or needs and cravings that children actually feel or experience. As a result, those who follow this line of thinking constantly examine children to discover their needs. Other progressives argue that not all felt needs are desirable or genuine; therefore, a curriculum should be based on "real" or "genuine" needs.[3]

When considering what an individual needs, one might consider how to fulfill some objective ("She needs a nutritious diet to maintain

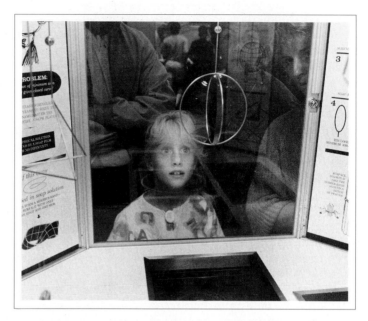

Learning materials can stimulate students to broaden their interests.

sound health"; or "He needs to learn to read so he can hold a job."). In these cases a need is only recognized as such if it fulfills a desired objective. Whether an objective is desirable is determined by a set of values or a philosophy; that is, objectives determine needs, not the converse. Once objectives are spelled out, the experiences required to achieve them can be selected.

A need is sometimes defined as a lack or deficiency. This is an unsatisfactory definition because many people lack things that they do not need or want (some people in Alaska lack lawnmowers; people in the tropics lack snowmobiles). Moreover, many deficiencies that people consider needs (the inability to afford a new car every year, for example) are culturally induced. Even the expression of physiological drives (hunger, thirst, sex) are influenced by the culture, since those drives can be sublimated or modified.

Educators frequently have used the term *need* and the expression "meeting the needs of students" as slogans; because "need" statements are general and ambiguous, they are suited to such purposes. For a need statement to mean something, one should specify the objective that the satisfaction of a need is expected to fulfill. The objective should also be proven worthwhile and its priority should be stated in relation to other worthwhile objectives. A philosophy of education provides the foundation for making these value decisions.[4]

Subject Matter. Scholars from various disciplines sometimes confer to determine curriculum priorities. From the subject-matter perspective, scholars believe they know best not only how subjects should be structured and organized but also what relative emphasis should be given to each in the curriculum. During the sixties, the structure-of-the-disciplines approach involved scholars in revising, updating, and reorganizing content and materials in the disciplines, especially mathematics and the natural sciences. It was found that if the curriculum were structured by subjects, the scholars could prescribe how specialists in their areas should be prepared. Because most students did not aspire to become mathematicians, scientists, or historians, scholars also attempted to design curriculums to show students, whatever their career aspirations, how to think like scholars in these disciplines so that they could grasp the discipline's structure and engage in organized inquiry.

Interestingly, many different subjects advance the claim of promoting reflective thinking: mathematics, physical science, philosophy, economics, and psychology. If reflective thinking is the only goal, or the most important one, then not all of these subjects are needed in the curriculum unless reflective thinking can be developed only by a study of all of them. If such is the case, what combination of these subjects will bring about the desired outcome? They probably will vary in importance. Decisions are further complicated by claims of multiple outcomes from the study of each discipline. If the study of English, for example, not only clarifies thought but also improves communication skills, two objectives are being advanced and one must determine the relative worth of each.

To create an effective curriculum from the subject-matter perspective, curriculum developers need to gather all the claims from the specialists, watching out for the tendency of scholars to "protect their turf" by extolling the supreme importance of their discipline and the lesser or even negligible importance of other disciplines. Developers then must discard claims that lack supportive evidence and give priority to certain learning outcomes. This last step is determined through knowledge of what schools should accomplish. Knowing what the disciplines have to offer does not answer the question because the curriculum developer must consider the curriculum as a whole, not just its separate parts or disciplines. However, once the question has been answered, the developer can decide the relative weight to give each discipline in the curriculum or even whether the curriculum will consist of disciplines or subjects at all. We can know what schools should accomplish only by developing a philosophy of education that will enable us to think clearly and systematically about this question.

A subject-based curriculum weights what each discipline can offer toward the overall educational goal.

Curriculum may
be structured
around the goal
of filling society's
needs.

The Larger Society.   Another curriculum perspective and a source of curriculum priorities are studies of contemporary life and societal demands. One approach to changing the curriculum to meet these new demands has been to give greater attention to the skills needed to handle adult tasks and responsibilities. Franklin Bobbitt, an early curriculum reformer, chose not to analyze traditional subjects to determine how they should be taught.[5] Nor did he establish a set of priorities, as did Herbert Spencer, by which to select knowledge designed to best prepare students for life activities.[6] Instead, Bobbitt suggested in the early part of the twentieth century that life activities be analyzed to develop a curriculum that will prepare youth for their adult responsibilities. He believed that a model of the ideal person would disclose how a citizen should participate in the community. This ideal model, he thought, could be constructed from a notion of common social functions. The task for curriculum developers was to determine ideal adult activities that would mold the future in a certain direction. Society should take the direction that would provide the greatest good for the greatest number of people; this good would be discovered by use of the scientific method and scientific surveys.

W. W. Charters followed Bobbitt's thought and contributed to curriculum development through **job analysis**.[7] He analyzed several occupations to determine the ideals and duties necessary to perform the occupation. For instance, the "ideals" of a clerk's duties would represent qualities such as the ability to question tactfully, friendliness, and punctuality. The job-analysis information was organized into working units and ordered in terms of its importance. Activities best learned outside of school were deleted, and the remaining material was arranged so that instruction was consistent with the way children learn. The best practices in handling these activities and ideals were collected and used as models for instruction.

The advantages of this approach include that the curriculum is directly related to social and occupational functions in the larger society, the gap between school and society is largely overcome, and students might be more motivated to learn through this approach than through a subject curriculum because they can make more connections with everyday life.

But to focus the curriculum on life activities or job analysis is to accept that the way these tasks are conducted is the way they *should* be conducted. Certainly most tasks can be improved, new tasks can be introduced, and others can be curtailed or eliminated. Breaking life functions and occupations into their specific activities might help the curriculum developer make new distinctions, but it can also be misleading when complex functions such as those surrounding effective citizenship are subdivided into specific acts. One can learn to perform these specific acts and still not be able to integrate them into thought and action. Good citizenship is not like baking a cake (for which directions can be specified); it involves knowledge of the issues, reflection and evaluation, and the motivation to act. Not only do the sum of the parts not equal the whole, but it is impossible to anticipate and teach for all the specific demands involved in complex life functions. Educators can develop only broad general abilities that can be used in diverse situations.

Activity and job analysis can furnish material to be used in the curriculum, but they cannot determine objectives or provide a philosophy about what is worthwhile. Scientific studies in education can provide information about different aims and objectives and the possible consequences of adopting one over another; but curriculum developers still need a philosophy of education to determine which objectives are of greatest worth.

This curriculum approach lacks a philosophical foundation.

Another example of developing a curriculum by focusing on the larger society is that of national preparedness. This emphasis was evident in the National Defense Education Act, passed one year after Sputnik was launched in 1957. The act provided funding for the teaching of science, mathematics, and foreign languages to enable the United States to keep up with the Soviet Union in the space race. In its report *A Nation at Risk,* the National Commission on Excellence in Education observed the educational practices of the Japanese and recommended that American schools institute a longer school day and school year, give the subject curriculum more depth, and require more homework.[8]

Sometimes national preparedness emphasizes using education to promote economic growth. James Hunt, former governor of North Carolina, claims that the United States has become less competitive and that our economic future is in danger.[9] U.S. students, he wrote in a 1989 article, suffer in comparison with students of other nations, and American curriculums are much less demanding than those of other nations. He says that to adequately prepare youth for jobs, schools must go beyond the basics and teach complex skills and the ability to learn how to learn. Our quality of life depends on the nation's investing more in human resources to achieve sound economic growth.

The close link that Hunt claims exists between education and the economy was not demonstrated in his article (although a more qualified relationship was discussed in Chapter 12 on finance). If the problems are as serious as Hunt suggests, probably more large-scale changes are needed than the ones he recommends. But preparation for societal needs still is not a solid basis for curriculum planning because societal problems can change rapidly, and the economy itself goes through cycles. Curriculum developers need a firmer foundation on which to build. A more serious problem, however, is that this perspective subordinates the learner's development to societal demands, making the schools a tool of the state—a characteristic of totalitarian states. If the needs of the larger society are used to determine curriculum, democratic safeguards are needed to prevent the establishment of authoritarian policies. Finally, economic growth emerges as a sole instrumental value, and intrinsic values are neglected.

Eclecticism. Balance is needed among the three perspectives—the learner, subject matter, and the larger society—although one perspective might temporarily take precedence over the others when certain deficiencies arise. These deficiencies could include low scores on standardized achievement tests, neglect of culturally different learners, inadequate programs for the disabled, neglect of the gifted, inadequate coverage of certain subjects, and lack of preparation for citizenship responsibilities. Greater balance also is needed between intrinsic and instrumental values, because instrumental values often will predominate if left unchecked.

An eclectic approach attempts to address all the concerns of the other curriculum perspectives.

Eclecticism can best be represented by Ralph Tyler's work, which came to be known as the Tyler Rationale.[10] The Tyler Rationale, which probably was the most influential approach to curriculum in the United States in the 1950s and 1960s, is eclectic in that it did not focus exclusively on one curriculum perspective, but used all of them. Tyler drew upon the work of Bobbitt and Charters, John Dewey, Jean Piaget, Edward L. Thorndike, George S. Counts, Boyd H. Bode, Hilda Taba, and Charles H. Judd. Tyler believed that anyone involved in curriculum development must answer certain basic questions:

1. What educational purposes should the school seek?
2. What educational experiences are likely to serve these purposes?
3. How can these educational experiences be organized effectively?
4. How can we determine whether these purposes are being served?

Tyler's eclecticism can be seen in his answer to the first question. To determine educational objectives, he would study learners, contemporary life outside the school, and suggestions from subject specialists. The resulting list of objectives would be screened in terms of the values embodied in the school's philosophy and of a psychology of learning to ensure that the objectives conform with conditions intrinsic to learning.

The Tyler Rationale is a linear, rational model that provides no assistance in determining the relative weight that should be given to the three sources of objectives. The philosophy is introduced later as a screen, but it is unclear what values would be used initially to determine what is worth considering in the three sources. In other words, one probably should begin with the school's philosophy to provide the values needed to assess the three sources. The Tyler Rationale also looks at curriculum making from the top down: experts and administrators plan the curriculum with little teacher or student participation. It also depicts curriculum as pre-planned and fixed—not fluid, ongoing, and subject to modification at any time.

▪ **PAUSE TO REFLECT**
Developing a Curriculum

- What kind of curriculum did your high school offer? Did it focus on the learner, subject matter, or society—or did it have an eclectic perspective? How could it have been improved to give you a more well-rounded education?

- Of the four perspectives discussed in this section, which do you think is the most defensible? Why? How would you use it to develop the ideal curriculum? Or would you shape a completely new perspective? What would that be?

Curriculum Criteria

In addition to the four perspectives and balance between intrinsic and instrumental values, certain criteria can be used in curriculum development to select content:

Significance. The material should contribute to the overall objectives of the curriculum. How, for instance, does a required course in physical education contribute to the overall objectives of the curriculum? This can be discerned by examining the objectives and assessing the outcomes of the program.

Learnability. Content should be appropriately placed, organized, and sequenced. The curriculum developer needs authoritative reports of the effectiveness of various curriculum materials at different grade levels and how they can be arranged to promote learning.

Authoritativeness. The content should be up-to-date and reflect the present state of knowledge in the disciplines. Usually there is a considerable time lag between the discovery of new knowledge and its widespread use in the curriculum. Similarly, a lag exists in removing recently disproved knowledge from the curriculum. Scholars also develop new ways to structure and organize knowledge and it can be many years before these new approaches are fully recognized and put into practice. (Highly bureaucratic school systems tend to resist innovation and take longer to accept new ideas.) Once the curriculum developer has an idea of the essential content, this criterion can be used to weed out material that should not be included.

Interest. The content should be related to the interests of learners who will use it so that students will become more involved and motivated. But if student interests are restricted and do not promote progress in learning, content and curricular experiences should be introduced to broaden and deepen student interests in areas they should become interested in. Ideally, the new material should relate meaningfully to students' current interests.

Feasibility. The curriculum needs to be implemented successfully. Curriculum developers should consider such variables as available resources, funding, faculty expertise, the political climate, and existing legislation that might advance or inhibit certain curricular provisions. National commissions cannot consider the variables in every school district, of course, so local educators must make such decisions.

■ CURRICULUM ORGANIZATION

Once content is selected, it must be organized. Organization includes determining the relative emphasis to be given the material, its order and sequence, and how it fits with other material.

Common Elements and Sequence

Certain common elements are used to structure the curriculum and provide organizational handles for the content: concepts, principles, theories, values, and skills. A **concept** is a generalized idea of a thing or class of things. Concepts are the building blocks of the disciplines. Examples are proton, neutron, electron (in science), cell (in biology), ego (in psychology), and social class, learning, instruction, and curriculum (in education). Another element is a **principle,** which is a fundamental rule or truth. Principles provide structure and regularity to the disciplines by stating certain uniform relations (for example, humans generally tend to repeat the pleasurable and avoid the displeasurable). A **theory** is a coherent group of propositions used to explain a class of phenomena. Theories seek to explain and predict phenomena; they are more highly developed in the physical sciences than other curricular areas. Evolutionary theory, quantum theory, and relativity theory can be found in the sciences; organizational theory, psychoanalysis, and behaviorism are examples in the social and behavioral sciences; and education has administrative, learning, and instructional theories, as well as theories generated from historical and philosophical studies. **Values** are statements of the worth, utility, or importance of something. Value is ascribed to things in terms of their utility (computers, automobiles), to character traits (loyalty, honesty, integrity), and to objects in terms of their aesthetic appeal (painting, sculpture). A **skill** is a developed aptitude or ability. A curriculum indicates the skills that are to be developed (typing, computer programming, surgery).

In addition to considering these common elements, curriculum developers need to determine sequencing. The logic of the subject largely dictates its order of exposition. Here are some sequencing rules observed in various subjects:

1. *Simple to complex.* This rule is commonly used in biology and chemistry and helps the student to better grasp the material. For instance, in the study of plants, students begin with simple observation, move on to classification, and finally to development of theories.

2. *Concrete to abstract.* This rule is observed in biology where one observes specific characteristics of specimens before developing hypotheses about what is observed.

3. *Expository order based on prerequisite learning.* The curriculum is built upon prerequisite knowledge; advanced material depends upon bringing forward and building on previous material. This sequence is used in subjects that contain laws and principles, such as physics, grammar, and geometry.

4. *Whole to part.* Geography frequently begins with the globe and progresses to studies of different regions and nations.

5. *Part to whole.* In biology one might study anatomy (the separate organs and structures of the organism) before investigating physiology (the study of how the parts and the total organism function).

6. *Chronological.* Used in history and literature, when the subjects logically should be learned in order of occurrence.

Organizational Patterns

The two chief methods of organizing the curriculum are respecting the integrity of the disciplines and using an interdisciplinary organization related more to the way students learn. A variety of patterns have been developed from these two approaches, and occasionally some patterns fall between the two.

Subject Curriculum. The **subject curriculum** is designed to maintain the integrity of the disciplines by organizing content in terms of subjects of instruction. The separate disciplines, such as history, English, and mathematics, remain intact. The study of these subjects is considered necessary because they represent the cultural heritage, and knowledge of them will best prepare students for adult responsibilities.

A subject curriculum is organized according to the inherent logic of the disciplines from which the subjects are selected.

The disciplines from which subjects are drawn consist of organized bodies of knowledge that employ certain methods of inquiry to uncover new knowledge. The disciplines are organized logically and systematically, hence, subjects of instruction are ordered to reflect this internal organization. Once the content is selected for a subject curriculum, it must be associated with the appropriate disciplines and then organized into subjects.

A problem that arises in organizing any curriculum is the content and time devoted to general education and the elective program. **General education** consists of experiences required of all students because such experiences are considered to be essential to fulfilling common objectives, such as becoming an educated person and developing good citizenship qualities. **Elective programs** cater to special interests, abilities, and aspirations and might consist of further study in any area, including vocational preparation. Most of the elementary curriculum is general education; whereas the secondary curriculum, especially grades ten through twelve, have both general and elective programs. Although the subject curriculum is the most commonly used organizational pattern for both general education and elective programs, other organizational patterns can be found, especially in elementary and middle schools.

The reasons for using a subject curriculum are that it is logical and systematic in its organization of knowledge; it ensures the transmission of the cultural heritage by developing essential knowledge; it develops the mind by providing students with substantive material to master; and, finally, both teachers and the public are geared to the subject curriculum and will provide the needed support to assure its success.

But critics claim that the organization of subject curriculums is based essentially on what scholars have found to be valuable in their research rather than on the way children learn. Because a curriculum is desirable only when it corresponds sufficiently with children's thinking and the way they learn, there is some doubt whether the subject curriculum best develops the mind and promotes effective citizenship. Although it is not always the case, instructional practices tend to emphasize rote learning and the massing of facts for test-taking, while they neglect critical thinking and transfer of training.

E D U C A T I O N A L I S S U E 14–1

Should the subject curriculum be the main organizational pattern for education?

Yes	No
1. It is logical and systematic, which makes teaching easier.	1. The logical organization fits the way scholars conduct research, not the way students learn.
2. Students acquire essential knowledge necessary for the transmission of the cultural heritage.	2. The subject curriculum does not necessarily best develop the mind or promote effective leadership.
3. Teachers and the public are most familiar with the subject curriculum and are more likely to support it than any other curriculum.	3. Sticking with a curriculum just because it is familiar can discourage innovative thinking that might develop new, superior ideas.

Structure-of-the-Disciplines Approach. This approach arose during the 1950s and 1960s as a result of the alleged obsolescence of curriculum content and instructional practices in the subject curriculum. While this newer approach retained subjects as a basis for organization, it revised and updated the content, introduced discovery learning, and de-emphasized rote learning in favor of teaching students to grasp the discipline's structure. Fundamental axioms, postulates, concepts and other building blocks of a discipline become the focus of learning so that students can comprehend the underlying structure, attempt to generate fruitful hypotheses, and perceive how scholars discover new knowledge. Advocates of this approach reassessed the concept of readiness and found that some concepts previously reserved for the later grades could be introduced earlier. Jerome Bruner said, "We begin with the assumption that any subject can be taught effectively in some intellectually honest form to any child at any stage of development."[11] Through renewed studies of children's cognitive developmental stages, experts could determine what concepts could be introduced at an earlier age. Surveys of elementary and secondary school principals indicated that, as a result of this approach, some subjects and concepts were being placed in earlier grades.[12]

While the evidence is mixed as to the effectiveness of discovery learning in comparison with other forms of learning,[13] the structure-of-the-disciplines approach is an improvement over the original subject curriculum in several important respects. It requires revision and updating of curriculum content; emphasizes understanding a discipline's structure rather than learning facts for their own sake; stresses critical thinking and intuitive judgments; and urges earlier mastery of concepts. As a result of these factors, students are likely to learn and retain more than they would in a subject curriculum.

Despite its promise, the structure-of-the-disciplines approach does have some shortcomings. The nature of life problems suggests that an interdisciplinary organization would be more effective in teaching students to cope with them because problems know no disciplinary bounds. Many social issues—race relations, war and peace, ecology, population growth—require interdisciplinary insights. Second, when working with subjects rather than interdisciplinary programs teachers and students tend to fail to examine the curriculum as a whole. Such examination is necessary if concepts are to be developed progressively and if there is to be proper continuity and articulation from one grade to the next. Third, this approach emphasizes cognitive learning and tends to neglect social, emotional, and moral development. This emphasis on cognitive development orients the approach to the academically talented; in fact, this curriculum usually was introduced to highly motivated children in superior schools and seldom introduced in schools in lower-class neighborhoods.[14] Fourth, children do not think like adults, much less like trained researchers, and to expect them to do so places unrealistic demands on children. Finally, this type of curriculum gives little attention to goals, other than a mastery of disciplines—and, as we saw earlier, such a goal is open to question.

An interdisciplinary structure gives students a broader conceptual framework for dealing with life beyond school.

Broad-Fields Curriculum. Some educators sought to overcome the shortcomings of the subject curriculum by organizing experiences in terms of the way children learn and avoiding the atomization of knowledge. An approach known as "correlation" or the **correlated curriculum** was proposed in the nineteenth century by the German educator Johann Friedrich Herbart. While correlation retains the subject curriculum, it attempts to interconnect the subjects. One subject is made central, and other subjects are related to it. In studying American history, for instance, material from geography, literature, and other related subjects might be introduced to provide greater understanding.

The **broad-fields curriculum,** which was introduced by the 1920s in American secondary schools and colleges, attempts to diverge from strict subject matter lines and provide a more unified curriculum. While the curriculum retains course organization, subject matter is drawn from two or more disciplines to create survey courses for general-education programs. Examples at the secondary level are the general science course, which usually includes material from biology, geology, and physical science, and the course in problems of American democracy, which uses material from various social sciences. Junior-high and middle schools have offered, in addition to the general-science course, broad-field courses in fine arts, mathematics, language arts, and social studies.

Broad-field proponents claim that such courses provide more opportunities to unify and integrate knowledge, relate more closely to student interests, and afford more opportunities for transfer of training. This curriculum organization, as used in general education, also is suited to the preparation of elementary teachers who need a broad perspective on the arts, natural sciences, and social sciences.

On the other hand, critics say, the broad-fields curriculum suffers from a lack of intellectual rigor, tends toward superficiality, and fails to cover topics adequately. Since particular methods of inquiry were developed in the organized disciplines, scholars tend to charge a lack of intellectual rigor when these methods are appropriated for purposes other than those for which they originally were designed. This curriculum probably can be considered superficial, though, because it does not treat any single discipline in depth. As for the adequate-coverage charge, advocates of the subject curriculum can be expected to believe that students must gain considerable specialized knowledge before a topic has been covered adequately.

Life-Functions Curriculum. This type of curriculum was discussed earlier in connection with the work of Bobbitt and Charters; but other significant programs have since developed along these lines. The **life-function curriculum,** developed by Florence Stratemeyer and associates, is a curriculum organized around persistent life situations.[15] They structured these situations on three broad categories: individual capacities; social participation; and ability to deal with environmental factors and forces. Certain learning tasks are listed under each. For instance, under "individual capacities" are health, intellectual power, moral choices, and aesthetic expression and appreciation. Each of

> Survey courses integrate material from several different disciplines.

these has different subheadings that call for growth and development. Health needs, for example, consist of satisfying physiological, emotional, and social needs as well as learning to avoid and care for illness and injury.

This curriculum more closely connects school experiences and life activities than do the previous curriculums. It breaks completely from subjects. Students no longer study subjects and attempt to apply them to life situations; instead they study the situations themselves. Because of this close connection, this curriculum would seem to facilitate transfer of training (assuming that teachers instruct for transfer). The problem of integration and articulation is less severe in this curriculum because all learning experiences are integrated with persistent life situations and these situations determine the appropriate tasks for each grade level.

The weaknesses of this curriculum are similar to those found in the programs developed by Bobbitt and Charters. The curriculum is based on the assumption that the tasks people currently perform are desirable and should be continued; hence, these tasks are accepted with little thought given to how they could be improved. The social structure remains unquestioned; the school's purpose, in short, is to turn out people who can fit into it. Moreover, the focus is on the present rather than on the more imperative need of preparing for the future. The persistent life situations addressed by this curriculum are usually middle-class situations found in American society; youth of different cultural and socioeconomic backgrounds, therefore, emerge ill-prepared for situations they probably will face.

Activity or Experience Curriculum. As a result of the progressive movement, many elementary schools use an activity or experience curriculum rather than a subject matter curriculum. The **activity curriculum** is based on the assumption that children learn best through experiential units developed from a knowledge of their needs and interests. The curriculum often calls for teacher-pupil planning in which teachers ask children about their needs. They use a problem-solving approach to determine tasks, with the teacher serving as a guide and resource person. (Some educators claim, however, that sufficient knowledge of needs and interests at different age levels is already available, rendering teacher-pupil planning unnecessary.) When the curriculum is preplanned (as most curriculums are), the needs and interests of the students facilitate learning by providing motivation.

Children are likely to find this curriculum more meaningful than the subject curriculum, diminishing motivational problems. The curriculum also is likely to serve a wide range of needs—not just intellectual needs. While it might be wise to begin with a curriculum built around children's interests to stimulate motivation, teachers at some point ought to move children toward what they *should* become interested in. (As we noted earlier, since a child's range of experience is limited, the school should broaden these experiences.) New learning should be connected to the growing interests of children, but the interests, themselves, should not dictate the curriculum.

As we have discussed, basing a curriculum on student needs raises all sorts of obdurate problems. To say that a need exists and that it should be fulfilled is to recognize that it exists to fulfill some objective. Whether an objective is desirable is determined by a set of values or the school's philosophy—not by an appeal to needs.

Core Curriculum. The **core curriculum** is an organizational plan developed during the Eight Year Study sponsored by the Progressive Education Association.[16] (The study, conducted between 1933 and 1941, compared the college performance of high school graduates from traditional schools with that of graduates from progressive schools. Progressive graduates performed as well as, if not better than, the traditional graduates.) While educators intended for this curriculum to be used at all levels of secondary education, it has been found almost exclusively in junior high schools. A core program is an interdisciplinary general-education program that employs block time—two or more hours—rather than the usual classroom periods. It centers on problems of social life or problems of American democracy and uses diverse curricular materials. Because the program involves knowledge of many disciplines, schools usually use a team-teaching approach. The problems surveyed in a core curriculum can require knowledge from the arts, literature, social studies, and the sciences. Students still enroll in vocational and elective courses within a regular class framework, but the heart of their studies is in the core curriculum.

One merit of the core curriculum is its use of problem situations, which are more likely to foster critical thinking than are traditional approaches. By concentrating on the problems of social life, student motivation is enhanced, and a closer connection is made between school concerns and the larger society. The curriculum also assigns a larger role to general education in the lives of students and the use of block time avoids the fragmentation that can be found in the traditional subject curriculum.

Proponents of the subject curriculum contend, however, that the core program leaves large gaps in coverage and fails to handle knowledge systematically; therefore, it fails to provide a grounding in essen-

> Basing curriculum on children's interests does not mean the teacher is not responsible for *extending* their interests.

In addition to implementation, teachers in a core curriculum have demanding intellectual responsibilities.

tial knowledge and skills and neglects the passing along of the cultural heritage. The core curriculum is designed to provide integrated knowledge, but teacher limitations can hinder achievement of that goal. The curriculum is more demanding of teachers than are the more traditional approaches, calling for considerable knowledge, flexibility, and originality. Teacher education seldom prepares teachers for working in such programs.

Humanistic Curriculum. A movement during the 1970s known as humanistic education sought to integrate the affective domain (emotions, attitudes, and values) with the cognitive domain to add more personal meaning to what is learned and to balance coverage of the neglected affective domain with coverage of the cognitive domain. The goal is to offer learners a greater range of choices and have them take responsibility for their choices. Some humanistic curriculums took the form of **values clarification,** a program that avoids indoctrination and focuses instead on a process of examining, clarifying, and accepting or rejecting values.

Gerald Weinstein and Mario Fantini held that teacher-pupil relations are most effectively developed and maintained when the content and methods of instruction have an affective base.[17] The irrelevance found in education, especially for children from disadvantaged backgrounds, stemmed from a failure to match teaching strategies to learning styles, unrelatedness of the material to the learner's knowledge, and the use of materials that ignore the learner's feelings and concerns.

Their first step in developing a humanistic curriculum is to identify the characteristics of the learners as a group and then identify their concerns. This is different from building on interests as the progressives did; interests are limited, and what pupils call interests are really based on concerns. Boys might be "interested" in racing cars, but their real concern is power. Concerns are deeper and more persistent than interests, and can provoke anxiety. Concerns usually fit into one of three broad categories: self-image, control over one's life, and disconnectedness (lack of desire to establish connections with others and society at large). Although children might share similar concerns, their manifestation depends on the social forces affecting them; therefore, the teacher needs to focus on the distinctive group expression of concerns to avoid selecting inappropriate content. The behavioral changes needed are suggested by the learner's concerns. If a child expresses a concern of powerlessness and later begins to take the initiative in overcoming obstacles, then desired behavioral changes are resulting. The teacher introduces "cognitive organizers" in the form of generalizations, principles, and concepts around which the curriculum is developed. These organizers are based on learner concerns and are designed to help learners cope more effectively. The "content vehicles" include not only conventional subjects but also media, classroom situations, out-of-school experiences, and the children themselves. To handle the content, children need basic skills, learning-how-to-learn skills, and self-awareness skills. Basic skills consist of the three Rs and oral communication; learning how to learn involves learning how to analyze problems and identify causes; and self-awareness skills enable the learner to effectively communicate emotional states. Teaching procedures are chosen for matching the learning styles of the group to styles that will have the desired outcomes for the affective domain. Ideally, the curriculum is evaluated continuously, examining the learner's behavior, content vehicles, cognitive skills, and teaching procedures.

The humanistic curriculum, though profiting from some progressive curricular patterns, avoids focusing exclusively on student interests, includes the cognitive domain, draws upon organized subjects as well as personal experiences, and emphasizes basic skills as well as other skills. It also can be a strong motivational tool by identifying and working with deeper student concerns and probably taps into the affective domain more fully than other curricular patterns studied.

The humanistic curriculum, however, requires special skills that most teachers lack and special-educational materials that might not be available. The curriculum also can place too much emphasis on the learner's concerns at the expense of society's needs. It also might focus too much on methods and techniques instead of appraising their consequences for learners.

Teachers may not be adequately trained to manage a humanistic curriculum.

In conclusion, although each curricular organizational pattern has strengths and weaknesses, curriculum developers need not choose a single pattern exclusively. For instance, the general-education program could use a broad-fields approach and the area of specialization could be organized by subjects or by the structure-of-the-disciplines approach. The use of a disciplinary or interdisciplinary approach would depend on one's goals, as well as beliefs about whether the purpose of schooling is for cognitive development or the development of the total person. An emphasis on cognitive development probably would incline the developers toward the disciplines, though other patterns could be used; to develop the whole person, the curriculum likely would use the humanistic curriculum and related interdisciplinary patterns. Which of the two the developers choose would depend upon the philosophy of education used as a foundation.

Organizing a Curriculum

- Using the organizational patterns discussed in this section, describe how your high-school curriculum was organized. What about your junior high or middle school? What would you have done differently? For instance, if the curriculum was organized by subjects, how could it have been supplemented with activity or humanistic elements?

- If you were in charge of developing a curriculum, which organizational pattern or patterns would you choose to work with? How would you attempt to overcome the disadvantages discussed here?

▪ CURRICULUM EVALUATION

A school system cannot select a curriculum until it decides what its educational objectives will be.

Once goals and priorities are clarified, instructional objectives and learning outcomes can be stated more precisely. A curriculum is not evaluated in general terms, such as stating that one curriculum is better than another. In other words, it makes no sense to ask whether the core curriculum is "better than" the subject curriculum. We should ask instead, "Which curriculum is better for what purposes and for what group of students?" Until objectives are clearly stated, a curriculum cannot be evaluated effectively. Certain constraints and limitations within each school system also need to be considered before adopting a curriculum. These constraints can include the administration, faculty, financial resources, physical facilities, and public support.

The nature of evaluation depends, first, on how curricular objectives are defined, and second, on the purposes for which the evaluation results are to be used. Objectives should be defined so that a school system can achieve them through the best efforts of the faculty. Standards are used to determine the extent to which the objectives have been fulfilled. Those standards, also used in curriculum construction, help determine effective teaching, and the degree to which students have achieved desired learning outcomes.

Evaluation determines the effectiveness of curriculum articulation, the capacity of personnel to work effectively with a new curriculum, the ability of students to grasp curricular concepts, and the relative effectiveness of the new curriculum compared with the old one in bringing about certain levels of achievement in specific areas. These and other inquiries are the usual targets of curriculum evaluation.

Because evaluation usually focuses on selected aspects of curriculum or instruction, evaluators must be clear about how the results of the evaluation will be used. The results of an evaluation might confirm the effectiveness of present policies or reveal the need for changes in administration, supervision, curriculum, or instruction.

Michael Scriven shows that the curriculum plan can be studied separately or in terms of its effects.[18] He calls the first type **intrinsic evaluation,** in which evaluators look at the curriculum in terms of its sequence, content accuracy, types of experiences used to understand the content, and the materials used. This type of evaluation relates to Figure 14–2, which shows the separation of curriculum and instruction.

Pay-off evaluation is undertaken after intrinsic evaluation, and examines the effects of the curriculum in practice. Evaluators can consider the effects the curriculum has not only on students but also on teachers, administrators, and parents. They can judge the differences between pre-instruction tests and post-instruction tests and the differences between experimental and control-group outcomes. Pay-off evaluation is usually used to determine short-term results of the curriculum; therefore, intrinsic evaluation is necessary to determine the overall significance of the curriculum.

Besides using standards to determine the extent to which objectives have been achieved, evaluators also can test the hypotheses on which the curriculum rests. In comparing the subject curriculum with curriculums that depart from subject organization, evaluators attempt to compare the learning outcomes of each type of curriculum. The Eight Year Study undertook such a systematic attempt to test hypotheses comparing students from traditional and progressive schools.[19]

A curriculum can be evaluated while it is being developed, or it can be examined for an overall estimate of its effectiveness. Scriven has referred to the first type as formative evaluation and the second type as summative evaluation.[20] **Formative evaluation** examines the curriculum at a predetermined stage of development, and changes, if necessary, are made on the basis of reliable evidence. In contrast, **summative evaluation** is used to reach general conclusions about the curriculum; the curriculum has been developed and can be compared with other curriculums.

Allan Ornstein and Francis Hunkins have conceived the overall process of evaluation in six steps, with the objective of gathering valuable information: (1) focusing on curricular phenomena to be evaluated; (2) collecting the information; (3) organizing the information; (4) analyzing the information; (5) reporting the information; and (6) recycling the information (reevaluation and reassessment).[21]

Evaluation should examine both the short-term and overall effects of a curriculum.

Evaluation is useful only if it is purposeful.

All curriculum evaluation ultimately is used to make more intelligent decisions about programs. Decision makers must first recognize what decisions need to be made and then have the staff collect and analyze information that will summarize the data needed to appraise and modify school policies that affect the curriculum.

▪ CURRICULAR INNOVATIONS

The field of education has seen several curricular and instructional innovations during recent years, each of which varies in scope and significance. For our purposes, we will focus on the innovations that relate more closely to curriculum, rather than those that pertain primarily to instruction and administration. An **innovation** is a new idea, method, or device that improves some aspect of the educational process. In this section, we will look at the innovations of middle schools, non-graded schools, open education, alternative schools, fundamental schools, and competency education. Some of these innovations are recent; others were introduced in the 1960s. Some innovations are widely used; others are less common but have influenced educational thought.

Middle Schools

The **middle school** was developed during the 1960s as a new organizational form and a new approach to educating pupils in grades six, seven, and eight (in some instances fifth or ninth grade is included). Proponents of the middle school believe that the junior high school is not entirely effective and advocate the use of separate buildings and special programs to educate pupils in these grades. The middle school is designed as a bridge between the world of childhood and adolescence, the transitional period in which existing programs are not considered sufficiently suited to the age group. The middle school seeks its own identity apart from the elementary school and the high school. The program features individualized study, team teaching, the integration of extracurricular activities into the formal curriculum, the use of a non-graded plan, and the development of interdisciplinary programs.

The middle school has a more distinctive curriculum of its own than does the junior high school.

The early growth of the middle school may have reflected impatience in turning the junior high school (founded in 1909) into a more responsive program. The junior high school was largely an administrative reorganization that gradually developed a curricular rationale. The middle school directs its attention to a period called "transescence"—a stage of development that begins before the onset of puberty and extends through the early stage of adolescence.[22]

Administrators sometimes have used middle schools to accommodate excessive enrollments from other schools. Besides the difficulties of providing a distinctive program and recruiting qualified teachers, school buildings geared to these programs are not always available. The middle-school movement also has met considerable resistance from junior high-school proponents. But the junior-high program suffers from a lack of research to validate its effectiveness over other middle-grade programs. The middle schools, on the other hand, have produced enough research to allow educators to begin identifying middle-grade practices.[23]

Non-Graded Schools

The principal feature of **non-graded schools** is that grade levels and all expectations associated with separate grades are eliminated. These schools offer individualized instruction and permit students to learn at their own rate of speed. The problems associated with promotion and retention are overcome, instruction no longer has to be geared to the hypothetical average student, and students no longer are delayed by slower classmates. Different age groups work together and learn from one another. For example, a child may be advanced in arithmetic but slower to grasp social studies; consequently, the child is placed with others who have similar abilities in the subjects and works with them in large and small groups. The students also spend time working alone.

Teachers, however, need special preparation to operate in these programs, and the demands can be greater than the demands in traditional graded plans. Most curricular materials are designed for graded schools and, therefore, teachers have to rely on programmed materials and related self-instructional devices. Moreover, many schools that claim to have made the transition to non-graded programs have not really done so. Instead, they merely have substituted homogeneous grouping within the same grade and left vertical curriculum organization and teaching practices unchanged.

> Non-graded schools tend to be more an ideal than a reality.

Open Education

This innovation arose in England and was adapted in the United States in the 1970s; it drew upon the findings of psychologists Susan Issacs and Jean Piaget. In **open education** the teacher instructs and guides learning in small groups or individually rather than instructing the class as a whole. Scheduling is flexible and many activities progress simultaneously. The abolition of a required curriculum enables students to make some decisions about their work. Grading is de-emphasized, students learn at their own pace and in terms of their own learning style, and the teacher is more of a diagnostician, guide, and stimulator. Above all, "the whole child" is recognized. Although open education shares similarities with progressive education, it differs in that it is used more in public than private schools, provides an active role for the teacher, and offers more of a planned environment than do child-centered progressive schools.

The chief difference between open-space schools and open education lies in the flexible architectural arrangements. Research into open-space schools has not found any real improvements in learning or teaching outcomes.[24] Any type of innovative program can exist in open-space or traditional classrooms. Merely changing the architectural design does not make a difference. Open education, however, does seem to have a positive influence on self-concept, attitude toward school, independence, creativity, and curiosity. In a study of ten schools, the researchers found higher achievement in schools that used traditional methods and higher self-concept in schools that used open education.[25] The different definitions of open education and the varied evaluative criteria make it difficult to arrive at conclusive evidence about its overall effectiveness.

Alternative Schools

Free Schools. One of the earliest forms of alternative schooling was the **free school,** which was usually small, private, and based on a belief in liberating the child. Free schools sprang up across the country in the late 1960s as parents attempted to create a new type of learning environment. Using city storefronts, old barns, barracks, abandoned churches, and people's homes, they tried to bring greater freedom of learning through humane principles. *Freedom* is a watchword among free-school advocates, even though the term is not always clearly defined or examined. While the majority of these schools are organized by middle-class white parents and attended by their children, integrated school settings occasionally can be found. The free schools mix progressive and libertarian methods, borrow child-development ideas from Piaget, and add some practices from English infant schools (schools that influenced the open-classroom innovation). School atmospheres range from free and easy to structured, but, generally, children are not pushed to acquire basic skills before they show a readiness to learn.

Most free schools have difficulty raising funds to keep going, and the average school closes down after about eighteen months. Financial instability and the more independent, idiosyncratic personalities of those who are drawn to establish free schools combine to offer further possible explanations for their transience. Free schools also are criticized for being accessible mainly to middle-class whites and for putting little emphasis on basic skills and vocational training. With these serious problems and the increased availability of alternatives in the public schools, free schools declined sharply in the 1970s.

Alternatives in Public Schools. Alternatives in public schools provide options to the traditional model or comprehensive high school to serve diverse educational needs within the community. Alternative schools tend to have more comprehensive goals than traditional schools, provide greater curricular flexibility, and usually are smaller and less bureaucratic than comprehensive high schools.

Alternative schools have several forms. Open schools feature individualized learning activities organized around interest centers. Schools without walls use the entire community for learning. In a large urban area, learning resources might be concentrated in educational parks that are accessible to every student in the city. Magnet schools promote desegregation and special programs not offered in the traditional high school. Street academies and "dropout centers" organize programs for a specific population. Multicultural schools stress ethnic and racial awareness and cultural pluralism. Science academies and schools for the performing arts appeal to students with special talents. Any of these alternative programs can be organized as a unit within a more traditional school.

The rules in alternative schools are usually fewer and clearer and there are higher levels of order and organization than in traditional schools.[26] Studies also have found that students in these programs have more favorable attitudes toward themselves, their teachers, and their schools than do students of traditional schools.[27] Nevertheless, much of the research on alternative schools is of limited value because it typically uses case studies focused on only one or two schools and few studies have compared the academic achievement of students in alternative schools with the achievement of students in traditional schools.

The variety of alternative schools makes it difficult to compare them and their effectiveness.

Magnet Schools

During the 1970s magnet schools were established to promote integration. These schools were designed to offer different types of programs that would stem "white flight" and attract students of different racial and ethnic backgrounds. Magnet schools can be found in many areas of the country, offering programs to students to meet admission criteria regardless of the neighborhoods in which they reside. The 1976 Amendments of the Emergency School Act (ESAA) provided funding

Some magnet schools are dedicated to preparation in the performing arts.

for magnet-school programs, and the Reagan administration used magnet schools for out-of-court settlement of desegregation cases.

Magnet-school programs have continued to diversify. The programs can be built around any one of the following themes: academics, the performing arts, special needs of the gifted and talented, vocations, communications and mass media, health professions, foreign languages, and commercial arts. Elementary magnet schools focus on a particular teaching style: open classroom, Montessori methods, or emphasis on basic skills.

The Houston Independent School District has created an extensive network of magnet schools, ranging from Petro-Chemical Careers Institute to a High School for Law Enforcement and Criminal Justice. This network has been instrumental in reducing segregation of black and Hispanic students and attracting white suburban students to city schools. Magnet schools also have promoted desegregation in Milwaukee. Magnet schools for the performing arts have been established in Philadelphia and Cincinnati.

While the quality of magnet schools varies widely, some studies show that these schools are effective.[28] They seem to foster a positive climate for learning and a commitment by faculty and students to the school's mission. Magnet schools offer voluntary desegregation but cannot, by themselves, overcome segregation problems. Districts that implement mandatory desegregation plans achieve more than three times the racial balance of districts implementing voluntary plans.[29] A lack of support for magnet schools in some districts from school board members, faculty, and especially parents have led to unimpressive results.[30] Criticisms also come from administrators of neighborhood schools who see magnet schools siphoning off the brightest students and isolating students by promoting elitism.

Fundamental Schools

A movement known as **back-to-basics** began in the 1970s and has grown rapidly. More than 5,000 **fundamental schools** exist in the United States ("fundamental" is the title given schools that emphasize basics) and their numbers are still growing. Some of the schools have a fundamental religious foundation. In contrast to most other innovations, the fundamental school was initiated by parents and local citizens who were alarmed over low scores of students on standardized tests, the devaluation of the high-school diploma, and what they considered excessive permissiveness in public schools.

Fundamental schools originated as a reaction to lowered standards in public education.

Fundamental schools stress the basics, strict discipline (which can include corporal punishment and detention), competition, letter grades, standardized testing, ability grouping, homework, and dress codes. Such schools also emphasize moral standards, courtesy, respect for adults, and patriotism. They teach logical reasoning, one's history and heritage, and government structure. In contrast to many alternative schools, students are rewarded for achievement but not for effort. The motives for establishing fundamental schools include overcoming permissiveness, transmitting the cultural heritage more effectively, improving test scores, and instilling religious values.

Fundamental schools have been recognized, though reluctantly, by leaders in the alternatives movement as a legitimate alternative to the prevailing model, even though the underlying ideas are not entirely new. If alternative schools are based on freedom of choice and if the interests and desires of many citizens can be fulfilled only in fundamental schools, then the fundamental school should be an option for parents.

The back-to-basics movement, however, produced improvement only in those mathematical abilities that are least important in an advanced technological society. Students' computational facility improved, but they failed to learn how to solve problems in mathematics.[31] The National Council of Teachers of Mathematics stresses the interdependence of three factors: (1) techniques should help learners focus on specific elements and solve problems on their own; (2) a variety of strategies to solve problems should be encouraged; and (3) students should learn to relate events to mathematical models.[32] Fundamental schools also offer a restricted curriculum that neglects the arts, affective education, vocational education, and full programs of extracurricular activities. With emphasis on drill and rote learning, critical thinking and creativity are neglected. Furthermore, declining test scores, which fundamentalists point to as a reason for gettingback to basics, might be linked to high teacher-pupil ratios, excessive television viewing, more low achievers remaining in school, and less family supervision rather than solely to dereliction of duty in public schools.

Competency Education

This grass-roots movement, initiated by parents, employees, and interested citizens, has pushed for minimum competency testing, starting with the public schools and extending to teacher education. Minimum competency tests have been approved for public schools in thirty-nine states.[33] Teachers in states such as Georgia, Tennessee, and Texas are required to teach prescribed sets of basic skills or "essential elements" on which students will be evaluated on standardized tests. When mandated, the basic skills constitute the major part of the curriculum. Competency tests for experienced teachers, to ensure that their skills are maintained, have been administered in Texas and are being considered in other states. Other competency tests include exit tests in teacher education.

Some citizens believe that incompetent students lacking basic reading and mathematical skills have been certified as competent by being awarded high-school diplomas and, in some cases, college degrees. They believe that the use of competency tests will increase achievement by motivating students to learn so they can attain certain goals and rewards. Proponents also say that certain competencies are needed not only by professionals but also by each high-school graduate who wants to function successfully in society. Though experts may differ as to specific competencies, they agree that a minimum level of achievement should be reached before a student is awarded a diploma. These competencies can be observed and measured in testing situations.

A primary criticism of competency testing is the potential danger that curriculums will be narrowed to "teach to the test."

Critics of competency testing worry that the tests might not be fair to students if it is sprung on them late in their program with little notice. They also are concerned that the test might discriminate against minority students. Also, school programs might have to be changed to prepare students for these competencies. Such changes run the risk of becoming the curriculum itself, which would severely reduce and narrow the curriculum. Teachers probably would teach mainly for the test, and the minimum would be in danger of becoming the maximum.

Mastery Learning

Mastery learning is based on the assumption that mastering a topic or a human behavior is theoretically possible for anyone if schools provide the optimum quality of instruction appropriate to each individual and enough time to master the subject. Mastery learning began with the work of Henry C. Morrison in the 1920s and continued in the 1960s with further studies by J. B. Carroll and Benjamin S. Bloom.

Carroll's model uses five variables: aptitude, perseverance, ability to understand instruction, quality of instruction, and opportunity for learning. Developers of a mastery strategy decide what will constitute mastery for a particular course, determine appropriate procedures, and decide how mastery will be evaluated. Bloom supplements regular instruction with frequent evaluation to determine student progress and uses alternative methods and materials. Objectives are stated behaviorally; students are assessed before instruction to determine their interests and abilities; instruction is adapted to the learner; difficulties are diagnosed frequently; prescriptions for improvement are offered; and students are assessed again after instruction. A variety of instructional procedures are selected; some are discarded and others are added, based on feedback from ongoing instruction. Students who fail to achieve mastery should be assessed to determine the problem and then given more time to gain mastery.

Mastery learning has several advantages. It works in virtually any level of schooling in any subject; potentially 90 percent of students can master a course; students can have a role in developing objectives; mastery can enhance a student's self-concept with a sense of accomplishment; and it promotes cooperation rather than competition for grades.

Mastery learning also has disadvantages. It is more appropriate for learning technical skills; grades become meaningless if most of the students receive the same grades; teachers are unprepared for mastery teaching because reliable tests for assessing the five variables are scarce; mastery learning is overly teacher-centered in that it ignores credit for student effort not reflected on tests; outcomes are overemphasized to the detriment of learning processes.

> Mastery learning is not appropriate for all types of knowledge.

Instructional Technology

Technology in education has grown rapidly in recent decades. Classrooms today might use audio tapes, audiovisual tapes, commercial and cable television, computer conferencing, microwave and satellite transmissions, and computer-based education programs. Two of the most potentially influential technologies are instructional television and computer-based education.

Instructional Television. Instructional television provides students with live or prerecorded television lectures or demonstrations. It can be used to enlarge slides, documents, and pictures; provide off-campus instruction; share firsthand field experiences; provide short demonstrations for videotapes; observe one's own behavior to improve performance (helpful in teacher training); and offer professionally prepared educational programs. Television also can provide instruction for students unable to attend classes (in conjunction with a study guide or syllabus); the broadcasts can be aired repeatedly at convenient times; students generally prefer television instruction to regular lectures; and viewers are able to see specimens, documents, and pictures more clearly.

Instructional television has some disadvantages. It provides no interaction or opportunities to raise questions (unless specific provisions are made for feedback); it is inferior to other media for music broadcasts; it requires a large audience to be cost effective; and some teachers are averse to using it. Furthermore, except in the early grades, students tend to prefer small-group discussion. Even though instructional television offers students little opportunity to raise questions and interact, it can be argued that it is at least as effective as other media and methods.

Computer-Based Education. Some observers believe that, within a few years, the ability to program and use microcomputers may be as important as the ability to read, write, type, drive, or use a telephone.

Automated teaching devices emerged in the 1920s with the first teaching machines, mechanical and electronic devices used for self-instruction, although they did not achieve popularity until the 1950s. Programmed materials supplanted these machines in the 1950s and 1960s. The emergence of computer-assisted instruction (CAI) in the late 1960s was heralded as a breakthrough, but its cost was prohibitive. The rapid spread of microcomputers can be attributed mostly to decreases in the cost of microtechnology. More than one million units can be found in elementary and secondary schools. Hardware development is outpacing software development and implementation, and the current microcomputers probably will be outdated in several years.

Microcomputers are valuable in several ways. They can involve the learner actively, provide immediate feedback, link with anything that responds to an electronic signal (videotape players, electronic musical equipment), and promote conceptual and abstract thinking.

Among the shortcomings, the quality of programs often is a problem because program development is time-consuming and expensive. Also, thousands of programs have limited instructional value. Other problems include the lack of teacher preparation in computer instruc-

Computer-based education actively involves learners with diverse stimuli.

tion; the reduction of personal contact and interpersonal communication; limited experiential learning, especially in young children; and the tendency of most software programs to restrict imagery and creative thinking by treating knowledge as linear, objective, determinate and finite.

Home Schooling

Home schooling, a young movement found in the United States and other countries, is allowed in thirty-eight states. In the early 1970s, 15,000 children were educated at home; today, that number has grown to more than 120,000—perhaps as many as 200,000.[34] Parents who prefer home instruction cite "drugs, sex, and Godlessness" in public schools as the reason for keeping their children home; others contend that public schools are ineffective in dealing with the disabled and the gifted. They share the belief that parents should be deeply involved in the education of their children.

Some states require attendance at a public or private school but do not authorize home instruction. Controversies have arisen in those states over what legally constitutes a "school." Some states have interpreted such statutes as precluding home instruction, while other states have authorized home education that meets state standards. Four states require home tutors to be certified, and five states require testing for mastery of basic skills.[35] Where home schooling is authorized, courts have differed over whether the state or the parents have the burden of proving that home-education programs are equivalent to public-school offerings.

One advantage of home schooling is that it permits parents to be in charge of their children's education. It also allows parents to shield their children from what they consider undesirable influences in public and nonpublic schools. Education in general also might benefit from home education. John Holt says home schooling can be considered a sort of research laboratory that can answer some vital questions that would unlikely be tested in public schools. Does frequent testing help or hinder children's learning? What would happen if students could read anything they liked and not be graded on it? What would be the effect of allowing students as much time as they desired on projects?[36]

> A major disadvantage of home schooling is the child's lack of social interaction with peers.

One serious disadvantage lies in states that have few, if any, regulations for home schooling. This means that parents, some of whom are not high-school graduates, are solely responsible for their child's education. Another disadvantage is that home schoolers have less opportunity to interact and learn from other children, and their social and emotional development might be arrested. Parents also cannot provide the quality of learning resources that schools can, such as science laboratories, libraries, computer facilities, and gymnasiums.

▪ **PAUSE TO REFLECT**
The Effect of Computers on Education

- Computers already have an important place in all levels of education; how do you envision computers affecting education in the future? Do you think they might someday replace the teacher as the main instructor in the classroom? Why or why not?

- How could computers and instructional television be used to help upgrade the quality of home schooling?

▪ Summary

- The curriculum can be conceptualized in one of three ways: as courses of study, as the sum of the learner's experiences under school influence, or as a systematic body of material with an organized plan for promoting formal instruction.

- A school district's *policy network* establishes and regulates the *curriculum development system,* the organizational framework for development, implementation, and evaluation of the curriculum.

- Curriculum developers derive general curricular objectives from the aims of the school system's educational philosophy. The curriculum goals and content vary depending on the educational philosophy adopted by a school.

- Curriculums usually are structured from one of four perspectives: the learner (based on the interests and needs of the students); the subject matter (based on the suggestions of scholars from various disciplines); the larger society (based on the skills needed to handle adult tasks and responsibilities); and eclecticism (based on a combination of the previous three perspectives).

- The criteria used to select a curriculum's content are significance (how the material contributes to the objectives of the curriculum); learnability (how effective the various curriculum materials are); authoritativeness (how up-to-date the knowledge is); interest (whether the students will be motivated by the material); and feasibility (how easily the curriculum can be implemented).

- Developers use certain common elements to structure the curriculum: concepts, principles, theories, values, and skills. They also determine how best to sequence the material from grade to grade. Some sequencing guidelines include *simple to complex* (chemistry); *concrete to abstract* (biology); *expository order based on prerequisite learning* (grammar); *whole to part* (geography); *part to whole* (anatomy and physiology); and *chronological* (history).

- Curriculums can be organized in several different ways, all of which either respect the integrity of the disciplines or use an interdisciplinary approach related more to the way students learn—or a little of both. Organizational patterns include *subject curriculum* (organized in terms of subjects of instruction); *structure-of-the disciplines approach* (organized around subjects, but emphasizing discovery learning and de-emphasizing rote learning); *broad-fields curriculum* (diverges from strict subject matter lines and offers a more unified curriculum); *life-functions curriculum* (organized around persistent life situations); *activity or experience curriculum* (organized in terms of experiential units based on students' needs and interests); *core curriculum* (an interdisciplinary general-education program); and *humanistic curriculum* (integrates the affective domain with the cognitive domain).

- Curriculum evaluation helps educators determine several factors: the effectiveness of curriculum articulation, the capacity of personnel to work with a new curriculum, the ability of students to grasp curricular concepts, and the relative effectiveness of a new curriculum compared with the old one.

- Curricular and instructional innovations include *middle schools* (designed to bridge the gap between childhood and adolescence for students in grades six through eight, and sometimes fifth and ninth grades); *non-graded schools* (designed to eliminate grade levels and all associated expectations); *open education* (abolishes a required curriculum and provides flexibility); *alternative schools* (sometimes known as "free schools," which mix progressive and libertarian methods); *alternatives in public schools* (adds educational options to the traditional or comprehensive high school); *magnet schools* (designed as a desegregation tool by attracting students from different racial and ethnic backgrounds); *fundamental schools* (emphasize back-to-basics); *competency education* (provides instruction in essential skills on which students are tested); *mastery learning* (focuses on helping students master certain subjects); *instructional technology* (includes instructional television and computer-based education); and *home schooling* (allows parents to educate their children at home.

▪ **Key Terms**

activity curriculum

alternative schools

back-to-basics

co-curriculum

concept

core curriculum

correlated curriculum

curriculum

curriculum development system

elective programs

formative evaluation

free schools

fundamental schools

general education

humanistic curriculum

innovation

intrinsic evaluation

job analysis

life-functions curriculum

mastery learning

middle school

non-graded schools

open education

pay-off evaluation

policy network

principle

skill

structure-of-the-disciplines approach

subject curriculum

summative evaluation

theory

values

values clarification

■ Discussion Questions

1. Evaluate the relative merits of the three ways of conceptualizing the curriculum.

2. What steps would one need to take in developing a curriculum?

3. How can curriculum evaluation be used to improve curriculum?

4. Of the different curricular innovations discussed in this chapter, which ones are likely to have the most influence on the curriculum during the 1990s? Explain the basis for your decision.

■ Learning Activities

1. In terms of your teaching field, show how you would develop a unit based on the ideas in this chapter.

2. Organize a classroom debate on the resolution "_____ is the most educationally sound." (Fill in the blank with a curricular organizational pattern.)

3. Investigate the curriculum experiments conducted in the Eight Year Study and report to class on your findings.

4. Interview educators in your local school district to determine how the district's curriculum is developed. How do state and federal guidelines and requirements influence that curriculum?

5. Trace the evolution of the curriculum in your local school district since 1960 by recording the major changes in the underlying philosophy, curriculum content, organization, and evaluation.

Suggested Readings

Kliebard, Herbert M. *The Struggle for the American Curriculum 1893–1958.* Boston: Routledge & Kegan Paul, 1986.

A historical study of significant curricular movements and influential educators.

McNeil, John D. *Curriculum: A Comprehensive Introduction,* 4th ed., Glenview, IL: Scott, Foresman, 1990.

Discusses different curriculum conceptions, curriculum development, theory, and issues.

Ornstein, Allan C., and Francis P. Hunkins. *Curriculum: Foundations, Principles, and Issues.* Englewood Cliffs, NJ: Prentice-Hall, 1988.

Systematically outlines contributions to curriculum of various foundation fields, the principles of curriculum development and evaluation, and current issues.

Rich, John Martin, ed. *Innovations in Education: Reformers and Their Critics*, 5th ed. Boston: Allyn and Bacon, 1988.

A selection of leading reformers and their critics, followed by prominent innovations, both pro and con.

Tanner, Daniel, and Laurel N. Tanner. *Curriculum Development: Theory Into Practice*, 2nd ed. New York: Macmillan, 1980.

An in-depth study of the curriculum field's emergence and its effect on current issues.

Notes

1. Ronald C. Doll, *Curriculum Improvement: Decision-Making and Process* (Boston: Allyn and Bacon, 1970), 21; J. Minor Gwynn and John B. Chase, Jr., *Curriculum Principles and Social Trends*, 4th ed. (New York: Macmillan, 1969), 216; and J. Galen Saylor and William M. Alexander, *Curriculum Planning for Modern Schools* (New York: Holt, Rinehart and Winston, 1966), 5.

2. For a discussion of programmatic definitions, see Israel Scheffler, *The Language of Education* (Springfield, IL: Charles C. Thomas, 1960), ch. 1.

3. This approach can be found in Educational Policies Commission, *Education for All American Youth* (Washington, DC: National Education Association, 1944).

4. More comprehensive critiques of the need concept can be found in Reginald D. Archambault, "The Concept of Need and Its Relation to Certain Aspects of Educational Theory," *Harvard Educational Review* 27 (1957): 38–62; and B. Paul Komisar, "'Need' and the Needs-Curriculum," in *Language and Concepts in Education*, eds. B. Othanel Smith and Robert H. Ennis (Chicago: Rand McNally, 1961), 24–42. A more sophisticated theory of needs than presented in this chapter is in Abraham Maslow's *Motivation and Personality* (New York: Harper & Row, 1954).

5. Franklin Bobbitt, *The Curriculum* (Boston: Houghton Mifflin, 1918).

6. Herbert Spencer, *Education: Intellectual, Moral, and Physical* (New York: James B. Millar and Co., 1884), ch. 1.

7. W. W. Charters, *Curriculum Construction* (New York: Macmillan, 1923).

8. National Commission on Excellence in Education, *A Nation at Risk: The Imperative for Educational Reform* (Washington, DC: U.S. Department of Education, 1983).

9. James B. Hunt, Jr., "Education for Economic Growth." In *Taking Sides: Clashing Views on Controversial Educational Issues*, 5th ed. Ed. James Wm. Noll (Guilford, CT: Dushkin, 1989), 118–25.

10. Ralph W. Tyler, *Basic Principles of Curriculum and Instruction* (Chicago: University of Chicago Press, 1950).

11. Jerome S. Bruner, *The Process of Education* (Cambridge, MA: Harvard University Press, 1960), 33.

12. Project on Instructional Program of the Public Schools, *The Principals Look at the Schools* (Washington, DC: National Education Association, 1962).

13. Richard E. Ripple and Desmond J. Drinkwater, "Transfer of Learning," in *Encyclopedia of Educational Research*, 5th ed. Ed. Harold E. Mitzel (New York: Free Press, 1982), 1947–55.

14. For this and other criticisms, see John I. Goodlad, *School Curriculum Reform* (New York: Fund for the Advancement of Education, 1964) and Theodore R. Sizer, "Reform Movement or Panacea?" *Saturday Review* 48 (1965), 52–54, 72.

15. Florence B. Stratemeyer, et al., *Developing a Curriculum for Modern Living* (New York: Bureau of Publications, Teachers College, Columbia University, 1947).

16. See H. H. Giles, S. P. MacCutcheon, and A. N. Zechiel, *Exploring the Curriculum* (New York: Harper & Row, 1942).

17. Gerald Weinstein and Mario D. Fantini, *Toward Humanistic Education: A Curriculum of Affect* (New York: Praeger Publishers, 1970).

18. Michael Scriven, "The Methodology of Evaluation," in *Curriculum: An Introduction to the Field*, eds. J. R. Gress and D. E. Purple (Berkeley, CA: McCutchan, 1978), 337–408.

19. Giles, et al., *Exploring the Curriculum;* E. R. Smith and Ralph W. Tyler, *Appraising and Recording Student Progress* (New York: Harper & Row, 1942).

20. Michael Scriven, "The Methodology of Evaluation," in *Perspectives of Curriculum Evaluation*, ed. Robert E. Stake (Chicago: Rand McNally, 1967), 39–83.

21. Allan C. Ornstein and Francis P. Hunkins, *Curriculum: Foundations, Principles, and Issues* (Englewood Cliffs, NJ: Prentice-Hall, 1988), 268.

22. D. H. Eichorn, *The Middle School* (New York: Center for Applied Research in Education, 1966), 3.

23. J. H. Johnston and G. C. Markle, eds., *Middle School Research Annual* (Laramie: University of Wyoming, Center for Research and Publications, 1979); and C. K. McCann, ed., *Perspectives on Middle School Research* (Cincinnati: University of Cincinnati, College of Education, 1980).

24. D. G. Armstrong, "Open Space vs. Self-Contained," *Educational Leadership* 32 (1975): 291–95.

25. A. Lukasevich and R. F. Gray, "Open Space, Open Education, and Pupil Performance," *Elementary School Journal* 79 (1978): 108–14.

26. E. J. Trickett, "Toward a Social-Ecological Conception of Adolescent Socialization: Normative Data on Contrasting Types of Public School Classrooms," *Child Development* 49 (1978): 408–14.

27. D. L. Duke and I. Muzio, "How Effective Are Alternative Schools? A Review of Recent Evaluations and Reports," *Teachers College Record* 79 (1978): 461–83.

28. Denis P. Doyle and Marsha Levine, "Magnet Schools: Choice and Quality in Public Education," *Phi Delta Kappan* 66 (1984): 265–69.

29. Mark Smylie, "Reducing Racial Isolation in Large School Districts: The Comparative Effectiveness of Mandatory and Voluntary Strategies," *Urban Education* 17 (1983): 77–83.

30. James Lowry Associates, *Survey of Magnet Schools* (Washington: National Institute of Education, 1984).

31. Curtis L. McNight, et al., *The Underachieving Curriculum* (Champaign, IL: Stipes, 1987).

32. National Council of Teachers of Mathematics, *An Agenda for Action: Recommendations for School Mathematics of the 1980s* (Reston, VA: The Council, 1983).

33. *Education Vital Signs,* Vol. II (Baltimore: National School Boards Association, 1986), chart I.

34. Patricia M. Lines, "An Overview of Home Instruction," *Phi Delta Kappan* 68 (1987): 510.

35. Patricia Lines, "Home Instruction," *Issuegram* No. 49, Education Commission of the States (1984).

36. John Holt, "Schools and Home Schoolers: A Fruitful Partnership," *Phi Delta Kappan* 64 (1983): 391–94.

■ PART SIX

FUTURISM AND EDUCATION ■

Part Six explores the future of American education (to the year 2000 and beyond) to involve the student's imagination and envision plans for a better future. This is accomplished by projecting future problems, offering scenarios, and developing vivid models and compelling future policies.

We bring our past to each present moment and project upon these moments our aspirations for the future. Our images of the future shape our experiences and fill them with hope or dread, anticipation or apprehension. Soothsayers since antiquity have hypnotized their followers with prophecies of bliss or catastrophe. Scientific and scholarly minds have addressed the future systematically since the 1960s and have developed a large body of futuristic studies that offer enlightened visions and alternative future scenarios.

Futurists can help form plausible visions of the future and provide projections that educators can use for planning and decision making. The magnitude of present social and educational problems requires renewed effort to generate realistic solutions and alternative future models to prepare education to meet the challenges of the twenty-first century.

Chapter 15 looks at the meaning of and requirements for education in a postindustrial society, the types and importance of futuristic studies, future educational trends, and the search for new educational futures.

■ CHAPTER 15

EDUCATION FACES ■
THE FUTURE

A LOOK AHEAD

The purpose of this chapter is to promote imaginative thinking about the future of education to the year 2000 and beyond. You will learn about:

- How a postindustrial society differs from an industrial society
- The role of education in a postindustrial society
- Techniques used in futuristics to gain a perspective of the future
- The significance of educational trends
- How the search for new educational futures might affect schooling

The future will not wait. While some people hold tightly to infrequent moments of joy, others seek an idyllic former age or anticipate future developments and devise ways to cope with them intelligently.

Families and schools always have had the task of preparing youth for the future, but this task is probably more difficult today. Rapid, unprecedented changes are sweeping society, and social institutions often prove ill-prepared in anticipating, planning, and coordinating these changes. The inadequacies of existing institutions and their beliefs and values are more vividly and forcefully publicized than ever because of electronic developments that have made instantaneous, worldwide communication possible. Citizens, scholars, and educators are joining forces to change those institutions and greet the future of education armed with timely, intelligent information.

■ THE CHALLENGES OF POSTINDUSTRIAL SOCIETY

Observers believe that the United States and other developed nations have entered a new age that is qualitatively different from the industrial age. It has several names, such as "postindustrial society," "technotronic society," "postmodern society," "post-civilized era," "third wave," and "electronic society." Several dramatic developments, most of which have occurred since World War II, have precipitated the shift from an industrial to a **postindustrial society**.

Postwar developments include the development of enormous nuclear arsenals, the beginning of the Cold War, and the promise of peaceful uses of atomic energy. The threat of nuclear warfare has altered international diplomacy significantly and has changed the face of warfare as a way to achieve political objectives.

The introduction of automation in industry has changed industrial relations and the worker's place in the economy. The development of digital and analog computers has made possible important advancements in research and engineering. Computers have been particularly valuable in the design and navigation of aircraft and rockets and in the development of computer sequences of operation for automatic machinery in industry. The successful exploration of space would not have been possible without such advances in computers. The space age began with the Soviet Union's launching of Sputnik in 1957 and has continued to more recent expeditions to the moon and with instrumental probes of planets in our solar system. The space age has provided important meteorological and scientific information as well as a new vision of the universe and humanity's place in it.

Vast biological changes promise to transform our world view as dramatically as the developments in the physical sciences did earlier in the century, and surely will raise far greater moral issues. Scientists are unraveling the intricacies of the genetic code, which could lead to the ability to alter inherited diseases and congenital characteristics and extend the average life expectancy.

The postindustrial age has witnessed a growing interdependence in economic life and in social, political, and educational aspects of society. The trend has been heightened by advancements in transportation and communication that are turning the world, in Marshall McLuhan's terms, into a "global village." Most technological changes in the past affected social life and value systems slowly over many decades. Today's changes, however, quickly and significantly affect the way people live and relate to one another, their beliefs and values. These rapid developments have created what Alvin Toffler has called "future shock," the "shattering stress and disorientation that we induce in individuals by subjecting them to too much change in too short a time."[1] Many people find it difficult to comprehend fully—much less cope with—these dramatic changes. Yet failure to adapt can be catastrophic for a society.

The emphasis in industrial societies is on the production of sufficient goods. Now that the economy has demonstrated the capacity to produce an overabundance of some goods, emphasis has shifted to services and equitable distribution of goods and resources. The focus is now on providing greater economic equality in an affluent society.

Daniel Bell envisions postindustrial society as embracing the shift to a service economy, the preeminence of the professional and technical class, and the centrality of theoretical knowledge as the source of innovation and policy development.[2] He suggests that while soldiers and landowners dominated in the preindustrial age and business owners dominated in industrial society, scientists and researchers will dominate in postindustrial society. In the move from industrial to postindustrial society, the locus of power shifts from the corporation to the university and research institute, and the role of new knowledge becomes preeminent.

However, some observers believe that a shortage of brain power threatens postindustrial advances such as the growth and vitality of the computer, electronics, and communications industries in the United States.[3] American leadership, they say, has failed to recognize the shift from a capital-intensive economy that plays down education to a knowledge-intensive economy. But the scrutiny of American education since the early 1980s, the large-scale changes introduced in many schools and colleges, and the greater involvement of business and political leaders in educational decisions does suggest increased awareness, however belated, of the problem.

> Society must learn to adapt more quickly to change than it has been required to do in the past.

> Knowledge may eventually determine society's dominant class.

FUTURISTICS ■

Futuristics is the attempt to gain a long-range perspective on the future using a variety of inquiry methods. Until the 1960s, when research institutes and government commissions got involved, little systematic effort had been devoted to forecasting and the development of futuristic techniques. Today's futurists (those who study the future) might use knowledge from the past to project into the future by assuming certain similarities or continuities between the two. Or they might assume that certain patterns of events recur periodically (as in economic cycles). Futurists also fashion creative notions about the future, such as ideas about a more healthful environment, leaving it to the policy makers to bring about needed changes.

It is likely that future problems will demand interdisciplinary solutions.

Future problems are difficult to define because they usually involve more than one discipline, such as population and environmental problems. The future is uncertain not only because it magnifies the uncertainties in present-day life but also because the future evolves from decisions yet to be made. Because of this, futuristics does not strive primarily for prediction but for a greater understanding of problems to be faced and possible alternative futures. Different futuristic techniques complement one another and can be used together. They also can be divided into intuitive techniques (primarily using imagination) and formalistic techniques (primarily using mathematical models). Futurists have many techniques from which to choose. Let us look at a few of the major ones.

Trend Extrapolation

In some respects futuristics in the 1960s was a reaction against trend extrapolation, or the view that the future is strictly determined by past events. Nevertheless, trend extrapolations are used to quantify various aspects of a problem, as in studies of population growth, energy consumption, and increases in the transportation of goods. **Trend extrapolation** assumes that forces at work in the past will also be found in the future. This technique does not allow for discontinuities or the unexpected. If the population of a city is increasing 3 percent annually, it is assumed that this rate of increase will continue, and future population projections are based on this rate. Demographers, city planners, and economists often use this technique in their forecasts.

To know what effect an event or trend might have on the future, we must know its underlying causes.

But the results of trend extrapolation can be misleading if the underlying causes of the change are unknown or if new changes occur. Growth sometimes does not follow the projected pattern, especially when breakthroughs in technology bring major changes in areas such as transportation and communication, or when new policies bring about changes, such as reduced birth rates in undeveloped nations.

Delphi Technique

The **Delphi technique** is a method of forecasting based on concerns of experts. A group of experts in a field develop forecasts individually; then the group collects and studies the results. The experts might revise their earlier forecasts or offer reasons for disagreeing with the others. The process continues until each individual understands all other positions and all have reached final conclusions on their individual positions. Generally, the Delphi technique engages experts in anonymous debate, and opinions are exchanged through an intermediary or moderator. In the first round, experts are asked when an event might take place. The answers are collected and justification is sought in the second round. The third and final round expects the participants to reassess their views in light of the views of others. A later form of this technique does not seek a consensus among experts or communicate final individual responses to everyone—it is handled through a questionnaire sent to a group of experts. The monitor summarizes questionnaire results and usually gives the experts a final chance to evaluate their responses.

> The Delphi technique calls for experts to draw on their imaginations as well as their knowledge.

An example of a modified Delphi approach in education involves an NEA panel composed of fifty selected leaders who were asked what they expected the world would be like at the turn of the century and how they believed educators should help people prepare for it.[4] Another example involves a survey of scholars in the natural and social sciences who were asked to identify concepts in their fields that they believed students should understand to survive the troubled years ahead.[5] The Delphi technique also has been used frequently in combination with other methods.

Scenarios

A **scenario** is a description of a future development at a given point in time. It is an imagined future in which one speculates about what would happen if certain things occurred. Once a question is posed, one begins to imagine various consequences of events. A scenario could be developed using Malthus's axiom that the means of subsistence increase by an arithmetic ratio while the population increases by a geometric ratio. If true, what world population conditions could be expected in the next twenty-five years? Or, if the school-of-choice movement (as presented in Chapter 11) grows throughout the nation during the 1990s, what scenario could be developed for public and nonpublic education?

A scenario can consist of a hypothetical situation in the future, with the major changes assumed to have taken place during the intervening years, and an account of anticipated actions by the chief parties involved in the situation. Scenarios can be used to avert or cope more effectively with future crises, such as the dangers of nuclear war, threats to international security, or environmental disturbances. Scenarios also can help mobilize people to plan and make more intelligent decisions about the future. Successful scenarios are multifaceted and holistic in their approach to the future, showing the interaction of many variables—social trends, political events, economic variables, and educational changes. By tracing the events that lead to a particular future point, one can understand what has to occur before the future development results. Some future events might be considered dangerous or undesirable; therefore, by imagining in detail how they might arise, experts can suggest steps to make them less probable or dangerous.

■ **PAUSE TO REFLECT**
A Scenario of Future School Systems

● It is the year 2005. The public-school system in the United States has been abolished and replaced by a fragmented system of secular private and parochial schools. What events would have to occur to bring about this scenario? Is it a desirable possibility? What suggestions would you make to encourage—or prevent—such a situation?

● If experts in the 1960s had been able to envision the state of education in the 1990s, would they have encouraged it? What suggestions do you think they might have made in an effort to shape the future?

Mapping Techniques

Mapping techniques use diagrams or flow charts to depict events, characteristics, and goals to be explored. The diagram might not actually supply any more information than a separate listing of the items; but a diagram provides a visual representation that indicates a pattern of relationships or choices that might not be apparent on a basic list. It also can show various future alternatives that might not be evident in a verbal description. Mapping techniques can be useful in formulating a sequence of events (as in planning a trip with many different stops), and in assessing multiple choices or options available.

Figure 15–1 shows a cross-impact or multiple-trend projection of future curriculums. Existing program E combines with educational reform proposals B, C, and D; program F combines with C and D reform proposals; program G combines with proposal D; and H remains independent of the new proposals. With such a diagram, experts can visualize the multiple combinations and more easily anticipate changes.

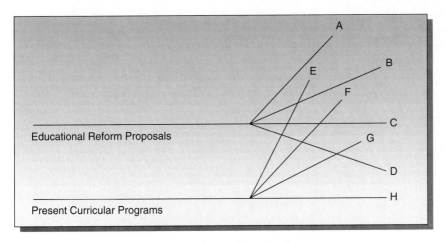

FIGURE 15–1 Cross-impact analysis of curriculums

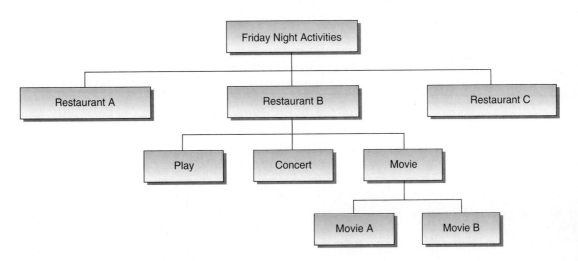

FIGURE 15–2 Entertainment decision

Suppose we are trying to decide where to go Friday night for entertainment. Assume the choice is dining in one of three different types of restaurants, to be followed by attending a play, a concert, or one of two movies. One can visualize in Figure 15–2 the various alternatives more clearly and more easily come to a decision based on a consideration of the different options. The chosen alternative then becomes a plan of action. In other situations, the alternatives might be vastly more complex and require the use of computers to determine the best choice.

Models, Simulations, and Games

A **model** provides an interpretation of phenomena through a form of analogy. A model might suggest ways to expand the theory that the model is a part of or that is embedded in the model. An established model can help a new theory gain acceptance if it resembles the model. Models can be "models of" or "models for." "Models of" are isomorphic, such as scale-model prototypes of new airplanes, whereas "models for" are more like hypotheses or assertions about the expected behavior of certain phenomena. The model might have negative and positive analogies; the negative analogies, which are misleading, are merely discarded. One example of a "model for" is using athletics to show, by an interpretive analogy, how discipline is somewhat like sports, games, and exercises. Economists often use "models of" to understand the nation's economy.

A **simulation** brings about changes in a static model over time. When children play with model airplanes, they create simulations of the airplane in flight. **Games** might be simulations of situations but also involve rule-governed behavior that regulates the players' moves or activities and determines what counts as "winning" or success within the framework of the game. A war game might involve several teams at military installations, government agencies, and research institutes using a nationwide network of teletypes and computers to simulate the Navy's role in a particular war. Games might also simulate international political affairs and projected crisis situations, leading to an assessment of the strength of nations under a stipulated set of conditions.

▪ FUTURE EDUCATIONAL TRENDS

We can anticipate major changes in education over this decade.

In the year 2000 education will retain many of its present attributes, but also will have taken on sharply divergent tendencies and new directions. Nationwide concern about education, influential national commission reports, state reform measures, and the activities of various interest groups are likely to bring about the biggest changes in American education in the 1990s. Here are some likely developments.

National Educational Standards

After an initial meeting in 1989 among President George Bush and the nation's governors, a follow-up meeting of the governors in early 1990 led to a vision of the nation's educational system for the year 2000. A package of six goals and twenty-one objectives was adopted, creating a direction for the nation's educational system. The National Governor's Association said that to have a strong and responsible democracy and a prosperous economy into the twenty-first century, the nation must reach these six educational goals by the year 2000:

1. All children in the United States will begin school ready to learn.

2. The high-school graduation rate will increase by at least 90 percent.

3. Students will leave grades four, eight, and twelve having demonstrated competency in challenging subject matter.

4. Students in the United States will be first in the world in mathematics and science achievement.

5. Every American citizen will be literate and possess the skills necessary to compete in a global economy and exercise citizenship responsibilities.

6. Every school in America will be free of violence and drugs and will provide a disciplined environment conducive to learning.[6]

These ambitious national goals do not emanate from the federal government (though they have the encouragement of the executive branch). They are not matters of federal legislation and largely will be pursued at the state level through the cooperation of the governors.

Even though states will continue to control educational policy, federal influence will not diminish.

Another sign of a movement toward national educational standards is the National Assessment, established by Congress under a National Assessment Education Board. The board, which operates the National Assessment fairly independently, voted to seek greater authority to make state-by-state reporting routine, institute international comparisons, and develop a list of what students in every grade should know in every subject. Because the goals set by the governors are broader than those of any single state, the National Assessment would measure progress toward achieving them. Some educators have accused the board of attempting to impose a national curriculum on the states.[7]

Chester Finn has proposed establishing national norms for minimum knowledge and skill levels that every student should acquire before completing compulsory education. Compulsory education, he says, should relate to attainment levels, not age levels. These norms should apply not only to basic skills but also to standard subjects ranging from mathematics to foreign languages. While the norms would apply to this core, schools would be free to differ from each other by developing programs outside the core. States and school dis-

It is possible that national standards of education will emerge.

tricts would be free to choose whether to adopt the norms. Finn recognizes that some will complain that the proposal leads to a national core curriculum, but he believes that this outcome would be better than the *de facto* national curriculum created by textbook publishers, testing companies, the television industry, national publications, and popular cultures.[8]

Other evidence of a move toward national standards includes the proposal by the Carnegie Task Force on Teaching as a Profession to create a National Board for Professional Teaching Standards by 1993. The board will be organized with a regional and state membership to establish high teacher standards and to certify teachers who meet the standards.[9] The board will consist of teachers, government officials,

There is a move toward national teacher certification.

business leaders, and representatives of higher education. Teachers will be evaluated on knowledge of their subject, teaching techniques, and an understanding of child development. National teaching credentials will be offered in twenty-nine fields. These national credentials will not replace state teaching certificates but will be in addition to state certification.[10] National certification scheduled to begin in 1993 is likely to carry more prestige than state certification, and not all teachers certified by the state are expected to qualify.

The national board proposed a national teachers certificate in lieu of a college degree in education. This decision is likely to place the movement at odds with 1,200 institutions that grant education degrees. Many educators think the national certificate would reduce the state's role in certification.[11] The American Association of Colleges for Teacher Education (AACTE), representing more than seven hundred institutions that prepare teachers, voted not to support the work of the national board because it believes the board's approach will lower the very quality it seeks to elevate by eliminating requirements of state certification and pedagogical preparation.[12]

Resistance to national norms for a core curriculum will probably be strongest, followed by opposition to national certification. The governors' plan to establish national goals generally has been well received, but some observers insist that a national assessment is needed to determine whether the goals are achieved. Therefore, the trend in the 1990s will be toward national plans of education and probably greater similarity to education in other nations.

Alex Inkeles and Larry Sirowy launched a study to determine whether the educational systems of nations are becoming more alike in thirty different dimensions. The evidence suggested that national education systems converge on common structures and practices. Some common factors include an increasingly complex administrative and financial structure; a national ministry, department, or office of education; and greater use of inspectors to ensure conformity to standards. Forces that lead to differences are historical traditions, political systems, and the level of economic development.[13]

EDUCATIONAL ISSUE 15–1

Should public schools adopt national educational standards?

Yes	**No**
1. Students would be more likely to receive an equal education.	1. The reduced state and local education would mean a less personal approach to education, fewer opportunities for innovation, and more bureaucracy.
2. National certification requirements would improve the quality of teachers.	2. Many teachers who qualify for state certificates likely would not qualify for national certificates, leading to disparities in pay and prestige that might foster frustration and resentment among teachers.
3. Adoption of a national education plan would make it easier to incorporate successful educational methods from other nations.	3. A suitable plan does not exist for evaluating the success of a national program.

Decline of Public Education

The development of schools of choice, voucher plans, and tuition tax credits (presented in earlier chapters) mark a decline in the central role of public schools in American education. Along these lines, the Wisconsin legislature passed a bill giving about 1,000 Milwaukee public-school students the option of attending nonsectarian private schools at state expense. The program was designed to last five years and permit the students to enroll in accredited nonpublic schools that agree to accept the state's per-pupil aid allotment. Most of the other states that permit students to attend private schools at public expense grant school districts a role in approving and monitoring the participation of private schools.[14]

Arthur C. Clarke projects that public education will become diffused throughout society. Though the public school still will exist, it will be only one facet of a diversity of systems, many of which will be privately operated.[15] Theodore Sizer believes that the system will fragment, and several different schooling methods will arise as public confidence in the present system erodes.[16]

One scenario envisions the passage of a tuition tax-credit law that leads to the rapid growth of private schools and funding cuts for public schools. Later, a voucher system is adopted as an alternative to tuition tax credits. A three-tier system results, with partially subsidized and selective schools for upper-class and upper-middle-class children, subsidized schools for the middle class, and no-frills public schools for the lower class. The scenario concludes that citizen groups will need to fight for public schools to save American democracy.[17]

One might argue that the movement toward national educational standards conflicts with this trend because the decline of public education signifies greater diversity. But national standards still would apply mainly to public education. The curriculum of most public schools probably would emphasize minimum competencies, compensatory education, fundamental skills, and some vocational preparation. Diverse, enriched, and alternative programs would be found more often in nonpublic schools.

Technology in Education

In a technotronic society technology is vital. Electronics can be expected to be involved in many innovations: computers to assist in medical diagnosis; access to library holdings on microfiche with readable computer printouts; ordinary books available to the blind as computers are programmed to convert printed English into natural-speech sounds; portable computer terminals and telephone-plus-computer systems that allow managers thousands of miles away to keep in touch with several employees simultaneously through computer terminals; and homes equipped with computer terminals for shopping, voting, and working at home.[18]

In the 1990s the home increasingly will become an "electronic cottage," but not to the extent that Alvin Toffler predicted.[19] Mainly it applies to young adults who are eager to advance in their careers and who prefer to work at home rather than in the traditional workplace of office and factory. Such work in the home includes monitoring distant manufacturing processes, typing electronic correspondence, writing pamphlets, or programming computers. In the electronic cottage,

Texas is the first state to allow some textbook funds to be used to purchase laser videodiscs.

parent-child relations will become more technocratic—structured, planned, hierarchal, and organized in terms of rules and standards.

Education technology will be expanded and perfected during the 1990s. Instructional and education television, interactive television, teleconferencing, dial-access systems for individualized instruction, microteaching, computer-assisted instruction, and computer-managed instruction will become common features of school systems.

Instruction follows the premise stated by Charles Weingartner that everything can be done better by adopting electronic information-handling systems. The computer, he claimed, is synergistic, and everyone can learn more efficiently by computer than by traditional instruction.[20]

Decades ago Lewis Mumford warned about the dangers of automation, but he has gone unheeded by the new experts. Mumford, looking at the historical record, insisted that autocracy and technology are the same, that they suppress variety and autonomy and pressure people to conform to the controls of the autocratic designer.[21] He said the media of communication, although an improvement over earlier, cruder models, fail to provide needed information about their own performance—or if the information is available, refuse to accept it by

There are fears that knowledge will become subordinate to technology.

blocking its transmission and attempting to cover up their own errors.[22] The system is interested only in quantitative increases; where automation has taken command, it has made dialogue, social cooperation, and moral evaluation difficult. Human beings need the freedom to accept, modify, or reject the new technology and should pursue the knowledge needed to make intelligent decisions.[23]

As Jacques Ellul said, contemporary individuals have no moral, intellectual, or spiritual reference point for judging technology because they were born into a technological society and are not fully conscious of the environment and the way it shapes them. In this environment the individual is prepared for professions that require a knowledge and use of technology; entertainment and advertising hypostasize the environment and depict leisure in terms of technological things and devices. In the end there is only one way to satisfy desires—the technological way.[24] And although technology frees humans from many restraints, it limits the range of fundamental choice. Choices are expressed in terms of objects and have no ethical content. What is to be produced or eliminated—the choice among investments that determine consumption—is not open to the consumer. The system reduces choices either to faster or slower growth. Thus both the choices and the intellectual systems are expressions or justifications of technology.[25]

But citizens of a technotronic society are not fully cognizant of these dangers because they have no firm place to stand apart from the system itself. Consequently, in the world of the 1990s criticism of technology will be considered in terms of growth patterns (insufficient growth in some sectors and overly rapid growth in others) or distribution of rewards (some claim that their compensation for services is inadequate). Society is rushing pell mell toward greater growth of technocracy and the encapsulation of citizens in the intellectual systems and life styles that emerge from and are consonant with this type of society. On the one hand, some prophecies did not materialize in the 1980s—economic collapse as a consequence of unmanageable population growth; alterations in the balance of power between the rich and poor nations as poor nations learned to wage nuclear war; and the inability to maintain industrial growth because of limited resources and pollution problems, leading to the destabilization of democracies and the rise of authoritarian states.[26] Yet no alternate technology, as urged in the 1970s and based on a steady-state economy and economically sound practices,[27] will be found or even seriously considered in the United States during the 1990s.

Global Education

More people are recognizing the importance of global education, and in light of international changes in political, economic, and educational conditions, global education probably will become more wide-spread. These developments are likely to begin in higher education and spread to secondary schools. A national survey of 3,000 college students by the Educational Testing Service found only a small proportion of college students have an adequate understanding of global situations and processes. At most, 5 percent of the four-year college programs are devoted to global knowledge. Political science textbooks lack an adequate global perspective. Moreover, the Department of Education spends less than 1.5 percent of its budget on international programs.[28]

> We must educate students to live in a global community.

A 1972 survey of fifty leaders suggested that educators need to develop a spirit of global community that respects multiethnic and multicultural differences at home and abroad.[29] Gordon M. Ambrich believes the focus of the 1990s will be on preparing students for a worldwide marketplace in which emphasis will be placed on foreign languages and citizenship responsibility in democratic government. He also believes that cross-national comparisons of education will be emphasized and that education will provide global action on peace-keeping and environmental problems.[30] Austin and Knight Kiplinger envision a college core curriculum in which courses will be placed in a global context regardless of the student's major. Most professions will require some knowledge of geography, economics, languages, and cultures.[31]

These changes already have begun in higher education. Stanford University offers seventeen courses with a global dimension, including a seminar on East-West economic relations. It also sends students on study trips to Japan, the Soviet Union, and Mexico.[32] Purdue University is adopting curriculum changes to internationalize the outlook of its students. Languages offered now include Japanese and Chinese, and Purdue has new affiliations in China and Europe. To become more marketable, engineering majors will take courses in foreign languages and general culture.[33]

Multiple Centers of Learning

Alvin Toffler believes that more learning will occur outside the class-room than inside. Compulsory schooling will be shortened, and young and old will mingle in learning activities. Work, which will begin earlier in life and also be found in the home, will become more interwoven with education. Because of these anticipated changes, the young will become less peer-oriented, less consumption-oriented, and not as hedonistically self-involved.[34]

The business community is heavily involved in providing its own educational programs. IBM spends two billion dollars annually for education within the company. Assembly-line workers are granted tuition vouchers through a joint program of the United Auto Workers and Ford to put toward earning college degrees. Ten million workers take courses each year. It is expected that by the year 2000 business will invest $80 billion to $100 billion a year in worker training and development, and at any given time 10 percent of the work force will be enrolled in job-training programs.[35] Corporate education in the United States already is the fastest-growing segment of the educational community. One can expect that people will pursue education throughout their lives.[36]

National public-service youth corps are likely to be established, replacing most of the federal student-aid program. Students seeking federal aid would be expected first to provide national or community service, such as joining the military, tutoring, or working in nursing homes or hospitals. An individual could earn vouchers to be applied to college, technical training, or even a down payment on a house.[37] Some observers see it becoming an expected public service year for youth that is devoted to community, state, or nation.[38]

▪ **PAUSE TO REFLECT**
National Public Service

- The idea of a national public-service youth corps opens up many possibilities for society. Other than the examples of public service discussed in this section, what other services could young people be asked to provide in a mandatory corps? Should such service come before or after college? Why?

- Do you think one year is long enough for young people to serve in a public-service corps? If not, how long should they serve? How could their experience supplement their education? How else would young people benefit from serving in such a corps?

Greater Family Choice and Participation

Families differ in the problems they face, not only because families confront different conditions and have varying degrees of resources for coping with those conditions, but also because families themselves differ. No single prescription could fit everyone because of the numerous types of families: two parent, married; two parent, contractual; gay or lesbian couple with children; one parent, divorced; one parent, separated; one parent, widowed; one parent, unmarried; grandparent and child; relatives and child; guardian and child.

By the year 2000 three kinds of American families are likely to dominate: families of first marriages, single-parent families, and families of remarriage (three-fourths of divorced people remarry). Cohabitation will become more widely accepted, but as a precursor to marriage rather than as an alternative.[39] The divorce rate is expected to decline, the growth in the number of single-person households will slow, and income inequality among families will increase.[40]

Thus the school-of-choice movement is likely to expand during the 1990s. While today's families, because of their structure or circumstances, are in a better position to take advantage of the increasingly available options, families of the future will have more choices in the education of their children. Home schooling will expand slowly because many parents lack the abilities to meet state guidelines or because of economic or health constraints. The growth of the Christian fundamental school movement is likely to continue. Other states also might follow Minnesota's lead and provide tuition tax credits. Some cities might pursue Milwaukee's plan to allow students to enroll in private schools at state expense (see page 585), although such plans are in danger of being struck down by the courts. And if Chicago's community-control plan is successful, similar plans probably will be tested elsewhere.

Families will have more choices in education and, thus, more involvement.

Public-school educators also will seek greater parent participation in the education of their children. One serious problem hindering such participation is that the divorce rate, the number of single-parent homes, and the proportion of married mothers of young children working outside the home have doubled since 1965. As a consequence, parents have less time and energy to devote to their children. Although many schools encourage parent participation in the primary grades, most schools do less to promote participation in higher grades. But plans are being introduced to change this situation. The state of Kentucky intends to install telephones in every classroom to make it easier for teachers and parents to maintain contact. Dade County, Florida, and St. Paul, Minnesota, are constructing elementary schools close to factories and office buildings to make it easier for parents to meet with teachers and attend school events.[41]

Some school districts are already trying to make it easier for parents to be more involved in their children's education.

More than 75 percent of working women are in childbearing years. Although 90 percent of employers with ten or more workers presently do not provide day care, John Naisbitt and Patricia Aburdene predict that day care will become a common employee benefit in the 1990s. They also expect that more employers will adopt creative policies for maternity leave.[42] Child care will need to improve dramatically—the United States ranks nineteenth in the world in preventing infant mortality. France, which ranks fourth, has national policies for child care, well-trained staffs, leadership from the government, support from

In the future, educators will encourage parents to play a greater role in their children's education.

business and industry, and free preschool programs for three-to-five year olds attended by 98 percent of the children.[43]

Because the welfare of children is crucial to the future of our children and the nation, government (at all levels), business, and health services will need to take a more active role in child care. As parents are given more options in the education of their children they also will need more assistance in selecting a school (through gathered information about school characteristics and available opportunities); in caring for their children more effectively (possibly through parent education); in gaining knowledge about human sexuality and birth control; and in supporting and participating intelligently in their child's education.

New Traits and Abilities

Major changes in society, the economy, and international relations will result in a need for new abilities, traits, and different educational preparation. About one million students, 25 percent of the high-school population, drop out annually, and another million have only marginal skills. By 1995 only 5 percent to 7 percent of the nation's jobs will be unskilled; by the year 2000 nearly a third will require a college degree.[44] Before they retire, workers of the 1990s can expect to change jobs ten times and careers three times.[45]

According to Arthur C. Clarke, more jobs will involve creating, transmitting, and processing ideas and information; therefore, schools will need to focus on how to think and how to learn.[46] The growth occupations are shifting to sectors that require high-level skills in problem-solving, communication, reading, writing, and mathematics.[47] John Naisbitt believes that we will need to return to the ideal of a generalist education. Those who overspecialize run the risk that their specialty will become obsolete; a generalist who is committed to lifelong education can change more readily. Long-range forecasting skills, Naisbitt believes, also will increase in value.[48] The volume of information will double every two years; therefore periodic upgrading of qualifications will become routine.[49] The education needed by productive citizens will go far beyond today's basics and emphasize problem-solving, thinking skills, and learning how to learn in a context that will cultivate broadly educated, flexible, and creative individuals.

> The need for lifelong committment to education will become more acute, and specialized skills may quickly become obsolete.

THE SEARCH FOR NEW EDUCATIONAL FUTURES ■

A group of scholars in the natural and social sciences have identified concepts in their fields that they believe students should understand if they are to survive in the years ahead. Basic concepts from the natural sciences include the carrying capacity of the Earth and the need to conserve, ecological holism and interdependence, threat of ecocide, entropy, scientific method, threat of explosive population growth, theory of evolution, unity, photosynthesis, and oxidation. Basic concepts from the social sciences include the proliferation of knowledge, learning how to learn, the systems approach, the need to develop a set of examined values, issues relating to freedom and responsibility, issues of equality and the law, and history. Other concepts from the social sciences include understanding the nature of power and national interests, free enterprise and enlightened self-interest, trade-offs, economic equity, the information economy, social fragmentation, voluntary frugality, cultural pluralism, and global community. Four basic issues were raised in both the natural and social sciences: human vulnerability, the need for more research, lifelong learning, and information overload.[50] Thus, futuristic studies can include a large and significant body of concepts. Such a futuristic curriculum would provide substantive and significant material for study and, along with an understanding of futuristic techniques, enable students to think more boldly and prepare more effectively for the future.

The decisions we make in the present help shape the future. That some people have disproportionate power to make decisions that affect us all suggests the importance of democratic, responsive institutions that guarantee basic freedoms and the constitutional rights of all. Donald Michael said, "All who create and use thinking about the future do so on the bases of values and images about what is real, valuable, and meaningful."[51] Although we grow up in a culture that helps us to make these determinations, and our thought is further shaped on these matters by social class, ethnicity, ideologies, family socialization, political socialization, and schooling, an individual's quest is usually to gain sufficient autonomy to make reasonably independent judgments. One can create value and meaning, but it helps to have a responsive environment. Many different outlooks, however, stand in the way. For example, the idea that "every event has a cause" was challenged by Pyrro (c. 360–270 B.C.) and the Pyrrhonists who held that it is impossible to know the nature of anything. Every statement can be countered by its contradictory, and neither is more convincing than the other. Later thinkers also have expressed this outlook, but in somewhat different form. The presupposition that a person's life can have purpose has been disputed by Calvinism and pessimism. Calvinism holds that each person's salvation or damnation is predetermined by God and that every event of one's life is predestined. Pessimists, such as Clarence Darrow and Leo Tolstoy, contend that death is better than life and nothing is really worth doing.

But the search for meaning and value can be found, as Viktor Frankl showed, under the most radically restrictive conditions, such as those found in a Nazi concentration camp, where individuals maintained their dignity by finding a meaning for their suffering and, therefore, meaning in life.[52] Individuals with terminal illnesses may be thought not to have a choice. They do, however. They have a choice of what Frankl calls "attitudinal values," the attitude they will take toward their suffering; if, in fact, the attitude they assume has a place for suffering in human existence, life can have a meaning for them until the very end.[53]

Because the future is in part created by decisions made today, individuals need to be creators as well as receivers of values. Therefore, a productive orientation to life is needed. This orientation is maintained by the full use of one's abilities, as well as by overcoming the natural and cultural forces that weaken productivity and despoil human creations. By cultivating a sense of identity and a productive orientation, one can avoid the stifling of human ability by the alienating forces in the larger society. To have the courage to make oneself whole in an uncertain universe is the height of the life-affirming spirit.

Our present values shape our thinking for the future.

■ Summary

- The industrial age in the United States has been replaced by what many observers call "postindustrial society," moving away from manufacture and toward service. Where business owners dominated in the industrial age, researchers and scientists dominate in the postindustrial age. The growing computer, electronics, and communications industries face a shortage of brain power; therefore, educators, business leaders, and politicians are studying the American educational system to determine the best path to take toward the future.

- *Futuristics* involves the attempt to gain perspective on the future through a variety of inquiry methods. *Trend extrapolation* anticipates the future based on past events. The *Delphi technique* depends on the opinions of experts to forecast the future. *Scenarios* involve imagining the future and figuring out what events would lead to such a scenario. *Mapping techniques* use diagrams or flow charts to help experts visualize events, characteristics, and goals to be explored. *Models* offer analogies of certain phenomena; *simulations* involve manipulation of models; and *games* can include simulations but also include rules.

- The growing concern about the future of American education is likely to bring about major changes in school systems by the year 2000. Some of those changes include a movement toward national educational standards, the decline of public education, the growth of technology in education, an emphasis on global education, the emergence of multiple centers of learning outside schools, greater family choice and participation in education, and the need for significant new traits and abilities.

- Scholars in the natural and social sciences have identified several concepts that they believe students need to understand to function effectively in the years ahead. The two sciences came up with many different concepts, but shared four basic ones: human vulnerability, the need for more research, lifelong learning, and information overload.

■ Key Terms

Delphi technique	postindustrial society
futuristics	scenario
games	simulation
mapping techniques	trend extrapolation
model	

■ Discussion Questions

1. What do industrial and postindustrial societies have in common? How do they differ?

2. What challenges are humans in a postindustrial society facing for the first time in history?

3. Of the six future trends identified, which do you believe will have the greatest effect on American education? Why?

4. What future trends, other than the six presented, do you believe will occur by the year 2000? Provide evidence to support your beliefs.

5. In studying the future, what futures studies will likely be the most useful?

6. What types of curriculum changes are needed to prepare students more effectively for the future?

■ Learning Activities

1. Imagine you are living in the year 2110. How would you characterize the early 1990s? Write down your thoughts and note any perspectives you have gained on the present.

2. Develop a scenario of American education in the year 2000. Depict it as vividly as you can. Present it in class and defend your vision.

3. Read some science fiction books and identify the most plausible and compelling scenarios you find of the future. Explain the basis of your selection.

4. Collect materials and information about futuristics programs (see World Future Society materials and other sources). Identify programs that you believe to be especially effective and present your findings to the class.

Suggested Reading

Clarke, Arthur C. *Arthur C. Clarke's July 20, 2019.* New York: Macmillan, 1986.

An imaginative and vivid foray into the future by a renowned science-fiction writer.

Didsbury, Howard J., Jr. *Student Handbook for the Study of the Future.* Washington, DC: World Future Society, 1979.

Designed to help the student gain a basic understanding of futuristics.

Kiplinger, Austin and Knight A. Kiplinger. *America in the Global '90s.* Washington, DC: Kiplinger Books, 1989.

Provides a generally optimistic picture of changes in America's economy, population, health, education, and job opportunities in the 1990s.

Marien, Michael and Lane Jennings, eds. *What I Have Learned: Thinking About the Future Then and Now.* New York: Greenwood Press, 1987.

Leading futurists assess their experiences in futuristics and convey insights into the future.

Toffler, Alvin. *The Third Wave.* New York: Bantam Books, 1981.

The author of *Future Shock* explains the new electronic age and its demands on various aspects of our lives, including education.

Wyant, Alice Chambers and O. W. Markley. *Information and the Future: A Handbook of Sources and Strategies.* New York: Greenwood Press, 1988.

Provides important information about key sources for studying the future.

Notes

1. Alvin Toffler, *Future Shock* (New York: Bantam, 1971), 2.
2. Daniel Bell, *The Coming of Post-Industrial Society* (New York: Basic Books, 1973).
3. James Botkin, Dan Dimancescu, and Ray Stata, *Global Stakes: The Future of High Technology in America* (Cambridge, MA: Ballinger, 1982).
4. Harold G. Shane, "The Views of 50 Distinguished World Citizens and Educators," in *1999: The World of Tomorrow,* ed. Edward Cornish, (Washington, DC: World Future Society, 1978), 105–10.
5. Harold G. Shane with M. Bernadine Tabler, *Education for a New Millenium: Views of 132 International Scholars* (Bloomington, IN: Phi Delta Kappa Educational Foundation, 1981).
6. "Text of Statement on Education Goals Adopted by Governors," *Education Week* (March 7, 1990): 16–17.
7. Edward B. Fiske, "The Struggle Begins Over Controlling How Education Will Be Evaluated," *The New York Times* (March 21, 1990): B7.
8. Chester E. Finn, Jr., "Why We Need a National Education Policy," *The Education Digest* (April 1990): 8–10.
9. Carnegie Forum on Education and the Economy, *A Nation Prepared: Teachers for the 21st Century* (Washington, DC: Carnegie Forum on Education and the Economy, 1986).
10. "National Teaching Licenses Aim at Upgrading," *Arkansas Gazette* (July 18, 1989): 6A.
11. "Education Degree Isn't a Requirement in Plan to Certify Teachers Nationally," *The Wall Street Journal* (July 10, 1989): A10.

12. Ann Bradley, "AACTE Decides Not to Support Teaching Board," *Education Week* (September 20, 1989): 1, 21.

13. Alex Inkeles and Larry Sirowy, "Convergent and Divergent Trends in National Educational Systems," *Social Forces* 62 (1983): 303–33.

14. William Snider, "Voucher System for 1,000 Pupils Adopted in Wisconsin," *Education Week* (March 28, 1990): 14.

15. Arthur C. Clarke, *Arthur C. Clarke's July 20, 2019* (New York: Macmillan, 1986), 78–79.

16. Quoted in "A Look Ahead: Education and the New Decade," *Education Week* (January 10, 1990): 29.

17. Robert A. Blume, "Toward Private Schools: Can We Save Public Education?" *The Humanist* 42 (January–February 1982): 16–19.

18. See Stephen Rosen, *Future Facts* (New York: Touchstone Books, 1976), ch. 7; and Alvin Toffler, *The Third Wave* (New York: Bantam Books, 1980), 194–207, 216–21.

19. Toffler, *The Third Wave*, 216–21.

20. Charles Weingartner, "No More Pencils, No More Books, No More Teachers' Dirty Looks." In *Educational Futures: Sourcebook I,* eds. F. Kierstead, J. Bowman, and C. Dede (Washington, DC: World Future Society, 1979), 71–82.

21. Lewis Mumford, *The Myth of the Machine: The Pentagon of Power* (New York: Harcourt Brace Jovanovich, 1970), graphics section.

22. Ibid., 183.

23. Ibid., 184–93.

24. Jacques Ellul, *The Technological Society* (New York: Continuum, 1980), 311–18.

25. Ibid., 319–25. For an opposing position, see Samuel C. Florman, *Blaming Technology* (New York: Saint Martin's Press, 1981).

26. Robert L. Heilbroner, *An Inquiry into the Human Prospect* (New York: Norton, 1975).

27. David Dickerson, *Alternative Technology and the Politics of Technical Change* (Glasgow: Fontana/Collins, 1974).

28. Advisory Task Force, Council on Learning, *Education and the World View: Final Task Force Report and Recommendations* (New Rochelle, NY: Change Magazine Press, 1981).

29. Shane, "The Views," 108.

30. Quoted in "A Look Ahead," 31.

31. Austin H. Kiplinger and Knight A. Kiplinger, *America in the Global 90s* (Washington, DC: Kiplinger Books, 1989), 157.

32. "Best Business Schools," *U.S. News & World Report* (March 19, 1990): 55–56.

33. "The Race is on to Ready Students for Globalization," *The New York Times* (March 26, 1990): 85.

34. Toffler, *The Third Wave*, 384.

35. Kiplinger and Kiplinger, *America*, 155.

36. Clarke, 79.

37. Kiplinger and Kiplinger, 159–60.

38. Paul F. Brandwein, *Memorandum: On Renewing Schooling and Education* (New York: Harcourt Brace Jovanovich, 1981).

39. Andrew Cherlin, "The American Family in the Year 2000," *The Futurist* 17 (1983): 7–14; American Council of Life Insurance, *The Shape of the American Family in the Year 2000.* (Washington, DC: The Council, 1982).

40. United Way Strategic Institute, "Nine Forces Reshaping America," *The Futurist* 24 (1990): 9–16.

41. Kenneth H. Bacon, "Many Educators View Involved Parents as Key to Children's Success in School," *The Wall Street Journal* (July 31, 1990): B1.

42. John Naisbitt and Patricia Aburdene, *Megatrends 2000* (New York: William Morrow, 1990), 231–34.

43. Fred M. Hechinger, "Why France Outstrips the United States in Nurturing its Children" *The New York Times* (August 1, 1990): B8.

44. Ellen Graham, "If Johnny Can't Read, the U.S. Can't Compete," *The Wall Street Journal*, Centennial Edition (June 27, 1989): A23.

45. "Measures of Change," *U.S. News & World Report* (December 25, 1989): 66–67.

46. Clarke, 76.

47. "A Look at the Economy," *The Washington Spectator* (April 15, 1990): 2.

48. John Naisbitt, *Megatrends* (New York: Warner Books, 1982), 95–96.

49. Kiplinger and Kiplinger, *America*, 161.

50. Shane with Tabler, *Educating for a New Millenium*.

51. Donald N. Michael, "The Futurist Tells Stories," in *What I Have Learned*, eds. Michael Marien and Lane Jennings (New York: Greenwood Press, 1987), 79.

52. Viktor Frankl, *Man's Search for Meaning* (New York: Washington Square Press, 1963).

53. Viktor Frankl, *The Doctor and the Soul* (New York: Knopf, 1955).

GLOSSARY ■

A priori knowledge: knowledge that is prior to and independent of sense experience.

Absolute purpose statement: a statement that would hold eternally, be immutable, and apply universally.

Absurd, the: the hiatus between the individual and the world, the actor and his or her setting.

Academic freedom: the liberty needed to develop and communicate knowledge in the academic community without administrative, political, ecclesiastical, and other forms of interference.

Academic sanctions: rewards granted by teachers when students learn content in accordance with rules employed by the teacher for content mastery; or punishment, administered when students fail to do so.

Acculturation: the process of learning about and adopting the cultural traits of another group.

Achieved status: a voluntarily assumed social position that reflects a measure of personal ability and accomplishment.

Activity curriculum: a form of curriculum organization based on the assumption that children learn best through experiential, rather than subject matter, units that are developed from a knowledge of their needs and interests.

Aesthetics: a branch of philosophy that analyzes standards and values in art and aesthetic experience.

Aim: a statement of purpose that applies internationally, nationally, or statewide in education.

Alternative schools: schools designed to provide options to the traditional model or comprehensive high school by offering more comprehensive goals, greater curricular flexibility, smaller enrollment and less bureaucracy.

Amalgamation: the blending of racial types through a lengthy period of inbreeding.

Anglo conformity: the period (about 1900) in which Anglo-Americans, the dominant group, sought to maintain the social institutions and cultural pattern of England.

Aristocratic education: education rooted in the belief that a certain class or group is superior and should be the only group to receive the benefits of a formal education.

Ascribed status: an involuntary social position assumed at birth or later in life.

Assimilation: the process by which individuals or groups voluntarily or involuntarily adopt the culture of another group, thereby losing their original identity.

Authority: power that is perceived as legitimate rather than coercive.

Authority, charismatic: the ability to inspire obedience and devotion in others as a result of extraordinary personal characteristics.

Authority, rational-legal: the granting of power to someone under a constitutional or other legal system; sometimes called "bureaucratic authority."

Authority, traditional: power based on respect for established cultural patterns. (Contrast with *Authority, charismatic* and *Authority, rational-legal.*)

Axiology: the study of values to determine their origins, meaning, characteristics, types, and epistemological status.

Back-to-basics: an educational movement that stresses learning the basics; it is the mission of fundamental schools.

Behaviorism: the belief that one's behavior is determined by environment, not heredity, and that education can contribute significantly to the shaping of the individual.

Bilingual education: a program in two languages that seeks to enable children to function effectively in an environment of two languages and two cultures.

Block grants: federal allocations that states or municipalities may spend as they choose as long as the intent of the legislation authorizing the grant is satisfied. (Contrast with *Categorical grants.*)

Boundary maintenance mechanisms: ways in which one culture tries to separate itself from another culture, usually a more dominant culture.

Broad-fields curriculum: a form of curriculum organization in which subject matter is drawn from two or more disciplines to provide survey courses for general education.

Bureaucracy: a large-scale organization designed to carry out complex tasks.

Busing: a means of equalizing educational opportunity by balancing the distribution of different races throughout the school system.

Calvinism: principles and practices associated with John Calvin's teachings, which were based on a stern moral code and influenced colonial education.

Career ladders: plans that offer teachers higher salaries for performing duties different from those of colleagues.

Caste system: a social stratification system based almost entirely on *ascribed status.*

Categorical grants: aid for specific purposes that frequently takes the form of federal grants that the state is required to match. (Contrast with *Block grants.*)

Censorship: the deliberate attempt to exclude materials that may damage the young, harm society, or offend the censor.

Certification: evidence that the applicant meets requisite standards for employment or further training.

Charismatic authority: See *Authority, charismatic.*

Child abuse: violence or mistreatment that causes physical or mental suffering to a child.

Classical conditioning: as discovered by Ivan Pavlov, it is a process by which an originally neutral stimulus comes to elicit a response.

Co-curriculum: activities outside the classroom that influence or relate to classroom learning activities.

Coherence theory of truth: the theory that a statement or belief is true if it is logically consistent with other statements accepted as true.

Collective bargaining: a means of power accommodation in which an attempt is made to resolve the conflict between two or more parties through compromise and concession.

Collective responsibility: the ascription of obligation to a group, organization, firm or governing body for an act or related series of acts that affect an individual or individuals, groups and, in some cases, society as a whole.

Common schools: schools under state auspices designed to teach a common body of knowledge to students of different social backgrounds.

Communication: a means of conveying thoughts and information through language and nonverbal behavior.

Community control of schools: schools run by lay school boards in the neighborhood, rather than the central administration.

Compensatory education: programs designed to meet the special educational needs of disadvantaged children from low-income families.

Competency-based teacher education: a teacher-preparation program, also known as performance-based teacher education, designed to train and test teachers in terms of exhibiting specific desirable abilities.

Competency education: the teaching of certain skills, abilities, and experiences needed by every high-school graduate to function successfully in society; schools generally are considered responsible for developing these competencies.

Complete skeptics: those who believe it is impossible to have knowledge of any sort.

Concept: a generalized idea of a thing or class of things.

Conditioning: the process of modifying the relation of a response to a stimulus to bring about a change in behavior.

Conflict: in a society, the struggle between contrasting and opposing groups.

Conflict theory, legal: a theory that questions for whom the legal system is functional and observes that it is not functional for some less powerful groups. It views the legal system as created by certain individuals and groups to protect their interests. (Contrast with *Functionalism, legal.*)

Conflict theory, social: Karl Marx's theory of inevitable conflict between capitalists and workers.

Contributory value: the value of a thing that is part of a whole that has value.

Control: the restraint or regulation of persons and things. Requires authority.

Core curriculum: a general education program that employs block time, is interdisciplinary, and centers on problems of social life in which diverse curricular materials are employed.

Corporal punishment: punishment inflicted directly to the body.

Correlated curriculum: a form of curriculum organization that retains subjects but attempts to interconnect them.

Correspondence theory of truth: the theory that a statement is true if what it refers to (corresponds to) exists.

Critical pedagogy: an educational philosophy that draws on neo-Marxism and promotes some of the goals of reconstructionism, including the creation of new social order.

Cultural ecology: the theory that explores the relationship between human culture and the physical environment.

Cultural lag: inconsistence within a culture resulting from the unequal rate of change in cultural elements.

Cultural pluralism: a state of peaceful coexistence in which different groups maintain their cultural differences after undergoing a period of adjustment.

Cultural relativism: a method by which different cultures are studied objectively without using the values of one culture to judge the worth of another.

Cultural traits: the smallest unit of a culture that can be listed and described; for example, the use of a stone ax to develop tools.

Cultural universals: practices and codes of conduct found in every culture.

Culture: an integrated pattern of human behavior that includes thought, speech, action, and artifacts and depends on the human capacity for learning and transmitting knowledge to succeeding generations.

Curriculum: a systematic body of material and an organized plan for the purpose of promoting formal instruction.

Curriculum development system: an organizational framework with assigned personnel for ongoing development, implementation, and evaluation of the curriculum.

Dame school: an early form of primary instruction that consisted of single women taking children into their homes to hear lessons.

De facto segregation: segregation enforced not by law but by fact, as in segregated patterns of housing. (Contrast with *De jure segregation.*)

Deism: a belief in God on rational grounds without reliance on authority or revelation.

De jure segregation: segregation by law or by government intent. (Contrast with *De facto segregation.*)

Delphi technique: a method of forecasting based on concerns of experts.

Determinism: the idea that all things in the universe are governed by causal laws.

Deviant behavior: social behavior that violates social norms and is subject to social sanctions, including legal sanctions.

Deviant subculture: a microculture made up of individuals in rebellion against the norm. (See *Microculture.*)

Dialectical materialism: the philosophy stemming from Marx and Engels that applies Hegel's dialectic to nature, history, and social processes.

Diffusion: the spread of cultural elements of one culture to another culture.

Discovery: the uncovering, recognizing, and understanding of something that exists.

Discrimination: unfair or unjust treatment of minorities just because they are minorities.

Dogma: a point of view, set of beliefs, or tenet put forth as authoritative without adequate grounds.

Dualism: belief in the existence of two independent, separate and irreducible realms, such as mind and matter.

Educational parks: areas that consolidate or cluster existing schools, broadening their attendance areas so that the school population becomes racially and economically mixed.

Educator: someone knowledgeable in the theory and practice of education who can apply that expertise in the classroom.

Egalitarianism: a belief in human equality in terms of human rights that advocates the removal of inequalities among people.

Elastic: a tax yield whose rate increases more rapidly than incomes. (Contrast with *Inelastic.*)

Elective programs: programs designed to appeal to special interests, abilities, and aspirations and might consist of further study in any area, including vocational preparation.

Empiricism: the school of thought that holds that all ideas are derived from experience and must be established by reference to experience alone.

Endogamy: marriage between people of the same social class.

Enlightenment: a movement in eighteenth century European thought that fostered a belief in natural law, universal order, and confidence in human reason.

Epistemology: a branch of philosophy that inquires about the nature, source, meaning, and limits of knowledge.

Equal outcomes: a school-reform theory that focuses on equalizing the achievements of all students.

Equal resources: a school-reform theory that advocates equalization of inputs in all school districts.

Equality: a mostly prescriptive concept based on the principle that all people should be treated similarly.

Essentialism: an educational movement that arose in the 1930s as a reaction against progressivism; it holds that both values and truth are rooted in and derived from objective sources, and its goals are to transmit the cultural heritage and develop good citizens.

Ethics: the branch of philosophy that inquires into morally right conduct and the morally good life.

Ethnic groups: a subculture that shares a common ancestry and culture.

Ethnic stratification: a relationship in which two or more groups have a dominant-subordinate relationship.

Ethnocentrism: the belief that one's way of life, attitudes, and customs are superior to those of other cultures.

Existentialism: a European philosophy that holds that metaphysics is inadequate to encompass, and account for, the variety and richness of human experience. Through existentialism, humans think not in terms of abstract philosophical ideas, but in terms of their own existence and what it entails.

Experimentalism: a pragmatic philosophy that espouses relativism rather than absolute truths and values. An experimentalist's idea of education would be one of reorganization, reconstruction, and transformation of experience.

Exploitation: the use of others for one's own advantage by violating their trust, manipulating their natural disabilities, or deliberately undermining their efforts in a joint undertaking.

Extrinsic value: the value of an object, quality, or act derived from the value of something else.

Family power-equalizing plan: proposes that several levels of quality be available in a community's schools, with each family free to choose the quality it wants for its children and be taxed accordingly.

Fatalism: the belief that all events happen the way they do no matter how we try to avoid them.

Feminization of teaching: a reference to the late nineteenth century when teaching changed from a predominantly male occupation to a predominantly female one.

Flat grant: a grant that specifies the amount given to local districts for each pupil.

Folkways: norms that do not evoke strong emotion and whose violation calls for only mild criticism or slight ridicule.

Force: mild or deliberate action to compel someone to do something—it does not cause physical harm or suffering.

Formal discipline theory: the theory that the mind is analogous to the muscles and can be strengthened by rigorous exercise by studying difficult subjects such as Latin and mathematics.

Formative evaluation: the examination of a curriculum at a predetermined stage of development; changes, if necessary, are made on the basis of reliable evidence. (Contrast with *Summative evaluation.*)

Foundation program: a state funding formula designed to overcome some inequities in local support and assure that all school districts can meet minimum standards.

Freedom from: an absence of restraint or coercion so that any restrictions on the individual would be an abrogation of that person's freedom.

Freedom to: the concept that one is not fully free to do something without the ability to perform an act.

Free schools: small, private schools that arose in the late 1960s based on the belief in liberating the child.

Frustration-aggression hypothesis: suggestion that aggressive behavior presupposes the existence of frustration that leads to some form of aggression.

Full-funding plan: a plan that mandates that the state specify per pupil funding levels for each classification of student and then imposes a uniform property tax to fund the plan.

Functionalism, legal: a theory that perceives the legal system as having several vital societal functions. The system seeks to promote order, stability, and provide justice impartially. (Contrast with *Conflict theory, legal.*)

Fundamental schools: schools that stress the basics, strict discipline, competition, letter grades, standardized testing, ability grouping, homework, and dress codes.

Futuristics: the attempt to gain a long-range perspective on the future by a variety of inquiry methods.

Games: a futuristics technique that might involve simulations of situations, but also includes rules.

General education: an approach to education that consists of experiences required of all students because such experiences are considered essential to fulfill certain common objectives.

General objective: a purpose statement that is more restricted in scope than an aim.

Hard determinism: the idea that one could not act other than the way he or she did.

Harm (in education): those conditions under the school's aegis which endanger well-being by rendering one temporarily or permanently incapable of benefitting from an education.

Helping professions: those professions that share the objective of helping others in need who are, for whatever reasons, unable fully to help themselves. They include teaching, medicine, nursing, law, social work, psychotherapy, and the ministry.

Hidden curriculum: the covert informal relations in home and school that influence learning, such as grades, norms, competition, social class background and prejudice.

Hopelessness: the feeling one arrives at if life's conditions are unbearable and he or she does not feel competent to change those conditions.

Human rights: basic rights to be enjoyed by all people; they are not based on merit or privilege.

Humanistic curriculum: a movement during the 1970s that sought to integrate the cognitive and affective domain in order to provide greater personal meaning in what is learned and to give the neglected affective domain parity with the cognitive domain.

Ideal: an archetypal idea. It is a conception of something in its perfection and, as such, is not literally attainable.

Idealism: the perception of the world as essentially mental, composed of Mind, Spirit, or Idea. (Contrast with *Realism.*)

Idealism, objective: the idea that the mental and spiritual character of existence is more comprehensive than finite minds.

Idealism, subjective: the idea that matter does not exist because physical things are ideas in the minds of perceivers.

Ideology: any system of ideas regarding philosophic, economic, political, or social beliefs.

Individual responsibility: the ascription of sole or primary obligation for an act or a related series of acts to one person.

Indoctrination: the process of instilling dogmas to the exclusion of contrary views and values.

Inelastic: a tax yield that increases at a slower rate than incomes. (Contrast with *Elastic.*)

Influence: to sway, affect, or alter another by indirect or intangible means.

Innovation: any new idea, method, or device used to improve some aspect of the educational process.

Institutionalized racism: practices legitimized by society that result in systematic discrimination against members of specific groups.

Instruction: planning, executing, and evaluating lessons.

Instructional objective: an objective that specifies the observable behavior the learner is expected to display during or after instruction.

Instrumental value: an extrinsic value often appealed to in education. For example, vocational education has instrumental value because it can help one find a good job.

Intangible personal property: property such as stocks, bonds, bank deposits, accounts receivable, insurance policies and mortgages. (Contrast with *Real property* and *Tangible personal property.*)

Integration: a move toward greater equality by reducing the separation between ethnic groups and encouraging them to work together.

Intentional tort: an act committed with the intent to inflict harm, such as assault, battery, or false imprisonment.

Intrinsic evaluation: the evaluation of a curriculum in terms of sequence, content accuracy, types of experience used to understand content, and the materials employed.

Intrinsic value: a value in and of itself; the value of a thing is not derived from anything else.

Invention: the process of creating new cultural elements.

Invidious discrimination: involves arbitrary unequal treatment in developing and enforcing rules or in distributing burdens. Rules and programs that arbitrarily exclude people from benefits or treat people unequally on grounds of race, sex, ethnicity, or religion would be invidiously discriminatory.

Job analysis: a plan to determine the ideals and duties necessary for successful performance in various occupations; those that could best be learned in school then would be presented in terms of the way children learn.

Judgmental injustice: the practice of unfairly judging people—as individuals, or by their activities and achievements.

Labeling: the practice of identifying a person with a particular trait; most often used in the negative, such as labeling a troubled child "deviant" or "delinquent."

Language: a system of formalized systems and signs used as a means of communication.

Latchkey children: youngsters who return from school to an empty home, usually because their parents work outside the home.

Latent social problem: a social condition that might go against a society's interests or values but which has yet to be acknowledged by the public as a problem.

Law: a prescribed rule of conduct or action formally recognized as binding by a controlling authority.

Legal system: a network of rules established for enforcing the laws.

Lenski's theory: the theory that social stratification is a sort of sociocultural evolution.

Libertarianism: a political philosophy that opposes big government and believes that all human beings should be free to make their own choices as long as they do not interfere with the choices of others. Libertarians would place the primary responsibility for education in the hands of parents.

Life chances: access to goods, services, and opportunities throughout the life cycle.

Life functions curriculum: a form of curriculum organization around persistent life situations, which is designed to provide a close connection between school experiences and life activities.

Linguistic relativity hypothesis: the idea that the unique grammatical form of language shapes the thoughts and perceptions of its users.

Logic: the branch of philosophy that studies correct thinking or rules of inference to arguments.

Logical empiricism: a modification of the verification principle of logical positivism, allowing confirmation of a statement.

Logical positivism: a scientific philosophy that held that philosophy should be reformulated to deal only with statements that can be verified; epistemology would become part of the empirical sciences, and metaphysical statements and ethics—whose statements cannot be verified—would be shifted to the arts.

Magnet schools: schools designed to promote integration by attracting students of different racial and ethnic backgrounds through special programs that appeal to diverse interests.

Mainstreaming: a plan by which handicapped children receive special education in the regular classroom as much as possible.

Manifest social problem: a social problem that has been denounced by the majority as harmful and in need of solution.

Mapping techniques: diagrams or flow charts that depict events, characteristics, and goals to be explored.

Mastery learning: a form of learning based on the assumption that the mastery of a topic or a human behavior is theoretically possible for anyone given the optimum quality of instruction appropriate to each individual and given the time needed for mastery.

Meritocratic system: a plan in which rewards are based on demonstrated achievement rather than political influence, nobility, wealth, race, gender, or other extraneous criteria.

Merit pay: a plan that rewards teachers with higher salaries for doing the same or a similar job better than their colleagues.

Metaethics: a branch of ethics that analyzes ethical language and the justification of ethical inquiry and judgments.

Metaphysics: a branch of philosophy that investigates the nature of the world or reality through reason.

Microculture: a system of attitudes, values, and modes of behavior, and life styles that are distinct but related to the dominant culture. Also known as "subculture."

Middle school: a plan for an approach to educating pupils in grades six, seven, and eight (in some instances fifth and ninth are also included). It often features individualized study, team teaching, the integration of extracurricular activities in the formal curriculum, a nongraded plan, and interdisciplinary programs.

Minimum competency test: a test that students in some states are required to pass before receiving a high school diploma.

Minority group: a category of people defined by physical or cultural characteristics and often subject to differential treatment.

Model: a technique used in futuristics to provide an interpretation of phenomena through a form of analogy.

Modeling-identification theory: a theory based on the principle of modeling and imitation; it emphasizes that learning takes place by observing the example of others.

Monism: a form of metaphysics that depicts the world as comprising essentially one thing, mental or otherwise.

Monocultural: a culturally exclusive position that reflects the traditions of only one culture, usually the dominant one.

Mores: norms that evoke strong emotions; violations of mores can lead to severe punishment within the community.

Multicultural education: a program designed to help individuals function effectively in their microculture, develop an appreciation of other cultures, gain cross-cultural competency, and reduce prejudice and discrimination.

Naive realism: the belief that the world is the way we perceive it and that no distinction needs to be made between the way the world seems to be and what the world really is.

Naturalistic fallacy: the process of deriving ethical statements from non-ethical statements; such as, "Humans possess the trait of rationality." (non-ethical statement); therefore, schools should seek to develop rationality (ethical or value statement).

"Nature-nurture" controversy: the conflict between the belief that intelligence is inherited and the belief that intelligence is affected by environment.

Negligence: the standard established by law to protect persons from unreasonable risks of harm.

Nongraded schools: grade levels and all expectations associated with separate grades are eliminated in order to individualize instruction and permit students to learn at their own rate of speed.

Nonpublic schools: schools not under the auspices of a government agency.

Nonverbal communication: all forms of communication that are neither spoken nor written.

Normative consensus: a condition that exists when there is widespread cultural agreement on mores and folkways.

Normative ethics: a branch of ethics that is concerned with what people ought to do.

Norms: rules that tell people what to do in a particular situation; guidelines for social action.

Objective, behavioral: See *Objective, instructional.*

Objective, general: a purpose statement that is at a different level and more restricted in scope than an aim. It applies to educational institutions, local school districts, curriculum areas, and subjects.

Objective, instructional: specifies the observable behavior the learner is expected to display during or after instruction. Also known as 'behavioral objective.

Open attendance: a plan designed to permit parents, at their own expense, to see that their children are transported to schools not operating at capacity enrollment.

Open education: an innovation that uses small groups and individual instruction, flexible scheduling, deemphasizes grading, and emphasizes the "whole child."

Operant conditioning: behavior modification developed by B. F. Skinner that offers a reward for some aspect of random behavior, with the reinforcement contingent upon the response.

Ordinary language analysis: a branch of analytic philosophy that addresses philosophical problems and puzzles in ordinary language, because that is where the problems arise.

Pairing: the joining of two schools so that they share the same attendance district; used to promote desegregation.

Participatory democracy: a political system that offers the widest possible participation of all citizens; stems from Jacksonian democracy. (Contrast with *Representative democracy.*)

Particularism: a way of relating to individuals based on whether their personalities and characteristics are attractive or unattractive. Professionals may indulge in particularism only in extraoccupational activities.

Partitioning: the splitting of a country into separate areas that house different ethnic groups.

Paternalism: coercive interference with an action or state of a person to protect or promote the subject's welfare.

Pay-off evaluation: the evaluation of a curriculum undertaken after intrinsic evaluation by examining the effects of curriculum in practice.

Peer group: egalitarian groups in which members share a common characteristic, such as age or ethnicity.

Perennialism: an educational philosophy that seeks to give new life to the philosophies of Plato, Aristotle, and Aquinas, and holds that the core beliefs of ancient and medieval culture apply directly to our own age.

Philosophy of education: a justifiable belief system about education that provides guidance in making everyday decisions.

Pluralism (metaphysics): a belief that the world is composed of many things.

Pluralist model: the view that in any complex organization there are likely to be many centers of power. (Contrast with *Power-elite model.*)

Policy network: a body of policy developed over a period of time to guide the daily operation of schools in a district.

Policy sanctions: rewards granted by educators when student behavior exemplifies compliance with the rules of the classroom and the school, or punishment administered when it fails to do so.

Postindustrial society: a period qualitatively different from industrial society in terms of a shift from manufacturing to service and knowledge industries.

Power: the ability to get someone to carry out one's will despite resistance.

Power-elite model: the view that a small proportion of the population at the top of the social hierarchy holds most of the power, while those at the bottom have very little. (Contrast with *Pluralist model.*)

Power-equalizing plan: a state plan that guarantees to each local school district in a state the same assessed valuation per pupil.

Pragmatism: an American philosophical movement based on interpreting ideas through their consequences.

Prejudice: an unfavorable opinion formed beforehand or without facts to support it.

Primary rules: rules that impose duties. They are commonly equated with laws. (See *Secondary rules.*)

Principle: a fundamental rule or truth.

Privacy: the right to be let alone, to enjoy solitude, intimacy, reasonable anonymity, and to reserve personal information.

Privileges: rights or immunities granted as peculiar benefits, advantages, or favors.

Procedural due process: a process that prohibits states from depriving anyone of "life, liberty, or property" without fair procedures.

Process philosophy: those philosophies that stress becoming rather than being, such as Dewey's and James' pragmatism.

Profession: an occupation that requires advanced education and the use of intellectual skills, promotes the public good, controls standards of entrance and exclusion, and enforces an ethical code.

Professional ethics: all issues involving principles of conduct for professionals in society.

Progressive tax: a tax in which the rates increase as the base amount increases.

Progressivism: an educational movement that differs from essentialism and perennialism in its view that the "whole child" should be educated, not just the mind.

Public: as opposed to private, refers to that which has no relation to a particular person or persons but concerns all members of the community without distinction.

Public-school choice plans: open enrollment plans that permit parents to enroll their children in public schools outside the geographical district; state funds are allocated to systems depending on their enrollment.

Race: a subspecies of homo sapiens distinguished by certain physical traits.

Racism: the belief that one racial category is innately superior or inferior to another.

Radical free will: an existentialist belief in a free will that includes a great range of human choices and total responsibility for one's choices.

Rationalism: the belief that reason is the primary source of knowledge and is superior to and independent of sense perception.

Rational-legal authority: See *Authority, rational-legal.*

Realism: a belief that there is an external world that exists independently of the observer and is not dependent on the mind for existence. (Contrast with *Idealism.*)

Realism, representative: a form of realism that distinguishes between sense data and the objects they represent.

Real property: land and the buildings and improvements on that land, all of which are fixed in one location. (Contrast with *Tangible personal property* and *Intangible personal property.*)

Reconstructionism: an educational movement that called for a new social order that would fulfill basic democratic values and harmonize the underlying forces of the modern world.

Reformation: sixteenth century religious movement aimed at reforming the Catholic church; led to the establishment of Protestantism and the growth of literacy.

Regressive tax: a tax in which the rates decrease when the base amount taxed decreases.

Relative purpose statement: a statement that is meaningful and desirable in a particular situation. (Contrast with *Absolute purpose statement* and *Subjective purpose statement.*)

Renaissance: the revival of art, literature, and learning in Western Europe during the fourteenth, fifteenth, and sixteenth centuries.

Representative democracy: a form of government in which the citizens determine who shall represent them in the election process. The view stems from Jeffersonian democracy. (Contrast with *Participatory democracy.*)

Rights: any claims against others recognized by law.

Rule: a generalization used to prescribe conduct, action, or usage.

Romanticism: a broad European movement that sought a simpler life and elevated feelings over intellect. The movement affected education, the arts, humanities, and the tenor of thought.

Sanctions: curtailment or withdrawal of teacher services to a district or state where teachers are not under contract.

Scenario: a technique used in futuristics that involves describing a future development at a given point in time.

School-based management: system that involves managers and teachers in joint planning, developing goals, and redefinition of teacher roles.

Secondary deviance: the uniting of rebellious individuals into a deviant subculture.

Secondary rules: rules about rules. They provide procedures for creating, modifying, and abrogating *primary rules.*

Segregation: the forced separation of one group from another and the establishment of rules or laws by which the dominant group maintains its control.

Selection: the process of choosing materials for a course or a curriculum that will help fulfill objectives and be appropriate to learners.

Self-actualizing: the idea that the purpose of life is to become all you can be.

Self-fulfilling prophecy: a situation that occurs when the teacher expects certain behaviors from the student and the student responds to those expectations.

Semiprofession: an occupation that resembles a profession but has a shorter training period, a less specialized and systematized body of knowledge, and less autonomy.

Sex discrimination: the denial of opportunity, reward, role, or privilege on the basis of sex.

Sexism: the belief that one sex is innately superior to another.

Sexual harassment: unwelcome sexual advances, requests for sexual favors, and other unwelcome verbal or physical conduct of a sexual nature.

Simulation: a futuristic technique designed to bring about change in a static model over time.

Skepticism, complete: the position that it is impossible to have knowledge of any sort.

Skill: a developed aptitude or ability.

Social class: the grouping of people of similar socioeconomic background.

Social-conflict analysis: a depiction of culture not as a well-integrated system but as a dynamic center of social conflict among categories of people.

Social disorganization: the disintegration of a society when its members cannot agree on a consistent set of norms and values.

Social mobility: changes of position within a social-stratification system.

Social sanctions: forms of rewards and punishments used to exercise social control.

Social stratification: a system by which categories of people are ranked in a hierarchy that differentiates them as superior or inferior.

Socialization: the process by which individuals acquire the knowledge, skills, and behavior that will make them active members of society.

Social problem: social condition that is widely considered undesirable.

Society: an aggregate of people that is self-sustaining, has a definite location and a long duration, and shares a way of life.

Sociobiology: an area of inquiry that seeks to explain the social organization of animals, including humans, in terms of biological characteristics.

Soft determinism: a form of determinism that recognizes causality and multiple causal forces, including one's own decisions.

Socratic method: a method of instruction used by Socrates in which questions are raised, points of view are elicited, and conclusions are drawn leading to a general truth or ideal.

Solipsism: the theory that no reality exists other than oneself and everything is the creation of one's consciousness.

Speech community: a group of people who speak the same language.

Status consistency: the degree to which members of the same class differ in status within that class.

Strict liability: a legal term that refers to an injury that occurs from the creation of an unusual hazard (e.g., storing dynamite).

Strike: a work stoppage while under contract to force an employer to comply with demands.

Structural-functional analysis: a view of society as a system of many different parts that work together to develop a stable social system.

Structural-functional theory: a sociological theory that explains the social structure in terms of the functions that the particular features fulfill in maintaining the system as a viable entity.

Structure-of-the-disciplines approach: a form of curricular organization that retained subjects but revised and updated content, introduced discovery learning, and taught students to grasp the discipline's structure.

Student subculture: a group of peers, often found in secondary schools.

Subculture: See *Microculture.*

Subject curriculum: designed to maintain the integrity of disciplines by organizing content in terms of subjects of instruction.

Subjective purpose statement: statement that applies only to an individual. (Contrast with *Relative purpose statement* and *Absolute purpose statement.*)

Substantive due process: a process that protects people against laws or rules that are overly vague, arbitrary, capricious, or unreasonable.

Substantive equality: a school-reform theory that advocates transforming society into a form of democratic socialism.

Summative evaluation: an evaluation approach used to reach some general conclusions about a curriculum. The curriculum has been developed and can be compared with other curriculums. (Contrast with *Formative evaluation.*)

Supply and demand (for teachers): the number of teachers available by level and field in relation to the need for teachers at local, state, and national levels.

Symbolic-interactionist theory: the theory that the self arises in childhood through the communication process that enables individuals to view themselves from the perspective of others.

Tabula rasa: the mind, as conceived by John Locke, as a blank slate on which experience writes. The concept was used against the belief in original sin.

Tangible personal property: property that has a value of its own and can be moved from place to place. It includes automobiles, jewelry, appliances, and household furniture. (Contrast with *Real property* and *Intangible personal property.*)

Tax yield: the ability of a tax to generate revenue.

Tenure: a continuing contract awarded to a faculty member after a successful period of probationary service.

Theory: a coherent group of propositions used to explain a class of phenomena.

Tort: a wrongful act that causes damage, loss, or injury to another.

Total institutions: a place of residence or work where individuals are cut off from the larger society for an appreciable period of time.

Tracking: the practice of subdividing students by ability or achievement level within and between curriculums.

Traditional authority: See *Authority, traditional.*

Training: the systematic practice in performance of a skill.

Trend extrapolation: a futuristics technique that assumes forces at work in the past also will be found in the future.

Tuition tax credits: a plan to enable parents who send their children to private or parochial schools to receive some federal income tax credit for tuition expenses.

Under class: members of the lower-lower class trapped in poverty generation after generation.

Universalism: a characteristic that professional service is expected to display; a professional is oriented toward clients in terms of general standards.

Value: the quality of a thing, process, or relationship which makes it desirable or undesirable.

Values: statements of the worth, utility, or importance of something.

Values clarification: a program that avoids indoctrination and instilling of a fixed set of values and is based instead on a valuing process for examining, clarifying, and accepting or rejecting values.

Violence: a sudden and extremely forceful act that causes physical harm and suffering.

Voucher plan: a plan designed to finance elementary and secondary education through certificates given by government to parents of school-age children.

Weighed-pupil approach: a method of school funding that provides cost differentials to compensate for the higher cost of educating some students because of their characteristics and the types of programs needed.

■ NAME INDEX ■

■ SUBJECT INDEX ■